CDX Learning Systems™

We support ASE
program certification
through

ASE NATEF

FUNDAMENTALS OF
Automotive Technology
Principles and Practice

SECOND EDITION

STUDENT WORKBOOK

World Headquarters
Jones & Bartlett Learning
5 Wall Street
Burlington, MA 01803
978-443-5000
info@jblearning.com
www.jblearning.com

Jones & Bartlett Learning books and products are available through most bookstores and online booksellers. To contact Jones & Bartlett Learning directly, call 800-832-0034, fax 978-443-8000, or visit our website, www.jblearning.com.

Substantial discounts on bulk quantities of Jones & Bartlett Learning publications are available to corporations, professional associations, and other qualified organizations. For details and specific discount information, contact the special sales department at Jones & Bartlett Learning via the above contact information or send an email to specialsales@jblearning.com.

Production Credits
General Manager: Douglas Kaplan
Executive Publisher: Vernon Anthony
Content Services Manager: Kevin Murphy
Senior Vendor Manager: Sara Kelly
Marketing Manager: Amanda Banner
Manufacturing and Inventory Control Supervisor: Amy Bacus
Composition and Project Management: Integra Software Services Pvt. Ltd.
Cover Design: Scott Moden
Rights & Media Specialist: Robert Boder
Media Development Editor: Shannon Sheehan
Cover Image (Title Page): © Umberto Shtanzman/Shutterstock
Printing and Binding: Sheridan Books
Cover Printing: Sheridan Books

ISBN: 978-1-284-11950-3

6048

Printed in the United States of America
22 21 20 19   10 9 8 7 6 5 4 3

Contents

Note to Students

This workbook was created to help you on your path to a career in the transportation industry. Employability basics covered early in the text will help you get and keep a job in the field. Essential technical skills are built in cover to cover and are the core building blocks of an advanced technician's skill set.

The textbook introduces "strategy-based diagnostics," a method used to solve technical problems correctly on the first attempt. The text covers every task the industry standard recommends for technicians, and will help you on your path to a successful career.

As you navigate this workbook, ask yourself, "What does a technician need to know and be able to do at work?"

This workbook is set up to answer that question. Each chapter starts by listing the technicians' tasks that are covered within the chapter. These are your objectives. The content of each chapter includes exercises to help you learn and remember each objective. As you study, continue to ask yourself that question. Gauge your progress by imagining yourself as the technician. Do you have the knowledge, and can you perform the tasks required at the beginning of each chapter? Combining your knowledge with hands-on experience is essential to becoming a Master Technician.

During your training, remember that the best thing you can do as a technician is learn to learn. This will serve you well because vehicles keep advancing, and good technicians never stop learning.

Stay curious. Ask questions. Practice your skills, and always remember that one of the best resources you have for learning is right there in your classroom . . . your instructor.

Best wishes and enjoy!
The CDX Automotive Team

Careers in Automotive Technology

At the start of each chapter you'll find the NATEF Tasks, Knowledge Objectives, and Skills Objectives from the textbook. These are your objectives as you make your way through the exercises in this workbook and the chapter in your textbook. The following activities have been designed to help you refresh your knowledge of the material in this chapter.

NATEF Tasks

There are no NATEF tasks for this chapter.

Knowledge Objectives

After reading this chapter, you will be able to:

- K01001 Outline the history of the automobile.
- K01002 Describe the modern automobile manufacturing process.
- K01003 Describe the careers in the automotive service sector.
- K01004 Describe each type of repair facility.
- K01005 Describe the importance of automotive industry certification and ongoing training.

Skills Objectives

There are no Skills Objectives for this chapter.

Matching

Match the following terms with the correct description or example.

A. Automotive Service Excellence (ASE)
B. Brake technician
C. Drivability technician
D. Heavy line technician
E. Lube technician
F. Service consultant/advisor
G. Shop foreman

_____ 1. Specializes in major engine, transmission, and differential overhaul and repair.

_____ 2. Carries out scheduled maintenance activities.

_____ 3. Supervisor who oversees the work of technicians and staff.

_____ 4. An independent, nonprofit organization dedicated to the improvement of vehicle repair through the testing and certification of automotive professionals.

_____ 5. Specializes in working on vehicle brake systems.

_____ 6. Diagnoses and identifies mechanical and electrical faults that affect vehicle performance and emissions.

_____ 7. A service worker who works with both customers and technicians.

Multiple Choice

Read each item carefully, and then select the best response.

_____ 1. Who is generally acknowledged to have invented the modern automobile around 1885?

A. Henry Ford
B. Karl Benz
C. Armand Peugeot
D. Charles Rolls

_____ **2.** Who is a repair shop's first point of contact for customers seeking vehicle repairs?
    A. Shop foreman
    B. Service consultant/advisor
    C. Drivability technician
    D. Service manager

_____ **3.** What type of technician might specialize in particular vehicle systems, such as engines, transmissions, or final drives?
    A. Shop foreman
    B. Light line technician
    C. Drivability technician
    D. Heavy line technician

_____ **4.** What type of technician diagnoses and repairs faults, replaces or overhauls brake systems, and tests the components of disc, drum, and power brake systems used on all types of vehicles?
    A. Light line technician
    B. Heavy line technician
    C. Brake technician
    D. Drivability technician

_____ **5.** What type of technician works with computer-controlled engine management systems to service, identify, and repair faults on electronically controlled vehicle systems such as fuel injection, ignition, antilock braking, cruise control, and automatic transmissions?
    A. Electrical technician
    B. Heavy line technician
    C. Shop foreman
    D. Service manager

_____ **6.** What type of technician regularly uses meters, oscilloscopes, circuit wiring diagrams, and solder equipment?
    A. Light line technicians
    B. Transmission specialist
    C. Electrical technicians
    D. Heavy line technicians

_____ **7.** Which of the following is a key skill of a service manager?
    A. Communicating
    B. Motivating
    C. Creating positive work environments
    D. All of the above

_____ **8.** What types of shops are usually independent and focus on one type of service, such as transmission service, electrical system repair, or emission system diagnosis?
    A. Dealerships
    B. Specialty shops
    C. Franchises
    D. Fleet shops

_____ **9.** Which of the following programs receives access to new vehicle technology as well as manufacturer service information to help prepare students for working on today's vehicles and technology?
    A. National Automotive Technicians Education Foundation
    B. Automotive Service Excellence
    C. Automotive Youth Educational Systems
    D. Advanced Engine Performance certification

_____ **10.** Technicians who handle refrigerants or work on AC systems are required to have what?
    A. Environmental Protection Agency Section 609 certification
    B. ASE Advanced Engine Performance certification
    C. NATEF refrigerant certification
    D. AYES certification

True/False

If you believe the statement to be more true than false, write the letter "T" in the space provided. If you believe the statement to be more false than true, write the letter "F."

_____ **1.** Today's vehicles are assembled on high-volume production lines, with robots used for many of the assembly processes, including welding seams.

_____ **2.** Heavy line technicians diagnose and replace the mechanical and electrical components of motor vehicles, such as gaskets, belts, hoses, timing belts, water pumps, radiators, alternators, and starters.

_____ **3.** Drivability technicians perform wheel alignments and wheel balancing, and they diagnose and replace faulty steering system components.

_____ **4.** In larger shops, roles may be assigned to separate electrical and drivability technicians, whereas in smaller shops, one technician could perform both roles.

_____ **5.** Electrical technicians test and replace faulty charging system components, starter motors, and related items such as batteries.

_____ **6.** Light line technicians use electronic test equipment, scan tools, pressure transducers, exhaust gas analyzers, lab scopes, meters, and circuit wiring diagrams to locate electrical, fuel, and emission systems faults.

_____ **7.** A service manager's job is to oversee technicians' work in order to ensure that customers receive quality repair work.

_____ **8.** Because dealership technicians are working on the latest vehicles, they are right at the cutting edge of technology.

_____ **9.** The automotive service industry in the United States is generally not subject to licensure requirements.

_____ **10.** The Automotive Youth Educational Systems (AYES) is an independent, nonprofit organization dedicated to the improvement of vehicle repair through the testing and certification of automotive professionals.

Fill in the Blank

Read each item carefully, and then complete the statement by filling in the missing word(s).

1. Henry Ford applied two concepts that helped make the Model T affordable for the masses, _____ and the _____ _____.

2. A(n) _____ _____ changes oil and filters and carries out lubrication, fluid inspection, fluid service, and tire rotations.

3. A(n) _____ _____ diagnoses, repairs, and services steering system components and suspension systems on all types of vehicles.

4. A(n) _____ _____ diagnoses, replaces, maintains, identifies faults with, and repairs electrical wiring and computer-based equipment in vehicles.

5. Electrical technicians use meters, oscilloscopes, test instruments, and circuit wiring diagrams to diagnose _____ _____.

6. A(n) _____ _____ works with computer-controlled engine management systems to service, identify, and repair faults on electronically controlled vehicle systems such as fuel injection, ignition, and automatic transmissions.

7. A(n) _____ _____ may also work on the other components of the drivetrain, including the drive shafts and differentials.

8. A(n) _____ _____ oversees the work of all types of technicians and staff, communicates with customers and external suppliers, and handles the various administrative duties involved with operating a business.

9. _____ are affiliated with a specific vehicle manufacturer.

10. To earn _____ _____, technicians are required to pass one or more ASE certification tests and have 2 years of qualifying work experience as a technician.

Review Questions

_____ **1.** When compared to early vehicles, modern vehicles do not have:
   A. as much sophistication and reliability.
   B. as much speed.
   C. as many maintenance requirements.
   D. as many convenience systems.

_____ **2.** Which of the following statements is true?
   A. "Interchangeability" meant that parts did not have to be custom built to match a particular car.
   B. Assembly line involved workers moving to the car as it was being assembled rather than bringing the car to the worker.
   C. The advent of mass production made automobiles available to only the wealthy.
   D. Efficiency in mass production is increased when parts are produced where the vehicle is being assembled.

_____ **3.** Advances in vehicle manufacturing technology have decreased the need for:
   A. large-scale parts manufacturers.
   B. high-volume production lines.
   C. large-scale investments.
   D. large amounts of labor.

_____ **4.** In "Just in Time" manufacturing:
   A. there is no need for scheduling.
   B. the manufacturer doesn't have to store large quantities of parts.
   C. parts are delivered a few months before assembly and in the order the supplier prefers.
   D. technology use is reduced in response to environmental pressures.

_____ **5.** Which of the following would be the most likely to program or reprogram (reflash) powertrain control modules (PCMs) using computerized equipment?
   A. Transmission specialists
   B. Brake technicians
   C. Drivability technicians
   D. Light line technicians

_____ **6.** All the statements below are true _except_:
   A. Service consultants work only with customers.
   B. A shop foreman is the supervisor in a shop.
   C. Service managers are responsible for the functioning of the entire service department.
   D. A shop foreman may also be responsible for hiring and training new workers.

_____ **7.** A technician wants to be at the cutting edge of technology. Which of repair facility would be the best fit for him or her?
   A. Franchise
   B. Fleet shop
   C. Independent shop
   D. Dealership

_____ **8.** Jiffy Lube outlets are examples of:
   A. dealerships.
   B. franchises.
   C. fleet shops.
   D. independent shops.

_____ **9.** Special certification is required for technicians who handle which of the following systems?
   A. Refrigerants and AC systems
   B. Computer-controlled systems
   C. Automatic transmission systems
   D. Engine management systems

_____ **10.** Which of the following organizations certify technicians in all areas of a vehicle?
   A. EPA
   B. ASE
   C. ASA
   D. AYES

ASE Technician A/Technician B Style Questions

_____ **1.** Tech A says that newer vehicles require less maintenance compared to older vehicles. Tech B says that major repairs are needed more frequently on newer engines. Who is correct?
 A. Tech A
 B. Tech B
 C. Both A and B
 D. Neither A nor B

_____ **2.** Tech A says that Henry Ford is credited with the invention of the gasoline engine. Tech B says that Carl Benz is credited with the invention of the automobile. Who is correct?
 A. Tech A
 B. Tech B
 C. Both A and B
 D. Neither A nor B

_____ **3.** Tech A says that the production of vehicles today requires a mix of robotic and human assembly. Tech B says that most of the parts on a vehicle are preassembled into unit assemblies before they reach the assembly line. Who is correct?
 A. Tech A
 B. Tech B
 C. Both A and B
 D. Neither A nor B

_____ **4.** Tech A says that only a certain few people will find jobs in the automotive industry. Tech B says the automotive industry offers numerous career choices. Who is correct?
 A. Tech A
 B. Tech B
 C. Both A and B
 D. Neither A nor B

_____ **5.** Tech A says that a technician can specialize in different areas based on his or her interest and ability. Tech B says that most specialty shops, such as transmission shops, primarily work on only one manufacturer's vehicles. Who is correct?
 A. Tech A
 B. Tech B
 C. Both A and B
 D. Neither A nor B

_____ **6.** Tech A says that the shop foreman is the frontline contact for customer relations. Tech B says that the service consultant typically reports directly to the business owner. Who is correct?
 A. Tech A
 B. Tech B
 C. Both A and B
 D. Neither A nor B

_____ **7.** Tech A says that dealership technicians generally have access to manufacturers' training courses. Tech B says that an independent shop works on a wide variety of vehicles that requires a broad skill level in technicians. Who is correct?
 A. Tech A
 B. Tech B
 C. Both A and B
 D. Neither A nor B

_____ **8.** Tech A says that AYES certifies technicians. Tech B says that having ASE certifications can make it easier to get a job. Who is correct?
 A. Tech A
 B. Tech B
 C. Both A and B
 D. Neither A nor B

_____ **9.** Tech A says that the maintenance intervals of a vehicle have changed very little since the creation of the automobile. Tech B says that manufacturers are predicting 25,000-mile (40,000 km) maintenance intervals. Who is correct?
  A. Tech A
  B. Tech B
  C. Both A and B
  D. Neither A nor B

_____ **10.** Tech A says that a technician can progress to different jobs within the industry. Tech B says that careers in the automotive industry include parts manager. Who is correct?
  A. Tech A
  B. Tech B
  C. Both A and B
  D. Neither A nor B

Introduction to Automotive Technology

At the start of each chapter you'll find the NATEF Tasks, Knowledge Objectives, and Skills Objectives from the textbook. These are your objectives as you make your way through the exercises in this workbook and the chapter in your text-book. The following activities have been designed to help you refresh your knowledge of the material in this chapter.

NATEF Tasks

There are no NATEF tasks for this chapter.

Knowledge Objectives

After reading this chapter, you will be able to:

- K02001 Identify vehicle body types and their characteristics.
- K02002 Describe vehicle chassis designs.
- K02003 List the functions of common vehicle systems.
- K02004 Describe general vehicle operation.
- K02005 Describe drivetrain layouts.
- K02006 Identify engine configurations.
- K02007 Describe transmission/transaxle and axle configurations.
- K02008 Explain how torque is applied.
- K02009 Describe the functions of transmissions and final drives.
- K02010 Distinguish between four-wheel and all-wheel drive.

Skills Objectives

There are no Skills Objectives for this chapter.

Matching

Match the following terms with the correct description or example.

A. Differential gear set   **F.** Piston engine
B. Four-wheel drive   **G.** Rotary engine
C. Horizontally opposed engine   **H.** Torque converter
D. In-line engine   **I.** Unibody design
E. Longitudinal   **J.** VR engine

_____ **1.** An engine in which the cylinders are arranged side by side in a single row.

_____ **2.** An internal combustion engine that uses cylindrical pistons moving back and forth in a cylinder to extract mechanical energy from chemical energy.

_____ **3.** A term used to describe an engine configuration that uses a single bank of cylinders staggered at a shallow 15-degree V.

_____ **4.** An engine that uses a triangular rotor turning in a housing instead of conventional pistons.

_____ **5.** A term used to describe the front-to-back engine orientation when mounted in the engine compartment.

_____ **6.** The arrangement of gears between two axles that allows each axle to spin at its own speed when the vehicle is going around a corner.

_____ **7.** A drivetrain layout in which the engine drive has either two wheels or four wheels depending on which mode is selected by the driver.

_____ **8.** A vehicle design that does not use a rigid frame to support the body. The body panels are designed to provide the strength for the vehicle.

_____ **9.** A device that is turned by the crankshaft and transmits torque to the input shaft of an automatic transmission.

_____ **10.** An engine with two banks of cylinders, 180 degrees apart, on opposite sides of the crankshaft. It is also called a flat engine or a boxer engine.

Multiple Choice

Read each item carefully, and then select the best response.

_____ **1.** Which vehicle design has an enclosed body with a maximum of four doors, and a trunk located in the rear of the vehicle accessible from a trunk lid?
   A. Coupe
   B. Sedan
   C. Hatchback
   D. Station wagon

_____ **2.** Which type of vehicle acts like both a full-size van and a pickup in that it has a heavier-duty chassis so it can carry heavier loads?
   A. Sedan
   B. Hatchback
   C. Sport utility vehicle
   D. Minivan

_____ **3.** What type of chassis design was first used in aircraft and then spread to automobiles?
   A. Unibody
   B. Body on frame
   C. Dual shell
   D. Steel ladder

_____ **4.** In which type of drivetrain layout are all four wheels driven by the engine all of the time?
   A. Front-wheel drive
   B. Rear-wheel drive
   C. All-wheel drive
   D. Four-wheel drive

_____ **5.** All of the following criteria are used to define the drivetrain layout, _except_:
   A. Engine position
   B. Transmission type
   C. Engine orientation
   D. Type of drive

_____ **6.** Which of the following engine designs is the most powerful compared to its overall dimensions, but more complicated and expensive than the other engines?
   A. V8
   B. Flat 6
   C. W12
   D. In-line 4

_____ **7.** Which type of engine uses a single bank of cylinders, staggered at a shallow 15-degree V within the bank?
   A. Horizontally opposed
   B. W
   C. V
   D. VR

_____ **8.** Which type of axle uses the engine's torque to turn the wheels (drive the vehicle) and at the same time support the weight of the vehicle?
   A. Live axle
   B. Dead axle
   C. Transaxle
   D. Solid axle

_____ **9.** The twisting force applied to a shaft is known as what?
  A. Play
  B. Torque
  C. Collar
  D. Give

_____ **10.** What designation is used when measuring torque?
  A. Foot-pound
  B. Inch-pound
  C. Newton meter
  D. Any of the above

True/False

If you believe the statement to be more true than false, write the letter "T" in the space provided. If you believe the statement to be more false than true, write the letter "F."

_____ **1.** Reducing the number of doors to the passenger compartment makes the vehicle structure more rigid.

_____ **2.** In some vehicles, known as roadsters, the roof can be a series of folding steel or fiberglass panels.

_____ **3.** A station wagon has an extended roof that goes all the way to the rear of the vehicle. It is similar to a van but not as tall.

_____ **4.** Body-on-frame is the term used when a vehicle body is mounted on a rigid frame or chassis.

_____ **5.** Some high-performance racing cars today have no chassis at all.

_____ **6.** Mechanical energy can be converted into chemical energy in two primary ways: through the operation of an internal combustion engine or through the operation of an electric motor.

_____ **7.** The suspension system makes the connection between the steering wheel and the road wheels so the driver can point the vehicle in the intended direction of travel.

_____ **8.** A drivetrain is classified by type, cylinder arrangement, number of cylinders/rotors, and total engine displacement in cubic inches or liters.

_____ **9.** Multi-cylinder internal combustion automotive engines are produced in four common configurations.

_____ **10.** V engines have two banks of cylinders sitting side by side in a V arrangement sharing a common crankshaft.

_____ **11.** Horizontally opposed engines are very powerful for their size, but they do not use conventional pistons that slide back and forth inside a straight cylinder.

_____ **12.** The automatic transmission uses a torque converter instead of a clutch.

_____ **13.** Part-time 4WD means the vehicle is usually driven in two-wheel drive and switched to full-time when needed by engaging the transfer case.

_____ **14.** A transfer case locks the driveshafts together and directs torque through them to both axles.

_____ **15.** All transfer cases use a viscous coupling to split the drive between the front and rear wheels.

Fill in the Blank

Read each item carefully, and then complete the statement by filling in the missing word(s).

1. A(n)_____ has only two doors.

2. A(n)_____ is available in three-door and five-door designs.

3. A(n) _____ is an automobile that can convert from having an enclosed top to having an open top by means of a roof that can be removed, retracted, or folded away.

4. A(n) pickup, or _____, carries and tows cargo.

5. A(n) _____ _____ _____ can easily be used to carry out functions that would otherwise require several different vehicles.

6. A(n) _____ is an underlying supporting structure for vehicles—similar to the skeleton of a human—on which additional components are mounted.

7. The _____ design is constructed of a large number of steel sheet metal panels that are precisely formed in presses and spot-welded together into a structural unit.

8. Stored _____ energy is converted to mechanical energy to propel a vehicle down the road.

9. As the pistons move up and down, they rotate the crankshaft, turning the _____ or flex plate, which is bolted to the engine crankshaft.

10. The _____ system evens out the road shocks caused by irregular road surfaces.

11. Manufacturers mount engines in one of two orientations, _____ and _____, depending on which design best fits the vehicle and the rest of the drivetrain.

12. In a piston engine, the way engine cylinders are arranged is called the engine _____.

13. _____ _____ engines are sometimes referred to as "flat" engines and are commonly found in 4- and 6-cylinder configurations.

14. Axles come in two configurations: _____ axle and _____ axle.

15. A vehicle with a manual transmission uses a _____ to engage and disengage the engine from the transmission.

Labeling

Label the following images with the correct terms.

1. Chassis, engines, and axles:

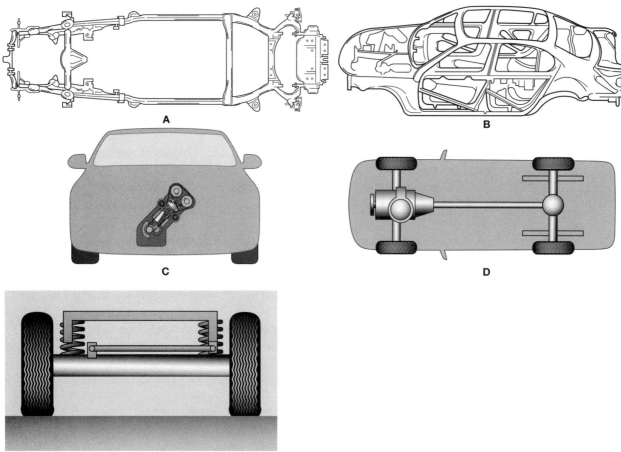

A. _____

B. _____

C. _____

D. _____

E. _____

2. Manual transmission clutch:

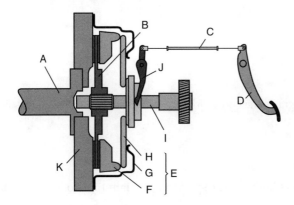

A. _____

B. _____

C. _____

D. _____

E. _____

F. _____

G. _____

H. _____

I. _____

J. _____

K. _____

3. Final drive assembly:

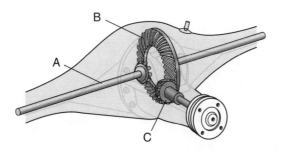

A. _____

B. _____

C. _____

Review Questions

_____ **1.** A hatchback typically has:
   A. 2 doors.
   B. 3 doors.
   C. 4 doors.
   D. 6 doors.

_____ **2.** A design that either partially or wholly integrates the bodywork into a single unit with the chassis is called:
   A. body-on-frame design.
   B. ladder-frame design.
   C. retool design.
   D. unibody design.

_____ **3.** Which of these systems creates and delivers high voltage sparks at the right time to ignite the air-fuel mixture in the combustion chamber?
   A. Emission system
   B. SRS system
   C. TPMS system
   D. Ignition system

_____ **4.** Which of these components multiples the torque from the engine by running it through a number of different gear ratios?
   A. Steering
   B. Suspension
   C. Transmission
   D. Piston

_____ **5.** Which of these does _not_ define the drivetrain layout?
   A. Engine position
   B. Engine capacity
   C. Engine orientation
   D. Number of driven axles

_____ **6.** Which of the following is true of a horizontally opposed configuration?
   A. The pistons are in two banks on both sides of a common crankshaft.
   B. The pistons are in two banks on opposite sides, forming a deep V with a common crankshaft at the base of the V.
   C. The pistons are in one bank, but form a shallow V within the bank.
   D. The pistons are in two VR banks in a deep V configuration with each other.

_____ **7.** Which of the following statements is true?
   A. Both live and dead axles drive the vehicle.
   B. Both live and dead axles support the weight of the vehicle.
   C. The dead axles use the engine's torque to turn the wheels.
   D. The lazy axles use the engine's torque to turn the wheels.

_____ **8.** All of the statements below are true _except_:
   A. Torque twists the gears in the transmission.
   B. Torque twists the gears in the final drive assembly.
   C. Torque turns the axles.
   D. Torque pushes the piston down.

_____ **9.** Choose the correct statement.
   A. A vehicle starting from rest needs less torque.
   B. The lower the gear selected, the lower the output torque transmitted.
   C. An automatic transmission uses a torque converter instead of a clutch.
   D. The driveshaft divides the torque to the axles.

_____ **10.** Which vehicles can switch from two-wheel to four-wheel drive by engaging the transfer case attached to the transmission?
   A. Front-wheel drive
   B. All-wheel drive
   C. Rear-wheel drive
   D. Four-wheel drive

ASE Technician A/Technician B Style Questions

_____ 1. Tech A says that most vehicles today are built with a ladder frame. Tech B says that most vehicles today do not have a full frame. Who is correct?
   A. Tech A
   B. Tech B
   C. Both A and B
   D. Neither A nor B

_____ 2. Tech A says that an SUV is typically a two-door convertible vehicle. Tech B says that many pickups come in two-door and four-door versions. Who is correct?
   A. Tech A
   B. Tech B
   C. Both A and B
   D. Neither A nor B

_____ 3. Tech A says that gasoline is energy in chemical form. Tech B says that chemical energy is converted to mechanical energy by the combustion process of an engine. Who is correct?
   A. Tech A
   B. Tech B
   C. Both A and B
   D. Neither A nor B

_____ 4. Tech A says that a live axle is an axle that drives the vehicle. Tech B says that a dead axle means that the axle can be steered. Who is correct?
   A. Tech A
   B. Tech B
   C. Both A and B
   D. Neither A nor B

_____ 5. Tech A says that the gear ratios in the transmission give the vehicle an extended operating range. Tech B says that the final drive assembly has various gear ratios that can be selected with a gearshift lever. Who is correct?
   A. Tech A
   B. Tech B
   C. Both A and B
   D. Neither A nor B

_____ 6. Tech A says that pushing on the brake pedal stops the vehicle by converting chemical energy into thermal energy. Tech B says that brake pedal pressure is transmitted to the brakes hydraulically. Who is correct?
   A. Tech A
   B. Tech B
   C. Both A and B
   D. Neither A nor B

_____ 7. Tech A says that one advantage of a mid-engine design is better weight distribution. Tech B says that the rear-engine design is commonly used in four-wheel drive vehicles. Who is correct?
   A. Tech A
   B. Tech B
   C. Both A and B
   D. Neither A nor B

_____ 8. Tech A says that the purpose of the battery is to charge the vehicle. Tech B says that in-line engines are generally easier to work on than V engines. Who is correct?
   A. Tech A
   B. Tech B
   C. Both A and B
   D. Neither A nor B

_____ **9.** Tech A says that a piston engine has a roughly triangular shaped rotor. Tech B says that V engines have horizontally opposed cylinders. Who is correct?

    A. Tech A

    B. Tech B

    C. Both A and B

    D. Neither A nor B

_____ **10.** Tech A says that the definition of torque is how far the crankshaft twists in degrees. Tech B says that torque can relate to tightness of bolts. Who is correct?

    A. Tech A

    B. Tech B

    C. Both A and B

    D. Neither A nor B

Introduction to Automotive Safety

At the start of each chapter you'll find the NATEF Tasks, Knowledge Objectives, and Skills Objectives from the textbook. These are your objectives as you make your way through the exercises in this workbook and the chapter in your textbook. The following activities have been designed to help you refresh your knowledge of the material in this chapter.

NATEF Tasks

- N03001 Identify general shop safety rules and procedures.
- N03002 Identify the location of the posted evacuation routes.
- N03003 Identify marked safety areas.
- N03004 Identify the location and the types of fire extinguishers and other fire safety equipment; demonstrate knowledge of the procedures for using fire extinguishers and other fire safety equipment.
- N03005 Identify the location and use of eyewash stations.
- N03006 Locate and demonstrate knowledge of safety data sheets (SDS).

Knowledge Objectives

After reading this chapter, you will be able to:

- K03001 Outline safe practices in the workplace.
- K03002 Describe how the Occupational Safety and Health Administration (OSHA) and the Environmental Protection Agency (EPA) impact the workplace.
- K03003 Describe the difference between a shop policy and a shop procedure.
- K03004 Identify workplace safety signs and their meanings.
- K03005 Identify hazards in the shop environment.
- K03006 Describe the standard safety equipment.
- K03007 Maintain a safe air quality in the workplace.
- K03008 List the safety precautions when working with electrical tools and equipment.
- K03009 Explain the safety importance of the shop layout.
- K03010 Describe how to reduce the risk of fires in the shop.
- K03011 Describe how to use firefighting equipment.
- K03012 Explain how to use an SDS.
- K03013 Describe how to properly dispose of used engine oil and other petroleum products.
- K03014 Describe shop safety inspections and hazards commonly found.

Skills Objectives

After reading this chapter, you will be able to:

- S03001 Safely clean and dispose of hazardous dust.

Matching

Match the following terms with the correct description or example.

- **A.** Environmental Protection Agency
- **B.** Hazardous environment
- **C.** Safety data sheet
- **D.** Occupational Safety and Health Administration
- **E.** Personal protective equipment
- **F.** Threshold limit value

_____ **1.** Equipment designed to protect the technician, such as safety boots, gloves, clothing, protective eyewear, and hearing protection.

_____ **2.** A sheet that provides information about handling, use, and storage of a material that may be hazardous.

_____ **3.** The maximum allowable concentration of a given material in the surrounding air.

_____ **4.** Government agency created to provide national leadership in occupational safety and health.

_____ **5.** A place where hazards exist.

_____ **6.** Federal government agency that deals with issues related to environmental safety.

Multiple Choice

Read each item carefully, and then select the best response.

_____ **1.** A safe work environment includes which of the following?
 A. A well-organized shop layout
 B. Good supervision
 C. Safety training
 D. All of the above

_____ **2.** Which federal government agency deals with issues related to environmental safety?
 A. SDS
 B. EPA
 C. OSHA
 D. NIOSH

_____ **3.** A document that describes the steps required to safely use the vehicle hoist is an example of?
 A. Regulation
 B. Policy
 C. Procedure
 D. Compliance

_____ **4.** A _____ can be used to identify hazards and risks within the work environment.
 A. risk analysis
 B. procedure
 C. vulnerability analysis
 D. threat assessment

_____ **5.** All of the following are components of safety signs, _except_:
 A. Signal word
 B. Background color
 C. Warning light
 D. Pictorial message

_____ **6.** Which signal word indicates a potentially hazardous situation, which, if not avoided, may result in minor or moderate injury?
 A. Danger
 B. Hazard
 C. Warning
 D. Caution

_____ **7.** A droplight that is designed in such a way that the electrical parts can never come into contact with the outer casing of the device is called?
 A. Grounded
 B. Ground fault
 C. Double-insulated
 D. Cordless

_____ **8.** What class of fires involves flammable liquids or gaseous fuels?
 A. Class A
 B. Class B
 C. Class C
 D. Class D

_____ **9.** To operate a fire extinguisher, you should follow which of the following acronyms?
    A. PULL
    B. PASS
    C. PAGE
    D. APES

_____ **10.** The concentration of hazardous material in the air you breathe in your shop must not exceed _____.
    A. The threshold limit value
    B. Ten percent
    C. Shop standards
    D. Fifteen percent

True/False

If you believe the statement to be more true than false, write the letter "T" in the space provided. If you believe the statement to be more false than true, write the letter "F."

_____ **1.** SDS refers to items of safety equipment like safety footwear, gloves, clothing, protective eyewear, and hearing protection.

_____ **2.** There is the possibility of an accident occurring whenever work is undertaken.

_____ **3.** Shop policies and procedures ensure that the shop operates according to OSHA and EPA laws and regulations.

_____ **4.** An OSHA document for the shop that describes how the shop complies with legislation is an example of a procedure.

_____ **5.** There are three standard signal words—danger, warning, and caution.

_____ **6.** Signal words on a warning sign allow the safety message to be conveyed to people who are illiterate or who do not speak the local language.

_____ **7.** Whenever a vehicle's engine is running, toxic gases are emitted from its exhaust.

_____ **8.** An engine fitted with a catalytic converter can be run safely indoors.

_____ **9.** Always keep circuit breaker and electrical panel covers open to provide easy access.

_____ **10.** The danger of a gasoline fire is always present in an automotive shop.

_____ **11.** Fire extinguishers are marked with pictograms depicting the types of fires that the extinguisher is approved to fight.

_____ **12.** Eye wash stations are used to flush the eye with potassium chloride in the event that you get foreign liquid or particles in your eye.

_____ **13.** In the United States it is required that workplaces have an SDS for every chemical that is on site.

_____ **14.** Always use compressed air to blow brake and clutch dust from components and parts before brake service.

_____ **15.** Used oil and fluids will often contain dangerous chemicals and impurities and need to be safely recycled or disposed of in an environmentally friendly way.

Fill in the Blank

Read each item carefully, and then complete the statement by filling in the missing word(s).

1. _____ _____ are a safe way of escaping danger and gathering in a safe place where everyone can be accounted for in the event of an emergency.

2. OSHA stands for the _____ _____ and _____ _____.

3. EPA stands for the _____ _____ _____.

4. It is the _____'s responsibility to know and follow the rules.

5. The signal word _____ indicates a potentially hazardous situation, which, if not avoided, could result in death or serious injury.

6. _____ are used to separate walkways and pedestrian traffic from work areas.

7. _____ _____ is extremely dangerous, as it is odorless and colorless and can build up to toxic levels very quickly in confined spaces.

8. All circuit breakers and fuses should be clearly _____ so you know which circuits and functions they control.

9. Three elements must be present at the same time for a fire to occur: _____, _____, and _____.

10. Class B fire extinguishers are designed for use on flammable liquids or gaseous fuels and are marked with a _____ _____.

11. _____ _____ are designed to smother a small fire and are very useful in putting out a fire on a person.

12. SDS stands for _____ _____ _____.

13. _____ bulbs present an extreme fire hazard if broken in the presence of flammable vapors or liquids.

14. Coming into frequent or prolonged contact with used _____ _____ can cause dermatitis and other skin disorders, including some forms of cancer.

15. Shop _____ _____ are valuable ways of identifying unsafe equipment, materials, or activities so they can be corrected to prevent accidents or injuries.

Labeling

Label the following images with the correct terms.

To operate a fire extinguisher, follow PASS:

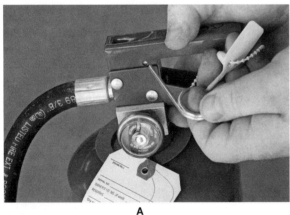

A

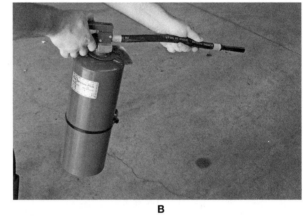

B

C

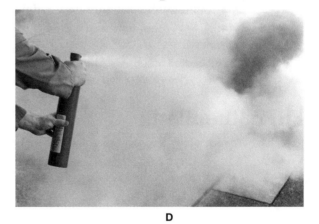

D

A. _____

B. _____

C. _____

D. _____

Skill Drills

Place the skill drill steps in the correct order.

1. Identifying Hazardous Environments:

_____ **A.** Check for air quality. There should be good ventilation and very little chemical fumes or smell. Locate the extractor fans or ventilation outlets, and make sure they are not obstructed in any way. Locate and observe the operation of the exhaust extraction hoses, pump, and outlets that are used on the vehicle's exhaust pipes.

_____ **B.** Familiarize yourself with the shop layout. There are special work areas that are defined by painted lines. These lines show the hazardous zone around certain machines and areas. If you are not working on the machines, you should stay outside the marked area.

_____ **C.** Identify flammable hazards. Find out where flammable materials are kept, and make sure they are stored properly.

_____ **D.** Identify caustic chemicals and acids associated with activities in your shop. Ask your supervisor for information on any special hazards in your particular shop and any special avoidance procedures, which may apply to you and your working environment.

_____ **E.** Check the location and types of fire extinguishers in your shop. Be sure you know when and how to use each type of fire extinguisher.

_____ **F.** Check the hoses and fittings on the air compressor and air guns for any damage or excessive wear.

2. Safely Cleaning Brake Dust:

_____ **A.** When performing any cleaning tasks on brake or clutch components, always wear a face mask, gloves, and eye protection.

_____ **B.** Turn on the wash station pump and paint the solution over the components to wet and clean the components and remove the dust.

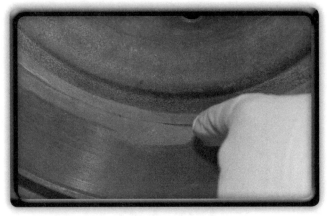

_____ **C.** Position the brake wash station under the bottom of the backing plate. When cleaning brakes, remove the brake drum and check for the presence of dust and brake fluid. When cleaning a clutch, position the wash station underneath the bell housing.

_____ **D.** Periodically dispose of the residue in an approved manner.

Review Questions

_____ **1.** All of the statements below with respect to emergency evacuation are true _except_:
   A. There should be only one clearly identified evacuation route to avoid confusion.
   B. Exits should be highlighted with signs that may be illuminated.
   C. There should be a prearranged safe place for gathering.
   D. Exits should never be chained closed or obstructed.

_____ **2.** Which of the following works toward finding the most effective ways to help prevent worker fatalities and workplace injuries and illnesses?
   A. EPA
   B. FDA
   C. OSHA
   D. ASA

_____ **3.** The list of steps required to get the same result each time a task or activity is performed is known as the:
   A. shop policy.
   B. shop regulations.
   C. shop procedure.
   D. shop system.

_____ **4.** The signal word that indicates a potentially hazardous situation, which, if not avoided, could result in death or serious injury is:
  A. danger.
  B. caution.
  C. warning.
  D. hazardous.

_____ **5.** Shop users other than those operating the welding machine or cutting torch can be protected from welding flash or injury by:
  A. sound insulated rooms.
  B. temporary barriers.
  C. adequate ventilation.
  D. painted lines.

_____ **6.** Which of these should not be used in a shop?
  A. Incandescent bulbs
  B. Extension cords
  C. Low-voltage tools
  D. Air-operated tools

_____ **7.** To operate a fire extinguisher, follow the acronym for fire extinguisher use: PASS, which stands for:
  A. Press, aim, squeeze, sweep.
  B. Pull, aim, shake, sweep.
  C. Press, aim, shake, sweep.
  D. Pull, aim, squeeze, sweep.

_____ **8.** All of the following statements regarding safety data sheets are true *except*:
  A. They should be consulted to learn how to use the product safely.
  B. If you are using more than one product, consult the SDS of only one of the products.
  C. They include information on chemical ingredients.
  D. All new SDS should be in a uniform format.

_____ **9.** Which of these should never be used to remove dust?
  A. Floor scrubbers
  B. Water hoses
  C. Compressed air
  D. Brake wash stations

_____ **10.** When disposing of used liquids:
  A. federal regulations need not be followed.
  B. incompatible liquids can be mixed together.
  C. impervious gloves are not needed.
  D. petroleum products can be mixed together.

ASE Technician A/Technician B Style Questions

_____ **1.** Tech A says that exposure to solvents may have long-term effects. Tech B says that accidents are almost always avoidable. Who is correct?
  A. Tech A
  B. Tech B
  C. Both A and B
  D. Neither A nor B

_____ **2.** Tech A says that after an accident you should take measures to avoid it in the future. Tech B says that it is okay to block an exit for a shop if you are actively working. Who is correct?
  A. Tech A
  B. Tech B
  C. Both A and B
  D. Neither A nor B

_____ **3.** Tech A says that both OSHA and the EPA can inspect facilities for violations. Tech B says that a shop safety rule does not have to be reviewed once put in place. Who is correct?
  A. Tech A
  B. Tech B
  C. Both A and B
  D. Neither A nor B

_____ **4.** Tech A says that all hazards can be removed from a shop. Tech B says that you should disconnect an air gun before inspecting it. Who is correct?
  A. Tech A
  B. Tech B
  C. Both A and B
  D. Neither A nor B

_____ **5.** Tech A says that both caution and danger signs indicate a potentially hazardous situation. Tech B says that an exhaust extraction hose is not needed if the vehicle is only going to run for a few minutes. Who is correct?
  A. Tech A
  B. Tech B
  C. Both A and B
  D. Neither A nor B

_____ **6.** Tech A says that if you are unsure of what personal protective equipment (PPE) to use to perform a job, you should just use what is nearby. Tech B says that air tools are less likely to shock you than electrically powered tools. Who is correct?
  A. Tech A
  B. Tech B
  C. Both A and B
  D. Neither A nor B

_____ **7.** Tech A says that PASS is an acronym used to help remember how to use a fire extinguisher. Tech B says that a class A fire extinguisher can only be used to fight an electrical fire. Who is correct?
  A. Tech A
  B. Tech B
  C. Both A and B
  D. Neither A nor B

_____ **8.** Tech A says that a safety data sheet (SDS) contains information on procedures to repair a vehicle. Tech B says that you only need an SDS after an accident occurs. Who is correct?
  A. Tech A
  B. Tech B
  C. Both A and B
  D. Neither A nor B

_____ **9.** Tech A says that one approved way to clean dust off brakes is with compressed air. Tech B says that some auto parts may contain asbestos. Who is correct?
  A. Tech A
  B. Tech B
  C. Both A and B
  D. Neither A nor B

_____ **10.** Tech A says that when cleaning brake and clutch components, the wash station should be placed directly under the component. Tech B says that you should follow state and local regulations when disposing of used oil. Who is correct?
  A. Tech A
  B. Tech B
  C. Both A and B
  D. Neither A nor B

Personal Safety

At the start of each chapter you'll find the NATEF Tasks, Knowledge Objectives, and Skills Objectives from the textbook. These are your objectives as you make your way through the exercises in this workbook and the chapter in your textbook. The following activities have been designed to help you refresh your knowledge of the material in this chapter.

NATEF Tasks

- N04001 Comply with the required use of safety glasses, ear protection, gloves, and shoes during lab/shop activities.
- N04002 Identify and wear appropriate clothing for lab/shop activities.
- N04003 Secure hair and jewelry for lab/shop activities.
- N04004 Utilize proper ventilation procedures for working within the lab/shop area.

Knowledge Objectives

After reading this chapter, you will be able to:

- K04001 Identify personal protective equipment and how it should be used.
- K04002 Describe the applications for hand protection.
- K04003 Describe the types of ear protection.
- K04004 Describe the types of breathing devices available.
- K04005 Describe the applications of eye protection.
- K04006 Apply injury protection practices.
- K04007 Describe proper lifting techniques.
- K04008 Describe the importance of maintaining a clean and orderly workspace.
- K04009 Explain the procedure when approaching an emergency.
- K04010 Explain the first aid procedures for bleeding, eye injuries, fractures, and burns.

Skills Objectives

There are no Skills Objectives for this chapter.

Matching

Match the following terms with the correct description or example.

A. Barrier cream
B. Complicated fracture
C. Ear protection
D. External bleeding
E. First-degree burns

F. Gas welding goggles
G. Heat buildup
H. Open fracture
I. Second-degree burns
J. Third-degree burns

_____ **1.** Protective gear worn when the sound levels exceed 85 decibels, when working around operating machinery for any period of time, or when the equipment you are using produces loud noise.

_____ **2.** Burns that show reddening of the skin and damage to the outer layer of skin only.

_____ **3.** Protective gear designed for gas welding; they provide protection against foreign particles entering the eye and are tinted to reduce the glare of the welding flame.

_____ **4.** A dangerous condition that occurs when a glove can no longer absorb or reflect heat and heat is transferred to the inside of the glove.

_____ **5.** The loss of blood from an external wound; blood can be seen escaping.

_____ **6.** Burns that involve blistering and damage to the outer layer of skin.

_____ **7.** A cream that looks and feels like a moisturizing cream but has a specific formula to provide extra protection from chemicals and oils.

_____ **8.** A fracture in which the bone is protruding through the skin or there is severe bleeding.

_____ **9.** Burns that involve white or blackened areas and damage to all skin layers and underlying structures and tissues.

_____ **10.** A fracture in which the bone has penetrated a vital organ.

Multiple Choice

Read each item carefully, and then select the best response.

_____ **1.** Proper footwear provides protection against which of the following?
   A. Chemicals
   B. Cuts
   C. Slips
   D. All of the above

_____ **2.** What type of gloves will protect your hands from burns when welding or handling hot components?
   A. Light-duty
   B. Leather
   C. Chemical
   D. General-purpose cloth

_____ **3.** What type of protectant prevents chemicals from being absorbed into your skin and should be applied to your hands before you begin work?
   A. Sunscreen
   B. Moisturizer
   C. Barrier cream
   D. Sanitizer

_____ **4.** What type of gloves should be used to protect your hands from exposure to greases and oils?
   A. Chemical
   B. Light-duty
   C. Leather
   D. General-purpose cloth

_____ **5.** When using a _____ always make sure the cartridge is the correct type for the contaminant in the atmosphere.
   A. dust mask
   B. welding helmet
   C. respirator
   D. all of the above

_____ **6.** The most common type of eye protection is a pair of safety glasses, which must be marked with _____ on the lens and frame.
   A. Z87.1
   B. PPE
   C. UV
   D. Polarized

_____ **7.** What type of protection can be worn instead of a welding mask when using or assisting a person using an oxyacetylene welder?
   A. Respirator
   B. Full face shield
   C. Safety glasses
   D. Gas welding goggles

_____ **8.** Which of the following is an example of a mechanical means of ventilation?
   A. Open door
   B. Exhaust extraction system
   C. Open window
   D. Both A and C

ew Questions

1. Neoprene gloves are ideal for protection from:
  A. dust.
  B. heavy materials.
  C. changing workplace temperatures.
  D. certain acids and other chemicals.

2. All of the following may pose a problem when working on rotating equipment *except*:
  A. gloves.
  B. hats.
  C. watches.
  D. rings.

3. Heat buildup is a factor to be aware of when wearing:
  A. leather gloves.
  B. cloth gloves.
  C. light-duty gloves.
  D. chemical gloves.

4. You can use a disposable dust mask to protect yourself against:
  A. asbestos dust.
  B. shop dust.
  C. chemical vapors.
  D. paint solvents.

5. All of the following statements are true *except*:
  A. When grinding, wear a pair of safety glasses underneath your face shield for added protection.
  B. Never wear tinted safety glasses indoors or in low light conditions.
  C. Wear safety glasses while in a work area only when you are working.
  D. Safety glasses have built-in side shields to help protect your eyes from the side.

6. Carry out housekeeping activities:
  A. only while working.
  B. only after the job is completed.
  C. only at the end of the day.
  D. both while working and after the job is completed.

7. When bending down to lift something, you should:
  A. bend over with straight legs.
  B. put your feet together.
  C. bend your knees.
  D. bend your back.

8. What should you do when an object punctures the victim's skin and becomes embedded in the victim's body?
  A. Apply direct pressure to the wound.
  B. Remove the object immediately.
  C. Start compression-only cycles.
  D. Apply a bulky dressing.

9. If a chemical splashes into the eye:
  A. apply a bulky dressing.
  B. rinse from the ear end of the eye.
  C. flush the eyes with warm water.
  D. do not attempt to remove it.

10. In the case of an open fracture, you may do all of the following *except*:
  A. push any protruding bone back in.
  B. apply ice or a cold pack if possible.
  C. cover the wound and exposed bone with a dressing.
  D. stabilize the injured part with your hands or a splint to prevent movement.

9. Before lifting anything, you can reduce the risk of injury by:
  A. breaking down the load into smaller quantities.
  B. seeking assistance.
  C. using a mechanical device.
  D. All of the above

10. In the event of an accident the first step is to:
  A. remove the injured person.
  B. perform first aid.
  C. survey the scene.
  D. call 9-1-1.

11. In the event of a medical emergency, always have a bystander call _____, unless you are alone.
  A. the fire department
  B. the shop owner
  C. 9-1-1
  D. The shop manager

12. What type of fracture involves bleeding or the protrusion of bone through the skin?
  A. Simple
  B. Open
  C. Complicated
  D. All of the above

13. What type of injury symptoms include pain or tenderness around the area, inability to move the joint, deformity of the joint, and swelling and discoloration over the joint?
  A. Sprain
  B. Strain
  C. Dislocation
  D. Open fracture

14. What type of burns show reddening of the skin and damage to the outer layer of skin only?
  A. First degree
  B. Second degree
  C. Third degree
  D. Fourth degree

15. Burns are caused by:
  A. electricity.
  B. excessive heat.
  C. chemicals.
  D. All of the above

True/False

If you believe the statement to be more true than false, write the letter "T" in the space provided. If you believe the statement to be more false than true, write the letter "F."

1. PPE includes clothing, shoes, safety glasses, hearing protection, masks, and respirators.

2. Leather gloves should always be worn when using solvents and cleaners.

3. Avoid picking up very hot metal with leather gloves because it causes the leather to harden, making it less flexible during use.

4. Light-duty gloves are designed for use in cold temperatures, particularly during winter, so that cold tools do not stick to your skin.

5. If a proper barrier cream is not available, use a standard moisturizer as a suitable replacement.

6. Ear protection that covers the entire outer ear usually has higher noise-reduction ratings than in-the-ear type.

7. A disposable dust mask should not be used if chemicals, such as paint solvents, are present in the atmosphere.

8. When grinding, you should wear a pair of safety glasses underneath your face shield for added protection.

_____ **9.** Tinted safety glasses are not designed to be worn outside in bright sunlight conditions.

_____ **10.** Ultraviolet radiation can burn your skin like a sunburn.

_____ **11.** Safety goggles provide much the same eye protection as safety glasses but with added protection against harmful chemicals that may splash up behind the lenses of glasses.

_____ **12.** Always remove watches, rings, and jewelry before starting work.

_____ **13.** When attending to an injured victim, never send for assistance until after administering CPR.

_____ **14.** If an object punctures the victim's skin and becomes embedded in the victim's body, remove the object and cover with a sterile dressing.

_____ **15.** Burns are classified as either superficial, partial thickness, or full thickness.

Fill in the Blank

Read each item carefully, and then complete the statement by filling in the missing word(s).

1. It is a good idea to keep a spare set of _____ _____ in the workshop in case a toxic or corrosive fluid is spilled on the ones you are wearing.

2. Your _____ _____ can protect you from bumping your head on a vehicle when the vehicle is raised on a hoist.

3. Never use _____ such as gasoline or kerosene to clean your hands.

4. There are two types of breathing devices: disposable _____ _____ and _____.

5. A(n) _____ has removable cartridges that can be changed according to the type of contaminant being filtered.

6. The light from a welding arc is very bright and contains high levels of _____ radiation.

7. It is necessary to use a full _____ _____ when using solvents and cleaners, or when working on a battery.

8. You should always think _____ _____ and then act safely.

9. In high-exposure situations, such as vehicles running in the shop, a mechanical means of _____ is required.

10. Good _____ is about always making sure the shop and your work surroundings are neat and kept in good order.

11. Bleeding is divided into two categories: internal and _____.

12. Symptoms of _____ _____ include bruising, a painful or tender area, coughing frothy blood, and vomiting blood.

13. If a chemical splashes into the eyes, you may be able to flush it out using a(n) _____ _____ _____.

14. Full-thickness burns, or _____-_____ burns, involve white or blackened areas and include damage to all skin layers and underlying structures and tissues.

15. If clothing is burning, have the victim roll on the ground using the _____, _____, and _____ method.

Labeling

Label the following images with the correct terms.

Level of burns:

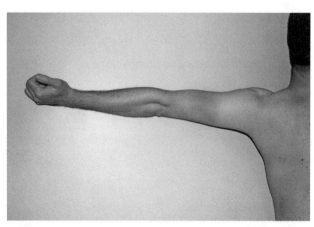

A. _____

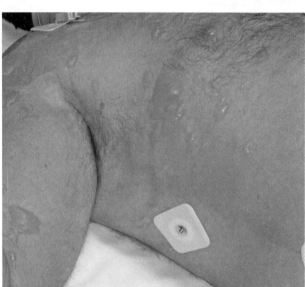

B. _____

© E. M. Singletary, MD. Used with permission.

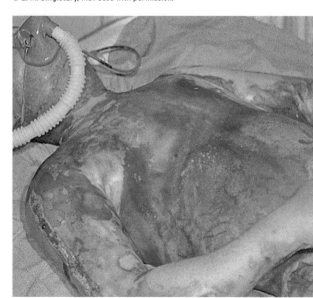

C. _____

Courtsty of AAOS

ASE Technician A/Technician B Style Questions

_____ **1.** Tech A says that personal protective equipment (PPE) does not include clothing. Tech B says that the PPE used should be based on the task you are performing. Who is correct?
   A. Tech A
   B. Tech B
   C. Both A and B
   D. Neither A nor B

_____ **2.** Tech A says that protective clothing that is not in good condition should be replaced. Tech B says that safety glasses are adequate to protect your eyes regardless of the activity. Who is correct?
   A. Tech A
   B. Tech B
   C. Both A and B
   D. Neither A nor B

_____ **3.** Tech A says that rings, watches, and other jewelry should be removed prior to working. Tech B says that you should always wear cuffed pants when working in a shop. Who is correct?
   A. Tech A
   B. Tech B
   C. Both A and B
   D. Neither A nor B

_____ **4.** Tech A says that proper footwear may include both leather and steel-toed shoes. Tech B says that when working in the shop, you only need to wear safety glasses if you are doing something dangerous. Who is correct?
   A. Tech A
   B. Tech B
   C. Both A and B
   D. Neither A nor B

_____ **5.** Tech A says that a hat can help keep your hair clean when working on a vehicle. Tech B says that chemical gloves should be used when working with solvent. Who is correct?
   A. Tech A
   B. Tech B
   C. Both A and B
   D. Neither A nor B

_____ **6.** Tech A says that you only need to worry about external bleeding because internal bleeding doesn't leak out. Tech B says that leather gloves help protect you from hot pieces of metal. Who is correct?
   A. Tech A
   B. Tech B
   C. Both A and B
   D. Neither A nor B

_____ **7.** Tech A says that one use of barrier creams is to make cleaning your hands easier. Tech B says that hearing protection only needs to be worn by people operating loud equipment. Who is correct?
   A. Tech A
   B. Tech B
   C. Both A and B
   D. Neither A nor B

_____ **8.** Tech A says that dust masks should be used when painting. Tech B says that a respirator should be used when the TLV for a chemical is exceeded. Who is correct?
   A. Tech A
   B. Tech B
   C. Both A and B
   D. Neither A nor B

_____ **9.** Tech A says that tinted safety glasses can be worn when working outside. Tech B says that welding can cause a sunburn. Who is correct?
  A. Tech A
  B. Tech B
  C. Both A and B
  D. Neither A nor B

_____ **10.** Tech A says that you should put tools away when done using them. Tech B says that a bystander can perform first aid. Who is correct?
  A. Tech A
  B. Tech B
  C. Both A and B
  D. Neither A nor B

Vehicle Service Information and Diagnostic Process

At the start of each chapter you'll find the NATEF Tasks, Knowledge Objectives, and Skills Objectives from the textbook. These are your objectives as you make your way through the exercises in this workbook and the chapter in your textbook. The following activities have been designed to help you refresh your knowledge of the material in this chapter.

NATEF Tasks

- N05001 Identify information needed and the service requested on a repair order.
- N05002 Complete work order to include customer information, vehicle identifying information, customer concern, related service history, cause, and correction.
- N05003 Review vehicle service history.
- N05004 Demonstrate use of the "3 Cs" (concern, cause, and correction).

Knowledge Objectives

After reading this chapter, you will be able to:

- K05001 Describe the purpose and use of owner's manuals.
- K05002 Describe the purpose and use of shop manuals/service information.
- K05003 Explain how TSBs are used.
- K05004 Explain how service campaigns and recalls are used.
- K05005 Describe the purpose and use of labor guides.
- K05006 Identify the purpose and use of a parts program.
- K05007 Describe the information and its use within a repair/work order.
- K05008 Describe the purpose and use of service history.
- K05009 Explain the purpose and application of VINs.
- K05010 Identify other vehicle information labels.
- K05011 Describe each step in strategy-based diagnosis.
- K05012 Explain how the "3 Cs" are applied in repairing and servicing vehicles.

Skills Objectives

After reading this chapter, you will be able to:

- S05001 Use an owner's manual to obtain vehicle information.
- S05002 Use a shop/repair manual while conducting a service or repair.
- S05003 Use a service information program while conducting a service or repair.
- S05004 Use a labor guide to estimate the cost or charge of conducting a service or repair.
- S05005 Use a parts program to identify and order the correct replacement parts for a service or repair.
- S05006 Use service history in the repair and service of vehicles.
- S05007 Locate the VIN and production date code.
- S05008 Decode a North American VIN.

Matching

Match the following terms with the correct description or example.

A. Belt routing label
B. Lemon law buyback
C. Refrigerant label
D. Service campaign and recall
E. Shop or service manual

F. Technical Service Bulletin (TSB)
G. Vehicle Emission Control Information (VECI) label
H. Title history
I. Vehicle Identification Number (VIN)
J. Vehicle Safety Certification (VSC) label

_____ 1. A detailed account of a vehicle's past.

_____ 2. A label that lists the type and total capacity of refrigerant that is installed in the air conditioning system.

_____ 3. Information issued by manufacturers to alert technicians of unexpected problems or changes to repair procedures.

_____ 4. A label that lists a diagram of the serpentine belt routing for the engine accessories.

_____ 5. A consumer protection law used in some states to identify a new vehicle that has undergone several unsuccessful attempts to repair the same fault.

_____ 6. A unique serial number that is assigned to each vehicle produced.

_____ 7. A label certifying that the vehicle meets the Federal Motor Vehicle Safety, Bumper, and Theft Prevention Standards in effect at the time of manufacture.

_____ 8. A corrective measure conducted by manufacturers when a safety issue is discovered with a particular vehicle.

_____ 9. Manufacturer's or after-market information on the repair and service of vehicles.

_____ 10. A label used by technicians to identify engine and emission control information for the vehicle.

Multiple Choice

Read each item carefully, and then select the best response.

_____ 1. What type of information publication comes in two types—factory and aftermarket?
A. Owner's manual
B. Service manual
C. Technical service bulletin
D. Labor guide

_____ 2. Who pays for the costs associated with a mandatory recall?
A. Consumer
B. Repair shop
C. Manufacturer
D. Insurance company

_____ 3. If a customer wants to know how much it will cost to replace a leaking intake manifold gasket on a particular vehicle, a technician can look up this procedure in the _____ to help estimate the cost.
A. owner's manual
B. labor guide
C. service manual
D. service information program

_____ 4. When determining labor costs, every tenth of an hour equal _____ minutes.
A. 4
B. 5
C. 6
D. 7

_____ 5. Initial information on a(n) _____ includes customer and vehicle details, along with a brief description of the customer's concern(s).
A. repair order
B. service bulletin
C. insurance claim
D. recall notice

_____ **6.** Which of the following is *not* required to determine the total cost of service?
  A. Labor costs
  B. Tax amounts
  C. Cost of gas and consumables used to service the vehicle
  D. Odometer reading

_____ **7.** The _____ can provide potential new owners of used vehicles an indication of how well the vehicle was maintained.
  A. service history
  B. owner's manual
  C. repair order
  D. service manual

_____ **8.** The vehicle identification number is designed for what type of motor vehicle?
  A. Trucks
  B. Motorcycles
  C. Cars
  D. All of the above

_____ **9.** The first character of a North American vehicle identification number indicates?
  A. Manufacturer
  B. Country of origin
  C. Model
  D. Body type

_____ **10.** Which of the 3 Cs stands for understanding the reason that there is a fault?
  A. Connect
  B. Check
  C. Cause
  D. Control

True/False

If you believe the statement to be more true than false, write the letter "T" in the space provided. If you believe the statement to be more false than true, write the letter "F."

_____ **1.** Usually a factory service manual is specific to one year and make of vehicle.

_____ **2.** The information found in shop manuals provides a systematic procedure and identifies special tools, safety precautions, and specifications relevant to the task.

_____ **3.** To use a technical service bulletin, you need to have a basic understanding of how to start and use a computer.

_____ **4.** A typical owner's manual contains step-by-step procedures and diagrams on how to identify if there is a fault and perform an effective repair.

_____ **5.** Online versions of labor guides can be updated as new models of vehicles are released or updates are made by the manufacturer.

_____ **6.** If you are replacing the brake pads on a vehicle with wheel locks, the customer should be charged for the extra time it takes to find the lock key and to remove and install the wheel locks.

_____ **7.** A labor guide is a computer application that is used to identify part numbers for vehicle components.

_____ **8.** Most manufacturers store all service history performed in their dealerships.

_____ **9.** The VIN is a 12-character identification code composed of letters and digits.

_____ **10.** The Vehicle Safety Certification label is used by technicians to identify engine and emission control information for the vehicle.

Fill in the Blank

Read each item carefully, and then complete the statement by filling in the missing word(s).

1. A(n) _____ _____ includes an overview of the controls and features of the vehicle; the proper operation, care, and maintenance of the vehicle; owner service procedures; and specifications or technical data.

2. _____ _____ programs are computer applications used to provide technical information for the repair and maintenance of vehicles.

3. _____ can be mandatory and enforced by law or voluntary in order to ensure the safe operation of the vehicle or damage to their business and product image.

4. When working on vehicles that have not been recalled, check to see if a _____ _____ _____ has been issued for that vehicle and type of repair.

5. _____ _____ software can be installed on the computer, accessed via the Internet using a browser, or run from a CD or DVD.

6. A(n) _____ indicates the customer's understanding of the problem with the vehicle.

7. The _____ section contains information about the methods of payment, which can be cash, credit card, or account.

8. A(n) _____ _____ tells you that the vehicle has been wrecked and suffered irreparable damage.

9. The _____ _____ _____ label certifies that the vehicle meets the Federal Motor Vehicle Safety, Bumper, and Theft Prevention Standards in effect at the time of manufacture.

10. The 3 Cs are an easy way to learn the fundamental steps in conducting repairs. They stand for _____, _____, and _____.

Labeling

Label the following images with the correct terms.

1. VIN standards:

A.

1	2	3	4	5	6	7	8	9	10	11	12	13	14	15	16	17
Manufacturer Identifier			Vehicle Attributes					Check Character	Model Year	Plant Code	Sequential Number					

B.

1	2	3	4	5	6	7	8	9	10	11	12	13	14	15	16	17
World Manufacturer Identifier (WMI)		Vehicle Descriptor System (VDS)						Vehicle Identifier System (VIS)								

A. _____

B. _____

2. Vehicle information labels:

A. _____

B. _____

C. _____

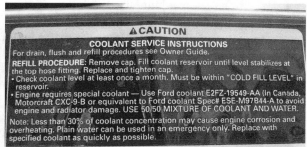

D. _____

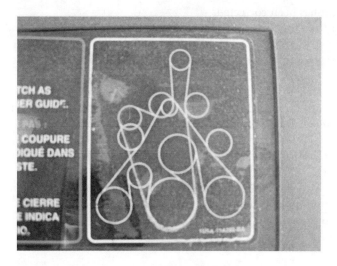

E. _____

Skill Drills

Read each item carefully, and then place each procedure in the correct sequence.

1. Using a Service Information Program:
   _____ **A.** The search engine will provide a list of possible matches for you to select from. If the initial search does not produce what you are looking for, try changing the search criteria. Keep searching until you find the information.
   _____ **B.** Enter the vehicle identification information into the system in the appropriate places: year, make, model, engine, and possibly VIN.
   _____ **C.** Log in to the application using the appropriate username and password.
   _____ **D.** Finally, once the general details for the item are displayed, gather the specific information on the specifications or repairs. You may need more than one piece of information.
   _____ **E.** Search for the information you require to perform the service or repair.
   _____ **F.** If necessary, start the computer and select the service information program.
   _____ **G.** Print out or write down the information needed. Put this on a clipboard and take it with you to perform the service or repair.

2. Using a Labor Guide:
   _____ **A.** Check for any "combination" time that would need to be added to the base job when a related job is also being completed.
   _____ **B.** Find the labor operation either by working your way through the menu tree or by typing a keyword into the search bar.
   _____ **C.** Calculate the total time and multiply it by the shop's hourly labor rate. You now have the correct figure to estimate the charge for the particular service.
   _____ **D.** Once you locate the labor operation, there are usually two columns that list the time. The first one is "warranty time." The second time listed is the "customer pay" time.
   _____ **E.** Decide what specific labor operations you need to locate. Make sure you know the year, make, model, engine, and any other pertinent details of the vehicle.
   _____ **F.** Enter the vehicle information into the system.
   _____ **G.** Check for any "additional" time. This is extra time needed to deal with situations that occur on a relatively common basis, such as vehicle-installed options that are not common to all vehicles, like wheel locks.
   _____ **H.** Log in to the labor estimating system.

3. Applying the 3 Cs:
   _____ **A.** Retest the vehicle to be sure the fault has been corrected.
   _____ **B.** Review the information you collect from the tests. To review effectively, you need to understand how the systems work and interact.
   _____ **C.** Identify and document the correction required, including work activities and parts required or used.
   _____ **D.** Make repairs or replace parts to complete the repair.
   _____ **E.** Identify and document the root cause of the concern. Research service information and perform tests to identify the cause of the problem. This may require a number of tests across multiple systems.
   _____ **F.** Using the 3 Cs, document the repair process required for a repair order.
   _____ **G.** Fill in the required repair order with details of the work conducted.
   _____ **H.** Identify and document the concern. This should be on the repair order. Obtain as much information as possible, as this will help you to understand the problem. Identify what the problem is and which vehicle systems are involved.
   _____ **I.** Always work safely and use the proper tools and correct personal protective equipment (PPE).

Review Questions

_____ 1. Vehicle security PIN codes can typically be found in the:
   A. shop manual.
   B. owner's manual.
   C. technical service bulletin.
   D. after-market manual.

_____ 2. A technical service bulletin may provide information on all of the following _except_:
   A. unexpected problems.
   B. updated parts.
   C. changes to repair procedures.
   D. the scheduled maintenance chart.

_____ 3. Which of these can be used in arriving at flat rate servicing costs?
   A. Service interval recommendations
   B. Shop manuals
   C. Labor guides
   D. Service warranty applications

_____ 4. All of the following statements about a parts program are true _except_:
   A. It can only be accessed by DVD.
   B. It can be used to directly place an order.
   C. It can provide information on the cost of a part.
   D. It provides options for search by multiple criteria.

_____ 5. When a vehicle comes into a shop for repair, detailed information regarding the vehicle should be recorded in the:
   A. service booklet.
   B. repair order.
   C. vehicle information label.
   D. shop manual.

_____ 6. The service history of the vehicle gives information on whether:
   A. the vehicle was serviced for the same problem more than once.
   B. the vehicle is going to break down again.
   C. the vehicle meets federal standards.
   D. the vehicle has Vehicle Safety Certification.

_____ 7. All of the following statements about the VIN are true _except_:
   A. It is a unique serial number.
   B. It deters auto theft.
   C. It helps in accessing title history.
   D. It is made up of 10 characters.

_____ 8. What does the 10th character of a North American VIN denote?
   A. Type of sear restraint
   B. Model year of manufacture
   C. Body type
   D. Name of the manufacturer

_____ 9. The first step in the strategy-based diagnostic process is to:
   A. research possible faults.
   B. verify the customer's concern.
   C. perform focused testing.
   D. verify the repair.

_____ 10. Which of the following is not one of the 3 Cs of vehicle repair?
   A. Cause
   B. Cost
   C. Concern
   D. Correction

ASE Technician A/Technician B Style Questions

_____ **1.** Tech A says that the owner's manual provides engine overhaul procedure information. Tech B says that engine oil capacity information for that specific vehicle is in the owner's manual. Who is correct?
   A. Tech A
   B. Tech B
   C. Both A and B
   D. Neither A nor B

_____ **2.** Tech A says that the cause of the customer concern should be recorded on the repair order. Tech B says that as long as you replace at least one part on a vehicle with a problem, you don't need to verify the repair. Who is correct?
   A. Tech A
   B. Tech B
   C. Both A and B
   D. Neither A nor B

_____ **3.** Tech A says that reviewing service history is an important part of diagnosis. Tech B says that "caution" is one of the 3 Cs. Who is correct?
   A. Tech A
   B. Tech B
   C. Both A and B
   D. Neither A nor B

_____ **4.** Tech A says that service information programs are extremely helpful, as the technician can use a laptop at the vehicle for quick access to repair procedures. Tech B says that a fault from the factory within the airbag system would likely trigger a recall. Who is correct?
   A. Tech A
   B. Tech B
   C. Both A and B
   D. Neither A nor B

_____ **5.** Tech A says that TSBs are typically updates to the owner's manual. Tech B says that TSBs are generally updated information on model changes that do not affect the technician. Who is correct?
   A. Tech A
   B. Tech B
   C. Both A and B
   D. Neither A nor B

_____ **6.** Tech A says that labor guides are used by the service writer to quote prices for a customer. Tech B says that labor guides allow more time for repairs made under warranty. Who is correct?
   A. Tech A
   B. Tech B
   C. Both A and B
   D. Neither A nor B

_____ **7.** Tech A says that strategy-based diagnosis is only used on faults you have never encountered before. Tech B says that a parts person needs to have basic computer operating skills. Who is correct?
   A. Tech A
   B. Tech B
   C. Both A and B
   D. Neither A nor B

_____ **8.** Tech A says that the repair order is just a piece of paper telling the technician what to do. Tech B says that the repair order is a legal and binding contract between the customer and the repair facility. Who is correct?
   A. Tech A
   B. Tech B
   C. Both A and B
   D. Neither A nor B

_____ **9.** Tech A says that customer authorization is again required if the repairs are more than a certain dollar amount or percentage above the original estimate. Tech B says that additional charges can be dealt with after the repair is complete, as the customer will be satisfied because more repairs have been completed. Who is correct?
   A. Tech A
   B. Tech B
   C. Both A and B
   D. Neither A nor B

_____ **10.** Tech A says that the VIN number on a vehicle can help identify which engine is installed in the chassis. Tech B says that the digits in the VIN number can be an identifier for information pertinent to that vehicle. Who is correct?
   A. Tech A
   B. Tech B
   C. Both A and B
   D. Neither A nor B

Tools

At the start of each chapter you'll find the NATEF Tasks, Knowledge Objectives, and Skills Objectives from the textbook. These are your objectives as you make your way through the exercises in this workbook and the chapter in your textbook. The following activities have been designed to help you refresh your knowledge of the material in this chapter.

NATEF Tasks

- N06001 Demonstrate safe handling and use of appropriate tools.
- N06002 Utilize safe procedures for handling of tools and equipment.
- N06003 Identify standard and metric designation.
- N06004 Demonstrate proper use of precision measuring tools (i.e., micrometer, dial-indicator, dial-caliper).
- N06005 Demonstrate proper cleaning, storage, and maintenance of tools and equipment.

Knowledge Objectives

After reading this chapter, you will be able to:

- K06001 Describe the safety procedures to take when handling and using tools.
- K06002 Describe how to properly lockout and tag-out faulty equipment and tools.
- K06003 Describe typical tool storage methods.
- K06004 Identify tools and their usage in automotive applications.
- K06005 Describe the type and use of wrenches.
- K06006 Describe the type and use of sockets.
- K06007 Describe the type and use of torque wrenches.
- K06008 Describe the type and use of pliers.
- K06009 Describe the type and use of cutting tools.
- K06010 Describe the type and use of Allen wrenches.
- K06011 Describe the type and use of screwdrivers.
- K06012 Describe type and use of magnetic pickup tools and mechanical fingers.
- K06013 Describe the type and use of hammers.
- K06014 Describe the type and use of chisels.
- K06015 Describe the type and use of punches.
- K06016 Describe the type and use of pry bars.
- K06017 Describe the type and use of gasket scrapers.
- K06018 Describe the type and use of files.
- K06019 Describe the type and use of clamps.
- K06020 Describe the type and use of taps and dies.
- K06021 Describe the type and use of screw extractors.
- K06022 Describe the type and use of pullers.
- K06023 Describe the type and use of flaring tools.
- K06024 Describe the type and use of riveting tools.
- K06025 Describe the type and use of measuring tapes.
- K06026 Describe the type and use of steel rulers.
- K06027 Describe the type and use of outside, inside, and depth micrometers.
- K06028 Describe the type and use of telescoping gauges.
- K06029 Describe the type and use of split ball gauges.
- K06030 Describe the type and use of dial bore gauges.
- K06031 Describe the type and use of vernier calipers.
- K06032 Describe the type and use of dial indicators.
- K06033 Describe the type and use of straight edges.

- K06034 Describe the type and use of feeler gauges.
- K06035 Describe the importance of proper cleaning and storage of tools.

Skills Objectives

There are no Skills Objectives for this chapter.

Matching

Match the following terms with the correct description or example.

A. Bottoming tap

B. Tube flaring tool

C. Cross-arm

D. Dead blow hammer

E. Dial bore gauge

F. Die stock

G. Rivet tool

H. Intermediate tap

I. Micrometer

J. Parallax error

K. Peening

L. Pullers

M. Measuring tape

N. Split ball gauge

O. Telescoping gauge

P. Dial indicators

Q. Vernier calipers

R. Wad punch

_____ **1.** It is used to flare the end of a tube so it can be connected to another tube or component.

_____ **2.** It is used to join a sheet metal to a stiffening frame.

_____ **3.** An accurate measuring device for inside bores, usually made with a dial indicator attached to it.

_____ **4.** An accurate measuring device for internal, external, and depth measurements that incorporates fixed and adjustable jaws.

_____ **5.** A thread-cutting tap designed to cut threads to the bottom of a blind hole.

_____ **6.** A gauge that expands and locks to the internal diameter of bores; a caliper or outside micrometer is used to measure its size.

_____ **7.** A type of hammer that has a cushioned head to reduce the amount of head bounce.

_____ **8.** An accurate measuring device for internal and external dimensions.

_____ **9.** It is used for measuring longer distances and is accurate to a millimeter or fraction of an inch.

_____ **10.** A description for an arm that is set at right angles or 90 degrees to another component.

_____ **11.** A type of punch that is hollow for cutting circular shapes in soft materials such as gaskets.

_____ **12.** One of a series of taps designed to cut an internal thread. Also called a plug tap.

_____ **13.** A term used to describe the action of flattening a rivet through a hammering action.

_____ **14.** They have a dial and needle where measurements are read, and can be used to measure the trueness of a rotating disc brake rotor.

_____ **15.** A generic term to describe hand tools that mechanically assist the removal of bearings, gears, pulleys, and other parts.

_____ **16.** A handle for securely holding dies to cut threads.

_____ **17.** A measuring device used to accurately measure small holes.

_____ **18.** A visual error caused by viewing measurement markers at an incorrect angle.

Multiple Choice

Read each item carefully, and then select the best response.

_____ **1.** What are straight edges made from?

    A. Hardened steel

    B. Pig iron

    C. Stainless steel

    D. Wrought iron

_____ **2.** Which of the following is a type of fastener?
   A. Bolt
   B. Nut
   C. Stud
   D. All of the above

_____ **3.** In the metric system, which of the following is measured by the distance between the peaks of threads in millimeters?
   A. Thread pitch
   B. Thread file
   C. Torque
   D. Thread count

_____ **4.** What type of wrench is also known as a tension wrench?
   A. Open-end wrench
   B. Ratcheting box-end wrench
   C. Torque wrench
   D. Pipe wrench

_____ **5.** Which of these can a straight edge be used for?
   A. To measure the width of gaps, such as the clearance between valves and rocker arms
   B. To measure the extent of warpage in the surface of a cylinder head
   C. To determine the runout on rotating shafts and surfaces
   D. To measure a bore directly by using telescoping pistons on a T-handle with a dial mounted on the handle

_____ **6.** A(n) _____ is the fastest way to spin a fastener on or off a thread by hand, but it cannot apply much torque to the fastener.
   A. breaker bar
   B. sliding T-handle
   C. speed brace
   D. lug wrench

_____ **7.** What type of plier is used for cutting wire and cotter pins?
   A. Diagonal
   B. Snap ring
   C. Flat-nosed
   D. Needle-nosed

_____ **8.** A screw or bolt with a cross-shaped recess requires a(n)_____.
   A. flat blade screwdriver
   B. offset screwdriver
   C. Phillips head screwdriver
   D. Allen wrench

_____ **9.** What type of screwdriver fits into spaces where a straight screwdriver cannot and is useful where there is not much room to turn it?
   A. Ratcheting screwdriver
   B. Impact driver
   C. Phillips head screwdriver
   D. Offset screwdriver

_____ **10.** What kind of tools are composed of a strong metal and used as a lever to move, adjust, or pry?
   A. Cold chisels
   B. Pry bars
   C. Drift punches
   D. Speed brace

_____ **11.** What type of file is thinner than other files, comes to a point, and is used for working in narrow slots?
   A. Warding file
   B. Triangular file
   C. Thread file
   D. Square file

_____ **12.** What type of file cleans clogged or distorted threads on bolts and studs?
  A. Triangular file
  B. Warding file
  C. Thread file
  D. Square file

_____ **13.** The name for this type of clamp comes from its shape, it can hold parts together while they are being assembled, drilled, or welded.
  A. J-clamp
  B. C-clamp
  C. D-clamp
  D. K-clamp

_____ **14.** What type of tap narrows at the tip to give it a good start in the hole where the thread is to be cut?
  A. Intermediate tap
  B. Taper tap
  C. Plug tap
  D. Bottoming tap

_____ **15.** What type of tool consists of three main parts: jaws, a cross-arm, and a forcing screw?
  A. Tap and die set
  B. Bench vice
  C. Flaring tool
  D. Gear puller

_____ **16.** What tool is used to measure the gap between a straight edge and the surface being checked for flatness?
  A. Steel rule
  B. Caliper
  C. Feeler gauge
  D. Split ball gauge

_____ **17.** Which of the following statement correctly describes a needle nose plier?
  A. It has metal pins that fit in the holes of a snap ring.
  B. It has long, pointed jaws and can reach into tight spots or hold small items that other pliers cannot.
  C. It can clamp a thing and lock it in place to hold it.
  D. It can cut through soft metal objects sticking out from a surface.

_____ **18.** Which driver gives the best grip on a screw or bolt and can easily get into tight spots?
  A. Impact driver
  B. Posidriv screwdriver
  C. Flat blade screwdriver
  D. Allen wrench

_____ **19.** Which hammer is used in conjunction with a chisel to cut off a bolt where corrosion has made it impossible to remove the nut?
  A. Steel hammer
  B. Ball-peen hammer
  C. Soft-faced hammer
  D. Sledgehammer

_____ **20.** Which of these is a special-purpose tool that is often used for moving components into place without damaging the item being moved?
  A. Dead blow hammer
  B. Hard rubber mallet
  C. Ball-peen hammer
  D. Sledgehammer

True/False

If you believe the statement to be more true than false, write the letter "T" in the space provided. If you believe the statement to be more false than true, write the letter "F."

_____ **1.** To identify tools and their usage in automotive applications, create a list of tools in your toolbox and identify their application for automotive repair and service.

_____ **2.** Thread pitch is a way of defining how much a fastener should be tightened.

_____ **3.** An advantage of the box-end wrench is that it can be easily used once the nut or bolt has been loosened a bit.

_____ **4.** Torque wrenches come in various types: beam style, clicker, dial, and electronic.

_____ **5.** The open-end wrench fits fully around the head of the bolt or nut and grips each of the six points at the corners just like a socket.

_____ **6.** Six- and 12-point sockets fit the heads of hexagonal shaped fasteners.

_____ **7.** Arc joint pliers, also called vice grips, are general-purpose pliers used to clamp and hold one or more objects.

_____ **8.** Allen wrenches are sometimes called hex keys.

_____ **9.** When a large chisel needs a really strong blow, it is time to use a dead blow hammer.

_____ **10.** When marks need to be drawn on an object like a steel plate to help locate a hole to be drilled, a drift punch can be used to mark the points so they will not rub off.

_____ **11.** A cold chisel gets its name from the fact it is used to cut cold metals, rather than heated metals.

_____ **12.** A bottoming tap is used when you need to cut threads to the very bottom of a blind hole and in holes that already have threads started that just need to be extended slightly.

_____ **13.** Always use a single flare if the tubing is to be used for higher pressures such as in a brake system.

_____ **14.** A tubing cutter is more convenient and neater than a saw when cutting pipes and metal tubing.

_____ **15.** A flare nut wrench can be easily used on extremely tight fasteners.

_____ **16.** Depth micrometers are used to measure inside dimensions.

_____ **17.** A drawback of the design of a beam-style torque wrench is that one has to be positioned directly above the scale to read it accurately. This can be a problem when working under the hood of a vehicle.

_____ **18.** A drift punch can be used to scribe intersecting lines between given points.

_____ **19.** A gasket scraper should be kept sharp and straight to make it easy to remove all traces of the old gasket and sealing compound.

_____ **20.** One should always inspect tools prior to use, and never use damaged tools.

Fill in the Blank

Read each item carefully, and then complete the statement by filling in the missing word(s).

1. _____ /_____ is an umbrella term that describes a set of safety practices and procedures that are intended to reduce the risk of technicians inadvertently using tools, equipment, or materials that have been determined to be unsafe.

2. There are three commonly used wrenches: the _____, the _____, and the _____.

3. A(n)_____ is a cylindrical piece of metal with a thread on one end and a hexagonal head on the other.

4. A _____ is used for cleaning out or even making key ways.

5. The most common types of punches are the _____, _____, _____, and _____.

6. A(n) _____ wrench has an open-end head on one end and a box-end head on the other end.

7. _____ is a hand tool designed to hold, cut, or compress materials.

8. End cutting pliers, also called _____, have a cutting edge at right angles to their length.

9. A(n) _____ _____ is used when a screw or a bolt is rusted/corroded in place or overtightened and needs a tool that can apply more force.

10. A(n) _____ _____ hammer is designed not to bounce back when it hits something.

11. _____ are used when the head of the hammer is too large to strike the object being hit without causing damage to adjacent parts.

12. A(n) _____ _____ has a hardened, sharpened blade and is designed to remove a gasket without damaging the sealing face of the component.

13. A screw _____ is a device designed to remove screws, studs, or bolts that have broken off in threaded holes.

14. To cut a brand new thread on a blank rod or shaft, a die held in a _____ _____ is used.

15. A measuring _____ is a flexible type of ruler and a common measuring tool.

16. A(n) _____ _____ can measure how round something is.

17. A(n) _____ _____ is used to measure the width of gaps, such as the clearance between valves and rocker arms.

18. The most common hammer in an automotive shop is the _____ _____.

19. _____ and _____ are very useful for grabbing items in tight spaces.

20. A _____ is a special-purpose tool used to install a hubcap.

Labeling

Label the following diagrams with the correct terms.

1. Anatomy of a socket:

A. _____
B. _____
C. _____
D. _____
E. _____
F. _____

2. Components of a flare tool:

A. _____
B. _____
C. _____
D. _____
E. _____
F. _____
G. _____

3. Anatomy of a rivet:

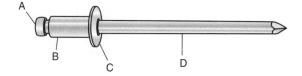

A. _____
B. _____
C. _____
D. _____

Skill Drills

Place the skill drill steps in the correct order.

1. Using Micrometers:

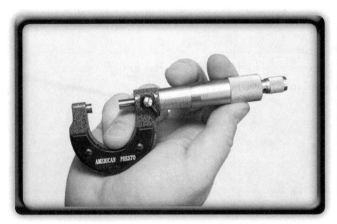

_____ **A.** In your right hand, hold the frame of the micrometer between your pinky, ring finger, and the palm of your hand, with the thimble between your thumb and forefinger.

_____ **B.** With your left hand, hold the part you are measuring, and place the micrometer over it.

_____ **C.** Select the correct size of micrometer. Verify that the anvil and spindle are clean and that it is calibrated properly. Clean the surface of the part you are measuring.

_____ **D.** Using your thumb and forefinger, lightly tighten the ratchet. It is important that the correct amount of force is applied to the spindle when taking a measurement. The spindle and anvil should just touch the component with a slight amount of drag when the micrometer is removed from the measured piece. Be careful that the part is square in the micrometer so the reading is correct. Try rocking the micrometer in all directions to make sure it is square.

2. Safe Procedures for Handling Tools and Equipment:

_____ **A.** Inspect tools and equipment for possible defects before starting work. Report and/or tag faulty tools and equipment according to shop procedures.

_____ **B.** Seek assistance if tools and equipment are too heavy or too awkward to be managed by a single person.

_____ **C.** Select and wear appropriate PPE for the tools and equipment being used.

3. Using Dial Indicators:

_____ **A.** Continue the rotation, making sure the needle does not go below zero. If it does, re-zero the indicator and remeasure the point of maximum variation.

_____ **B.** Rotate the part one complete turn and locate the low spot. Zero the indicator.

_____ **C.** Find the point of maximum height and note the reading. This will indicate the runout value.

_____ **D.** Select the gauge type, size, attachment, and bracket that fit the part you are measuring. Mount the dial indicator firmly to keep it stationary.

_____ **E.** Adjust the indicator so that the plunger is at 90 degrees to the part you are measuring and lock it in place.

Review Questions

_____ **1.** Specialty tools:
   A. should not be shared among technicians.
   B. should have tag-out practices for regular storage.
   C. should be put in the proper storage space after each use.
   D. can be used for purposes they were not designed for.

_____ **2.** A set of safety practices and procedures that are intended to reduce the risk of technicians inadvertently using tools that have been determined to be unsafe is known as:
   A. lockout.
   B. shop policy.
   C. equipment storage procedure.
   D. PPE maintenance.

_____ **3.** Which of these wrenches can be awkward to use once the nut or bolt has been loosened a bit?
   A. Open-end
   B. Flare nut
   C. Combination
   D. Box-end

_____ **4.** Oil filters should be installed using:
   A. an oil filter wrench.
   B. a flare nut wrench.
   C. your hand.
   D. arc joint pliers.

_____ **5.** When tightening lug fasteners, an impact wrench should:
   A. always be used.
   B. never be used.
   C. be used in difficult-to-access positions.
   D. never be used in high-torque settings.

_____ **6.** Which of these would you use for a wider grip and a tighter squeeze on parts too big for conventional pliers?
   A. Diagonal cutting pliers
   B. External snap ring pliers
   C. Arc joint pliers
   D. Combination pliers

_____ **7.** When a large chisel needs a really strong blow, use a:
   A. sledgehammer.
   B. hard rubber mallet.
   C. dead blow hammer.
   D. ball-peen hammer.

_____ **8.** Which style of torque wrench is the simplest and least expensive?
   A. Clicker
   B. Dial
   C. Beam
   D. Electronic

_____ **9.** The depth of blind holes in housings can best be measured using a:
   A. measuring tape.
   B. steel rule.
   C. dial bore gauge.
   D. vernier calipers.

_____ **10.** All of the following are good practices _except_:
   A. replacing cleaning products when they lose their effectiveness.
   B. discarding solvents into the sewage system immediately after use.
   C. using chemical gloves when using any cleaning material.
   D. wearing a respirator when using toxic cleaning chemicals.

ASE Technician A/Technician B Style Questions

_____ **1.** Tech A says that knowing how to use tools correctly creates a safe working environment. Tech B says that a flare nut wrench is used to loosen very tight bolts and nuts. Who is correct?
   A. Tech A
   B. Tech B
   C. Both A and B
   D. Neither A nor B

_____ **2.** Tech A says that lockout is designed to secure a vehicle after all work on it has been completed. Tech B says that tag-out is used when a tool is no longer fit for use and identifies what is wrong with it. Who is correct?
   A. Tech A
   B. Tech B
   C. Both A and B
   D. Neither A nor B

_____ **3.** Tech A says that torque wrenches need to be calibrated periodically to ensure proper torque values. Tech B says that when using a clicker-style torque wrench, keep turning the torque wrench ⅛–¼ turn to make sure the bolt is properly tightened. Who is correct?
   A. Tech A
   B. Tech B
   C. Both A and B
   D. Neither A nor B

_____ **4.** Tech A says that when using a micrometer, a "standard" is used to hold the part you are measuring. Tech B says that the micrometer spindle should be firmly closed against the anvil prior to storage. Who is correct?
   A. Tech A
   B. Tech B
   C. Both A and B
   D. Neither A nor B

_____ **5.** Tech A says that a box-end wrench is more likely to round the head of a bolt than an open-end wrench. Tech B says that 6-point sockets and wrenches will hold more firmly when removing and tightening bolts. Who is correct?
   A. Tech A
   B. Tech B
   C. Both A and B
   D. Neither A nor B

_____ **6.** Tech A says that it is usually better to pull a wrench to tighten or loosen a bolt. Tech B says that pushing a wrench will protect your knuckles if the wrench slips. Who is correct?
   A. Tech A
   B. Tech B
   C. Both A and B
   D. Neither A nor B

_____ **7.** Tech A says that a feeler gauge is used to measure the diameter of small holes. Tech B says that a feeler gauge and straight edge are used to check surfaces for warpage. Who is correct?
   A. Tech A
   B. Tech B
   C. Both A and B
   D. Neither A nor B

_____ **8.** Tech A says that a dead blow hammer reduces rebound of the hammer. Tech B says that a dead blow hammer should be used with a chisel to cut the head of a bolt off. Who is correct?
   A. Tech A
   B. Tech B
   C. Both A and B
   D. Neither A nor B

_____ **9.** Tech A says that gaskets can be removed quickly and safely with a hammer and sharp chisel. Tech B says that extreme care must be used when removing a gasket on an aluminum surface. Who is correct?
   A. Tech A
   B. Tech B
   C. Both A and B
   D. Neither A nor B

_____ **10.** Tech A says that when using a file, apply pressure to file in the direction of the cut and no pressure when pulling the file back. Tech B says that file cards are used to file uneven surfaces. Who is correct?
   A. Tech A
   B. Tech B
   C. Both A and B
   D. Neither A nor B

Power Tools and Equipment

At the start of each chapter you'll find the NATEF Tasks, Knowledge Objectives, and Skills Objectives from the textbook. These are your objectives as you make your way through the exercises in this workbook and the chapter in your textbook. The following activities have been designed to help you refresh your knowledge of the material in this chapter.

NATEF Tasks

There are no NATEF tasks for this chapter.

Knowledge Objectives

After reading this chapter, you will be able to:

- K07001 Explain when and how batteries are charged and jump-started.
- K07002 Identify and describe the main categories of power tools.
- K07003 Identify and describe the use of air tools.
- K07004 Identify and describe the use of electric power tools.
- K07005 Describe the application and use of soldering tools.
- K07006 Identify and describe the use of cleaning tools and equipment.
- K07007 Identify and describe the use of a hydraulic press.
- K07008 Identify and describe the use of welding and cutting equipment.
- K07009 Identify and describe the use of chassis dynamometers.

Skills Objectives

After reading this chapter, you will be able to:

- S07001 Charge a battery.
- S07002 Jump-start a vehicle.
- S07003 Use an air nozzle.
- S07004 Use an air impact wrench.
- S07005 Use an air drill.
- S07006 Use an air hammer.
- S07007 Use a bench grinder.
- S07008 Use an angle grinder.
- S07009 Use soldering tools.
- S07010 Use a pressure washer.
- S07011 Use a spray wash cabinet.
- S07012 Use a solvent tank.
- S07013 Use a brake washer.
- S07014 Use a sand or bead blaster.
- S07015 Purge an oxyacetylene torch.
- S07016 Set up an oxyacetylene torch.
- S07017 Use an oxyacetylene torch for heating.
- S07018 Use a welding tip for welding.
- S07019 Use a welding tip for brazing.
- S07020 Use a cutting torch.
- S07021 Use a plasma cutter.
- S07022 Use a wire feed welder.

Matching

Match the following terms with the correct description or example.

A. Drill press

B. Chassis dynamometer

C. Automatic oilers

D. Morse taper

E. Wire feed welder

F. Cutting torch

G. Oxyacetylene torch

_____ 1. It is designed to regularly oil an air tool or air equipment so it does not have to be done manually before or during its use.

_____ 2. This equipment allows for accurate drilling with more control than is offered by a portable drill, which, although convenient, can be difficult to guide accurately.

_____ 3. It is a system for securing drill bits to drills.

_____ 4. It is used by technicians to cut a wrench to shorten it so it will fit into a tight space.

_____ 5. It is used to heat, braze, weld, and cut metal.

_____ 6. A welding machine that automatically feeds the filler wire by operating a trigger mechanism on a welding gun.

_____ 7. A machine with rollers that allows a vehicle to attain road speed and load while sitting still in the shop.

Multiple Choice

Read each item carefully, and then select the best response.

_____ 1. Which tool uses electricity and compressed gas to produce a stream of high-temperature gas to cut metal?

A. Oxyacetylene torch

B. Plasma cutter

C. Wire feed welder

D. Straight grinder

_____ 2. Which device is used with sensors and test instruments to create simulated load conditions and diagnose any faults while in the shop?

A. Air hammer

B. Cleaning gun

C. Rattle gun

D. Chassis dynamometer

_____ 3. Which of these describes an air drill?

A. A compressed air-powered drill used to drill holes

B. A tool powered by compressed air with various hammer and cutting attachments

C. A compressed air device that emits a fine stream of compressed air for drying or cleaning parts

D. A portable grinder for grinding or cutting metal

_____ 4. Which of the following is a cutting tool?

A. Air hammer

B. Air drier

C. Air nozzle

D. Air ratchet

_____ 5. Which process uses a charged battery from a vehicle to provide electrical energy to start another vehicle that has a discharged or dead battery?

A. Jump starting

B. Charging

C. Discharging

D. Recharging

_____ 6. Which of the following correctly describes the function of an air drier?

A. It can drill holes, grind, polish, and clean parts.

B. It is fitted to compressed air systems to remove the moisture or water from the compressed air that is a result of compressing air from the atmosphere, which contains water in the form of humidity.

     C. It is used for blowing dirt and debris out of holes, for example, around spark plugs prior to removing them.

     D. It is used to control the flow of compressed air.

_____ **7.** Which correctly describes the function of a solvent tank?

     A. They are cleaning tanks filled with a suitable solvent to clean parts by removing oil, grease, dirt, and grime.

     B. They wash brake dust from wheel brake units and their components.

     C. They spray low-temperature, low-pressure cleaning solutions onto parts inside a sealed cabinet.

     D. They spray high-temperature, high-pressure cleaning solutions onto parts inside a sealed cabinet.

_____ **8.** Which tool is used for heating to remove a ring gear from a flywheel?

     A. Drill chuck

     B. Fire feed welder

     C. Oxyacetylene torch

     D. Cleaning gun

_____ **9.** A sand blaster is used to_____.

     A. clean paint, corrosion, or dirt from metal parts

     B. clean greasy residue from brake units

     C. wash brake dust from wheel brake units

     D. to clean parts inside a sealed cabinet

_____ **10.** Which tool is used to press off an axle bearing using several tons of force?

     A. Hydraulic press

     B. Flashback arrestors

     C. Blowgun

     D. None of the above

True/False

If you believe the statement to be more true than false, write the letter "T" in the space provided. If you believe the statement to be more false than true, write the letter "F."

_____ **1.** When charging a battery, fast charging a battery is less stressful on the battery than slow charging.

_____ **2.** An air ratchet works well where there isn't much room to swing a ratchet handle.

_____ **3.** Air hammers have a similar cycling rate as a jackhammer.

_____ **4.** A drill press allows for accurate drilling with more control than is offered by a portable drill.

_____ **5.** Soapy water is a good cleaning agent for most brake components.

Fill in the Blank

Read each item carefully, and then complete the statement by filling in the missing word(s).

1. _____ are very useful for tuning engines.

2. Heating using an oxyacetylene torch is used to loosen rusted _____ to help remove them.

3. _____ are automated and act like a dishwasher for parts.

4. As air drills are powered by air and not electricity, they are safer to use in an environment where _____ are present.

5. A _____ is used to take the wheels off a car to replace the tire.

6. Smart chargers incorporate _____ to monitor and control the charge rate, so the battery receives the correct amount of charge depending on its state of charge.

7. A _____ provides backup power to retain electronic memory settings in the vehicle's computer systems.

8. A _____ has a high-pressure nozzle that focuses high-pressure water (possibly over 2000 psi [13,790 kPa]) to quickly clean accumulated dirt and grease from components.

9. _____ is a mixture of metals with low melting points that is used to join metals together.

10. A _____ is a spring-loaded valve installed on oxyacetylene torches as a safety device to prevent flame from entering the torch hoses.

Labeling

Label the following images with the correct terms.

   1. Types of Air Driers:

A. _____

B. _____

   2. Types of Air Tools:

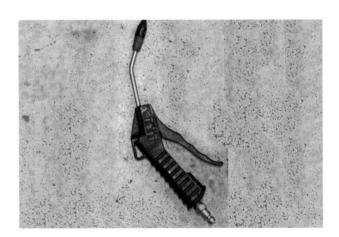

A. _____

B. _____

Skill Drills

Place the skill drill steps in the correct order.

1. Using Air Nozzles:

_____ **A.** The air nozzle is used to blast dirt and debris out of confined spaces. To avoid injury, be sure to wear eye and ear protection whenever you use the air nozzle.

_____ **B.** Do *not* use the air nozzle to dust yourself off because you risk injury. Be sure to direct the air jet away from yourself and away from anyone else who may be working nearby.

_____ **C.** Fit an OSHA-approved air nozzle to the end of the air hose. Make sure there are no air leaks.

2. Using Air Impact Wrenches:

_____ **A.** Continue to remove or install the fastener by squeezing the trigger only long enough to get the job done. Release the trigger before getting to the end as it takes time for the impact wrench to slow down; otherwise the nut could fly off the end of the stud, or if tightening, you could end up over tightening.

_____ **B.** Select the properly sized impact gun and socket, and inspect them for damage.

_____ **C.** Adjust the direction of spin—forward or backward—with the selector.

_____ **D.** Place the impact wrench fully over the bolt or nut and give the trigger a quick squeeze to verify that the impact wrench is turning the correct direction.

_____ **E.** Turn the valve to increase or reduce the torque to match the needs of the fastener. If removing lug nuts, adjust it toward the upper middle torque setting. If running a nut back on a stud, adjust it toward the lowest torque setting. You can always readjust it if you end up needing more torque.

_____ **F.** Lubricate the gun if an automatic oiler is not installed in the system.

3. Using Air Drills:

_____ **A.** Select the properly sized air drill and drill bit, inspect them for damage, and lubricate the gun if an automatic oiler is not installed in the system.

_____ **B.** Continue to operate the air drill by squeezing the trigger only long enough to get the job done.

_____ **C.** Turn the valve to increase or reduce the torque to match the needs of the job. **(There is no image associated with this step.)**

_____ **D.** Adjust the direction of spin—forward or backward—with the selector.

_____ **E.** Place the air drill into position and hold it firmly. Give the trigger a quick squeeze to verify that the air drill is turning the correct direction and does not slip. **(There is no image associated with this step.)**

Review Questions

_____ **1.** All of the following statements with respect to jump-starting are true *except*:
  A. Charge the dead vehicle 5 to 10 minutes before trying to start the vehicle.
  B. Jumper leads with surge protectors reduce the risk of damage to sensitive electronic devices.
  C. Read the owner's manual for both vehicles before jump-starting.
  D. Always use a fully charged battery to jump-start a frozen battery.

_____ **2.** Which of these is true of an air impact wrench?
  A. It always spins in the clockwise direction.
  B. It can apply only minimal torque.
  C. It should never be used for final tightening of lug nuts.
  D. It does not need special hardened impact sockets.

_____ **3.** Which of these is used for driving and cutting?
   A. Air hammer
   B. Air ratchet
   C. Air nozzle
   D. Air drill

_____ **4.** When grinding metal using a bench grinder:
   A. stop and dip it regularly into the water pot.
   B. do not leave a gap between the tool rest and wheel.
   C. stand off to the side of the wheel.
   D. grind on the side of the wheel.

_____ **5.** When soldering non-electrical connections, what should be used as the flux-cleaning agent?
   A. Rosin
   B. Water
   C. Acid
   D. Gasoline

_____ **6.** Which of these is true of a spray wash cabinet?
   A. It removes paint under high pressure.
   B. It increases the frequency of cleaning solution changes.
   C. It does not leavy dirty residue on parts.
   D. It does not produce harmful waste.

_____ **7.** All of the following are good practices when operating a hydraulic press *except*:
   A. remove guards around the press for smooth operation.
   B. wear thick clothing or a snug-fitting leather apron.
   C. only use approved press plates and adapters.
   D. never wear loose clothing.

_____ **8.** Which of these is a good choice as a cleaning agent for brake components?
   A. Kerosene
   B. Soapy water
   C. Plain water
   D. Solvent

_____ **9.** The advantage of using rose bud tips is that they:
   A. are best used on small heating jobs.
   B. are efficient under low pressure.
   C. can weld thicker materials.
   D. lower the chance of flashback.

_____ **10.** Chassis dynamometers are very useful for:
   A. grinding down metals.
   B. cleaning accumulated dirt.
   C. testing vehicle performance.
   D. driving a drill bit.

ASE Technician A/Technician B Style Questions

_____ **1.** Tech A says that it is safe to use an air nozzle to blow dust off you or your coworker. Tech B says that OSHA-approved nozzles lower the tip pressure by venting some of the air for safety reasons. Who is correct?
   A. Tech A
   B. Tech B
   C. Both A and B
   D. Neither A nor B

_____ **2.** Tech A says that you should always wear ear protection when using an air hammer. Tech B says that standard wall sockets can be safely used with impact wrenches. Who is correct?
   A. Tech A
   B. Tech B
   C. Both A and B
   D. Neither A nor B

_____ **3.** Tech A says that when soldering electrical wires, rosin flux must be used. Tech B says that a heat dam is used to prevent heat from traveling to the electronic component when you are soldering. Who is correct?
  A. Tech A
  B. Tech B
  C. Both A and B
  D. Neither A nor B

_____ **4.** Tech A says that air tools and equipment require a regular application of a lubricating oil to reduce wear and tear. Tech B says that some compressed air systems use an inline water trap that needs to be drained periodically. Who is correct?
  A. Tech A
  B. Tech B
  C. Both A and B
  D. Neither A nor B

_____ **5.** Tech A says that one of the first things to do when purging an acetylene torch is to turn off the valves on both bottles. Tech B says that when setting the line pressures on an acetylene torch, the acetylene should always be adjusted so it is above 15 psi (103.42 kPa). Who is correct?
  A. Tech A
  B. Tech B
  C. Both A and B
  D. Neither A nor B

_____ **6.** Tech A says that when using a bench grinder, the tool rest should be no more than 1/8" (3.2 mm) or half the thickness of the metal you are grinding, away from the grinding wheel. Tech B says that when using a bench grinder, the piece you are grinding needs to be cooled periodically. Who is correct?
  A. Tech A
  B. Tech B
  C. Both A and B
  D. Neither A nor B

_____ **7.** Tech A says that when you jump-start a vehicle, a spark typically occurs when making the last jumper cable connection. Tech B says that all four of the jumper cable connections should be made at the battery terminals. Who is correct?
  A. Tech A
  B. Tech B
  C. Both A and B
  D. Neither A nor B

_____ **8.** Tech A says that an air nozzle can be used to safely blow brake dust from brake parts. Tech B says that brake wash stations use strong acid as a cleaning solution. Who is correct?
  A. Tech A
  B. Tech B
  C. Both A and B
  D. Neither A nor B

_____ **9.** Tech A says that gaskets can be removed quickly and safely with a portable grinder and high-speed grinding stone. Tech B says that extreme care must be used when removing a gasket on an aluminum surface. Who is correct?
  A. Tech A
  B. Tech B
  C. Both A and B
  D. Neither A nor B

_____ **10.** Tech A says that a wire feed welder is used to braze components together. Tech B says that sunglasses should be used when watching someone weld with a wire feed welder. Who is correct?
  A. Tech A
  B. Tech B
  C. Both A and B
  D. Neither A nor B

Fasteners and Thread Repair

At the start of each chapter you'll find the NATEF Tasks, Knowledge Objectives, and Skills Objectives from the textbook. These are your objectives as you make your way through the exercises in this workbook and the chapter in your textbook. The following activities have been designed to help you refresh your knowledge of the material in this chapter.

NATEF Tasks

- N08001 Perform common fastener and thread repair, to include: remove broken bolt, restore internal and external threads, and repair internal threads with thread insert.

Knowledge Objectives

After reading this chapter, you will be able to:

- K08001 Identify threaded fasteners and describe their use.
- K08002 Identify standard and metric fasteners.
- K08003 Describe how bolts are sized.
- K08004 Describe thread pitch and how it is measured.
- K08005 Describe bolt grade.
- K08006 Describe the types of bolt strength required.
- K08007 Describe nuts and their application.
- K08008 Describe washers and their applications.
- K08009 Describe the purpose and application of thread-locking compounds.
- K08010 Describe screws and their applications.
- K08011 Describe the torque-to-yield and torque angle.
- K08012 Describe how to avoid broken fasteners.
- K08013 Identify situations where thread repair is necessary.

Skills Objectives

- S08001 Perform common fastener and thread repair.

Matching

Match the following terms with the correct description or example.

A. Thread pitch
B. Threaded fasteners
C. Tensile strength
D. Millimeters
E. Proof load
F. 12.9
G. Metric fasteners

_____ 1. Fasteners that are primarily designed to clamp objects together.
_____ 2. Fasteners that can be identified by the grade number cast into the head of the bolt.
_____ 3. The coarseness of any thread.
_____ 4. Unit of measure of the thread pitch in the metric system.
_____ 5. The strongest grade in metric bolt grades.

_____ **6.** The maximum tension that the fastener can withstand without being torn apart or the maximum stress used under tension (lengthwise force) without causing failure.

_____ **7.** An applied tensile load that the fastener must support without exceeding the elastic phase, which is the point up to which the bolt returns to its original point when tension is removed.

Multiple Choice

Read each item carefully, and then select the best response.

_____ **1.** Which fastener must withstand sheer stresses?
  A. Wheel lug
  B. Bolt
  C. Rivet
  D. Roll pin

_____ **2.** What does a ½" bolt size mean?
  A. The bolt has a head that fits into a ½" socket.
  B. The diameter of the bolt head is ½ millimeter.
  C. The distance across the outside diameter of the bolt's threads measures ½" in diameter.
  D. The length of the bolt from the end of the bolt to the bottom of the head is ½ millimeter.

_____ **3.** What is the measure of a material's ability to withstand a twisting load, usually expressed in terms of torque, in which the fastener fails by being twisted off about its axis?
  A. Toughness
  B. Fatigue strength
  C. Proof load
  D. Torsional strength

_____ **4.** The ability of a material to deform before it fractures is known as _____.
  A. ductility
  B. toughness
  C. torsional strength
  D. fatigue strength

_____ **5.** A material's ability to absorb impact or shock loading is known as _____.
  A. proof load
  B. toughness
  C. ductility
  D. fatigue strength

_____ **6.** Which type of washer is a piece of steel cut in a circular shape with a hole in the middle for the bolt or stud to fit through?
  A. Flat washer
  B. Lock washer
  C. Star washer
  D. Fender washer

_____ **7.** Which type of washer is used sometimes to stop the rotation of the nut above?
  A. Star washer
  B. Lock washer
  C. Flat washer
  D. Fender washer

_____ **8.** Which liquid is put on the threads of a bolt or stud to hold the nut that is threaded over it?
  A. Antiseize compound
  B. Thread-locking compound
  C. Gorilla glue
  D. Loctite glue

_____ **9.** Which of these is a way to avoid a broken bolt?
  A. Use an antiseize compound
  B. Fasten it counterclockwise
  C. Use penetrating oil
  D. Apply thread-locking compound

_____ **10.** Which is the most precise method to tighten TTY bolts and is essentially a multistep process?
    A. Torque-to-yield
    B. Torque angle
    C. Torque
    D. None of the above

True/False

If you believe the statement to be more true than false, write the letter "T" in the space provided. If you believe the statement to be more false than true, write the letter "F."

_____ **1.** Thread repair is used in situations where it is possible to replace a damaged thread.

_____ **2.** Rusted fasteners are a cause of broken bolts.

_____ **3.** Self-tapping screws are used in applications where there is a need to hold plastic and metal ornamentation to the vehicle.

_____ **4.** Antiseize compounds keep threaded fasteners from becoming corroded together or seized due to galling.

_____ **5.** Flat washers are used with conventional nuts and in applications that create a lot of vibration.

_____ **6.** Higher grade bolts can be used in all applications.

_____ **7.** Torque is the best method to ensure that a bolt is tightened enough as to give the proper amount of clamping force.

_____ **8.** Locking nuts are used when there is a chance of the nut vibrating loose.

_____ **9.** Generally, the higher the grade of the bolt, the higher is the shear strength.

_____ **10.** Trim screws are used to attach things to sheet metal.

Fill in the Blank

Read each item carefully, and then complete the statement by filling in the missing word(s).

1. A _____ is used to fasten components together, but these are usually driven by a screwdriver with a Philips or slotted head.

2. _____ means that a fastener is torqued to, or just beyond, its yield point.

3. If the fastener doesn't loosen after applying penetrating oil, you may need to _____ the component to help break up the rust or corrosion.

4. The _____ of a bolt is measured from the end of the bolt to the bottom of the head.

5. Metric bolt grades are typically grade _____ to grade _____.

6. _____ is the maximum load that can be supported prior to fracture, when applied at a right angle to the fastener's axis.

7. _____ are used with a cotter pin to keep them from moving once they are installed.

8. The aim of _____ is to restore the thread to a condition that restores the fastening integrity.

9. _____ are used to hold door panels, trim pieces, and other small components to the vehicle.

10. A _____ withstands tension stresses by clamping the head gasket between the cylinder head and block so that combustion pressures can be contained in the cylinder.

Labeling

Label the following diagrams with the correct terms.

Types of lock nuts:

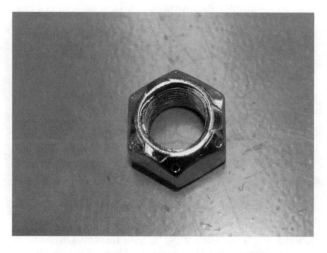

A. _____

B. _____

Skill Drills

Place the skill drill steps in the correct order.

1. Using a Torque Angle Gauge with a Torque Wrench:

_____ **A.** Tighten the bolt to the specified torque. If the component requires multiple bolts or fasteners, make sure to tighten them all to the same torque value in the sequence and steps that are specified by the manufacturer.

_____ **C.** Install the torque angle gauge over the head of the bolt, and then put the torque wrench on top of the gauge and zero it, if necessary.

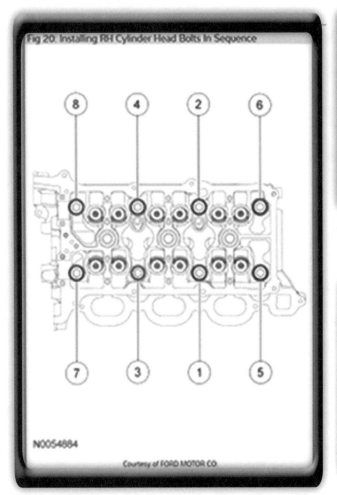

Fig 20: Installing RH Cylinder Head Bolts In Sequence

N0054884

Courtesy of FORD MOTOR CO.

_____ **D.** Turn the torque wrench the specified number of degrees indicated on the angle gauge.

_____ **B.** Check the specifications. Determine the correct torque value (ft-lb or N·m) and sequence for the bolts or fasteners you are using. Also, check the torque angle specifications for the bolt or fastener, and whether it involves one step or more than one step.

_____ **E.** If the component requires multiple bolts or fasteners, make sure to tighten them all to the same torque angle in the sequence that is specified by the manufacturer. Some torquing procedures could call for four or more steps to complete the torquing process properly.

2. Conducting Thread Repair:

_____ **A.** Inspect the condition of the threads, and determine the repair method.

_____ **B.** Determine the type and size of the thread to be repaired. Thread pitch gauges and vernier calipers may be used to measure the thread.

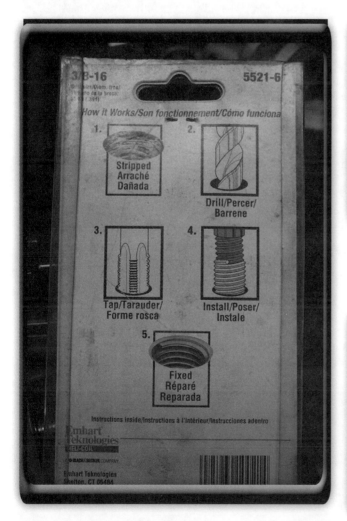

_____ **C.** Always refer to the manufacturer's manual for specific operating instructions.

_____ **D.** Prepare materials for conducting the repair: dies and taps or a drill bit and drill; cutting oil, if required; and inserts.

_____ **E.** Select the correctly sized tap or die if conducting a minor repair. Run the die or tap through or over the thread; be sure to use cutting lubricant.

Review Questions

_____ 1. Which of these are threaded fasteners?
    A. C-clips
    B. Trim screws
    C. Cotter pins
    D. Solid rivets

_____ 2. All of the following statements are true _except_:
    A. Metric bolts can be identified by the grade number on the top of the bolt heads.
    B. Measuring units of standard bolts use a fractional number–based system.
    C. Standard bolts can be identified by the hash marks on the top of the bolt heads.
    D. Measuring units of metric bolts use a roman number–based system.

_____ 3. In an 8 mm bolt, 8 mm refers to the:
    A. length of the bolt.
    B. size of the bolt head.
    C. threads' outer diameter.
    D. number of threads per inch.

_____ 4. The easiest way to identify the TPI is to:
    A. use a vernier caliper.
    B. count the number of threads.
    C. measure distance from peak to peak.
    D. use a thread pitch gauge.

_____ 5. A bolt has 3 hash marks on its head. What is its grade?
    A. 2
    B. 5
    C. 6
    D. 8

_____ 6. Which nut is made with a deformed top thread?
    A. Lock nut
    B. J nut
    C. Castle nut
    D. Specialty nut

_____ 7. When you want a nut or bolt to hold tight such that it needs heat to be removed with a socket and ratchet, you should use a(n):
    A. lubricant.
    B. blue thread-locking compound.
    C. antiseize compound.
    D. red thread-locking compound.

_____ 8. Which of these has a fluted tip to drill a hole into the base material so that there is no need for a pilot hole?
    A. Machine screw
    B. Self-tapping screw
    C. Trim screw
    D. Sheet metal screw

_____ 9. Torque-to-yield bolts:
    A. should be tightened using torque angle.
    B. can be reused multiple times.
    C. cannot be torqued beyond the elastic phase.
    D. do not get stretched.

_____ 10. All of the following are ways to avoid breaking a bolt when removing it _except_:
    A. using penetrating oil with bolts that are rusted or corroded in place.
    B. applying maximum force in both directions.
    C. first checking whether it is a left-hand bolt.
    D. as a last resort, you may heat up the bolt that is rusted or corroded in place.

ASE Technician A/Technician B Style Questions

_____ 1. Tech A says that most metric fasteners can be identified by the grade number cast into the head of the bolt. Tech B says that standard bolts can generally be identified by hash marks cast into the head of the bolt indicating the bolt's grade. Who is correct?
   A. Tech A
   B. Tech B
   C. Both A and B
   D. Neither A nor B

_____ 2. Two technicians are discussing bolt sizes. Tech A says that the diameter of a bolt is measured across the flats on the head. Tech B says that the length of a bolt is measured from the top of the head to the bottom of the bolt. Who is correct?
   A. Tech A
   B. Tech B
   C. Both A and B
   D. Neither A nor B

_____ 3. Tech A says that a standard grade 5 bolt is stronger than a standard grade 8 bolt. Tech B says that a metric grade 12.9 bolt is stronger than a metric grade 4.6 bolt. Who is correct?
   A. Tech A
   B. Tech B
   C. Both A and B
   D. Neither A nor B

_____ 4. Tech A says that torque-to-yield head bolts are tightened to, or just past, their yield point. Tech B says that the yield point is the torque at which the bolt breaks. Who is correct?
   A. Tech A
   B. Tech B
   C. Both A and B
   D. Neither A nor B

_____ 5. Tech A says that some locking nuts have a nylon insert that has a smaller diameter hole than the threads in the nut. Tech B says that castle nuts are used with cotter pins to prevent the nut from loosening. Who is correct?
   A. Tech A
   B. Tech B
   C. Both A and B
   D. Neither A nor B

_____ 6. Tech A says that antiseize compound is a type of thread-locking compound. Tech B says that thread-locking compounds acts like very strong glue. Who is correct?
   A. Tech A
   B. Tech B
   C. Both A and B
   D. Neither A nor B

_____ 7. Tech A says that flat washers act as a bearing surface, making it so that the bolt achieves the expected clamping force at the specified torque. Tech B says that lock washers are usually considered single use and should be replaced rather than reused. Who is correct?
   A. Tech A
   B. Tech B
   C. Both A and B
   D. Neither A nor B

_____ 8. Tech A says that a common method for repairing damaged internal threads is a thread insert. Tech B says that a thread file is used to repair the threads on the inside of a bolt hole. Who is correct?
   A. Tech A
   B. Tech B
   C. Both A and B
   D. Neither A nor B

_____ **9.** Tech A says that if a bolt breaks off above the surface, you might be able to remove it using locking pliers or curved jaw Channellock pliers. Tech B says that a hammer and punch can sometimes be used to remove a broken bolt. Who is correct?
   A. Tech A
   B. Tech B
   C. Both A and B
   D. Neither A nor B

_____ **10.** Tech A says that when using a Heli-Coil to repair a damaged thread, the Heli-Coil is welded into the bolt hole. Tech B says that when using a solid sleeve type of insert, the damaged threads need to be drilled out with the correct size drill bit. Who is correct?
   A. Tech A
   B. Tech B
   C. Both A and B
   D. Neither A nor B

Vehicle Protection and Jack and Lift Safety

At the start of each chapter you'll find the NATEF Tasks, Knowledge Objectives, and Skills Objectives from the textbook. These are your objectives as you make your way through the exercises in this workbook and the chapter in your textbook. The following activities have been designed to help you refresh your knowledge of the material in this chapter.

NATEF Tasks

- N09001 Identify purpose and demonstrate proper use of fender covers, mats.
- N09002 Identify and use proper placement of floor jacks and jack stands.
- N09003 Identify and use proper procedures for safe lift operation.
- N09004 Ensure vehicle is prepared to return to customer per school/company policy (floor mats, steering wheel cover, etc.).

Knowledge Objectives

After reading this chapter, you will be able to:

- K09001 Explain the precautions and procedures to prevent vehicle damage while conducting repairs.
- K09002 Describe ways that vehicles can be damaged during service and their prevention.
- K09003 Describe the application, purpose, and safe use of lifting equipment.
- K09004 Describe the purpose and use of jacks and stands.
- K09005 Describe the purpose and use of vehicle hoists.
- K09006 Describe the purpose and use of vehicle inspection pits.
- K09007 Explain how to prepare a vehicle for customer pickup.

Skills Objectives

After reading this chapter, you will be able to:

- S09001 Use fender, seat, floor, and steering wheel covers.
- S09002 Lift and secure a vehicle with a floor jack and jack stands.
- S09003 Lift a vehicle using a two-post hoist.
- S09004 Lift a vehicle using a four-post hoist.
- S09005 Use an engine hoist to lift an engine.
- S09006 Use a vehicle inspection pit.
- S09007 Prepare a vehicle for customer pickup.

Matching

Match the following terms with the correct description or example.

A. Four-post hoist	**E.** Single-post hoist
B. Hydraulic jack	**F.** Two-post hoist
C. Pneumatic jack	**G.** Vehicle inspection pit
D. Safe working load	

_____ **1.** A type of vehicle jack that uses compressed gas or air to lift a vehicle.

_____ **2.** A type of vehicle jack that uses oil under pressure to lift vehicles.

_____ **3.** A trench permanently fitted into the floor of the shop to allow easy work access to the vehicle's underside.

_____ **4.** The maximum safe lifting load for lifting equipment.

_____ **5.** A type of vehicle hoist that uses two parts (one on each side of vehicle) and four arms to lift the vehicle.

_____ **6.** A type of vehicle hoist that uses a single central platform to lift a vehicle.

_____ **7.** A type of hoist onto which a vehicle is driven, that uses two long, narrow platforms to lift the vehicle.

Multiple Choice

Read each item carefully, and then select the best response.

_____ **1.** It is good practice for the service advisor to perform a(n) _____ with the customer to point out any existing damage or missing components on the vehicle.
- **A.** detailed inspection
- **B.** vehicle walk-around
- **C.** audit
- **D.** performance analysis

_____ **2.** Battery electrolyte contains acid, which can be cleaned up by neutralizing it with which of the following materials?
- **A.** An alkaline
- **B.** Engine oil
- **C.** Gasoline
- **D.** Water

_____ **3.** There are three main types of mechanisms that provide the lifting action for vehicle jacks including all of the following, _except_:
- **A.** Hydraulic
- **B.** Pneumatic
- **C.** Electric
- **D.** Mechanical

_____ **4.** What type of jack is mounted on four wheels, two of which swivel to provide a steering mechanism?
- **A.** Bottle jack
- **B.** Sliding bridge jack
- **C.** Floor jack
- **D.** Scissor jack

_____ **5.** Often used on farms, what type of jack is designed to lift, winch, clamp, pull, and push?
- **A.** High-lift jack
- **B.** Scissor jack
- **C.** Sliding bridge jack
- **D.** Bottle jack

_____ **6.** What type of jack uses compressed air to either operate a large ram or inflate an expandable air bag to lift the vehicle?
- **A.** Bottle jack
- **B.** Air jack
- **C.** High-lift jack
- **D.** Floor jack

_____ **7.** Which lifting device is useful for raising a vehicle to a height that removes the need for the technician to bend down?
- **A.** Engine hoist
- **B.** Jack stand
- **C.** Farm jack
- **D.** Vehicle hoist

_____ **8.** What type of hoist comes in two configurations—symmetrical and asymmetrical?
- **A.** Four-post hoist
- **B.** Two-post hoists
- **C.** Farm hoist
- **D.** Single-post hoists

_____ **9.** The engine or component to be lifted is attached to the lifting arm of an engine hoist by which of the following?
- **A.** Sling
- **B.** Rope

       C. Lifting chain

       D. Either A or C

_____ **10.** The size of the vehicle jack you use will be determined by:

       A. the length of the axles.

       B. the length of the vehicle.

       C. the weight of the vehicle.

       D. the type of vehicle.

True/False

If you believe the statement to be more true than false, write the letter "T" in the space provided. If you believe the statement to be more false than true, write the letter "F."

_____ **1.** Customers expect their vehicles to be treated with care and respect while in your shop.

_____ **2.** Fender, carpet, seat, and steering wheel covers should be the first thing on and the last thing removed when working on vehicles.

_____ **3.** Never place tools in your back pocket.

_____ **4.** Only the most skilled and experienced drivers available should be allowed to test-drive higher performance vehicles.

_____ **5.** When multiple pieces of lifting equipment are used, the safe working load is determined by the highest rated piece of equipment.

_____ **6.** Vehicle jacks may be used to support the weight of the vehicle during any task that requires you to get underneath any part of the vehicle.

_____ **7.** High-lift jacks are usually fitted in pairs to four-post hoists as an accessory to allow the vehicle to be lifted off the drive-on hoist runways.

_____ **8.** Tall jack stands are used to stabilize a vehicle up on a hoist that is having a heavy component, such as a transaxle, removed or installed.

_____ **9.** Since the vehicle rests on its wheels on the four-post hoist, the wheels cannot be removed, unless the hoist is fitted with sliding bridge jacks.

_____ **10.** Every vehicle hoist in the shop must have a built-in mechanical locking device so that the vehicle hoist can be secured at the chosen height after the vehicle is raised.

Fill in the Blank

Read each item carefully, and then complete the statement by filling in the missing word(s).

  1. _____ _____ are a protective layer used to cover the fenders when work is conducted around the engine bay.

  2. If spills do occur, be sure to clean them up thoroughly using appropriate methods, which can usually be found in the _____ _____ sheets for each material.

  3. Special _____ materials in granular form can be used to absorb liquid spills such as engine oil.

  4. Often _____ _____ will be used by someone directing you to maneuver the vehicle.

  5. When using lifting equipment always maintain some _____ _____ as an extra safety margin.

  6. Lifting equipment should be periodically _____ and _____ to make sure it is safe.

  7. A(n) _____ jack is a portable jack that usually has either a mechanical screw or a hydraulic ram mechanism that rises vertically from the center of the jack as the handle is operated.

  8. _____ two-post hoists have arms that are of approximately equal length so that the vehicle is roughly centered lengthwise between the posts.

  9. The lifting arm of the _____ _____ is moved by a hydraulic cylinder and is adjustable for length.

 10. A(n) _____ _____ _____ allows the technician to access the underside of the vehicle without the need for a hoist or jacks to raise the vehicle.

Labeling

Label the following images with the correct terms.

1. Jacks:

A. _____

B. _____

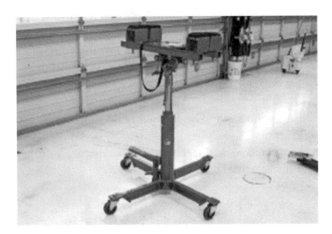

C. _____

2. Hoists:

A. _____

B. _____

Skill Drills

Place the skill drill steps in the correct order.

   1. Applying Fender Covers, Seat Covers, Floor Mats, and Steering Wheel Covers:

_____ **A.** Position the fender covers and floor mats so they provide adequate protection. Ensure that fender covers and floor mats stay in position, providing protection while the vehicle is in the shop.

_____ **B.** Remove fender covers and floor mats prior to customer pickup.

_____ **C.** Install the floor mat on the floor so that it covers as much of the floor as possible. Also make sure it doesn't interfere with the throttle, brake, or clutch pedals.

_____ **D.** Select appropriate protective covers for the vehicle and type of repair. Inspect the covers for rocks, metal, or fluids that would damage the vehicle

_____ **E.** Install the steering wheel cover so that it covers as much of the steering wheel as possible without interfering with any controls.

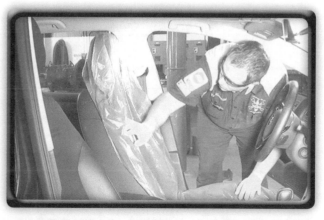

_____ **F.** Position the seat cover so it covers both the back and bottom of the seat. Make sure it hangs over all of the edges and will stay in place.

2. Lifting and Securing a Vehicle with a Vehicle Jack and Jack Stands:

_____ **A.** When the repairs are complete, use the jack to raise the vehicle off the jack stands. Slide the jack stands from under the vehicle. Make sure no one goes under the vehicle or puts any body parts under the vehicle since the jack could fail or slip.

_____ **B.** Position the vehicle on a flat, solid surface. Put the vehicle into neutral or park and set the parking brake. Place wheel chocks in front of and behind the wheels that are not going to be raised off the ground.

_____ **C.** Roll the vehicle jack under the vehicle, and position the lifting pad correctly under the frame or cross member. Turn the jack handle clockwise, and begin pumping the handle up and down until the lifting pad touches and begins to lift the vehicle.

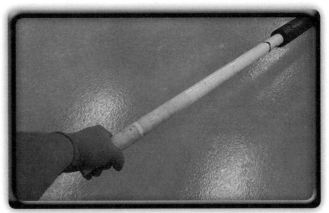

_____ **D.** Slide the two jack stands underneath the vehicle and position them to support the vehicle's weight. Slowly turn the jack handle counterclockwise to open the release valve and gently lower the vehicle onto the jack stands.

_____ **E.** Once the wheels lift off the floor, stop and check the placement of the lifting pad under the vehicle to make sure there is no danger of slipping. Double-check the position of the wheel chocks to make sure they have not moved. If the vehicle is stable, continue lifting it until it is at the height at which you can safely work under it.

_____ **F.** Slowly turn the jack handle counterclockwise to gently lower the vehicle to the ground. Return the jack, jack stands, and wheel chocks to their storage area before you continue working on the vehicle.

_____ **G.** Place one jack stand on each side of the vehicle at the same point, and adjust them so that they are both the same height.

_____ **H.** Check the manufacturer's labels on the jack and stands. Make sure they are rated higher than the weight you are lifting. If in doubt, ask your instructor.

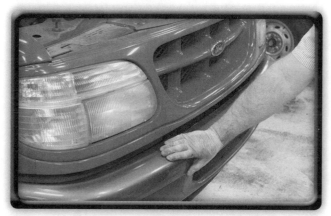

_____ **I.** When the vehicle has settled onto the jack stands, lower the vehicle jack completely, and remove it from under the vehicle. Gently push the vehicle sideways to make sure it is secure. Repeat this process to lift the other end of the vehicle.

3. Lifting a Vehicle Using a Two-Post Hoist:

_____ **A.** Prepare to use the two-post hoist. Check the hoist and check the vehicle clearance. Carefully drive the vehicle so that it is centered between the two posts, left and right.

_____ **B.** Before the two-post hoist is lowered, remove all tools and equipment from the area and wipe up any spilled fluids. Raise the hoist to unlock the lift before lowering it. Make sure no one is near the vehicle before lowering it. Once the vehicle is on the ground, remove the lifting arms and drive it away.

_____ **C.** Make sure no one is near the vehicle and then raise the vehicle until the wheels are a couple of inches off the floor. Check the position of the lifting pads, and shake the vehicle gently to confirm that it is stable.

_____ **D.** Position the lifting pads under the vehicle lifting points. Make sure the lifting pads are adjusted to the same height for both sides of the vehicle. Move to the operating controls and raise the two-post hoist just far enough to come into contact with the vehicle.

_____ **E.** Also ensure that it is positioned properly, front to back, for the type of hoist and vehicle you are using. Leave the vehicle in neutral, and apply the emergency brake.

_____ **F.** Lift the vehicle to slightly above working height, and then lower it onto the locks or safety device.

Review Questions

_____ **1.** A vehicle walk-around with the customer before repair:
    A. avoids customer dissatisfaction.
    B. ensures personal safety.
    C. is mandated by federal regulations.
    D. decreases repair cost to the customer.

_____ **2.** All of the following statements are true _except_:
    A. Seat covers prevent staining.
    B. The engine bay is prone to accidental damage.
    C. Avoid putting your hands on painted surfaces.
    D. Fender covers prevent denting.

_____ **3.** Acid spills can be cleaned up using:
    A. absorbent granules.
    B. alkalines.
    C. water-soaked rags.
    D. solvents.

_____ **4.** When multiple pieces of lifting equipment are used, the SWL is:
    A. the sum of the SWLs of the individual pieces.
    B. that of the piece with the highest rating.
    C. that of the piece with the lowest rating.
    D. the average of the SWLs of the pieces with the highest and lowest ratings.

_____ **5.** Which piece of equipment is typically used to jack a vehicle one wheel at a time?
    A. Floor jack
    B. Bottle jack
    C. Scissor jack
    D. Sliding bridge jack

_____ **6.** All of the following statements are correct _except_:
    A. Jack stands should be gripped by the top and bottom when moving them.
    B. Jack stands should only be used for loads less than the rating indicated on them.
    C. Jack stands should always be used as a pair.
    D. Jack stands must be used on solid, hard surfaces only.

_____ **7.** Which of the following statements is true?
    A. If the end of the vehicle is heavier than the lifting capacity, use wood or steel blocks to support the vehicle.
    B. If the vehicle is loaded, use bricks or concrete blocks to support the vehicle.
    C. The size of vehicle jack to be used will be determined by the weight of the vehicle to be lifted.
    D. The lifting capacity of the vehicle jacks in most shops is about five tons.

_____ **8.** Four-post hoists are most often used for:
    A. lifting engines.
    B. lifting vehicles for wheel alignment services.
    C. lifting vehicles to remove the wheels.
    D. removing an engine from the engine bay.

_____ **9.** All of the following are good practices when using the vehicle inspection pit _except_:
    A. You should get someone inside the vehicle inspection pit to help guide you as you drive over it.
    B. Ensure that there are no obstacles in the vehicle inspection pit or its surrounding area.
    C. Before using the vehicle inspection pit, check its lighting.
    D. Get out of the vehicle and check that it is correctly positioned on the platform.

_____ **10.** All of the following should be done post-repair _except_:
    A. go back through the vehicle and look for tools.
    B. ensure that no damage to the vehicle has been sustained during repair.
    C. look for worn tires and wiper blades.
    D. check that all fingerprints have been removed.

ASE Technician A/Technician B Style Questions

_____ 1. Tech A says that you should always deal with the customer's valuables according to company policy. Tech B says that you should protect a customer's vehicle by waxing it when you are finished working on it. Who is correct?
  A. Tech A
  B. Tech B
  C. Both A and B
  D. Neither A nor B

_____ 2. Tech A says that it is a good practice to perform a walk-around inspection of the vehicle with the customer. Tech B says that fender covers prevent the fenders from becoming dented when the engine is being worked on. Who is correct?
  A. Tech A
  B. Tech B
  C. Both A and B
  D. Neither A nor B

_____ 3. Tech A says that a vehicle jack can be used to support the vehicle while working under it. Tech B says that a jack stand automatically adjusts to the vehicle's height. Who is correct?
  A. Tech A
  B. Tech B
  C. Both A and B
  D. Neither A nor B

_____ 4. Tech A says that hoists should be inspected and certified periodically. Tech B says that safety locks do not need to be applied before working under the vehicle unless you will be working for more than 10 minutes. Who is correct?
  A. Tech A
  B. Tech B
  C. Both A and B
  D. Neither A nor B

_____ 5. Tech A says that an engine hoist can lift more weight when the legs and arm are extended. Tech B says that the bolts used to mount an engine to a stand should complete at least six turns. Who is correct?
  A. Tech A
  B. Tech B
  C. Both A and B
  D. Neither A nor B

_____ 6. Tech A says that gasoline vapors are lighter than air, so inspection pits do not have a fire hazard like above ground hoists. Tech B says that you should never exceed the lifting capacity of the hoist. Who is correct?
  A. Tech A
  B. Tech B
  C. Both A and B
  D. Neither A nor B

_____ 7. Tech A says that you should always ensure that the vehicle has enough ground clearance before driving on a lift. Tech B says that you should center the vehicle on the lift before raising it. Who is correct?
  A. Tech A
  B. Tech B
  C. Both A and B
  D. Neither A nor B

_____ 8. Tech A says that you should always inspect a hydraulic lifting device for leaks and operation before using it. Tech B says that all mechanical safety locks on a hoist should be in place before getting under the vehicle. Who is correct?
  A. Tech A
  B. Tech B
  C. Both A and B
  D. Neither A nor B

_____ **9.** Tech A says that an engine sling should have an angle between 120 and 150 degrees. Tech B says that all slings and lifting chains should be inspected for damage prior to use. Who is correct?
  A. Tech A
  B. Tech B
  C. Both A and B
  D. Neither A nor B

_____ **10.** Tech A says that you should have a coworker help guide you onto an inspection pit. Tech B says that the lights should be on in the pit before driving over it. Who is correct?
  A. Tech A
  B. Tech B
  C. Both A and B
  D. Neither A nor B

CHAPTER

10

Vehicle Maintenance Inspection

At the start of each chapter you'll find the NATEF Tasks, Knowledge Objectives, and Skills Objectives from the textbook. These are your objectives as you make your way through the exercises in this workbook and the chapter in your textbook. The following activities have been designed to help you refresh your knowledge of the material in this chapter.

NATEF Tasks

- N10001 Check and refill diesel exhaust fluid (DEF). (MLR/AST/MAST)
- N10002 Inspect, service, or replace air filters, filter housings, and intake duct work. (MLR/AST/MAST)
- N10003 Verify operation of the instrument panel engine warning indicators. (MLR/AST/MAST)

Knowledge Objectives

After reading this chapter, you will be able to:

- K10001 Explain the systems to be inspected when performing an underhood inspection.
- K10002 Describe what fluids are used in the typical modern automobile.

Skills Objectives

After reading this chapter, you will be able to:

- S10001 Perform an underhood inspection.
- S10002 Check and adjust engine oil level; perform oil and filter change.
- S10003 Measure the freeze protection level of coolant.
- S10004 Check the level and condition of brake and clutch fluid.
- S10005 Check the level and condition of power steering fluid.
- S10006 Check the level and condition of automatic transmission fluid.
- S10007 Check the level and condition of windshield washer fluid.
- S10008 Inspect the engine drive belts and hoses.
- S10009 Perform an exterior vehicle inspection.
- S10010 Inspect and replace the wiper blades.
- S10011 Inspect the windshield.
- S10012 Inspect the exterior lights.
- S10013 Inspect the tires.
- S10014 Perform an in-vehicle inspection.
- S10015 Check the operation of the brake pedal.
- S10016 Check the operation of the parking brake.
- S10017 Check the operation of the horn.
- S10018 Inspect the interior lights.
- S10019 Perform an under-vehicle inspection.
- S10020 Inspect under the vehicle for fluid leaks.

Matching

Match the following terms with the correct description or example.

- **A.** Body Control Module (BCM)
- **B.** Coolant
- **C.** CV joint
- **D.** Diesel Exhaust Fluid (DEF)
- **E.** Hydrometer
- **F.** Hygroscopic
- **G.** Oil-life monitoring (OLM) system

_____ 1. A property of a substance or liquid that causes it to absorb moisture (water), as a sponge absorbs water.

_____ 2. A type of universal joint used on the drive axles or half-shafts of a vehicle. Usually refers to front-wheel drive vehicles.

_____ 3. A system that displays the useful life remaining in the engine oil.

_____ 4. An onboard computer that controls many vehicle functions including the vehicle interior and exterior lighting, horn, door locks, power seats, and windows.

_____ 5. The resulting mixture when anti-freeze concentrate is mixed with water.

_____ 6. A tool that measures the specific gravity of a liquid.

_____ 7. A mixture of urea and water that is injected into the exhaust system of a late-model diesel-powered vehicle to reduce exhaust nitrogen oxide emissions.

Multiple Choice

Read each item carefully, and then select the best response.

_____ 1. If the oil in an engine's lubrication system is too high, the oil will be struck by the crankshaft and will:
   A. burn.
   B. smoke.
   C. coagulate.
   D. foam.

_____ 2. Do not remove the _____ when the engine is warm or hot.
   A. oil dipstick
   B. radiator cap
   C. filter housing cover
   D. transmission dipstick

_____ 3. The anti-freeze protection level can be checked with which of the following?
   A. Hydrometer
   B. Hydroscope
   C. Refractometer
   D. Either A or C

_____ 4. If an automatic transmission does not have a dipstick, the fluid level is checked using a _____ on the side of the transmission.
   A. master cylinder
   B. reservoir
   C. fill plug
   D. sight glass

_____ 5. Some late-model diesel-powered vehicles use a fluid called _____, which is injected into the exhaust stream to reduce oxides of Nitrogen during certain driving conditions.
   A. diesel exhaust fluid
   B. oxide reducer
   C. nitrous oxide
   D. octane booster

_____ 6. What type of drive belt has a flat profile with a number of grooves running lengthwise along the belt?
   A. V-type
   B. Serpentine type
   C. Variable diameter type
   D. Toothed

_____ 7. The _____ is the most important component driven by the drive belt, and the engine will quickly overheat if the belt breaks or comes off.
   A. alternator
   B. air conditioning compressor
   C. water pump
   D. power steering pump

_____ 8. What is the shininess on the surface of a belt where it comes in contact with the pulley called?
   A. Shine
   B. Gloss
   C. Soaking
   D. Glazing

_____ 9. What device on a multiport fuel-injected vehicle is typically located in a rectangular box within the air induction system?
   A. Fuel filter
   B. Air cleaner
   C. Serpentine belt
   D. Carburetor

_____ 10. What type of fluid is normally green, orange, or yellow in color?
   A. DOT 4
   B. Power steering fluid
   C. Coolant
   D. Automatic transmission fluid

True/False

If you believe the statement to be more true than false, write the letter "T" in the space provided. If you believe the statement to be more false than true, write the letter "F."

_____ 1. Component damage or failure is often caused by a lack of maintenance or low fluid level in the related system.

_____ 2. Always check engine oil with the engine on.

_____ 3. If the brake fluid level gets too low, air can be pulled into the hydraulic system.

_____ 4. Most brake fluids are dark or black.

_____ 5. Some automatic transmissions do not have a dipstick.

_____ 6. Transmission fluid is added through the transmission reservoir.

_____ 7. Many newer vehicles have transmissions that are considered sealed and lubricated for the life of the vehicle.

_____ 8. There are two types of accessory drive belts: the V-type and the serpentine type.

_____ 9. The engine should be hot when inspecting radiator hoses.

_____ 10. The warning lamps perform a self-check each time the ignition is switched on or the engine is cranked.

Fill in the Blank

Read each item carefully, and then complete the statement by filling in the missing word(s).

1. Nearly all of the _____ in a vehicle, except some used in automatic transmissions/transaxles get old and wear out, requiring replacement.

2. The level of _____ in an engine's lubrication system is critical to the engine's operation.

3. Engine _____ must be controlled to prevent overheating and to maintain proper exhaust emission levels.

4. A hydraulic braking system depends on a special fluid called _____ _____.

5. When checking power steering fluid levels the engine should be _____ and the fluid hot.

6. Driving in dusty or wet conditions may require that the _____ _____ _____ be checked more often.

7. Engine _____ _____ are used to operate the various accessories on the engine, such as the water pump, power steering pump, air conditioner compressor, and alternator.

8. _____ that exceed a certain number per inch in a belt indicate that the belt may soon fail and should be replaced.

9. The _____ _____ should flex at the hinge and be held firmly against the windshield by the wiper arm spring.

10. The _____ _____ acts as a lever to increase the force applied to the brake assemblies by the driver.

Labeling

Label the following diagrams with the correct terms.

Power steering fluid reservoir:

A. _____

B. _____

Skill Drills

Place the skill drill steps in the correct order.

1. Changing the Air Filter:

_____ **A.** On carbureted or throttle body injected engines, remove the top of the air filter by unscrewing the wing nut, and remove the air filter.

_____ **B.** Inspect the air cleaner element by holding the filter element up to light and looking through it. If it is bright with no tears or cracks, it can be reused. If it is dark or damaged in any way, it will need to be replaced.

_____ **C.** Place the new air filter inside the filter housing. Make sure it is aligned properly on both sides.

_____ **D.** Clean the inside of the air filter housing to make sure the new air filter will seal properly when fitted. Also inspect the housing and any ducts for cracks. If the air filter is being replaced, obtain a new air filter and compare it with the old one to ensure that they are exactly the same.

_____ **E.** On fuel-injected engines, unlatch or unscrew the filter housing fasteners to remove the air filter. It may be necessary to loosen the clamps and hoses on the induction tubing to remove the filter housing cover.

_____ **F.** Replace the cover of the air filter housing and tighten the latches, screws, or wing nut until completely closed. Reinstall any induction tubing or clamps.

2. Performing a Visual Inspection on the Vehicle's Exterior:

_____ **A.** Check exterior component and system operation. Check the body condition to make sure all the body components are secure. Look for loose plastic trim.

_____ **B.** Prepare the vehicle. Park the vehicle in a well-lit area. Turn the engine off and unlock the doors and trunk or rear hatch.

_____ **C.** Inspect the external mirrors to ensure that they are secure and not broken.

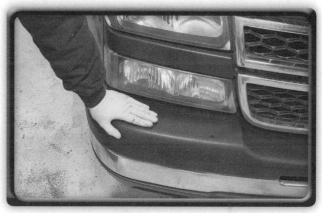

_____ **D.** Push and pull on the bumpers or fenders to ensure that they are secure.

_____ **E.** Open and close doors to check that they are operating correctly.

_____ **F.** Walk around the vehicle, observing any obvious items that need attention.

3. Checking and Replacing the Windshield Wiper Blades:

_____ **A.** Wet the windshield with a hose or with the washers and switch the wipers on. If the windshield is being wiped cleanly, do not replace the wiper blades. If the wiper blades are not wiping the glass evenly or are smearing, replace the blades.

_____ **B.** Obtain and install the appropriate replacement blades. Test the wiper blades.

_____ **C.** Check the windshield wiper blades. Lift the wiper arm away from the windshield and inspect the condition of the blades. Look for damage or loss of resilience in the material.

_____ **D.** Remove the blade assembly.

_____ **E.** Place a folded up fender cover under the wiper blade you are working on to protect the windshield.

_____ **F.** Once the wiper blade is installed, test them for proper operation.

Review Questions

_____ **1.** All of the following statements are true *except*:
    A. Engine oil level should be checked preferably at every other fuel stop.
    B. If the engine oil level is too high, it will foam.
    C. When checking engine oil level, hold the dipstick vertically to read it.
    D. If the oil level is too low or too high, the engine bearings can be damaged.

_____ **2.** Removing the radiator cap when the engine is warm or hot may cause the coolant to:
    A. evaporate and decrease in quantity.
    B. cool down.

    C. be contaminated.

    D. boil and spray out.

_____ **3.** The antifreeze protection level can be checked with an antifreeze:

    A. hydrometer.

    B. tachometer.

    C. OLM system.

    D. hydraulic pump.

_____ **4.** Most brake fluids:

    A. are black in color.

    B. do not wear out.

    C. absorb water from the atmosphere.

    D. do not decrease in quantity.

_____ **5.** In which of these states should the automatic transmission fluid level be checked?

    A. Engine running and the fluid cold

    B. Engine idling and the fluid hot

    C. Engine running and in drive gear

    D. Engine idling and in reverse gear

_____ **6.** A delayed shift into reverse could indicate that the transmission/transaxle fluid:

    A. level is too high.

    B. is contaminated.

    C. is cold.

    D. level is low.

_____ **7.** The belt causing drive belt squeal can be spotted by:

    A. replacing the tensioner.

    B. squirting some water on the belt.

    C. turning on the air conditioner.

    D. loosening the belt.

_____ **8.** The following statements are true *except*:

    A. While checking, operate the wipers when they are dry.

    B. The wiper blades should be checked as part of the exterior inspection.

    C. Never bend the arms to make better contact with the windshield.

    D. The wiper blade should be flexible and not torn.

_____ **9.** All of the following systems should be checked as part of an under-vehicle inspection *except*:

    A. the exhaust system.

    B. the electrical system.

    C. the driveshaft.

    D. the steering area.

_____ **10.** Which of these is normally reddish in color?

    A. Engine oil

    B. Brake fluid

    C. Automatic transmission fluid

    D. Manual transmission fluid

ASE Technician A/Technician B Style Questions

_____ **1.** Tech A says that engine oil should be checked with the engine idling. Tech B says that the vehicle should be on a level surface when checking the oil level. Who is correct?

    A. Tech A

    B. Tech B

    C. Both A and B

    D. Neither A nor B

_____ **2.** Tech A says that coolant freeze protection can be measured with a hydrometer. Tech B says that coolant freeze protection can be measured with a refractometer. Who is correct?

    A. Tech A

    B. Tech B

     C. Both A and B

     D. Neither A nor B

_____ **3.** Tech A says that most brake fluids absorb water from the atmosphere. Tech B says that brake fluid should be changed every two to four years. Who is correct?

     A. Tech A

     B. Tech B

     C. Both A and B

     D. Neither A nor B

_____ **4.** Tech A says that improper handling of a windshield wiper can lead to a broken windshield. Tech B says that dishwashing detergent works well as washer fluid. Who is correct?

     A. Tech A

     B. Tech B

     C. Both A and B

     D. Neither A nor B

_____ **5.** While servicing an automatic transaxle–equipped vehicle, Tech A says that some of these vehicles do not have a transaxle dipstick. Tech B says that the lines between "full" and "add" on the dipstick are usually about 1 qt (0.95 liters). Who is correct?

     A. Tech A

     B. Tech B

     C. Both A and B

     D. Neither A nor B

_____ **6.** Tech A says to test new wiper blades against a dry windshield to ensure they seat properly. Tech B says that if the wiper blade don't seat properly, bend the arms to make better contact with the windshield. Who is correct?

     A. Tech A

     B. Tech B

     C. Both A and B

     D. Neither A nor B

_____ **7.** Tech A says that Stretch Fit belts apply an appropriate amount of tension to the belt over its useful life. Tech B says that any cracks in a belt mean it needs to be replaced. Who is correct?

     A. Tech A

     B. Tech B

     C. Both A and B

     D. Neither A nor B

_____ **8.** Tech A says that the minimum pressure the tires should be inflated to is listed on the tire sidewall. Tech B says that the specified tire pressure is listed on the tire placard, usually located on the driver's door pillar. Who is correct?

     A. Tech A

     B. Tech B

     C. Both A and B

     D. Neither A nor B

_____ **9.** Tech A says that changes to how far the brake pedal travels can be an indicator of problems in the hydraulic system. Tech B says that high-pitched scraping noises or heavy grinding noises during braking could indicate a worn brake lining. Who is correct?

     A. Tech A

     B. Tech B

     C. Both A and B

     D. Neither A nor B

_____ **10.** Tech A says that when the engine is started, the amber anti-lock brake system (ABS) warning lamp should come on, stay on for a few seconds, and then go off, indicating a successfully completed preliminary self-check. Tech B says that if a fault is detected in the system, the warning lamp will stay illuminated. Who is correct?

     A. Tech A

     B. Tech B

     C. Both A and B

     D. Neither A nor B

Communication and Employability Skills

At the start of each chapter you'll find the NATEF Tasks, Knowledge Objectives, and Skills Objectives from the textbook. These are your objectives as you make your way through the exercises in this workbook and the chapter in your textbook. The following activities have been designed to help you refresh your knowledge of the material in this chapter.

NATEF Certification Standards

Personal Standards (see Standard 7.9)

1. Reports to work daily on time; able to take directions and motivated to accomplish the task at hand.
2. Dresses appropriately and uses language and manners suitable for the workplace.
3. Maintains appropriate personal hygiene.
4. Meets and maintains employment eligibility criteria, such as drug/alcohol-free status and clean driving record.
5. Demonstrates honesty, integrity, and reliability.

Work Habits/Ethic (see Standard 7.10)

1. Complies with workplace policies/laws.
2. Contributes to the success of the team, assists others, and requests help when needed.
3. Works well with all customers and coworkers.
4. Negotiates solutions to interpersonal and workplace conflicts.
5. Contributes ideas and initiative.
6. Follows directions.
7. Communicates (written and verbal) effectively with customers and coworkers.
8. Reads and interprets workplace documents; writes clearly and concisely.
9. Analyzes and resolves problems that arise in completing assigned tasks.
10. Organizes and implements a productive plan of work.
11. Uses scientific, technical, engineering, and mathematics principles and reasoning to accomplish assigned tasks.
12. Identifies and addresses the needs of all customers, providing helpful, courteous, and knowledgeable service and advice as needed.

Knowledge Objectives

After reading this chapter, you will be able to:

- K11001 Describe active listening.
- K11002 Describe the components of the listening process.
- K11003 Describe how empathy should be used when listening.
- K11004 Describe how nonverbal feedback should be used during listening.
- K11005 Describe how verbal feedback should be used during listening.
- K11006 Discuss effective speaking strategies.
- K11007 Describe each type of question and its application.
- K11008 Describe proper telephone skills.
- K11009 Describe how to give and receive instructions.
- K11010 Describe how to communicate in a team.
- K11011 Describe employability skills.
- K11012 Describe the requirements for employment.
- K11013 Describe the employment requirements for appearance and environment.
- K11014 Describe the requirements for management of time.
- K11015 Describe the customer service skills needed for employment.
- K11016 Describe effective reading skills.

- K11017 Describe reading comprehension.
- K11018 Describe the process of researching and using information.
- K11019 Use effective writing skills.
- K11020 Describe the characteristics of good written business correspondence.

Skills Objectives

After reading this chapter, you will be able to:

- S11001 Complete a repair order.
- S11002 Complete a shop safety inspection form.
- S11003 Complete a defective equipment report.
- S11004 Complete an accident report.
- S11005 Complete a vehicle inspection form.
- S11006 Complete a lockout/tagout form.

Multiple Choice

Read each item carefully, and then select the best response.

_____ 1. The first step in good communication is:
   - **A.** nonverbal communication.
   - **B.** asking good questions.
   - **C.** providing feedback.
   - **D.** active listening.

_____ 2. Attempting to see a situation from someone else's point of view is known as which of the following?
   - **A.** Sympathy
   - **B.** Empathy
   - **C.** Nonverbal communication
   - **D.** Feedback

_____ 3. Phrases such as "I see" or "Tell me more" that indicate you are paying attention are examples of a(n)_____?
   - **A.** validating statement
   - **B.** supporting statement
   - **C.** closed question
   - **D.** open question

_____ 4. Statements like "Go on" and "Give me an example" that let the speaker know you would like more detail because you are genuinely interested in finding a solution are examples of a(n)_____?
   - **A.** validating statement
   - **B.** supporting statement
   - **C.** closed question
   - **D.** open question

_____ 5. What type of question usually begins with the words when or where?
   - **A.** Open questions
   - **B.** Yes/no questions
   - **C.** Closed questions
   - **D.** Good questions

_____ 6. What aspect of our physical appearance creates the first impression made in any encounter?
   - **A.** Clothes
   - **B.** Hairstyle
   - **C.** Demeanor
   - **D.** All of the above

_____ 7. Looking through the table of contents, introduction, conclusion, headings, and index until we find what we are looking for is the quickest way to use what type of reading?
   - **A.** Absorbing
   - **B.** Comprehending
   - **C.** Selective
   - **D.** Quick

_____ **8.** Which of the following is like conducting an investigation?
  A. Reading
  B. Researching
  C. Comprehending
  D. Skimming

_____ **9.** What online reference organization consists of over 85,000 active members, with more than 2 million years of combined experience, who share their knowledge with each other on over a dozen forums?
  A. International Automotive Technicians Network
  B. National Association for Stock Car Auto Racing
  C. Occupational Safety and Health Administration
  D. National Automotive Parts Association

_____ **10.** Which of the following should you do when you come across any defective equipment?
  A. Tag the defective item
  B. Complete a defective equipment report
  C. Notify your supervisor
  D. All of the above

True/False

If you believe the statement to be more true than false, write the letter "T" in the space provided. If you believe the statement to be more false than true, write the letter "F."

_____ **1.** Learning and applying good communication skills will save you time and help you avoid or get through tricky situations.

_____ **2.** Most people tend to believe the actual words expressed over the nonverbal message you are sending.

_____ **3.** Your body position, eye contact, and facial expression can all set the direction of a conversation.

_____ **4.** Speaking is often referred to as a science.

_____ **5.** Closed questions allow individuals to answer with a simple yes or no.

_____ **6.** Nonverbal communication is not possible during a phone conversation.

_____ **7.** Being part of a team allows us to complement each other's strengths and weaknesses.

_____ **8.** If you have to take customers into the shop, always escort them, and be sure to keep them safe.

_____ **9.** Routinely texting your friends or taking personal calls during work hours is stealing from your employer.

_____ **10.** The CSI rating is reported each month and used to evaluate individual technicians and the entire service facility.

_____ **11.** The person who wants the job done right will probably be very keen to have the repairs finished on schedule.

_____ **12.** The faster you try to read, the more you are likely to be able to concentrate on the meaning.

_____ **13.** A repair order can become a legal document that will be used by the court to determine if the shop has any liability in a lawsuit situation.

_____ **14.** Safety inspection forms are a way of keeping up on routine maintenance tasks such as changing the oil or replacing the belt of an air compressor.

_____ **15.** If a problem is noticed with a piece of equipment, the lockout/tagout procedure should be followed.

Fill in the Blank

Read each item carefully, and then complete the statement by filling in the missing word(s).

1. Mental _____ are thoughts and feelings that interfere with our listening, such as our own assumptions, emotions, and prejudices.

2. As a person is speaking to you, you need to provide _____ feedback, which indicates to the speaker that you are engaged in what he or she is saying.

3. _____ feedback includes very simple spoken signals that can enhance the conversation and let the person know you comprehend.

4. Before speaking, take a moment to consider that your _____ of _____ reveals a lot about your feelings and adds significant meaning to your message.

5. A(n) _____ question encourages people to speak freely so we can gather facts, insights, and opinions from them.

6. When taking a _____ _____ for someone else, make sure you have the caller's name and organization, contact details, the date and time of the call, and a summary of the caller's message.

7. _____ should contain information about who, what, when, where, and why, and direction on how a task should be completed.

8. Good _____ skills involve setting a clear vision of the goals, empowering each team member to contribute his or her best efforts, and recognizing each team member's strengths and weaknesses.

9. Our _____ is the image we present of ourselves to the public.

10. _____ means showing up on time (typically 5–10 minutes early to get ready to start work at the appointed time).

11. _____ reading is reading only the parts we need to know. This method is useful when looking for a particular piece of information.

12. Before you spend too much time researching information, it is important that you _____ the problem.

13. When completing a repair order these elements constitute what are called the three Cs: _____, _____, and _____.

14. If someone is injured in the workplace a(n) _____ _____ should be completed by those involved, both the victim and witnesses, if possible.

15. When performing a(n) _____, you need to check that all major components and systems are operational, secured, and safe in accordance with the vehicle manufacturer's recommendations.

Skill Drills

Read each item carefully, and then place the procedure in the correct sequence.

Properly identifying faulty equipment:

_____ **A.** Power tools that have been identified as faulty, due to failure of parts, should also be tagged and set aside. The tool can only be used again after an authorized agent has made the repair.

_____ **B.** Basic workshop tools that are broken or worn should be replaced. Make sure you tag the tool as faulty or broken and do not use it until you buy a replacement. Then discard the tool.

_____ **C.** Remove the keys and lock the vehicle, if appropriate. Attach a tag to the keys that identifies the vehicle they belong to. Store the keys in the key organizer, and notify your supervisor.

_____ **D.** Isolation tags are also used on disabled vehicles or vehicles undergoing a repair. In this case, you will have to locate and complete the "Disabled Vehicle" warning notice. Write the license number of the vehicle and the nature of the defect. Write your name and then the date and time you completed the notice. Attach the notice to the steering wheel or driver's window.

Review Questions

_____ **1.** When speaking with customers, they tend to believe your:
    A. verbal messages only.
    B. verbal messages over nonverbal messages.
    C. nonverbal messages only.
    D. nonverbal messages over verbal messages.

_____ **2.** A good practice when listening to a customer is to:
    A. fold your arms.
    B. stand upright.
    C. have your hands in your pockets.
    D. look at the damaged part of the car.

_____ **3.** Which of these is a good way to start a conversation with a customer?
    A. Yes-or-no questions
    B. Closed questions
    C. Open questions
    D. Validating questions

_____ **4.** If there is a need to keep someone on hold for an extended time:
   A. offer to call them back.
   B. pass on the receiver to someone else to keep the caller engaged.
   C. ask them to call you back.
   D. check if they are holding the line every few minutes.

_____ **5.** Which of these are basic job-keeping skills?
   A. Technical skills
   B. Employability skills
   C. Communication skills
   D. Problem-solving skills

_____ **6.** A person's first impression about you is typically based on your:
   A. technical skills.
   B. educational qualifications.
   C. appearance.
   D. problem-solving skills.

_____ **7.** After you have spotted a potentially relevant TSB for specific symptoms, the best reading method is:
   A. comprehending reading.
   B. absorbing reading.
   C. selective reading.
   D. skimming.

_____ **8.** All of the following statements are true *except*:
   A. Customer service has a direct impact on the ability of employers to hire employees.
   B. When interacting with the customer, take notes that will help to diagnose the problem.
   C. Helping coworkers is unrelated to customer satisfaction.
   D. The same customer may have different needs at different times.

_____ **9.** Which of the following sources is comparatively more subjective and therefore less reliable?
   A. Automotive educational sources
   B. People with direct experience of the same problem
   C. Technical assistance services
   D. Computer databases

_____ **10.** Choose the correct statement.
   A. The spell-check feature will identify all spelling errors.
   B. Express your anger when dealing with an upset customer.
   C. Use technical jargon when addressing customers.
   D. Structure your letter logically.

ASE Technician A/Technician B Style Questions

_____ **1.** Tech A says that repair orders are legal documents, so they have to be filled out accurately and carefully. Tech B says that ensuring the repair order is well written, clear, and concise promotes a professional reputation. Who is correct?
   A. Tech A
   B. Tech B
   C. Both A and B
   D. Neither A nor B

_____ **2.** Tech A says that you shouldn't inspect a vehicle that is in for a repair unless the customer requests it. Tech B says that performing an inspection in addition to a repair can lead to discovery of additional concerns. Who is correct?
   A. Tech A
   B. Tech B
   C. Both A and B
   D. Neither A nor B

_____ **3.** Tech A says that the proper way to listen to a customer is to maintain eye contact with the customer in between taking notes. Tech B says that talking with customers about the concern is usually a waste of time. Who is correct?
   A. Tech A
   B. Tech B
   C. Both A and B
   D. Neither A nor B

_____ **4.** Tech A says that a good summary of integrity is "doing the right thing." Tech B says that if you are ever working on a vehicle and seem to have hit a dead end in diagnosis, don't be afraid to discuss the symptoms with other technicians around you. Who is correct?
   A. Tech A
   B. Tech B
   C. Both A and B
   D. Neither A nor B

_____ **5.** Tech A says that maintaining an appearance of neatness is important as it conveys to the customer the idea of careful, professional technicians. Tech B says that a dirty and cluttered shop indicates to customers that the shop gets a lot of quality work done. Who is correct?
   A. Tech A
   B. Tech B
   C. Both A and B
   D. Neither A nor B

_____ **6.** Tech A says you can use the skimming technique when researching information to locate it quickly. Tech B says that diagnostic trouble charts provide a great way to narrow down faults without missing any steps in the procedure. Who is correct?
   A. Tech A
   B. Tech B
   C. Both A and B
   D. Neither A nor B

_____ **7.** Tech A says that an example of an open question is "What kind of problem are you having?" Tech B says that an example of a closed question is "Would you like us to go ahead with the repair?" Who is correct?
   A. Tech A
   B. Tech B
   C. Both A and B
   D. Neither A nor B

_____ **8.** Tech A says that one customer who has a bad experience stemming from a misdiagnosed repair due to a technician's failure to listen has more of an effect on the repair shop than several good and happy customers. Tech B says that it is only one customer who is unhappy, and because this person paid the bill, all is well. Who is correct?
   A. Tech A
   B. Tech B
   C. Both A and B
   D. Neither A nor B

_____ **9.** Tech A says that routinely texting your friends or taking personal calls during work hours is generally okay with most employers. Tech B says that being punctual means arriving early so you are ready to begin work at the appointed time. Who is correct?
   A. Tech A
   B. Tech B
   C. Both A and B
   D. Neither A nor B

_____ **10.** Tech A says that the three Cs are "customer, complaint, and condition." Tech B says that the three Cs are "concern, cause, and correction." Who is correct?
   A. Tech A
   B. Tech B
   C. Both A and B
   D. Neither A nor B

Motive Power Types— Spark-Ignition (SI) Engines

At the start of each chapter you'll find the NATEF Tasks, Knowledge Objectives, and Skills Objectives from the textbook. These are your objectives as you make your way through the exercises in this workbook and the chapter in your textbook. The following activities have been designed to help you refresh your knowledge of the material in this chapter.

NATEF Tasks

There are no NATEF tasks for this chapter.

Knowledge Objectives

After reading this chapter, you will be able to:

- K12001 Describe the principles of physics that allow internal combustion engines to operate.
- K12002 Explain the difference between external combustion engines and internal combustion engines.
- K12003 Explain the relationships among pressure, temperature, and volume.
- K12004 Describe force, work, and power, and how they are measured.
- K12005 Describe the operation of the four-stroke engine.
- K12006 Explain the five events common to all internal combustion engines.
- K12007 Explain bore, stroke, displacement, and compression ratio.
- K12008 Describe how the Atkinson and Miller cycle engines differ from conventional four-stroke engines.
- K12009 Identify and describe the purpose of four-stroke engine components.
- K12010 Describe the major components in a short block assembly.
- K12011 Describe the functions and components of the cylinder head.
- K12012 Describe the difference between a cam-in-block engine and an overhead cam (OHC) engine.
- K12013 Describe the valve train, its components, and their function.
- K12014 Describe intake and exhaust manifold.
- K12015 Describe the operation of two-stroke engines.
- K12016 Explain the differences between two- and four-stroke engines.
- K12017 Describe the operation of the rotary engine.
- K12018 Explain the basic principles of operation and components of the rotary spark-ignition engine.

Skills Objectives

There are no Skills Objectives for this chapter.

Matching

Match the following terms with the correct description or example.

A.	Volumetric efficiency	K.	Ignition
B.	Bottom dead center (BDC)	L.	Lobe
C.	Cam	M.	Compression stroke
D.	Camshaft	N.	Power
E.	Atkinson cycle	O.	Reed valve
F.	Cylinder bore	P.	Spark ignition (SI) engine
G.	Blowby gas	Q.	Torque
H.	Exhaust stroke	R.	Valve margin
I.	Fulcrum	S.	Dual overhead cam (DOHC)
J.	Horsepower	T.	Work

_____ **1.** The hole in the engine block that the piston fits into.

_____ **2.** An engine that relies on an electrical spark to ignite the air and fuel mixture.

_____ **3.** A design in a V-engine that includes four cams; also called a twin cam engine.

_____ **4.** The stroke of piston during which the exhaust valve is open and the piston is moving from bottom dead center to top dead center to push exhaust gas out of the cylinder.

_____ **5.** The stroke of the piston during which air and fuel is being compressed into a small area prior to ignition.

_____ **6.** The flat surface on the outer edge of the valve head between the valve head and the valve face.

_____ **7.** An engine cycle that uses a longer effective exhaust stroke than intake stroke to reduce exhaust emissions.

_____ **8.** The amount of twisting force applied in a turning application, usually measured in foot-pounds.

_____ **9.** The egg-shaped lobe machined to a shaft used to cause opening and closing of the valves of a four-stroke cycle engine.

_____ **10.** The result of combustion gases leaking past the compression rings and getting into the crankcase.

_____ **11.** A half-round bearing that the rocker moves on as a bearing surface.

_____ **12.** The position of the piston at the end of its stroke when it is closest to the crankshaft.

_____ **13.** The part of the engine that activates the valve train by using lobes riding against lifters.

_____ **14.** The lighting of the fuel and air mixture in the combustion chamber.

_____ **15.** The result of force creating movement.

_____ **16.** The rate or speed at which work is done.

_____ **17.** A ratio, given as a percentage, of the amount of air actually inducted at a given engine speed at full throttle compared to the internal engine displacement.

_____ **18.** A small flexible metal plate that covers the inlet port of a two-stroke engine and opens and closes to let air and fuel into the crankcase.

_____ **19.** An amount of work performed in a given time.

_____ **20.** The raised portion on a camshaft; used to lift the lifter and open the valve.

Multiple Choice

Read each item carefully, and then select the best response.

_____ **1.** The steam engine and the Stirling engine are examples of what kind of engine?

    A. Internal combustion engine

    B. External combustion engine

    C. Rotary engine

    D. Reciprocating piston engine

_____ **2.** Which of the following types of fuel contains latent heat energy?

    A. Diesel

    B. Ethanol

    C. Hydrogen

    D. All of the above

_____ **3.** The effort to produce a push or pull action is referred to as _____.

    A. power

    B. work

    C. force

    D. torque

_____ **4.** The unit of measurement for torque in the metric system is _____.

    A. ft-lb

    B. Newton meters

    C. horsepower

    D. rpms

_____ **5.** How many radians are there in the circumference of a circle?

    A. 1

    B. 3.14

    C. 6.28

    D. Depends on the radius of the circle

_____ **6.** The _____ occurs as extreme force moves the piston from TDC to BDC with both valves remaining closed.

    A. power stroke

    B. compression stroke

    C. intake stroke

    D. exhaust stroke

_____ **7.** The distance the piston travels from TDC to BDC, or from BDC to TDC, is called the _____.

    A. throw

    B. piston stroke

    C. displacement

    D. compression ratio

_____ **8.** The displacement of an engine can be altered by changing the _____.

    A. cylinder bore

    B. piston stroke

    C. number of cylinders

    D. all of the above

_____ **9.** The Miller cycle engine and the Atkinson cycle engine are both variations on the traditional _____ engine.

    A. two-stroke SI

    B. four-stroke SI

    C. external combustion engine

    D. rotary engine

_____ **10.** The cylinder head is constructed of _____.

    A. cast iron

    B. magnesium

    C. steel

    D. stainless steel

_____ **11.** An internal combustion engine uses _____ that slide up and down in the valve guides.

    A. poppet valves

    B. cams

    C. pushrods

    D. tappets

_____ **12.** What type of engines use pushrods to transfer the camshaft's lifting motion to the valves by way of rocker arms on top of the cylinder head?

    A. Flathead engines

    B. Cam-in-block engines

    C. Overhead cam

    D. Dual overhead cam (DOHC) engines

_____ **13.** Which part rides on the camshaft lobes to actuate the pushrods, rocker arms, and valves?

    A. Tappets

    B. B Ramps

    C. Lifters

    D. Either A or C

_____ **14.** A unit of measurement of work is _____.

    A. watt

    B. ft-lb per second

    C. newton

    D. ft-lb per minute

_____ **15.** A machined surface on the back of the valve head is known as the valve _____.

    A. face

    B. margin

    C. keeper

    D. stem

_____ **16.** The valve train operates off of the camshaft, and the part that rides against the cam lobe is the _____.

    A. valve stem

    B. valve lifter

    C. rocker arm

    D. fulcrum

_____ **17.** A _____ is a locking device that keeps the valve retained by the valve spring seat.

    A. lobe

    B. fulcrum

      C. valve stem
      D. valve keeper

_____ **18.** The _____ engine has enough clearance between the pistons and the valves so in the event the timing belt breaks any valve that is hanging all the way open will not contact the piston, thus preventing engine damage.
      A. interference
      B. rotary
      C. freewheeling
      D. stirling

_____ **19.** The intake system of a two-stroke engine is called a _____ system.
      A. multiport
      B. vane-type
      C. piston port
      D. phaser

_____ **20.** The _____ engine is also called the "Wankel" engine because it was improved upon by Felix Wankel for automotive use in the 1940s.
      A. two-stroke
      B. four-stroke
      C. interference
      D. rotary

True/False

If you believe the statement to be more true than false, write the letter "T" in the space provided. If you believe the statement to be more false than true, write the letter "F."

_____ **1.** The internal combustion engine has almost completely replaced the external combustion engine and has been around for well over a century.

_____ **2.** Compression-ignition engines do not use spark plugs.

_____ **3.** Pressure and volume are inversely related; as one rises, the other falls.

_____ **4.** Force is measured in ft-lb per second or ft-lb per minute.

_____ **5.** Movement must occur to produce torque.

_____ **6.** A turbocharger or supercharger will increase an engine's volumetric efficiency well above 100%.

_____ **7.** When the piston in the cylinder is at a position closest to the crankshaft, it is said to be at top dead center.

_____ **8.** The power stroke starts with the exhaust valve closed, the intake valve(s) opening, and the piston moving from TDC to BDC.

_____ **9.** The block deck is the machined surface of the block farthest from the crankshaft.

_____ **10.** Increasing the diameter of the bore or increasing the length of the stroke will produce a larger piston displacement.

_____ **11.** Moving of the piston from bottom dead center (BDC) to top dead center (TDC) or TDC to BDC is known as a stroke.

_____ **12.** A long block replacement includes the engine block from below the head gasket to above the oil pan.

_____ **13.** In a naturally aspirated engine, air almost never completely fills the combustion chamber while the engine is running.

_____ **14.** The oil pump of an engine resides at its bottom end assembly.

_____ **15.** Intake and exhaust valves may all be actuated by a single camshaft, or there may be two camshafts per head, called dual overhead cam engines.

_____ **16.** Roller-equipped rocker arms are used on many new engines as they reduce friction and increase engine efficiency.

_____ **17.** The two-stroke engine differs from an ICE in the method of air induction and exhaust used.

_____ **18.** If valve clearance is too large, the valve can be held open longer than it should be.

_____ **19.** Variable valve timing allows cam timing to be adjusted during engine operation.

_____ **20.** The rotary engine is not an internal combustion engine.

Fill in the Blank

Read each item carefully, and then complete the statement by filling in the missing word(s).

1. The branch of physical science that deals with heat and its relation to other forms of energy such as mechanical energy is generally defined as _____.

2. The gasoline _____ engine uses a crankshaft to convert the reciprocating movement of the pistons in their cylinder bores into rotary motion at the crankshaft.

3. Heating a gas in a sealed container will _____ the pressure in the container.

4. One _____ equals 550 ft-lb per second, or 33,000 ft-lb per minute.

5. A(n) _____ describes how many radius distances there are in the circumference of a circle.

6. The _____ is the output side of the engine's breathing apparatus.

7. When the piston in a cylinder is at the position farthest away from the crankshaft, it is at _____ _____ _____.

8. Internal combustion engines are designated by the amount of space their pistons displace as they move from TDC to BDC, which is called _____ _____.

9. The process of removing burned gases from the cylinder through the use of moving airflow pulling or extracting the gases out is known as _____.

10. The _____ _____ is the single largest part of the engine.

11. A(n) _____ is a weighted assembly that stores kinetic energy from each power stroke and helps keep the crankshaft turning through nonpower strokes.

12. The _____ _____ connects the piston to the crankshaft and transfers piston movement and combustion pressure to the crankshaft rod journals.

13. The _____ _____ _____ is an oil control ring that keeps lubricating oil on the cylinder wall and out of the combustion chamber.

14. The housing of a rotary engine is made of _____ alloy.

15. Up until the 1950s, many engines had their valves installed in the engine block. Such engines are called _____ engines.

16. _____ is the amount of slack between the cam and the lifter in a bucket-style OHC engine.

17. There are usually two spark plugs fixed to the housing that enable combustion to occur; these are referred to as _____ and _____ spark plugs.

18. When the piston reaches TDC of the compression stroke, the air-fuel mixture is ignited and burns rapidly at up to about _____ °F or _____ °C.

19. In a _____-_____ engine, the inlet and exhaust ports are opened and closed by the movement of the piston.

20. A(n) _____ _____ is the circular movement around the perimeter of another circle.

Labeling

Label the following diagrams with the correct terms.

1. External combustion engines:

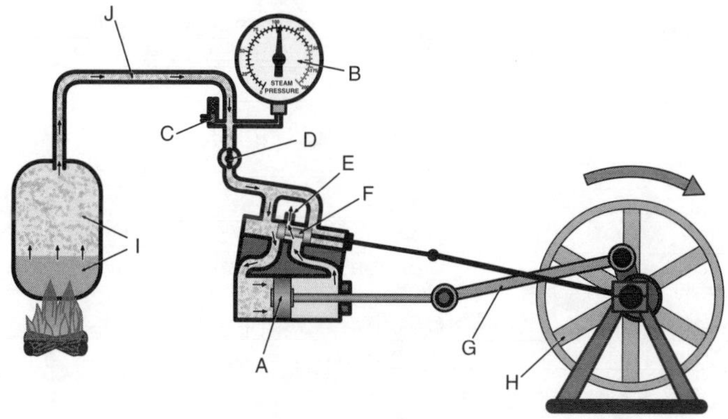

Steam engine

A. _____

B. _____

C. _____

D. _____

E. _____

F. _____

G. _____

H. _____

I. _____

J. _____

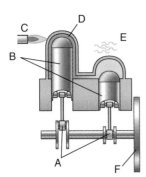

Stirling engine

A. _____

B. _____

C. _____

D. _____

E. _____

F. _____

2. Temperature changes pressure:

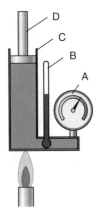 

A: As temperature increases, the pressure increases

B: As temperature decreases, the pressure decreases

A. _____

B. _____

C. _____

D. _____

3. Volume affects pressure:

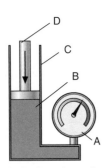 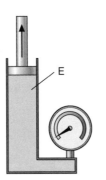

A: As the volume decreases, the pressure increases

B: As the volume increases, the pressure decreases

A. _____

B. _____

C. _____

D. _____

E. _____

4. The basic four-stroke cycle:

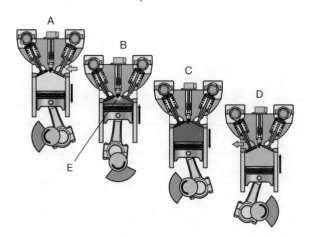

A. _____

B. _____

C. _____

D. _____

E. _____

5. Engine block:

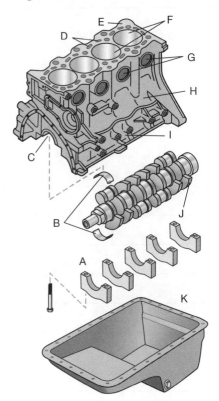

A. _____

B. _____

C. _____

D. _____

E. _____

F. _____

G. _____

H. _____

I. _____

J. _____

K. _____

6. Basic parts of the crankshaft:

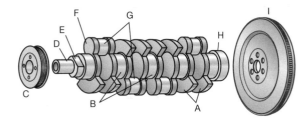

A. _____

B. _____

C. _____

D. _____

E. _____

F. _____

G. _____

H. _____

I. _____

7. Piston and piston rings:

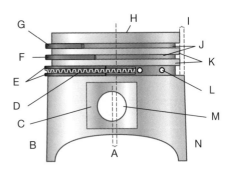

A. _____

B. _____

C. _____

D. _____

E. _____

F. _____

G. _____

H. _____

I. _____

J. _____

K. _____

L. _____

M. _____

N. _____

8. Two-stroke reed valve operation:

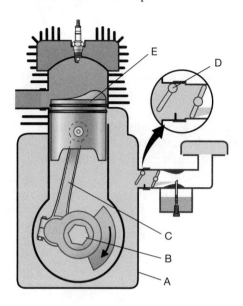

A. _____

B. _____

C. _____

D. _____

E. _____

9. Operation of a rotary engine:

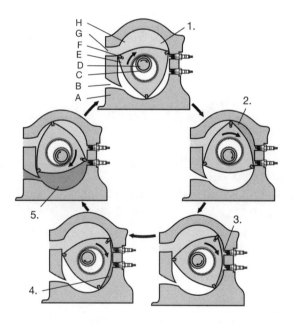

1. _____

2. _____

3. _____

4. _____

5. _____

A. _____

B. _____

C. _____

D. _____

E. _____

F. _____

G. _____

H. _____

Review Questions

_____ 1. When compared to internal combustion engines:
  A. the output of Stirling engines can be easily varied.
  B. steam engines take relatively less time to generate pressure.
  C. steam engines do not present an explosion hazard under too much pressure.
  D. Stirling engines run almost silently.

_____ 2. Choose the correct statement.
  A. For pressure to increase, either temperature must decrease or volume must be increased.
  B. For pressure to increase, either temperature or volume must be increased.
  C. For pressure to increase, either temperature must increase or volume must be decreased.
  D. For pressure to increase, either temperature or volume must be decreased.

_____ 3. The effort to produce a push or pull action is referred to as:
  A. force.
  B. power.
  C. work.
  D. torque.

_____ 4. Which event occurs when the piston reaches TDC of the compression stroke?
  A. Ignition
  B. Compression stroke
  C. Exhaust
  D. Intake

_____ 5. The displacement of an engine can be altered by changing all of the below _except_:
  A. cylinder bore.
  B. type of fuel.
  C. piston stroke.
  D. number of cylinders.

_____ 6. In the Miller and Atkinson cycle engines:
  A. compression stroke is longer and expansion stroke is shorter.
  B. the combustion chamber is slightly bigger.
  C. the compression pressure at ignition is greater than in a conventional engine.
  D. compression stroke is shorter and expansion stroke is longer.

_____ 7. Which of these converts the reciprocating movement of the pistons into rotary motion?
  A. Camshaft
  B. Flywheel
  C. Crankshaft
  D. Piston ring

_____ 8. Proper power output and low-emissions operation of the engine is ensured by:
  A. using pistons with an iron coating.
  B. timing the valve opening to the piston position.
  C. keeping the combustion pressure in check by letting it into the crankcase.
  D. decreasing the number of valves per cylinder.

_____ 9. The two-stroke engine differs from the four-stroke engine in all the below aspects _except_:
  A. the events involved in the operation of the engine.
  B. the emissions produced by the engine.
  C. the method of air induction and exhaust.
  D. their production costs and size.

_____ 10. Which of the following statements is true with respect to a rotary engine?
  A. The rotor is mounted in a cylindrical housing.
  B. There is no reciprocating motion.
  C. The engine produces one power pulse per rotor rotation.
  D. The engine produces more vibration when compared to other ICEs.

ASE Technician A/Technician B Style Questions

_____ **1.** Tech A says that as volume decreases, pressure increases. Tech B says that when temperature increases, pressure decreases. Who is correct?
   A. Tech A
   B. Tech B
   C. Both A and B
   D. Neither A nor B

_____ **2.** Tech A says that horsepower is a measurement simply of the amount of work being performed. Tech B says that horsepower can be calculated by multiplying torque by rpm and dividing by 5252. Who is correct?
   A. Tech A
   B. Tech B
   C. Both A and B
   D. Neither A nor B

_____ **3.** Tech A says that in a four-stroke engine, the piston travels to TDC four times to complete the cycle. Tech B says that in a four-stroke engine, the air-fuel mixture is ignited once every two strokes. Who is correct?
   A. Tech A
   B. Tech B
   C. Both A and B
   D. Neither A nor B

_____ **4.** Tech A says that spark ignition typically occurs before TDC. Tech B says that spark ignition typically occurs during the intake stroke. Who is correct?
   A. Tech A
   B. Tech B
   C. Both A and B
   D. Neither A nor B

_____ **5.** Tech A says that valve overlap occurs between the exhaust stroke and the intake stroke. Tech B says that valve overlap occurs to assist in scavenging the cylinder. Who is correct?
   A. Tech A
   B. Tech B
   C. Both A and B
   D. Neither A nor B

_____ **6.** Tech A says that compression ratio is the comparison of the volume above the piston at BDC to the volume above the piston at TDC. Tech B says that scavenging of the exhaust gases occurs once the exhaust valve closes. Who is correct?
   A. Tech A
   B. Tech B
   C. Both A and B
   D. Neither A nor B

_____ **7.** Tech A says that the weight of the flywheel smoothes out the engine's power pulses. Tech B says that the flexplate and torque converter perform this same function. Who is correct?
   A. Tech A
   B. Tech B
   C. Both A and B
   D. Neither A nor B

_____ **8.** Tech A says that an interference engine is designed so that the pistons can hit the valves if the timing belt breaks. Tech B says that the shape of the cam lobe determines how long and far the valves are held open. Who is correct?
   A. Tech A
   B. Tech B
   C. Both A and B
   D. Neither A nor B

_____ **9.** Tech A says that blowby gases occur when compression and combustion gases leak past the piston rings. Tech B says that the upper two piston rings are oil control rings. Who is correct?

    A. Tech A

    B. Tech B

    C. Both A and B

    D. Neither A nor B

_____ **10.** Tech A says that the principle of thermal expansion is what pushes the piston down the cylinder on the power stroke. Tech B says that the crankshaft pulls the piston down the cylinder on the compression stroke. Who is correct?

    A. Tech A

    B. Tech B

    C. Both A and B

    D. Neither A nor B

Engine Mechanical Testing

At the start of each chapter you'll find the NATEF Tasks, Knowledge Objectives, and Skills Objectives from the textbook. These are your objectives as you make your way through the exercises in this workbook and the chapter in your textbook. The following activities have been designed to help you refresh your knowledge of the material in this chapter.

NATEF Tasks

- N13001 Perform engine absolute manifold pressure tests (vacuum/boost); determine needed action.
- N13002 Perform cylinder power balance test; determine needed action.
- N13003 Perform cylinder cranking and running compression tests; determine needed action.
- N13004 Perform cylinder leakage test; determine needed action.
- N13005 Diagnose abnormal engine noises or vibration concerns; determine needed action.
- N13006 Inspect engine assembly for fuel, oil, coolant, and other leaks; determine needed action.

Knowledge Objectives

After reading this chapter, you will be able to:

- K13001 Explain how engine mechanical testing is part of the SBD process.
- K13002 Identify engine testing tools and their purpose.
- K13003 Approximate engine condition based on cranking sound.
- K13004 Approximate engine condition using engine vacuum.
- K13005 Describe the purpose of a cylinder power balance test.
- K13006 Evaluate cylinder cranking and running compression.
- K13007 Evaluate possible causes of cylinder leakage.
- K13008 Describe the variety of engine noises and vibrations and how to locate them.
- K13009 Describe the process for identifying various types and causes of engine fluid leaks.
- K13010 Describe how consumption of oil or coolant not due to external leaks may be determined by the color of the exhaust.

Skills Objectives

After reading this chapter, you will be able to:

- S13001 Perform a cranking sound diagnosis test.
- S13002 Test engine vacuum using a vacuum gauge.
- S13003 Test engine vacuum using a pressure transducer.
- S13004 Perform a cylinder power balance test.
- S13005 Perform a cranking compression test.
- S13006 Perform a running compression test.
- S13007 Perform a cylinder leakage test.
- S13008 Perform a fluid leak inspection.

Matching

Match the following terms with the correct description or example.

- **A.** Compression tester
- **B.** Cylinder leakage tester
- **C.** Data link connector (DLC)
- **D.** Pressure transducer
- **E.** Vacuum gauge

_____ 1. The connector through which the scan tool communicates to the vehicle's computers; it will display the readings from the various sensors and can retrieve trouble codes, freeze-frame data, and system monitor data.

_____ 2. A device used to measure the amount of compression pressure a cylinder can generate.

_____ 3. A device used to measure the amount of vacuum an engine can generate during various operating conditions.

_____ 4. A device that pumps air into the cylinder and measures the percentage of air that is leaking out of the cylinder.

_____ 5. A device used to measure engine vacuum and display it graphically on a lab scope.

Multiple Choice

Read each item carefully, and then select the best response.

_____ 1. What tool, available in both standard and electronic versions is used by technicians to listen to unusual noises in a vehicle?
   A. Microphone
   B. Stethoscope
   C. Sound transducer
   D. Amplifier

_____ 2. When using fluorescent dye to help locate the leak, the dye can only be seen under what kind of light?
   A. Fluorescent
   B. Infrared
   C. Ultraviolet
   D. Incandescent

_____ 3. Many newer vehicles are programmed with a _____ capability that effectively shuts off the fuel injectors as long as the throttle is held to the floor before the ignition key is turned to the run or crank position.
   A. time delay
   B. cold start
   C. crank mode
   D. clear flood

_____ 4. A low and steady reading gauge reading during a vacuum test indicates:
   A. everything is good.
   B. possible late valve or ignition timing.
   C. possible worn rings.
   D. burned or leaking valve.

_____ 5. The typical vacuum reading for a properly running engine at idle is a steady _____ of vacuum.
   A. 10" to 12"
   B. 17" to 21"
   C. 4" to 8"
   D. 20" to 23"

_____ 6. Using a pressure transducer and _____ is a similar process to using a vacuum gauge, except it is much more accurate and allows you to look at the vacuum graphically.
   A. lab scope
   B. stethoscope
   C. amp probe
   D. monitor

_____ 7. Which test identifies which cylinder(s) are not operating properly and gives a general indication of each cylinder's overall health?
   A. Vacuum gauge test
   B. Cylinder leakage test
   C. Pressure transducer test
   D. Power balance test

_____ 8. In which test is a high-pressure hose hand threaded into the spark plug hole of the cylinder to be tested and then connected to the compression gauge?
   A. Power balance test
   B. Vacuum gauge test

    C. Cranking or running compression test
    D. Cylinder leakage test
_____ **9.** What test checks an engine's ability to move air into and out of the cylinder?
    A. Running compression test
    B. Vacuum gauge test
    C. Power balance test
    D. Running compression test
_____ **10.** Black exhaust is an indication of:
    A. coolant leak.
    B. excessive rich fuel mixture.
    C. burning engine oil.
    D. blown head gasket.

True/False

If you believe the statement to be more true than false, write the letter "T" in the space provided. If you believe the statement to be more false than true, write the letter "F."

_____ **1.** Mechanical testing starts with a good visual inspection.
_____ **2.** A mechanic could diagnose a burned valve with just a piece of bubble gum and its wrapper.
_____ **3.** The smell of a leaking fluid can give you a clue as to its source.
_____ **4.** Seals leak only when the engine is running.
_____ **5.** You can disable the ignition system so that it will crank but not start.
_____ **6.** A sharp oscillation back and forth in the needle or a dip in the vacuum gauge reading could relate to a problem such as a restricted exhaust system.
_____ **7.** Using a vacuum gauge is much more accurate than using a pressure transducer and lab scope.
_____ **8.** Disabling a cylinder that is not operating correctly will not produce much, if any rpm drop.
_____ **9.** A cranking compression test is performed when indications show a misfiring or dead cylinder that is not caused by an ignition or fuel problem.
_____ **10.** A rod bearing makes an evenly spaced single knock while a main bearing generally makes a double knock.

Fill in the Blank

Read each item carefully, and then complete the statement by filling in the missing word(s).

1. Engine mechanical testing uses a series of tests to assess the mechanical _____ of the engine.
2. Sometimes adding a special fluorescent _____ to the fluid will help locate a leak.
3. If one or more cylinders have _____ _____, the engine will run rough, in many cases misleading the customer to request a "tune-up."
4. A(n) _____ _____ can be used so that the vacuum gauge can be connected and, at the same time, vacuum can still be supplied to the existing component.
5. A vacuum _____ reading shows the difference between outside atmospheric pressure and the amount of manifold pressure in the engine.
6. During an engine vacuum test, all vacuum gauges are calibrated to, and all instructions and readings are referenced to _____ _____.
7. The purpose of the _____ _____ test is to see whether the cylinders are creating equal amounts of power and, if not, to isolate the problem to a particular cylinder or cylinders.
8. When a low-compression cylinder is found, you should put a couple squirts of oil into the spark plug hole, crank the engine a few turns, and recheck the compression. if the compression rises significantly, the problem is typically worn _____ _____.
9. The _____ _____ test is performed by leaving all of the spark plugs in the engine except for the one in the cylinder that you are testing.
10. The _____ _____ test is performed on a cylinder with low compression to determine the severity of the compression leak and where the leak is located.

Labeling

Label the following images with the correct terms.

Testing tools:

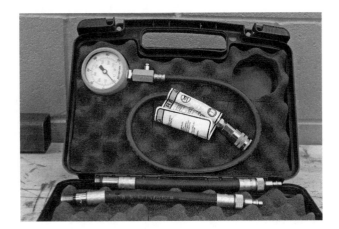

A. _____

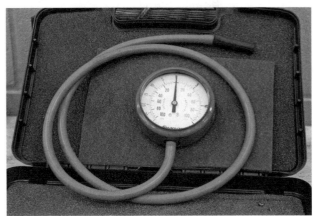

B. _____

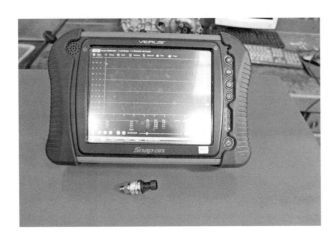

C. _____

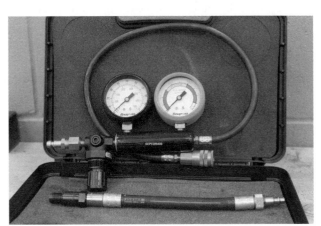

D. _____

Skill Drills

Place the skill drill steps in the correct order.

1. Performing a Fluid Leak Inspection by Looking under the Hood:

_____ **A.** Check for engine oil leaks or seepage at the valve covers, intake manifold, cam seal, and so on.

_____ **B.** Check for power steering leaks at the power steering pump, lines, and steering box or rack and pinion.

_____ **C.** Raise the hood and make sure it is secure. Check for any coolant leaks. Check the radiator, radiator hoses, heater hoses, water pump, heater control valve, and any coolant lines.

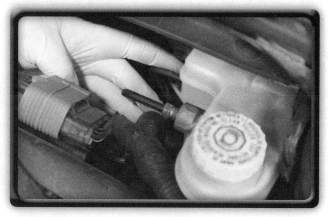

_____ **D.** Check the master cylinder brake lines. Check the rear seal of the brake master cylinder, looking for signs of seepage between the master cylinder and the vacuum booster.

2. Performing a Fluid Leak Inspection by Looking under the Vehicle:

_____ **A.** Inspect the front and rear differentials if equipped.

_____ **B.** Inspect for transmission and transaxle leaks.

_____ **C.** Inspect for engine oil leaks around the front main seal, oil pan, oil filter, oil pressure switch, and rear main seal.

_____ **D.** Safely raise the vehicle, using a hoist. Check for any coolant seepage or leakage on each side of the block around the soft plugs.

3. Testing Engine Vacuum Using a Pressure Transducer:

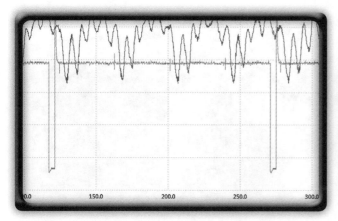

_____ **A.** Start the engine and let it idle. Adjust the lab scope so that the screen captures the vacuum pulses for all of the cylinders. Observe the vacuum trace.

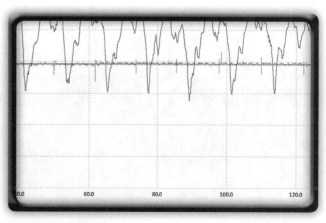

_____ **B.** Snap accelerate the engine by opening and closing the throttle, and compare the trace to known good readings.

_____ **C.** Connect the second channel of the lab scope to the ignition system so it can identify cylinder 1.

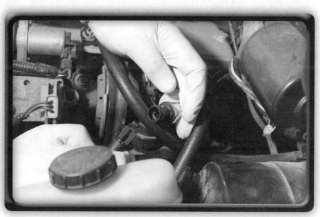

_____ **D.** Connect the pressure transducer to the intake manifold and the lab scope.

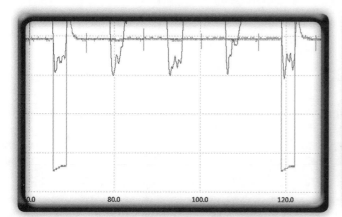

_____ **E.** Hold the throttle steady at 1200–1500 rpm and compare the trace to known good readings.

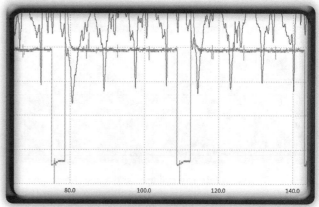

_____ **F.** Then hold the throttle steady at 2500 rpm, and compare the trace to known good readings.

4. Performing a Cylinder Power Balance Test:

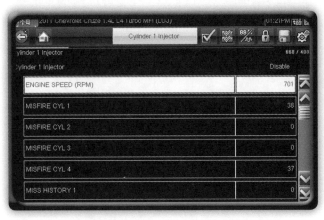

_____ **A.** Using the method chosen to disable cylinders, disable the first cylinder and record the rpm. (Do not leave the cylinder disabled for more than a few seconds.)

_____ **B.** Visually inspect the engine to determine the best method to disable the cylinders. If necessary, disable the idle control system. Start the engine and allow it to idle. Record the idle rpm.

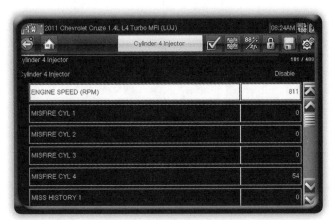

_____ **C.** Reactivate the cylinder and allow the engine to run for approximately 10 seconds to stabilize. Repeat the steps on each of the cylinders and record your readings. Determine any necessary action.

Chapter 13   Engine Mechanical Testing

5. Performing a Running Compression Test:

_____ **A.** Remove the spark plug on the cylinder that you are testing and ground the spark plug wire.

_____ **B.** Have your partner quickly snap the throttle open for about 1 second and then quickly close it. (Make sure the key can be turned off quickly if the throttle sticks.) Record the reading. Repeat the process on the other cylinders. Determine any necessary action.

_____ **C.** Install the proper hose and compression tester into the spark plug hole. Start the engine, allow it to idle, press and release the bleed valve, and record the reading.

Review Questions

_____ **1.** All of the following statements are true with respect to engine mechanical testing *except*:
   A. It helps to determine what major engine work is needed.
   B. It is an integral part of preventive maintenance.
   C. The tests start off broad and narrow down as each test is performed.
   D. Testing needs to be done before tune-up parts are replaced.

_____ **2.** Which of these measures engine vacuum or pressure and displays it graphically on a lab scope?
   A. Pressure transducer
   B. Cylinder leakage tester
   C. Vacuum gauge
   D. Stethoscope

_____ **3.** When performing a cranking sound diagnosis, a cylinder with no compression produces a(n):
   A. even cranking sound.
   B. slow cranking sound.
   C. uneven cranking sound.
   D. fast cranking sound.

_____ **4.** When performing vacuum testing using a vacuum gauge, a steady reading of 17" to 21" of vacuum indicates:
   A. a burned valve.
   B. possible worn rings.
   C. possible late valve timing.
   D. a good reading.

_____ **5.** All of the following are advantages of using a pressure transducer rather than a vacuum gauge *except*:
   A. greater accuracy.
   B. easier identification of the specific cylinder.
   C. measuring higher pressures.
   D. ability to see the levels graphically.

_____ **6.** During a cylinder power balance test, when a cylinder that is not operating correctly is disabled, it:
   A. produces a large rpm drop.
   B. does not produce much, if any, rpm drop.
   C. produces the same rpm drop as when disabling a correctly operating cylinder.
   D. will not be compensated for by the PCM.

_____ **7.** For the cranking compression test to be completely accurate, it is recommended that the engine:
   A. be at operating temperature.
   B. spark plugs be connected.
   C. battery be fully discharged.
   D. throttle be closed.

_____ **8.** When doing the cylinder leakage test, it is acceptable to have a small amount of leakage past the:
   A. head gasket.
   B. intake valve.
   C. exhaust valve.
   D. piston rings.

_____ **9.** A light ticking noise could be caused by a problem in the:
   A. main bearing.
   B. connecting rod bearing.
   C. valve lifter.
   D. piston skirt.

_____ **10.** All of the following are helpful in identifying the source of a liquid leak *except*:
   A. the smell of the fluid.
   B. the part on which the fluid is dripping.
   C. the addition of a fluorescent dye.
   D. the color of the fluid.

ASE Technician A/Technician B Style Questions

_____ **1.** Tech A says that a cranking sound diagnosis can be used to diagnose components in the ignition system. Tech B says that a cranking sound diagnosis can indicate differences in compression. Who is correct?
   A. Tech A
   B. Tech B
   C. Both A and B
   D. Neither A nor B

_____ **2.** Tech A says that a power balance test is a good way to narrow a misfire down to a particular cylinder(s). Tech B says that a cylinder power balance test measures the volumetric efficiency of the cylinder being tested. Who is correct?
   A. Tech A
   B. Tech B
   C. Both A and B
   D. Neither A nor B

_____ **3.** Tech A says that a cranking compression wet test can indicate whether the cylinder has worn piston rings. Tech B says that the throttle should be held wide open during a cranking compression test. Who is correct?
   A. Tech A
   B. Tech B
   C. Both A and B
   D. Neither A nor B

_____ **4.** Tech A says that low compression on a single cylinder will cause an engine not to start. Tech B says that low compression on a single cylinder means that the engine can be fixed with a tune-up. Who is correct?
   A. Tech A
   B. Tech B
   C. Both A and B
   D. Neither A nor B

_____ **5.** Tech A says that a cylinder leakage test is performed on a cylinder with low compression to determine the severity of the leak and where it is located. Tech B says that most manufacturers consider up to 50% cylinder leakage acceptable. Who is correct?
   A. Tech A
   B. Tech B
   C. Both A and B
   D. Neither A nor B

_____ **6.** Tech A says that a scan tool connected to the data link connector (DLC) will report cylinder pressures during a cylinder power balance test. Tech B says that a scan tool will perform a cylinder power balance test and report whether the rings or valves have failed. Who is correct?
   A. Tech A
   B. Tech B
   C. Both A and B
   D. Neither A nor B

_____ **7.** Tech A says that when performing a cylinder leakage test, the piston should be positioned at bottom dead center. Tech B says that a blown head gasket would generally leak past the exhaust valve. Who is correct?
   A. Tech A
   B. Tech B
   C. Both A and B
   D. Neither A nor B

_____ **8.** Tech A says that a vacuum gauge needle that dips 4–8" rhythmically can indicate a burned valve. Tech B says that a stethoscope can be used to determine the source of unusual engine noises. Who is correct?
   A. Tech A
   B. Tech B
   C. Both A and B
   D. Neither A nor B

_____ **9.** Tech A says that if the exhaust has a bluish tint, it indicates that engine is burning coolant. Tech B says that black exhaust indicates a rich fuel mixture. Who is correct?

   A. Tech A

   B. Tech B

   C. Both A and B

   D. Neither A nor B

_____ **10.** Tech A says that a bad cam lobe or broken valve spring will show up during a running compression test. Tech B says that when performing a cylinder leakage test, the engine must be running during the test. Who is correct?

   A. Tech A

   B. Tech B

   C. Both A and B

   D. Neither A nor B

Engine Lubrication Theory

At the start of each chapter you'll find the NATEF Tasks, Knowledge Objectives, and Skills Objectives from the textbook. These are your objectives as you make your way through the exercises in this workbook and the chapter in your textbook. The following activities have been designed to help you refresh your knowledge of the material in this chapter.

NATEF Tasks

There are no NATEF tasks in this chapter.

Knowledge Objectives

After reading this chapter, you will be able to:

- K14001 Describe the composition, functions, additives, types, and certifying bodies of lubricating oils.
- K14002 Describe the functions of lubricating oil.
- K14003 Describe the common additives in lubricating oil.
- K14004 Describe the types of oil.
- K14005 Describe the certifying bodies and their standards for engine oil.
- K14006 Identify and describe the purpose of lubrication system components.
- K14007 Describe wet sump and dry sump systems.
- K14008 Identify and describe the purpose of the pickup tube assembly.
- K14009 Describe the types and functions of oil pumps.
- K14010 Describe the operation of the oil pressure relief valve.
- K14011 Describe the purpose and function of oil filters.
- K14012 Describe the purpose and function of spurt holes and oil galleries.
- K14013 Describe the purpose and function of oil coolers.
- K14014 Describe the purpose and function of oil indicators.
- K14015 Describe the purpose and function of oil monitoring systems.
- K14016 Describe the types of lubrication systems.
- K14017 Describe the function of pressure-fed lubrication systems.
- K14018 Describe the function of splash lubrication systems.
- K14019 Describe the function of two-stroke premix lubrication systems.
- K14020 Describe the function of two-stroke oil injection lubrication systems.

Skills Objectives

There are no Skills Objectives in this chapter.

Matching

Match the following terms with the correct description or example.

A. Antifoaming agents	**H.** Gelling
B. Bypass filter	**I.** Hydro-cracking
C. Corrosion inhibitors	**J.** Hydrogenating
D. Crescent pump	**K.** Lubrication system
E. Detergents	**L.** Oil cooler
F. Dispersants	**M.** Oil slinger
G. Extreme loading	**N.** Oxidation inhibitor

O. Polyalphaolefin (PAO)

P. Rotor-type oil pump

Q. Scavenge pump

R. Synthetic blend

S. Viscosity index improver

T. Windage tray

_____ **1.** A thickening effect of oil in cold weather, wax content in base stock mineral oil makes it worse.

_____ **2.** A device used on small engines, located on the crankshaft or driven by the camshaft. It works to fling oil up onto moving engine parts.

_____ **3.** Oil additives that keep contaminants held in suspension in the oil, to be removed by the filter or when the oil is changed.

_____ **4.** A plate that bolts onto the bottom of the engine between the crankshaft and the oil pan, helping to keep the crankshaft from contacting the engine oil.

_____ **5.** A system of parts that work together to deliver lubricating oil to the various moving parts of the engine.

_____ **6.** A pump used with a dry sump oiling system to pull oil from the dry sump pan and move it to an oil tank outside the engine.

_____ **7.** Oil additives that help to keep carbon from sticking to engine components.

_____ **8.** A blend of conventional engine oil and pure synthetic oil.

_____ **9.** An oil filter system that only filters some of the oil.

_____ **10.** A process in which group 2 and group 3 oils are refined with hydrogen at much higher temperatures and pressures.

_____ **11.** An oil pump that uses a crescent-shaped part to separate the oil pump gears from each other, allowing oil to be moved from one side of the pump to the other.

_____ **12.** An oil additive that resists a change in viscosity over a range of temperatures.

_____ **13.** An oil additive that helps keep hot oil from combining with oxygen to produce sludge or tar.

_____ **14.** Oil additives that keep acid from forming in the oil.

_____ **15.** An oil pump that uses rounded gears to squeeze oil through.

_____ **16.** Oil additives that keep oil from foaming as it moves through the engine.

_____ **17.** A man-made base stock (synthetic) used in place of mineral oil. Oil molecules are more consistent in size, and no impurities are found in this oil since it is made in a lab.

_____ **18.** Large amount of pressure placed on two bearing surfaces to press oil from between them.

_____ **19.** A process used during refining of crude oil. Hydrogen is added to crude oil to create a chemical reaction to take out impurities such as sulfur.

_____ **20.** A device that takes heat away from engine oil by passing it near either engine coolant or outside air.

Multiple Choice

Read each item carefully, and then select the best response.

_____ **1.** What kind of oil varies in color from a dirty yellow to dark brown to black and can be thin like gasoline or a thick oil- or tarlike substance?
   A. Lubricating oil
   B. Motor oil
   C. Grease
   D. Crude oil

_____ **2.** _____ is a measure of how easily a liquid flows.
   A. Pour point
   B. Viscosity
   C. Solidity
   D. Reluctance

_____ **3.** What kind of additive coats parts with a protective layer so that the oil resists being forced out under heavy load?
   A. Extreme-pressure additives
   B. Viscosity index improver
   C. Pour point depressants
   D. Dispersants

_____ **4.** Which oil certifying body sets minimum performance standards for lubricants, including engine oils?
   A. American Petroleum Institute
   B. American Society of Automotive Engineers
   C. International Lubricant Standardization and Approval Committee
   D. Japanese Automotive Standards Organization

_____ **5.** The letter *W* in an SAE viscosity rating stands for _____.
   A. water content
   B. winter viscosity
   C. wax content
   D. weight

_____ **6.** Which of the following organizations sets classification standards for motorcycle engines, both two-stroke and four-stroke?
   A. American Society of Automotive Engineers
   B. Association des Constructeurs Européens d'Automobiles
   C. Japanese Automotive Standards Organization
   D. International Lubricant Standardization and Approval Committee

_____ **7.** The American Petroleum Institute classifies oils into _____ groups.
   A. three
   B. four
   C. five
   D. six

_____ **8.** What type of oil can be man-made or highly processed petroleum?
   A. Group 1
   B. Synthetic
   C. Conventional
   D. Blended

_____ **9.** Lubrication oil is stored in the _____.
   A. oil slinger
   B. pickup tube
   C. oil gallery
   D. oil sump

_____ **10.** Flat pieces of steel placed around the oil pump pickup in the oil pan to prevent oil from surging away from the pickup during cornering, braking, and accelerating are called _____.
   A. windage trays
   B. baffles
   C. crescents
   D. barriers

_____ **11.** In a _____ oil pump, the driving gear meshes with a second gear; as both gears turn, their teeth separate, creating a low-pressure area.
   A. geared
   B. crescent
   C. rotor-type
   D. spline-type

_____ **12.** The spin-on type oil filter has a(n) _____ that fits into a groove in the base of the filter.
   A. garter spring
   B. O-ring
   C. plastic cap
   D. compression ring

_____ **13.** Passageways called _____ allow oil to be fed to the crankshaft bearings first, then through holes drilled in the crankshaft to the connecting rods.
   A. pickup tubes
   B. sumps
   C. oil jackets
   D. galleries

_____ **14.** On most small four-stroke horizontal-crankshaft engines, a _____ on the bottom of the connecting rod scoops up oil from the crankcase for the bearings.
  A. crescent pump
  B. dipper
  C. rotor
  D. strainer

_____ **15.** Some high-performance vehicles have a _____ located close to the crankshaft, inside the oil pan, fitted to prevent churning of the oil by the rotation of the crankshaft.
  A. windage tray
  B. scavenge pump
  C. baffle
  D. oil sump

True/False

If you believe the statement to be more true than false, write the letter "T" in the space provided. If you believe the statement to be more false than true, write the letter "F."

_____ **1.** Clearances, such as those between the crankshaft journal and crankshaft bearing, fill with lubricating oil so engine parts move or float on layers of oil instead of directly on each other.

_____ **2.** Two-stroke oil is different than engine oil, and the two cannot be substituted for each other.

_____ **3.** Oxidation allows air bubbles to form in the engine oil, reducing the lubrication quality of oil and contributing to the breakdown of the oil.

_____ **4.** The International Lubricant Standardization and Approval Committee requires that the oil provide increased fuel economy over a base lubricant.

_____ **5.** If you are servicing a European vehicle, it is advised that you do not go by any API recommendations; instead, make sure the oil meets the recommended JASO rating specified by the manufacturer.

_____ **6.** One of the impurities found in all crude oil is wax, which is removed during refining and is used for candle wax.

_____ **7.** Type 4 synthetic lubricating oil is not a true synthetic.

_____ **8.** On a wet sump lubricating system, the oil pan holds the entire volume of the oil required to lubricate the engine.

_____ **9.** The bypass filtering system is more common on diesel engines and is used in conjunction with a full-flow filtering system.

_____ **10.** The oil pressure sensor is also commonly called a sending unit since it sends a signal to the light, gauge, or message center in the dash.

_____ **11.** Oil monitoring systems are used to inform the driver when the oil needs to be changed.

_____ **12.** Oil would be good for thousands of miles longer in a vehicle driven in stop-and-go traffic with long periods of idling than if it were driven in moderate temperatures for long distances.

_____ **13.** Because there is no oil storage sump under the engine, the engine can be mounted much lower in a dry sump system.

_____ **14.** Most two-stroke gasoline engines use a specified gasoline–oil mixture for lubrication.

_____ **15.** Some two-stroke gasoline engines use an oil injection system that does not require the oil and gasoline be mixed manually.

Fill in the Blank

Read each item carefully, and then complete the statement by filling in the missing word(s).

1. _____ oil is distilled from crude oil and used as a base stock.

2. _____ occurs between all surfaces that come into contact with each other.

3. Base stock derived from crude oil will not retain its viscosity if the temperature gets cold enough, so viscosity _____ improvers are added to the stock.

4. The American _____ _____ symbol is the donut symbol located on the back of the oil bottle.

5. _____ oils flow easily during cold engine start-up but do not thin out as much as the engine and oil come up to operating temperature.

6. Using the wrong _____ can void the customer's warranty, leaving the customer, or your shop, responsible for repairs.

7. Group 2 and group 3 API classified oils are refined with _____ at much higher temperatures and pressures, in a process known as hydro-cracking.

8. Crude oil is broken down into _____ oil, which is then combined with additives to enhance the lubricating qualities.

9. True synthetic oils are based on man-made _____, commonly polyalphaolefin oil, which is a man-made oil base stock.

10. Oil is drawn through the oil pump _____ from the oil sump by an oil pump.

11. In a(n) _____ _____ system, the oil is not stored under the engine in an oil pan.

12. Between the oil sump and oil pump is a(n) _____ _____ with a flat cup and a wire mesh strainer immersed in the oil.

13. In a rotor-type oil pump, outside atmospheric pressure forces oil into the pump, and the oil fills the spaces between the _____ _____.

14. An oil pressure _____ _____ stops excess pressure from developing.

15. The location of the _____-_____ filter right after the oil pump ensures that all of the oil is filtered before it is sent to the lubricated components.

16. Some connecting rods have oil _____ holes that are positioned to receive oil from similar holes in the crankshaft.

17. Oil _____ systems are used to inform the driver when the oil needs to be changed.

18. Modern vehicle engines use a pressure, or _____-_____, lubrication system where the oil is forced throughout the engine under pressure.

19. Diesel fuel has more _____ thermal units of heat energy than gasoline, so it produces more heat when it is ignited, placing more stress on the engine's moving parts.

20. A two-stroke engine may require a 40:1 mixture, which is 40 parts _____ to 1 part oil.

Labeling

Label the following diagrams with the correct terms.

1. The lubrication system:

A. _____
B. _____
C. _____
D. _____
E. _____
F. _____
G. _____
H. _____
I. _____

2. Oil pump types:

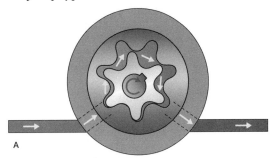

A

B

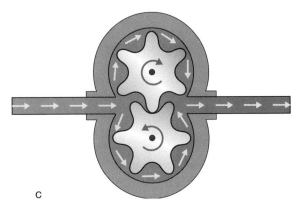

C

A. _____

B. _____

C. _____

3. Full-flow filtering system:

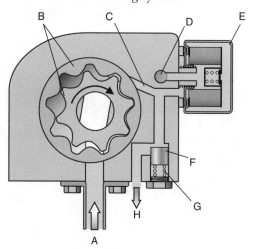

A. _____

B. _____

C. _____

D. _____

E. _____

F. _____

G. _____

H. _____

4. Bypass filtering system:

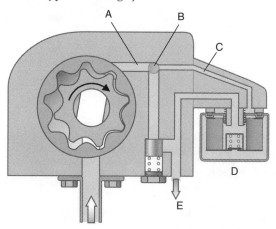

A. _____

B. _____

C. _____

D. _____

E. _____

5. Oil injection system in a two-stroke engine:

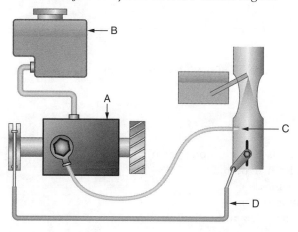

A. _____

B. _____

C. _____

D. _____

Review Questions

_____ 1. Lubricating oil performs all of the following functions *except*:
   A. cleaning.
   B. powering.
   C. sealing.
   D. cooling.

_____ 2. Which of these additives reduces carbon deposits on parts such as piston rings and valves?
   A. Oxidation inhibitors
   B. Corrosion inhibitors
   C. Detergents
   D. Dispersants

_____ 3. All of the following are advantages of synthetic oil over conventional oil *except*:
   A. cost effectiveness.
   B. better low temperature viscosity.
   C. fewer wax impurities.
   D. operation at higher temperatures.

_____ 4. Which of these provides stringent classifications formulated for engine oils used in European vehicles?
   A. SAE
   B. API
   C. ILSAC
   D. ACEA

_____ 5. Choose the correct statement.
   A. A dry sump system stores oil in a tank outside of the engine.
   B. A wet sump system uses a scavenge pump and pressure pump.
   C. The wet sump system is the best fit during aggressive driving conditions.
   D. The dry sump system is the best fit in low performance applications.

_____ 6. Which of these is most likely to cause low engine oil pressure over time?
   A. Oil is thicker than it should be.
   B. Oil pump is creating excessive flow.
   C. Oil leaks inside the engine have become excessive.
   D. Oil pump is of the wrong type.

_____ 7. Oil nozzles have fairly small holes that can become plugged by old, dirty oil fairly easily. Therefore:
   A. change the nozzles periodically.
   B. add oil periodically.
   C. change the oil regularly.
   D. add detergents to the oil regularly.

_____ 8. Different types of oil pressure sensors/switches can do all of the following *except*:
   A. add oil to the oil pan.
   B. activate a warning light.
   C. register on a gauge.
   D. turn on a warning message.

_____ 9. Which of the following statements is true of a splash lubrication system?
   A. Oil that is splashed around usually comes from an oil pump.
   B. It can lubricate all of the parts on bigger engines.
   C. Diesel engines use only the splash lubrication system.
   D. Oil is thrown around and gets into spaces that need lubrication.

_____ 10. In a two-stroke engine oil injection system:
   A. oil and fuel are mixed manually.
   B. the oil pump is designed to deliver the correct amount of oil.
   C. oil and fuel are premixed to manufacturers' specifications.
   D. it only injects oil if you forgot to mix oil with the gas.

ASE Technician A/Technician B Style Questions

_____ **1.** Tech A says that one function of oil is to clean. Tech B says that one function of oil is to cushion. Who is correct?
   A. Tech A
   B. Tech B
   C. Both A and B
   D. Neither A nor B

_____ **2.** Two techs are discussing 5W20 oil. Tech A says the "W" stands for "weight." Tech B says the "W" stands for "Winter." Who is correct?
   A. Tech A
   B. Tech B
   C. Both A and B
   D. Neither A nor B

_____ **3.** Tech A says that the higher the viscosity number, the thicker the oil. Tech B says that most modern vehicles use single weight oil. Who is correct?
   A. Tech A
   B. Tech B
   C. Both A and B
   D. Neither A nor B

_____ **4.** Tech A says that spin-on oil filters use a square-cut rubber O-ring to seal the base of the filter to the engine block. Tech B says that some oil filters use a replaceable paper filter cartridge. Who is correct?
   A. Tech A
   B. Tech B
   C. Both A and B
   D. Neither A nor B

_____ **5.** Tech A says that API's "S" rating means it should only be used in supercharged engines. Tech B says that C rated oil is certified for use for cars, and not trucks. Who is correct?
   A. Tech A
   B. Tech B
   C. Both A and B
   D. Neither A nor B

_____ **6.** Tech A says that most oil pumps are of the positive displacement style. Tech B says that oil pumps are designed to deliver more oil than is needed for an engine. Who is correct?
   A. Tech A
   B. Tech B
   C. Both A and B
   D. Neither A nor B

_____ **7.** Tech A says that the oil-life monitor calculates the expected life of the oil and displays it to the driver. Tech B says that an oil pressure regulator boosts the oil pressure at high engine rpm. Who is correct?
   A. Tech A
   B. Tech B
   C. Both A and B
   D. Neither A nor B

_____ **8.** Tech A says that oil pressure is increased when bearing clearances increase. Tech B says that the faster the oil pump turns, the more oil that is pumped. Who is correct?
   A. Tech A
   B. Tech B
   C. Both A and B
   D. Neither A nor B

_____ **9.** Tech A says that a full-flow oil filter filters all of the oil going to the bearings. Tech B says that a bypass filter bypasses the pump so that any particles in the oil won't damage the pump. Who is correct?

    A. Tech A

    B. Tech B

    C. Both A and B

    D. Neither A nor B

_____ **10.** Tech A says that an oil gallery is what keeps the oil in storage at the bottom of the engine. Tech B says that spurt holes spray oil onto some parts such as timing chains. Who is correct?

    A. Tech A

    B. Tech B

    C. Both A and B

    D. Neither A nor B

Lubrication System Service

At the start of each chapter you'll find the NATEF Tasks, Knowledge Objectives, and Skills Objectives from the textbook. These are your objectives as you make your way through the exercises in this workbook and the chapter in your textbook. The following activities have been designed to help you refresh your knowledge of the material in this chapter.

NATEF Tasks

- N15001 Perform engine oil and filter change; use proper fluid type per manufacturer specification. (MLR/AST/MAST)
- N15002 Perform oil pressure tests; determine needed action. (AST/MAST)
- N15003 Inspect, test, and replace oil temperature and pressure switches and sensors. (AST/MAST)
- N15004 Inspect auxiliary coolers; determine needed action. (AST/MAST)

Knowledge Objectives

After reading this chapter, you will be able to:
- K15001 Identify and describe the purpose of lubrication system tools.

Skills Objectives

After reading this chapter, you will be able to:
- S15001 Perform lubrication system inspection, maintenance, diagnosis, and repair.
- S15002 Check the engine oil.
- S15003 Drain the engine oil.
- S15004 Replace oil filters.
- S15005 Refill the engine oil.
- S15006 Diagnose lubrication system faults.
- S15007 Inspect auxiliary coolers; determine necessary action.

Matching

Match the following terms with the correct description or example.

A. Drag
B. Digital multimeter (DMM)
C. Dipstick
D. Oil level sensor
E. Mechanic's stethoscope
F. Fluorescent dye
G. Oil pressure sending unit socket

_____ 1. Used to check and display the engine oil level on the instrument panel of a vehicle.
_____ 2. The slowing down of the crankshaft when it strikes the oil in the crankcase.
_____ 3. Used to pinpoint noises from the engine.
_____ 4. A useful tool to remove and install oil pressure sending units.
_____ 5. Used to test wiring and sensors of the oil warning light or gauge.
_____ 6. It is specially made to find engine oil leaks.
_____ 7. Used to check the level of engine oil.

Multiple Choice

Read each item carefully, and then select the best response.

_____ 1. When checking oil level, the dipstick should be held _____.
   A. horizontally
   B. vertically
   C. inclined
   D. inverted

_____ 2. What is the color of the engine oil when it is contaminated only with coolant or water?
   A. Blue
   B. Black
   C. Milky gray
   D. Red

_____ 3. A(n) _____ lists physical properties of oil such as viscosity, condensed water, fuel dilution, antifreeze, acids, metal content, and oil additives.
   A. sensor substitution box
   B. oil analysis
   C. pre-delivery inspection
   D. dipstick

_____ 4. Engine oil is normally changed after the engine _____.
   A. is cranked
   B. crankcase is pressurized
   C. is fully warmed up
   D. blowby is reduced

_____ 5. Failure to change engine oil results in _____.
   A. drag
   B. sludge formation
   C. power loss
   D. knocking

_____ 6. A(n) _____ can be used to determine if an engine noise is related to low oil pressure or if it is a result of worn parts with improper running clearances.
   A. oil pressure gauge
   B. dipstick
   C. sensor substitution box
   D. oil level sensor

_____ 7. Identify the reason for low levels of engine oil.
   A. Excess oil is added to the engine.
   B. The oil may have burnt off.
   C. Oil pressure may be too high.
   D. Too many suspended particles are present in the oil.

_____ 8. In an engine, drag can _____.
   A. reduce leaks
   B. result in less fuel consumption
   C. induce improper running clearances
   D. cause a loss of power

_____ 9. If oil pressure goes too low, oil pressure information is fed back to the warning light to issue the operator a warning by the _____.
   A. auxiliary cooler
   B. oil pressure gauge
   C. sensor substitution box
   D. oil sensors

_____ 10. Testing oil pressure sensors usually involves substituting the specified resistance with a(n) _____.
   A. oil pressure gauge
   B. memory minder
   C. microprocessor
   D. resistor substitution box

True/False

If you believe the statement to be more true than false, write the letter "T" in the space provided. If you believe the statement to be more false than true, write the letter "F."

_____ **1.** The engine lubrication system requires periodic inspection, maintenance, diagnosis, and repair.

_____ **2.** All modern vehicles are equipped with an engine oil dipstick.

_____ **3.** Oil will suspend particles as the engine wears.

_____ **4.** Removing old contaminated oil helps to make the engine last longer.

_____ **5.** Engine replacement is less expensive than an extensive oil change.

Fill in the Blank

Read each item carefully, and then complete the statement by filling in the missing word(s).

1. _____ involves checking the level, condition, and service life of the engine oil.

2. _____ involves changing the oil, filter, and resetting the oil-life monitor, if applicable.

3. Oil level is typically checked with a dipstick located _____ _____ _____ _____.

4. A(n) _____ _____ _____ tells the percentage of oil life remaining before a change is needed.

5. Milky gray engine oil can be caused by a bad head gasket, cracked head, or _____ _____ _____ _____.

6. _____ _____ are designed to filter out particles that find their way into the oil.

7. _____ _____ occurs when the new O-ring in the new filter is installed over the old O-ring.

8. The use of _____ _____ _____ reduces the amount of waste generated from used spin-on filters.

9. Oil leaking from seals of _____ _____ _____ will typically sling oil in a circle.

10. A(n) _____ _____ _____ _____ is used to diagnose gauge problems by substituting precise resistances in the gauge circuit and comparing the gauge reading to the specifications.

Labeling

Label the following images with the correct terms.

1. Tools for lubrication system maintenance:

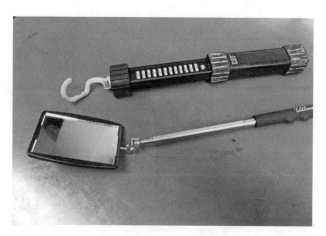

A. _____

B. _____

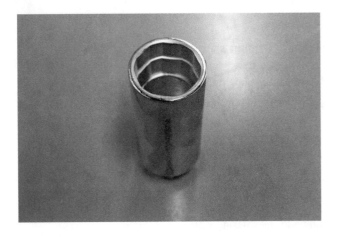

C. _____

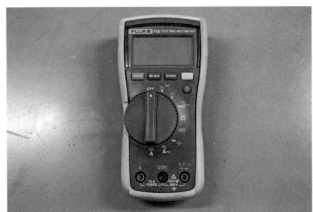

D. _____

E. _____

F. _____

Skill Drills

Test your knowledge of skill drills by filling in the correct words in the photo captions.

   1. Check the Engine Oil:

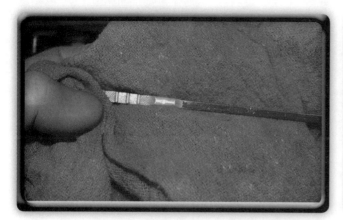

_____ **A.** Locate the dipstick. With the engine off, remove the dipstick, catching any drops of oil on a rag, and wipe it clean. Observe the markings on the lower end of the stick, which indicate the "full" and "add" marks or specify the "safe" zone.

_____ **B.** If additional oil is needed, estimate the amount by checking the service manual guide to the dipstick markings. Unscrew the filler cap at the top of the engine, and using a funnel to avoid spillage, turn the oil bottle so the spout is on the high side of the bottle, and gently pour the oil into the engine. Recheck the oil level.

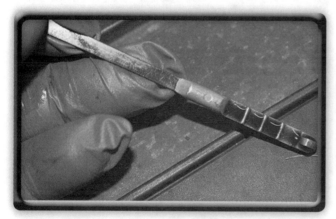

_____ **C.** Replace the dipstick and push it back down into the sump as far as it will go. Remove it again, and hold it level while checking the level indicated on the bottom of the stick. If the level is near or below the "add" mark, then you will need to determine if the engine just needs topped up to the full level with fresh oil or replaced with new oil and oil filter.

_____ **D.** Replace the oil filler cap, and check the dipstick again to make sure the oil level is now correct.

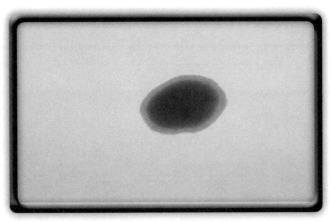

_____ **E.** Check the oil monitoring system, oil sticker, or service record to determine if the oil needs changed. (Some oil monitoring systems show the percentage of life left in the oil.)

_____ **F.** Check the oil for any conditions such as unusual color or texture. Report these to your supervisor.

2. Replacing a Spin-On Filter:

_____ **A.** Remove the filter.

_____ **B.** Confirm you have the correct replacement filter. Smear a little oil on the surface of the new O-ring.

_____ **C.** Screw in the filter until it just starts, and ensure that it cannot be pulled off. Then turn the filter by hand until the filter lightly contacts the base. Be careful not to cross-thread the oil filter.

_____ **D.** Clean the seating area on the oil filter adapter so that its surface can seal properly. Make sure the O-ring from the removed filter is not still stuck to the mounting surface like in this picture.

_____ **E.** Position a drain pan to catch any oil that will leak from the filter.

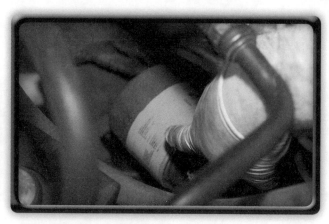

_____ **F.** Check for new filter availability. Locate the filter being changed. It will usually be located on the side of the engine block or at an angle underneath the engine. Select the proper oil filter wrench.

3. Refilling Engine Oil:

_____ **A.** Refer to the owner's manual or the service information, and install a static sticker.

_____ **B.** If the oil pressure is good, turn the engine off and check underneath the vehicle to make sure no oil is leaking from the oil filter or drain plug.

_____ **C.** Reset the maintenance reminder system to remind the owner when the next oil change is due.

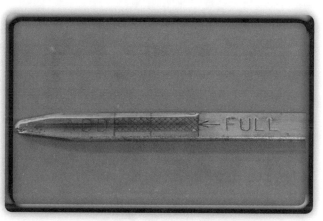

_____ **D.** With a level vehicle, check the oil level again with the dipstick. It may be necessary to top off the engine by adding a small quantity of oil to compensate for the amount absorbed by the new filter. Do not overfill.

_____ **E.** Start the engine and check the oil pressure indicator on the dash. If the oil pressure is inadequate, stop. Do not continue to run the engine.

_____ **F.** Research the correct grade and the quantity of oil you will need. Position the spout on the high side of the bottle. Pour the oil into the funnel slowly enough to avoid the risk of blowback or overflow. Fill the engine only to the level indicated on the engine dipstick. Replace the filler cap.

Review Questions

_____ **1.** The tools for lubrication system maintenance include all of the following *except*:
   A. a compression tester.
   B. an oil filter wrench
   C. a sensor substitution box.
   D. a pressure gauge.

_____ **2.** Which of these is the best guide to knowing when to change the oil?
   A. Dipstick
   B. Oil-life monitor
   C. Oil level sensor
   D. Pressure gauge

_____ **3.** If the oil on the dipstick looks milky gray, it is possible that there is water (or coolant) being mixed into the oil. This could have been caused by any of the following *except*:
   A. a bad head gasket.
   B. a cracked head.
   C. a leaky oil cooler.
   D. a leaky fuel injector.

_____ **4.** Choose the correct statement with respect to oil change.
   A. Normal use and severe use have the same oil change intervals.
   B. When draining oil, the oil should be cold.
   C. The drain plug should be tightened with maximum force to prevent oil leak.
   D. The engine should be fully warmed up when draining oil.

_____ **5.** When installing a spin-on oil filter, failure to lube the O-ring will:
   A. lead to double gasketing.
   B. damage the threads on the adapter.
   C. cause it to bind and roll out of the oil filter groove.
   D. damage the threads on the adapter.

_____ **6.** During replacement, when compared with a spin-on filter, in a cartridge filter:
   A. all parts get replaced.
   B. it is easier to properly dispose of the oil.
   C. a greater amount of waste is generated.
   D. reuse is minimal.

_____ **7.** Excessive oil results in all of the following *except*:
  A. low oil pressure.
  B. high oil pressure.
  C. drag.
  D. foaming.

_____ **8.** Which of these is used to test the electrical circuits of oil pressure sensors and gauges?
  A. A resistance substitution box
  B. An oil pressure gauge
  C. A florescent dye check kit
  D. A stethoscope

_____ **9.** If oil pressure is higher than specifications:
  A. there may be excessive clearance in the engine bearings.
  B. the oil pump may be worn.
  C. the engine is noisy.
  D. the oil pressure regulator might be sticking.

_____ **10.** Low oil pressure reading on the instrument panel can be caused by all of the following except:
  A. worn crankshaft bearings.
  B. worn oil pump gears and housing.
  C. oil pressure regulator spring too strong.
  D. Faulty oil pressure sensor.

ASE Technician A/Technician B Style Questions

_____ **1.** Tech A says that when changing the spin-on oil filter, you need to verify that the old O-ring was removed with the filter. Tech B says that the O-ring on the new filter should be dry when the filter is screwed on. Who is correct?
  A. Tech A
  B. Tech B
  C. Both A and B
  D. Neither A nor B

_____ **2.** Tech A says that the engine oil drain plug typically needs to be replaced with a new one at each oil change. Tech B says that engine oil drain plugs must be tightened with a torque wrench when they are installed. Who is correct?
  A. Tech A
  B. Tech B
  C. Both A and B
  D. Neither A nor B

_____ **3.** Tech A says that the oil pressure will typically be low if the oil level is at the "add" line on the dipstick. Tech B says that worn engine bearings could cause low oil pressure. Who is correct?
  A. Tech A
  B. Tech B
  C. Both A and B
  D. Neither A nor B

_____ **4.** Tech A says that it takes about 1 quart of oil to raise the oil level from "add" to "full." Tech B says that it takes about 1 pint to raise it that much. Who is correct?
  A. Tech A
  B. Tech B
  C. Both A and B
  D. Neither A nor B

_____ **5.** Tech A says that if the oil pressure reads low, the oil pressure sending unit may need to be replaced. Tech B says that if the oil pressure is low, the oil pressure should be measured using a separate pressure tester. Who is correct?
  A. Tech A
  B. Tech B
  C. Both A and B
  D. Neither A nor B

_____ **6.** Tech A says that when draining the engine oil, the engine should be fully cold for best results. Tech B says that the engine should be running when checking the engine oil level. Who is correct?

  A. Tech A
  B. Tech B
  C. Both A and B
  D. Neither A nor B

_____ **7.** Tech A says that after changing the engine oil and filter, you should apply a static sticker to remind the owner when the next oil change is due. Tech B says that you should reset the maintenance reminder system to remind the owner when the next oil change is due. Who is correct?

  A. Tech A
  B. Tech B
  C. Both A and B
  D. Neither A nor B

_____ **8.** Two techs are discussing engine oil leaks. Tech A says that oil pressure sending units are common leaks. Tech B says that oil leaking from seals of rotating parts typically slings oil in a circle. Who is correct?

  A. Tech A
  B. Tech B
  C. Both A and B
  D. Neither A nor B

_____ **9.** Tech A says that many oil pressure sensors are typically variable resistors that change resistance based on pressure changes. Tech B says that a sensor substitution box can be used in place of the sensor while observing the reaction of the oil pressure gauge on the dash. Who is correct?

  A. Tech A
  B. Tech B
  C. Both A and B
  D. Neither A nor B

_____ **10.** Two techs are discussing oil coolers. Tech A says that when inspecting oil-to-water type coolers, look for mixing of the fluids: oil in the coolant, and coolant in the oil. Tech B says that when inspecting oil-to-air type coolers, look for oil in the coolant only. Who is correct?

  A. Tech A
  B. Tech B
  C. Both A and B
  D. Neither A nor B

Cooling System Theory

At the start of each chapter you'll find the NATEF Tasks, Knowledge Objectives, and Skills Objectives from the textbook. These are your objectives as you make your way through the exercises in this workbook and the chapter in your textbook. The following activities have been designed to help you refresh your knowledge of the material in this chapter.

NATEF Tasks

There are no NATEF tasks for this chapter.

Knowledge Objectives

After reading this chapter, you will be able to:

- K16001 Describe the methods of heat transfer.
- K16002 Describe cooling system configurations and their operation.
- K16003 Describe engine coolant and its required properties.
- K16004 Describe how pressure affects the boiling point of coolant.
- K16005 Describe the cause and concerns of electrolysis in a cooling system.
- K16006 Describe how centrifugal force is used in a cooling system.
- K16007 Describe the operation of a rotary engine cooling system.
- K16008 Identify and describe the purpose of each of the cooling system components.
- K16009 Describe the types of coolant and their properties.
- K16010 Describe the purpose, function, and components of a radiator.
- K16011 Describe the purpose and function of the surge tank and recovery system.
- K16012 Describe the purpose and function of the thermostat.
- K16013 Describe the purpose and function of the water pump.
- K16014 Describe the types, purpose, and function of cooling fans.
- K16015 Describe the purpose and function of coolant hoses.
- K16016 Describe the types, purpose, and function of drive belts and tensioners.
- K16017 Describe the type, purpose, and function of temperature indicators.
- K16018 Describe the purpose and function of water jackets and core plugs.
- K16019 Describe the purpose and function of the heater core, control valve, and air doors/actuators.

Skills Objectives

There are no Skills Objectives for this chapter.

Matching

Match the following terms with the correct description or example.

- **A.** Coolant
- **B.** Coolant control valve
- **C.** Cooling hoses
- **D.** Cross-flow radiator
- **E.** Down-flow radiator
- **F.** Ethylene glycol
- **G.** Heat dissipation
- **H.** Overflow tank

- **I.** Propylene glycol
- **J.** Radiator
- **K.** Radiator hoses
- **L.** Rotor housing
- **M.** Surge tank
- **N.** Thermo-control switch
- **O.** Thermostat
- **P.** Water jackets

_____ **1.** A device that takes hot coolant and cools it by passing heat energy to the surrounding air.

_____ **2.** Flexible hoses that connect the stationary components of the cooling system such as the heater core and radiator to the engine, which is mounted on flexible mounts.

_____ **3.** Regulates the flow of coolant, allowing coolant to flow from the engine to the radiator when the engine is running at its operating temperature.

_____ **4.** The engine block of the rotary engine. The rotor moves within it.

_____ **5.** The passages in the engine block and cylinder head that surround the cylinders, valves, and ports.

_____ **6.** Rubber hoses that connect the radiator to the engine. Because they are subject to pressure, they are reinforced with a layer of fabric, typically nylon.

_____ **7.** A fluid that contains antifreeze mixed with water.

_____ **8.** A temperature-sensitive switch that is mounted into the radiator or into a coolant passage on the engine to control electric fan operation.

_____ **9.** The spreading of heat over a large area to increase heat transfer.

_____ **10.** A valve that blocks off coolant flow to keep hot water from entering the heater core when less heat is requested by the operator.

_____ **11.** A chemical used as antifreeze. It is labeled as a nontoxic antifreeze.

_____ **12.** A radiator that uses cooling tubes that run horizontal with tanks on each end. This design allows lower hood profile for better vehicle aerodynamics.

_____ **13.** A tank used to catch any coolant that is released from the radiator cap (works like a catch can).

_____ **14.** A chemical used as antifreeze that provides the lower freezing point of coolant and raises the boiling point. It is a toxic antifreeze.

_____ **15.** A sealed tank that captures coolant coming from the head that has turned to steam and changes the steam back to coolant to be reused by the cooling system.

_____ **16.** A radiator that uses cooling tubes that run vertically. This design requires a higher hood profile.

Multiple Choice

Read each item carefully, and then select the best response.

_____ **1.** Heat transfers through liquids and gases by a process called _____.
   A. conduction
   B. convection
   C. radiation
   D. transference

_____ **2.** Engines have an ideal operating temperature somewhere around _____, give or take 20°F, depending on the vintage of the vehicle.
   A. 200°F
   B. 212°F
   C. 250°F
   D. 325°F

_____ **3.** The circulation of coolant is controlled by the _____.
   A. water pump
   B. radiator temperature sensor
   C. air temperature
   D. thermostat

_____ **4.** The best coolant is a _____ balance of water and antifreeze, making it an ideal coolant for both hot and cold climates and providing adequate corrosion protection.
   A. 60/40
   B. 40/60
   C. 50/50
   D. 70/30

_____ **5.** A force pulling outward on a rotating body is known as _____.
   A. roll
   B. convection
   C. centrifugal force
   D. spin

_____ **6.** Coolant absorbs heat by _____ from the engine and becomes hotter.
   A. conduction
   B. convection
   C. radiation
   D. all of the above

_____ **7.** As coolant moves through the hottest part of an engine with a reverse-flow design, steam tends to form and get stuck at the head cooling passages; this problem was fixed by adding a(n) _____.
   A. overflow tank
   B. cooling fan
   C. surge tank
   D. recirculation pump

_____ **8.** What type of belt is used to drive the water pump and other accessories on the front of the engine?
   A. V-belt
   B. Serpentine belt
   C. Toothed belt
   D. Any of the above

_____ **9.** _____ are used around the radiator fan to help draw air through the entire radiator core and not just in front of the fan blades.
   A. Fins
   B. Baffles
   C. Shrouds
   D. Ducts

_____ **10.** The _____ is called a fan clutch since it can engage and disengage the cooling fan from the pulley.
   A. torque connector
   B. viscous coupler
   C. thermo-control switch
   D. electric solenoid

_____ **11.** The _____ is typically located on the water pump and connects to the intake manifold on many V-configured engines, such as a V6 or V8.
   A. bypass hose
   B. upper hose
   C. lower hose
   D. throttle body coolant line

_____ **12.** A _____ belt has a flat profile with a number of small V-shaped grooves running lengthwise along the inside of the belt.
   A. V-type
   B. serpentine
   C. stretch
   D. toothed

_____ **13.** The _____ operates by using a signal sent from a coolant temperature sensor located on the engine in a coolant passage.
   A. temperature gauge
   B. thermostat
   C. warning light
   D. both A and C

_____ **14.** The aluminum, brass, or steel plugs designed to seal the openings left from the casting process where the casting sand was removed are called _____.
   A. core plugs
   B. soft plugs
   C. expansion plugs
   D. all of the above

_____ **15.** What type of coolant contains a mixture of inorganic and organic additives?
   A. Organic acid technology
   B. Inorganic acid technology
   C. Hybrid organic acid technology
   D. Poly organic acid technology

True/False

If you believe the statement to be more true than false, write the letter "T" in the space provided. If you believe the statement to be more false than true, write the letter "F."

_____ **1.** Heat is transferred from one solid to another by a process called radiation.

_____ **2.** No matter how efficiently fuel burning occurs, and no matter the size of the engine, the heat energy generated never completely transforms into kinetic energy.

_____ **3.** Some newer vehicles have a coolant heat storage system that uses a vacuum-insulated container similar to a Thermos bottle.

_____ **4.** Water alone is by far the best coolant there is, since it can absorb a larger amount of heat than most other liquids.

_____ **5.** Ethylene glycol is a chemical that resists freezing but is not toxic and is used in nontoxic antifreezes.

_____ **6.** Because atmospheric pressure is lower at higher elevations, the boiling temperature of a liquid in an unsealed system is higher.

_____ **7.** In an automotive cooling system, electrolysis is possible when the coolant breaks down and becomes more acidic.

_____ **8.** Vehicle coolant prevents an engine from overheating while in use.

_____ **9.** Air-cooled engines use a fan to direct air through and over the cooling fins, which increases the cooling capacity.

_____ **10.** All engines operate best when they are at their full operating temperature.

_____ **11.** The hottest part of any engine is the cylinder head, since this is where the combustion chamber is located.

_____ **12.** Radiator hoses connect the water pump and engine to the heater core. They carry heated coolant to the heater core to be used to heat the passenger compartment.

_____ **13.** In both the cross-flow and the down-flow radiator designs, the core is built of the same components.

_____ **14.** The thermostat is a spring-loaded valve that is controlled by a wax pellet located inside the valve.

_____ **15.** Thermo-control switches often use a bimetallic strip that consists of two different metals or alloys laminated back to back that expand and contract at different rates.

_____ **16.** Some radiator hoses, especially lower hoses, have a spiral wire inside to keep the hose from collapsing during heavy acceleration when the water pump is drawing a lot of water from the radiator.

_____ **17.** The bottom radiator hose is typically attached to the thermostat housing, which allows the heated coolant to enter the inlet side of the radiator.

_____ **18.** The heater control valve, if used, controls the flow of coolant to the heater core to control the temperature of the air desired by the operator.

_____ **19.** Coolant can be easily identified according to its color, which may be anything from green or purple to yellow/gold, orange, blue, or pink.

_____ **20.** Poly organic acid technology coolant contains a proprietary blend of corrosion inhibitors and provides up to 7 years or 250,000 miles of protection.

Fill in the Blank

Read each item carefully, and then complete the statement by filling in the missing word(s).

1. Heat is _____ energy. It cannot be destroyed; it can only be transferred.

2. Heat is transferred through space by a process called _____.

3. The principle that heat always moves from hot to cold is known as the second law of _____.

4. Coolant is a mixture of water and _____-_____, which is used to remove heat from the engine.

5. _____ glycol is a chemical that resists freezing but is very toxic to humans and animals.

6. A liquid under pressure higher than atmospheric pressure has a _____ boiling point than when that liquid is at atmospheric pressure.

7. The radiator of a vehicle is made of materials such as _____, _____, or _____.

8. In a typical _____-_____ design, coolant starts from the radiator and flows through the radiator outlet hose to the thermostat and then to the water pump.

9. The _____ is usually made of copper, brass, or aluminum tubes with copper, brass, aluminum, or plastic tanks on the sides or top for coolant to collect in.

10. _____ coolers are used to cool automatic transmission fluid, power steering fluid, EGR gasses, and compressed intake air.

11. One way to prevent coolant from boiling is to use a radiator _____ cap.

12. The coolant _____ system consists of an overflow bottle, a sealed radiator pressure cap, and a small hose connecting the bottle to the radiator neck.

13. The _____ _____ is usually belt driven from a pulley on the front of the crankshaft.

14. Engine-driven _____ _____ may be located on the water pump shaft, or in a few cases it may be attached directly to the engine crankshaft.

15. The bottom or lower _____ _____ is connected between the outlet of the radiator and the inlet of the water pump.

16. A(n) _____ belt looks like an ordinary serpentine belt but is found on vehicles without a tensioner.

17. _____ are used to keep the drive belt tight around the pulleys to ensure the least amount of slippage without causing damage to component bearings.

18. Temperature _____ can come in two forms: a temperature gauge or a temperature light located in the instrument cluster.

19. The _____ _____ is simply a small radiator that is mounted inside the heater box in the passenger compartment.

20. Air doors are moved by one of three methods: cable, vacuum actuator, or an electric _____, called a stepper motor.

Labeling

Label the following diagrams with the correct terms.

1. Heat transfer:

A. _____

B. _____

C. _____

D. _____

2. Heat loss in a gasoline engine:

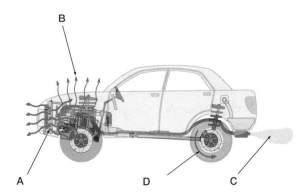

A. _____

B. _____

C. _____

D. _____

3. Types of radiators:

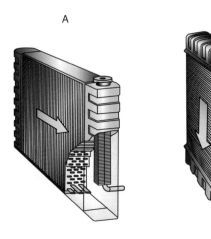

A. _____

B. _____

4. Coolant recovery system:

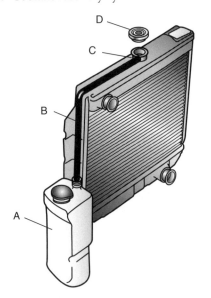

A. _____

B. _____

C. _____

D. _____

5. Thermostat valve:

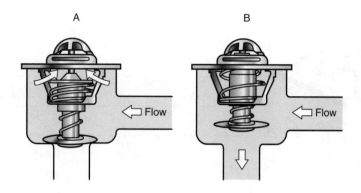

A. _____

B. _____

6. Water pump:

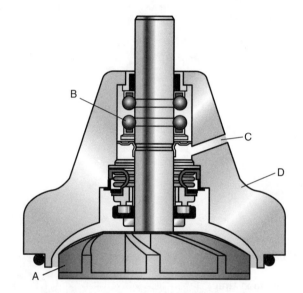

A. _____

B. _____

C. _____

D. _____

7. Hydraulically operated cooling fan:

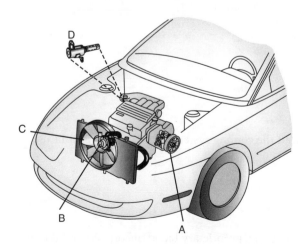

A. _____

B. _____

C. _____

D. _____

8. Cooling system:

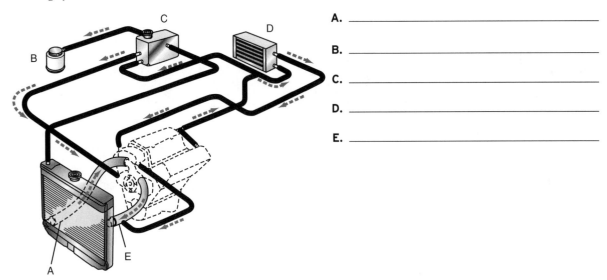

A. _____

B. _____

C. _____

D. _____

E. _____

Review Questions

_____ **1.** The movement of heat through space is known as:
   A. conduction.
   B. radiation.
   C. convection.
   D. evaporation.

_____ **2.** The coolant heat storage system:
   A. uses a condenser.
   B. prevents the engine from overheating on hot days.
   C. increases hydrocarbon exhaust emissions.
   D. preheats the engine when the vehicle is started the next time.

_____ **3.** A coolant serves all of the following purposes *except*:
   A. preventing an engine from overheating while in use.
   B. keeping the engine from freezing while not in use in cold climates.
   C. reducing friction in the moving parts of the engine.
   D. preventing corrosion of the parts in the cooling system.

_____ **4.** When pressurizing coolant:
   A. its boiling point increases.
   B. the cooling system becomes heavier.
   C. the radiator becomes bigger.
   D. engine efficiency decreases.

_____ **5.** Which of these is used to force coolant throughout the cooling system in order to transfer heat energy?
   A. Water pump
   B. Thermostat
   C. Radiator
   D. Cooling fan

_____ **6.** Coolants based on which of these technologies contain a proprietary blend of corrosion inhibitors and are claimed to be compatible with most other types of coolant?
   A. IAT
   B. HOAT
   C. POAT
   D. OAT

_____ 7. The surface area that dissipates heat is increased by the use of:
   A. soft plugs.
   B. fins.
   C. hood insulation.
   D. drain plugs.

_____ 8. The surge tank:
   A. regulates coolant temperature.
   B. prevents coolant leak.
   C. reduces engine noise.
   D. removes gas from the system.

_____ 9. All of the following statements are true of a thermostat _except_:
   A. It regulates the flow of coolant.
   B. It is a spring-loaded valve controlled by a wax pellet.
   C. When the engine is cold, the valve is open; when hot, the valve closes.
   D. When installing the thermostat, the jiggle valve should be in the uppermost position.

_____ 10. Which hose allows the water pump to circulate the water in the engine when the thermostat is closed, but not when it is open.
   A. Bypass hose
   B. Throttle body coolant line
   C. Overflow hose
   D. Radiator hose

ASE Technician A/Technician B Style Questions

_____ 1. Tech A says that the cooling system is designed to keep the engine as cool as possible. Tech B says that heat travels from cold objects to hot objects. Who is correct?
   A. Tech A
   B. Tech B
   C. Both A and B
   D. Neither A nor B

_____ 2. Tech A says that the thermostat is open until the engine warms up, and then it closes. Tech B says that a faulty radiator cap can be the cause of boiling coolant. Who is correct?
   A. Tech A
   B. Tech B
   C. Both A and B
   D. Neither A nor B

_____ 3. Tech A says that when 100% antifreeze is used in the cooling system, the protection level is approximately −70°F. Tech B says that 100% antifreeze will cool the engine better than 100% water. Who is correct?
   A. Tech A
   B. Tech B
   C. Both A and B
   D. Neither A nor B

_____ 4. Tech A says that some drive belts are of a stretch fit design and are not adjustable. Tech B says that automatic belt tensioners never wear out. Who is correct?
   A. Tech A
   B. Tech B
   C. Both A and B
   D. Neither A nor B

_____ 5. Tech A says that the design of a surge tank system helps to purge air from the cooling system. Tech B says that the overflow tank adds coolant to the radiator when the engine is hotter than normal. Who is correct?
   A. Tech A
   B. Tech B
   C. Both A and B
   D. Neither A nor B

_____ **6.** Tech A says that when you find coolant hoses collapsed after the engine cools down, the radiator pressure cap has likely failed. Tech B says that the thermostat may have a bleed valve that should be accurately positioned when the thermostat is replaced. Who is correct?
   A. Tech A
   B. Tech B
   C. Both A and B
   D. Neither A nor B

_____ **7.** Tech A says that electric cooling fans are used to cause a large airflow over the radiator when the engine is cold. Tech B says that electric cooling fans are used to cause a large airflow over the radiator at low vehicle speeds. Who is correct?
   A. Tech A
   B. Tech B
   C. Both A and B
   D. Neither A nor B

_____ **8.** Tech A says that there are a number of coolant types that each has its own life span. Tech B says that mixing of coolants is generally okay, as all coolants use the same chemical base. Who is correct?
   A. Tech A
   B. Tech B
   C. Both A and B
   D. Neither A nor B

_____ **9.** Tech A says that coolant leaking out of the water pump weep hole means the pump is operating normally. Tech B says that the water pump uses centrifugal force to circulate coolant. Who is correct?
   A. Tech A
   B. Tech B
   C. Both A and B
   D. Neither A nor B

_____ **10.** Tech A says that raising the pressure on the cooling system raises the boiling point of the coolant. Tech B says that air-cooled engines operate within a more consistent and ideal temperature range. Who is correct?
   A. Tech A
   B. Tech B
   C. Both A and B
   D. Neither A nor B

Cooling System Service

At the start of each chapter you'll find the NATEF Tasks, Knowledge Objectives, and Skills Objectives from the textbook. These are your objectives as you make your way through the exercises in this workbook and the chapter in your textbook. The following activities have been designed to help you refresh your knowledge of the material in this chapter.

NATEF Tasks

- N17001 Inspect and/or test coolant; drain and recover coolant; flush and refill cooling system; use proper fluid type per manufacturer specification; bleed air as required. (MLR/AST/MAST)
- N17002 Inspect, replace, and/or adjust drive belts, tensioners, and pulleys; check pulley and belt alignment. (MLR/AST/MAST)
- N17003 Inspect engine cooling and heater system hoses and pipes; determine needed action. (MLR/AST/MAST)
- N17004 Remove, inspect, and replace thermostat and gasket/seal. (MLR/AST/MAST)
- N17005 Identify causes of engine overheating. (AST/MAST)
- N17006 Perform cooling system pressure and dye tests to identify leaks; check coolant condition and level; inspect and test radiator, pressure cap, coolant recovery tank, heater core, and galley plugs; determine needed action. (MLR/AST/MAST)
- N17007 Verify engine operating temperature; determine needed action. (MLR/AST/MAST)
- N17008 Inspect and test fan(s), fan clutch (electrical or mechanical), fan shroud, and air dams determine needed action. (AST/MAST)
- N17009 Inspect and test heater control valve(s); perform needed action. (AST/MAST)
- N17010 Remove and replace radiator. (AST/MAST)
- N17011 Determine procedure to remove, inspect, reinstall, and/or replace heater core. (AST/MAST)

Knowledge Objectives

There are no knowledge objectives in this chapter.

Skills Objectives

After reading this chapter, you will be able to:

- S17001 Diagnose cooling system faults.

Matching

Match the following terms with the correct description or example.

A. Centrifugal force
B. Electrolysis
C. Hydrometer
D. Ethylene glycol
E. Glazing
F. An infrared temperature gun
G. Wire or spring clamp

_____ 1. The process of pulling metals apart by using electricity.

_____ 2. It is highly toxic to humans and animals.

_____ 3. It is the force pulling outward on a rotating body.

_____ 4. It is the shine on the surface of a belt.

_____ 5. It is not adjustable and is fitted and removed with special hose clamp pliers.

_____ 6. It is used to test coolant mixture and freeze protection by testing the specific gravity of the coolant.

_____ 7. It can be used to measure the operating temperature of the engine.

Multiple Choice

Read each item carefully, and then select the best response.

_____ 1. A(n) _____ can tell the proportions of antifreeze and water in a coolant mix.
  A. refractometer
  B. infrared temperature gun
  C. litmus paper
  D. electronic pH tester

_____ 2. A serpentine belt can be checked with a(n) _____.
  A. adjuster tool
  B. refractometer
  C. hydrometer
  D. plastic wear gauge

_____ 3. Checking pulley alignment is done with a _____ across the face of the pulleys when replacing an accessory drive belt.
  A. plastic wear gauge
  B. straightedge
  C. belt tension gauge
  D. serpentine belt gauge

_____ 4. _____ are designed to be operated without a tensioner.
  A. V-belts
  B. Flat belts
  C. Stretch Fit belts
  D. Rope belts

_____ 5. A _____ is a hose that has become brittle and will break and leak.
  A. swollen hose
  B. hardened hose
  C. soft hose
  D. cracked hose

_____ 6. A _____ is a hose that has become very weak and is in danger of ballooning or bursting.
  A. soft hose
  B. swollen hose
  C. cracked hose
  D. hardened hose

_____ 7. Identify the tool that is used to test coolant mixture and freeze protection by testing the fluid's ability to bend light.
  A. Hydrometer
  B. Coolant system pressure tester
  C. Borescope
  D. Refractometer

_____ 8. A(n) _____ is used to check for electrical problems such as cooling fan and temperature gauge issues.
  A. refractometer
  B. voltmeter
  C. gas analyzer
  D. scan tool

_____ 9. A _____ can be used to read DTCs related to cooling system operation.
  A. scan tool
  B. voltmeter
  C. gas analyzer
  D. hydrometer

_____ 10. Coolant leak into the combustion chamber will produce _____ from the engine exhaust.
  A. particulate
  B. black smoke
  C. smog
  D. white smoke

True/False

If you believe the statement to be more true than false, write the letter "T" in the space provided. If you believe the statement to be more false than true, write the letter "F."

_____ **1.** A proper way of disposing coolant is to dump it into a storm drain or down a shop floor drain.

_____ **2.** Antifreeze has a lower specific gravity than water.

_____ **3.** Cracks in a belt indicate that immediate replacement is needed.

_____ **4.** Stretch Fit belts can last up to 10 years or 150,000 miles.

_____ **5.** A clutch fan is inspected in the same way as the mechanical fan.

Fill in the Blank

Read each item carefully, and then complete the statement by filling in the missing word(s).

1. _____ is the reaction of different metals to an acid solution to produce electricity.

2. Testing of the coolant's _____ can be performed with a test strip or electronic tester.

3. A _____ hose is a hose that has lost its reinforcement and is swelling under pressure.

4. A _____ hose is a hose that has cracked and will soon start to leak.

5. A(n) _____ _____ _____ _____
_____ is used to apply pressure to the cooling system to diagnose leakage complaints.

6. _____ _____ _____ _____
_____ are used to test the acid-to-alkalinity balance of the coolant.

7. A _____ _____ _____ _____
_____ is used to check whether the serpentine belt grooves are worn past their specifications.

8. A _____ is used for examining internal passages for evidence of a coolant leak.

9. A _____ _____ _____ _____ is used to
detect exhaust gases in the cooling system due to a leak.

10. _____ _____ _____ _____ control the
flow of coolant to the heater core.

Labeling

Identify the correct component as shown in the following illustrations.

1. Radiator hose problems:

A. _____

B. _____

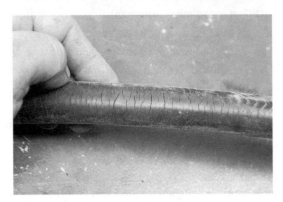

C. _____

2. Tools for diagnosing and servicing the engine cooling system:

A. _____

B. _____

Skill Drills

Test your knowledge of skill drills by filling in the correct words in the photo captions.

1. Using a Hydrometer to Test the Freeze Point of the Coolant:

_____ **A.** Remove the pressure cap. Place the hydrometer tube in the coolant, and squeeze the ball on top.

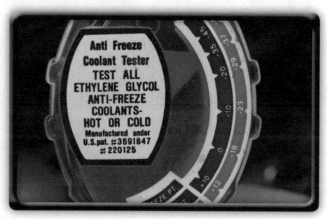

_____ **B.** Hold the tool vertical. Read the scale to verify the freeze protection of the coolant. Return coolant sample to the radiator or surge tank.

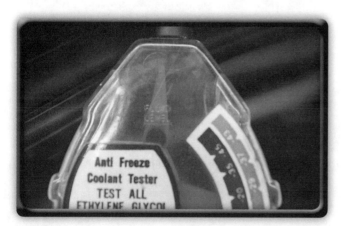

_____ **C.** Release the ball to pull a coolant sample into the hydrometer. Verify it is above the minimum level in the tester.

2. Using a Refractometer to Test the Freeze Point of the Coolant:

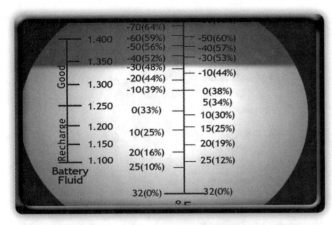

_____ **A.** Hold the refractometer roughly level under a light, look through the viewfinder, and read the scale to verify the freeze protection of the coolant.

_____ **B.** Remove the pressure cap. Be sure the cooling system is cool first.

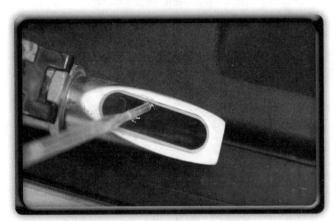

_____ **C.** Determine the type of antifreeze, and verify that the refractometer is designed to be used with it. Place a few drops of coolant on the sample plate on the top of the tool.

3. Draining and Refilling Coolant:

_____ **A.** Remove the block drain plugs, and allow the coolant to drain into the pan.

_____ **B.** Refill the cooling system with the proper coolant mix after closing the drain plugs. Start the engine and verify the proper level. Dispose of coolant in an approved way.

_____ **C.** Locate the radiator drain plug, if equipped, and place a catch pan marked for coolant underneath the drain valve. Drain the radiator into the catch pan.

Review Questions

_____ 1. A refractometer is used to test:
   A. coolant pH.
   B. the freeze protection of the coolant.
   C. electrolysis.
   D. coolant level.

_____ 2. Draining and refilling the coolant is necessary in all of the following cases _except_ when:
   A. a customer requests it.
   B. the pH is out of specification.
   C. the coolant is contaminated.
   D. the coolant level is low.

_____ 3. Choose the correct statement.
   A. Belts should be inspected when the engine is running.
   B. Tears or split belts are serviceable.
   C. A bottomed out belt will slip and squeal.
   D. Always replace belts with cracks..

_____ 4. The best way to remove hoses from heater cores is:
   A. to slit them and peel them off.
   B. pry them off with a screwdriver.
   C. twist the hose off.
   D. to heat them mildly.

_____ 5. A borescope is used:
   A. for examining internal passages for evidence of a coolant leak.
   B. to check belt tension.
   C. to check the temperature of air exiting the heating ducts.
   D. to activate the cooling fan through bidirectional controls.

_____ 6. When testing the cooling system for leaks using a pressure tester:
   A. ensure there is only 50% coolant or water.
   B. the radiator cap need not be tested.
   C. do not adjust the pressure when the engine heats up.
   D. look for both internal and external leaks.

_____ 7. The engine's operating temperature can be verified using all of the following _except_ a:
   A. dash gauge.
   B. refractometer.
   C. scan tool.
   D. temperature gun.

_____ 8. If the vehicle only overheats while stopped, it is likely an issue with the:
   A. heater core.
   B. thermostat.
   C. cooling fan.
   D. coolant.

_____ 9. When removing a radiator:
   A. do not disconnect automatic transmission cooler lines.
   B. inspect the cooling system hoses and clamps.
   C. do not drain the coolant.
   D. use the same container to hold transmission fluid and coolant.

_____ 10. All of the following should be checked for coolant leaks when pressure testing a cooling system _except_:
   A. Soft plugs.
   B. Heater core.
   C. Thermostat housing.
   D. clutch fan.

ASE Technician A/Technician B Style Questions

_____ **1.** Tech A says that most coolants are designed to last the life of the vehicle. Tech B says that a hydrometer can be used to test the freeze point of coolant. Who is correct?
   A. Tech A
   B. Tech B
   C. Both A and B
   D. Neither A nor B

_____ **2.** Tech A says that the thermostat may have an air bleed that must be positioned properly when the thermostat is replaced. Tech B says that the thermostat housing must be flush against the mating surface or the ear may break off when tightening the bolts. Who is correct?
   A. Tech A
   B. Tech B
   C. Both A and B
   D. Neither A nor B

_____ **3.** Tech A says that coolant leaks can be located by performing a pressure test on the system. Tech B says that when pressure testing the cooling system, you should pressurize it to at least 10 psi (69 kPa) above the radiator cap pressure rating. Who is correct?
   A. Tech A
   B. Tech B
   C. Both A and B
   D. Neither A nor B

_____ **4.** Tech A says that the radiator cap should be pressure tested as part of a cooling system diagnosis. Tech B says that the water pump weep hole could be the source of a coolant leak. Who is correct?
   A. Tech A
   B. Tech B
   C. Both A and B
   D. Neither A nor B

_____ **5.** Tech A says that the engine operating temperature can be tested with an infrared temp gun. Tech B says that it can be tested with a scan tool. Who is correct?
   A. Tech A
   B. Tech B
   C. Both A and B
   D. Neither A nor B

_____ **6.** Tech A says that an electric fan that runs all the time can cause the engine to overheat. Tech B says a refractometer is used to turn a clutch fan on and off. Who is correct?
   A. Tech A
   B. Tech B
   C. Both A and B
   D. Neither A nor B

_____ **7.** Tech A says that one coolant test is a coolant electrolysis test. Tech B says that a thermostat that is stuck open will cause the engine to run cooler than it should. Who is correct?
   A. Tech A
   B. Tech B
   C. Both A and B
   D. Neither A nor B

_____ **8.** Tech A says that there are a number of coolant types and each has its own life span. Tech B says that mixing of coolants is generally okay because all coolants use the same chemical base. Who is correct?
   A. Tech A
   B. Tech B
   C. Both A and B
   D. Neither A nor B

_____ **9.** Tech A says that when replacing cooling system hoses, it may be best to slit the hose rather than trying to twist it off. Tech B says that cooling system hoses only need to be changed when they start leaking. Who is correct?

A. Tech A

B. Tech B

C. Both A and B

D. Neither A nor B

_____ **10.** Two technicians are discussing cooling system hose replacement. Tech A says to make sure that the hose clamps get installed just inside the flared or barbed segment of the fitting, not on top of it. Tech B says that it is good practice to install new hose clamps at the same time as new hoses. Who is correct?

A. Tech A

B. Tech B

C. Both A and B

D. Neither A nor B

Engine Removal and Replacement

At the start of each chapter you'll find the NATEF Tasks, Knowledge Objectives, and Skills Objectives from the textbook. These are your objectives as you make your way through the exercises in this workbook and the chapter in your textbook. The following activities have been designed to help you refresh your knowledge of the material in this chapter.

NATEF Tasks

- N18001 Remove and reinstall engine on a newer vehicle equipped with OBD; reconnect all attaching components and restore the vehicle to running condition. (MAST)

Knowledge Objectives

After reading this chapter, you will be able to:

- K18001 Describe the purpose of individual engine removal tool.
- K18002 Explain the safety concerns when removing and installing engines.

Skills Objectives

After reading this chapter, you will be able to:

- S18001 Disconnect the topside components.
- S18002 Relieve fuel pressure and remove fuel lines.
- S18003 Disconnect the battery.
- S18004 Disconnect electrical components and wire harnesses.
- S18005 Disconnect the front accessories.
- S18006 Disconnect and/or remove radiator.
- S18007 Remove accessories and brackets.
- S18008 Disconnect the underside components.
- S18009 Drain remaining fluids.
- S18010 Disconnect exhaust system components.
- S18011 Remove starter.
- S18012 Disconnect torque converter.
- S18013 Disconnect transmission/transaxle.
- S18014 Remove the engine.
- S18015 Remove engine using an engine hoist.
- S18016 Remove engine using a subframe jack.
- S18017 Install the engine.
- S18018 Reconnect motor mounts.
- S18019 Perform start-up and break-in of the engine.
- S18020 Perform prestart engine checks.
- S18021 Perform initial engine break-in.
- S18022 Perform DTC inspection and necessary module updates.

Matching

Match the following terms with the correct description or example.

- **A.** Date link connector (DLC)
- **B.** Diagnostic trouble code (DTC)
- **C.** Malfunction indicator light (MIL)
- **D.** Subframe

_____ **1.** A mount attached to the vehicle that is used to support the engine and transaxle assembly.

_____ **2.** An underdash connector for connecting a diagnostic scanner.

_____ **3.** A dash light usually indicating the presence of a diagnostic trouble code or malfunction.

_____ **4.** A code set by the computer indicating system or component malfunction.

Multiple Choice

Read each item carefully, and then select the best response.

_____ **1.** If the engine will need to be pulled from the top of the engine compartment, you will need to use a(n) _____.

    A. scissor jack

    B. sling bridge

    C. engine hoist

    D. single-post hoist

_____ **2.** Which tool is used to support the engine during engine mount removal in a front-wheel drive vehicle?

    A. Engine support bar

    B. FWD engine hoist

    C. Engine sling

    D. Transmission jack

_____ **3.** The first step in the engine removal process is to remove the _____.

    A. tires

    B. hood

    C. transmission

    D. muffler

_____ **4.** What is the minimum number of computers in the operational system of a modern vehicle?

    A. 3

    B. 4

    C. 5

    D. 10

_____ **5.** Which of these is used to monitor engine data and diagnostic trouble codes (DTCs)?

    A. Scan tool

    B. Warning light

    C. Dashboard display

    D. Microprocessor

_____ **6.** To begin the exhaust removal process, identify the _____ that need to be removed or disconnected.

    A. brackets

    B. oxygen sensors

    C. pipes

    D. bolts

_____ **7.** The point where the engine and the transmission/transaxle are mounted is called the _____, and the starter is usually bolted to it.

    A. torque converter

    B. subframe

    C. bell housing

    D. starter mount

_____ **8.** When using an engine hoist you must use at least _____ bolts, and make sure they screw in at least five full turns.

    A. seven

    B. grade 5

    C. six inch

    D. grade 3

_____ **9.** When reinstalling the torque converter make sure to pour enough _____ into the torque converter to fill it about halfway.
  A. power steering fluid
  B. coolant
  C. motor oil
  D. transmission fluid

_____ **10.** What should you do during start-up if the gauges indicate overheating or low oil pressure?
  A. Add oil
  B. Check the wiring
  C. Shut it down
  D. Tap the gauges

True/False

If you believe the statement to be more true than false, write the letter "T" in the space provided. If you believe the statement to be more false than true, write the letter "F."

_____ **1.** Some engines have pulling brackets that allow the chains to be attached by hooks when pulling the engine.

_____ **2.** Most engines in rear-wheel drive vehicles are best removed from the bottom of the engine compartment.

_____ **3.** You can block off and seal the fuel supply line from the fuel tank by using a vacuum hose plug compatible with gasoline.

_____ **4.** An automobile may have as many as 70 separate microprocessors onboard.

_____ **5.** When disconnecting the battery, remove the positive terminal of the battery first.

_____ **6.** In late-model vehicles, the electrical plug ends are interchangeable so you need to label them before disconnecting.

_____ **7.** Always make sure the engine is cool before removing the radiator cap.

_____ **8.** You must separate the transmission/transaxle from the engine before the transmission is supported and the engine is on the hoist.

_____ **9.** Before starting an engine after installation you should verify that the brake pedal is not spongy.

_____ **10.** There are significant differences in timing methods from one decade to another.

Fill in the Blank

Read each item carefully, and then complete the statement by filling in the missing word(s).

1. A(n) _____ _____ light is a dash light that indicates the presence of a diagnostic trouble code or a malfunction such as dead engine cylinders.

2. If the engine is removed from the _____ of the engine compartment, the engine and transaxle are usually removed as a unit attached to the engine cradle.

3. Always put _____ first in each step of the engine removal and installation process.

4. You will need to relieve the pressure on the _____ system before disconnecting the lines.

5. If power is removed from some electronic components such as radios and navigation devices, they will not work until the proper _____ _____ is keyed into it.

6. Before disconnecting electrical wire harness plug ends, it is a good idea to _____ _____.

7. The _____ _____ is normally located where the engine and the transmission/transaxle are mounted together.

8. A _____ is a mount used to support the engine and transaxle assembly and is attached to the vehicle.

9. An important task to complete after you have started a replaced engine is connecting a diagnostic scan tool to the _____ _____ connector.

10. If you find that a _____ _____ _____ was set during the engine break-in period, you should diagnose and correct the condition.

Labeling

Label the following images with the correct descriptions.

1. Engine removal tool:

A. _____

2. Front accessories disconnection: radiator

A. _____

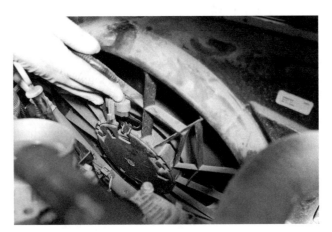

B. _____

C. _____

Review Questions

_____ 1. Which of these tools is used when removing the engine from a rear wheel drive vehicle?
  A. Scan tool
  B. Transmission jack
  C. Engine support bar
  D. FWD engine hoist

_____ 2. Removing engines are likely to pose all of the below safety hazards *except*:
  A. crushing fingers due to engine slips.
  B. fluids and chemicals spraying into your eyes.
  C. sharp edges of parts causing cuts.
  D. flash burns from arc welders.

_____ 3. During topside disconnection:
  A. always remove the hood irrespective of the degree to which it opens.
  B. maintain the fuel pressure in the fuel system.
  C. disable the electrical system by disconnecting the battery.
  D. retain the fluids in the engine.

_____ 4. When disconnecting a battery:
  A. have the unlock codes of the antitheft system available.
  B. remove the positive terminal of the battery first.
  C. lay the tools on the battery for easy use.
  D. ensure that all other components are disconnected.

_____ 5. When removing accessory components that are mounted to the engine:
  A. remove all the brackets.
  B. always disconnect the hydraulic lines.
  C. place all attachment bolts separate from the components.
  D. take pictures to remind you of bracket locations and positions.

_____ 6. During the exhaust system removal process, the exhaust pipe and component routing should be checked to:
  A. prevent leaks.
  B. improve their efficiency.
  C. determine the best places to disconnect.
  D. avoid emission of toxic gases.

_____ 7. For front-wheel drive vehicles in which the engine is being removed from the bottom, all of the below may be removed along with the engine *except*:
  A. transaxle.
  B. radiator.
  C. cradle.
  D. axles.

_____ 8. Until the transmission is supported and the engine is supported by the hoist, do not try to:
  A. drain engine fluids.
  B. remove the radiator.
  C. separate the transmission from the engine.
  D. disconnect the battery.

_____ 9. When reinstalling the torque converter, push in and turn the torque converter. We can make sure it fully engages into the front pump when we feel:
  A. four distinct clunks.
  B. three distinct clunks.
  C. two distinct clunks.
  D. single clunk.

_____ 10. As part of prestart engine checks, it is essential to do all of the below *except*:
  A. checking all fluid levels, especially the engine oil and coolant levels.
  B. checking that the battery terminals are clean and connected firmly.
  C. checking all auxiliary components for proper installation.
  D. checking the ignition timing with a timing light.

ASE Technician A/Technician B Style Questions

_____ **1.** Tech A says that one of the most important steps in performing an engine removal and installation procedure is to research the appropriate service information. Tech B says that researching service information is a waste of time. Who is correct?
   A. Tech A
   B. Tech B
   C. Both A and B
   D. Neither A nor B

_____ **2.** Tech A says that engines in most RWD vehicle are removed from the top. Tech B says that before an engine fails, there are usually warning signs such as dash warning lights indicating low oil pressure, high operating temperature, or abnormal engine noises. Who is correct?
   A. Tech A
   B. Tech B
   C. Both A and B
   D. Neither A nor B

_____ **3.** Tech A says that when disconnecting the battery, remove the positive terminal from the battery first. Tech B says that it is often easier to disconnect main wire harnesses at their central connector instead of at the end of each branch. Who is correct?
   A. Tech A
   B. Tech B
   C. Both A and B
   D. Neither A nor B

_____ **4.** Tech A says that a fuel injection system automatically relieves pressure when the engine is turned off. Tech B says that you need to relieve fuel pressure from most fuel-injected vehicles before disconnecting the lines. Who is correct?
   A. Tech A
   B. Tech B
   C. Both A and B
   D. Neither A nor B

_____ **5.** Tech A says that if refrigerant removal is necessary, air-conditioning refrigerant must be removed with an approved recycling machine. Tech B says that if refrigerant removal is needed, it is much better to release it into the atmosphere because modern refrigerants are safe. Who is correct?
   A. Tech A
   B. Tech B
   C. Both A and B
   D. Neither A nor B

_____ **6.** Tech A says to remove the radiator cap so that coolant will be able to flow more freely out of the drain plug. Tech B says that the lower radiator hose needs to be disconnected if there is no drain valve or plug at the bottom of the radiator. Who is correct?
   A. Tech A
   B. Tech B
   C. Both A and B
   D. Neither A nor B

_____ **7.** Tech A says that after starting the engine, it should be revved higher than 4000 rpm for a few minutes to break in the rings. Tech B says that after initial break-in, connect a diagnostic scan tool to the DLC and check for DTCs. Who is correct?
   A. Tech A
   B. Tech B
   C. Both A and B
   D. Neither A nor B

_____ **8.** Tech A says that a technician needs to make sure an engine hoist is rated for the lifting capacity needed for the engine being removed. Tech B says that when installing a clutch in an engine with a manual transmission, a clutch alignment tool is needed. Who is correct?
   A. Tech A
   B. Tech B

    C. Both A and B

    D. Neither A nor B

_____ **9.** Tech A says to check all fluid levels before starting a newly installed engine, especially the engine oil and coolant levels. Tech B says that once started, the engine should be checked for external leaks. Who is correct?

    A. Tech A

    B. Tech B

    C. Both A and B

    D. Neither A nor B

_____ **10.** Tech A says that a torque converter should engage at three different levels as it is being installed in a transmission. Tech B says that the torque converter requires an alignment tool when installing it in the transmission. Who is correct?

    A. Tech A

    B. Tech B

    C. Both A and B

    D. Neither A nor B

19 Cylinder Head Components

At the start of each chapter you'll find the NATEF Tasks, Knowledge Objectives, and Skills Objectives from the textbook. These are your objectives as you make your way through the exercises in this workbook and the chapter in your textbook. The following activities have been designed to help you refresh your knowledge of the material in this chapter.

NATEF Tasks

- N19001 Remove cylinder head; inspect gasket condition; install cylinder head and gasket; tighten according to manufacturer's specification and procedures. (AST/MAST)
- N19002 Clean and visually inspect a cylinder head for cracks; check gasket surface areas for warpage and surface finish; check passage condition. (AST/MAST)
- N19003 Inspect valves and valve seats; determine needed action. (MAST)
- N19004 Inspect valve guides for wear; check valve stem-to-guide clearance; determine needed action. (MAST)
- N19005 Inspect valve springs for squareness and free height comparison; determine needed action. (MAST)
- N19006 Inspect pushrods, rocker arms, and rocker arm pivots and shafts for wear, bending, cracks, looseness, and blocked oil passages (orifices); determine needed action. (AST/MAST)
- N19007 Inspect and/or measure camshaft for runout, journal wear, and lobe wear. (MAST)
- N19008 Inspect camshaft bearing surface for wear, damage, out-of-round, and alignment; determine needed action. (MAST)

Knowledge Objectives

After reading this chapter, you will be able to:

- K19001 Identify cylinder head configuration and components.
- K19002 Describe unique features of an OHV cylinder head.
- K19003 Describe unique features of an SOHC cylinder head.
- K19004 Describe unique features of a DOHC cylinder head.
- K19005 Describe individual cylinder head components.
- K19006 Describe the various cylinder head designs.
- K19007 Explain the function of the valve assemblies.
- K19008 Describe valves and their related components.
- K19009 Describe common valve arrangements.
- K19010 Describe the operation of intake and exhaust valves.
- K19011 Describe valve spring assemblies and their purpose.
- K19012 Describe valve guides and seals.
- K19013 Describe valve seats and their purpose.
- K19014 Explain the role of the camshaft in engine operation.
- K19015 Define the terms used in camshaft specifications.
- K19016 Describe how valve timing affects engine operation.
- K19017 Explain how and why valve timing is altered in variable valve timing engines.
- K19018 Explain the operation of valve train components.
- K19019 Describe the operation of the different types of lifters.
- K19020 Describe the purpose and types of pushrods.
- K19021 Describe the purpose and types of rocker arms.
- K19022 Explain the function and application of gaskets, seals, and sealants.
- K19023 Describe the purpose and types of head gaskets.
- K19024 Describe the purpose and types of seals.
- K19025 Describe the purpose and types of sealants.
- K19026 Describe the process of removing, inspecting, and diagnosing cylinder heads and related components.

Skills Objectives

After reading this chapter, you will be able to:

■ S19001 Reassemble a cylinder head.

Matching

Match the following terms with the correct description or example.

<table>
<tr><td>**A.** Anisotropic</td><td>**H.** Flat tappet</td><td>**O.** Valve face</td></tr>
<tr><td>**B.** Bedding-in</td><td>**I.** Head gasket</td><td>**P.** Valve guide</td></tr>
<tr><td>**C.** Camshaft follower</td><td>**J.** Keeper groove</td><td>**Q.** Valve keeper</td></tr>
<tr><td>**D.** Canted valves</td><td>**K.** L-head</td><td>**R.** Valve margin</td></tr>
<tr><td>**E.** Concentricity</td><td>**L.** Poppet valve</td><td>**S.** Valve stem</td></tr>
<tr><td>**F.** Flame front</td><td>**M.** Pushrod</td><td>**T.** Valve train</td></tr>
<tr><td>**G.** Flame propagation</td><td>**N.** Quench or squish area</td><td></td></tr>
</table>

_____ **1.** A device used to keep the valve spring retainers attached to the valve while in the cylinder head.

_____ **2.** A cam-operated, spring-loaded mushroom-type valve used to control intake into, and exhaust out of, the combustion chamber.

_____ **3.** The process of a valve wearing into the valve seat and creating a positive seal around the whole diameter.

_____ **4.** The portion of the valve between the valve face and the valve head.

_____ **5.** The portion of the valve that does the actual sealing to the valve seat.

_____ **6.** An object that has unequal physical properties along its various axes. Used in head gaskets to pull heat laterally from the edge surrounding the combustion chamber to the water jacket.

_____ **7.** A camshaft specifically designed to push on flat bottom lifters (nonroller types). It typically has a higher rolling resistance than the roller-style camshafts.

_____ **8.** A system encompassing all of the parts used in the opening and closing of the valves.

_____ **9.** The movement of the flame through the combustion chamber during the combustion process.

_____ **10.** A valve arrangement in the cylinder head where the valves are at an angle to the cylinder bore, this can make for a straighter path for air to flow into and out of the intake and exhaust ports.

_____ **11.** The front edge of the burning air/fuel mixture in the combustion chamber.

_____ **12.** The long shaftlike portion of the valve.

_____ **13.** A long, often hollow, metal tube that transfers the force from the valve lifter to the rocker arm assembly.

_____ **14.** A term used to describe a valve seat where the valve seat and valve stem share a common center. In this design, the valve can seal against the seat no matter how it is rotated.

_____ **15.** A thin piece of material, often a multilayered, bimetallic sheet used to seal the cylinder head assembly to the engine block.

_____ **16.** The narrow area between the top of the piston at top dead center and the cylinder head.

_____ **17.** A groove machined into the top of the valve stem near the tip of the valve that is used to "lock in" the valve keepers to help retain the valve spring onto the valve assembly.

_____ **18.** A slider or roller placed in direct contact with the lobes of the OHC camshaft that pushes on the tip of the valve to open it.

_____ **19.** A hole machined into the cylinder head or a hollow metal tube pressed into the cylinder head in which the valve stem rides, holding the stem in the proper position within the cylinder head.

_____ **20.** A type of four-stroke internal combustion engine having both intake and exhaust valves located in one side of the engine block, which are operated by lifters actuated by a single camshaft.

Multiple Choice

Read each item carefully, and then select the best response.

_____ **1.** The cylinder head caps off the top of the _____.
   A. carburetor
   B. head gasket
   C. combustion chamber
   D. intake port

_____ **2.** Which type of engine has valves that are positioned in the cylinder head assembly directly over the top of the piston, operated by a camshaft that is located in the cylinder block?
   A. Overhead valve engine
   B. Overhead cam engine
   C. Dual overhead cam engine
   D. None of the above

_____ **3.** In the cylinder head, swirl is initially created by the shape and angle of the _____.
   A. intake valves
   B. combustion chamber
   C. quench area
   D. intake port

_____ **4.** What type of combustion chamber is shaped like an inverted antique bathtub?
   A. Hemispherical
   B. Oval
   C. Wedge
   D. Elliptical

_____ **5.** The portion of the valve stem that comes in direct contact with the rocker arm, cam follower, or bucket lifter is called the _____.
   A. valve stem
   B. valve tip
   C. keeper
   D. valve margin

_____ **6.** What type of valve stem seals are used in today's engines?
   A. O-ring
   B. Umbrella-style
   C. Positive
   D. Integral

_____ **7.** When the valve and seat are machined about 1 degree different than each other for sealing purposes the difference is called _____.
   A. bedding-in
   B. concentricity
   C. positive seal
   D. interference angle

_____ **8.** Which term refers to how far the intake lobe is offset from the exhaust lobe?
   A. Lobe separation angle
   B. Lobe interference angle
   C. Lobe profile
   D. Lobe nose

_____ **9.** The _____ closes the valve and holds the valve firmly against the valve seat.
   A. rocker arm
   B. valve spring
   C. push rod
   D. camshaft lobe

_____ **10.** The metal spring wrapped circularly around the inside of a seal that applies a small, constant pressure to keep the lip in contact with the rotating part it is sealing is called the _____.
   A. keeper
   B. seal spring
   C. garter spring
   D. retainer spring

True/False

If you believe the statement to be more true than false, write the letter "T" in the space provided. If you believe the statement to be more false than true, write the letter "F."

_____ **1.** The dual overhead valve engine contains two camshafts per cylinder head.

_____ **2.** The valve keeper actuates a valve by pivoting near the center and pushing on the tip of the valve stem to open it.

_____ **3.** GDI refers to gasoline injected directly into the combustion chamber just above the piston.

_____ **4.** The use of smaller intake and exhaust ports allows the engine to develop more torque at low engine speeds.

_____ **5.** The valve spring is compressed when the valve is closed.

_____ **6.** The intake valve does not get as hot as the exhaust valve does.

_____ **7.** Integral valve guides can be removed and replaced as needed for repairs.

_____ **8.** In some cases intake valve angles are different than exhaust valve angles.

_____ **9.** Solid valve lifters are constructed as a centrally located plunger inside a hollow cylindrical body.

_____ **10.** A camshaft follower performs the same basic function as a rocker arm.

_____ **11.** Valve float is a condition that occurs when the valves cannot be closed by the valve springs as fast as is needed before the next stroke.

_____ **12.** Valve keepers lock the valve stem to the retainer.

_____ **13.** Gaskets are used to seal the rotating parts of an engine.

_____ **14.** When RTV is applied, it has the consistency of a gel, and as it sets, it becomes rubbery.

_____ **15.** The presence of a crack in a cylinder head automatically condemns it to the scrap bin.

Fill in the Blank

Read each item carefully, and then complete the statement by filling in the missing word(s).

1. Cylinder heads can be made of cast _____ or _____ alloy.

2. A(n) _____ combustion chamber has the intake valve on one side of the chamber and the exhaust valve on the other.

3. The _____ _____ is responsible for moving air and fuel through the engine.

4. The portion of the valve between the valve face and the valve head is called the valve _____.

5. A poppet valve must be able to stand up to both the _____ pressure trying to pull the valve apart and the _____ pressure trying to force it into the valve seat.

6. The non-replaceable _____ valve guide is cast into the cylinder head when the cylinder head is formed and is machined into the casting.

7. The _____ _____ is the part of the cylinder head that mates with the face of the valve when it is fully closed.

8. The _____ is the highest point of the cam lobe and determines how far the valve opens.

9. _____ refers to how long the valve is held open.

10. If the camshaft is located on top of and centered over the valves, the engine will use _____ - _____ lifters.

11. A _____ _____ is a lever that actuates a valve by pivoting inward near the center, and pushing on the tip of the valve to open it.

12. The valve spring _____ is used along with valve keepers to hold the valve spring in place, centered on the valve stem.

13. _____ form a seal by being compressed between stationary parts where liquid or gases could pass.

14. The most widely used seal for rotating parts is the _____ - _____ dynamic oil seal.

15. _____ _____ is capable of adhering to many different surfaces, including felt, cork, metal, paper, rubber, and asbestos gaskets.

Labeling

Label the following diagrams with the correct terms.

1. Dual overhead cam (DOHC) engine:

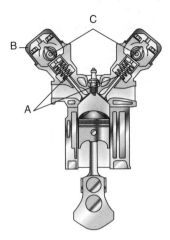

A. _____

B. _____

C. _____

2. Valve train:

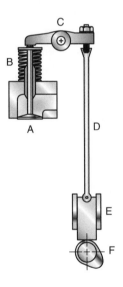

A. _____

B. _____

C. _____

D. _____

E. _____

F. _____

3. Parts of the valve:

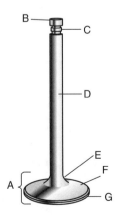

A. _____

B. _____

C. _____

D. _____

E. _____

F. _____

G. _____

4. Valve-to-valve seat interference angle:

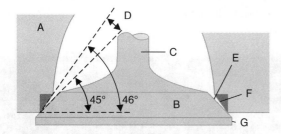

A. _____

B. _____

C. _____

D. _____

E. _____

F. _____

G. _____

5. Bucket-style lifters:

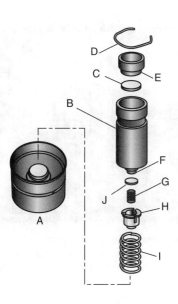

A. _____

B. _____

C. _____

D. _____

E. _____

F. _____

G. _____

H. _____

I. _____

J. _____

Skill Drills

Test your knowledge of skill drills by filling in the correct words in the photo captions.

   1. Removing Cylinder Heads:

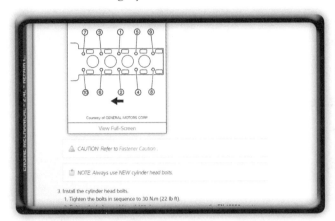

Step 1: Research the procedure for _____ the cylinder head(s) in the appropriate service information. Determine whether the head bolts are torque-to-yield (TTY) bolts. If so, you will need to discard them and replace them with new TTY bolts upon reassembly. Determine if the head bolts need to be _____ in a specified sequence.

Step 2: Before the _____ come off, put an identifying mark on at least one of the heads. Follow the specified procedure to remove all of the head _____, and set them aside.

Step 3: If dealing with a _____ _____ that is stuck to the head and block surface, reinstall two corner head bolts _____ or _____ turns in their respective holes.

Step 4: If the engine is mounted on an engine stand, check that the _____ _____ is in your engine stand. Insert a _____ _____ or a long breaker bar handle into one of the intake port openings of the head, and give it a firm push.

Step 5: Remove the safety bolts from the _____ and carefully lift it.

Step 6: Inspect the _____ _____ visually for any unusual conditions.

2. Inspecting Valves and Valve Seats:

Step 1: Inspect each valve for signs of _____, _____, and excessive face, stem, and tip wear. If found, replace the valves with new ones.

Step 2: Inspect each valve seat for signs of burning, leakage, or excessive wear. If found, the seat must be _____ or _____.

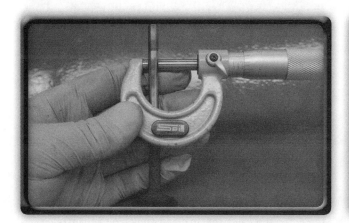

Step 3: Using a micrometer, measure each valve stem diameter in _____ places where the valve rides in the valve guide, and _____ your answers.

Step 4: Measure the valve _____ with a machinist's rule and record your readings.

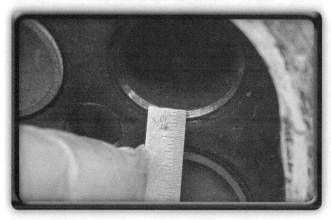

Step 5: Measure the _____ of the valve seats and record your readings.

Step 6: Compare readings to the _____, and determine needed actions.

Application	Specification
Intake Valves	
Face Angle	46°
Face Runout (Maximum)	.0015" (.038 mm)
Head Diameter	1.396–1.399" (35.47–35.53 mm)
Minimum Margin	.010" (.25 mm)
Length	4.227" (107.29 mm)
Tip-To-Groove Distance	.1346" (3.420 mm)
Stem Diameter	.2331–.2339" (5.921–5.941 mm)
Installed Height [1]	.9787–1.002" (24.86–25.62 mm)

3. Reassembling a Cylinder Head:

Step 1: Ensure that all _____ and _____ have been cleaned, checked for defects, and replaced if necessary. If any _____ are found, correct them now.

Step 2: Dip the _____ stem that is about to be installed in _____ engine oil or use the appropriate assembly lubrication.

Step 3: Insert the corresponding valve into the valve guide, and place the _____ sleeve over the grooves near the end of the valve stem.

Step 4: Dip the valve seal in clean engine oil and install it down over the _____ top of the valve guide assembly, using a(n) _____ if necessary.

Step 5: Remove the protective sleeve and place the valve _____ and _____ over the installed valve.

Step 6: Compress the valve spring and retainer with the valve spring _____, and install the valve keepers. Be sure the _____ are locked into their groove before releasing _____ on the valve spring compressor. Repeat this process for the remaining valves.

4. Inspecting and/or Measuring the Camshaft:

Step 1: Inspect the camshaft journals and _____ for obvious damage or wear. If found, replace the camshaft. Install the _____ on a set of V-blocks so that two specified cam journals are resting in the Vs.

Step 2: Set the _____ indicator so it is engaged on one of the other cam journals _____.

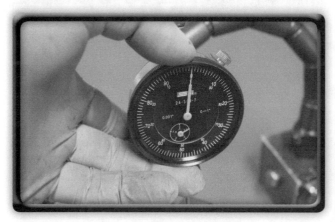

Step 3: Rotate the _____ until the dial indicator reads the _____ point, and zero the dial.

Step 4: Rotate the camshaft until the dial indicator reads the _____ point, and record the reading. Continue rotating the camshaft to verify that the needle does not go _____ zero. If it does, zero it again, and _____ the runout. Perform this process on all of the remaining journals, and compare to the runout specifications.

Step 5: Using a _____, measure each journal in two places _____ degrees apart to determine any out-of-round condition. Record your readings, and compare to the specifications.

Step 6: Reset the dial indicator so it is engaged on one of the cam lobes perpendicularly.

Step 7: _____ the camshaft until the dial indicator reads the lowest point, and zero the dial.

Step 8: Rotate the camshaft until the dial indicator reads the _____ point, and record the reading. Continue to rotate the camshaft to verify that the needle does not go _____ zero. If it does, zero it again, and remeasure the lobe.

Step 9: Measure each of the remaining _____ _____, and compare your readings to specifications.

5. Assembling Cam Follower/Rocker Arm–Style Heads:

Step 1: _____ the rocker arm pivot points and the valve tips using engine assembly _____ or clean engine _____.

Step 2: Install the rocker arms into the _____ points and over the tip of the valve.

Step 3: Lubricate the _____ arm where the camshaft lobe will ride using engine _____ lube or clean engine oil. Lubricate the camshaft bearings, journals, and cam lobes with engine _____ lube or clean engine oil. Install the camshaft into the camshaft bearings.

Step 4: Install the camshaft _____ _____. Tighten the support cap bolts finger tight, and torque the bolts to the manufacturer's specification.

Step 5: Use a _____ _____ to measure the valve clearance following the manufacturer's recommended procedure.

Step 6: Adjust the valve clearance to the manufacturer's specifications. Be sure to _____ the adjustment jam nut to prevent the clearance from _____.

Review Questions

_____ 1. The smaller water jackets in aluminum cylinder heads:
   A. reduce the heat generated by combustion.
   B. increase the chance of localized hot spots.
   C. prevent them from overcooling the engine.
   D. prevent them from overheating the engine.

_____ 2. As the camshaft rotates, the lifter rises and transfers the motion to the:
   A. camshaft lobe.
   B. pushrod.
   C. rocker arm.
   D. tappet.

_____ 3. Which of these is primarily used to block holes used in the original casting and machining of the head?
   A. Valve springs
   B. Cam seals
   C. Valve stem seals
   D. Soft plugs

_____ 4. The technician observes that the valves are arranged in a straight line positioned along the tapered angle. This typical arrangement is found in which of the following cylinder head designs?
   A. Wedge combustion chamber
   B. Oval combustion chamber
   C. Hemispherical combustion chamber
   D. Gas direct injection cylinder head

_____ 5. Which component in the valve train assembly determines the opening and closing of valves?
   A. Camshaft lobe
   B. Valve keeper
   C. Valve spring
   D. Valve retainers

_____ 6. Valve springs are checked for all of the following EXCEPT:
   A. Valve spring squareness
   B. Valve spring installed pressure
   C. Valve spring length
   D. Valve spring thickness

_____ 7. When the valve stem clearance is excessive, there is:
   A. a valve that is burned.
   B. more oil passing through the guide.
   C. less smoke emission from exhaust pipe.
   D. less oil consumption.

_____ 8. All of the statements below are true EXCEPT:
   A. The timing of the valves is controlled by the physical shape and position of the cam lobes on the cam shaft.
   B. Racing engines are designed to minimize the effect of the column inertia encountered at higher rpm.
   C. Valve timing is critical to the proper operation of the ICE.
   D. On variable valve timing engines, the valve timing can be modified to provide the best operating conditions.

_____ 9. Which of the following is a simple sealing device used to seal stationary and slowly rotating or sliding shafts?
   A. Garter spring
   B. Lip-type dynamic oil seal
   C. O-rings
   D. Multilayer steel (MLS) head gasket

_____ 10. All of the statements below are true EXCEPT:
   A. Cylinder head gaskets can be repaired and reused.
   B. Most cylinder head problems can be repaired by a cylinder head machinist.
   C. Cast iron cylinder heads can be magnafluxed to locate cracks.
   D. The cylinder head is subject to a variety of problems that can affect engine function.

ASE Technician A/Technician B Style Questions

_____ **1.** Tech A says that variable valve timing allows the engine's piston displacement to be increased or decreased. Tech B says that in-block cams usually include variable valve timing. Who is correct?
   A. Tech A
   B. Tech B
   C. Both A and B
   D. Neither A nor B

_____ **2.** Tech A says that DOHC engines use two camshafts in each head. Tech B says that cylinder head flatness can be measured with a straightedge and feeler blade. Who is correct?
   A. Tech A
   B. Tech B
   C. Both A and B
   D. Neither A nor B

_____ **3.** Tech A says that the head gasket is designed to provide a seal between the head and the block. Tech B says that most head gaskets require that you coat them with special sealers before installation. Who is correct?
   A. Tech A
   B. Tech B
   C. Both A and B
   D. Neither A nor B

_____ **4.** Tech A says that pent-roof heads are of the cross-flow design, but typically with four or five valves. Tech B says that GDI heads typically have the spark plug centrally located and the fuel injector offset to one side. Who is correct?
   A. Tech A
   B. Tech B
   C. Both A and B
   D. Neither A nor B

_____ **5.** Tech A says that an interference angle is the difference in angle between the valve face and valve seat. Tech B says an interference angle is the point where the cam lobe contacts the lifter. Who is correct?
   A. Tech A
   B. Tech B
   C. Both A and B
   D. Neither A nor B

_____ **6.** Tech A says that soft plugs allow the head or block to expand and contract without cracking. Tech B says that soft plugs are designed to prevent damage to the head or block whenever coolant freezes. Who is correct?
   A. Tech A
   B. Tech B
   C. Both A and B
   D. Neither A nor B

_____ **7.** Tech A says that valve seals are designed to prevent combustion gases from entering the valve train area. Tech B says that valve retainers hold the valve in the spring. Who is correct?
   A. Tech A
   B. Tech B
   C. Both A and B
   D. Neither A nor B

_____ **8.** Tech A says that valve springs close the valves. Tech B says that turbulence in the combustion area creates a better burn of the air-fuel mixture. Who is correct?
   A. Tech A
   B. Tech B
   C. Both A and B
   D. Neither A nor B

_____ **9.** Tech A says that when the lifter is on the base circle of the cam lobe, the valve is closed. Tech B says that the cam-in-block lifter rides directly against the valve. Who is correct?
   A. Tech A
   B. Tech B
   C. Both A and B
   D. Neither A nor B

_____ **10.** Tech A says that when cleaning the gasket mating surface on a cast iron head a metal gasket scraper can be used. Tech B says that when cleaning the gasket mating head on an aluminum head, use only plastic or nylon scrapers. Who is correct?
   A. Tech A
   B. Tech B
   C. Both A and B
   D. Neither A nor B

Engine Block Components

At the start of each chapter you'll find the NATEF Tasks, Knowledge Objectives, and Skills Objectives from the textbook. These are your objectives as you make your way through the exercises in this workbook and the chapter in your textbook. The following activities have been designed to help you refresh your knowledge of the material in this chapter.

NATEF Tasks

- N20001 Disassemble engine block; clean and prepare components for inspection and reassembly. (MAST)
- N20002 Deglaze and clean cylinder walls. (MAST)
- N20003 Inspect crankshaft for straightness, journal damage, keyway damage, thrust flange and sealing surface condition, and visual surface cracks; check oil passage condition; measure end play and journal wear; check crankshaft position sensor reluctor ring (where applicable); determine needed action. (MAST)
- N20004 Inspect main and connecting rod bearings for damage and wear; determine needed action. (MAST)
- N20005 Identify piston and bearing wear patterns that indicate connecting rod alignment and main bearing bore problems; determine needed action. (MAST)
- N20006 Inspect and measure cylinder walls/sleeves for damage, wear, and ridges; determine needed action. (MAST)
- N20007 Inspect and measure piston skirts and ring lands; determine needed action. (MAST)
- N20008 Inspect auxiliary shaft(s) (balance, intermediate, idler, counterbalance and/or silencer); inspect shaft(s) and support bearings for damage and wear; determine needed action; reinstall and time. (MAST)

Knowledge Objectives

After reading this chapter, you will be able to:

- K20001 Describe the block and its related components.
- K20002 Describe how engine blocks are manufactured.
- K20003 Describe the engine block construction.
- K20004 Describe the function of the oil pan.
- K20005 Describe the features and function of the cylinders.
- K20006 Describe the features and function of the pistons.
- K20007 Describe the features and function of the piston rings.
- K20008 Describe the features and function of the connecting rods.
- K20009 Explain the function of the rotating assembly.
- K20010 Describe the features and functions of the crankshaft.
- K20011 Describe the features and function of friction bearings.
- K20012 Describe the features and function of flywheels, flexplates, and harmonic balancers.
- K20013 Describe the features and function of crankshaft seals.
- K20014 Describe the purpose and function of balance shafts.

Skills Objectives

After reading this chapter, you will be able to:

- S20001 Remove the oil pan.
- S20002 Drain the block.
- S20003 Disassemble the block underside.
- S20004 Remove the oil pump and tray.
- S20005 Label and remove the piston assemblies.
- S20006 Remove the crankshaft and bearings.
- S20007 Remove passage plugs.
- S20008 Clean the components.

- S20009 Prepare cylinder block for reuse.
- S20010 Inspect the cylinder block.

Matching

Match the following terms with the correct description or example.

A. Back clearance
B. Bearing crush
C. Billet
D. Core plug
E. Crank core
F. Deck
G. Expander

H. Fillet
I. Accessory drive pulley
J. Gravity pouring
K. Interference fit
L. Magnafluxing
M. Mallory metal
N. Piston slap

O. Reciprocation
P. Rod beam
Q. Sintering process
R. Tang
S. Water jacket
T. Welch plug

_____ 1. The area of connecting rod between the big and small ends.

_____ 2. A round circular metal disc attached to the front of the engine crankshaft with a rubber/fiber belt that helps operate automotive accessories.

_____ 3. The force created to seat the bearing by the extra bearing material when the ends of the bearing inserts touch each other and are forced against each other.

_____ 4. An engine noise caused by excessive clearance between the piston skirt area and the cylinder wall.

_____ 5. A part of the bearing insert that helps to lock the bearing insert into the bearing saddles and caps.

_____ 6. The part of an oil control ring that holds the ring against the cylinder wall.

_____ 7. A soft, round, metal disc pressed into the engine block to plug a water jacket or oil passageway.

_____ 8. A metal hardening process in which the metal is fused together without melting.

_____ 9. The roughly shaped steel piece that has been cast or forged but has not undergone its final machining.

_____ 10. A metal cap for the holes that are used to remove core sand used during the casting process.

_____ 11. A tungsten alloy of copper and nickel that is used as a metal substitute added to the crankshaft counterweight for balancing purposes.

_____ 12. The radius portion of an inside corner that reduces stress at the corner.

_____ 13. A passageway for coolant to flow inside the engine block that is formed when the block is cast.

_____ 14. The casting process used for creating metal parts.

_____ 15. The area or space behind the piston rings when the rings are in the piston ring grooves.

_____ 16. The back-and-forth movement of the piston assembly inside the cylinder.

_____ 17. An electromagnetic process used to locate cracks in ferrous engine blocks and cylinder heads and other ferrous metal parts.

_____ 18. The rough, unfinished crankshaft assembly that has just left the foundry or forging area.

_____ 19. The surface area at the top of the engine block against which the cylinder head seals.

_____ 20. A fastening between two parts that is activated by friction after the two parts are pushed together.

Multiple Choice

Read each item carefully, and then select the best response.

_____ 1. The largest part of the engine and the main supporting structure for all engine parts is the _____.
A. chassis
B. crankshaft
C. engine block
D. main bearing cradle

_____ 2. Sometimes called a boxer engine, these engines have cylinders that are positioned side to side.
A. Two-stroke engine
B. Horizontally opposed engine
C. Rotary engine
D. Diesel engine

_____ 3. The most popular piston coating, black moly is made of _____ coating on the piston skirt.
   A. molybdenum disulfide
   B. cast aluminum
   C. cast iron
   D. tungsten alloy

_____ 4. When casting an engine block all of the following structures are used to provide rigidity to the casting while reducing overall engine weight, *except*:
   A. Pillars
   B. Ribs
   C. Fillets
   D. Webs

_____ 5. The job of the _____ is to extract the thermal energy from the burning fuel and convert it into mechanical energy, which can be used to power the vehicle.
   A. camshaft
   B. valve train
   C. piston
   D. connecting rod

_____ 6. The tubular structure that connects the piston to the top of the connecting rod is called the _____.
   A. piston pin
   B. connecting pin
   C. wrist pin
   D. Either A or C

_____ 7. The difference between the volume in the combustion chamber above the piston when the piston is at bottom dead center and the volume of the combustion chamber above the piston when the piston is at top dead center is called the _____.
   A. power stroke
   B. compression ratio
   C. range
   D. combustion volume

_____ 8. What type of piston ring prevents excessive oil from working up into the combustion chambers?
   A. Oil control rings
   B. Fire rings
   C. Compression rings
   D. Expander rings

_____ 9. Which type of connecting rod is the most common?
   A. Cast rod
   B. Powdered metal
   C. Aluminum rod
   D. Forged rod

_____ 10. The main role of the _____ is to convert the up-and-down strokes of the pistons into rotary motion.
   A. connecting rod
   B. crankshaft
   C. camshaft
   D. flywheel

_____ 11. The heavy metal disc that bolts to the rear of the crankshaft of all engines equipped with a manual transmission/transaxle is called the _____.
   A. harmonic balancer
   B. flex plate
   C. camshaft
   D. flywheel

_____ 12. Also known as the crankshaft damper, this part is located on the front of the crankshaft assembly; its function is to reduce vibration from the crankshaft and piston assembly.
   A. Flywheel
   B. Harmonic balancer

     C. Flex plate

     D. None of the above

_____ **13.** To address the problem of second-order vibration, engine manufacturers have developed a _____ with counterweights spaced so as to cancel out the inherent vibrations.

     A. balance shaft

     B. flywheel

     C. harmonic balancer

     D. fluid damper

_____ **14.** A cutting tool that will cut into the metal ridge and carbon buildup at the top of the cylinder and remove the lip is called a _____.

     A. honing stone

     B. wedge

     C. chamfer bore

     D. ridge reamer

_____ **15.** Cracks in cast iron parts can be detected by using an electromagnetic process called _____.

     A. electroplating

     B. Zyglo™

     C. magnafluxing

     D. ferropolarization

True/False

If you believe the statement to be more true than false, write the letter "T" in the space provided. If you believe the statement to be more false than true, write the letter "F".

_____ **1.** A wet sleeve is called so because coolant from the cooling system circulates against the wet sleeve's outer surface.

_____ **2.** The most common methods used for engine block casting are the green sand, shell, and lost foam processes.

_____ **3.** Main bearing caps can be fastened using a two-, four-, or eight-bolt design.

_____ **4.** In a dry sleeve only the outer surface is in direct contact with the coolant in the water jacket that surrounds the cylinder.

_____ **5.** The wrist pin design can be a floating pin or a press-fit pin.

_____ **6.** With the stronger hypereutectic piston, the higher compression ratios that create hotter exhaust gases and higher pressures can be used without piston damage.

_____ **7.** Piston rings are not a complete circle; they are split and must have a specified piston ring end gap.

_____ **8.** The main journals are ground to manufacturer specifications from the crank core.

_____ **9.** Crankshafts can be machined out of a billet, which is a solid piece of metal.

_____ **10.** Most crankshafts use Mallory metal journal surfaces to give good wear qualities.

_____ **11.** An engine block made of aluminum alloy is lighter than one made of cast iron.

_____ **12.** In automatic transmission engines, a flex plate is used instead of a flywheel.

_____ **13.** In engines that use a timing chain or timing gears, the front main seal is located in a housing bolted to the front of the engine block.

_____ **14.** The harmonic balancer is attached to the crankshaft using a Woodruff key or a square key and center bolt.

_____ **15.** The harmonic balancer is used to cancel out second-order vibrations in the engine.

Fill in the Blank

Read each item carefully, and then complete the statement by filling in the missing word(s).

1. A(n) _____ _____ vibration occurs at twice the engine rpm.

2. Some engines use an integrated _____ _____ _____ that has all the main caps cast in a single supporting structure.

3. The _____ _____ sleeve is not held in place by an interference fit; instead, it has a flange at the top of the cylinder that is used to lock the sleeve into the engine block.

4. The most common piston arrangement has two thin _____ ring grooves and one larger _____ ring groove.

5. Piston slap occurs when there is too great a clearance between the _____ and the _____ _____.

6. The most popular piston coating is a black _____.

7. A compression ring must have _____ _____ inside the piston groove to accommodate heat expansion of the piston.

8. The _____ _____ connects the piston to the crankshaft.

9. As the crankshaft rotates, the crankshaft _____ rotates on bearing inserts inside the connecting rod's big end.

10. Down the center of the connecting rod mold, there is an imperfection separating one half of the rod from the other referred to as a _____ _____.

11. Connecting rods are attached to offset journals called _____.

12. Main bearing caps mate to _____ _____, located at the bottom of the engine block.

13. The crank throws, also called rod journals are offset from the centerline of the crankshaft; the amount of offset determines the _____ _____.

14. The crankshaft requires a _____ _____, which limits the end play movement of the crankshaft.

15. The two most popular _____ _____ in use are the trimetal and the bimetal types.

Labeling

Label the following diagrams with the correct terms.

    1. The engine block of an overhead cam engine:

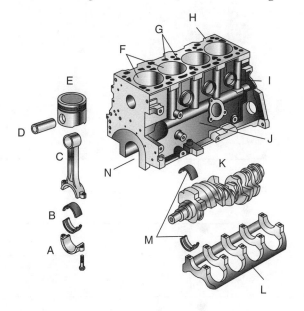

A. _____

B. _____

C. _____

D. _____

E. _____

F. _____

G. _____

H. _____

I. _____

J. _____

K. _____

L. _____

M. _____

N. _____

2. A horizontally opposed engine:

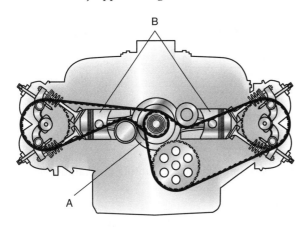

A. _____

B. _____

3. Cylinder sleeves:

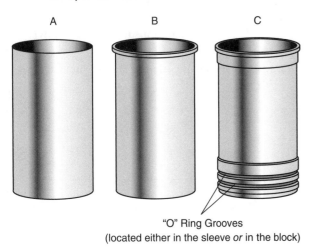

"O" Ring Grooves
(located either in the sleeve *or* in the block)

A. _____

B. _____

C. _____

4. Oil passageway drilled in the crankshaft:

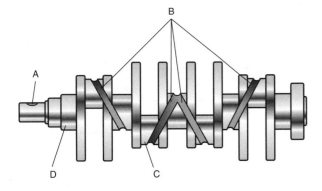

A. _____

B. _____

C. _____

D. _____

5. Bearing wear patterns:

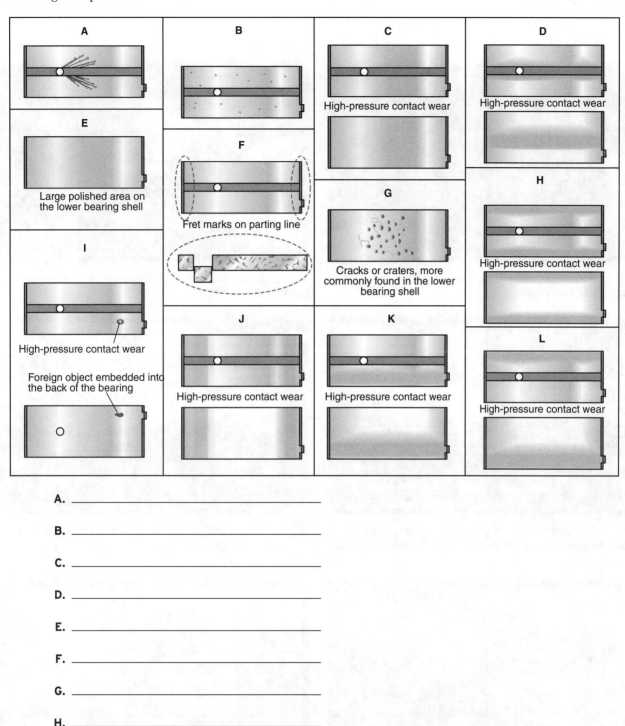

A. _____

B. _____

C. _____

D. _____

E. _____

F. _____

G. _____

H. _____

I. _____

J. _____

K. _____

L. _____

Skill Drills

Place the skill drill steps in the correct order.

1. Inspecting the Crankshaft:

_____ **A.** Visually inspect the crankshaft for cracks; magnaflux, if necessary.

_____ **B.** Measure the rod and journals using a micrometer, and record your findings.

_____ **C.** Make sure the oil passages are clear. Check the crankshaft position sensor reluctor ring to make sure there is no damage.

_____ **D.** Visually inspect the square-cut or Woodruff key and keyway for damage.

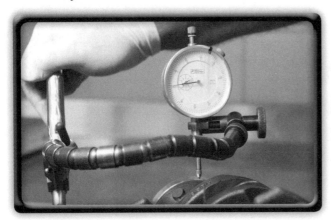

_____ **F.** Check the crankshaft for straightness with a dial indicator.

_____ **G.** Visually inspect the thrust flange, bolt holes, and rear seal surface for nicks or scratches.

2. Removing and Replacing the Floating Piston Pin:

_____ **A.** Position the piston so it is in the proper relationship to the connecting rod (see service information).

_____ **B.** Install the second snap ring, and move the piston and connecting rod, rocking the rod back and forth to ensure that it moves freely and smoothly.

_____ **C.** Push on the wrist pin to separate the wrist pin from the piston and connecting rod.

_____ **D.** Install the floating pin design. Lubricate the wrist pin hole on the piston and the small end of the connecting rod along with the wrist pin. Using your snap ring pliers, install one snap ring on the piston.

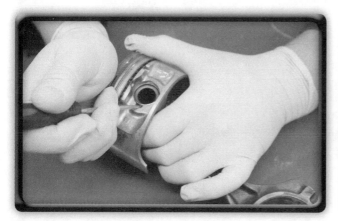

_____ **E.** Using the proper snap ring pliers that fit the holes in the snap ring, remove both snap rings.

_____ **F.** Using a bore gauge or inside micrometer, measure the inside of the small end of the connecting rod. Record the clearance.

_____ **G.** Place the small end of the connecting rod between the piston pin bosses. Using your fingers or a wrist pin driver, push the wrist pin through the piston and small end of the rod until it stops against the snap ring.

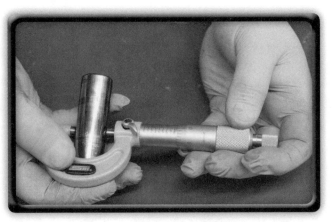

_____ **H.** Using an outside micrometer, measure the piston pin outside diameter and record your findings.

3. Inspecting and Measuring the Cylinder Walls/Sleeves:

_____ **A.** Measure each cylinder at the top, center, and bottom, 90 degrees across the thrust side and pin side at each level. Compare the readings to specifications.

_____ **B.** If there is obvious scoring or damage, then the block will need to be machined.

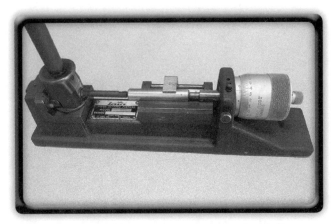

_____ **C.** If there is no obvious damage, set a dial bore gauge to the specified standard cylinder bore size.

4. Inspecting and Measuring Piston Skirts:

_____ **A.** Measure the diameter of the bottom of the piston skirt. It should never be smaller than the previous measurement. If the measurement is smaller, then the piston has a collapsed skirt, and the piston must be replaced.

_____ **B.** With the piston inverted, measure the diameter of the piston skirt even with the center of the wrist pin, and compare to specifications. Replace the pistons if necessary.

5. Deglazing and Cleaning a Cylinder Wall:

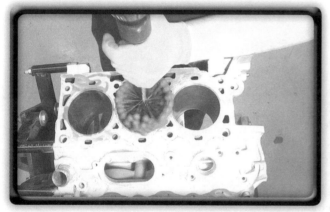

_____ **A.** Using the drill with the attached flex hone, stroke up and down in the cylinder that you are honing for approximately 10 to 15 seconds at a speed at which you get a good crosshatch.

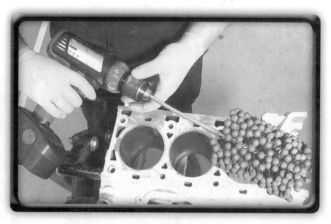

_____ **B.** Using a drill, attach the proper-sized flex hone.

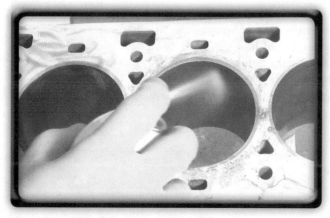

_____ **C.** Use a rag to wipe the cylinder out so you can inspect the cylinder walls.

_____ **D.** Carefully insert the hone, and apply honing oil to the cylinder walls.

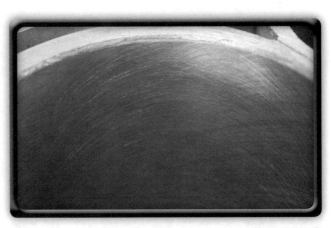

_____ **E.** Clean the block in a spray cabinet, followed by using soap and water with a cylinder brush. Finish by drying and applying protectant.

_____ **F.** Inspect the crosshatch on the cylinders. Repeat until a good crosshatch pattern is achieved.

Review Questions

_____ **1.** The bottom of the crankcase is sealed off by the:
  A. oil pump.
  B. crankshaft bearings.
  C. oil pan.
  D. flexplate.

_____ **2.** When removing the pistons from the block:
  A. remove them out the bottom of the block.
  B. remove them after removing the crankshaft from the block.
  C. use large pliers to pull them out of the cylinders.
  D. check for an excessive amount of cylinder ridge.

_____ **3.** Which of these functions is related the most to a piston?
  A. It converts thermal energy into mechanical energy.
  B. It transfers movement of the cam lobe to the valve.
  C. It prevents the engine from overheating.
  D. It reduces vibrations during engine operation.

_____ **4.** Compression rings are designed to:
  A. seal the piston and the cylinder wall.
  B. scrape excessive oil from the walls and release it back to the crankcase as needed.
  C. to hold a small amount of lubrication oil to lubricate the piston and cylinder walls.
  D. decrease compression to prevent engine damage.

_____ **5.** Choose the correct answer.
  A. The top end of the connecting rod is where the large rod bearings are inserted.
  B. Powdered metal rods have a vert smooth surface finish.
  C. Forged connecting rods are made of metallurgically bonded metal alloy.
  D. Connecting rods transfer motion and force from the piston to the crankshaft.

_____ **6.** Which of these converts the reciprocating motion of the piston into rotary motion?
  A. The upper part of the engine block
  B. The piston rings
  C. The balance shafts
  D. The crankshaft

_____ **7.** All of the below are likely causes of bearing wear _except_:
  A. insufficient oil.
  B. improper assembly.
  C. overcooling.
  D. poor cleaning during rebuild.

_____ **8.** The flexplate and fly wheel are similar in that both:
   A. have a torque converter bolted to them.
   B. are mounted to the end of the crankshaft.
   C. are of similar weight.
   D. are used in automatic transmission engines.

_____ **9.** The balance shaft serves to:
   A. increase the compression ratio.
   B. decrease cylinder wear.
   C. increase fuel efficiency.
   D. reduce vibrations from engine operation.

_____ **10.** Increased wear pattern on diagonally opposite sides of the piston indicates:
   A. a bent connecting rod.
   B. problems in the main bearing bores.
   C. problems in the rod bearing inserts.
   D. wear in the rear seals.

ASE Technician A/Technician B Style Questions

_____ **1.** Tech A says that the upper portion of the block contains the cylinders and pistons. Tech B says that the lower section of the engine block forms the crankcase. Who is correct?
   A. Tech A
   B. Tech B
   C. Both A and B
   D. Neither A nor B

_____ **2.** Tech A says that most pistons use one compression ring and one oil control ring. Tech B says that most pistons are made of steel to withstand the heat of combustion. Who is correct?
   A. Tech A
   B. Tech B
   C. Both A and B
   D. Neither A nor B

_____ **3.** Tech A says that each main bearing in the engine is fitted with a thrust bearing. Tech B says that thrust bearings limit the end play of the crankshaft. Who is correct?
   A. Tech A
   B. Tech B
   C. Both A and B
   D. Neither A nor B

_____ **4.** Tech A says that using a thicker head gasket would lower the compression ratio. Tech B says that the effective compression ratio is affected by valve timing. Who is correct?
   A. Tech A
   B. Tech B
   C. Both A and B
   D. Neither A nor B

_____ **5.** Tech A says that a piston is manufactured slightly oval in shape. Tech B says that the piston pin is slightly oval in shape to allow for heat expansion and lubrication. Who is correct?
   A. Tech A
   B. Tech B
   C. Both A and B
   D. Neither A nor B

_____ **6.** Tech A says that cylinder walls are manufactured with a slight taper so that the piston rings will make a tighter seal at TDC. Tech B says that ceramic piston coatings assist in the control of piston temperature, which allows for tighter bore clearances and greater engine efficiency. Who is correct?
   A. Tech A
   B. Tech B
   C. Both A and B
   D. Neither A nor B

_____ **7.** Tech A says that fractured rods have a unique mating surface and that only the cap that was fractured from that rod is the one that will fit that rod. Tech B says that a powdered metal rod is less expensive, lighter, and as strong as a forged rod. Who is correct?
  A. Tech A
  B. Tech B
  C. Both A and B
  D. Neither A nor B

_____ **8.** Tech A says that when grinding main journals, an undersized main bearing will be required. Tech B says that the main bearing journals should be measured for minimum diameter, out-of-round, and taper. Who is correct?
  A. Tech A
  B. Tech B
  C. Both A and B
  D. Neither A nor B

_____ **9.** Tech A says that a failed harmonic balancer can cause a crankshaft to break. Tech B says that the crankshaft rod journals are typically measured using a dial indicator. Who is correct?
  A. Tech A
  B. Tech B
  C. Both A and B
  D. Neither A nor B

_____ **10.** Tech A says that main and rod bearings are glued in place with special bearing cement. Tech B says that main and rod bearings are held in place by a precise amount of "bearing crush." Who is correct?
  A. Tech A
  B. Tech B
  C. Both A and B
  D. Neither A nor B

Engine Machining

At the start of each chapter you'll find the NATEF Tasks, Knowledge Objectives, and Skills Objectives from the textbook. These are your objectives as you make your way through the exercises in this workbook and the chapter in your textbook. The following activities have been designed to help you refresh your knowledge of the material in this chapter.

NATEF Tasks

There are no NATEF tasks for this chapter.

Knowledge Objectives

After reading this chapter, you will be able to:

- K21001 Explain the purpose of engine machining.
- K21002 Explain the cylinder block machining processes.
- K21003 Explain how surface finish is important to the head gasket sealing surfaces.
- K21004 Explain the procedure for boring and honing the cylinder bores.
- K21005 Explain the process for resizing the main bearing bores.
- K21006 Describe the process of machining crankshafts and connecting rods.
- K21007 Describe the crankshaft refinishing process.
- K21008 Explain the process of resizing the connecting rods.
- K21009 Explain the process for machining the cylinder heads.
- K21010 Explain the process of detecting cracks.
- K21011 Explain the process of pressure testing a cylinder head.
- K21012 Explain the process of servicing overhead cam bearings.
- K21013 Explain the valve grinding process.
- K21014 Explain valve guide service.
- K21015 Explain valve seats service.
- K21016 Describe the process of balancing an engine.

Skills Objectives

There are no Skills Objectives for this chapter.

Matching

Match the following terms with the correct description or example.

A. Ball hone   **D.** Cubic boron nitride cutter   **G.** Interference angle

B. Bob weights   **E.** Engine block deck   **H.** Nitriding

C. Crosshatch   **F.** Induction hardening

_____ **1.** A metal surface-hardening process using nitrogen and high temperatures.

_____ **2.** An engine block resurfacing tool used on cast iron parts.

_____ **3.** Weights used during the balancing process to mimic the exact weight of the piston and connecting rod weights for that particular rod bearing journal.

_____ **4.** The portion of the engine cylinder block the head gasket lies on and the cylinder head is bolted to.

_____ **5.** A pattern of lines placed at angles to each other, appearing as a series of Xs across a surface.

_____ **6.** A process for hardening metal by using a magnetic field to quickly heat up the surface and then suddenly cooling it in water, oil, or another chemical.

_____ **7.** An assembly of metal rods, with abrasive stones attached, that is inserted into the cylinder and spun to break the glazing off the cylinder walls and make a new crosshatched pattern.

_____ **8.** The angle formed between the valve face and the valve seat; usually it is ½ to 1 degree.

Multiple Choice

Read each item carefully, and then select the best response.

_____ **1.** What type of engine block cutting bit would you choose for an aluminum engine block?
   A. Tungsten carbide cutter
   B. Polycrystalline diamond cutter
   C. Ball hone
   D. Cubic boron nitride cutter

_____ **2.** What type of engine block cutting bit would you choose for a cast iron engine block?
   A. Ball hone
   B. Polycrystalline diamond cutter
   C. Tungsten carbide cutter
   D. Cubic boron nitride cutter

_____ **3.** Dry cylinder sleeves require the cylinder to be bored out an additional 0.002" to 0.0025", this extra machining is called _____.
   A. overbore
   B. sleeve clearance
   C. interference fit
   D. taper

_____ **4.** A long bar used to position and align a single-point tool, such as an engine block boring machine is called a(n)_____.
   A. boring bar
   B. reference bar
   C. engine block dowel
   D. mainline bar

_____ **5.** What term refers to the finish produced when the crosshatch scratches have been worn away, leaving the cylinder smooth and shiny and unable to retain oil?
   A. Glazing
   B. Enameled
   C. Hone
   D. Varnished

_____ **6.** To correct a bore alignment issue, the engine block must be _____.
   A. line bored
   B. ball honed
   C. line honed
   D. either A or C

_____ **7.** What process adds materials to the journal by melting and spraying molten metal onto the crankshaft journal surface so there is material that can be ground?
   A. Submerged arc welding
   B. Plasma welding
   C. Spray welding
   D. Chrome plating

_____ **8.** This process takes that sharp edge at the top of the oil hole and makes it more like a 45-degree angle.
   A. Chamfering
   B. Honing
   C. Polishing
   D. Reaming

_____ **9.** A good way to check the valve seat contact on the valve is to use _____.
  A. dry-erase marker
  B. plastigauge
  C. prussian blue
  D. either A or C

_____ **10.** Weights used during the balancing process that are used to mimic the exact weight of the piston and connecting rod weights for that particular rod bearing journal are called _____.
  A. rotating weights
  B. lead shot
  C. bob weights
  D. reciprocating weights

True/False

If you believe the statement to be more true than false, write the letter "T" in the space provided. If you believe the statement to be more false than true, write the letter "F".

_____ **1.** It is best to leave machining to the Automotive Service Excellence (ASE) Master Certified Machinist professionals.

_____ **2.** A 60-Ra finish is smoother than a 30-Ra finish.

_____ **3.** With some of the newer CNC-style machines, engine block measurements are taken from the top of the engine block dowel pinhole.

_____ **4.** Bob weights are used to simulate the weight of the reciprocating components and are fitted to the crank journals.

_____ **5.** A portable boring bar should not be used on modern thinner-walled engine blocks.

_____ **6.** A good crosshatch helps to trap the oil and retain it in the cylinder bores where it is needed.

_____ **7.** The presence of even a small crack in the cylinder head automatically condemns the cylinder head to the scrap bin.

_____ **8.** Nitriding produces a harder, more durable surface than induction hardening.

_____ **9.** The press-fit wrist pin is typically held in place with a snap ring on each side of the piston pin boss.

_____ **10.** Pressure testing is normally used on cast iron cylinder heads since the magnaflux process cannot be used.

_____ **11.** Overhead cam engines have camshafts that typically ride in removable bearings in the cylinder head.

_____ **12.** Knurling is when a bit with a spiral groove is threaded through or run through the valve guide.

_____ **13.** When using grinding stones, a three-angle grind is typically used to properly form the valve seat.

_____ **14.** Some engines are internally balanced, while others are externally balanced.

_____ **15.** Reciprocating weight is the amount of weight that is moving in a circular motion.

Fill in the Blank

Read each item carefully, and then complete the statement by filling in the missing word(s).

1. _____ _____ average is a measure of how rough a surface is at the microscopic level.

2. The desired procedure in surfacing the engine block's deck is to surface the engine block parallel to the _____ where the crankshaft is installed.

3. The computer _____ _____ machine is a tool that uses computer programs to automatically execute a series of machining operations.

4. Using _____ allows the original size of pistons to be used, restoring the factory bore dimensions.

5. Hone stones are used to smooth out the surface of the cylinder walls, leaving a unidirectional finish also known as a _____ pattern.

6. Bore alignment can be checked for straightness by using a straightedge with a _____ _____.

7. _____ _____ are valve seats that have been heat treated to make them more robust and capable of withstanding the severe demands of today's engines and fuels.

8. Powdered metal connecting rods are _____ _____ to ensure perfect alignment.

9. Before any machining can begin after the disassembly and cleaning of the cylinder head, the cylinder head should be _____ or dye checked to locate any external cracks.

10. A cylinder head can be surfaced using a surface grinder using a stone wheel or a _____ - _____ surfacer using a CBN or a PCD cutting bit.

Labeling

Label the following diagrams with the correct terms.

1. Measuring the deck height from the setting fixture:

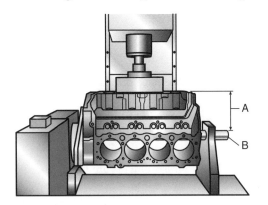

A. _____

B. _____

2. Cylinder sleeves:

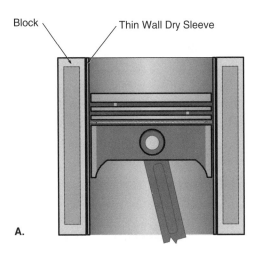

A.

A. _____

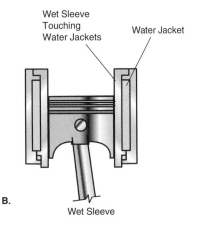

B.

B. _____

3. Cam bores using removable bearing caps:

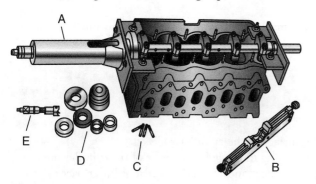

A. _____

B. _____

C. _____

D. _____

E. _____

4. Valve seat with proper angles:

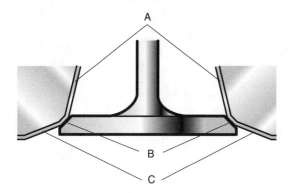

A. _____

B. _____

C. _____

5. Engine balancing:

A. _____

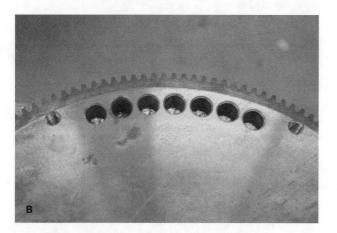

B. _____

Review Questions

_____ 1. When resurfacing an engine block surface, the machinist determines exactly how much metal to take off by measuring the:
   A. depth of the dowel pinholes.
   B. surface roughness of the cylinder head.
   C. height of the dowel pins.
   D. thickness of the head gasket.

_____ 2. Choose the correct statement regarding crosshatch.
   A. It does not allow oil to be trapped on the surface of the cylinder walls.
   B. The desired pattern can be achieved by adjusting the speed and stroke of the cylinder hone.
   C. If a steeper-angled X pattern is needed, move the stones up and down at a slower pace.
   D. If the angle gets too flat, the compression will be too low.

_____ 3. The ball hone:
   A. restores cylinder size.
   B. simply reapplies the crosshatching.
   C. is done when there is considerable wear and tear.
   D. does not remove glazing.

_____ 4. What must be done when correcting a main bore alignment issue?
   A. the crank journals must first be made smaller.
   B. the cylinders must be bored oversize.
   C. the pistons must be replaced with oversize pistons.
   D. main caps should be cut.

_____ 5. During crankshaft grinding, the:
   A. main and rod journals can be ground to different sizes.
   B. rod and main journals must be cut to the same undersize.
   C. main journals that are worn are the only ones that should be ground.
   D. crankshaft is ground slightly bigger than its original size.

_____ 6. A small crack in a cylinder head can be fixed by:
   A. boring it oversize.
   B. milling the surface.
   C. welding.
   D. sealing.

_____ 7. Which of these can be used to check for internal cracks?
   A. Magnaflux testing using dry method
   B. Dye checking
   C. Pressure testing
   D. Magnaflux testing using wet method

_____ 8. If the cam bores are misaligned, you should first:
   A. machine the bore in a process similar to line boring of the main bearing journals.
   B. straighten the head if it is warped.
   C. weld the cam bores and remachine them to the proper size.
   D. simply increasing the bore size.

_____ 9. During valve grinding, the:
   A. valve and grinding stone rotate in the opposite directions.
   B. grinding stone moves side to side.
   C. valve and grinding stone rotate in the same direction.
   D. valve is held in place and does not move.

_____ 10. Knurling is:
   A. reaming the guide oversize and using a valve with an oversized valve stem.
   B. when a bit with a spiral groove is threaded through or run through the valve guide.
   C. installing a thin-walled aluminum liner.
   D. installing a thick-walled guide that is made of aluminum.

ASE Technician A/Technician B Style Questions

_____ **1.** Tech A says that failure analysis will assist the technician in determining whether it is more cost effective to replace rather than repair an engine. Tech B says that when an engine fails under warranty, the manufacturer may want it back for complete analysis of why it failed. Who is correct?
   A. Tech A
   B. Tech B
   C. Both A and B
   D. Neither A nor B

_____ **2.** Tech A says that Ra is critical in the machining process to ensure head gasket sealing. Tech B says that a Ra rating of 0–1 is the best sealing surface. Who is correct?
   A. Tech A
   B. Tech B
   C. Both A and B
   D. Neither A nor B

_____ **3.** Tech A says that full floating pistons use keepers to retain the piston pin. Tech B says that some piston pins are press fitted in the rod. Who is correct?
   A. Tech A
   B. Tech B
   C. Both A and B
   D. Neither A nor B

_____ **4.** Tech A says that when measurement of the cylinder bore is out of specifications, just install an oversized piston. Tech B says that 0.030" over and 0.060" over are two common piston sizes. Who is correct?
   A. Tech A
   B. Tech B
   C. Both A and B
   D. Neither A nor B

_____ **5.** Tech A says that after boring the cylinders oversize, the cylinder bore will have to be honed. Tech B says that you should always bore out the block as big as possible. Who is correct?
   A. Tech A
   B. Tech B
   C. Both A and B
   D. Neither A nor B

_____ **6.** Tech A says that the main bore alignment can be checked with a straightedge and feeler blade. Tech B says that the main bore can be straightened by resurfacing the bottom of the main bearing caps and then resizing the main bore. Who is correct?
   A. Tech A
   B. Tech B
   C. Both A and B
   D. Neither A nor B

_____ **7.** Tech A says that valves must be replaced if the margin is below the minimum specified. Tech B says that the valves must be replaced if the stems are not within specifications. Who is correct?
   A. Tech A
   B. Tech B
   C. Both A and B
   D. Neither A nor B

_____ **8.** Tech A says that some valve seats can be replaced. Tech B says that newer style valve seats are made of soft materials, so they don't create as much wear on the valves. Who is correct?
   A. Tech A
   B. Tech B
   C. Both A and B
   D. Neither A nor B

_____ **9.** Tech A says that valve stem height is measured with the valve in the head and seated fully. Tech B says that there should be a minimum of 0.060" of clearance between coils of a valve spring when fully compressed. Who is correct?

    A. Tech A

    B. Tech B

    C. Both A and B

    D. Neither A nor B

_____ **10.** Tech A says that when balancing an engine, bob weights are used to simulate the weight of the engine block. Tech B says that balancing a crankshaft can include removing or adding weight to the crankshaft. Who is correct?

    A. Tech A

    B. Tech B

    C. Both A and B

    D. Neither A nor B

Engine Assembly

At the start of each chapter you'll find the NATEF Tasks, Knowledge Objectives, and Skills Objectives from the textbook. These are your objectives as you make your way through the exercises in this workbook and the chapter in your textbook. The following activities have been designed to help you refresh your knowledge of the material in this chapter.

NATEF Tasks

- N22001 Assemble engine block. (MAST)

Knowledge Objectives

After reading this chapter, you will be able to:

- K22001 Describe the application and use of various types of adhesives/sealers.

Skills Objectives

After reading this chapter, you will be able to:

- S22001 Perform all preassembly actions and measurements.
- S22002 Prepare the crankshaft and block for preassembly.
- S22003 Perform piston, ring, and block clearance checks.
- S22004 Install the pistons on the connecting rods.
- S22005 Perform a temporary test buildup and related measurements of the engine.
- S22006 Install main bearings, and measure the clearances.
- S22007 Install the crankshaft, and measure the clearance.
- S22008 Assemble the piston and rod assemblies.
- S22009 Measure rod bearing clearance.
- S22010 Check piston-to-deck and piston-to-valve clearance.
- S22011 Perform final assembly of the short block.
- S22012 Clean and paint the engine.
- S22013 Install soft plugs and oil gallery plugs.
- S22014 Install the crankshaft.
- S22015 Install the piston rings.
- S22016 Install the pistons in the block, and measure side clearance.
- S22017 Install the cylinder head and valve train.
- S22018 Install the head gaskets.
- S22019 Install the cylinder heads.
- S22020 Assemble the valve train, and adjust the valves.
- S22021 Install the oil pickup, oil pump, and oil pan, and prime the engine.
- S22022 Install the oil pan and timing cover.
- S22023 Install the external components.
- S22024 Install the intake manifold.
- S22025 Install the other external components.
- S22026 Install the accessories.
- S22027 Inspect and replace camshaft drive belts and chains.
- S22028 Establish camshaft position sensor indexing.
- S22029 Inspect and replace valve stem seals on an assembled engine.

Matching

Match the following terms with the correct description or example.

A. Degree wheel   **D.** Torque angle

B. Outside micrometer   **E.** Torque-to-yield

C. Pip mark

_____ **1.** A tightening procedure in which a bolt is designed to be slightly elastic when tightened; the elastic bolt retains an even pressure on the head gasket.

_____ **2.** A precision measuring instrument meant to measure the outside of components. It is usually accurate to 0.0001" (0.0025 mm).

_____ **3.** A disc with 360 one-degree markings near its outer edge; it bolts to the front of the crankshaft and is used to check valve and cam timing.

_____ **4.** A small indent or dimple on the piston ring that indicates which side of the ring is installed upward. It is also used on some timing sprockets.

_____ **5.** A tightening procedure in which a bolt is torqued to a set torque value and then tightened using a measured angle instead of a torque value. Example: A bolt is torqued to 40 ft-lb and then tightened another 90 degrees.

Multiple Choice

Read each item carefully, and then select the best response.

_____ **1.** Which tool would you use to measure piston size?
     A. Depth gauge
     B. Inside micrometer
     C. Bore gauge
     D. Outside micrometer

_____ **2.** Which tool would you use to measure cylinder size?
     A. Feeler gauge
     B. Outside micrometer
     C. Bore gauge
     D. Tape measure

_____ **3.** What tool is used to measure the width of the ring end gap?
     A. Steel rule
     B. Feeler gauge
     C. Inside micrometer
     D. Gap tool

_____ **4.** In which piston design is the pin retained by a pair of snap rings?
     A. Floating pin
     B. Semi-floating pin
     C. Semi-press-fit
     D. Press-fit

_____ **5.** If you need to check the bearing clearance with the crankshaft installed, then you should use a(n) _____.
     A. outside micrometer
     B. bore gauge
     C. feeler gauge
     D. plastic gauging material

_____ **6.** All of the following tools may be used to measure the inside diameter of the main bearing bore, _except_:
     A. Inside micrometer
     B. Snap gauge
     C. Feeler gauge
     D. Bore gauge

_____ **7.** An extruded plastic thread that comes in different sizes, used to check clearances between parts is called _____.
   A. prussian blue
   B. plastigauge
   C. teflon tape
   D. clearance tape

_____ **8.** Which of the following is typically the size you cut a piece of plastic gauge?
   A. Half the bearing's width
   B. Just short of the bearing's width
   C. A quarter the bearing's width
   D. One-fifth of the bearing width's

_____ **9.** If any of the head bolts go into holes that extend into the _____, it is essential to put some nonhardening sealer on the threads of the bolts to keep the coolant from leaking past the threads.
   A. water jacket
   B. engine block
   C. water pump
   D. wet sleeve

_____ **10.** The _____ may be located in the oil pan, on the side of the block, or in the timing cover.
   A. timing chain
   B. oil pump
   C. crankshaft
   D. camshaft

True/False

If you believe the statement to be more true than false, write the letter "T" in the space provided. If you believe the statement to be more false than true, write the letter "F".

_____ **1.** Measuring the piston-to-cylinder wall clearance and the piston ring end gap ensures that the machining was performed properly.

_____ **2.** Some snap rings are directional, which means they must be installed with the correct side facing the wrist pin.

_____ **3.** Most main bearings can be cleaned with denatured alcohol.

_____ **4.** Before using a micrometer to measure the crankshaft, it is important to make sure the crankshaft is clean and free of oil and grease.

_____ **5.** The same method used to check main bearing clearances can be used to check the rod bearing clearance.

_____ **6.** Piston-to-valve clearance of a performance camshaft can be checked using the clay method or the dial indicator method.

_____ **7.** Any threaded plugs such as the rear oil gallery plugs should be coated with Teflon tape prior to installation.

_____ **8.** Never reuse torque-to-yield bolts, as they will likely fail in use.

_____ **9.** Most engines use a composition-type gasket that requires sealant on both sides.

_____ **10.** The torque angle method is a more precise way than the torque-to-yield method of torquing a standard fastener to a predetermined tension.

_____ **11.** On OHC engines, the timing chains or belts are installed after the cylinder head is installed.

_____ **12.** Use a thin coat of RTV silicone when installing neoprene gaskets with multi-sealing edges.

_____ **13.** One way to pre-oil the engine is to spin the oil pump with a drill attached to the pump drive.

_____ **14.** The camshaft and drive belt/chain assembly link the valve train system to the crankshaft and determine the right time in the engine cycle for the valves to open and close.

_____ **15.** It is sometimes necessary to replace the valve stem seals on an assembled engine.

Fill in the Blank

Read each item carefully, and then complete the statement by filling in the missing word(s).

1. Before installing piston rings on the piston, you need to check the _____ _____ _____.

2. The _____-_____ pin moves freely in the piston bore but is press-fit in the connecting rod bore.

3. It is very important to perform a _____ _____ _____ of the rotating assembly; it will determine if additional machining or exchange of any parts will be necessary.

4. To insert the main bearing, start the _____ of the bearing into the matching slot of the main bearing saddle.

5. If the thrust bearing is not a flange thrust bearing, _____ will need to be applied to the back side of the bearing to hold the bearing in place until the crankshaft is installed or the main cap is installed.

6. Use a(n) _____ _____ to measure each main bearing journal.

7. When you subtract the crankshaft main journal readings from the main bearing bore readings, the difference will give you the _____ _____.

8. Checking the thrust bearing end play can be done with a _____ _____ after the crankshaft is installed.

9. Most engines have a specification for piston height as compared to the cylinder block _____.

10. Once the piston rings are aligned and lubricated, they need to be compressed with a _____ _____ so they will fit into the cylinder.

11. OHC chain drives typically are of the _____ _____ style, which looks a lot like a bicycle chain.

12. _____ is an extruded plastic thread that can be used to check the main bearing clearance by squishing it between the crankshaft journal and bearing insert.

13. To help hold the gaskets in place, you can use a product made by 3M called _____ _____, which is contact cement in a liquid or spray form.

14. There is a sequence that must be followed during installation of oil pans and _____ _____ since the parts can overlap one another.

15. Most newer engines do not have an adjustable _____ _____ sensor, so indexing is usually needed only on sensors that can be manually adjusted.

Labeling

Fill in the blanks with the correct descriptions below.

1. Piston checks:

A. _____

B. _____

C. _____

D. _____

1. Measuring the piston-to-cylinder clearance using a bore gauge
2. Checking compression ring end gap
3. Measuring a piston
4. Squaring up piston rings

2. Installing main bearings:

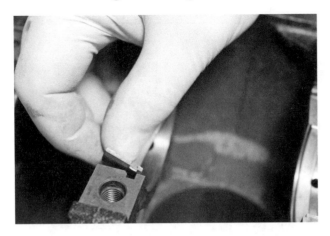

A. _____   B. _____

   1. Oil hole lined up
   2. Installing main bearing insert

Skill Drills

Test your knowledge of skill drills by filling in the correct words in the photo captions.

   1. Checking Piston-to-Valve Clearance (Clay Method):

Step 1: _____ the valve train for the number _____ cylinder. If using hydraulic lifters, install _____ valve springs.

Step 2: Make balls using soft clay, one for each valve. Stick them to the _____ in the valve reliefs that are cut into the _____ of the piston, and coat the clay with clean engine oil.

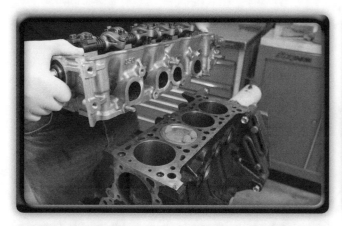

Step 3: Make sure the crank and cam are positioned properly, most likely with the timing marks lined up on each. Place the head gasket and cylinder head on the _____. Tighten all the _____ bolts to about 15 ft-lbs (20.3 N·m).

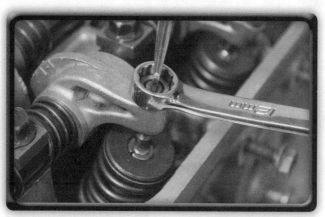

Step 4: Install the valve train and adjust the valves to the specified _____, or if using hydraulic lifters, zero _____.

Step 5: Carefully rotate the _____ until you see the exhaust and _____ valves open and close two times each.

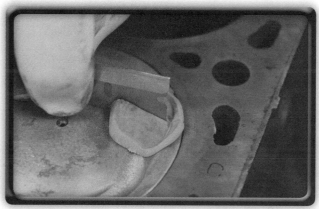

Step 6: Remove the valve train and head. Cut each piece of _____ and remove half. Measure the distance from the piston to the top of the valve imprint with a ruler or the _____ end of a dial caliper.

2. Installing Engine Plugs:

Step 1: Start with the _____ block sitting on the floor with the rear area facing _____. Apply a small amount of _____ to the threaded oil gallery plugs and screw them in.

Step 2: Clean the edges of the _____ water jacket holes before you install the _____ plugs.

Step 3: Coat the soft plug with a nonhardening _____. Wipe it thin and even, being careful not to leave any bare spots.

Step 4: Carefully tap in each _____ _____ using an impact socket and hammer.

Step 5: Turn the block over so that the _____ is facing up, and select a punch that is smaller than the inner _____ of the front oil gallery plugs. Wipe sealer evenly around each plug, and tap it in until it is 1/16" (1.6 mm) below the rim.

Step 6: Turn the block on its side. Clean, apply _____, and install the soft plugs in the side of the block, making sure not to miss any.

3. Installing the Heads:

Step 1: Clean all the head bolt threads and _____. Use sealer on any bolts that extend into the _____ _____. Lubricate the threads and under the heads on other bolts, if specified.

Step 2: Clean the deck surface of the block and head, and install the head gaskets. Look for any _____ _____ _____ or _____ labels on the head gaskets.

Step 3: On OHC _____ _____, make sure the crankshaft is set to the _____ position before installing the head.

Step 4: On OHC engines, make sure the camshaft is set to the specified position before installing the _____. Failure to do so could lead to _____ or _____ valves.

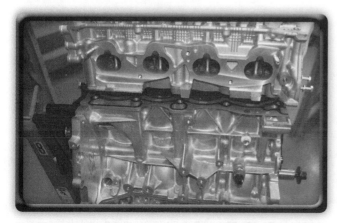

Step 5: Gently lay the head over the alignment _____ of the block, and start threading in the bolts. If _____-_____ -_____ head bolts are used, tighten each bolt in the speci- fied sequence to the specified torque. Torquing may need to be performed in several stages.

Step 6: Install the torque angle gauge, and tighten each bolt in the specified sequence to the specified angle. If torquing _____ head bolts, torque them in the specified sequence in three increments, resetting the torque wrench and increasing by _____-_____ each time.

4. Pre-oiling the Engine:

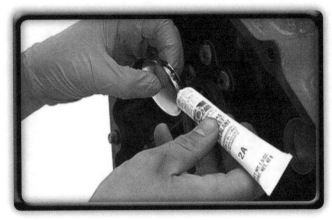

Step 1: Install the rear camshaft _____ and rear main seal, if not installed yet.

Step 2: Install the oil filter. _____ the rubber seal of the oil filter with a little engine oil, and _____ it on hand tight. Also install a manual pressure gauge.

Step 3: Fill the crankcase with the type and _____ of engine oil recommended in the repair information. If the oil pump is driven by the distributor, use a drill to _____ the oil pump.

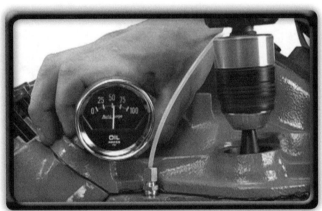

Step 4: Check that oil is reaching the _____ _____. You may need to rotate the engine two turns to get oil to flow to each valve.

Step 5: If the oil pump is driven by the crankshaft, use a pressurized _____-_____ to pressurize the _____ system.

Step 6: Once the engine has been pre-oiled, install the _____ _____.

5. Inspecting and Replacing the Camshaft and Drive Belt/Chain:

Step 1: Determine all specifications for timing chain or belt _____ assembly according to the manufacturer of the engine assembly being serviced. Remove all _____. Remove all components that cover the timing chain/belt assembly, such as the harmonic balancer, water pump, alternators, and power steering pump.

Step 2: Remove the camshaft timing chain/belt cover. Inspect the _____ for _____ _____, and replace if worn. Look for causes for the worn cover.

Timing mark lined up with head surface

Step 3: With the timing chain/belt cover off and the timing gears and belts/chains in full view, turn the engine over _____ to line up the timing marks of the crankshaft and camshaft _____ with the appropriate marks on the block and head.

Step 4: Inspect the belt/chain and measure for _____, and replace if not within specifications. Measure the _____ between tensioners, if applicable, and replace if not within specifications.

Step 5: Remove the _____ or _____ following the specified procedure. Use the proper cam holding tool, if specified, to prevent damage to valves.

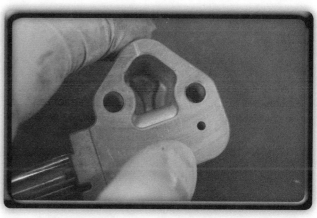

Step 6: If the tensioner is _____ operated, check the oil passages to the _____ for clogs or buildup of dirt sludge, and clean or replace according to recommendations.

Step 7: Inspect any guide pulleys for smooth _____ on their bearings, and replace if damaged. With the chain/belt removed, inspect the cam sprockets visually for wear, cracking, and damage. Inspect _____ for backlash and end play, if applicable, on the vehicle.

Step 8: On engines with any type of variable valve timing, check components for worn and damaged parts on the gears, inspect any _____ _____ _____ for leaks, and perform other tests on components according to the manufacturer's recommendations.

Step 9: Reassemble the timing chain/belt assembly. Turn the crankshaft _____ complete revolutions by hand, and recheck the timing marks and belt/chain tension. _____ components following the specified procedure.

Review Questions

_____ 1. Most engines use a composition-type head gasket that:
   A. requires special head gasket sealer on both sides of the gasket.
   B. needs antiseize applied to both sides.
   C. can be reused more than once.
   D. does not require sealant on either side.

_____ 2. The preferred method for installing a semi-floating wrist pin is to use a:
   A. sealant.
   B. hammer.
   C. rod heater.
   D. welding machine.

_____ 3. All of the below statements are true with respect to a temporary test buildup EXCEPT:
   A. It should always include the piston rings or a rear main seal for the crankshaft.
   B. It will determine if additional machining will be necessary.
   C. It should include the cylinder heads and the valve train.
   D. It will determine if exchange of any parts will be necessary.

_____ **4.** Which of these should be used to check the bearing clearance with the crankshaft installed?
   A. Micrometer
   B. Bore gauge
   C. Plastigauge
   D. Feeler gauge

_____ **5.** When installing the crankshaft, to prevent oil leak from the rear of the block:
   A. paint the surface in a double coat.
   B. use a dab of silicone sealer.
   C. use plugs to close any openings.
   D. temporarily solder together the parts in the rear of the block.

_____ **6.** When the piston is installed:
   A. the piston rings must be aligned in their proper positions to minimize blowby gases.
   B. ensure lubricants or oil is not present.
   C. the crankshaft should be positioned so its journal is at top dead center.
   D. hammer the piston hard into the cylinder until you do not feel any resistance.

_____ **7.** RTV should not be used on:
   A. paper gaskets.
   B. fiber gaskets.
   C. thermostat housing gaskets.
   D. neoprene gaskets with multi-sealing edges.

_____ **8.** When establishing camshaft position sensor indexing:
   A. use a labscope.
   B. use a micrometer.
   C. use Plastigauge.
   D. use a feeler blade and straight edge.

_____ **9.** When using this torque angle method of tightening head bolts, the bolts are torqued to a minimal specification, say 20 ft-lb, and then:
   A. loosened and reinstalled in a different hole.
   B. bent over so they don't loosen.
   C. locked in place with either a cotter pin or safety wire.
   D. tightened a further specified number of degrees.

_____ **10.** When replacing valve seals on an assembled engine, which of these is used to hold the valves closed while the valve spring is off?
   A. A special sleeve
   B. Compressed air
   C. An adhesive
   D. A wrench

ASE Technician A/Technician B Style Questions

_____ **1.** Tech A says that measuring piston ring end gap in the cylinder bore will verify that the rings are properly sized for the bore. Tech B says that measuring piston-to-cylinder bore clearance determines the compression ratio of the cylinder. Who is correct?
   A. Tech A
   B. Tech B
   C. Both A and B
   D. Neither A nor B

_____ **2.** Tech A says that semi-floating wrist pins can be pressed into the rods. Tech B says that a rod heater can be used to install semi-floating wrist pins. Who is correct?
   A. Tech A
   B. Tech B
   C. Both A and B
   D. Neither A nor B

_____ **3.** Tech A says that the bearing tang's purpose is to be used as a balance pad that can be ground, if needed, to lighten the bearing. Tech B says that bearing tangs are designed to prevent the bearing from spinning in its bore. Who is correct?

    A. Tech A

    B. Tech B

    C. Both A and B

    D. Neither A nor B

_____ **4.** Tech A says that the wider the Plastigauge is squished out, the smaller the bearing clearance. Tech B says that you should turn the crankshaft one full turn after the bearing cap is torqued in place when using Plastigauge. Who is correct?

    A. Tech A

    B. Tech B

    C. Both A and B

    D. Neither A nor B

_____ **5.** Tech A says that after installing piston rings on the piston, the ring gaps should be lined up with each other. Tech B says that the oil control ring typically is positioned closest to the head of the piston. Who is correct?

    A. Tech A

    B. Tech B

    C. Both A and B

    D. Neither A nor B

_____ **6.** Tech A says that rod bearings are held in place by the torque of the rod bolts crushing the bearing into the big end of the rod bore. Tech B says that one of the connecting rod bearings act as a thrust bearing for the engine. Who is correct?

    A. Tech A

    B. Tech B

    C. Both A and B

    D. Neither A nor B

_____ **7.** Tech A says that when installing a performance camshaft, the cam-to-lifter clearance should be measured and recorded. Tech B says that when installing a performance camshaft, piston-to-valve clearance should be checked. Who is correct?

    A. Tech A

    B. Tech B

    C. Both A and B

    D. Neither A nor B

_____ **8.** Tech A says that when installing the rod caps on a rod, the bearing tangs should be on the same side of the rod. Tech B says that when installing the piston and rod into the block, rod bolt protectors should be used. Who is correct?

    A. Tech A

    B. Tech B

    C. Both A and B

    D. Neither A nor B

_____ **9.** Tech A says that torque-to-yield head bolts are special bolts that are reusable. Tech B says that head bolts should be torqued in only one step to provide the proper bolt stretch. Who is correct?

    A. Tech A

    B. Tech B

    C. Both A and B

    D. Neither A nor B

_____ **10.** Tech A says that the use of some RTV sealants to seal components on an engine can damage the oxygen sensor. Tech B says that it is common to use a heavy-duty reversible drill to spin the oil pump to pre-lube the engine. Who is correct?

    A. Tech A

    B. Tech B

    C. Both A and B

    D. Neither A nor B

Automatic Transmission Fundamentals

At the start of each chapter you'll find the NATEF Tasks, Knowledge Objectives, and Skills Objectives from the textbook. These are your objectives as you make your way through the exercises in this workbook and the chapter in your textbook. The following activities have been designed to help you refresh your knowledge of the material in this chapter.

NATEF Tasks

There are no NATEF tasks for this chapter.

Knowledge Objectives

After reading this chapter, you will be able to:

- K23001 Describe the types and operation of automatic transmissions.
- K23002 Describe the operation of each type of automatic transmission.
- K23003 Describe the operation of a torque converter.
- K23004 Describe the purpose and function of a torque converter.
- K23005 Identify the components of a torque converter, and describe their function.
- K23006 Describe the various modes of operation of a torque converter.
- K23007 Identify the components used to lock up a converter, and describe their function.
- K23008 Describe the purpose and function of a transmission heat exchanger.
- K23009 Describe automatic transmission geartrain components and their operation.
- K23010 Describe the operation of the automatic transmission geartrain.
- K23011 Identify and describe automatic transmission gear set styles.
- K23012 Describe planetary gear sets and their operation.
- K23013 Describe the methods used to hold and drive automatic transmission gears.
- K23014 Describe the components of an automatic transmission and their function.
- K23015 Describe the qualities and additives of automatic transmission fluid.
- K23016 Describe purpose, types, and function of front pumps.
- K23017 Describe the purpose and function of the flexplate and ring gear.
- K23018 Describe the purpose and function of the case, extension housing, and pan.
- K23019 Describe each type of gasket and seal.
- K23020 Describe the purpose and function of the parking pawl assembly.
- K23021 Describe the purpose and function of standard and compound planetary gears.
- K23022 Describe the different types of thrust washers and thrust bearings used in an automatic transmission.
- K23023 Describe the bushings used in an automatic transmission.
- K23024 Describe the purpose and function of automatic transmission holding devices.
- K23025 Describe the purpose and operation of brake bands and servos.
- K23026 Describe the purpose and function of multidisc clutches.

Skills Objectives

There are no Skills Objectives for this chapter.

Matching

Match the following terms with the correct description or example.

A. Extension housing
B. Front hydraulic pump
C. Gear ratio
D. Helical-cut gear
E. One-way clutch

F. Planetary gears
G. Ravigneaux gear set
H. Simpson gear set
I. Spur gear
J. Thrust bearing

_____ **1.** A type of gear in which the teeth of the gear are cut in a straight line down the axis of the gear.

_____ **2.** A hydraulic pump used to supply lubrication oil and hydraulic pressure to the different components inside the automatic transmission.

_____ **3.** A type of gear in which the teeth are cut in a spiral down the axis of the gear.

_____ **4.** Also known as a Torrington bearing, it is a type of flat needle roller bearing with the rollers placed radially around the center of the bearing.

_____ **5.** The small gears in a planetary gear set that revolve around the sun gear; also known as pinion gears.

_____ **6.** A component of the automatic transmission housing that covers the output shaft of the transmission. The extension housing also supports the end of the driveshaft and may hold components such as the vehicle speed sensor, speedometer drive assembly, and governor assembly.

_____ **7.** A type of compound planetary gear set that uses two different sun gears and two different-diameter planets while only using one ring gear.

_____ **8.** The ratio of the size or teeth of one gear compared to the size or teeth of a mating gear.

_____ **9.** A type of gear set with two planetary gear sets that share a common sun gear.

_____ **10.** A type of holding device used by an automatic transmission to stop the movement of one component of a planetary gear set. It allows free spinning in one direction but will lock up when the part attempts to spin in the opposite direction.

Multiple Choice

Read each item carefully, and then select the best response.

_____ **1.** Transmissions that use two pulleys that change diameter in response to vehicle load and speed are known as_____.
    A. dual-clutch transmissions
    B. continuously variable transmissions
    C. power-splitting transmissions
    D. automatic transmissions

_____ **2.** With which type of hybrid drive train does the engine have two or more devices to power the transmission?
    A. Series hybrid
    B. Parallel hybrid
    C. Dual-clutch
    D. Continuously variable

_____ **3.** Early automatic transmissions used a _____ rather than a torque converter.
    A. fluid coupler
    B. flywheel
    C. transaxle
    D. countershaft

_____ **4.** In its simplest form, a single-stage torque converter has three elements including all of the following, _except_:
    A. Turbine
    B. Impeller
    C. Fluid coupler
    D. Stator

_____ **5.** The _____ has a small set of curved blades attached to a central hub and is positioned between the impeller and the turbine.
   A. fluid coupler
   B. pinion
   C. servo
   D. stator

_____ **6.** An operating condition where the turbine is stationary and the engine throttle is wide open, making the rotational speed of the impeller as high as possible is called _____.
   A. stall
   B. torque
   C. choke
   D. turbo

_____ **7.** Automatic transmission vehicles use a(n) _____, sometimes called a transmission cooler, in one tank of the radiator.
   A. evaporator
   B. heat exchanger
   C. blend box
   D. condenser

_____ **8.** The difference in diameter between the driving gear and the driven gear is known as _____.
   A. leverage
   B. torque conversion
   C. gear ratio
   D. reduction

_____ **9.** What type of gears are often used to change the direction of power flow by 90 degrees?
   A. Helical-cut gears
   B. Sun gears
   C. Planetary gears
   D. Hypoid gears

_____ **10.** A friction-lined steel belt that wraps around the outside of a drum inside the automatic transmission is called a _____.
   A. band
   B. clutch
   C. pinion
   D. strap

_____ **11.** Which of the following torque converter parts are similar in construction?
   A. Turbine and stator
   B. Impeller and stator
   C. Housing and impeller
   D. Turbine and impeller

_____ **12.** Which of the following should never be used to lubricate an internal transmission seal?
   A. ATF fluid
   B. Grease
   C. Petroleum jelly
   D. Automatic transmission assembly lubricant

_____ **13.** What type of transmission seals come in several styles—continuous, butt cut, scarf cut, and step joint?
   A. Lip seals
   B. Square-cut seals
   C. Teflon seals
   D. O-rings

_____ **14.** Which of the following is an example of a compound planetary gear set?
   A. Ravigneaux gear set
   B. Continuously variable transmission
   C. Simpson gear set
   D. Both A and C

_____ **15.** What component is used in automatic transmissions to convert the hydraulic pressure acting on a piston to a mechanical force that is then applied to a brake band?
   A. Pinions
   B. Servos
   C. Simpson gears
   D. Fluid couplers

True/False

If you believe the statement to be more true than false, write the letter "T" in the space provided. If you believe the statement to be more false than true, write the letter "F".

_____ **1.** An automatic transmission can select and shift gears without input from the driver.

_____ **2.** In a manual transmission, engine torque is controlled by two, typically wet, clutches.

_____ **3.** Modern transmissions no longer use fluid couplers.

_____ **4.** During acceleration or hill climbing, the turbine slows, and at the same time the driver increases engine power, causing the impeller to speed up.

_____ **5.** Planetary gears are held together in a planet carrier.

_____ **6.** Helical-cut gears tend to be much louder and do not offer as much strength as the other types of gears.

_____ **7.** Automatic transmission fluids are typically dyed purple for easy identification.

_____ **8.** On a manual transmission there is no flywheel; there is a thin, lightweight steel flexplate.

_____ **9.** If the tangs or flats are not engaged properly and the transmission is reinstalled into the vehicle, the front pump will be destroyed when the engine is first started.

_____ **10.** A basic planetary gear set has a sun gear, which meshes with planetary gears, also called planet pinions.

_____ **11.** A direct drive, or 1:1 ratio, is obtained by locking together any two members of the planetary gear set.

_____ **12.** Thrust bearings are a friction type of bearing similar to engine main bearings, they can be made of plastic or steel coated with a bronze bearing material.

_____ **13.** There are three types of clutches: multidisc, one-way and dog clutches.

_____ **14.** All bands inside an automatic transmission are externally contracting types.

_____ **15.** Multidisc clutches can hold or drive members of the planetary gear set.

Fill in the Blank

Read each item carefully, and then complete the statement by filling in the missing word(s).

1. _____-_____ transmissions are a newer type of automatic transmission that uses two clutches, either wet or dry, in place of a standard torque converter to connect the engine to the transmission.

2. In a _____ hybrid drive train, the electric motor is not typically able to propel the vehicle on its own. This electric motor is often placed between the engine and the transmission.

3. A series-parallel hybrid drive train uses what is called a _____-_____ transmission.

4. The _____ _____ is mounted between the engine and the transmission, in the same place as a manual transmission clutch.

5. A _____ _____ is basically two fans facing each other.

6. The _____ has a large number of vanes attached to the torque converter housing to form the driving member.

7. Combining rotary flow and vortex flow produces a progressive circular, or spiraling, motion known as _____ flow.

8. Planetary gears revolve inside a larger _____ gear that wraps around the outside of the whole planetary gear set.

9. _____ gears were used in early transmissions due to ease of manufacturing and lower cost.

10. _____ clutches are unique in that they not only can be used to hold a member of the planetary gear set, but they are the only type of component that can be used to drive a member of the planetary gear set.

11. One-way clutches can be either one-way _____ or _____.

12. A(n) _____ _____ vane pump reduces the pumping load on the engine when the transmission requires less fluid to be pumped.

13. When the driver shifts the transmission into park, a lever, called a _____ _____, is forced into notches cut into a hardened steel drum on the output shaft of the transmission.

14. The _____ _____ bushing is used to support the torque converter and sees the largest amount of wear in the transmission.

15. The number of plates installed determines the _____ _____ of the clutch.

Labeling

Label the following diagrams with the correct terms.

1. Torque converter mounted between the engine and the transmission:

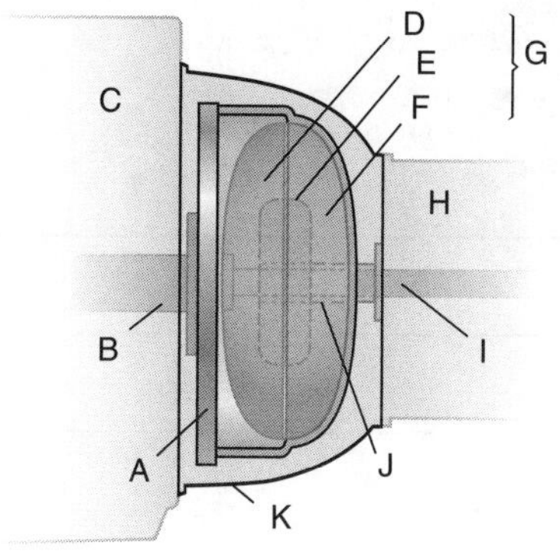

A. _____
B. _____
C. _____
D. _____
E. _____
F. _____
G. _____
H. _____
I. _____
J. _____
K. _____

2. Fluid flow through a torque converter:

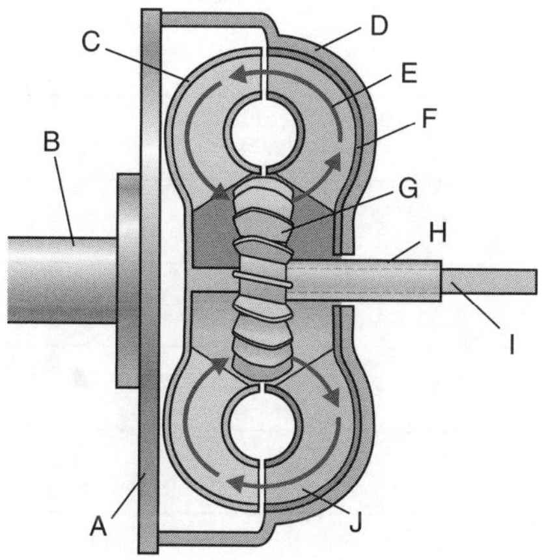

A. _____
B. _____
C. _____
D. _____
E. _____
F. _____
G. _____
H. _____
I. _____
J. _____

3. Simple planetary gear set:

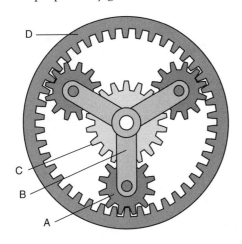

A. _____

B. _____

C. _____

D. _____

4. Gear set styles:

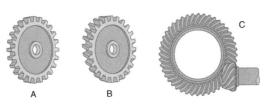

A. _____

B. _____

C. _____

5. A hypoid gear arrangement:

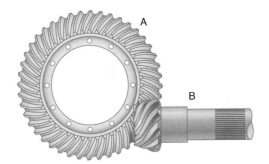

A. _____

B. _____

6. Typical transmission band:

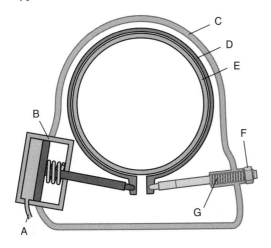

A. _____

B. _____

C. _____

D. _____

E. _____

F. _____

G. _____

7. Vane pump:

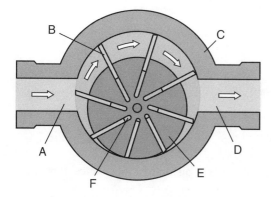

A. _____

B. _____

C. _____

D. _____

E. _____

F. _____

Review Questions

_____ **1.** Which of these transmissions uses two, either wet or dry, clutches in place of a standard torque converter to connect the engine to the transmission?
   A. Continuously variable transmissions
   B. Power-splitting transmissions
   C. Dual-clutch transmissions
   D. Parallel hybrid transmission

_____ **2.** A torque converter does all of the following *except*:
   A. enables the transmission to automatically couple and uncouple from the engine when needed.
   B. allows the engine to idle at a stop, even though the transmission is still in gear.
   C. multiplies torque from the engine to the input shaft of the transmission under certain driving conditions.
   D. transmits lower amounts of torque when driving away from a stop.

_____ **3.** When there is a large difference between the speed of the impeller and the turbine:
   A. maximum torque multiplication occurs.
   B. the vehicle is coasting.
   C. torque multiplication falls to zero.
   D. fluid flow from the turbine vanes is relatively low.

_____ **4.** What is achieved when the transmission fluid first runs through the external cooler and then through the cooler in the radiator?
   A. It increases the viscosity of the transmission fluid.
   B. It prevents overcooling of the transmission fluid.
   C. It draws heat away from the fluid in the transmission pan.
   D. It prevents overheating of the transmission fluid.

_____ **5.** Any gear ratio of less than 1:1 is considered an overdrive ratio. Overdrive ratios are typically used to:
   A. increase engine speed.
   B. increase fuel economy.
   C. increase engine noise.
   D. increase engine wear.

_____ **6.** Planetary gears are held in place by a:
   A. sun gear.
   B. ring gear.
   C. planet carrier.
   D. turbine.

_____ **7.** Which of the below additives allows the automatic transmission fluid to remain thin when the temperature is cold and prevents the fluid from becoming too thin as the transmission fluid warms up?
   A. Seal conditioners
   B. Detergents
   C. Antifoam
   D. Viscosity modifiers

_____ **8.** Which of these reduces the pumping load on the engine when the transmission requires less fluid to be pumped?
  A. Gear pump
  B. Variable displacement vane pump
  C. Crescent pump
  D. Rotor pump

_____ **9.** All of the below can be used to lubricate seals *except*:
  A. grease.
  B. petroleum jelly.
  C. automatic transmission assembly lubricant.
  D. automatic transmission fluid.

_____ **10.** Which of these converts the hydraulic pressure acting on a piston to a mechanical force that is then applied to a brake band?
  A. Seals
  B. Springs
  C. Servos
  D. Pinions

ASE Technician A/Technician B Style Questions

_____ **1.** Tech A says that the first gear of a transmission results in a large increase in torque, but a major decrease in speed. Tech B says that the reverse gear of a transmission results in a torque increase with a speed reduction. Who is correct?
  A. Tech A
  B. Tech B
  C. Both A and B
  D. Neither A nor B

_____ **2.** Tech A says that spur gears create more thrust motion than helical gears. Tech B says that helical cut gears are noisier than straight-cut gears. Who is correct?
  A. Tech A
  B. Tech B
  C. Both A and B
  D. Neither A nor B

_____ **3.** Tech A says that the impeller is splined to the input shaft. Tech B says that the stator is fixed solidly to the torque converter housing. Who is correct?
  A. Tech A
  B. Tech B
  C. Both A and B
  D. Neither A nor B

_____ **4.** Tech A says that a parallel hybrid drivetrain has two or more different devices to power the transmission. Tech B says that power-splitting transmissions use two adjustable pulleys and a heavy metal belt. Who is correct?
  A. Tech A
  B. Tech B
  C. Both A and B
  D. A nor B

_____ **5.** Tech A says that most automatic transmissions use planetary gear sets. Tech B says that planetary gear sets are often combined together to create the needed gear ratios for a transmission. Who is correct?
  A. Tech A
  B. Tech B
  C. Both A and B
  D. Neither A nor B

_____ **6.** Tech A says that the torque converter hub drives the front pump in an automatic transmission. Tech B says that the turbine shaft drives the front pump. Who is correct?
  A. Tech A
  B. Tech B

   C. Both A and B
   D. Neither A nor B

_____ **7.** Tech A says that multidisc clutches are used to drive or hold planetary gear components. Tech B says that bands are used to drive planetary gear components. Who is correct?
   A. Tech A
   B. Tech B
   C. Both A and B
   D. Neither A nor B

_____ **8.** Tech A says that bands allow components to freewheel in one direction, and lock up in the other direction. Tech B says that some servos are the "pressure release" type. Who is correct?
   A. Tech A
   B. Tech B
   C. Both A and B
   D. Neither A nor B

_____ **9.** Tech A says that the front pump only operates when the turbine is rotating. Tech B says that a torque converter clutch locks the turbine to the converter housing when applied. Who is correct?
   A. Tech A
   B. Tech B
   C. Both A and B
   D. Neither A nor B

_____ **10.** Tech A says that the torque converter can multiply the amount of torque transmitted from the engine to the transmission. Tech B says that the torque converter allows the engine to idle when the vehicle stops in traffic. Who is correct?
   A. Tech A
   B. Tech B
   C. Both A and B
   D. Neither A nor B

24 Hydraulic Fundamentals

At the start of each chapter you'll find the NATEF Tasks, Knowledge Objectives, and Skills Objectives from the textbook. These are your objectives as you make your way through the exercises in this workbook and the chapter in your textbook. The following activities have been designed to help you refresh your knowledge of the material in this chapter.

NATEF Tasks

- N24001 Diagnose transmission/transaxle gear reduction/multiplication concerns using driving, driven, and held member (power flow) principles. (AST/MAST)

Knowledge Objectives

After reading this chapter, you will be able to:

- K24001 Explain the principle of Pascal's law and how it relates to the operation of an automatic transmission.
- K24002 Identify the hydraulic system components and their function.
- K24003 Describe the types and function of automatic transmission filters.
- K24004 Describe the types and function of front pumps.
- K24005 Describe the types and function of pressure regulators.
- K24006 Describe the types and function of application devices.
- K24007 Describe the types and function of hydraulic valves.
- K24008 Describe the types and function of spool valves.
- K24009 Describe the types and function of solenoid valves.
- K24010 Describe the types and function of check valves.
- K24011 Describe the types and function of orifices and accumulators.
- K24012 Describe the use of clutch and band application charts.

Skills Objectives

There are no Skills Objectives for this chapter.

Matching

Match the following terms with the correct description or example.

A. Electronic pressure control solenoid
B. Mechanical pressure control regulator valve
C. Pascal's law
D. Separator plate
E. Spool valve
F. Surface filter

_____ 1. Sometimes called a spacer plate, a thin sheet metal plate installed between the valve body and the transmission case.

_____ 2. A type of valve commonly used in automatic transmissions that resembles the spool that thread or fishing line comes on.

_____ 3. One of the fundamental physics principles behind the operation of an automatic transmission, this law states that if fluid is placed in a confined space, pressure will be transferred equally in all directions inside the space.

_____ 4. A filter that is a simple screen mechanism to catch dirt and other particles in the hydraulic oil as it passes through.

_____ 5. A solenoid used to regulate line pressure on a computerized transmission.

_____ 6. A spool valve and spring assembly that are used to control the amount of line pressure in a transmission.

Multiple Choice

Read each item carefully, and then select the best response.

_____ **1.** One of the fundamental physics principles behind the operation of an automatic transmission is called _____.
  A. Ohm's law
  B. Pascal's law
  C. Faraday's principle
  D. Newton's law

_____ **2.** If 100 psi hydraulic pressure is applied to a piston with a surface area of 3 in^2, the output force will be
  A. 300 lb
  B. 300 psi
  C. 103 lb
  D. 103 psi

_____ **3.** If 100 psi of pressure is applied to a piston that has an area of 5 in^2, what will the resulting force be?
  A. 500 psi
  B. 50 psi
  C. 100 lbs.
  D. 500 lbs.

_____ **4.** A piston that has a radius of 1.75" would have an area of _____.
  A. 5.495 in^2
  B. 9.616 in^2
  C. 4.808. in^3
  D. 3.525 in^2

_____ **5.** If 100 psi is applied to a piston with a radius of 2" the total force output of the piston will be _____.
  A. 2,512 lbs.
  B. 628 lbs^2
  C. 100 psi
  D. 1,256 lbs.

_____ **6.** The hydraulic pump used in modern automatic transmissions is referred to as a _____.
  A. front pump
  B. rotor vane pump
  C. t-pump
  D. gear displacement pump

_____ **7.** The _____ operates back and forth inside of a bore in the valve body or the front pump.
  A. separator plate
  B. gear shift
  C. spool valve
  D. PEC valve

_____ **8.** Which of the following components are pulse-width modulated?
  A. EPC solenoid
  B. Spool valve
  C. Gear pump
  D. All of the above

_____ **9.** In an automatic transmission, which of the following devices can be used to hold a member of the planetary gear set?
  A. Multidisc clutch
  B. Band
  C. One-way roller or sprag
  D. All of the above

_____ **10.** Which of the following is an electromagnetic valve?
  A. Manual valve
  B. Solenoid valve
  C. Check valve
  D. Shift valve

True/False

If you believe the statement to be more true than false, write the letter "T" in the space provided. If you believe the statement to be more false than true, write the letter "F".

_____ **1.** Fluids are noncompressible and therefore transmit force effectively.

_____ **2.** If 125 psi of pressure is applied to a piston that has an area of 4 in^2 the resulting force will be 250 lb.

_____ **3.** A piston with a radius of 0.75" has a diameter of 2.5".

_____ **4.** Some vehicles have both an internal and an external transmission filter.

_____ **5.** Inside the transmission, there is often a magnet stuck to the transmission pan.

_____ **6.** Aluminum pump housings tend to resist wear very well and require replacement less often than cast iron pump housings.

_____ **7.** Internal filters can be of two types: surface filter or depth filter.

_____ **8.** A 50% pulse width modulation means that the valve is open 50% of the time and closed 50% of the time.

_____ **9.** A small piece of lint can cause a valve to stick in position and not operate, affecting the operation of the transmission.

_____ **10.** Accumulators are used to dampen the application of clutches and bands.

Fill in the Blank

Read each item carefully, and then complete the statement by filling in the missing word(s).

1. Pascal's law states that if we place fluid in a confined space, _____ will be transferred equally in all directions inside the space.

2. A(n) _____ type transmission filter is often a simple fine-mesh screen made out of metal or a plastic such as polyester.

3. A(n) _____ type transmission filter has a thick filter medium that the fluid must pass through.

4. Fluid pressure in an automatic transmission needs to be _____ to help control the quality of the shift.

5. When rebuilding a clutch pack, the _____ needs to be carefully inspected for cracks.

6. The majority of automatic transmission control valves are located inside the _____ _____.

7. Shift valves direct the flow of hydraulic oil to a clutch or band on upshift when they are moved by hydraulic pressure called _____ _____.

8. _____ valves can be one of two types in an automatic transmission: one-way or two-way.

9. _____ are often used in conjunction with spool valves to restrict fluid flow for timing purposes or to prevent valve fluctuations.

10. Manufacturer's clutch and band application charts are sometimes referred to as a _____ chart.

Labeling

Identify the correct component as shown in the following illustrations.

1. Transmission filters:

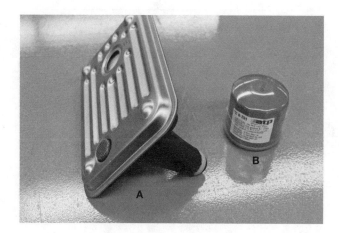

A. _____

B. _____

2. Mechanical pressure control regulator valve:

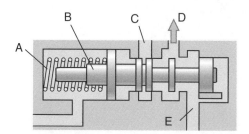

A. _____

B. _____

C. _____

D. _____

E. _____

3. EPC solenoid and fluid passages to and from the valve:

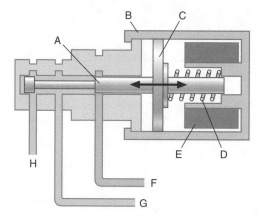

A. _____

B. _____

C. _____

D. _____

E. _____

F. _____

G. _____

H. _____

4. Accumulator operation in a servo circuit:

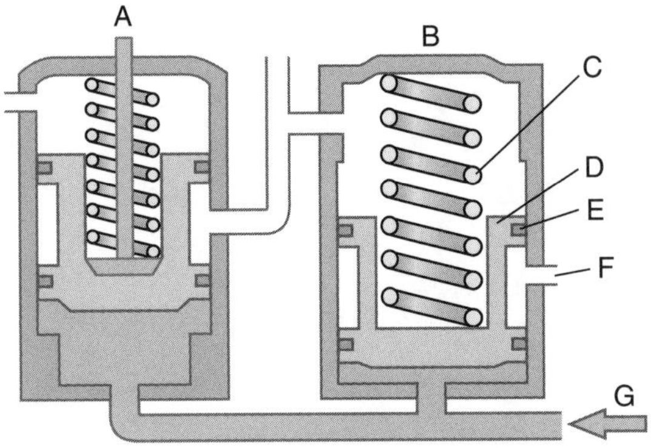

A. _____

B. _____

C. _____

D. _____

E. _____

F. _____

G. _____

Review Questions

_____ **1.** Pascal's law states that if we place fluid in a confined space, pressure will:
   A. be transferred equally in all directions inside the space.
   B. be higher at the end of the space.
   C. be lower at the end of the space.
   D. vary at various points inside the space.

_____ **2.** The hydraulic system of an automatic transmission includes all of the following *except*:
   A. a sump or pan.
   B. a filter.
   C. a front pump.
   D. a bushing.

_____ **3.** Depth filters may be made of:
   A. metal.
   B. felt.
   C. plastic.
   D. polyester.

_____ **4.** A pressure regulator valve ensures that:
   A. minimal clamping pressure is applied on clutches and bands at all times.
   B. engine load and rpm do not affect transmillsion shift points.
   C. the pressures are reduced during cruise, when less clutch and band holding power is needed.
   D. fluid pressure and line pressure stay uniformly high during all driving conditions.

_____ **5.** Which of these is used to regulate line pressure on computerized transmissions?
   A. EPC solenoid
   B. Multidisc clutches
   C. Check valves
   D. Accumulators

_____ **6.** When rebuilding a clutch pack, the piston needs to be carefully inspected for:
   A. clearance.
   B. expansion.
   C. contraction.
   D. cracks.

_____ **7.** Which of these valves is directly connected to the gearshift mechanism in the vehicle?
   A. Shift valve
   B. Manual valve
   C. Solenoid valve
   D. Check valve

_____ **8.** Which of these is often used in conjunction with check balls and spool valves to restrict fluid flow for timing purposes?
  A. Lip seal
  B. Accumulator
  C. Orifice
  D. Pressure regulator valve

_____ **9.** Accumulators are used to:
  A. dampen the application of clutches and bands.
  B. direct fluid under the proper pressure to the appropriate places in the transmission.
  C. regulate line pressure.
  D. prevent valve fluctuations.

_____ **10.** A clutch and band application chart helps to:
  A. obtain a clearer problem description from the customer.
  B. better record the problem on a repair order.
  C. identify a problem _before_ you pull the transmission.
  D. verify which transmission you are working on.

ASE Technician A/Technician B Style Questions

_____ **1.** Tech A says that band and clutch application charts can help to diagnose faults in a transmission. Tech B says that 100 psi of pressure on a 2-square-inch piston results in 50 lb of force. Who is correct?
  A. Tech A
  B. Tech B
  C. Both A and B
  D. Neither A nor B

_____ **2.** Tech A says that one benefit of using hydraulic pressure is that it is not affected by leaks in the system. Tech B says that hydraulic pressure is the same in all directions within a closed container. Who is correct?
  A. Tech A
  B. Tech B
  C. Both A and B
  D. Neither A nor B

_____ **3.** Tech A says that a mechanical pressure regulator exhausts excess fluid back to the transmission pan. Tech B says that if the transmission pan is removed, the magnet must be replaced. Who is correct?
  A. Tech A
  B. Tech B
  C. Both A and B
  D. Neither A nor B

_____ **4.** Tech A says that one type of front pump is a variable displacement pump. Tech B says that the front pump is turned by the torque converter hub. Who is correct?
  A. Tech A
  B. Tech B
  C. Both A and B
  D. Neither A nor B

_____ **5.** Tech A says that spring tension against a spool valve regulates system pressure. Tech B says that a 50% pulse width modulation means the valve is closed 50% of the time. Who is correct?
  A. Tech A
  B. Tech B
  C. Both A and B
  D. Neither A nor B

_____ **6.** Tech A says that transmission failures can be caused by failed lip seals preventing full pressure from being applied to the clutches. Tech B says that orifices are designed to speed up the movement of a valve. Who is correct?
  A. Tech A
  B. Tech B
  C. Both A and B
  D. Neither A nor B

_____ **7.** Tech A says that park is obtained by mechanically locking one band and one clutch together. Tech B says that spool valves tend to be self-cleaning. Who is correct?
   A. Tech A
   B. Tech B
   C. Both A and B
   D. Neither A nor B

_____ **8.** Tech A says that multi-plate clutches must have a specified amount of clearance when they are installed. Tech B says that there should be no clearance when they are installed because the clutch would slip. Who is correct?
   A. Tech A
   B. Tech B
   C. Both A and B
   D. Neither A nor B

_____ **9.** Tech A says that bands are a type of hydraulic valve. Tech B says that servos are devices used to allow free movement in one direction and lock up in the other direction. Who is correct?
   A. Tech A
   B. Tech B
   C. Both A and B
   D. Neither A nor B

_____ **10.** Tech A says that accumulators are used to filter contaminates. Tech B says that accumulators are used to soften clutch engagement. Who is correct?
   A. Tech A
   B. Tech B
   C. Both A and B
   D. Neither A nor B

Hydraulically Controlled Transmission

CHAPTER

25

At the start of each chapter you'll find the NATEF tasks, Knowledge Objectives, and Skills Objectives from the textbook. These are your objectives as you make your way through the exercises in this workbook and the chapter in your textbook. The following activities have been designed to help you refresh your knowledge of the material in this chapter.

NATEF Tasks

There are no NATEF tasks for this chapter.

Knowledge Objectives

After reading this chapter, you will be able to:

- K25001 Describe purpose and function of hydraulically controlled transmission components.
- K25002 Describe line pressure and how it is controlled.
- K25003 Describe the purpose and function of the governor valve.
- K25004 Describe the purpose and function of the vacuum modulator.
- K25005 Describe the purpose and function of the throttle valve.
- K25006 Describe the purpose and function of the kickdown valve.
- K25007 Identify and describe the function of shift valves.
- K25008 Describe the purpose and function of the secondary regulator valve.
- K25009 Describe the operation of the hydraulically controlled transmission.
- K250010 Describe the operation of the transmission in park.
- K250011 Describe the operation of the transmission in first gear.
- K250012 Describe the operation of the transmission in second gear.
- K250013 Describe the operation of the transmission in third gear.
- K250014 Describe the operation of the transmission in reverse.

Skills Objectives

There are no Skills Objectives for this chapter.

Matching

Match the following terms with the correct description or example.

A. Governor pressure
B. Modulator pressure
C. Reverse boost valve

D. Throttle valve
E. Throttle valve pressure
F. Vacuum modulator

_____ **1.** A component of the pressure regulator valve that increases line pressure when the vehicle is in reverse.

_____ **2.** The pressure created by the throttle valve that is proportional to throttle opening.

_____ **3.** The pressure created by the governor, which is used to make the shift valves upshift and is proportional to vehicle speed.

_____ **4.** A device on a hydraulically controlled transmission that converts engine manifold vacuum into an engine load signal called modulator pressure.

_____ **5.** A pressure used to delay transmission upshifting based upon engine load. It may also be used to raise line pressure to more firmly apply bands and clutches under higher engine loads.

_____ **6.** A type of spool valve that is connected to the throttle that creates a pressure proportional to throttle opening and is used to delay upshifting based on throttle opening.

Multiple Choice

Read each item carefully, and then select the best response.

_____ 1. A hydro-mechanical valve that produces a variable pressure, based on vehicle speed is called a _____.
   A. flex plate
   B. servo
   C. spool valve
   D. governor

_____ 2. The variable pressure produced by a governor is called _____.
   A. line pressure
   B. governor pressure
   C. output pressure
   D. negative pressure

_____ 3. A type of governor in which the assembly uses two valves, a primary valve and a secondary valve is called _____.
   A. multi-valve governor
   B. output shaft-mounted governor
   C. staged governor
   D. in-line governor

_____ 4. _____ is created by regulating hydraulic pressure that is generated in the front pump.
   A. Intake pressure
   B. Manifold vacuum
   C. Line pressure
   D. Throttle pressure

_____ 5. When engine vacuum is high, a vacuum modulator produces _____.
   A. very high modulator pressure
   B. low modulator pressure
   C. high modulator pressure
   D. zero modulator pressure

_____ 6. If the diaphragm on a vacuum modulator becomes ripped, what might the customer complain of?
   A. White exhaust smoke
   B. Dark exhaust smoke
   C. Delayed or harsh shifting
   D. Either A or C

_____ 7. Some hydraulically controlled transmissions use a(n) _____ in place of, or in addition to, a vacuum modulator.
   A. staged governor
   B. kickdown valve
   C. throttle valve
   D. orifice

_____ 8. On older hydraulically controlled transmissions, what device allows the transmission to downshift when you press the accelerator to the floor in order to accelerate faster?
   A. Modulator
   B. Kickdown valve
   C. Governor
   D. Servo

_____ 9. How high may line pressure be in reverse gear?
   A. As high as 200 psi
   B. As high as 300 psi
   C. As high as 400 psi
   D. As high as 500 psi

_____ 10. In which gear are governor pressure and modulator pressure/throttle valve pressure not used?
   A. First gear
   B. Second gear
   C. Third gear
   D. Reverse

True/False

If you believe the statement to be more true than false, write the letter "T" in the space provided. If you believe the statement to be more false than true, write the letter "F".

_____   **1.** Automobile manufacturers in the United States no longer produce fully hydraulically controlled transmissions.

_____   **2.** The case-mounted governor is mounted in line with the output shaft.

_____   **3.** Placing weaker springs in the governor will cause a delay in the transmission shift.

_____   **4.** Governors have trouble accurately measuring ground speed when the vehicle is moving slowly.

_____   **5.** A manual transmission can vary its shift points based on engine load.

_____   **6.** When an engine is operating under a light load, the engine manifold vacuum is low or even zero.

_____   **7.** The throttle valve has a rubber diaphragm that is compressed to the bottom of the housing by a large spring when there is no engine vacuum.

_____   **8.** Replacement vacuum modulators are often adjustable to fine-tune the shift timing.

_____   **9.** Throttle valve cables and linkages are a critical adjustment on a hydraulically controlled transmission.

_____   **10.** Fluid leaving the transmission pan can be extremely hot, so it first goes to the transmission cooler.

Fill in the Blank

Read each item carefully, and then complete the statement by filling in the missing word(s).

1. Both hydraulic and electronic transmissions with multi-plate clutches and bands use _____ _____ to apply the bands and clutches.

2. The governor is supplied with line pressure and then uses _____ force to vary the governor pressure in proportion to vehicle speed.

3. Springs behind the weights help to _____ the governor to the particular engine that is installed in the vehicle.

4. A(n) _____-_____ governor enables more precise control of governor pressure and, therefore, the transmission shift.

5. When engine vacuum is _____, the modulator produces a low modulator pressure.

6. As the throttle opening increases, throttle _____ _____ increases.

7. In some transmissions the kickdown valve is called a _____ valve.

8. A _____ can be located on the output shaft or in the transmission case.

9. A(n) _____ _____ will either block or allow the passage of line pressure to a particular clutch or band in order to apply the gear.

10. The _____ valve uses a simple spring-loaded valve that dumps fluid above the intended pressure back to the oil pan.

Labeling

Identify the correct component as shown in the following illustrations.

1. Hydraulic diagram of a governor valve: vehicle maximum speed:

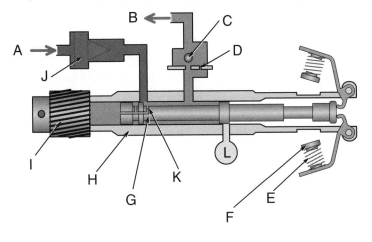

A. _____

B. _____

C. _____

D. _____

E. _____

F. _____

G. _____

H. _____

I. _____

J. _____

K. _____

2. Hydraulic throttle valve: under load (throttle partially open):

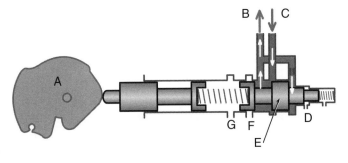

A. _____

B. _____

C. _____

D. _____

E. _____

F. _____

G. _____

3. Secondary pressure regulator valve showing a hydraulic circuit:

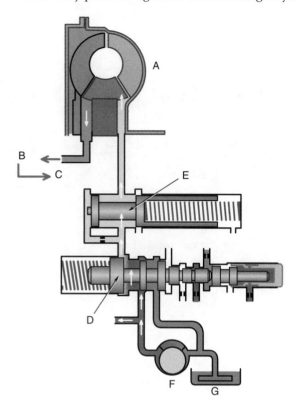

A. _____

B. _____

C. _____

D. _____

E. _____

F. _____

G. _____

4. Hydraulic diagram of a simple shift valve:

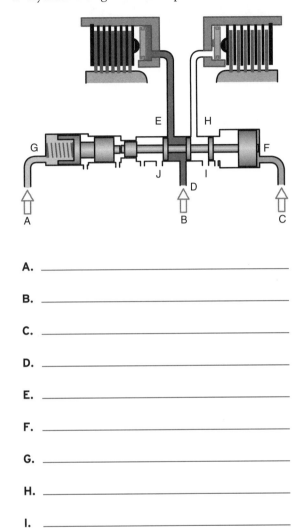

A. _____

B. _____

C. _____

D. _____

E. _____

F. _____

G. _____

H. _____

I. _____

J. _____

Review Questions

_____ **1.** Harsh-shifting transmission could be caused:
A. when the line pressure is too high during normal cruising speeds.
B. when the line pressure is too low during low cruising speeds.
C. when the line pressure is too high during high cruising speeds.
D. if the line pressure is too low during normal cruising speeds.

_____ **2.** The device that varies incoming line pressure using centrifugal force is known as:
A. vacuum modulator.
B. reverse boost valve.
C. governor.
D. throttle valve.

_____ **3.** The vacuum modulator converts the engine vacuum signal into:
A. engine pressure.
B. line pressure.

C. governor pressure.

D. modulator pressure.

4. All of the following statements are true *except*:

A. Throttle valves are located inside the transmission valve body.

B. As the throttle opening increases, throttle valve pressure decreases.

C. Increased throttle pressure delays the upshift.

D. Decreased throttle pressure allows upshifts.

5. Which of the following has multiple lands designed to block or allow line pressure to pass to a band or clutch in order to apply the gear?

A. Kickdown valve

B. Throttle valve

C. Modulator valve

D. Shift valve

6. When the manual valve is in park position, the line pressure:

A. is able to flow past the valve to all other components of the transmission.

B. is sent to apply the parking pawl.

C. is not able to flow past the valve to any other components of the transmission.

D. increases to full pressure so it will be ready to apply a band or clutch.

7. If an automatic transmission only had a governor, and no throttle valve or vacuum modulator, what is the shift most lilely to be like?

A. No difference since the throttle valve and vacuum modulator valve don't affect shift timing.

B. The transmission would shift later with greater engine load.

C. The transmission would shift earlier with greater engine load.

D. It would shift at the same point no matter what the engine load is.

8. Governor pressure and modulator pressure/throttle valve pressure are exhausted directly to the transmission pan while in _____.

A. 3rd gear.

B. 2nd gear.

C. 1st gear.

D. reverse gear.

9. When the governor pressure becomes great enough to overcome the spring pressure and the modulator/throttle valve pressure in the 2–3 shift valve, line pressure is allowed to flow to:

A. the 3rd gear clutch or band.

B. the 2nd gear clutch or band.

C. the 1st gear clutch or band.

D. the reverse gear clutch or band.

10. Which gear needs higher line pressure, and the modulator/throtle valve pressure are not used?

A. first gear.

B. second gear.

C. third gear.

D. reverse.

ASE Technician A/Technician B Style Questions

1. Tech A says that a vacuum modulator converts an engine vacuum signal into a hydraulic pressure signal. Tech B says that the manual valve is moved by governor pressure to force a shift. Who is correct?

A. Tech A

B. Tech B

C. Both A and B

D. Neither A nor B

2. Tech A says that governor pressure is controlled by torque converter rpm. Tech B says that governor pressure is controlled by output shaft speed. Who is correct?

A. Tech A

B. Tech B

    C. Both A and B
    D. Neither A nor B

_____ 3. Tech A says that reciprocating force controls governor pressure. Tech B says that centrifugal force controls governor pressure. Who is correct?
    A. Tech A
    B. Tech B
    C. Both A and B
    D. Neither A nor B

_____ 4. Tech A says that modifying governor weights will alter transmission shifting. Tech B says that excessive modification of the governor weights may cause the transmission to not shift. Who is correct?
    A. Tech A
    B. Tech B
    C. Both A and B
    D. Neither A nor B

_____ 5. Tech A says that the converter and cooler operate at line pressure. Tech B says that line pressure causes the manual valve to move during upshifts and downshifts. Who is correct?
    A. Tech A
    B. Tech B
    C. Both A and B
    D. Neither A nor B

_____ 6. Tech A says that the throttle valve is controlled by a cable or linkage hooked to the engine throttle linkage. Tech B says that a misadjusted throttle valve cable can prevent wide-open throttle (WOT) on an engine. Who is correct?
    A. Tech A
    B. Tech B
    C. Both A and B
    D. Neither A nor B

_____ 7. Tech A says that line pressure is reduced during light throttle conditions to improve fuel economy. Tech B says that as the engine speeds up in rpm, the transmission line pressure gradually reduces to maintain clutch pack pressure. Who is correct?
    A. Tech A
    B. Tech B
    C. Both A and B
    D. Neither A nor B

_____ 8. Tech A says that when governor pressure on one side of a shift valve overcomes spring pressure and throttle pressure on the other side, an upshift occurs. Tech B says when reverse boost pressure on one side of the reverse valve overcomes governor pressure on the other side, shift into reverse occurs. Who is correct?
    A. Tech A
    B. Tech B
    C. Both A and B
    D. Neither A nor B

_____ 9. Tech A says that line pressure in an automatic transmission is controlled by engine rpm. Tech B says that modulator pressure changes with engine vacuum. Who is correct?
    A. Tech A
    B. Tech B
    C. Both A and B
    D. Neither A nor B

_____ 10. Tech A says that in reverse, governor pressure regulates line pressure. Tech B says that in reverse, modulator pressure regulates line pressure. Who is correct?
    A. Tech A
    B. Tech B
    C. Both A and B
    D. Neither A nor B

Electronically Controlled Transmission

At the start of each chapter you'll find the NATEF tasks, Knowledge Objectives, and Skills Objectives from the textbook. These are your objectives as you make your way through the exercises in this workbook and the chapter in your textbook. The following activities have been designed to help you refresh your knowledge of the material in this chapter.

NATEF Tasks

There are no NATEF tasks for this chapter.

Knowledge Objectives

After reading this chapter, you will be able to:

- K26001 Describe the purpose and function of electronically controlled transmission components.
- K26002 Describe the purpose and function of transmission sensors.
- K26003 Describe the purpose and function of the vehicle speed sensor.
- K26004 Describe the purpose and function of the input shaft speed sensor.
- K26005 Describe the purpose and function of the transmission oil temperature sensor.
- K26006 Describe the purpose and function of transmission pressure switches.
- K26007 Describe the purpose and function of the line pressure sensor.
- K26008 Describe the purpose and function of the manual lever position switch.
- K26009 Describe the purpose and function of the overdrive switch.
- K26010 Describe the purpose and function of transmission-related engine sensors.
- K26011 Describe the purpose and function of the throttle position sensor.
- K26012 Describe the purpose and function of the accelerator pedal position sensor.
- K26013 Describe the purpose and function of the engine coolant temperature sensor.
- K26014 Describe the purpose and function of the manifold absolute pressure sensor.
- K26015 Describe the purpose and function of the mass airflow sensor.
- K26016 Describe the purpose and function of the crankshaft position sensor.
- K26017 Describe the purpose and function of the brake on/off switch.
- K26018 Describe the purpose and function of the manual upshift/downshift control system.
- K26019 Describe the purpose and function of the electronic actuators.
- K26020 Describe the purpose and function of the electronic pressure control solenoid.
- K26021 Describe the purpose and function of the shift solenoids.
- K26022 Describe the purpose and function of the torque converter clutch solenoid.
- K26023 Describe the operation of the electronically controlled transmission system.
- K26024 Describe the purpose and operation of the powertrain control module/transmission control module.
- K26025 Describe the purpose and function of electronic shift programs.

Skills Objectives

There are no Skills Objectives for this chapter.

Matching

Match the following terms with the correct description or example.

- **A.** Crankshaft position (CKP) sensor
- **B.** Electronic pressure control (EPC) solenoid
- **C.** Engine coolant temperature (ECT) sensor
- **D.** Manifold absolute pressure (MAP) sensor
- **E.** Manual lever position (MLP) switch
- **F.** Mass airflow (MAF) sensor

G. Line pressure sensor
H. Throttle position sensor (TPS)
I. Torque converter clutch (TCC)

J. Transmission control module (TCM)
K. Transmission fluid temperature (TFT) sensor
L. Vehicle speed sensor (VSS)

_____ **1.** A sensor used by the PCM to measure vehicle speed. It is often located in the transmission extension housing.

_____ **2.** A vacuum sensor that is attached to the intake manifold by a passageway or vacuum hose. The sensor measures engine intake manifold pressure to determine engine load and sends a corresponding signal to the PCM.

_____ **3.** A pulse-width–modulated solenoid used to control transmission line pressure in an automatic transmission.

_____ **4.** A sensor located in the air intake system that is used to measure the mass of the air flowing into the engine.

_____ **5.** A type of variable resistor used inside the transmission to monitor oil temperature.

_____ **6.** A sensor that changes resistance based upon coolant temperature, also known as a thermistor.

_____ **7.** A hydraulically operated clutch located inside the torque converter that applies at predetermined conditions and stops torque converter slippage.

_____ **8.** A type of potentiometer used by the PCM to measure throttle angle.

_____ **9.** A variable resistor sensor used to monitor line pressure.

_____ **10.** A sensor used by the PCM to monitor engine speed. It can be one of three types of sensors—Hall effect, magnetic pickup, or optical.

_____ **11.** A switch that is used by the PCM to tell which gear range the driver has selected with the shift lever.

_____ **12.** A computer module that controls the transmission operation. It may be integrated into the PCM.

Multiple Choice

Read each item carefully, and then select the best response.

_____ **1.** In a fully electronically controlled transmission, the shift points are controlled by the _____.
 A. powertrain control module
 B. driver
 C. transmission control module
 D. either A or C

_____ **2.** In a computerized transmission, the governor is replaced by a _____.
 A. manual lever position switch
 B. vehicle speed sensor
 C. shift solenoid
 D. crankshaft position sensor

_____ **3.** Most vehicle speed sensors are a type of sensor called a _____.
 A. magnetic pickup
 B. potentiometer
 C. magnetic reluctance sensor
 D. either A or C

_____ **4.** What type of electrical wave pattern is produced by a reed switch?
 A. DC square wave
 B. AC sine wave
 C. AC triangle wave
 D. DC sine wave

_____ **5.** What type of sensor is a line pressure sensor?
 A. Thermistor
 B. Transducer
 C. Magnetic pickup
 D. Potentiometer

_____ 6. Which of the following is another name for the input shaft speed sensor?
    A. Torque converter speed sensor
    B. Turbine speed sensor
    C. Impeller speed sensor
    D. Shift time sensor

_____ 7. What type of sensor is used on drive-by-wire vehicles to determine the driver's intent as related to acceleration/deceleration?
    A. Throttle position sensor
    B. Vehicle speed sensor
    C. Input shaft speed sensor
    D. Acceleratorpedal position sensor

_____ 8. What type of sensors use a flexible silicon chip within a sealed chamber that changes resistance when pressure flexes the chip?
    A. Manifold absolute pressure sensor
    B. Line pressure sensor
    C. Throttle position sensor
    D. Mass airflow sensor

_____ 9. Crankshaft position sensors are what type of sensor?
    A. Pickup-style sensor
    B. Hall-effect sensor
    C. Optical-style sensor
    D. Any of the above

_____ 10. Many four-speed automatic transmissions use two _____ to control the transmission.
    A. transducers
    B. shift solenoids
    C. potentiometers
    D. electronic pressure control solenoids

True/False

If you believe the statement to be more true than false, write the letter "T" in the space provided. If you believe the statement to be more false than true, write the letter "F".

_____ 1. Fully computer-controlled transmissions allow manufacturers to install smaller transmissions into vehicles.

_____ 2. Most vehicle manufacturers have integrated the transmission control module into the construction of the powertrain control module.

_____ 3. As the teeth of the reluctor wheel get closer to the iron core, a negative voltage is produced. As the tooth moves away, the voltage becomes positive.

_____ 4. Magnetic pickup sensors do not need a separate wire to supply them with a reference voltage.

_____ 5. Some powertrain control modules compare the input shaft speed sensor to the output shaft speed sensor to determine gear ratios.

_____ 6. If the transmission oil is hotter, the PCM will allow higher engine rpm before shifting the transmission and allow more time for the transmission to complete the shift.

_____ 7. When there is no pressure in a hydraulic circuit, a transmission pressure switch is closed, and when pressure is applied, it opens.

_____ 8. An engine coolant temperature sensor cannot accurately read engine temperature when the coolant level is low.

_____ 9. Mass airflow sensors measure airflow in grams per square inch.

_____ 10. On some newer vehicles, the brake switch is used to put the transmission into neutral while idling at a stoplight.

_____ 11. Many manufacturers recommend using overdrive when pulling a trailer or heavy loads.

_____ 12. Shift solenoids are typically an electromagnetic type of valve that is either open or closed.

_____ 13. A solenoid with a 25% pulse-width modulation is off 25% of the time and on 75% of the time.

_____ 14. In time, the powertrain control module learns how a particular driver uses the vehicle.

_____ 15. A newer powertrain control module can apply logic to the operating conditions it sees.

Fill in the Blank

Read each item carefully, and then complete the statement by filling in the missing word(s).

1. The powertrain control module receives various _____ from the engine and transmission to determine the shift timing and the firmness of the shift.

2. A(n) _____ _____ _____ is sometimes called an output shaft speed sensor.

3. A(n) _____ changes its resistance based upon its temperature.

4. A(n) _____ varies its resistance based on its position.

5. The _____ _____ temperature sensor is installed in an engine coolant passage, often near the thermostat housing on an engine.

6. To meet more stringent emission standards, most vehicles come equipped with a _____ _____ sensor, rather than a MAP sensor, to measure engine load.

7. The _____ _____ _____ switch is often mounted directly on the transmission case where the shift linkage connects to the transmission.

8. _____-_____ _____ means that the solenoid is only on for a percentage of the time.

9. In many transmissions the solenoid allows hydraulic oil to flow to a _____ _____ that moves, allowing line pressure to flow past and engage the clutch or band.

10. Early torque converters always had some slippage, so in the late 1970s and early 1980s manufacturers added a _____-_____ _____ to the torque converter.

11. The _____ _____ section of the powertrain control module is responsible for sending the proper reference voltage to many of the sensors.

12. The _____ _____ typically send either simple on/off signals or pulse-width–modulated signals to the actuators, depending on the actuator being controlled.

13. Identification of _____ means identifying unusual ambient conditions in which the vehicle is operating.

14. By having a completely _____-controlled transmission and engine, the PCM is able to reduce the amount of torque being produced by the engine right before the transmission shifts.

15. A fail-safe or _____-_____ mode allows a vehicle to be driven even if the computer for the transmission or the part of the PCM that controls the transmission fails.

Labeling

Label the following diagrams with the correct terms.

1. Input shaft speed sensor versus output shaft speed sensor:

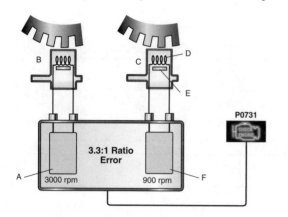

A. _____

B. _____

C. _____

D. _____

E. _____

F. _____

2. A common brake on/off switch wiring diagram:

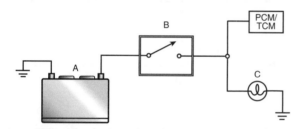

A. _____

B. _____

C. _____

3. A pulse-width–modulated pattern of an electronic pressure control (EPC) solenoid (ground side switched):

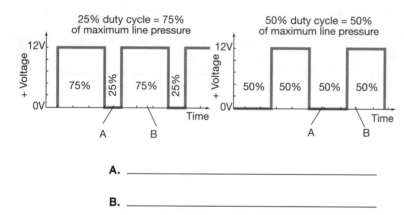

A. _____

B. _____

4. Simplified hydraulic diagram for a transmission in which the shift solenoids indirectly operate the clutches or bands in first gear:

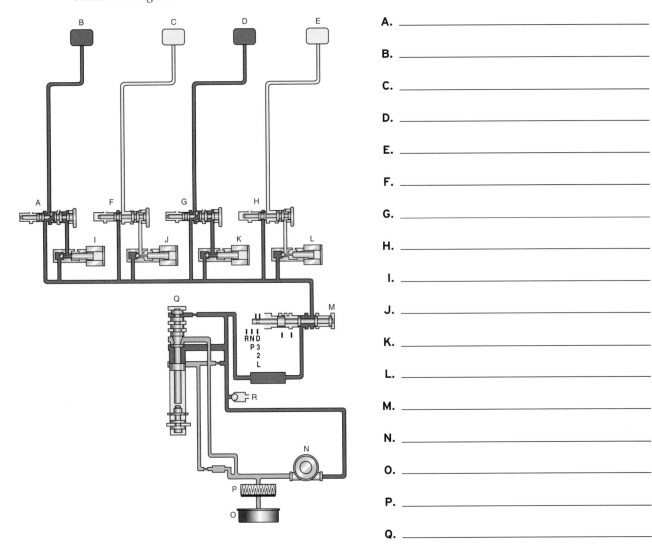

A. _____

B. _____

C. _____

D. _____

E. _____

F. _____

G. _____

H. _____

I. _____

J. _____

K. _____

L. _____

M. _____

N. _____

O. _____

P. _____

Q. _____

R. _____

Review Questions

_____ 1. All of the following statements are true with respect to vehicle speed sensor (VSS) *except*:
   A. It is responsible for sending the vehicle speed information to the vehicle speedometer.
   B. It is sometimes called an output shaft speed sensor.
   C. Most VSSs are a type of sensor called a magnetic pickup, or magnetic reluctance, sensor.
   D. It replaces the vacuum modulator on a computerized transmission.

_____ 2. All the following statements are true *except*:
   A. In a fully hydraulically controlled transmission, the shift points are controlled by vehicle's powertrain control module (PCM).
   B. In the fully electronically controlled transmission, the shift points are controlled by the vehicle's powertrain control module (PCM) or transmission control module (TCM).
   C. In the fully electronically controlled transmission, the shift points are controlled by the transmission governor.
   D. On a hydraulically controlled transmission, the computer can react to the increased load only *after* the transmission shifts.

_____ 3. Transmission pressure switches are:
   A. open when there is pressure.
   B. used to determine what gear the transmission is operating in.
   C. present in the dashboard.
   D. used to determine the temperature of the transmission fluid.

_____ 4. Which of the following is a pressure transducer?
   A. Electric-only propulsion
   B. Manual lever position (MLP) switch
   C. Overdrive switch
   D. Line pressure sensor

_____ 5. Which of the following is installed in an engine coolant passage, often near the thermostat housing on an engine?
   A. MAF sensor
   B. ECT sensor
   C. MAP sensor
   D. CKP sensor

_____ 6. All of the following statements are true *except*:
   A. The PCM or the TCM is the brain in the system.
   B. The PCM monitors the TPS sensor along with the VSS to determine a driver's driving pattern.
   C. Slippery conditions require a gear ratio that enhances the traction of the vehicle.
   D. Increasing the amount of torque being transmitted to the transmission reduces transmission wear.

_____ 7. Which of the following is used by the PCM to tell which gear range the driver has selected with the shift lever?
   A. Manual lever position switch
   B. Reed switch
   C. Line pressure sensor
   D. Throttle position sensor

_____ 8. Choose the correct statement with respect to limp-in mode.
   A. It is when the transmission can only operate in one forward gear.
   B. It is a sensor used by the PCM to monitor engine speed.
   C. It is a sensor that changes resistance based upon coolant temperature.
   D. It is a type of speed sensor that uses a magnetic field to open and close a movable set of contacts.

_____ 9. An electromechanical device used to control oil flow to bands and clutches in an automatic transmission is the:
   A. torque converter clutch.
   B. throttle position sensor.
   C. shift solenoid.
   D. potentiometer.

_____ **10.** All the following statements describing VSS are true *except*:

    A. The types of VSS are magnetic pickup and reed switch.

    B. An input shaft speed sensor is similar to a VSS and relays its signal to the PCM.

    C. It relays vehicle speed information to the speedometer.

    D. It is primarily used to determine functionality of emissions-related components.

ASE Technician A/Technician B Style Questions

_____ **1.** Tech A says that electronically controlled automatic transmissions improve fuel economy over hydraulically controlled transmissions. Tech B says that electronically controlled transmissions also reduce emissions. Who is correct?

    A. Tech A

    B. Tech B

    C. Both A and B

    D. Neither A nor B

_____ **2.** A vehicle comes in only operating in 3rd gear. Tech A says the transmission will need to be replaced. Tech B says that the transmission may be operating in limp-in mode. Who is correct?

    A. Tech A

    B. Tech B

    C. Both A and B

    D. Neither A nor B

_____ **3.** Tech A says that reed switches produce an AC signal. Tech B says that a magnetic VSS can be diagnosed by observing the pattern on a lab scope and comparing it to a known good pattern. Who is correct?

    A. Tech A

    B. Tech B

    C. Both A and B

    D. Neither A nor B

_____ **4.** Tech A says that transmissions with an input shaft speed sensor and a vehicle speed sensor (VSS) can use this information to determine shift solenoid failure. Tech B says the input shaft speed sensor is also called a turbine speed sensor. Who is correct?

    A. Tech A

    B. Tech B

    C. Both A and B

    D. Neither A nor B

_____ **5.** Tech A says that delayed shifts could be caused by a malfunctioning TPS. Tech B says that the crankshaft position sensor is used to indicate engine speed. Who is correct?

    A. Tech A

    B. Tech B

    C. Both A and B

    D. Neither A nor B

_____ **6.** Tech A says that the ECT sensor and the TFT sensor cause a delay in shifting when they indicate cold temperatures. Tech B says that the ECT and the TFT should read substantially different temperatures after sitting overnight. Who is correct?

    A. Tech A

    B. Tech B

    C. Both A and B

    D. Neither A nor B

_____ **7.** Tech A says that the EPC solenoid controls line pressure. Tech B says that if an EPC fails, it will default to minimum line pressure. Who is correct?

    A. Tech A

    B. Tech B

    C. Both A and B

    D. Neither A nor B

_____ **8.** Tech A says that in limp-in mode, even if the computer for the transmission fails, the vehicle will still be drivable. Tech B says that if the PCM fails, the EPC solenoid will mechanically default to maximum line pressure to prevent clutch and band slippage. Who is correct?

    A. Tech A

    B. Tech B

    C. Both A and B

    D. Neither A nor B

_____ **9.** Tech A says that pressure switches are used in electronically controlled transmissions to indicate which gear the transmission is operating in. Tech B says that the brake on/off switch signals the PCM to disengage the TCC. Who is correct?

    A. Tech A

    B. Tech B

    C. Both A and B

    D. Neither A nor B

_____ **10.** Tech A says that electronically controlled automatic transmissions can vary their gear ratios based upon winter weather conditions. Tech B says that on a vehicle with traction control, the transmission will change shift programming to assist when slippery conditions are encountered. Who is correct?

    A. Tech A

    B. Tech B

    C. Both A and B

    D. Neither A nor B

Servicing the Automatic Transmission/Transaxle

At the start of each chapter you'll find the NATEF tasks, Knowledge Objectives, and Skills Objectives from the textbook. These are your objectives as you make your way through the exercises in this workbook and the chapter in your textbook. The following activities have been designed to help you refresh your knowledge of the material in this chapter.

NATEF Tasks

- N27001 Check fluid level in a transmission or a transaxle equipped with a dipstick. (MLR/AST/MAST)
- N27002 Check fluid level in a transmission or a transaxle not equipped with a dipstick. (MLR/AST/MAST)
- N27003 Check transmission fluid condition; check for leaks. (MLR)
- N27004 Diagnose fluid loss and condition concerns; determine needed action. (AST/MAST)
- N27005 Drain and replace fluid and filter(s); use proper fluid type per manufacturer specification. (MLR/AST/MAST)
- N27006 Identify and interpret transmission/transaxle concerns, differentiate between engine performance and transmission/transaxle concerns; determine needed action. (AST/MAST)
- N27007 Diagnose noise and vibration concerns; determine needed action. (MAST)
- N27008 Diagnose electronic transmission/transaxle control systems using appropriate test equipment and service information. (MAST)
- N27009 Perform stall test; determine needed action. (AST/MAST)
- N27010 Perform pressure tests (including transmissions/transaxles equipped with electronic pressure control); determine needed action. (MAST)
- N27011 Inspect for leakage; replace external seals, gaskets, and bushings. (MLR/AST/MAST)
- N27012 Inspect, replace, and align powertrain mounts. (MLR/AST/MAST)
- N27013 Perform lock-up converter system tests; determine needed action. (AST/MAST)
- N27014 Inspect, adjust, and/or replace external manual valve shift linkage, transmission range sensor/switch, and/or park/neutral position switch. (MLR/AST/MAST)

Knowledge Objectives

After reading this chapter, you will be able to:

- K27001 Describe the strategy-based diagnostic process as it relates to automatic transmissions.
- K27002 Describe the safety and precautions needed when diagnosing automatic transmissions.
- K27003 Describe the methods of testing automatic transmissions during diagnosis.
- K27004 Describe the process of test-driving a vehicle during diagnosis of the transmission.

Skills Objectives

After reading this chapter, you will be able to:

- S27001 Perform maintenance tasks on an automatic transmission.
- S27002 Perform transmission in-vehicle diagnosis.
- S27003 Perform in-vehicle transmission repairs.

Matching

Match the following terms with the correct description or example.

A. Bidirectional control
B. Cooler flow test
C. Hydraulic pressure test

D. Air checking
E. Noise, vibration, and harshness (NVH) test
F. Powertrain mount

_____ 1. A test to measure for any audible noises, vibrations, and harsh operation. It can be completed by the technician with or without the aid of a tester. The tester is used to pinpoint the exact frequencies of the noise and vibrations.

_____ 2. A rubber or metal bracket used to secure the engine and transmission into the vehicle. Some vehicles use hydraulic or electrohydraulic powertrain mounts.

_____ 3. The ability to command different solenoids and actuators "on" and "off" to check their operation.

_____ 4. The use of compressed air to check clutch and servo operation on transmissions during and after assembly.

_____ 5. The placement of a specialty-measuring device into the transmission cooler line to measure fluid flow to the cooler.

_____ 6. The use of a hydraulic pressure gauge to measure the amount of hydraulic pressure produced in each gear range.

Multiple Choice

Read each item carefully, and then select the best response.

_____ 1. How much fluid does it take to raise the level from the bottom of the crosshatched area or add mark to the full mark on most transmission dipsticks?
A. Half-pint
B. Quart
C. Pint
D. Gallon

_____ 2. When raised in the air on a hoist, a vehicle's speed should never be allowed to exceed _____ mph on the speedometer.
A. 10
B. 25
C. 35
D. 45

_____ 3. What type of test checks the pump operation, the pressure regulator, and the seals and gaskets inside the transmission?
A. Air check
B. NVH test
C. Hydraulic pressure test
D. Cooler flow test

_____ 4. What feature makes a high-quality aftermarket scan tool or factory scan tool better than a code reader?
A. Live data
B. Reads DTCs
C. Bidirectional control
D. Both A and C

_____ 5. During which test is the vehicle placed in a gear with the emergency brake fully applied and the brake pedal firmly held?
A. Hydraulic pressure test
B. Stall test
C. NVH test
D. Preload test

_____ 6. Which of the following describes the appearance of clutch material in the bottom of a transmission pan?
A. Sparkly
B. Dark residue
C. Fine sediment collected on the magnet
D. Darkish red with a burnt smell

_____ 7. Replacement of which of the following requires the removal of the driveshaft and the extension housing?
A. Speed sensor seal
B. Extension housing bushing
C. Pan gasket
D. All of the above

_____ **8.** A loud thump when the accelerator is applied in drive or reverse and again when the brake pedal is applied may indicate a _____.
   A. broken powertrainmount
   B. dry extension-housing bushing
   C. transmission fluid leak
   D. bad shift sensor

_____ **9.** If the _____ is not adjusted properly, the transmission position indicator will not be set correctly and the customer will not know which gear the vehicle is in.
   A. speed sensor
   B. shift sensor
   C. linkage
   D. lock-up torque converter

_____ **10.** Which of the following best describes the appearance of metallic material in the bottom of a transmission pan?
   A. Sparkly
   B. Dark residue
   C. Coarse sediment collected on the magnet
   D. Darkish red with a burnt smell

_____ **11.** When testing hydraulic pressure, the line pressure should be highest in the _____ range.
   A. second gear
   B. first gear
   C. reverse gear
   D. third gear

_____ **12.** Which of the following is a good first step in the diagnosis of any transmission concern?
   A. Scan for computer codes
   B. Test drive
   C. Check fluid level and condition
   D. Flush the transmission fluid

_____ **13.** Which of the following tests checks the pump operation, the pressure regulator, and the seals and gaskets inside the transmission?
   A. Scan tool test
   B. Hydraulic pressure test
   C. Fluid level check
   D. Converter flow check

_____ **14.** Which is the first step in a strategy-based diagnostic process to properly diagnose a transmission?
   A. Verify the customer's concern
   B. Researching possible faults and gathering information
   C. Focused testing
   D. Performing the repair

_____ **15.** How long should the engine and transmission be allowed to cool down between tests of the different gear ratios?
   A. For about an hour
   B. For about 30 seconds
   C. For about 2 minutes
   D. For about 2 hours 30 seconds

_____ **16.** Which is the correct way to determine if a modern transmission fluid requires replacement?
   A. It has a slightly burnt smell.
   B. It is of a darker red color.
   C. It forms a dark-centered fluid spot on a paper towel.
   D. It disperses on a paper towel.

_____ **17.** Which is the third step in a strategy-based diagnostic process to properly diagnose a transmission?
   A. Focused testing
   B. Performing the repair
   C. Verify the customer's concern
   D. Researching possible faults and gathering information

_____ **18.** Identify the rule that needs to be followed when performing a stall test.
 A. Check all engine and transmission fluid levels before performing the test.
 B. Do not perform the test for more than 2 minutes.
 C. Tests between different gear ratios can be performed at a stretch without breaks.
 D. The vehicle should be at a higher than normal operating temperature before performing the test.

_____ **19.** Which of the following statements is true about the elimination of transmission dipstick in some vehicles?
 A. The fluid level can be checked with the vehicle in gear.
 B. It provides one less entry point for dirt and contaminants to enter the transmission.
 C. It causes a vehicle owner to overfill the transmission.
 D. The process of checking the service information for the proper fluid level check procedure can be avoided.

_____ **20.** When checking a line pressure of 140 psi, selecting a gauge that can read up to _____ can help obtain an accurate reading.
 A. 400 psi
 B. 1000 psi
 C. 150 psi
 D. 100 psi

True/False

If you believe the statement to be more true than false, write the letter "T" in the space provided. If you believe the statement to be more false than true, write the letter "F."

_____ **1.** Some vehicles do not have a transmission dipstick.

_____ **2.** The stall test to check torque converter operation is not recommended by all manufacturers to diagnose a transmission problem.

_____ **3.** Some modern transmission fluids are darker red when they are brand new and even have a slightly burnt smell to them.

_____ **4.** The presence of a small amount of clutch material or metal in the bottom of the pan indicates a serious transmission problem.

_____ **5.** Scanning the powertrain control module for trouble codes will indicate the specific transmission problem.

_____ **6.** Transmissions operate much differently when they are placed under a load, such as driving up a hill, than they do sitting in a shop on a hoist.

_____ **7.** A hydraulic pressure test puts maximum load on the engine, transmission, and brake system.

_____ **8.** A stall test should not be performed for more than 5 seconds, as severe transmission damage can occur.

_____ **9.** Low line pressure can be a sign of a stuck pressure regulator valve or failed EPC solenoid.

_____ **10.** The fluid in the transmission has to be at the proper level and in good condition and must be the fluid specified by the manufacturer.

_____ **11.** Test tools called NVH analyzers can help pinpoint noises in a vehicle while the vehicle is driven.

_____ **12.** None of the transmission tests require the vehicle to be driven while in the air on a hoist.

_____ **13.** When fluids leak, they travel downward due to gravity and typically toward the back of the vehicle because of air movement during driving.

_____ **14.** Powertrain mounts can be of the rubber style or the hydraulic style.

_____ **15.** Wearing insulated gloves can help prevent a technician from being severely cut by sharp edges under a vehicle such as cotter pins and sheet metal shrouds.

_____ **16.** The vehicle should be at a normal operating temperature before performing a stall test.

_____ **17.** The hydraulic control system uses an electrical solenoid valve to direct fluid away from, or to, the TCC assembly.

_____ **18.** A quick check under the vehicle can help identify the cause of undesirable transmission operation in the vehicle.

_____ **19.** A gauge that reads up to 150 psi (1034 kPa) would be more accurate than one that reads up to 400 psi (2758 kPa) when one is expecting a reading of 120 psi (827 kPa) pressure of the hydraulic system.

_____ **20.** To avoid leaks caused by loose bolts in an extension housing, the bolts can be tightened beyond their specifications to ensure proper sealing.

Fill in the Blank

Read each item carefully, and then complete the statement by filling in the missing word(s).

1. When fluids leak, they travel _____ due to gravity and typically toward the _____ of the vehicle.

2. If a transmission leak is hard to locate, place a leak detection _____ in the transmission fluid.

3. The new way to check the quality of transmission fluid is to take a few drops and place them on a clean _____ _____.

4. During the _____-_____, it is critical to place the transmission in the same operating conditions as the customer stated the problem occurred in.

5. Most manufacturers do not recommend _____ testing on late-model vehicles, as it can damage the transmission.

6. Generally, line pressure should be highest in the _____ gear range.

7. The process of removing the transmission pan to check for clutch material, metal, and other debris or contaminants is called _____ _____.

8. Some hydraulic powertrain _____ use a computer-controlled electronic control valve that can open an alternate passageway or vary the size of the orifice.

9. The lock-up torque converter contains a _____ _____ _____ that forces the turbine and impeller to match speeds.

10. Usually on hydraulically controlled transmissions, the PCM will not set a DTC except in the case of an _____ _____ or a _____ _____ for the TCC circuit.

11. Many factory scan tools give the technician _____ control of the transmission.

12. A(n) _____ _____ _____ uses a flowmeter on the cooler circuit of the hydraulic system of the transmission to help identify poor pump performance.

13. A(n) _____ _____ is a quick check under the hood or under the vehicle to visually identify problems that can be causing undesirable transmission operation.

14. The _____ feature of a scan tool should be used to record information when performing a test-drive to monitor electronic components inside and outside of the transmission.

15. On transmissions with a dipstick, transmission fluid should be checked at least at every _____ _____.

16. A _____ _____ checks the torque converter operation and also checks the transmission for slippage by operating the engine at full throttle.

Labeling

Identify the correct component as shown in the following illustrations.

1. A typical lock-up converter cutaway:

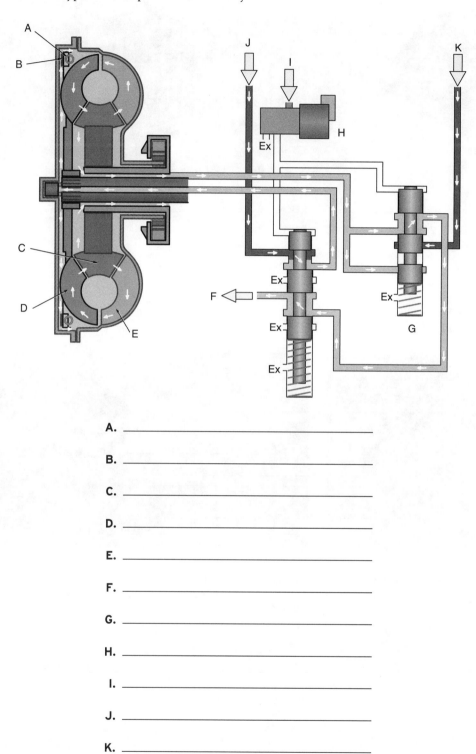

A. _____

B. _____

C. _____

D. _____

E. _____

F. _____

G. _____

H. _____

I. _____

J. _____

K. _____

2. Powertrain mounts:

A.

B.

A. _____

B. _____

Skill Drills

Place the skill drill steps in the correct order.

    1. Draining and Replacing Fluid and Filter:

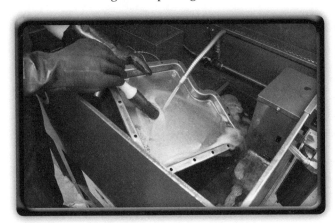

_____ **A.** Clean the pan and the magnet thoroughly in a parts washer. Dry the pan with a lint-free shop towel or compressed air. Check that the sealing surface of the pan is flat. See your supervisor if it is not.

_____ **B.** Put the new gasket on the transmission pan, clean the transmission sealing surface, and place the pan onto the transmission. Start all of the bolts before tightening.

_____ **C.** Hold the pan against the transmission with one hand while loosening the remaining bolts a few turns. Slowly allow the transmission pan to tilt downward so transmission fluid flows into the drain pan. Once most of the fluid has been drained, remove the remaining bolts the rest of the way.

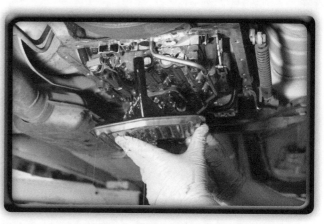

_____ **D.** If equipped, remove any bolts or clips holding the transmission filter in place, and lower the filter.

_____ **E.** Lower the vehicle and install about 75% of the correct new fluid. Start the vehicle and check the fluid level. Add fluid as necessary to bring it to the bottom of the safe or add mark. While your foot is firmly depressing the brake pedal, place the gear selector in each of the gear ranges. Check the fluid level and top off as necessary. Raise the vehicle, and check for any leaks.

_____ **F.** Safely raise and support the vehicle on the hoist. Place a drain pan with a large transmission drain funnel under the transmission pan. If the transmission has a drain plug, remove it, and place it to the side to prevent losing it. Be careful: The transmission fluid will be hot. If the transmission does not have a drain plug, loosen and remove all of the bolts except for two or three that are next to each other in a corner.

_____ **G.** Compare the new filter and transmission gasket to the old one to make sure they are correct. If the filter kit came with a new filter gasket or grommet, install the new one to prevent air leaks and possible transmission damage.

_____ **H.** Lower the pan and inspect it for nonferrous metal and old clutch material. Metal is sparkly, and clutch material is a dark residue in the bottom of the pan. The presence of some clutch material is normal. Also, inspect the magnet in the pan (if equipped). A small amount of metal is normal.

_____ **I.** Install the new filter, and torque any retaining bolts to the manufacturer's specifications.

2. Stall Testing:

_____ **A.** Check engine and transmission fluid levels. If the vehicle does not have a tachometer, place a tachometer on the engine. Place a large fan in front of the vehicle's radiator to help cool the radiator and transmission fluid.

_____ **B.** Release the throttle and place the vehicle into neutral. Record the stall speed. Cool the engine down for 30 seconds. Continue testing the remaining gear ranges (R, D4, D3, D2, D1). Compare your results with the manufacturer's specifications.

_____ **C.** Start the vehicle and allow it to reach operating temperature. Make sure the test area is clear of bystanders. Firmly apply the emergency brake, depress the brake pedal, and place the vehicle into a gear.

_____ **D.** Look up the service information to determine whether a stall test is recommended; if so, follow the procedure. Place wheel chocks in front of and behind the wheels to help prevent vehicle movement.

_____ **E.** Gradually press the throttle all the way to the floor to increase the engine rpm to the stall speed for a maximum of five seconds while firmly holding the brake pedal, and note the rpm.

3. Performing Pressure Tests:

_____ **A.** Install a transmission pressure tester(s) capable of measuring the maximum pressure into the test port(s) on the transmission.

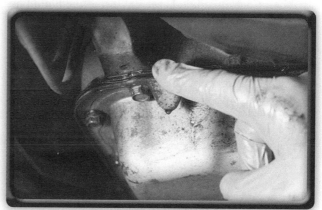

_____ **B.** Clean off any transmission fluid that dripped onto the transmission, restart the vehicle to check for leaks, and top off, if necessary.

_____ **C.** Start the engine, and place the vehicle in the specified operating conditions to monitor the pressures (e.g., transmission hot, in drive, idling). Record the pressure(s).

_____ **D.** Shut off the engine, remove the transmission pressure tester(s), seal the threads, and reinstall the test port plug(s).

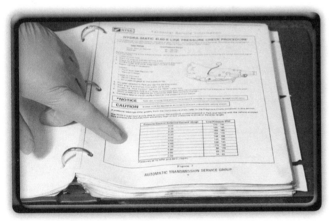

_____ **E.** Research the transmission's specified hydraulic pressures. Verify the correct transmission fluid level in the transmission. Place a drain pan under the transmission and remove the correct pressure test port plug(s).

4. Checking Fluid Level and Inspecting Fluid Loss:

_____ **A.** If the transmission has a large amount of transmission fluid or engine oil covering it, pour a leak detection dye in the transmission fluid, and use an ultraviolet light to look for fresh transmission fluid leaking.

_____ **B.** Inspect the transmission for signs of leakage.

_____ **C.** Look up the procedure for checking the transmission fluid level in the appropriate service information, and check the level.

5. Performing a Lock-Up Converter Test:

_____ **A.** Check the TCC circuit for power and ground at the TCC connector. If full power and ground are not available at the TCC connector, locate the open or high resistance, using the voltmeter to measure voltage drop.

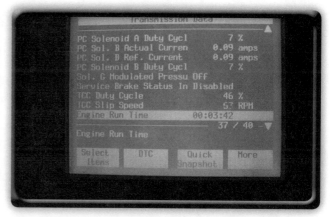

_____ **B.** Scan the vehicle to identify any TCC-related DTCs the PCM has, and record. Follow the diagnostic procedure for the DTC. Test drive the vehicle and observe the operation of the TCC circuit and the TCC slippage on the scan tool. If not within specifications, check for loose wiring or connections.

_____ **C.** If power and ground are available at the TCC connector on the transmission, measure the resistance of the solenoid through the TCC connector. If out of specifications, the transmission will have to be drained and the pan removed to test the wires and solenoid. If the solenoid is not within specification, replace the solenoid.

_____ **D.** If power and ground are available to the TCC connector, and the TCC resistance is within specifications, the TCC solenoid will have to be removed and checked to see if the valve is actually opening and closing. Apply power and ground to the solenoid while attempting to blow air through the solenoid. If the solenoid operates properly, the problem may be in the TCC itself.

Review Questions

_____ **1.** As part of general transmission maintenance, all of the following should be done *except*:
  A. checking transmission fluid.
  B. disassembling and checking the transmission.
  C. locating leaks.
  D. replacing filters.

_____ **2.** When diagnosing problems in the transmission:
  A. assume the fault.
  B. ignore the customer's point of view.
  C. take a quick decision based on visual inspection.
  D. use accurate service information.

_____ **3.** When using a scan tool to monitor electronic components inside and outside of the transmission during a road test, which of the following precautions has to be taken?
  A. Wear insulated gloves and arm sleeves.
  B. Check if tires are in balance.
  C. Do not use the movie feature of a scan tool.
  D. Do not drive with a scan tool in front of an airbag.

_____ **4.** When a customer describes a slipping transmission as a complaint, what test is the best way to verify?
  A. Fluid test
  B. Visual inspection
  C. Road test
  D. Scan of computer for codes

_____ **5.** Which test stresses the drivetrain so much that many manufacturers do not recommend performing it?
  A. Hydraulic pressure test
  B. Stall test
  C. Fluid test
  D. Road test

_____ **6.** To check the pump operation, what test should the technician conduct?
  A. Leak check
  B. Air checking
  C. NVH test
  D. Hydraulic pressure test

_____ **7.** All of the following can be replaced during in-vehicle transmission repairs *except*:
  A. vehicle speed sensor.
  B. shift solenoids.
  C. sun gear.
  D. extension housing bushing.

_____ **8.** Having access to what would allow the technician to test-drive the vehicle in the repair shop?
  A. Scan tool
  B. Pressure tester
  C. Chassis dynamometer
  D. Modulator

_____ **9.** All of the following are very critical while doing a test-drive *except*:
  A. avoiding testing the transmission in different gear ranges.
  B. recording the results for further analysis.
  C. testing the transmission during light, medium, and hard acceleration.
  D. testing the transmission in many different operating conditions.

_____ **10.** Which of these is an invaluable tool for testing a TCC on an electronically controlled transmission?
  A. Pressure gauge
  B. Factory scan tool
  C. NVH analyzer
  D. Specialty tool

ASE Technician A/Technician B Style Questions

_____ **1.** Tech A says that the fluid level in many automatic transmissions is checked with the engine idling and the transmission in park. Tech B says that some manufacturers don't provide a dipstick to check the automatic transmission fluid (ATF) level. Who is correct?
   A. Tech A
   B. Tech B
   C. Both A and B
   D. Neither A nor B

_____ **2.** Tech A says that increasing the transmission fluid level from the add mark to the full mark typically requires a quart of fluid, just like with engine oil. Tech B says that when checking for automatic transmission fluid leaks, you should also remove the radiator cap and look for ATF in the radiator, Who is correct?
   A. Tech A
   B. Tech B
   C. Both A and B
   D. Neither A nor B

_____ **3.** Tech A says that when checking the fluid level on the dipstick, always read the highest level on either side. Tech B says that when reinstalling the pan, start all of the bolts before tightening any of them. Who is correct?
   A. Tech A
   B. Tech B
   C. Both A and B
   D. Neither A nor B

_____ **4.** Tech A says that when changing the fluid and filter, the presence of a small amount of clutch material in the pan is normal. Tech B says that if the pan gasket is leaking, you should tighten the pan bolts about a quarter turn at a time until the leak stops. Who is correct?
   A. Tech A
   B. Tech B
   C. Both A and B
   D. Neither A nor B

_____ **5.** Tech A says that powertrain mounts hold the powertrain firmly in place and prevent the engine from moving at all. Tech B says that the life of rubber powertrain mounts is reduced by being saturated with oil from a leak. Who is correct?
   A. Tech A
   B. Tech B
   C. Both A and B
   D. Neither A nor B

_____ **6.** Tech A says that performing a stall test can reveal slippage within the torque converter or transmission. Tech B says that a stall test can damage some transmissions and should not be performed on all transmissions. Who is correct?
   A. Tech A
   B. Tech B
   C. Both A and B
   D. Neither A nor B

_____ **7.** Tech A says that using a scan tool to momentarily activate the TCC, with the engine idling in drive and the brakes applied, is a typical troubleshooting task. Tech B says that diagnosis is a waste of time on a faulty transmission because it will be rebuilt anyway. Who is correct?
   A. Tech A
   B. Tech B
   C. Both A and B
   D. Neither A nor B

_____ **8.** Tech A says that when checking line pressure, the engine should be off. Tech B says that low line pressure can be caused by a worn pump. Who is correct?
   A. Tech A
   B. Tech B

    C. Both A and B

    D. Neither A nor B

_____ **9.** Tech A says that low line pressure can be caused by a plugged transmission vent. Tech B says that high line pressure is caused by a restricted filter. Who is correct?

    A. Tech A

    B. Tech B

    C. Both A and B

    D. Neither A nor B

_____ **10.** Tech A says that commanding shift solenoids on and off, one at a time, is an example of focused testing. Tech B says that test driving the vehicle is an example of verifying the customer's concern. Who is correct?

    A. Tech A

    B. Tech B

    C. Both A and B

    D. Neither A nor B

Rebuilding the Automatic Transmission/Transaxle

At the start of each chapter you'll find the NATEF Tasks, Knowledge Objectives, and Skills Objectives from the textbook. These are your objectives as you make your way through the exercises in this workbook and the chapter in your textbook. The following activities have been designed to help you refresh your knowledge of the material in this chapter.

NATEF Tasks

- N28001 Remove and reinstall transmission/transaxle and torque converter; inspect engine core plugs, rear crankshaft seal, dowel pins, dowel pin holes, and mounting surfaces. (AST/MAST)
- N28002 Inspect converter flex (drive) plate, converter attaching bolts, converter pilot, converter pump drive surfaces, converter end play, and crankshaft pilot bore. (AST/MAST)
- N28003 Inspect, leak test, flush, and/or replace transmission/transaxle oil cooler, lines, and fittings. (AST/MAST)
- N28004 Measure transmission/transaxle end play and/or preload; determine needed action. (MAST)
- N28005 Disassemble, clean, and inspect transmission/transaxle. (MAST)
- N28006 Inspect, measure, and reseal oil pump assembly and components. (MAST)
- N28007 Inspect and measure planetary gear assembly components; determine needed action. (MAST)
- N28008 Inspect bushings; determine needed action. (MAST)
- N28009 Inspect, measure, and/or replace thrust washers and bearings. (MAST)
- N28010 Inspect one-way clutches, races, rollers, sprags, springs, cages, retainers; determine needed action. (MAST)
- N28011 Inspect oil delivery circuits, including seal rings, ring grooves, and sealing surface areas, feed pipes, orifices, and check valves/balls. (MAST)
- N28012 Inspect case bores, passages, bushings, vents, and mating surfaces; determine needed action. (MAST)
- N28013 Inspect clutch drum, piston, check-balls, springs, retainers, seals, friction plates, pressure plates, and bands; determine needed action. (MAST)
- N28014 Measure clutch pack clearance; determine needed action. (MAST)
- N28015 Air test operation of clutch and servo assemblies. (MAST)
- N28016 Inspect, measure, clean, and replace valve body (includes surfaces, bores, springs, valves, switches, solenoids, sleeves, retainers, brackets, check valves/balls, screens, spacers, and gaskets). (MAST)
- N28017 Inspect, measure, repair, adjust, or replace transaxle final drive components. (MAST)
- N28018 Assemble transmission/transaxle. (MAST)

Knowledge Objectives

There are no knowledge objectives in this chapter.

Skills Objectives

After reading this chapter, you will be able to:

- S28001 Install and seat the torque converter to engage drive/splines.
- S28002 Perform final checks after installation.

Matching

Match the following terms with the correct description or example.

A. Free play
B. Morse-style chain
C. Preload
D. Whetstone
E. Transaxles
F. Brinelling

_____ **1.** A type of flat stone used to sharpen knives and other cutting tools.

_____ **2.** Further pressure applied to bearing-supported parts after all the free play is taken up.

_____ **3.** The damage found in the race from a high bearing load.

_____ **4.** The amount of movement between two mating parts.

_____ **5.** Transmission with an integrated final drive unit.

_____ **6.** A heavy-duty chain constructed of many links and held together with pins.

Multiple Choice

Read each item carefully, and then select the best response.

_____ **1.** Identify the tool that can be used for checking torque converter end play.
   A. Refractometer
   B. Dial indicator
   C. Straightedge
   D. Borescope

_____ **2.** What is the typical specification for torque converter end play?
   A. 0.010" to 0.020"
   B. 0.060" to 0.070"
   C. 0.030" to 0.050"
   D. 0.080" to 0.090"

_____ **3.** A transmission cooler can be cleaned by using a(n) _____.
   A. aerosol flushing kit
   B. antifreeze
   C. gas analyzer
   D. hydrometer

_____ **4.** _____ measures the amount of free play not only in the bearing but also in the gear train inside the transmission.
   A. Feeler gauge
   B. Brinelling
   C. End play
   D. Air test

_____ **5.** Bearing end play is checked by placing the transmission so that the input shaft is _____.
   A. horizontal
   B. inclined
   C. balanced
   D. vertical

_____ **6.** Pump gear-to-housing clearance can be measured with a _____.
   A. straightedge
   B. feeler gauge
   C. vernier caliper
   D. screw gauge

_____ **7.** Which of the following statements with respect to variable displacement vane pump design is true?
   A. It results in less pumping losses.
   B. It increases fluid foaming.
   C. It allows for fixed pumping chambers.
   D. It increases the chances of wear.

_____ 8. Identify the clearance above which the bushings inside the transmission require replacement.
    A. 0.001"
    B. 0.008"
    C. 0.005"
    D. 0.003"

_____ 9. A _____ should be used to check the thickness of a thrust washer.
    A. dial indicator
    B. vernier caliper
    C. feeler gauge
    D. micrometer

_____ 10. A(n) _____ must be able to stop the rotation of an object in one direction but allow the object to spin freely in the opposite direction.
    A. accumulator
    B. sprag clutch
    C. extension housing
    D. servo

True/False

If you believe the statement to be more true than false, write the letter "T" in the space provided. If you believe the statement to be more false than true, write the letter "F."

_____ 1. Before reusing a torque converter, the internal end play of the converter must be checked.

_____ 2. The aerosol can in an aerosol flushing kit can be reused for different transmissions.

_____ 3. Free play is also called preload.

_____ 4. The same methods for quickly checking a gear pump can be used on the rotor pump.

_____ 5. Planetary gear sets usually do not require service when rebuilding a transmission.

_____ 6. Even a small degree of scratching on the face of a thrust washer is not acceptable.

_____ 7. Aluminum pistons are more prone to cracking.

Fill in the Blank

Read each item carefully, and then complete the statement by filling in the missing word(s).

1. The sealing rings of vane pump are usually made from _____ _____ or _____.

2. The design of a variable displacement vane pump allows the pump chambers to have a _____ volume during low engine speeds, and _____ chambers during higher engine speeds.

3. The first check for inspecting planetary gears or the planet carrier is to check for _____.

4. The clearance of a transmission bushing can also be checked with a _____-_____ feeler gauge.

5. If the thrust bearings or washers are worn, _____ _____ of components inside the transmission can occur, affecting their operation.

6. Sprag clutches must be serviced as a _____ _____ if any damage is found.

7. The sealing surfaces of the transmission case need to be checked with a precision _____.

8. Clutch packs that are rebuilt outside of the transmission are typically _____ _____ before installation.

9. In transaxles, the power from the transmission portion of the transaxle needs to be transferred to _____ _____ portion of the transaxle.

10. In a gear-style transaxle assembly, power is transferred from the transmission planetary gears to the _____ through a set of helically cut gears.

Labeling

Label the following diagrams with the correct terms.

1. Power transfer type:

A.

B.

A. _____

B. _____

Skill Drills

Place the skill drill steps in the correct order.

1. Inspecting the Converter and Flexplate:

_____ **A.** Remove the bolts securing the flexplate to the crankshaft.

_____ **B.** Inspect the pump drive tangs for damage.

_____ **C.** Inspect the torque converter pilot, crankshaft pilot bore, and rear main seal for signs of damage.

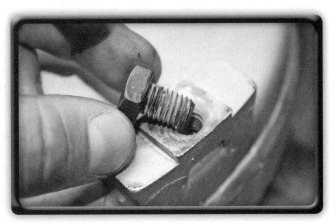

_____ **D.** Inspect the torque converter mounting pads for damage.

_____ **E.** Inspect the bolts and bolt holes for the flexplate to crankshaft and flexplate to torque converter.

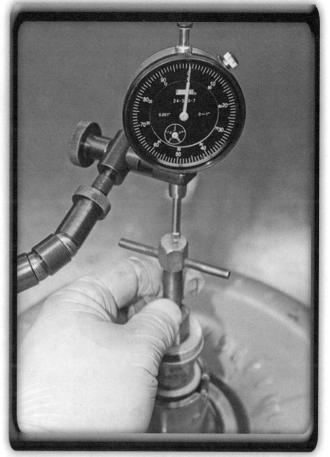

_____ **F.** Install the required tool into the turbine to check for torque converter end play. Use a dial indicator to measure the amount of turbine movement.

2. Inspecting and Flushing Cooler Lines:

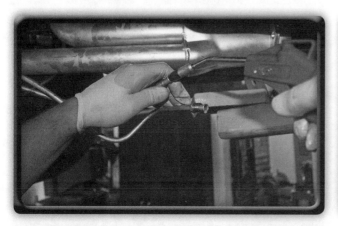

_____ **A.** Using compressed air, blow into one cooler line while catching the residue in a container as it comes out the other line. Switch directions and repeat.

_____ **B.** Look up the recommended transmission cooler service method. Remove the fluid cooler lines from the transmission if the transmission is still in the vehicle.

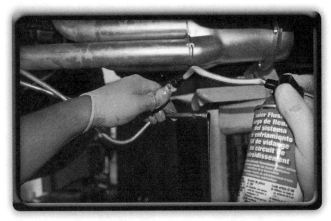

_____ **C.** Start the flush machine or aerosol can, and allow it to run the recommended time. If necessary, switch directions on the lines so they can be flushed in the other direction.

_____ **D.** Install the cooler flush machine or aerosol can lines onto the transmission cooler lines so that the flow is in the reverse direction.

_____ **E.** Reinstall the lines onto the transmission, or cap them if the transmission is removed from the vehicle. After properly filling the transmission with fluid, start the vehicle and inspect the lines and fittings for any signs of leakage. Check inside the radiator for signs of the transmission cooler leaking into the radiator.

_____ **F.** Remove the flush machine, and blow out the lines again so no residue remains inside the lines.

3. Measuring Transmission End Play or Preload:

_____ **A.** Pull up on the input shaft or push up on the output shaft, depending on the transmission, and record the dial indicator movement. This measurement is the input shaft end play.

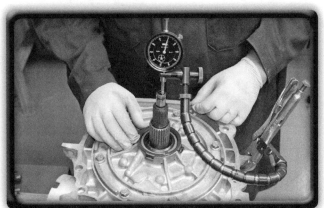

_____ **B.** Research the specified procedure, and note any special tools required. Mount the transmission in a fixture with the input shaft vertical. Install a dial indicator onto the top edge of the input shaft. Set the indicator needle to zero.

_____ **C.** Release the input shaft. The dial indicator should return to zero. If it does not, reset and measure again.

4. Inspecting Bushings:

_____ **A.** Measure the inside diameter of the bushing, and compare to the manufacturer's specifications. Replace any bushings that are not within specifications and/or that show signs of wear.

_____ **B.** Inspect each bushing in the transmission for pitting, scoring, or scratches.

_____ **C.** Research the proper procedure and specifications for checking bushings. Wipe the bushing dry with a lint-free shop towel.

5. Inspecting One-Way Roller and Sprag Clutch Assemblies :

_____ **A.** Research the proper service procedure for one-way roller or sprag clutch assemblies, and disassemble them.

_____ **B.** Inspect the faces of the sprags and the race for signs of scoring or damage. If any damage is found, replace the one-way roller or sprag.

_____ **C.** Inspect each roller and race for signs of pitting, scoring, or brinelling.

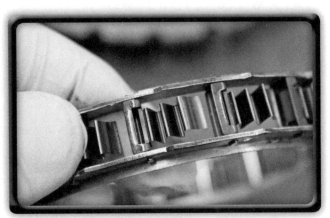

_____ **D.** Inspect the folded springs on the one-way roller for cracks or broken springs.

_____ **E.** Reassemble the one-way roller or sprag, lubricate with transmission fluid, and test the operation of the one-way roller or sprag.

Review Questions

_____ **1.** All of the following statements are true with respect to the bolts and nuts securing the torque converter to the flexplate except:
   A. All of the engine's power pulses and torque are transmitted through three or four bolts to the torque converter.
   B. If any bolts are found to be damaged, replace only the damaged bolts.
   C. If the converter uses nuts, inspect the threads of the studs on the converter for thread damage.
   D. If the studs are damaged, the converter will need to be replaced.

_____ **2.** Transmission coolers can be cleaned by:
   A. an aerosol flushing kit.
   B. compressed air.
   C. detergents.
   D. rust inhibitors.

_____ **3.** When disassembling a transmission, it is good to disassemble it into its unit assemblies because it helps in all of the following except:
   A. preventing missed steps.
   B. preserves the warranty.
   C. locating faults.
   D. remembering how the parts go back together.

_____ **4.** Discoloration of the planetary gears or the planet carrier is most likely a sign of:
   A. incorrect clearance.
   B. a gear that is loose on its shaft.
   C. slightly over full fluid level.
   D. a failed lubrication circuit.

_____ **5.** Which of these should be used to identify fluid passages through the case when inspecting fluid delivery circuits?
   A. Scan tool
   B. Mirror and light
   C. Transmission case diagram
   D. Telescoping gauge

_____ **6.** A drum that is not badly scored (lightly worn) should:
   A. still be replaced.
   B. be refinished using emery cloth.
   C. be used as is.
   D. be used with more lubrication.

_____ **7.** If the clutch pack has too little clearance, the clutch:
   A. will drag when it is disengaged.
   B. may slip.
   C. will have a very harsh engagement.
   D. piston needs to be replaced.

_____ **8.** How many engagements should you feel when installing a torque converter?
   A. One
   B. Two
   C. Three
   D. Four

_____ **9.** Choose the correct statement.
   A. Planetary gear sets are generally replaced with new once during a transmission rebuild.
   B. Fluid flow in an automatic transmission does not affect the operation of the transmission.
   C. Bands should always be replaced with new bands during a transmission overhaul.
   D. When rebuilding an automatic transmission, all clutch assemblies should be rebuilt.

_____ **10.** After the transmission is installed properly into the vehicle, approximately what percentage of the total transmission fluid should be added to the transmission?
  A. 100%
  B. 50%
  C. 75%
  D. 25%

ASE-Type Technician A/Technician B Style Questions

_____ **1.** Two technicians are discussing transmission end play. Tech A says that if the end play is insufficient, it may cause premature wear on the thrust bearings. Tech B says that transmissions with incorrect end play may have been reassembled incorrectly. Who is correct?
  A. Tech A
  B. Tech B
  C. Both A and B
  D. Neither A nor B

_____ **2.** Tech A says that one crescent-type front pump measurement uses a feeler blade between the outer gear and pump body. Tech B says that a micrometer is used to measure the width of the crescent. Who is correct?
  A. Tech A
  B. Tech B
  C. Both A and B
  D. Neither A nor B

_____ **3.** Tech A says that to determine whether roller type thrust bearings need to be replaced, they should be measured with a micrometer. Tech B says that to determine whether thrust washers are worn excessively, they should be measured with a micrometer and compared to specifications. Who is correct?
  A. Tech A
  B. Tech B
  C. Both A and B
  D. Neither A nor B

_____ **4.** Tech A says that a one-way roller clutch will work fine if assembled in either direction. Tech B says that sprag clutches must be serviced as a complete unit if any damage is found. Who is correct?
  A. Tech A
  B. Tech B
  C. Both A and B
  D. Neither A nor B

_____ **5.** Tech A says that when rebuilding a multidisc clutch, the steels should be checked for flatness, and their thickness should be measured. Tech B says that it is common to reuse the clutch piston's lip seals. Who is correct?
  A. Tech A
  B. Tech B
  C. Both A and B
  D. Neither A nor B

_____ **6.** Tech A says that clutch pack clearance should be checked with a micrometer. Tech B says that any clearance in the clutch pack means that the clutch discs are worn out. Who is correct?
  A. Tech A
  B. Tech B
  C. Both A and B
  D. Neither A nor B

_____ **7.** Tech A says that after rebuilding a clutch, it needs to be air checked before the clutch plates are installed. Tech B says that clutches that are rebuilt outside of the transmission are typically air tested before installing them back in the transmission. Who is correct?

A. Tech A

B. Tech B

C. Both A and B

D. Neither A nor B

_____ **8.** Tech A says that when assembling a transmission, the components should be lubricated with the correct automatic transmission fluid or transmission assembly lube. Tech B says that the transmission end play needs to be measured after the front pump is installed. Who is correct?

A. Tech A

B. Tech B

C. Both A and B

D. Neither A nor B

_____ **9.** Tech A says that the torque converter should be bolted to the flexplate before installing the transmission. Tech B says that when installing the torque converter, three separate engagements with their mating parts must be felt. Who is correct?

A. Tech A

B. Tech B

C. Both A and B

D. Neither A nor B

_____ **10.** Tech A says that when inspecting the torque converter, you need to check the snout of the converter where the seal and bushing rides for excessive wear. Tech B says that the internal end play of the converter must be checked. Who is correct?

A. Tech A

B. Tech B

C. Both A and B

D. Neither A nor B

Hybrid and Continuously Variable Transmissions

At the start of each chapter you'll find the NATEF tasks, Knowledge Objectives, and Skills Objectives from the textbook. These are your objectives as you make your way through the exercises in this workbook and the chapter in your textbook. The following activities have been designed to help you refresh your knowledge of the material in this chapter.

NATEF Tasks

- N29001 Describe the operational characteristics of a hybrid vehicle drivetrain. (MLR/AST/MAST)
- N29002 Describe the operational characteristics of a continuously variable transmission (CVT). (MLR/AST/MAST)

Knowledge Objectives

After reading this chapter, you will be able to:

- K29001 Describe the purpose and function of idle stop systems.
- K29002 Describe the purpose and function of torque smoothing systems.
- K29003 Describe the purpose and function of regenerative braking.
- K29004 Describe the purpose and function of torque assist.
- K29005 Describe the purpose and function of electric-only propulsion.
- K29006 Describe the operational characteristics of various models of hybrid vehicles.
- K29007 Describe the purpose and function of belt alternator starter systems.
- K29008 Describe the purpose and function of the Honda Integrated Motor Assist system.
- K29009 Describe the purpose and function of the Honda two-motor hybrid powertrain.
- K29010 Describe the purpose and function of the Toyota and Lexus hybrid powertrain.
- K29011 Describe the purpose and function of the Ford hybrid powertrain.
- K29012 Describe the purpose and function of the two-mode hybrid powertrain.
- K29013 Describe the function of the VDP CVT.
- K29014 Describe the function of the toroidal CVT.

Skills Objectives

There are no Skills Objectives for this chapter.

Matching

Match the following terms with the correct description or example.

A. Belt alternator starter (BAS)
B. Continuously variable transmission (CVT)
C. Electronic continuously variable transmission (ECVT)
D. Integrated motor assist (IMA)
E. Toroidal CVT
F. Variable-diameter pulley (VDP)

_____ 1. A type of CVT that uses two pulleys with moveable sheaves, allowing the effective diameter of the pulleys to change, resulting in variable gear ratios.

_____ 2. A type of hybrid drive system that uses a belt-driven alternator/starter that operates on 42 volts.

_____ 3. A type of hybrid transmission that often uses two electric motors in combination with an ICE. The two electric motors and the ICE transfer power through a planetary gear set, allowing an infinite amount of gear ratios.

_____ 4. A type of transmission that has no fixed gear ratios; the transmission can infinitely change the gear ratio within its operational design.

_____ **5.** A Honda hybrid drive system that uses a moderate-sized electric motor installed between the engine and the transmission.

_____ **6.** A type of CVT that uses moveable rollers in contact with input and output drive discs. The rollers transfer power from one drive disc to the other. Their position determines the effective gear ratio.

Multiple Choice

Read each item carefully, and then select the best response.

_____ **1.** When the powertrain control module shuts off the hybrid engine at a stoplight, it is an example of _____ .
- **A.** torque smoothing
- **B.** regenerative braking
- **C.** torque assist
- **D.** idle stop

_____ **2.** What ability can a hybrid employ to smooth out the power pulses of the internal combustion engine and create a flatter torque output curve?
- **A.** Torque assist
- **B.** Torque smoothing
- **C.** Idle stop
- **D.** Regenerative braking

_____ **3.** When a conventional vehicle is being stopped, most of the kinetic energy of the vehicle's movement is converted into _____ .
- **A.** heat
- **B.** electricity
- **C.** electromagnetic energy
- **D.** all of the above

_____ **4.** What ability of a hybrid engine reduces the need to use the internal combustion engine at lower rpms by using an electric motor to help propel the vehicle from a stop?
- **A.** Torque smoothing
- **B.** Kinetic braking
- **C.** Torque assist
- **D.** Integrated propulsion

_____ **5.** What hybrid system is classified as a parallel hybrid because the electric motor is operating at the same time as the gasoline engine?
- **A.** Two-mode
- **B.** Integrated motor assist
- **C.** Belt alternator starter
- **D.** Continuously variable

_____ **6.** What type of transaxle can be used in combination with the integrated motor assist system?
- **A.** Automatic transmission
- **B.** Manual transmission
- **C.** Continuously variable transmission
- **D.** All of the above

_____ **7.** What type of hybrid uses a system voltage of 300 volts to power two electric motor/generators housed inside the transmission case?
- **A.** Belt alternator starter
- **B.** Integrated motor assist
- **C.** Two-mode
- **D.** None of the above

_____ **8.** The Toyota and Lexus hybrids are classified as _____ because either the internal combustion engine or the electric motor/generator can propel the vehicle, or both can be used together.
- **A.** series-parallel hybrid
- **B.** parallel hybrid
- **C.** series hybrid
- **D.** integrated hybrid

_____ **9.** All of the following are basic types of CVTs commonly used in production vehicles, *except*:
   A. Variable-diameter pulley
   B. Integrated motor assist
   C. Toroidal
   D. Electronic continuously variable

_____ **10.** Which continuously variable transmission design is currently limited in production due to its high manufacturing costs?
   A. Electronic continuously variable
   B. Variable-diameter pulley
   C. Toroidal
   D. All of the above

True/False

If you believe the statement to be more true than false, write the letter "T" in the space provided. If you believe the statement to be more false than true, write the letter "F."

_____ **1.** Automobile manufacturers have had hybrid vehicles and vehicles with continuously variable transmissions in mass production for more than 20 years.

_____ **2.** Mechanical brakes can be used to recapture kinetic energy while braking.

_____ **3.** Hybrid vehicles are able to maintain a higher gas mileage rating during highway driving than in stop-and-go traffic.

_____ **4.** An electric motor is capable of creating its maximum torque as soon as it begins spinning.

_____ **5.** On many full hybrids, the vehicle can operate at low speeds using the electric motor only.

_____ **6.** Currently, Honda Integrated Motor Assist hybrids cannot drive using the electric motor only.

_____ **7.** The gasoline engine does not run during the second mode of a two-mode hybrid.

_____ **8.** Some of the early CVTs in Europe used a stiff rubber belt, as do many snowmobiles and all-terrain vehicles.

_____ **9.** As the vehicle gains speed, the input pulley diameter of the VDP decreases, while the output pulley diameter increases.

_____ **10.** Continuously variable transmissions require special transmission fluid.

Fill in the Blank

Read each item carefully, and then complete the statement by filling in the missing word(s).

1. Many hybrid vehicles that use idle stop have a small, electric transmission _____ _____ used to prevent a delay in the engagement of the transmission when the vehicle is restarted.

2. On a hybrid vehicle, when the driver initiates a stop, the electric motor becomes a _____.

3. The _____ _____ _____ system uses a 42-volt battery.

4. The _____-_____ hybrid was a joint venture by the General Motors, Chrysler, and BMW companies to create a hybrid system that could be used on trucks and larger luxury vehicles.

5. Toyota and Lexus hybrids use voltages from _____ to _____ volts, depending on the application.

6. The only major difference between the Ford hybrid and the Toyota hybrid is that rather than having the two electric motor/generators directly connected to the ring gear and the sun gear, they are attached through a set of _____ _____.

7. Each of the VDP pulleys has two movable drive faces called _____.

8. The _____ _____ is made up of hundreds of transversely mounted steel plates that are held in place with several steel bands running longitudinally around the edge of the plates.

9. The _____ CVT design uses two curved discs—an input disc and an output disc.

10. Most manufacturers use a limited number of _____ _____ _____ and a set of planetary gears that allow the continuously variable transmission to operate in reverse.

Labeling

Label the following diagrams with the correct terms. For diagram 1, also include engine status.

1. Planetary gear operation during deceleration:

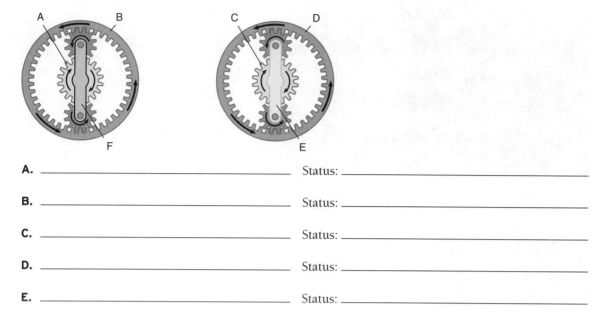

A. _____ Status: _____

B. _____ Status: _____

C. _____ Status: _____

D. _____ Status: _____

E. _____ Status: _____

F. _____ Status: _____

2. Cutaway of a Ford hybrid transmission:

A. _____

B. _____

C. _____

D. _____

E. _____

F. _____

3. A VDP CVT—two sheaves that are moveable:

A. _____

B. _____

C. _____

D. _____

4. The changing sizes of the input and output pulleys:

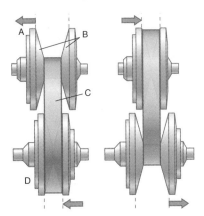

A. _____

B. _____

C. _____

D. _____

5. A toroidal CVT (the transmission on the left is in high torque multiplication ratio, the transmission on the right is in an overdrive ratio):

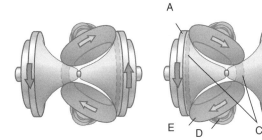

A. _____

B. _____

C. _____

D. _____

E. _____

Review Questions

_____ 1. Which function uses a small, electric transmission hydraulic pump that prevents a delay in the engagement of the transmission?
  A. Torque smoothing
  B. Idle start
  C. Regenerative braking
  D. Electric-only propulsion

_____ 2. What is helpful on small three- and four-cylinder engines with respect to compression and power impulses?
  A. Electric-only propulsion
  B. Belt alternator starter
  C. Torque assist
  D. Torque smoothing

_____ 3. All of the following statements are true _except_:
  A. regenerative braking system turns the generator and creates electricity to charge the high-voltage battery.
  B. regenerative brakes can develop great amount of stopping power.
  C. regenerative braking system is an opportunity to recharge the battery.
  D. regenerative braking system makes hybrids ideal for delivery vehicles and city transit buses.

_____ 4. Which of these functions makes it so that the overall displacement of the ICE can be reduced?
  A. Torque smoothing
  B. Torque assist
  C. Electric-only propulsion
  D. Regeneration

_____ 5. All of the following systems are considered as full hybrid that can be classified as a series-parallel hybrid _except_:
  A. Integrated motor assist (IMA)
  B. Honda two-motor hybrid systems.
  C. Toyota and Lexus hybrid systems.
  D. Ford hybrid powertrain.

_____ 6. During idle-stop:
  A. the engine idles while the vehicle is stopped.
  B. the engine stops while the vehicle is stopped.
  C. the high-voltage battery is charged when the vehicle is stopped.
  D. the engine charges the high-voltage battery while it idles.

_____ 7. All of the following statements with respect to i-MMD are true _except_:
  A. it is a direct drive powertrain with no shifts.
  B. its unique feature is that there is no real transmission.
  C. it utilizes a four-speed gear box.
  D. the propulsion motor is permanently coupled to the direct drive system.

_____ 8. Torque smoothing:
  A. adds power when high torque is required.
  B. use an electric motor to help smooth out the power pulses of the ICE.
  C. is used to smooth out road vibration at high speed.
  D. is used during regeneration to smooth out the electrical pulsations going to the high-voltage battery.

_____ 9. Which system uses the combination of two electric motor/generators and an ICE driven through a specially designed planetary gear set(s), which creates an infinite number of gear ratios?
  A. Honda Integrated Motor Assist (IMA)
  B. Two-mode hybrid
  C. Toyota and Lexus hybrids
  D. Honda Intelligent Multi-Mode Drive

_____ 10. The variable-diameter pulley CVT:
  A. as the vehicle gains speed, the input pulley diameter increases while the output pulley diameter decreases.
  B. as the vehicle gains speed, the input pulley diameter decreases while the output pulley diameter increases.

C. prevents high torque multiplication.

D. has no effect on the gear ratio.

ASE Technician A/Technician B Style Questions

_____ 1. Tech A says that hybrid vehicles have two power sources such as an internal combustions engine and an electric motor. Tech B says that most hybrid vehicles utilize regenerative braking to help improve fuel economy. Who is correct?

A. Tech A

B. Tech B

C. Both A and B

D. Neither A nor B

_____ 2. Tech A says that it is critical to have the proper safety equipment before working on a hybrid vehicle. Tech B says that hybrid vehicles use safety interlocks to prevent technician injury so it is no longer necessary to use protective gloves. Who is correct?

A. Tech A

B. Tech B

C. Both A and B

D. Neither A nor B

_____ 3. Tech A says that hybrid vehicles do not need a transmission since they have two power sources. Tech B says that some hybrid transmissions have a small electric fluid pump for when the transmission is in idle/stop mode. Who is correct?

A. Tech A

B. Tech B

C. Both A and B

D. Neither A nor B

_____ 4. Tech A says that BAS vehicles use an alternator to help slow the vehicle as well as act as a starter. Tech B says that the BAS alternator can be used to propel the vehicle independent of the ICE. Who is correct?

A. Tech A

B. Tech B

C. Both A and B

D. Neither A nor B

_____ 5. Tech A says that the transmission in a Toyota hybrid has a separate gear to provide reverse. Tech B says that Toyota hybrids use a VDP CVT transmission. Who is correct?

A. Tech A

B. Tech B

C. Both A and B

D. Neither A nor B

_____ 6. Tech A says that on a vehicle with a VDP CVT, when the vehicle starts from a stop, the input pulley has a small diameter while the output pulley has large diameter. Tech B says that VDP CVTs typically use a separate electric motor for reverse. Who is correct?

A. Tech A

B. Tech B

C. Both A and B

D. Neither A nor B

_____ 7. Tech A says that some CVTs require a heating system to warm the transmission fluid during cold weather operation. Tech B says that CVTs use conventional automatic transmission fluid. Who is correct?

A. Tech A

B. Tech B

C. Both A and B

D. Neither A nor B

_____ **8.** Tech A says that VDP CVTs use a steel belt made up of hundreds of transversely mounted steel plates. Tech B says that some VDP CVTs are programmed to give the feel of shift points. Who is correct?

    A. Tech A

    B. Tech B

    C. Both A and B

    D. Neither A nor B

_____ **9.** Tech A says that two-mode hybrid vehicles uses two motor/generators along with an ICE to propel the vehicle. Tech B says that at low speeds, the two-mode hybrid vehicle can operate off one motor only. Who is correct?

    A. Tech A

    B. Tech B

    C. Both A and B

    D. Neither A nor B

_____ **10.** Tech A says that the Honda IMA system uses a thin electric motor in place of a conventional flywheel or flexplate. Tech B says that the Honda IMA system can operate on the electric motor only. Who is correct?

    A. Tech A

    B. Tech B

    C. Both A and B

    D. Neither A nor B

Manual Transmission/ Transaxle Principles

At the start of each chapter you'll find the NATEF tasks, Knowledge Objectives, and Skills Objectives from the textbook. These are your objectives as you make your way through the exercises in this workbook and the chapter in your textbook. The following activities have been designed to help you refresh your knowledge of the material in this chapter.

NATEF Tasks

There are no NATEF tasks for this chapter.

Knowledge Objectives

After reading this chapter, you will be able to:

- K30001 Give an overview of manual drivetrains and their history.
- K30002 Explain the principles of operation of manual transmissions.
- K30003 Explain the principles of mechanical advantage.
- K30004 Explain the principles of gear ratios.
- K30005 Explain the principles of power flow.
- K30006 Describe the operation of a manual transmission drivetrain.
- K30007 Explain the operation of a vehicle equipped with a manual transmission.
- K30008 Describe the purpose and function of manual drivetrain components.
- K30009 Describe the purpose and function of shafts, gears, and bearings.
- K30010 Describe the purpose and function of the clutch system.
- K30011 Describe the purpose and function of the transmission/transaxle.
- K30012 Describe the purpose and function of the transfer case.
- K30013 Describe the purpose and function of the final drive assembly.
- K30014 Describe the purpose and function of drive axles.

Skills Objectives

There are no Skills Objectives for this chapter.

Matching

Match the following terms with the correct description or example.

A.	Brake pedal	**K.**	Radial load
B.	Axial load	**L.**	Rotational speed
C.	Dead axle	**M.**	Shaft
D.	Drive axle	**N.**	Solid rear axle
E.	Drivetrain	**O.**	Solid axle
F.	Gear set	**P.**	Splined
G.	Helical gears	**Q.**	Spur gears
H.	Independent suspension drive axle	**R.**	Closed clutch safety switch
I.	Live axle	**S.**	Transfer case
J.	Power flow	**T.**	Transmission

_____ 1. Gears that have angled teeth that are cut on an angle to the shaft.

_____ 2. An assembly that houses a variety of gear sets that allow the vehicle to be driven at a wider range of speeds and terrain conditions than would be possible without a transmission.

_____ **3.** The load that is perpendicular to a shaft, usually controlled by bearings or bushings.

_____ **4.** Gears with straight-cut gear teeth.

_____ **5.** A type of axle that has a one-piece axle housing, so the action of hitting a bump with one wheel affects the other wheel.

_____ **6.** A component that allows the starter motor to crank the engine over when the driver turns the key to the crank position.

_____ **7.** The component that supplies the power from the final drive to the wheels.

_____ **8.** Typically, a shaft and gear that have parallel grooves machined in them so they mate with each other and lock together rotationally.

_____ **9.** A type of drive axle that powers the wheels attached to it.

_____ **10.** The load applied in line with a shaft. It can be controlled with thrust bearings.

_____ **11.** An assembly used in four-wheel drive vehicles to transmit power to either two wheels only or all four wheels.

_____ **12.** The component assemblies that transmit power from the engine all the way to the drive wheels.

_____ **13.** The path that power takes from the beginning of an assembly to the end. In a transmission, power flow changes as different gears are selected by the driver.

_____ **14.** The foot-operated pedal used by the driver to stop the vehicle's motion.

_____ **15.** The speed at which an object rotates, measured in revolutions per minute (rpm).

_____ **16.** An axle that supplies no power to the wheels.

_____ **17.** A type of axle that is not flexible, with splines on one end to fit the final drive unit and a flange on the other end to power the wheel.

_____ **18.** Two or more gears that are in mesh with each other.

_____ **19.** A type of rear suspension system that allows each wheel on the axle to move independently of the other.

_____ **20.** The long, narrow component that carries one or more gears or has gears machined into it.

Multiple Choice

Read each item carefully, and then select the best response.

_____ **1.** In 1894, Louis René Panhard and Émile Levassor, designed a(n) _____.
  A. rear-wheel drive carriage
  B. synchromesh transmission
  C. automatic transmission
  D. multi-gear manual transmission

_____ **2.** Which of the following people connected an engine to a transmission and created a live rear axle by using a metal axle shaft supported by bushings in 1898?
  A. C. E. Duryea
  B. Louis Renault
  C. Henry Ford
  D. Ferdinand Porsche

_____ **3.** In 1928, Cadillac introduced the first _____.
  A. synchromesh transmission
  B. front-wheel drive automobile
  C. planetary gear set
  D. multi-gear transmission

_____ **4.** The amplification of the input force by trading distance moved for greater output force is the definition of _____.
  A. ratio
  B. mechanical advantage
  C. power flow
  D. rotational speed

_____ **5.** Given a 4:1 mechanical advantage, if a person pushes the lever down with a force of 100 pounds, the force the lever generates against the rock is _____.
  A. 140 lb.
  B. 40 lb.

    C. 400 lb.

    D. 4 lb.

_____ **6.** If the drive gear has 15 teeth and the driven gear has 30 teeth, then the gear ratio is _____.

    A. 2:1

    B. 800 lb.

    C. 1:4

    D. 4 lb.

_____ **7.** The path in which power is transmitted through a series of components is called _____.

    A. linkage

    B. power flow

    C. drivetrain

    D. transmission

_____ **8.** Which term relates to layouts where the transmission and final drive are integrated into a common assembly and is usually used on front-wheel drive vehicles?

    A. Differential

    B. Drivetrain

    C. Torque converter

    D. Transaxle

_____ **9.** What transmits power from the transmission to the final drive assembly on rear-wheel drive vehicles?

    A. Clutch plate

    B. Transaxle

    C. Driveshaft

    D. Live axle

_____ **10.** Flexible drive axles are called _____.

    A. radial axles

    B. dead axles

    C. half-shafts

    D. shafts

_____ **11.** If a drive gear has 20 teeth and its driven gear has 40 teeth, what is the mechanical advantage of the gear set?

    A. 4:2

    B. 4:1

    C. 3:1

    D. 2:1

_____ **12.** Grooves may be cut into the shafts to accommodate _____, which are used for holding the gears in the proper position on the shaft once the gears are installed.

    A. thrust washers

    B. spurs

    C. snap rings

    D. either A or C

_____ **13.** What component(s) allow the axles to turn at different speeds when the vehicle is cornering or turning?

    A. Constant velocity joints

    B. Universal joints

    C. Differential assembly

    D. Transfer case

_____ **14.** If one wheel is stuck in the snow or ice a(n) _____ allows both of the rear wheels to supply power to the ground in order to continue forward motion.

    A. transfer case

    B. limited slip differential

    C. transaxle

    D. open differential

_____ **15.** Which is the driven gear in a final drive assembly?

    A. Ring gear

    B. Side gear

    C. Sliding gear

    D. Pinion gear

True/False

If you believe the statement to be more true than false, write the letter "T" in the space provided. If you believe the statement to be more false than true, write the letter "F."

_____ **1.** Prior to 1898, vehicles were either belt or chain driven.

_____ **2.** If the output force is four times greater than the input force, the input distance moved is two times greater than the output distance.

_____ **3.** As the gear ratio decreases, the output speed increases.

_____ **4.** The clutch pedal is used for acceleration or deceleration of the engine.

_____ **5.** The final drive assembly incorporates a set of differential gears arranged so they sit between the two axles.

_____ **6.** Shafts are used to support gears and are machined precisely to accommodate bearings and individual gears.

_____ **7.** Splines allow shafts and gears to have greater rotational speeds, while at the same time minimizing metal-to-metal friction, which contributes to increased fuel economy and longer transmission life.

_____ **8.** The only difference between the transmission and the transaxle is that the transaxle incorporates the final drive assembly in its construction.

_____ **9.** Transmissions/transaxles are rated by the manufacturers for how much twisting force, measured in foot-pounds, they can handle.

_____ **10.** The main components of a manual transmission are shafts, gears, bearings, and the clutch assembly.

Fill in the Blank

Read each item carefully, and then complete the statement by filling in the missing word(s).

1. In the _____ differential assembly, power is supplied to both wheels equally only when each tire maintains traction.

2. A(n) _____ _____ applies a friction device between the gear and the shaft to match the gear speed to the shaft speed.

3. _____ are normally expressed as the equivalent of the first number to 1.

4. A gear set in which the _____ gear has half as many teeth as the _____ gear has a gear ratio of 2:1.

5. The _____ system is the medium by which the driver can connect and disconnect the engine from the transmission, resulting in the vehicle's forward or rearward movement.

6. The final _____ _____ gives the final gear reduction to the drivetrain and powers the drive wheels through axles.

7. The driveshaft uses _____ _____, which allow the driveshaft to change angles due to the movement of the suspension relative to the body.

8. Both front-wheel drive and rear-wheel drive vehicles use _____ _____ to power the wheels.

9. Depressing the clutch pedal closes the contacts of the _____ _____ switch.

10. _____ are round parts with teeth cut on the outside perimeter.

11. In a manual transmission vehicle, the component that locks the engine and transmission together is the _____ system.

12. The _____ _____ takes the power from the transmission and directs it to one or both axles, depending on the mode selected.

13. With the _____ _____ assembly, if one wheel is stuck in the snow or ice, the other wheel cannot supply power.

14. The _____ _____ drive axle uses one half-shaft axle for each of the two wheels.

15. A(n) _____ _____ allows the wheels to freely rotate on the axle assembly and do not drive the wheels.

Labeling

Label the following diagrams with the correct terms.

1. Power flow in a transmission:

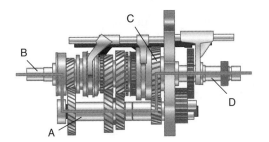

A. _____

B. _____

C. _____

D. _____

2. Typical final drive assembly:

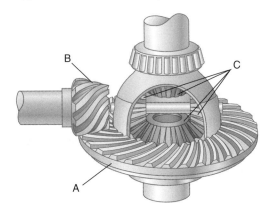

A. _____

B. _____

C. _____

3. Typical driveshaft:

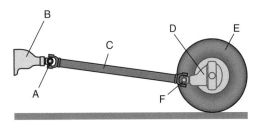

A. _____

B. _____

C. _____

D. _____

E. _____

F. _____

4. Axial-loaded thrust washer:

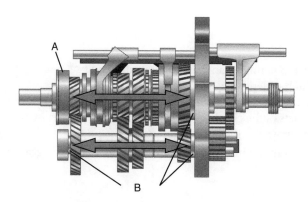

A. _____

B. _____

5. Clutch components designed to connect and disconnect power to the transmission:

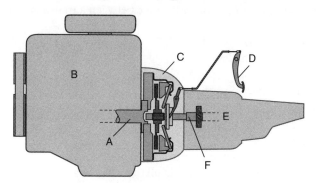

A. _____

B. _____

C. _____

D. _____

E. _____

F. _____

Review Questions

_____ **1.** The manual transmission receives power from the engine by way of the:
   A. driveshaft.
   B. clutch assembly.
   C. gear set.
   D. final drive.

_____ **2.** Mechanical advantage can be used to generate a larger output force, but it requires a(n):
   A. increase in input distance and speed.
   B. decrease in input distance and increase in speed.
   C. increase in input distance and decrease in speed.
   D. decrease in input distance and speed.

_____ **3.** If a driven gear has 40 teeth and the drive gear has 10 teeth, what is the gear ratio of this arrangement?
   A. 1:5
   B. 1:4
   C. 5:1
   D. 4:1

_____ **4.** In manual transmission, which of these determines the path of the power flow from the countershaft to the output shaft?
   A. Gears
   B. Transmission/transaxle
   C. Engine
   D. Input shaft

_____ **5.** The driver can increase and decrease the amount of power the engine develops using the:
   A. accelerator pedal.
   B. differential gears.
   C. clutch pedal.
   D. final drive assembly.

_____ **6.** All of the following statements with respect to manual transmission are true _except_:
   A. gears can be applied only when the clutch is depressed.
   B. when in gear, releasing the clutch connects the engine to the transmission.
   C. releasing the clutch pedal closes the contacts of the clutch safety switch.
   D. the transmission provides the best pulling power in the lowest gear.

_____ **7.** Which of these are used for holding the gears in the proper position on the shaft once the gears are installed?
   A. Parallel grooves in a shaft
   B. Shoulders
   C. Snap rings and thrust washers
   D. Bearings

_____ **8.** Which of the following statements is correct with respect to the difference between a transmission and a transaxle?
   A. A transmission is typically used in front-wheel drive vehicles.
   B. A transaxle is typically used in rear-wheel drive vehicles.
   C. The final drive assembly is incorporated in transmission construction.
   D. The final drive assembly is incorporated in transaxle construction.

_____ **9.** All of the following statements are true _except_:
   A. the transfer case is typically mounted to the rear of the transmission.
   B. the transfer case can only be operated mechanically.
   C. the transfer case takes the power from the transmission and directs it to one or both axles.
   D. the transfer case system requires that the front wheels be powered at all times.

_____ **10.** Choose the correct statement.
   A. The differential assembly does not allow the wheels on an axle to rotate at different speeds.
   B. Technically, "differential assembly" is the other name for "final drive assembly."
   C. The two varieties of differential assembly are open and closed.
   D. Without the differential assembly, the tires would bind, skip, hop, and slide when going around a corner.

ASE Technician A/Technician B Style Questions

_____ **1.** Tech A says that friction bearings are made up of balls and rollers. Tech B says that nonfriction bearings are in sliding contact between moving surfaces. Who is correct?
   A. Tech A
   B. Tech B
   C. Both A and B
   D. Neither A nor B

_____ **2.** Tech A says that a gear set in which the input gear has half as many teeth as the output gear has a ratio of 3:1. Tech B says that gears with the same number of teeth have a ratio of 1:1. Who is correct?
   A. Tech A
   B. Tech B
   C. Both A and B
   D. Neither A nor B

_____ **3.** Tech A says that the countershaft is splined to fit into the hub in the clutch disc. Tech B says that the output shaft has gears that are meshed with the countershaft gears. Who is correct?
   A. Tech A
   B. Tech B
   C. Both A and B
   D. Neither A nor B

_____ **4.** Tech A says that bearing axial loads are in line with the shaft. Tech B says that bearing radial loads occur because the gears have a tendency to push each other apart as torque is transmitted between them. Who is correct?

   A. Tech A
   B. Tech B
   C. Both A and B
   D. Neither A nor B

_____ **5.** Tech A says that the final drive is used to provide an increase in the rotational speed of the axles. Tech B says that the final drive is used to provide an increase of torque to the axles. Who is correct?

   A. Tech A
   B. Tech B
   C. Both A and B
   D. Neither A nor B

_____ **6.** Tech A says that a gear set that has a drive gear with 9 teeth and a driven gear with 27 teeth has a gear ratio of 3:1. Tech B says that the drive gear is also called the output gear. Who is correct?

   A. Tech A
   B. Tech B
   C. Both A and B
   D. Neither A nor B

_____ **7.** Tech A says that a transfer case is designed to transfer torque from the engine to the transmission. Tech B says that a transfer case is used on FWD vehicles. Who is correct?

   A. Tech A
   B. Tech B
   C. Both A and B
   D. Neither A nor B

_____ **8.** Tech A says that dead axles allow the wheels to freely rotate on the axle assembly and do not drive the wheels. Tech B says that the ring gear and pinion gear are part of the final drive assembly. Who is correct?

   A. Tech A
   B. Tech B
   C. Both A and B
   D. Neither A nor B

_____ **9.** Tech A says that an open differential allows both of the rear wheels to supply power to the ground even if one wheel loses traction. Tech B says that a live axle powers the wheels attached to it. Who is correct?

   A. Tech A
   B. Tech B
   C. Both A and B
   D. Neither A nor B

_____ **10.** Tech A says that the differential assembly provides a means for the inside and outside wheels to turn at different speeds when going around a corner. Tech B says that the differential assembly provides smooth shifts and reduces gear "grinding" by matching gear speeds. Who is correct?

   A. Tech A
   B. Tech B
   C. Both A and B
   D. Neither A nor B

The Clutch System

At the start of each chapter you'll find the NATEF tasks, Knowledge Objectives, and Skills Objectives from the textbook. These are your objectives as you make your way through the exercises in this workbook and the chapter in your textbook. The following activities have been designed to help you refresh your knowledge of the material in this chapter.

NATEF Tasks

- N31001 Inspect clutch pedal linkage, cables, automatic adjuster mechanisms, brackets, bushings, pivots, and springs; perform needed action. (AST/MAST)
- N31002 Bleed clutch hydraulic system. (AST/MAST)
- N31003 Diagnose clutch noise, binding, slippage, pulsation, and chatter; determine needed action. (AST/MAST)
- N31004 Inspect flywheel and ring gear for wear, cracks, and discoloration; determine needed action. (AST/MAST)
- N31005 Measure flywheel runout and crankshaft end play; determine needed action. (AST/MAST)
- N31006 Inspect and/or replace clutch pressure plate assembly, clutch disc, release (throw-out) bearing, linkage, and pilot bearing/bushing (as applicable). (AST/MAST)

Knowledge Objectives

After reading this chapter, you will be able to:

- K31001 Explain the purpose and function of a clutch.
- K31002 Describe the purpose and function of the clutch components.
- K31003 Describe the purpose and function of the flywheel.
- K31004 Describe the purpose and function of pressure plates.
- K31005 Describe the purpose and function of clutch discs.
- K31006 Describe the purpose and function of the throw-out bearing and clutch fork.
- K31007 Describe the purpose and function of the pilot bearing.
- K31008 Describe the purpose and function of clutch operating mechanisms.
- K31009 Describe the purpose and function of cable operating mechanisms.
- K31010 Describe the purpose and function of hydraulic clutch mechanisms.
- K31011 Describe the purpose and function of linkage operated systems.
- K31012 Describe the safety and hazard concerns related to clutch repair.
- K31013 Identify common tools used in clutch repair.
- K31014 Describe the required clutch preventive maintenance procedures.

Skills Objectives

After reading this chapter, you will be able to:

- S31001 Perform clutch maintenance and repair.
- S31002 Perform a clutch replacement.
- S31003 Remove and replace a transmission/transaxle.
- S31004 Inspect the engine block, crankshaft, crankshaft seal, and soft plugs.

Matching

Match the following terms with the correct description or example.

A. Carrier
B. Clutch binding
C. Clutch disc
D. Clutch fork
E. Flywheel ring gear
F. Coil spring pressure plate

G. Crankshaft end play
H. Diaphragm pressure plate
I. Driven center plate
J. clutch chatter
K. Friction facing
L. Fulcrum ring
M. Pilot bearing

N. Push-type clutch
O. Pressure plate
P. Quadrant ratchet
Q. Release mechanisms
R. Multi-plate clutch
S. Slave cylinder
T. Slippage

_____ 1. The bearing or bushing that supports the front of the transmission input shaft.

_____ 2. The friction disc that is held firmly against the flywheel by a pressure plate and transfers power from the flywheel to the transmission input shaft.

_____ 3. A type of pressure plate that uses coil springs to provide the clamping force.

_____ 4. A condition in which two surfaces are in firm contact with each other slide.

_____ 5. The material riveted to each side of the clutch disc that mates to the flywheel and pressure plate. Used to provide friction and a wear surface for the clutch assembly.

_____ 6. The amount of forward and rearward movement of the crankshaft in the main bearings.

_____ 7. The device used in some cable-operated clutches to provide self-adjustment as the clutch disc wears.

_____ 8. The component in a hydraulically operated clutch that converts hydraulic pressure to mechanical movement at the clutch fork.

_____ 9. The center component of the clutch assembly, with friction material riveted on each side. Also called a clutch plate or friction disc.

_____ 10. Components that operate the clutch. Usually included are the throw-out bearing and the clutch fork. Some manufacturers include the operating system.

_____ 11. A slightly conical, spring steel plate used to provide the clamping force for the clutch assembly.

_____ 12. The part of the throw-out bearing assembly that holds the bearing.

_____ 13. A clutch assembly that is comprised of two or more clutch plates and used to increase the torque-carrying capacity of the clutch.

_____ 14. The part of the clutch linkage that operates the throw-out bearing.

_____ 15. A condition in which the clutch shudders when the clutch pedal is released and the vehicle starts to move forward.

_____ 16. A condition in which the clutch disc is dragging, leading to grinding gears during gear shifts and possibly clutch chatter.

_____ 17. A steel ring that is used as a pivot point for the diaphragm spring in the pressure plate.

_____ 18. Large, round, externally toothed gear that is usually press fit to the outer diameter of the flywheel and used along with the starter to crank the engine over.

_____ 19. The assembly that applies and removes the clamping force on the clutch disc.

_____ 20. A typical clutch system used in modern vehicles where the clutch fork pushes the release bearing forward to release the friction facing from the pressure plate.

Multiple Choice

Read each item carefully, and then select the best response.

_____ 1. The amount of torque a clutch can transmit is dependent upon which of the following?
  A. Diameter of the clutch
  B. Coefficient of friction
  C. Total spring force
  D. All of the above

_____ 2. The _____ is able to connect to and disconnect from the engine's flywheel through the operation of the clutch.
  A. crankshaft
  B. input shaft

    C. pilot bearing
    D. output shaft

_____ **3.** The main purpose of the _____ is to smooth out the power pulses from the pistons during the power strokes.
    A. pressure plate
    B. throw-out bearing
    C. flywheel
    D. clutch disc

_____ **4.** Which of the following is a type of flywheel?
    A. One-piece
    B. Harmonic
    C. Dual mass
    D. Both A and C

_____ **5.** Refinishing the flywheel moves the pressure plate toward the engine and away from the throw-out bearing, increasing _____.
    A. free-play
    B. clutch chatter
    C. runout
    D. fuel economy

_____ **6.** The snout of the input shaft rides on the _____.
    A. throw-out bearing
    B. hub
    C. pilot bearing
    D. flywheel

_____ **7.** Which of the following is a type of clutch operating mechanism?
    A. Linkage style
    B. Hydraulic
    C. Cable style
    D. All of the above

_____ **8.** A(n) _____ pressure plate consists of a pressed steel cover, a pressure plate with a machined flat surface, a number of spring steel drive straps, and the diaphragm spring.
    A. single-plate
    B. diaphragm
    C. coil spring
    D. multi-plate

_____ **9.** What condition can usually be identified while driving the vehicle in fourth gear while accelerating?
    A. Clutch vibration
    B. Slippage
    C. Worn pilot bearing
    D. Clutch binding

_____ **10.** A shuddering feeling as the clutch pedal is being released is known as _____.
    A. clutch chatter
    B. torsional vibration
    C. clutch binding
    D. driveline vibration

True/False

If you believe the statement to be more true than false, write the letter "T" in the space provided. If you believe the statement to be more false than true, write the letter "F."

_____ **1.** Automotive manual transmission clutches are wet clutches.

_____ **2.** Both output shaft torque and speed can be increased at the same time.

_____ **3.** The output shaft is connected directly to the wheels through the drivetrain components and cannot be disconnected.

_____ **4.** The function of the dual mass flywheel is to absorb torsional crankshaft vibrations.

_____ **5.** Coil spring pressure plate clutches require less pedal effort to operate.

_____ **6.** The clutch throw-out bearing and clutch fork work together to compress the pressure plate springs when the clutch pedal is pressed.

_____ **7.** Some vehicles do not require a pilot bearing.

_____ **8.** In a cable-style clutch control system the slave cylinder is located directly behind the throw-out bearing and pushes directly on it.

_____ **9.** Excessive slippage from a misadjusted clutch can contribute to overheating of the clutch components and pedal pulsations.

_____ **10.** Use compressed air to blow off clutch parts such as the flywheel, pressure plate, clutch plate, transmission, or engine bell housings.

Fill in the Blank

Read each item carefully, and then complete the statement by filling in the missing word(s).

1. The _____ allows the driver to engage and disengage the engine from the transmission while operating the vehicle.

2. Two or more clutch plates can be used to form a _____-_____ clutch, increasing the number of facings and the torque capacity.

3. The _____ _____ bolts onto the flywheel.

4. The flywheel _____ _____ enables the starter motor drive gear to crank the engine over.

5. The _____ _____ flywheel improves the engine's fuel economy by smoothing out the power pulses and focusing them in the direction of engine rotation.

6. The diaphragm pressure plate is located inside the clutch cover on two _____ _____, held in place by a number of rivets passing through the diaphragm.

7. The clutch disc is also called a _____ _____ _____ or a friction disc.

8. The throw-out bearing carrier slides on the sleeve of the front _____ _____ that extends from the front of the transmission.

9. The _____ is generally screwed into the bell housing and is usually replaceable.

10. The clutch progressively transmits _____ from the engine to the transmission.

11. Older technology clutch operating systems used a series of levers with an equalizing mechanism called a(n) _____ _____.

12. A worn _____ _____ can make a howling or squeaking sound.

13. _____ _____ are rotational fluctuations caused by out-of-balance, misaligned, worn, or bent driveline components.

14. A _____ _____ tool is used to center the clutch plate between the flywheel and the pressure plate during the installation of the pressure plate.

15. As the clutch wears, the _____ _____ becomes thinner.

Labeling

Label the following diagrams with the correct terms.

1. Standard light vehicle clutch:

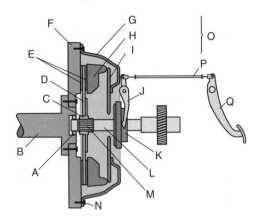

A. _____

B. _____

C. _____

D. _____

E. _____

F. _____

G. _____

H. _____

I. _____

J. _____

K. _____

L. _____

M. _____

N. _____

O. _____

P. _____

Q. _____

2. Releasing the clutch pedal:

Driven Unit Disengaged

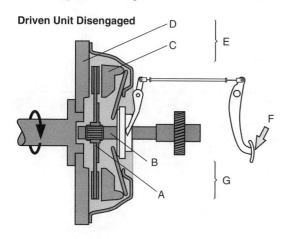

Driven Unit Engaged

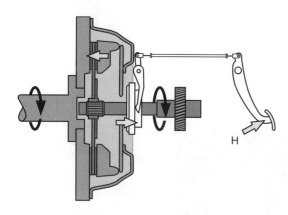

A. _____

B. _____

C. _____

D. _____

E. _____

F. _____

G. _____

H. _____

3. Two types of dual mass flywheels:

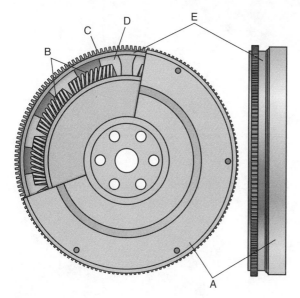

A. _____

B. _____

C. _____

D. _____

E. _____

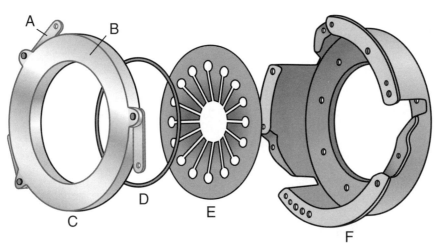

F. _____

G. _____

H. _____

I. _____

J. _____

K. _____

4. Diaphragm pressure plate:

A. _____

B. _____

C. _____

D. _____

E. _____

F. _____

5. Coil spring pressure plate:

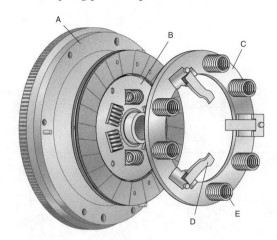

A. _____

B. _____

C. _____

D. _____

E. _____

6. Clutch disc components:

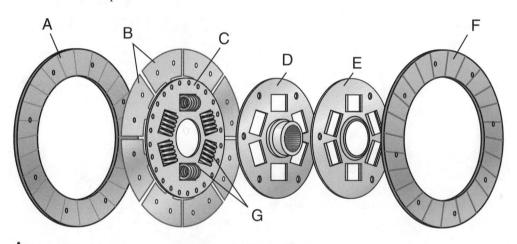

A. _____

B. _____

C. _____

D. _____

E. _____

F. _____

G. _____

7. Waved springs:

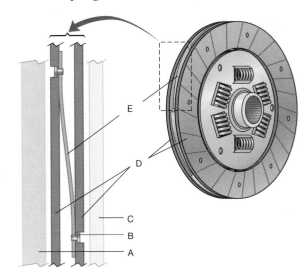

A. _____

B. _____

C. _____

D. _____

E. _____

8. Cable-operated clutch:

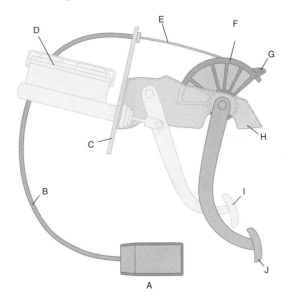

A. _____

B. _____

C. _____

D. _____

E. _____

F. _____

G. _____

H. _____

I. _____

J. _____

9. Hydraulic clutch control:

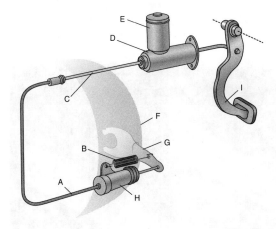

A. _____

B. _____

C. _____

D. _____

E. _____

F. _____

G. _____

H. _____

I. _____

10. Linkage-operated system:

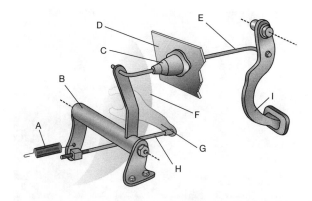

A. _____

B. _____

C. _____

D. _____

E. _____

F. _____

G. _____

H. _____

I. _____

Skill Drills

Place the skill drill steps in the correct order.

    1. Checking and Adjusting a Linkage Style Clutch:

_____ **A.** Check the clutch linkage components under the hood for the same signs of wear or damage as the components under the dash.

_____ **B.** Measure the clutch pedal free-play. Perform any adjustments as necessary, following the manufacturer's procedure.

_____ **C.** Following the specified procedure, inspect the clutch linkage parts for damaged, worn, bent, or missing components. Look for signs of binding, looseness, and excessive wear. Start with the clutch pedal assembly and inspect all components under the dash. Operate the clutch pedal, and inspect all components under the dash.

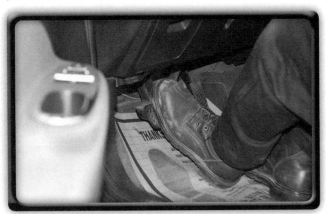

_____ **D.** Start the vehicle and depress the clutch. The clutch should engage at the proper height and have the proper free-play. Make a gear selection to ensure the gears do not clash going into mesh.

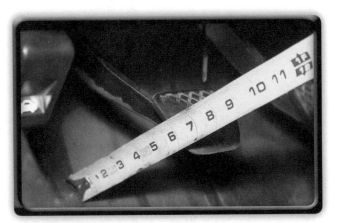

_____ **E.** Measure the clutch pedal height. Compare your reading to the specifications and determine any necessary actions to correct any fault.

2. Checking and Adjusting a Hydraulic Clutch:

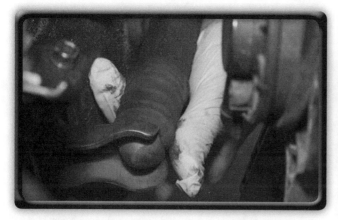

_____ **A.** Check the boot on the slave cylinder for seepage, which may indicate a leaking slave cylinder piston seal.

_____ **B.** Inspect the clutch master cylinder for correct fluid level, and test the quality of the fluid.

_____ **C.** Check clutch pedal height. Measure clutch pedal free-play using a tape measure. Compare your readings to the specifications, and determine any necessary actions to correct any fault.

_____ **D.** Check that all hydraulic lines are not kinked or leaking at their connections. This will require that the system be repaired and bled of any air. Check all rubber hoses for dry rot, bulges, or leaks. Make sure all hydraulic components are secure in their mountings.

_____ **E.** Inspect all line connections to the master cylinder.

3. Removing and Reinstalling a Transmission/Transaxle:

_____ **A.** If the vehicle is equipped with a hydraulic clutch, reinstall the slave cylinder and bleed and/or adjust if necessary.

_____ **B.** Check that all electrical wires, connectors, linkages, and other removed components are properly installed and adjusted. Place exhaust hose(s) over the exhaust pipe(s) and set the parking brake.

_____ **C.** Lightly lubricate input shaft splines to ensure that there is no binding upon entering the clutch disc hub. Position all wires, hoses, and tubes out of the way and in their specified positions. Secure them temporarily if necessary.

_____ **D.** Disconnect the drive shaft or axles and secure them from hanging. Disconnect all wires, tubes, and hoses that may be present and inspect for damage. Disconnect the clutch and shifter linkage and inspect for wear or damage. Secure the transmission with a transmission jack and remove any transmission mounts.

_____ **E.** Prepare the transmission to be reinstalled. Ensure that the release (throw-out) bearing and clutch fork are properly installed and the clutch disc is centered in the pressure plate. If specified, lubricate the pilot bushing/bearing.

_____ **F.** Following the specified procedure for the specific type of transmission/transaxle, remove the transmission/transaxle from the vehicle. At this time, you may want to overhaul the transmission/transaxle or perform other tasks such as inspecting and replacing the clutch assembly or replacing the rear crankshaft main seal.

_____ **G.** Research the procedures and specifications. Ensure that bolts, clips, and fasteners are kept in containers. Make sure the vehicle is secure on the lift. If necessary, drain the transmission fluid to avoid spills on the floor that may cause a safety hazard.

_____ **H.** Following the specified procedure for the specific type of transmission/transaxle, reinstall the transmission/transaxle. Tighten all fasteners to the proper torque. If the vehicle is equipped with a cable- or linkage-style clutch release system, reinstall and adjust it for the proper free-play.

_____ **I.** Refill the transmission/transaxle to the proper level with the specified fluid.

4. Inspecting the Flywheel and Ring Gear:

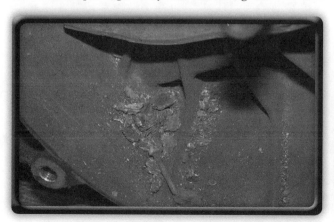

_____ **A.** Clean up any clutch dust and debris, using an approved method for disposing of hazardous dust.

_____ **B.** Inspect the ring gear for wear, chipped teeth, and cracks. If teeth are worn in one area, it may also be necessary to replace the starter drive.

_____ **C.** Inspect the starter drive, as it may have been damaged from a faulty ring gear.

_____ **D.** Inspect the flywheel for wear, hot spots, bluing, and cracks. Use of a straightedge can give a preliminary check for flatness.

_____ **E.** Follow the specified procedure to remove the pressure plate and clutch disc. Remove the pressure plate bolts evenly, backing each bolt out one turn at a time to avoid warping the pressure plate. Have an assistant hold the pressure plate and clutch disc as they are being removed.

_____ **F.** Check that the ring gear is secure on the flywheel.

5. Installing a Clutch Assembly:

_____ **A.** Following the specified procedure, install the pilot bushing/bearing, if removed. Lubricate it with the specified lubricant, if applicable.

_____ **B.** Following the specified procedure, install the clutch disc and pressure plate. Use an appropriate clutch alignment tool to ensure proper positioning of the clutch disc.

_____ **C.** Check the release (throw-out) bearing and linkage for damage or binding. Check the pilot bearing/ bushing for damage and its cavity. Determine any necessary action(s) for correcting failures, or replace any worn parts with new/remanufactured components.

_____ **D.** Research the procedure. Inspect the pressure plate assembly for worn springs or diaphragm and also for irregularities associated with any kind of failure, including hot spots. Inspect the clutch disc for loose dampening springs or rubber blocks, and check the condition of the rivets.

_____ **E.** Tighten the pressure plate bolts down evenly by tightening each bolt a turn or two, one at a time, until the pressure plate is evenly seated on the flywheel surface. Torque each pressure plate bolt according to the specified torque and sequence. Install the release (throw-out) bearing and linkage in the bell housing.

_____ **F.** Following the specified procedure, install the flywheel. Be sure to torque the flywheel bolts in the proper sequence.

Review Questions

_____ **1.** All of the following statements are true with respect to clutch principles *except*:
   A. increasing the friction of the clutch disc decreases the torque-carrying ability.
   B. increasing the diameter of the clutch increases its torque capacity.
   C. increasing the number of clutch discs increases torque capacity.
   D. increasing the spring force clamping the parts together increases torque capacity.

_____ **2.** Which of these parts compress the pressure plate springs?
   A. The clutch fork and the pilot bearing
   B. The clutch throw-out bearing and the pilot bearing
   C. The clutch throw-out bearing and clutch fork
   D. The clutch fork and the clutch disc

_____ 3. Which of these components smoothens out the power pulses from the pistons during the power strokes?
   A. Pressure plate spring
   B. Flywheel
   C. Clutch disc
   D. Throw-out bearing

_____ 4. The clamping force to clamp the clutch disc, allowing it to transmit torque, is provided by the:
   A. flywheel.
   B. clutch pedal.
   C. pressure plate.
   D. clutch fork.

_____ 5. A clutch disc allows engine torque to transmit from the flywheel and pressure plate to the:
   A. transmission input shaft.
   B. front bearing retainer.
   C. axles.
   D. pilot bearing.

_____ 6. All of the following statements are true _except_:
   A. the throw-out bearing and clutch fork work together.
   B. the throw-out bearing rotates with the pressure plate.
   C. the clutch fork rotates with the pressure plate.
   D. the throw-out bearing includes a thrust bearing in its assembly.

_____ 7. All of the following are types of clutch operating systems _except_:
   A. hydraulic style.
   B. cable style.
   C. linkage style.
   D. clutch fork.

_____ 8. In some cable-operated clutch vehicles, which device provides self-adjustment as the clutch disc wears?
   A. Single-plate clutch
   B. Clutch fork
   C. Quadrant ratchet
   D. Bell crank

_____ 9. What is clutch pedal free-play?
   A. The distance the clutch pedal moves the master cylinder piston.
   B. The distance the clutch pedal moves before the master cylinder piston moves.
   C. The distance from the floor where the clutch engages.
   D. The distance the clutch pedal moves for the clutch to be fully disengaged.

_____ 10. Which of these tools is used to center the clutch plate between the flywheel and the pressure plate during the installation of the pressure plate?
   A. Flywheel wrench
   B. Dial indicator
   C. Clutch alignment tool
   D. Transmission jack

ASE Technician A/Technician B Style Questions

_____ 1. Tech A says that the pressure plate friction surface rides on the flywheel friction surface to transmit torque. Tech B says that the flywheel can either be flat or stepped. Who is correct?
   A. Tech A
   B. Tech B
   C. Both A and B
   D. Neither A nor B

_____ 2. Tech A says that insufficient clutch pedal clearance (free play) can cause gear clashing when shifting. Tech B says that when the engine is idling and the clutch pedal is released, the friction disc should stop rotating. Who is correct?
   A. Tech A
   B. Tech B

    C. Both A and B

    D. Neither A nor B

_____ 3. Tech A says that hot spots on the flywheel are a result of excessive heat. Tech B says that a pulsation in a clutch pedal could be due to uneven clutch pressure plate levers. Who is correct?

    A. Tech A

    B. Tech B

    C. Both A and B

    D. Neither A nor B

_____ 4. Tech A says that a leaking rear main seal can cause clutch chatter. Tech B says that the throw-out bearing rides directly on the clutch disc. Who is correct?

    A. Tech A

    B. Tech B

    C. Both A and B

    D. Neither A nor B

_____ 5. Tech A says that the flywheel runout can be checked with a dial indicator. Tech B says that when checking flywheel runout, it is good practice to also check crankshaft end play. Who is correct?

    A. Tech A

    B. Tech B

    C. Both A and B

    D. Neither A nor B

_____ 6. Tech A says that clutch slippage can be a result of excessively strong pressure plate spring(s). Tech B says that when replacing the friction disc, it is good practice to also replace the pressure plate. Who is correct?

    A. Tech A

    B. Tech B

    C. Both A and B

    D. Neither A nor B

_____ 7. Tech A says that the pilot bearing can be a needle-style bearing. Tech B says that the pilot bearing can be a brass bushing style. Who is correct?

    A. Tech A

    B. Tech B

    C. Both A and B

    D. Neither A nor B

_____ 8. Tech A says that a bad pilot bearing can cause a whirring noise when the clutch pedal is released. Tech B says that many ring gears are press fit onto the flywheel. Who is correct?

    A. Tech A

    B. Tech B

    C. Both A and B

    D. Neither A nor B

_____ 9. Tech A says that waved springs between the clutch facings results in a smoother engagement of the clutch when starting from a stop. Tech B says that the heavy torsional coil springs in the clutch disc clamp the clutch disc between the flywheel and pressure plate. Who is correct?

    A. Tech A

    B. Tech B

    C. Both A and B

    D. Neither A nor B

_____ 10. Two technicians are discussing clutch operating systems. Tech A says that most hydraulic clutches need to be adjusted periodically. Tech B says that cable clutches use a slave cylinder to operate the clutch fork. Who is correct?

    A. Tech A

    B. Tech B

    C. Both A and B

    D. Neither A nor B

Manual Transmissions/ Transaxles Basic Diagnosis and Maintenance

At the start of each chapter you'll find the NATEF tasks, Knowledge Objectives, and Skills Objectives from the textbook. These are your objectives as you make your way through the exercises in this workbook and the chapter in your textbook. The following activities have been designed to help you refresh your knowledge of the material in this chapter.

NATEF Tasks

- N32001 Describe the operational characteristics of an electronically controlled manual transmission/transaxle. (MLR/AST/MAST)
- N32002 Check fluid condition; check for leaks; determine needed action. (MLR/AST/MAST)
- N32003 Drain and refill manual transmission/transaxle and final drive unit; use proper fluid type per manufacturer specification. (MLR/AST/MAST)
- N32004 Diagnose noise concerns through the application of transmission/transaxle power flow principles. (MAST)
- N32005 Diagnose hard shifting and jumping out of gear concerns; determine needed action. (MAST)
- N32006 Diagnose transaxle final drive assembly noise and vibration concerns; determine needed action. (MAST)

Knowledge Objectives

After reading this chapter, you will be able to:

- K32001 Describe the geartrain and the way it is shifted.
- K32002 Describe gear terminology and calculate gear ratios.
- K32003 Describe gear selection and mechanisms.
- K32004 Describe the purpose and function of bearings, thrust washers, gaskets, and seals.
- K32005 Describe the purpose and function of bearings and thrust washers.
- K32006 Describe the purpose and function of seals and gaskets.
- K32007 Describe the differences in design between a transmission and a transaxle.
- K32008 Describe the internal operation of transmissions/transaxles.
- K32009 Describe the internal operation of a transmission.
- K32010 Describe the internal operation of a transaxle.

Skills Objectives

After reading this chapter, you will be able to:

- S32001 Perform preventive maintenance on manual transmissions/transaxles.
- S32002 Diagnose common concerns on transmissions/transaxles.
- S32003 Diagnose drive train concerns.
- S32004 Diagnose electronically controlled transmission/transaxle.

Matching

Match the following terms with the correct description or example.

A. Blocking ring
B. Detent mechanism
C. Direct drive
D. Gear ratio
E. Gear reduction
F. Gradient resistance

G. Helix
H. Hydraulic actuator
I. Idler gear
J. Interlock mechanism
K. Overdrive
L. Paddle

M. Pocket bearing
N. Roller bearing
O. Selector gate
P. Shift fork

Q. Spring-loaded key
R. Synchronizer
S. Thrust washer
T. Torque multiplication

_____ **1.** A bronze or steel washer that acts as a wear surface and can be used to adjust end play.

_____ **2.** A hydraulically controlled cylinder that engages or disengages the clutch pedal.

_____ **3.** The increase of torque.

_____ **4.** A long cylindrical roller held in position by a cage.

_____ **5.** The curve created by a smooth spiral and used in the angle of gear teeth and coil springs.

_____ **6.** A part of the synchronizer that helps hold the synchronizer collar in position.

_____ **7.** A synchronizer part that increases or decreases a gear's speed to match shaft speed so that the synchronizer sleeve can lock the gear to the shaft.

_____ **8.** A gear used in between two gears to change the direction of the rotation of the driveshaft or drive axles in the transmission.

_____ **9.** The ratio of the number of turns that a drive gear must complete to turn the driven gear one turn.

_____ **10.** The use of a small gear to drive a large gear. The result is an increase in torque but a decrease in speed.

_____ **11.** Resistance encountered when a vehicle travels up a hill, requiring torque to be applied to overcome it.

_____ **12.** A roller in the rear of the input shaft that supports the front of the main shaft.

_____ **13.** A condition in which the input shaft and output shaft are locked together and turning at the same rate of speed.

_____ **14.** A gear in which the output speed is faster than the input speed.

_____ **15.** A mechanism that moves the synchronizer sleeve to lock the gear to the main shaft.

_____ **16.** A mechanical device that prevents engagement of two different gears at the same time.

_____ **17.** An assembly that allows for the selection of gears without grinding by matching the speed of the two assemblies.

_____ **18.** A shifting mechanism or electronic control usually attached to the steering wheel.

_____ **19.** The mechanism that holds or helps hold the shift rail into position to ensure that the gear does not pop out when selected and to let the driver feel when a shift is completed.

_____ **20.** The U-shaped cutaway in shift shafts that the shifter lever fits into.

Multiple Choice

Read each item carefully, and then select the best response.

_____ **1.** If the driven gear has 20 teeth and the drive gear has 5 teeth, the gear ratio is _____.
   A. 1:4
   B. 5:1
   C. 4:1
   D. none of the above

_____ **2.** What type of gear simply transfers motion and does not have an effect on the gear ratio of the input to output gears?
   A. Drive gear
   B. Driven gear
   C. Overdrive gear
   D. Idler gear

_____ **3.** The set of shafts that are connected to the shift forks are called the _____.
   A. synchronizer
   B. selector shift rail
   C. selector gate
   D. gear shift lever

_____ 4. The _____ engages the dog teeth on the selected gear and transmits torque from the gear to the output shaft.
   A. selector gate
   B. shift fork
   C. synchronizer sleeve
   D. detent mechanism

_____ 5. The fifth gear/ _____ engages in a groove in the synchronizer sleeve of the reverse gear synchronizer.
   A. detent mechanism
   B. reverse shift fork
   C. interlock mechanism
   D. selector gate

_____ 6. What device does the powertrain control module engage to prevent the manual transmission from being shifted into reverse gear at speeds above 5 mph?
   A. Lockout solenoid
   B. Blocking ring
   C. Interlock mechanism
   D. Hydraulic actuator

_____ 7. Which type of loads are applied along the length of the components?
   A. Radial
   B. Linear
   C. Thrust
   D. Horizontal

_____ 8. Washers that can be used to provide for adjustment of end play or preload are called _____.
   A. thrust washers
   B. selective thickness shims
   C. flanges
   D. tapered washers

_____ 9. What type of seals are designed with helical flutes molded into the sealing lip and must be installed with the correct direction of shaft rotation?
   A. Hydrodynamic
   B. O-ring
   C. Fiber
   D. RTV

_____ 10. What type of gear design reduces gear noise and distributes the load more evenly?
   A. Spur
   B. Pinion
   C. Helical
   D. Spline

_____ 11. A(n) _____ is used to synchronize the speeds of the gear and shaft before engagement.
   A. baulk-ring synchromesh unit
   B. vehicle speed sensor
   C. blocker ring synchromesh unit
   D. either A or C

_____ 12. The tapered cut on the teeth of the gear, blocker ring, and sleeve is called a _____.
   A. spur
   B. chamfer
   C. pinion
   D. mesh

_____ 13. A _____ is sometimes referred to as a semiautomatic or automated manual transmission.
   A. dual-clutch transmission
   B. transaxle synchromesh unit
   C. baulk-ring synchromesh unit
   D. direct drive transmission

_____ **14.** When the shifter will not move smoothly into the desired gear and requires excessive force by the driver to force it into gear it is called _____.
  A. grinding
  B. detent
  C. hard shifting
  D. slippage

_____ **15.** What tool is used to check input or output shaft end play?
  A. Feeler gauge
  B. Dial indicator
  C. Micrometer
  D. Outside caliper

True/False

If you believe the statement to be more true than false, write the letter "T" in the space provided. If you believe the statement to be more false than true, write the letter "F."

_____ **1.** When two gears are in mesh, one is a drive (output) gear. The other, providing the turning action, is the driven (input) gear.

_____ **2.** The terms _output gear_ and _drive gear_ have the same meaning.

_____ **3.** Fourth gear is normally a gear ratio of 1:1, or direct drive.

_____ **4.** The overall gear ratio is the gearbox ratio multiplied by the final drive ratio.

_____ **5.** Selector gates are the parts that actually move the components that change the gears selected inside the transmission.

_____ **6.** The interlock mechanism's function is ensuring that two gears cannot be selected at the same time.

_____ **7.** Thrust loads try to force the gears and shafts apart.

_____ **8.** Thrust washers are plain bearings, meaning they have no rollers.

_____ **9.** In transaxle designs, the drive is transferred through the clutch unit to a primary or input shaft.

_____ **10.** Fifth gear is always the lowest of the gear ratios in forward.

_____ **11.** A low gear ratio also gives the greatest amount of torque multiplication.

_____ **12.** Grinding or clashing noises during upshifts and downshifts are fairly common on manual transmissions.

_____ **13.** Clicking noises in any gear selection are typically related to a tooth of a gear that is damaged on the main shaft, input shaft, or countershaft.

_____ **14.** A visual inspection should always be performed when diagnosing the manual transmission.

_____ **15.** All transmissions use the same fluid.

Fill in the Blank

Read each item carefully, and then complete the statement by filling in the missing word(s).

1. _____ resistance is the resistance caused by tires contacting the road and wind resistance against the vehicle while rolling down the highway.

2. Gears with the same number of teeth rotate at the same rate of speed, resulting in _____ _____.

3. Different gear _____ are used inside the transmission to achieve varied torque to accelerate the vehicle.

4. _____ _____ trains have two or more pairs of gears in constant mesh so that they rotate together.

5. A(n) _____ _____ allows the driver to manually select gears via a gearshift mechanism.

6. Each selector shift rail has a _____ mechanism, usually in the form of a spring-loaded steel ball held in the casing.

7. Many newer manual transmissions are equipped with electronic _____ _____ systems, which use an electronic solenoid to prevent the transmission from being shifted into reverse while the vehicle is in forward motion.

8. _____ roller bearings can be caged, or they can be a loose number assembled to operate directly on a hardened gear or shaft.

9. _____ roller bearings are normally used in pairs and can sustain heavy radial and thrust loads in either direction.

10. _____ gears use straight-cut teeth for more coverage and heavy-duty operation.

11. Vehicle _____ _____ are mounted in the transmission case and are used to generate a signal based on the vehicle's speed that is sent to the PCM and/or speedometer.

12. A(n) _____-_____ transaxle uses electric solenoid valves to hydraulically engage and disengage each clutch.

13. The _____ is used to ensure proper engagement of gears without grinding.

14. Service consultants may use a _____ _____ to help the customer express all of the conditions related to the concern.

15. A _____ _____ is used to press bearings from the transmission shafts or to remove synchronizer sleeves.

Labeling

Label the following diagrams with the correct terms.

1. The idler gear is a gear used to change the direction of the rotation of shafts and is used to provide a reverse:

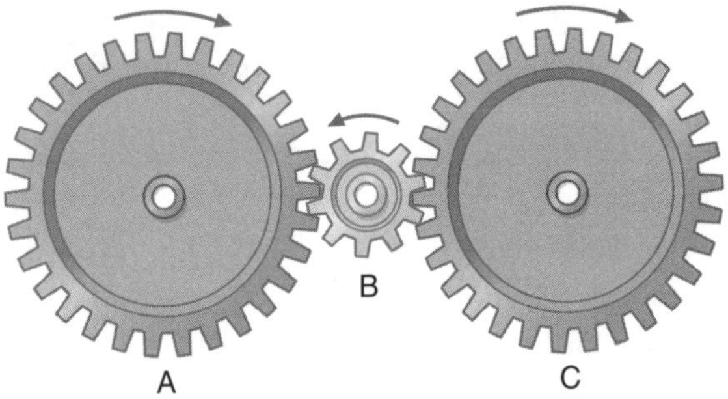

A. _____

B. _____

C. _____

2. The interlock mechanism:

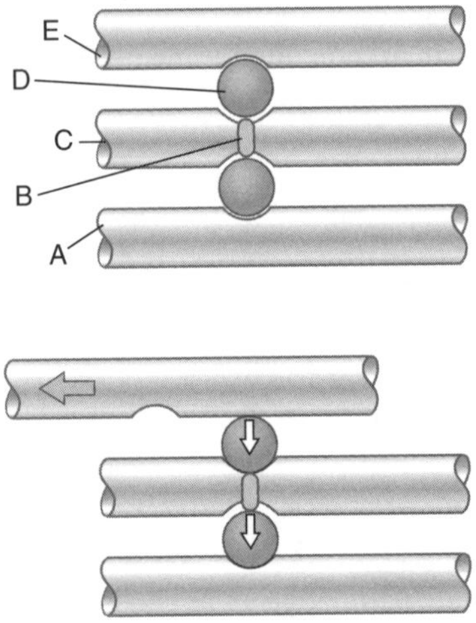

A. _____

B. _____

C. _____

D. _____

E. _____

3. Single-row ball bearings:

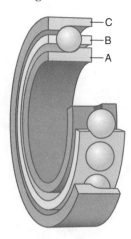

A. _____

B. _____

C. _____

4. Roller bearings:

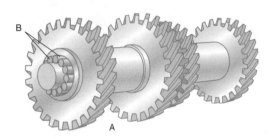

A. _____

B. _____

5. Caged roller bearings:

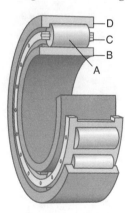

A. _____

B. _____

C. _____

D. _____

6. Tapered roller bearings:

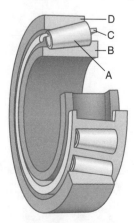

A. _____

B. _____

C. _____

D. _____

7. Pinion gear:

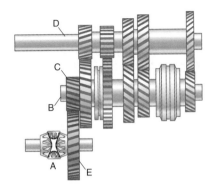

A. _____

B. _____

C. _____

D. _____

E. _____

8. Power flow through a transmission:

First gear:

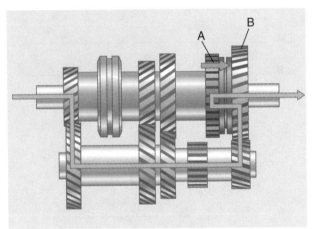

A. _____

B. _____

Second gear:

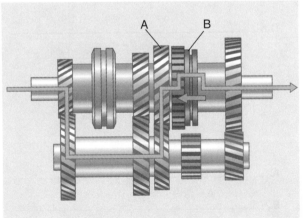

A. _____

B. _____

Third gear:

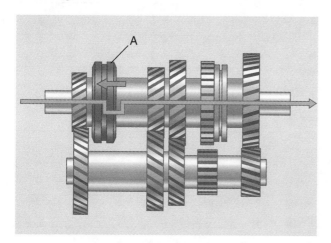

A. _____

B. _____

Fourth gear:

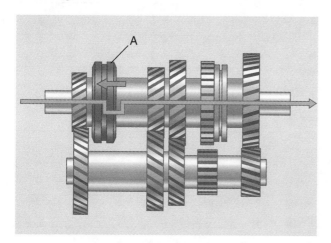

A. _____

9. Baulk-ring syncromesh unit:

Blocker ring teeth line up with the dog teeth to allow smooth engagement of the sleeve:

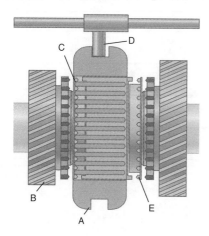

A. _____

B. _____

C. _____

D. _____

E. _____

Blocker ring teeth out of alignment, which allows the blocker ring to bring the gear to the same speed:

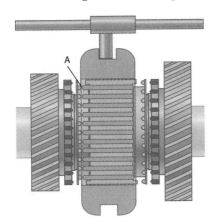

A. _____

10. Dual-clutch transmission layout:

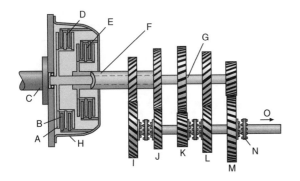

A. _____

B. _____

C. _____

D. _____

E. _____

F. _____

G. _____

H. _____

I. _____

J. _____

K. _____

L. _____

M. _____

N. _____

O. _____

Skill Drills

Test your knowledge of skill drills by filling in the correct words in the photo captions.

1. Checking the Fluid Level of a Manual Transmission:

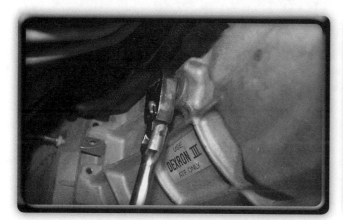 

Step 1: Safely raise and support the vehicle on the lift so that it is level. Inspect the _____ for leaks. Remove the filler plug, using the proper _____. Inspect the filler plug and fill hole for _____ _____, and replace/repair if necessary.

Step 2: If the gearbox fluid begins to _____ _____ as the filler plug is removed, let the gearbox fluid seek its own level before _____ the filler plug. The gearbox fluid level should be at the _____ of the filler plug hole.

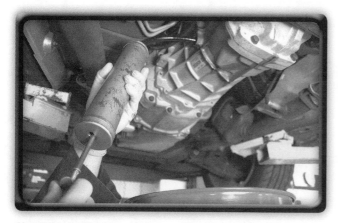

Step 3: If the fluid level is low, refill with the specified fluid, reinstall the filler plug, and wipe the area around the filler plug hole with a clean _____ _____. Tighten the filler plug to the specified _____.

2. Checking and Adjusting the Differential/Transfer Case Fluid Level:

Step 1: Safely raise and support the vehicle. Inspect the differential and transfer case for leaks. Position a clean _____ pan under the filler plug. Remove the _____ _____, using the proper tool. Inspect the filler plug threads for _____, and replace if necessary.

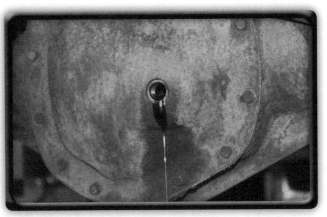

Step 2: If the fluid begins to run out as the filler plug is removed, let the fluid seek its own _____ before reinstalling the filler plug. The fluid level should be at the bottom of the _____ _____ _____.

Step 3: If the _____ _____ is low, refill with the specified fluid, reinstall the filler plug, and _____ the area around the filler plug hole with a clean shop towel. _____ the filler plug to the specified torque.

3. Changing the Gearbox Fluid:

Step 1. Safely _____ and _____ the vehicle, using an approved lift. Obtain a clean drain pan to put the used _____ in.

Step 2: Inspect the _____ for leaks.

Step 3: Remove the drain plug from the _____ of the transmission, being careful of the _____ gearbox fluid. Let gearbox fluid drain until it has stopped running. If necessary, drain the _____ _____ assembly in the same manner.

Step 4: Replace the _____ _____(s) and tighten to specification, and _____ the fill plug(s).

Step 5: Refill the transmission and final drive to the proper level using _____-approved gearbox fluid. _____ the fill plug(s), and tighten to the proper torque. Wipe away any spillage. _____ _____ the vehicle. If necessary, put the vehicle back on the lift, and check for any leaks.

4. Identifying the Cause of Fluid Loss in a Transmission:

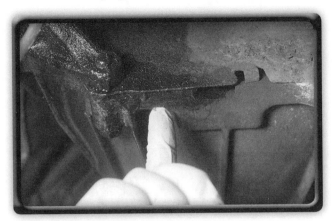

Step 1. Safely raise and support the vehicle. Look for leaks in the transmission _____ _____ to the engine block (front seal).

Step 2: Look for leaks in the transmission _____ outlet. Look for leaks in all case _____ areas.

Step 3: Look for leaks in the _____ tail shaft _____.

Step 4: Inspect for transmission case _____, such as _____ and _____.

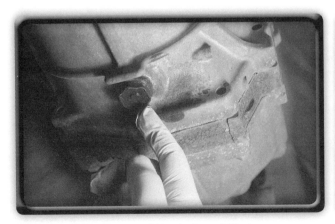

Step 5: Look for _____ at the drain and fill plugs.

Step 6: Check the gear fluid level. If excess level is found, let the excess drain into a container. If the fluid is more than ¼" (6 mm) below the _____ of the threaded hole, add new fluid of the correct _____ and type.

Review Questions

_____ 1. Choose the correct statement with respect to direct drive rotation.
   A. The input gear turns faster than the output gear.
   B. The output gear turns faster than the input gear.
   C. The input shaft and output shaft are locked together.
   D. The turning effort of the output gear is higher than the effort applied by the input gear.

_____ 2. For a gear ratio of 4:1, the output torque is 300 ft-lb. What would be the input torque?
   A. 1200 ft-lb
   B. 600 ft-lb
   C. 150 ft-lb
   D. 75 ft-lb

_____ 3. Which of the below engages with the dog teeth on the selected gear and transmits torque from the gear to the output shaft?
   A. Synchronizer sleeve
   B. Selector gate
   C. Shift forks
   D. Shift rails

_____ 4. All of the following statements are true _except_:
   A. pocket bearings sit in the pocket of the input shaft.
   B. pocket bearings support the front of the input shaft.
   C. pocket bearings are generally not used in rear-wheel drive transmissions.
   D. pocket bearings are roller bearings.

_____ 5. What type of bearing is best used to sustain radial and thrust loads?
   A. Cylindrical roller bearing
   B. Tapered roller bearing
   C. Needle roller bearing
   D. Pin roller bearing

_____ 6. All of the following statements are true except:
   A. gear fluid is splashed inside the casing while the transmission shafts rotate.
   B. oil seals prevent fluid leakage.
   C. oil seals prevent dirt and moisture from entering into the transmission.
   D. the helical flutes in the seal prevent the fluid from going back into the transmission.

_____ 7. In transaxle designs, the drive is transferred through the clutch unit to a(n):
   A. primary shaft.
   B. secondary shaft.
   C. counter shaft.
   D. alternate shaft.

_____ 8. Which of these is used to synchronize the speeds of gear and shaft before engagement?
   A. Vehicle speed sensor
   B. Blocker ring synchromesh unit
   C. Sliding reverse idler
   D. Constant-mesh reverse gear

_____ 9. Choose the correct answer.
   A. All manual transmissions use the same lubricating fluid.
   B. Ensure that the gearbox fluid is not warm during gearbox fluid change.
   C. If gearbox fluid levels are too low, aeration of the fluid will be present.
   D. Inspect the transmission for leaks when changing gearbox fluid.

_____ 10. Which of these could be related to hard shifting?
   A. Power flow through the countershaft
   B. A gear that is damaged on the main shaft
   C. Fluid level to high.
   D. The alignment of the bell housing

ASE Technician A/Technician B Style Questions

_____ 1. Tech A says that in a conventional transmission, the gears freewheel around the main shaft until they are locked to it by the synchronizer. Tech B says that when not engaged, main shaft gears slide away from the counter gears until they are no longer in mesh. Who is correct?
   A. Tech A
   B. Tech B
   C. Both A and B
   D. Neither A nor B

_____ 2. Tech A says that the speed ratio and the torque transferred depend on the gear selected in a transmission. Tech B says that first gear is always the lowest of the gear ratios in forward. Who is correct?
   A. Tech A
   B. Tech B
   C. Both A and B
   D. Neither A nor B

_____ 3. Tech A says that the dual-clutch arrangement requires two input shafts. Tech B says that the dual clutches are always controlled by a clutch pedal. Who is correct?
   A. Tech A
   B. Tech B
   C. Both A and B
   D. Neither A nor B

_____ 4. Tech A says that an overdrive gear ratio means the input gear turns faster than the output gear. Tech B says that overdrive ratios provide less torque output than underdrive ratios. Who is correct?
   A. Tech A
   B. Tech B
   C. Both A and B
   D. Neither A nor B

_____ 5. Tech A says that if a noise is caused by a set of worn gears, it will normally be loudest in that gear while driving under a load. Tech B says that if the bearings on the input shaft, countershaft, or main shaft are worn, either front or rear, a growling noise will result when stopped in gear. Who is correct?
   A. Tech A
   B. Tech B
   C. Both A and B
   D. Neither A nor B

_____ 6. Tech A says that some manual transmissions use two input shafts and two clutches. Tech B says that many manual transmissions now use planetary gear sets. Who is correct?
   A. Tech A
   B. Tech B
   C. Both A and B
   D. Neither A nor B

_____ 7. Tech A says that blocker rings prevent the vehicle from rolling when parked. Tech B says that engine torque is transferred from the dog teeth through the synchronizer sleeves. Who is correct?
   A. Tech A
   B. Tech B
   C. Both A and B
   D. Neither A nor B

_____ 8. Tech A says that if gearbox fluid begins to run out as the filler plug is removed, the technician must add the same amount back in. Tech B says that blocker rings have fine grooves that cut through the oil on the tapered cone of the matching gear. Who is correct?
   A. Tech A
   B. Tech B
   C. Both A and B
   D. Neither A nor B

_____ **9.** Tech A says that a broken detent spring can cause the transmission to pop out of gear. Tech B says that a broken interlock pin can cause the transmission to go into two gears at the same time? Who is correct?
  A. Tech A
  B. Tech B
  C. Both A and B
  D. Neither A nor B

_____ **10.** Tech A says that some manufacturers specify automatic transmission fluid to be used in their manual transmissions. Tech B says that some manufacturers specify engine oil to be used in their manual transmissions. Who is correct?
  A. Tech A
  B. Tech B
  C. Both A and B
  D. Neither A nor B

33 Manual Transmission Overhaul

At the start of each chapter you'll find the NATEF Tasks, Knowledge Objectives, and Skills Objectives from the textbook. These are your objectives as you make your way through the exercises in this workbook and the chapter in your textbook. The following activities have been designed to help you refresh your knowledge of the material in this chapter.

NATEF Task

- N33001 Disassemble, inspect, clean, and reassemble internal transmission/transaxle components.

Knowledge Objectives

After reading this chapter, you will be able to:

- K33001 Describe the things you need to know before rebuilding a transmission.
- K33002 List and identify the tools used for rebuilding transmissions.
- K33003 Describe the things necessary to prepare for disassembly of the transmission.

Skills Objectives

After reading this chapter, you will be able to:

- S33001 Inspect transmission case and components.
- S33002 Inspect the gaskets and seals.
- S33003 Inspect and reinstall the synchronizer assembly.
- S33004 Inspect and service lubrication devices.
- S33005 Inspect and service the shift cover.
- S33006 Inspect and service shift linkages.
- S33007 Remove and replace the transaxle final drive.
- S33008 Remove and service transaxle final drive pinion gears.
- S33009 Reassemble the transmission.
- S33010 Measure and adjust transmission end play/preload.

Matching

Match the following terms with the correct description or example.

A. Blocking ring   **D.** Oil slinger
B. Concentricity   **E.** Overhauling
C. End play

_____ **1.** The roundness of a hole.
_____ **2.** Slows down or speeds up the gear to match the main shaft speed to allow smooth shifts.
_____ **3.** A device that rides partially in the transmission fluid and flings oil to lubricate the internal workings of the transmission.
_____ **4.** The process of refurbishing the transmission to like-new condition.
_____ **5.** Refers to the input or output shaft fore and aft movement in the transmission.

Multiple Choice

Read each item carefully, and then select the best response.

_____ **1.** A thorough inspection of all gasket surfaces is important to prevent _____.
   A. out-of-round conditions
   B. blocker ring wear
   C. premature leakage of transmission fluids
   D. oil slinger wear

_____ **2.** Identify the tool used to check for concentricity of all seal surface openings.
   A. Seal driver
   B. Outside micrometer
   C. Bushing driver kit
   D. Dial caliper

_____ **3.** Identify the components that allow for the smooth shifting of the transmission.
   A. Synchronizer assemblies
   B. Countershafts
   C. Tail shafts
   D. Extension housings

_____ **4.** The presence of _____ particles in transmission fluid may indicate that the blocking rings are excessively worn.
   A. blue-colored
   B. gold-colored
   C. magnetic
   D. rubber

_____ **5.** When removing the shift cover and mechanism of a manual transmission, the transmission should be in _____ for easier reassembly.
   A. second gear
   B. reverse gear
   C. first gear
   D. neutral

_____ **6.** Identify the gear that drives the differential ring gear located inside the transaxle assembly.
   A. Worm gear
   B. Spider gear
   C. Pinion gear
   D. Sun gear

_____ **7.** End play is typically set by using _____ to ensure that the correct clearance is present.
   A. preselected spacers
   B. feeler gauges
   C. sprags
   D. regulators

_____ **8.** The need for end play and preload adjustments can be an indicator of _____.
   A. transmission fluid leak
   B. washer wear
   C. oil slinger crack
   D. synchronizer sleeve chipping

_____ **9.** _____ ensures that enough pressure is placed on the transmission bearing to keep the shaft from moving around, but not so much that the bearing will run hot and begin to fail.
   A. Blocking ring
   B. Synchronizer assembly
   C. Preload
   D. Pinion ring gear

_____ **10.** Identify one of the first tasks to be performed when servicing a manual transmission.
   A. Removing the synchronizer hub from the transmission.
   B. Inspecting the speedometer gear and retainer.
   C. Draining the transmission fluid.
   D. Obtaining and reading all manufacturer publications and service information.

True/False

If you believe the statement to be more true than false, write the letter "T" in the space provided. If you believe the statement to be more false than true, write the letter "F."

_____ 1. A bound-up shift boot that causes the transmission to pop out of gear requires a teardown and inspection of the manual transmission.

_____ 2. Even basic-level transmission rebuild kits include gaskets, seals, synchronizer rings, bearings, and sometimes even shafts.

_____ 3. On removal of the transmission, it is necessary to remove the shift linkage and associated parts.

_____ 4. The removal procedure of the transaxle final drive is specific to each vehicle.

_____ 5. If the pinion gear located inside the transaxle assembly needs to be replaced, then it is necessary to also replace the ring gear.

_____ 6. Measuring end play is critical to ensure that the transmission stays in service for a long time.

_____ 7. Incorrect end play and bearing preload will only reduce transmission efficiency and not result in transmission failure.

_____ 8. An advantage of modern manual transmissions is that their disassembly and reassembly do not require special tools.

_____ 9. The rebuilding of a transmission/transaxle is fairly simple and can be performed by a novice technician without any prior training.

_____ 10. When rebuilding a transmission/transaxle, it is always a good practice to replace the gaskets and seals.

Fill in the Blank

Read each item carefully, and then complete the statement by filling in the missing word(s).

1. The transmission mating surfaces, such as the main case and output shaft housing, should be checked with a _____ and _____ _____ to make sure both surfaces are flat.

2. A(n) _____ _____ ensures that oil is directed toward the front bearing and oil is returned to the transmission case.

3. _____ _____ and gear contact patterns are crucial to the longevity of the transaxle.

4. When measuring and adjusting end play and preload, _____ or _____ clearances can be used to determine whether gears and shafts need to be replaced or reused.

5. During a transmission rebuild, if it is found to be cheaper to use a replacement transmission, then the transmission may have to be reassembled for a _____ _____.

6. _____ _____ can be sent to a local laboratory to be analyzed for contamination or chemical breakdown to help determine the origin of a transmission failure.

7. The loss of _____ _____ in an oil pump can result in transmission damage.

8. During disassembly, _____ unknown parts is a good idea to ensure that they are reassembled correctly.

9. A _____ _____ _____ needs to be performed to determine if a remanufactured unit is to be used rather than rebuilding the transmission.

10. Improper end play and preload adjustments lead to misalignment of _____ _____.

Skill Drills

1. Inspecting and Servicing an Oil Pump:

_____ **A.** Replace any parts that have wear or etching. Reassemble the oil pump in the transmission case and check clearances. Any oil slingers should be replaced as necessary with the gaskets and seals.

_____ **B.** Start by removing the oil pump from the transmission case, following the specified procedure. Inspect all gears for excessive wear and clearances, and replace as necessary.

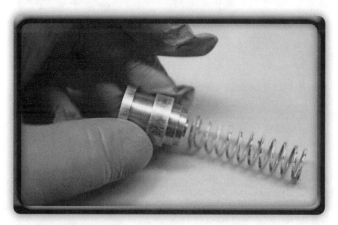

_____ **C.** Inspect the regulator piston for wear and etching in the bore.

2. Inspecting and Servicing the Shift Cover:

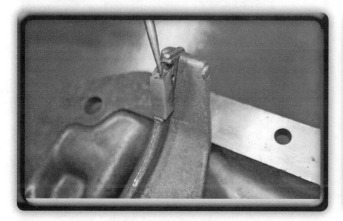

_____ **A.** Check all shifter forks for wear in the gear selector slots. If the gearshift fork inserts are worn or cracked, they should be replaced before the installation of the shift cover.

_____ **B.** As the shift rails are being installed, check all detent springs and balls for damage, and replace as necessary.

_____ **C.** Lubricate all main shift control shafts with petroleum jelly before installation.

_____ **D.** If an O-ring is present that is used to seal the cover to the output shaft housing, it should be replaced.

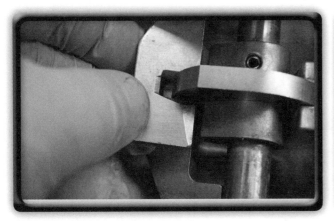

_____ **E.** Check the gear selector interlock sleeve for excessive wear and binding. If necessary, clean or replace.

_____ **F.** If roll pins are used to secure shift forks or sleeves, inspect for tightness and replace as necessary by driving the pin out and replacing with a new one. If the new pin fits loosely in the case, the case may be damaged and will have to be replaced or repaired.

_____ **G.** Secure a new shift cover gasket, usually by using a dab of RTV sealer, and install the shift cover. Some transmissions use RTV without an additional gasket, as does the transmission in the picture. Follow the manufacturer's directions to ensure a leakfree repair. Make sure the shift forks line up with the corresponding gears.

_____ **H.** Install the shift lever, and check that all gears can be shifted without binding.

3. Inspecting and Servicing Shift Linkages:

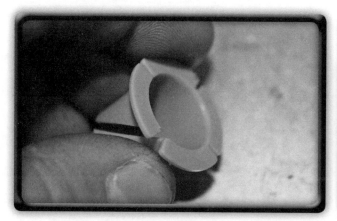

_____ **A.** If the vehicle has plastic or brass bushings, inspect them for excessive wear and replace as necessary.

_____ **B.** Inspect linkage rod ends for excessive wear from abuse. Inspect the rods for abnormal shape, which can occur as a result of driver abuse.

_____ **C.** Inspect mounting brackets for excessive wear and looseness, and replace as necessary. Check all sensors and solenoids.

_____ **D.** Inspect the mechanical linkage for worn or elongated holes where the bushings ride.

_____ **E.** Inspect the cable linkage for fraying and stretching.

_____ **F.** Lay all the associated parts out on a bench, if possible, to get a clear picture for inspection. Clean off the dirt and grease in order to properly inspect.

4. Measuring and Adjusting End Play/Preload:

_____ **A.** If an adjustment is necessary, remove the front bearing retaining cover. Remove the front bearing race, which may expose any existing shims.

_____ **B.** Install the correct shims to bring the end play into specifications. Reinstall the front bearing retainer and gasket. Torque the bolts to the manufacturer's specifications.

_____ **C.** Grab the output shaft and raise it upward until the end play is totally removed; doing so will give you an accurate reading. Record the measurement and compare with the manufacturer's specifications. Most are usually around 0.005" to 0.025" (0.127 to 0.635 mm).

_____ **D.** Once the transmission assembly is together, turn the transmission case on its end, and mount a dial indicator on the end of the output shaft. Rotate the dial indicator to zero.

Review Questions

_____ **1.** When diagnosing transmission failure, gear oil can be analyzed for contamination or chemical breakdown by:
   A. sending it to a local laboratory.
   B. doing chemical analysis in the shop.
   C. sending a sample to the manufacturer.
   D. sending a sample to the dealer.

_____ **2.** Which of these tools is required to pull differential case bearings?
   A. Push-type bearing puller
   B. An old bearing race
   C. Chain-style vice grips
   D. Snap ring pliers

_____ **3.** Which tool is required to remove rear bearing race from the transmission case?
   A. Brass drift and hammer
   B. Seal driver
   C. Gear pullers
   D. Impact screw driver

_____ **4.** Damaged synchronizer units as well as other shift mechanism problems may manifest as:
   A. sloppy or loose shifting.
   B. excessive noise.
   C. transmission fluid leak.
   D. vehicle breakdown.

_____ **5.** All of the following statements with respect to disassembly of the transmission are true *except*:
   A. obtain and read all manufacturer publications and service information.
   B. diagnose the possible causes.
   C. ensure proper tools are available for disassembly and assembly.
   D. ensure that all transmission case components are replaced.

_____ **6.** All of the following statements with respect to overhauling a transmission are true *except*:
   A. transmission case components should be cleaned and inspected.
   B. when in doubt about the reusability of a case component, do not replace it.
   C. perform a cost analysis for the customer.
   D. if rebuilding will cost more than a remanufactured unit, the customer should be informed.

_____ **7.** Choose the correct statement.
   A. Always reuse gaskets and seals.
   B. Sealants should not be used in transmissions.
   C. Gasket surfaces don't need to be cleaned because the new gasket will seal any residual gasket material.
   D. Check the main case and output shaft housing with a straightedge and feeler gauge.

_____ **8.** A good place to start when inspecting for synchronizer wear and damage is when the:
   A. transmission fluid is drained from the transmission.
   B. transmission is being assembled.
   C. vehicle is running.
   D. transmission endplay is measured and adjusted.

_____ **9.** Choose the correct statement.
   A. The transaxle final drive can be removed without disassembling the transaxle.
   B. The pinion gear is part of the input shaft of the transaxle.
   C. The pinion gear drives the differential ring gear, located inside the transaxle assembly.
   D. Do not replace the ring gear if the pinion gear has to be replaced.

_____ **10.** All of the following statements referring to transmission end play/preload are true *except*:
   A. end play and preload adjustments are a necessary part of the disassembly and assembly of the transmission.
   B. end play is the movement back and forth of the input or output shaft.
   C. Washer wear or bearing failure causes the shaft to walk back and forth in the case.
   D. axial or radial clearances should not determine whether gears and shafts are to be replaced or reused.

ASE Technician A/Technician B Style Questions

_____ **1.** Tech A says when performing a rebuild of a transmission, proper tool usage is vital. Tech B says special tools and equipment may be required to disassemble and reassemble modern manual transmissions.
   A. Tech A
   B. Tech B
   C. Both A and B
   D. Neither A nor B

_____ **2.** Tech A says specialty tools must be used to ensure that damage is not done to the parts that do not need to be replaced. Tech B says damaging components because of lack of knowledge and skill is keeping the customer's or shop owner's interests in mind.
   A. Tech A
   B. Tech B
   C. Both A and B
   D. Neither A nor B

_____ **3.** A manual transmission case is being inspected for an overhaul. Tech A says a close inspection of all vital parts is necessary to complete a manual transmission. Tech B says you should check the transmission case for cracks and porosity.
   A. Tech A
   B. Tech B
   C. Both A and B
   D. Neither A nor B

_____ **4.** Tech A says sloppy or loose shifting, or jumping out of gear can indicate a damaged oil slinger. Tech B says a good place to start when inspecting for synchronizer wear and damage is after you have reassembled the transmission.
   A. Tech A
   B. Tech B
   C. Both A and B
   D. Neither A nor B

_____ **5.** End play is being checked on a manual transmission. Tech A says measuring end play is critical to ensure that the transmission stays in service for a long time. Tech B says end play and preload adjustments are a necessary part of the disassembly and assembly of the transmission.
   A. Tech A
   B. Tech B
   C. Both A and B
   D. Neither A nor B

_____ **6.** A transmission is being disassembled. Tech A says organization during disassembly is not important. Tech B says you should perform a thorough inspection of the outside of the transmission, looking for any obvious signs of the failure or any other damage.
   A. Tech A
   B. Tech B
   C. Both A and B
   D. Neither A nor B

_____ **7.** Diagnosis of a manual transmission is being discussed. Tech A says diagnosis involves a thorough understanding of the customer complaint. Tech B says once the concern is fully understood, the technician needs to verify the concern.
   A. Tech A
   B. Tech B
   C. Both A and B
   D. Neither A nor B

_____ **8.** Tech A says a troubleshooting chart will not help you track the customer concern to the specific fault inside the transmission. Tech B says it is not necessary to test drive the vehicle, but verify the customer concern.
   A. Tech A
   B. Tech B
   C. Both A and B
   D. Neither A nor B

_____ **9.** A synchronizer hub is being inspected. Tech A says to inspect the blocking rings for wear, which can be seen on the friction side of the ring. Tech B says on transmissions that give blocking ring clearance specifications, measure the clearance with a feeler blade.
   A. Tech A
   B. Tech B
   C. Both A and B
   D. Neither A nor B

_____ **10.** Shift linkages are being discussed. Tech A says if the vehicle has plastic or brass bushings, replacement is not necessary. Tech B says it is not necessary to inspect the mechanical linkage for worn or elongated holes where the bushings ride.
   A. Tech A
   B. Tech B
   C. Both A and B
   D. Neither A nor B

Driveshafts, Axles, and Final Drives

At the start of each chapter you'll find the NATEF Tasks, Knowledge Objectives, and Skills Objectives from the textbook. These are your objectives as you make your way through the exercises in this workbook and the chapter in your textbook. The following activities have been designed to help you refresh your knowledge of the material in this chapter.

NATEF Tasks

- N34001 Check fluid condition; check for leaks; determine needed action. (MLR/AST/MAST)
- N34002 Check shaft balance and phasing; measure shaft runout; measure and adjust driveline angles. (AST/MAST)
- N34003 Diagnose universal joint noise and vibration concerns; perform needed action. (AST/MAST)
- N34004 Measure drive axle flange runout and shaft end play; determine needed action. (AST/MAST)
- N34005 Inspect and replace drive axle wheel studs. (MLR/AST/MAST)
- N34006 Remove and replace drive axle shafts. (AST/MAST)
- N34007 Inspect and replace drive axle shaft seals, bearings, and retainers. (AST/MAST)
- N34008 Inspect, service, and/or replace shafts, yokes, boots, and universal/CV joints. (MLR/AST/MAST)
- N34009 Diagnose noise and vibration concerns; determine needed action. (MAST)
- N34010 Diagnose drive axle shafts, bearings, and seals for noise, vibration, and fluid leakage concerns; determine needed action. (MAST)
- N34011 Diagnose noise, slippage, and chatter concerns; determine needed action. (MAST)
- N34012 Diagnose constant-velocity (CV) joint noise and vibration concerns; determine needed action. (AST/MAST)
- N34013 Inspect and replace companion flange and/or pinion seal; measure companion flange runout. (AST/MAST)
- N34014 Inspect ring gear and measure runout; determine needed action. (MAST)
- N34015 Remove, inspect, and/or reinstall drive pinion and ring gear, spacers, sleeves, and bearings. (MAST)
- N34016 Disassemble, inspect, measure, and/or replace differential pinion gears (spiders), shaft, side gears, side bearings, thrust washers, and case. (MAST)
- N34017 Measure and adjust drive pinion depth. (MAST)
- N34018 Measure and adjust drive pinion bearing preload. (MAST)
- N34019 Reassemble and reinstall differential case assembly; measure runout; determine needed action. (MAST)
- N34020 Check ring and pinion tooth contact patterns; perform needed action. (MAST)
- N34021 Clean and inspect differential case; check for leaks; inspect housing vent (MLR/AST/MAST)
- N34022 Measure rotating torque; determine needed action. (MAST)

Knowledge Objectives

After reading this chapter, you will be able to:

- K34001 Describe rear-wheel drive and front-wheel drive layout.
- K34002 Describe the layout and function of rear-wheel drive systems.
- K34003 Describe the layout and function of front-wheel drive systems.
- K34004 Describe the purpose and function of driveshafts, axles, and half-shafts.
- K34005 Describe the types, purpose, and function of axles and half-shafts.
- K34006 Describe the types, purpose, and function of rear-wheel drive solid axles.
- K34007 Describe the types, purpose, and function of half-shafts.
- K34008 Describe the purpose and function of joints and couplings in driveshafts and axles.
- K34009 Describe the types, purpose, and function of universal joints.
- K34010 Describe the types, purpose, and function of constant-velocity joints.
- K34011 Describe the purpose and function of final drives/differentials.
- K34012 Explain the purpose and function of rear-wheel final drives.
- K34013 Explain the purpose and function of limited slip differentials.
- K34014 Describe the purpose and function of front-wheel drive differentials.

Skills Objectives

After reading this chapter, you will be able to:

- S34001 Perform driveline and axle inspection and repair.
- S34002 Perform final drive and axle diagnosis.
- S34003 Perform final drive inspection and repair.
- S34004 Inspect and reinstall limited slip differential components.

Matching

Match the following terms with the correct description or example.

A. Beam-type axle

B. Double Cardan joint

C. Full floating axle

D. Backlash

E. Crush sleeve

F. Hooke's joint

_____ **1.** A collapsible spacer between the bearings that provides a means of maintaining a preset torque on the pinion nut.

_____ **2.** The amount of movement between the pinion teeth and the ring gear teeth.

_____ **3.** A type of joint that uses two Cardan joints housed in a short carrier.

_____ **4.** A joint that consists of a steel cross with four hardened bearing journals, mounted on needle rollers in hardened caps

_____ **5.** A rear-wheel drive axle assembly that has a solid tube incorporating the differential gears.

_____ **6.** An axle that does not support any weight and if removed, the vehicle will still roll on its wheels.

Multiple Choice

Read each item carefully, and then select the best response.

_____ **1.** A _____ joint is used to transmit torque through wider angles and without the change of velocity that occurs in U-joints.

    A. single Cardan

    B. tripod

    C. constant-velocity

    D. double Cardan

_____ **2.** _____ is the relationship of the driveshaft to the component that the driveshaft attaches.

    A. Driveline angularity

    B. Backlash

    C. End play

    D. Preload

_____ **3.** A _____ joint does not slide to allow for shaft lengthening or shortening.

    A. constant-velocity

    B. fixed-type

    C. tripod

    D. universal

_____ **4.** In a _____, the centerline of the pinion is below the centerline of the ring gear.

    A. worm gear

    B. sun gear

    C. planetary gear

    D. hypoid bevel gear

_____ **5.** _____ is a type of fixed constant-velocity joint that has been modified so that it will allow a limited amount of plunge capability.

    A. Single Cardan joint

    B. Tripod joint

    C. Rzeppa joint

    D. Double Cardan joint

_____ **6.** Identify the axle that carries the weight of the vehicle and if removed, there is no way to connect the wheel to the vehicle.
  A. Full floating axle
  B. Three-quarter floating axle
  C. Stub axle
  D. Semi-floating axle

_____ **7.** A _____ is a part of a two-piece driveshaft that is splined and allows for a change in length of the shaft as the suspension compresses and rebounds.
  A. slip yoke
  B. companion flange
  C. hypoid gear
  D. lug stud

_____ **8.** Identify the condition in which a vehicle pulls to one side during hard acceleration.
  A. Oversteer
  B. Torque steer
  C. Understeer
  D. Pitch

_____ **9.** A _____ has three equally spaced fingers shaped like a star and allows in-and-out movement of the shaft while allowing flexing.
  A. Rzeppa joint
  B. universal joint
  C. Cardan joint
  D. tulip joint

_____ **10.** _____ assemblies enclose the final drive gears, differential gears, and axle shafts into one housing.
  A. Beam-type axle
  B. Sprag clutch
  C. Extension housing
  D. Servo

True/False

If you believe the statement to be more true than false, write the letter "T" in the space provided. If you believe the statement to be more false than true, write the letter "F."

_____ **1.** In a helical-geared limited slip differential, there are no clutches.

_____ **2.** A sliding spline driveshaft can slide on itself to increase or decrease in length.

_____ **3.** In vehicles with an independent rear suspension, the final drive unit is mounted on the chassis frame.

_____ **4.** The ring and pinion gear set allows the transfer of power 180 degrees.

_____ **5.** The driveshaft is typically made from metal tubing material.

_____ **6.** The U-joint is capable of working at a maximum angle of 9 degrees without vibration and additional wear.

_____ **7.** In a one-piece driveshaft, the yokes can be moved easily.

_____ **8.** A dead axle does not provide any drive capabilities.

_____ **9.** A speedy sleeve is designed slightly oversize to maintain lubrication integrity.

_____ **10.** Driveline angularity is critical to making sure U-joints are working at their proper angle.

Fill in the Blank

Read each item carefully, and then complete the statement by filling in the missing word(s).

1. A splined flange that transmits power from the driveshaft to the pinion gear is called the _____ flange.

2. Driveline angularity is measured in _____.

3. A _____ - _____ limited slip differential responds very quickly to changes in traction and does not bind from friction in turns or lose its effectiveness.

4. In a(n) _____ mounted engine, the front of the engine faces the front of the vehicle.

5. A(n) _____ - _____ joint is used as the inner half-shaft joint to accommodate for changes in shaft length when traveling on different types of terrain.

6. A(n) _____ _____ is splined to the axle shaft and meshes with the spider gears and allows the axles to rotate at their own speeds when cornering and turning.

7. A(n) _____ _____ driveshaft is a two-piece driveshaft that is joined in the middle with splines.

8. An aftermarket repair kit that consists of a thin metal sleeve that fits tightly over the seal surface of the axle is called a(n) _____ _____.

9. In a(n) _____ _____ engine, the front of the engine faces the side of the vehicle.

10. _____ _____ are fitted at the front and rear ends of the driveshafts to allow for up-and-down suspension movement.

Labeling

Label the following diagrams with the correct terms.

1. Components of a rear-wheel driveshaft:

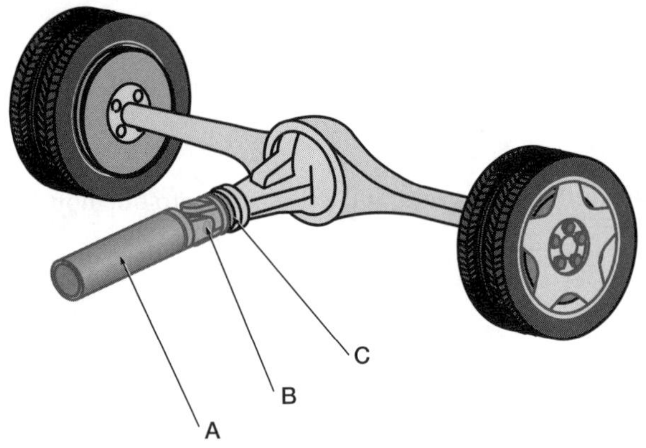

A. _____

B. _____

C. _____

2. Components of a differential:

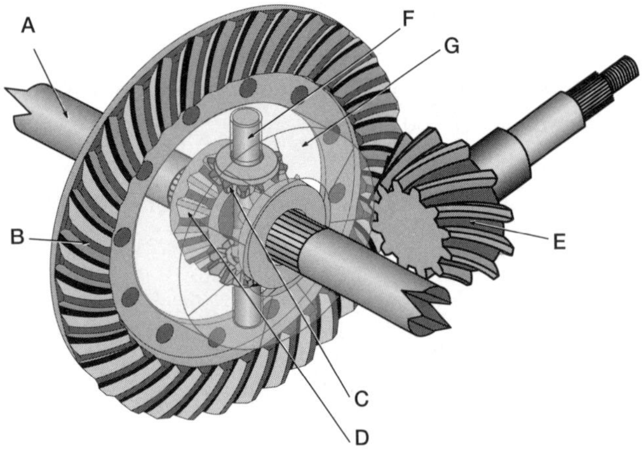

A. _____

B. _____

C. _____

D. _____

E. _____

F. _____

G. _____

3. Components of a clutch-style limited slip differential:

A. _____

B. _____

C. _____

D. _____

E. _____

F. _____

i. _____

ii. _____

Skill Drills

Place the skill drill steps in the correct order.

1. Inspecting Fluid Leakage:

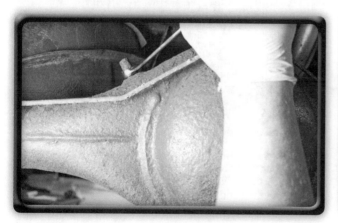

_____ **A.** Check and clean the breather or vent for any obstructions that may cause a pressure buildup to occur.

_____ **B.** Check the fluid level for lack of fluid or overfilling of the differential, as either one can indicate that a leak is present.

_____ **C.** Put the vehicle on an approved lift, and make sure it is secure. Visually inspect around the housing where the axle seats for any seepage.

_____ **D.** Inspect the pinion flange for any seepage.

_____ **E.** If necessary, remove the rear wheels and install a dial indicator on the axle flange to check for any distortion.

_____ **F.** Check the differential rear cover for a leaking gasket, if so equipped, and tighten if loose or replace as necessary.

2. Inspecting Half-Shaft Components:

_____ **A.** Apply the lubrication grease that comes with the new CV joint. Tighten the boot clamp to ensure that grease will not be lost. This applies to both sides of the half-shaft. Reinstall the half-shaft, following the manufacturer's guidelines.

_____ **B.** Clamp the entire half-shaft into a soft-jawed vise, and make sure it is secure. Remove the retaining clamps from the CV boot. Slide the boot down the shaft, paying attention to the condition of the boot.

_____ **C.** Wipe out as much grease as possible to be able to access the retaining ring from the CV joint itself. If there is a retaining ring present, remove the retaining ring with the appropriate tool. When the retaining ring is removed, remove the CV joint from the half-shaft, and inspect the splines on the end of the half-shaft. This also applies to the other end of the half-shaft.

_____ **D.** Inspect the old joint to gain an accurate assessment of the failure to prevent a reoccurrence of this failure. Reinstall the new CV joint onto the shaft splines as required.

3. Inspecting the Ring Gear and Measuring Runout:

_____ **A.** Rotate the ring gear slowly, paying attention to the dial, and compare the reading with specifications. Determine any necessary actions.

_____ **B.** Clean off the flat side of the ring gear to remove any excess oil. Attach a dial indicator to the differential housing near the area of the ring gear. Zero out the indicator so an accurate reading can be taken.

_____ **C.** Rotate the ring gear by installing a socket and a ratchet to the pinion companion flange nut. Load the ring gear up by wedging a screwdriver or equivalent in order to get an accurate reading.

4. Removing, Inspecting, and Reinstalling the Drive Pinion:

_____ **A.** Install the new bearings (and any necessary shims), using the press, and make sure they are seated correctly.

_____ **B.** Install the bearing splitter on the differential case bearings, and press these off using a press.

_____ **C.** Remove the pinion bearing by installing it in a press with a bearing splitter. Pump the handle and watch the bearing start to move and come off.

_____ **D.** Install the new pinion bearing (and any proper shims) by pressing the new bearing back on in the same fashion.

5. Adjusting Backlash of a Removable Carrier Differential:

_____ **A.** Thread the bearing adjusting nuts into the cap and housing threads, being careful not to cross-thread the adjusters (slight bearing preload for test).

_____ **B.** Attach a dial indicator to the housing. Set the dial indicator on the ring gear teeth, and zero out the dial indicator. Rock the ring gear back and forth, and take a measurement.

_____ **C.** Snug the bolts on the bearing caps.

_____ **D.** Install the ring gear/differential assembly and bearing cones and caps.

_____ **E.** Set the backlash to the manufacturer's specifications by alternately turning the adjuster nuts until the reading falls into the manufacturer's reading. Torque the bearing cap bolts to specifications.

Review Questions

_____ **1.** All of the following statements describing rear-wheel drive systems are true *except*:
   A. the ring and pinion gear set allows the transfer of power 90 degrees.
   B. the engine and transmission are transversely mounted at the front.
   C. drive from the engine is transmitted to a rear axle assembly by a propeller shaft.
   D. splines of the slip yoke mate to the splines on the transmission output shaft.

_____ **2.** Choose the correct statement.
   A. Most front-engine front-wheel drive vehicles use a longitudinal-mounted engine.
   B. Front-wheel drive power reaches the rear wheels through the transaxle.
   C. In a transverse-mounted engine, the front of the engine is facing the front of the vehicle.
   D. Power is transmitted in a straight line from the engine through the transaxle and out to the front axles.

_____ **3.** What is done to prevent twisting of long driveshafts from the torque output?
   A. Thicker metal is used.
   B. It is held in place by reinforcements.
   C. The length of the tube is decreased.
   D. Two or more sections may be used.

_____ **4.** The front section of the two-piece driveshaft is supported at its rear end by a:
   A. differential bearing.
   B. carrier bearing.
   C. U-joint.
   D. pocket bearing.

_____ **5.** Which of the following axles uses a single roller bearing between the hub and the outside of the axle housing?
   A. Semi-floating axle
   B. Full floating axle
   C. Floating axle
   D. Three-quarter floating axle

_____ **6.** Choose the correct statement.
   A. The driveshafts are connected directly to the final drive gears inside the transaxle.
   B. Half-shafts have an inner and an outer CV joint.
   C. Front-wheel drive transaxle typically places the final drive directly in the center of the vehicle.
   D. The intermediate shaft makes it so that both half-shafts are of different length from left to right.

_____ **7.** All of the following statements with respect to universal joints are true *except*:
  A. needle bearings fit between the ends of the cross and the caps, allowing the caps to rotate smoothly.
  B. in Hooke's joints, change in the angular velocity increases as the angle of the joint decreases.
  C. a double Cardan joint is considered as a CV joint under normal drive line angles.
  D. the ball-and-socket assembly keeps each Cardan joint at an equal angle, thereby canceling the change in velocity.

_____ **8.** Which type of joint has an inner race, six steel ball bearings, a bearing cage, and an outer race?
  A. Rzeppa joint
  B. Fixed-type joint
  C. Tulip joint
  D. Universal joint

_____ **9.** Choose the correct statement.
  A. The differential assembly provides the final gear reduction necessary for drivetrain operation.
  B. The differential assembly takes the power from the transmission and sends it to the wheels.
  C. The differential assembly is housed within the final drive assembly.
  D. The differential assembly is another name for the complete final drive assembly.

_____ **10.** All of the following statements referring to limited slip differentials are true *except*:
  A. the limited slip differential gives normal differential action and permits the outer wheel to turn faster than the inner wheel.
  B. the clutch-style limited slip differential uses a multi-plate clutch pack between each side gear and the differential case.
  C. the Torsen differential is to multiply the torque available from the wheel that is losing traction and turn it over to the slower turning wheel with better traction.
  D. helical-geared limited slip differentials do not respond very quickly to changes in traction.

ASE Technician A/Technician B Style Questions

_____ **1.** Tech A says that axle seals are a common source of solid axle fluid leaks. Tech B says that pinion seals are a common source of solid axle fluid leaks. Who is correct?
  A. Tech A
  B. Tech B
  C. Both A and B
  D. Neither A nor B

_____ **2.** Tech A says that the angle of the rear axle assembly companion flange should be perpendicular to the transmission output shaft. Tech B says that U-joints should be 45 degrees out of phase from one another to minimize vibration. Who is correct?
  A. Tech A
  B. Tech B
  C. Both A and B
  D. Neither A nor B

_____ **3.** Tech A says that a driveshaft center bearing is used on a vehicle with a short driveshaft. Tech B says that a driveshaft center bearing has a rubber insert that can deteriorate. Who is correct?
  A. Tech A
  B. Tech B
  C. Both A and B
  D. Neither A nor B

_____ **4.** Tech A says that if a CV boot is torn, it can typically be replaced without replacing the entire joint or shaft. Tech B says that worn CV joints can make a clicking noise when driving while making a tight turn. Who is correct?
  A. Tech A
  B. Tech B
  C. Both A and B
  D. Neither A nor B

Chapter 34 Driveshafts, Axles, and Final Drives

345

5. Tech A says that the gear tooth contact pattern can be taken using Prussian blue. Tech B says that the convex side of the ring gear is the coast side. Who is correct?
   A. Tech A
   B. Tech B
   C. Both A and B
   D. Neither A nor B

6. Tech A says that excessive ring gear runout could be the result of debris caught between the ring gear and the differential case during assembly. Tech B says that excessive ring gear runout could indicate bad bearings on the differential case housing. Who is correct?
   A. Tech A
   B. Tech B
   C. Both A and B
   D. Neither A nor B

7. Tech A says that the clutch-style limited slip differential uses a multi-plate clutch pack between each side gear and the differential case. Tech B says that if the clutch discs are worn, rotating torque will be higher than specifications. Who is correct?
   A. Tech A
   B. Tech B
   C. Both A and B
   D. Neither A nor B

8. Tech A says that pinion bearing preload is measured with a dial indicator. Tech B says that pinion bearing preload positions the bearings such that the pinion gear is held firmly in place but still allows smooth rotation of the gear. Who is correct?
   A. Tech A
   B. Tech B
   C. Both A and B
   D. Neither A nor B

9. Tech A says that on the full floating axle, there are two tapered roller bearings between the hub and the outside of the axle housing. Tech B says that a semi-floating axle, the axle supports the weight of the vehicle and is also subject to bending forces as the vehicle corners. Who is correct?
   A. Tech A
   B. Tech B
   C. Both A and B
   D. Neither A nor B

10. Tech A says that CV joints can make a clicking or popping noise when they are going bad. Tech B says that U-joints are typically used on FWD axles to provide torque through all angles of steering. Who is correct?
    A. Tech A
    B. Tech B
    C. Both A and B
    D. Neither A nor B

35 Four-Wheel Drive/ All-Wheel Drive

At the start of each chapter you'll find the NATEF Tasks, Knowledge Objectives, and Skills Objectives from the textbook. These are your objectives as you make your way through the exercises in this workbook and the chapter in your textbook. The following activities have been designed to help you refresh your knowledge of the material in this chapter.

NATEF Tasks

- N35001 Diagnose noise, vibration, and unusual steering concerns; determine needed action. (MAST)
- N35002 Identify concerns related to variations in tire circumference and/or final drive ratios. (AST/MAST)
- N35003 Diagnose, test, adjust, and/or replace electrical/electronic components of four-wheel drive systems. (MAST)
- N35004 Inspect, adjust, and repair shifting controls (mechanical, electrical, and vacuum), bushings, mounts, levers, and brackets. (AST/MAST)
- N35005 Disassemble, service, and reassemble transfer case and components. (MAST)
- N35006 Inspect locking hubs; determine needed action. (AST/MAST)

Knowledge Objectives

After reading this chapter you will be able to:

- K35001 Describe the purpose, function, and difference between four-wheel drive and all-wheel drive systems.
- K35002 Describe four-wheel drive layout.
- K35003 Describe all-wheel drive layout.
- K35004 Describe the purpose and function of 4WD and AWD transfer cases.
- K35005 Describe the purpose and function of the 4WD transfer case.
- K35006 Describe the purpose and function of the AWD transfer case.
- K35007 Describe the purpose and function of 4WD driveshafts, axles, and locking hubs.
- K35008 Describe the purpose and function of 4WD driveshafts.
- K35009 Describe the purpose and function of drive axles.
- K35010 Describe the purpose and function of 4WD locking hubs.

Skills Objectives

- S35001 Perform diagnosis and repair on 4WD components.
- S35002 Remove and reinstall transfer case.

Matching

Match the following terms with the correct description or example.

A. Viscous coupling
B. Locking hubs
C. 4WD high range
D. Power take-off
E. 4WD low range

_____ 1. A device attached to the transmission that is gear driven and can be used to run accessories such as winches and towing equipment.

_____ 2. A silicone clutch assembly used in AWD differentials to provide a slight amount of differential action for control of axle rotational speeds.

_____ 3. Four-wheel drive front axle hubs that are manually locked or unlocked by turning the knob on the hub.

_____ 4. Power is transmitted to the front and rear drive axles at normal drive speed.

_____ 5. A power transfer option that provides a gear reduction inside the transfer case and results in higher torque to the front and rear drive axles.

Multiple Choice

Read each item carefully, and then select the best response.

_____ **1.** A _____ is used to move power from the transfer case to the front and rear drive axles.
   A. driveshaft
   B. differential
   C. power take-off
   D. viscous coupling

_____ **2.** Identify the power transfer option that sends power only to the rear wheels.
   A. Neutral
   B. Two-wheel drive
   C. 4WD high range
   D. 4WD low range

_____ **3.** Identify the power transfer option in which no power is transmitted to either axle.
   A. 4WD high range
   B. Neutral
   C. Two-wheel drive
   D. 4WD low range

_____ **4.** In part-time 4WD vehicles, differentials are _____.
   A. fitted to the rear axle assembly
   B. fitted to the front axle assembly
   C. fitted to both the front and rear axle assemblies
   D. replaced by a torque convertor

_____ **5.** Identify the component that allows the rear wheels of a 4WD vehicle to rotate at different speeds when the vehicle is turning, while continuing to transmit an equal turning effort to each wheel.
   A. Sprag clutches
   B. Torque converters
   C. U-joints
   D. Differential gears

_____ **6.** A power transfer unit is used on vehicles that are primarily _____.
   A. FWD
   B. RWD
   C. 2WD
   D. AWD

_____ **7.** The transfer case is typically bolted to the _____.
   A. front driveshaft
   B. locking hub
   C. side of the transaxle
   D. rear of the transmission

_____ **8.** The power take-off is typically bolted to the _____.
   A. front driveshaft
   B. locking hub
   C. side of the transaxle
   D. rear of the transmission

_____ **9.** A(n) _____ locks the driveshafts together using a mechanical sleeve that slides over the splines on both shafts.
   A. mechanical differential lock
   B. electromagnetic clutch
   C. traction control system
   D. viscous coupler

_____ **10.** Identify a true statement with respect to a mechanical differential lock.
   A. It allows for little slippage in the transfer case.
   B. It should be disengaged before driving on high-traction surfaces.
   C. It should not be used on slippery surfaces.
   D. It is not effective in low-traction conditions.

True/False

If you believe the statement to be more true than false, write the letter "T" in the space provided. If you believe the statement to be more false than true, write the letter "F."

_____ **1.** The ability to drive all of the wheels enhances a vehicle's ability to connect the engine's power to the ground.

_____ **2.** AWD used in conjunction with traction control and stability control enhances acceleration and handling characteristics when driving aggressively.

_____ **3.** 4WD low range should only be selected when driving at fast vehicle speeds.

_____ **4.** When making a turn, the front wheels of a vehicle travel the same distance as the rear wheels.

_____ **5.** The tasks performed by transfer cases and power take-off units are totally different.

_____ **6.** Gear drive transfer cases tend to be noisier than chain drives transfer cases.

_____ **7.** In AWD high range, the differential lock is disengaged.

_____ **8.** The Torsen style differential is very effective in low-traction conditions.

_____ **9.** Rear axles in 4WD vehicles are just like solid rear axles in 2WD vehicles.

_____ **10.** If the 4WD system is electronically controlled, typical diagnosis might start with connecting a scan tool and reading any current codes.

Fill in the Blank

Read each item carefully, and then complete the statement by filling in the missing word(s).

1. 4WD _____ _____ causes the vehicle to move slowly while the engine turns at a higher rpm.

2. In a four-wheel drive layout, to transfer power to the movable hubs, _____ - _____ must be used in the axle shafts that are splined to the hubs.

3. A transfer case is used on vehicles that are primarily _____.

4. The AWD transfer case is bolted to the output of the _____.

5. A(n) _____ _____ unit is used between the front and rear driveshafts to act as a limited slip differential and drive both axles if one is slipping.

6. The _____ _____ uses gears similar to the gears in final drives for splitting torque to each axle as long as the tires maintain traction.

7. In computer-controlled transmissions, the _____ _____ _____ manages line pressures, shift functions, etc., and even incorporates a self-healing adjustment capability.

8. _____ hubs disconnect the hubs from the axle shafts and prevent rotation of the FWD components.

9. Many manufacturers require the circumference of all tires to be within _____" of each other.

10. The number of teeth of the pinion and ring gear can be used to calculate the _____ _____ gear ratios.

Labeling

Label the following diagrams with the correct terms.

1. Components of a freewheeling hub assembly:

Free Position

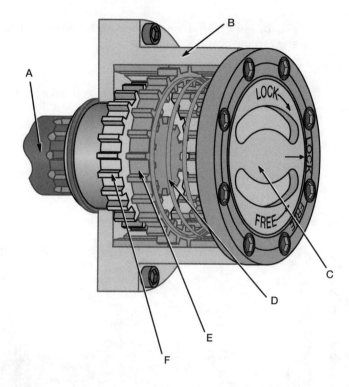

A. _____

B. _____

C. _____

D. _____

E. _____

F. _____

Skill Drills

Place the skill drill steps in the correct order.

1. Identifying Concerns Related to Variations in Tire Circumference and/or Final Drive Ratios:

_____ **A.** Check the differentials for correct ratios, which may require removal of the inspection cover. The number of teeth of the pinion and ring gear is often written on the ring gear's outer perimeter so that the ratio can be calculated.

_____ **B.** If necessary, measure the circumference of the tires and compare to each other. They should be within 0.25" (6.4 mm) of each other.

_____ **C.** If the vehicle is equipped with ABS and you can access the data stream, connect the appropriate scan tool and test-drive the vehicle. Compare each wheel speed sensor reading to the others. They should be within 0.2 mph (0.3 kph) of one another.

_____ **D.** Consult the manufacturer's service information for any necessary procedures to further diagnose the fault.

_____ **E.** Check all tires for mismatches or unusual wear, and set the tire pressures to specifications.

2. Inspecting, Adjusting, and Repairing Shifting Controls:

_____ **A.** Perform a visual inspection of all mechanical linkages or mounting brackets for any damage or excessive wear of bushings or grommets.

_____ **B.** Raise the vehicle with an approved vehicle hoist, and make sure it is secure. Check the manufacturer's publications for proper procedures for inspection of any special parts.

_____ **C.** Check for any codes that may be present by using a scan tool on the vehicle.

_____ **D.** Inspect any hoses that are dry rotted or cracked on any vacuum-operated components.

_____ **E.** Refer to the service information for proper diagnosis of any electrical components that are in question.

_____ **F.** Make any necessary adjustments to linkages or cables if they are loose or have been replaced.

_____ **G.** After all repairs have been made, road test the vehicle to ensure that it was repaired properly.

3. Reassembling the Transfer Case and Components:

_____ **A.** Reinstall the chain and driven sprocket.

_____ **B.** Reinstall the 4WD shift fork and collar into the case. Make sure the shift rod is installed in the correct position in the case.

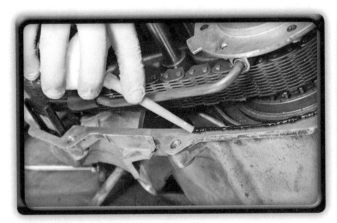

_____ **C.** Apply a thin bead of RTV to one case half. Reassemble the two halves of the case, and torque.

_____ **D.** Reinstall output flange yokes and torque to specification.

_____ **E.** Reinstall the planetary gear set into the case. Reinstall any snap rings holding the planetary gear set.

_____ **F.** Reinstall the output shaft into the case. Make sure the shift collars line up properly on the shaft.

_____ **G.** Reinstall the high/low shift fork and collar into the case.

_____ **H.** Reassemble the oil pump assembly and pickup tube.

_____ **I.** Reinstall all electrical sensors and switches.

Review Questions

_____ 1. Choose the correct statement.
   A. A transfer case is mounted to the front of the transmission.
   B. Driveshafts are used to move power from the transfer case to the front and rear drive axles.
   C. When making a turn, the rear wheels travel a greater distance than the front wheels.
   D. The ring and pinion gears allow the front wheels to rotate at different speeds.

_____ 2. Which of the following is a device designed to split the power from the transmission to both the front and the rear drive axles when four-wheel drive is selected?
   A. Clutch
   B. Transfer case
   C. Driveshaft
   D. CV joint

_____ 3. Which of these perform the same task of splitting power between the front and rear axles?
   A. Transfer cases and PTOs
   B. Output shaft and PTOs
   C. CV joints and PTOs
   D. Output shaft and CV joints

_____ 4. Choose the correct statement.
   A. Chain drive transfer cases tend to be noisier than gear drives.
   B. When the planetary gear carrier is in motion, a lower gear ratio results.
   C. Power comes into the transfer case directly from the engine flywheel and moves to the rear input shaft.
   D. The idler shaft contains two gears: a high-speed gear and a low-speed gear.

_____ 5. Which of the following devices squeezes the clutches together by applying a magnetic force on the clutch discs?
   A. Torsen-style clutch
   B. Mechanical differential lock
   C. Electromagnetic clutch
   D. Viscous coupling

_____ 6. All of the following statements are true _except_:
   A. axles may be either solid or half-shafts, depending on whether the vehicle uses an independent suspension or not.
   B. a viscous coupler uses two sets of clutch plates that are alternated front to back.
   C. the PTO determines when to switch from two-wheel drive to four-wheel drive.
   D. the degree of locking achieved depends on the severity of the wheel slippage occurring.

_____ 7. In four-wheel drive applications, which of the following components transfers the drive from the transfer case (torque splitter) to the final drive units at the front and rear axle assemblies?
   A. Driveshafts
   B. Drive axle
   C. Electromagnetic clutch
   D. Vacuum motor

_____ 8. All of the following statements are true _except_:
   A. when lock is selected on a manually locking hub, it acts on a sleeve.
   B. the sleeve slides in and out to lock the two splined components together.
   C. freewheeling hubs disconnect the hubs from the axle shafts and prevent rotation of the front-wheel drive components.
   D. in a four-wheel drive range, the drive is transmitted from the transfer case to the transmission.

_____ 9. Under which of these conditions must the driver get out of the vehicle and turn the locking hub knobs located on the front wheels to lock in the front drive axles?
   A. Hot weather conditions
   B. Dry weather conditions
   C. Inclement weather conditions
   D. Heavy traffic

_____ **10.** All of the following statements are true *except*:
   A. the automatic hub is factory installed on many newer vehicles.
   B. when four-wheel drive is activated, the front axle is not transmitting power.
   C. when "free" mode is selected, the compressed spring pushes the sleeve out of engagement.
   D. reversing the motion of the axle shafts will unbind the sleeve.

ASE Technician A/Technician B Style Questions

_____ **1.** Tech A says that when making a turn, the front wheels travel a greater distance than the rear wheels. Tech B says that in off-road conditions, differences in speed between the front and rear driveshafts can be absorbed through slippage of the tires on the ground. Who is correct?
   A. Tech A
   B. Tech B
   C. Both A and B
   D. Neither A nor B

_____ **2.** Tech A says that AWD vehicles have a differential in the middle of the drivetrain. Tech B says that many AWD vehicles incorporate a viscous clutch in the center differential. Who is correct?
   A. Tech A
   B. Tech B
   C. Both A and B
   D. Neither A nor B

_____ **3.** Tech A says that all front wheel hubs lock automatically. Tech B says that all front wheel hubs lock manually. Who is correct?
   A. Tech A
   B. Tech B
   C. Both A and B
   D. Neither A nor B

_____ **4.** Tech A says that some front differentials are operated by a vacuum motor. Tech B says that some front differentials are operated by electric motors. Who is correct?
   A. Tech A
   B. Tech B
   C. Both A and B
   D. Neither A nor B

_____ **5.** Tech A says that part-time 4WD does not use a transfer case. Tech B says that AWD vehicles can safely drive with all four wheels on pavement. Who is correct?
   A. Tech A
   B. Tech B
   C. Both A and B
   D. Neither A nor B

_____ **6.** Tech A says that constant-velocity joints are used on some 4WD vehicles. Tech B says that a slip joint is part of a driveshaft. Who is correct?
   A. Tech A
   B. Tech B
   C. Both A and B
   D. Neither A nor B

_____ **7.** Tech A says that electric actuators are used for things like engaging 4WD or locking the axles together. Tech B says that sensors send signals directly to electric actuators to cause them to operate. Who is correct?
   A. Tech A
   B. Tech B
   C. Both A and B
   D. Neither A nor B

_____ **8.** Tech A says that some transfer cases have a chain inside them to transfer torque to the wheels. Tech B says that some transfer cases have a belt inside them to transfer torque to the wheels. Who is correct?
   A. Tech A
   B. Tech B

      C. Both A and B

      D. Neither A nor B

_____ **9.** Tech A says that the PCM/TCM compensates for different size tires as long as the tires on the front match each other, and the tires on the rear match each other. Tech B says that many manufacturers require the circumference of ALL tires to be within 0.25" (6.4 mm) of each other. Who is correct?

      A. Tech A

      B. Tech B

      C. Both A and B

      D. Neither A nor B

_____ **10.** Tech A says that freewheeling hubs disconnect the hubs from the axle shafts. Tech B says that freewheeling hubs disconnect the wheels when steering around corners. Who is correct?

      A. Tech A

      B. Tech B

      C. Both A and B

      D. Neither A nor B

Wheels and Tires Theory

At the start of each chapter you'll find the NATEF Tasks, Knowledge Objectives, and Skills Objectives from the textbook. These are your objectives as you make your way through the exercises in this workbook and the chapter in your textbook. The following activities have been designed to help you refresh your knowledge of the material in this chapter.

NATEF Tasks

There are no NATEF tasks in this chapter.

Knowledge Objectives

After reading this chapter, you will be able to:

- K36001 Explain the principles of tire distortion and center of gravity.
- K36002 Describe the functions and features of wheels and tires.
- K36003 Describe purpose, function, and types of a wheel and wheel lug nuts/studs.
- K36004 Describe the components of a vehicle's tire.
- K36005 Decipher the tire markings on the sidewall of each tire.
- K36006 Describe the common safety features found on today's tires.
- K36007 Describe the purpose, function, and types of tire pressure monitoring systems.
- K36008 Describe the purpose and function of run-flat tires.
- K36009 Describe the purpose and function of self-sealing tires.
- K36010 Describe the purpose and function of space saver spare tires.

Skills Objectives

There are no Skills Objectives in this chapter.

Matching

Match the following terms with the correct description or example.

A. Centrifugal switch	F. Drop center
B. Aspect ratio	G. EH2 rim
C. Cornering force	H. Extended Mobility Technology
D. Casing plies	I. Flat seat without washer
E. Asymmetric tread pattern	J. Lug nuts

_____ 1. A tread pattern that differs on each side and is usually directional.

_____ 2. A network of cords that give the tire shape and strength; also known as casing cords.

_____ 3. The force between the tread and the road surface as a vehicle turns.

_____ 4. The ratio of sidewall height to section width of a tire.

_____ 5. A wheel design with part of the center section of the wheel a smaller diameter than the rest.

_____ 6. A switch that is only activated when centrifugal forces are placed on a vehicle.

_____ 7. Tires with thick sidewalls that allow the tire to be driven on even when it has no air pressure.

_____ 8. Nuts that secure the wheel onto the wheel studs.

_____ 9. The specialized rim design that is used with some run-flat tires.

_____ 10. A type of lug nut that is flat where it bolts to the wheel.

Multiple Choice

Read each item carefully, and then select the best response.

_____ **1.** Identify the part of the wheel that the tire seals against.
  A. Carcass
  B. Bead seat
  C. Inner liner
  D. Capply

_____ **2.** Identify the tread pattern that is designed to rotate in only one direction and has one side that must face outward to ensure that the tire performs as designed under operating conditions.
  A. Directional and asymmetric tread pattern
  B. Directional tread pattern
  C. Symmetric tread pattern
  D. Nondirectional tread pattern

_____ **3.** _____ is a condition in which the plane of the hub mounting surface is positioned toward the brake side
  or back of the wheel centerline.
  A. Positive offset
  B. Zero offset
  C. Centerline offset
  D. Negative offset

_____ **4.** Identify the condition in which a vehicle's front slip angles are larger than the rear slip angles.
  A. Neutral steer
  B. Understeer
  C. Oversteer
  D. Negative steer

_____ **5.** _____ is a condition in which the plane of the hub mounting surface is positioned toward the outside or front of the wheel centerline.
  A. Positive offset
  B. Zero offset
  C. Centerline offset
  D. Negative offset

_____ **6.** A tire with two or more layers of casing plies and cord loops running radially from bead to bead is called a _____.
  A. radial tire
  B. bias tire
  C. metal tire
  D. solid tire

_____ **7.** Identify the part of the wheel that is the outer circular lip of the metal on which the inside edge of the tire is mounted.
  A. Capply
  B. Bead seat
  C. Carcass
  D. Rim

_____ **8.** The pressure on the wheel that pushes it toward the outside or inside of the rim as the vehicle makes a turn is called the _____.
  A. cornering force
  B. side force
  C. centrifugal force
  D. rolling force

_____ **9.** _____ strength is a measure of how strong a material is as it is being pulled apart.
  A. Compressive
  B. Frictional
  C. Shear
  D. Tensile

_____ **10.** Identify the standardized grading system that indicates how well a tire will maintain contact with the road surface when wet.

  A. Speed rating
  B. Temperature grade
  C. Traction grade
  D. Load index

True/False

If you believe the statement to be more true than false, write the letter "T" in the space provided. If you believe the statement to be more false than true, write the letter "F."

_____ **1.** In radial tires, ply rating denotes the actual number of plies.

_____ **2.** The air pressure inside a tire gives the tire shape when the weight of the vehicle is sitting on it.

_____ **3.** Tires on many vehicles are inflated to about 42 pounds per square inch (psi).

_____ **4.** Without the resistance created by friction, side force will cause a vehicle to continue in a straight line.

_____ **5.** Cornering force is indirectly proportional to slip angle.

_____ **6.** Slip angles depend on the weight distribution within the vehicle, the wheelbase, the tire track, and the overall length of the vehicle.

_____ **7.** Acceleration puts more weight on the front wheels, while deceleration puts more weight on the rear wheels of a vehicle.

_____ **8.** The actual position of a vehicle's center of gravity depends on the location of the engine and transmission.

_____ **9.** Wheel offset can be only be either positive or negative.

_____ **10.** Most lug nuts and studs are manufactured as right-hand threads.

Fill in the Blank

Read each item carefully, and then complete the statement by filling in the missing word(s).

  1. In a wheel with negative offset, _____ _____ refers to the side of the wheel that
is farthest from the drop center.

  2. A(n) _____ _____ tire is constructed in a latticed, crisscrossing structure, with alternate plies crossing over each other and laid with the cord angles in opposite directions.

  3. A(n) _____ TPMS is a type of automated tire pressure monitoring system that measures tire pressure and possibly temperature via a sensor installed inside each wheel.

  4. A(n) _____ TPMS is a type of automated tire pressure monitoring system that uses the anti-lock braking system of a vehicle to measure the difference in the rotational speed of the four wheels, to determine tire pressure.

  5. _____ tread pattern is nonspecific and allows the tire to be placed on any wheel of a vehicle.

  6. _____ _____ _____ is the diameter of the imaginary circle drawn through the center of the wheel bolt holes.

  7. _____ _____ is a rating system that denotes the number of belt layers, or plies, that make up the tire carcass.

  8. _____ _____ is the distance across the rim from one rim flange to the other.

  9. A tire's sideways distortion that makes a vehicle follow a path at an angle to the direction the road wheel is pointing is called the _____ _____.

  10. _____ tread pattern is the same tread pattern on both sides of the tire and is typically nondirectional.

Labeling

Label the following diagrams with the correct terms.

1. Types of tire inflation:

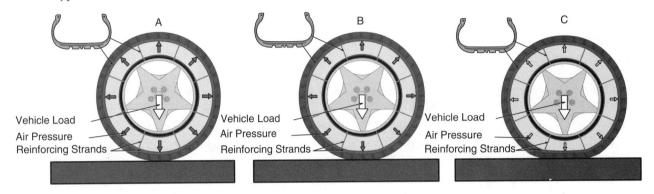

A. _____

B. _____

C. _____

2. Types of wheel offset:

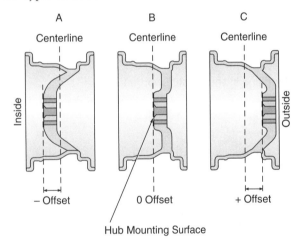

A. _____

B. _____

C. _____

3. Types of wheel retaining stud and nuts:

A. _____

B. _____

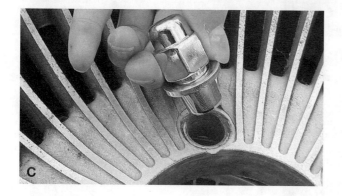

C. _____

D. _____

4. Parts of a tire:

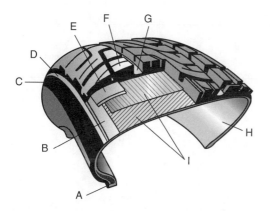

A. _____

B. _____

C. _____

D. _____

E. _____

F. _____

G. _____

H. _____

I. _____

5. Types of tread designs:

A. _____

B. _____

C. _____

D. _____

E. _____

Review Questions

_____ **1.** All of the following statements are true *except*:
   A. the front slip angles are larger than the rear slip angles in an understeer condition.
   B. the rear slip angles are larger than the front slip angles in an understeer condition.
   C. the rear slip angles are larger than the front slip angles in an oversteer condition.
   D. The front and the rear tires have equal amounts of slip angles in a neutral steer condition.

_____ **2.** In a typical rear-wheel drive vehicle, the weight distribution is approximately:
   A. 25% aft and 75% fore.
   B. 60% fore and 40% aft.
   C. 40% fore and 60% aft.
   D. 25% fore and 75% aft.

_____ **3.** Which type of rims have a slight ridge, or hump, at the inside edge of the bead ledges that helps to hold the tire beads in place when the tire goes flat?
   A. Multi-piece alloy rims
   B. Spinning rims
   C. Semi-drop well rims
   D. Safety-type drop-center rims

_____ **4.** Which type of lug nut is placed toward the rim and fits into a matching taper in the rim to help center the wheel on the lug studs?
   A. Tapered seat
   B. Flat seat with washer
   C. Flat seat without washer
   D. Ball seat

_____ **5.** Which of the following tread designs actually pumps water out from under the tire, bringing it in direct contact with the surface of the road?
   A. Symmetric tread pattern
   B. Asymmetric tread pattern
   C. Directional tread pattern
   D. Nondirectional tread pattern

_____ **6.** Which of the following speed rating designations is rated for speeds above 149 mph (240 kph)?
   A. V
   B. Z
   C. Y
   D. W

_____ **7.** Which of the following allows a vehicle to be driven for a reasonable amount of time when the tire pressure is low or empty?
  A. TPMS
  B. Run-flat tire
  C. Self-sealing tire
  D. Space-saving tire

_____ **8.** All of the following statements are true in the case of TPMS *except*:
  A. it monitors the tires for low air pressure and alerts the driver when pressure in one or more tires is lower than the designated thresholds.
  B. the TPMS adds air to tires which has slow leaks so that tire pressure is maintained.
  C. the indirect TPMS utilizes the anti-lock braking systems (ABS) to measure the difference in the rotational speed of the four wheels to detect low pressure in tires.
  D. the direct TPMS uses a sensor with an antenna in each wheel that wirelessly relays the information it senses to receivers located within the vehicle.

_____ **9.** All of the following statements are true in describing run-flat tires *except*:
  A. run-flat tires are not compatible with conventional rims.
  B. run-flat tires enable the driver to continue the journey within specified speed and distance limits.
  C. run-flat tires support the vehicle's weight when it is rotating with a total air loss.
  D. run-flat tire sidewalls are normally much thinner than the sidewalls of traditional tires.

_____ **10.** A tire constructed with a flexible and malleable lining inside the tire around the inner tubeless membrane is known as a:
  A. bias-ply tire.
  B. radial tire.
  C. self-sealing tire.
  D. tubeless tire.

ASE Technician A/Technician B Style Questions

_____ **1.** Tech A says that most wheels have a drop center or deep well that is used in installing a tire on the wheel. Tech B says that the drop center or deep well is used to prevent the tire from coming off the wheel in the case of low tire pressure. Who is correct?
  A. Tech A
  B. Tech B
  C. Both Tech A and B
  D. Neither Tech A nor B

_____ **2.** Tech A says that all wheels must be torqued to prevent wheels from loosening up and falling off. Tech B says that all wheels must be torqued to prevent over-tightening, which can weaken lug studs and warp brake rotors. Who is correct?
  A. Tech A
  B. Tech B
  C. Both Tech A and B
  D. Neither Tech A nor B

_____ **3.** Tech A says that tires are marked with a date code listing the date the tires should be discarded. Tech B says that any tires with a three-digit date code should be discarded because they are too old to be safely in service. Who is correct?
  A. Tech A
  B. Tech B
  C. Both Tech A and B
  D. Neither Tech A nor B

_____ **4.** Tech A says that a TPMS system can save fuel over time. Tech B says that a TPMS will help prevent blowouts. Who is correct?
  A. Tech A
  B. Tech B
  C. Both Tech A and B
  D. Neither Tech A nor B

_____ **5.** Tech A says that the center of gravity on a vehicle is located at the vehicle body's lowest point. Tech B says that having a low center of gravity makes a vehicle handle better. Who is correct?
A. Tech A
B. Tech B
C. Both Tech A and B
D. Neither Tech A nor B

_____ **6.** Tech A says that oversteer is when the front slip angles are larger than the rear slip angles. Tech B says that understeer is when the rear slip angles are larger than the front slip angles. Who is correct?
A. Tech A
B. Tech B
C. Both Tech A and B
D. Neither Tech A nor B

_____ **7.** Tech A says that the "P" in "P225/70, R15" means "the tire's inflation pressure in kPa." Tech B says that the "T" in "T135R16" means "temporary." Who is correct?
A. Tech A
B. Tech B
C. Both Tech A and B
D. Neither Tech A nor B

_____ **8.** Tech A says that a direct TPMS system uses a pressure sensor located in each wheel. Tech B says that an indirect TPMS system uses wires to connect the pressure sensor located in each wheel to the PCM. Who is correct?
A. Tech A
B. Tech B
C. Both Tech A and B
D. Neither Tech A nor B

_____ **9.** Tech A says that radial ply tires have much more flexible sidewalls than bias-ply tires because of their construction. Tech B says that bias-ply tires have a more durable construction than radial tires. Who is correct?
A. Tech A
B. Tech B
C. Both Tech A and B
D. Neither Tech A nor B

_____ **10.** Tech A says that most lug nuts and studs are right-hand threaded, which means they tighten when turned clockwise. Tech B says that some lug nuts and studs are left-handed, which means they tighten when turned counterclockwise. Who is correct?
A. Tech A
B. Tech B
C. Both Tech A and B
D. Neither Tech A nor B

Servicing Wheels and Tires

At the start of each chapter you'll find the NATEF Tasks, Knowledge Objectives, and Skills Objectives from the textbook. These are your objectives as you make your way through the exercises in this workbook and the chapter in your text-book. The following activities have been designed to help you refresh your knowledge of the material in this chapter.

NATEF Tasks

- N37001 Inspect tire condition; identify tire wear patterns; check for correct tire size and application (load and speed ratings), and adjust air pressure as listed on the tire information placard/label; determine needed action. (MLR/AST/MAST)
- N37002 Rotate tires according to manufacturer's recommendation including vehicles equipped with tire pressure monitoring systems (TPMS). (MLR/AST/MAST)
- N37003 Dismount, inspect, and remount tire on wheel; balance wheel and tire assembly. (MLR/AST/MAST)
- N37004 Demonstrate knowledge of steps required to remove and replace sensors in a tire pressure monitoring system (TPMS) including relearn procedure. (MLR/AST/MAST)
- N37005 Dismount, inspect, and remount tire on wheel equipped with tire pressure monitoring system sensor. (MLR/AST/MAST)
- N37006 Diagnose wheel/tire vibration, shimmy, and noise; determine needed action. (AST/MAST)
- N37007 Diagnose tire pull problems; determine needed action. (AST/MAST)
- N37008 Inspect tire and wheel assembly for air loss; perform needed action. (MLR/AST/MAST)
- N37009 Repair tire following vehicle manufacturer approved procedure. (MLR/AST/MAST)
- N37010 Measure wheel, tire, axle flange, and hub runout; determine needed action. (AST/MAST)
- N37011 Identify indirect and direct tire pressure monitoring system (TPMS); verify operation of instrument panel lamps. (MLR/AST/MAST)

Knowledge Objectives

After reading this chapter, you will be able to:

- K37001 Describe the types of tire maintenance tasks and their purpose.
- K37002 Describe the purpose and process of maintaining proper tire inflation.
- K37003 Describe the purpose and process of rotating tires.
- K37004 Describe the purpose and process of balancing wheels.
- K37005 Describe the purpose and process of maintaining TPMS sensors.
- K37006 Identify the tools used for servicing tires.
- K37007 Describe some of the common issues with wheels and tires.

Skills Objectives

After reading this chapter, you will be able to:

- S37001 Perform tire maintenance and repair procedures.
- S37002 Perform wheel and tire diagnosis.

Matching

Match the following terms with the correct description or example.

- **A.** Static imbalance
- **B.** Bar
- **C.** Road force imbalance
- **D.** Dynamic imbalance
- **E.** Match mounting
- **F.** Tire inflation pressure

_____ 1. Causes the wheel assembly to turn inward and outward with each half revolution.

_____ 2. The process of matching up the tire's highest point with the rim's lowest point.

_____ 3. Results from a heavy spot on a tire.

_____ 4. Occurs when the wheel or tire is not concentric or when the tire's sidewall has uneven stiffness.

_____ 5. A metric unit of measure for pressure.

_____ 6. The amount of air pressure in the tire that provides it with load-carrying capacity.

Multiple Choice

Read each item carefully, and then select the best response.

_____ 1. _____ is the process of matching the tire's lightest point with the rim's heaviest point.
- **A.** Match mounting
- **B.** Weight matching
- **C.** Static mounting
- **D.** Dynamic matching

_____ 2. The proper tire pressure for a vehicle is measured in _____.
- **A.** psi
- **B.** N/mm
- **C.** Watts
- **D.** cubic centimeter

_____ 3. Identify a true statement with respect to nitrogen fills.
- **A.** Nitrogen permeates rubber at a much faster rate than air.
- **B.** Nitrogen reacts with the rubber to improve sealing.
- **C.** Nitrogen increases the possibility of blowouts.
- **D.** Nitrogen does not cause rust and corrosion on steel or aluminum.

_____ 4. To meet the standards for proper nitrogen fill, the nitrogen level in the tire must be at _____ or higher.
- **A.** 85%
- **B.** 80%
- **C.** 95%
- **D.** 99%

_____ 5. What is the color of valve stem caps used to identify nitrogen-filled tires?
- **A.** Black
- **B.** Green
- **C.** Red
- **D.** Gray

_____ 6. Generally, it is recommended to rotate the tires on vehicles approximately every _____.
- **A.** 5000 miles
- **B.** 10000 miles
- **C.** 15000 miles
- **D.** 1000 miles

_____ 7. At what speed will an out-of-balance tire usually cause the vehicle to vibrate?
- **A.** 90 and 110 mph
- **B.** 10 and 30 mph
- **C.** 110 and 140 mph
- **D.** 50 and 70 mph

_____ 8. _____ imbalance occurs when the wheel or tire is not concentric.
- **A.** Dynamic
- **B.** Static
- **C.** Road force
- **D.** Radial

_____ 9. When dynamically balancing a tire using an off-car balancer, _____.
- **A.** the tire is run up against a roller
- **B.** the wheel and tire assembly is mounted on the balancer

      C. the tire's imbalance is measured when the tire is stationary

      D. the width of the tire is not taken into consideration

_____ **10.** Weights come in _____ increments.

      A. 5-gram

      B. 20-gram

      C. 10-gram

      D. 15-gram

True/False

If you believe the statement to be more true than false, write the letter "T" in the space provided. If you believe the statement to be more false than true, write the letter "F."

_____ **1.** Match mounting reduces a tire's radial runout.

_____ **2.** The goal of a wheel alignment is to restore proper handling along with extending the life of the tires.

_____ **3.** Tire manufacturers list the minimum safe inflation pressure on the tire sidewall.

_____ **4.** The term "cold" related to tire pressure reading relates to the outside temperature a tire is in.

_____ **5.** Tire manufacturers mandate the use of nitrogen as an inflation gas.

_____ **6.** Static balancing does not take into consideration that the tire has width.

_____ **7.** Static balancing can also be used to balance tires on today's vehicles.

_____ **8.** A wheel that is perfectly in balance statically and dynamically cannot feel like an out-of-balance tire.

_____ **9.** It is good practice to always use new wheel weights when balancing a tire.

_____ **10.** Generally, a damaged TPMS sensor will require the entire TPMS sensor unit to be replaced.

Fill in the Blank

Read each item carefully, and then complete the statement by filling in the missing word(s).

1. _____ imbalance tends to cause the tire to move purely up and down.

2. A(n) _____ _____ gauge is used to measure the air pressure within a tire.

3. Vehicle manufacturers determine the tire inflation pressure based on the vehicle's designed
_____ _____ and _____ _____.

4. To get an accurate pressure reading, the tires must be checked when _____.

5. _____ _____ _____ is the removal and relocation of each tire/wheel assembly on the vehicle.

6. _____ imbalance can cause the tire to move side to side as well as up and down.

7. _____ valve cores should not be used in TPMS sensors that use an aluminum valve stem.

8. One bar is equivalent to _____ psi.

9. Recommended tire pressures are located on the vehicle's _____ _____.

10. Most tire manufacturers indicate the tire's highest point with a _____ dot and the tire's lightest point with a _____ dot.

Labeling

Label the following diagrams with the correct terms.

1. Types of tire rotation sequence:

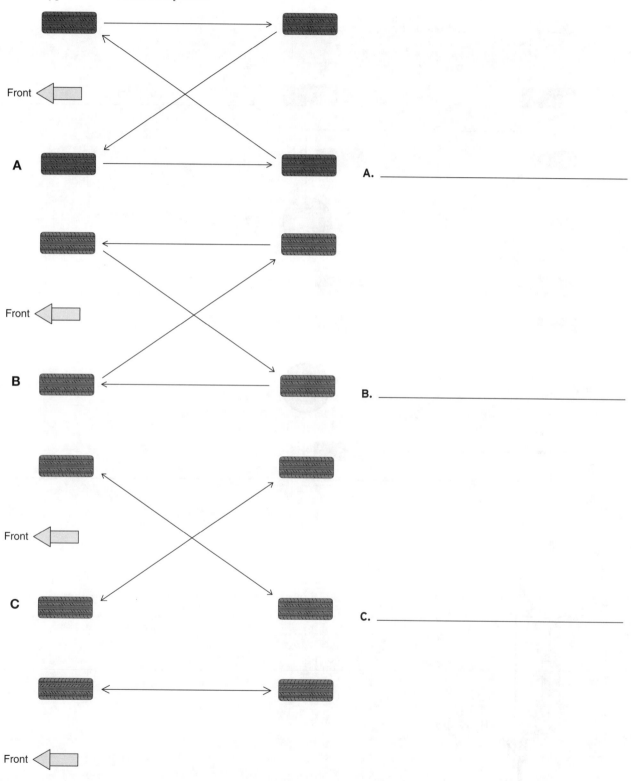

A. _____

B. _____

C. _____

D. _____

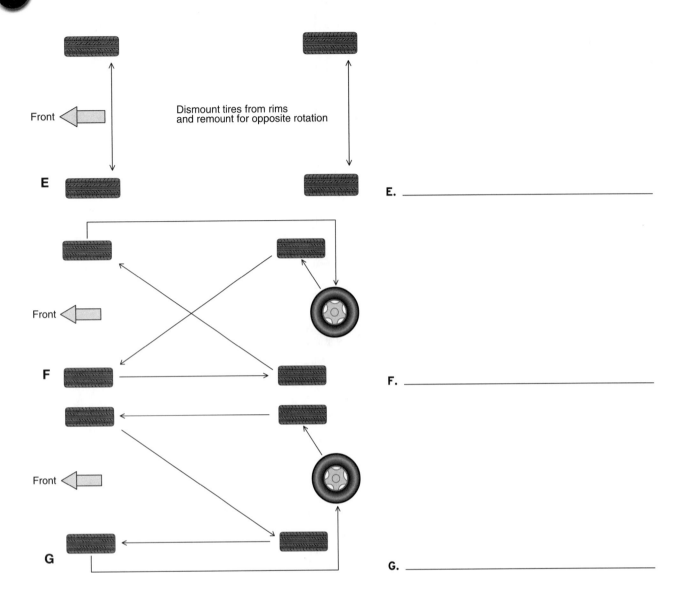

Dismount tires from rims
and remount for opposite rotation

Front

E

E. _____

Front

F

F. _____

Front

G

G. _____

2. Types of imbalance:

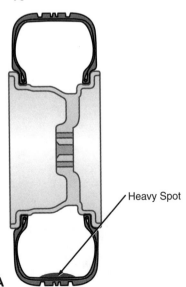

Heavy Spot

A

A. _____

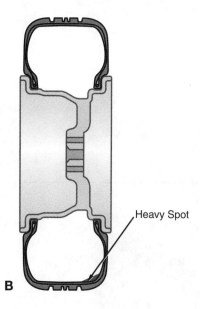

Heavy Spot

B

B. _____

3. Tire repair tools and equipment:

A

A. _____

B

B. _____

C

C. _____

D

D. _____

E

E. _____

F

F. _____

G. _____

H. _____

I. _____

J. _____

K. _____

L. _____

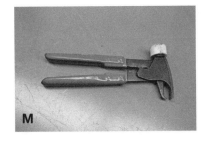

M. _____

N. _____

4. Types of tire pressure gauges:

A.

B. _____

Skill Drills

Place the skill drill steps in the correct order.

1. Using a Tire Pressure Gauge:

_____ **A.** Reset the dial pressure gauge to zero by pressing the button on the neck of the dial.

_____ **B.** Repeat the procedure for all wheels. Remember to replace the valve cap on each wheel as you go.

_____ **C.** Remove the valve cap from the tire valve. Fit the pencil gauge to the valve. Make sure the graduated sleeve is seated into the gauge body, and then push the tire gauge chuck firmly onto the head of the valve. Read the scale and add up the numbers.

_____ **D.** Attach the dial pressure gauge to the top of the valve. Adjust your hand pressure and angle so that no air escapes from the valve. When the needle has jumped, remove the dial pressure gauge from the valve, and read the dial.

2. Checking for Tire Wear Patterns:

_____ **A.** Check the tread wear patterns with the vehicle's service information to indicate the types of wear that have occurred.

_____ **B.** Spin the wheel and see if it is running true. If it is wobbling as it rotates, report it to your supervisor.

_____ **C.** Check the tread wear depth. Inspect the wear indicator bars. Tires should have at least 1/16" (2 mm) of tread remaining. If the tread is worn down to that level or below, the tires are unserviceable and must be replaced.

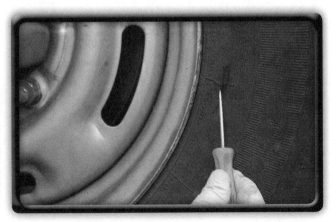

_____ **D.** Inspect the sidewalls of the tires for signs of weather cracking and gouges from impacts with blunt objects. Carefully examine the tread area for separation. This is usually identified as bubble sunder the tread area.

_____ **E.** Look for signs of wear on all tires, including the spare. Check the air pressure in the tires.

_____ **F.** Inspect the tires for embedded objects in treads and remove them. If anything penetrates the tread, mark the hole with a tire crayon.

3. Rotating the Tires:

_____ **A.** Remove the tire and wheel from the vehicle. Rotate the tires to the new specified position.

_____ **B.** Remove the lug nuts and place them in a convenient place such as the arm of the hoist.

_____ **C.** Reinstall the lug nuts by hand, at least two full turns, making sure the correct side of the lug nut is facing the wheel. Do not put the nut or stud into the socket of an impact wrench and power them on directly. Tighten the lug nuts to the correct torque in the proper tightening sequence, as specified in the service information.

_____ **D.** Prepare the vehicle by removing any hubcaps or lug nut covers. If using hand tools, break loose the lug or wheel nuts while some of the weight is still on the ground, and then raise the vehicle to a comfortable working position.

Review Questions

_____ 1. Which of the following is a clear indicator that the tire is at the end of its legal life?
   A. Out-of-balance conditions
   B. Tread depth above the level of built-in wear indicators
   C. Low tire pressure
   D. Tread depth below the level of built-in wear indicators

_____ 2. Wheel alignment is normally checked and adjusted under all of the following conditions *except*:
   A. when there is abnormal tire wear.
   B. when the steering parts are replaced.
   C. when the oil is changed.
   D. when new tires are put on the vehicle.

_____ 3. The cold inflation pressure of a tire is determined based on the:
   A. type of transmission in the vehicle.
   B. type of gas in the tire.
   C. vehicle's design load limit.
   D. engine capacity of the vehicle.

_____ 4. The typical procedure to remove any existing oxygen from an air-filled tire before filling nitrogen into it is to:
   A. completely deflate it and then inflate it to high pressure.
   B. inflate and deflate it more than once to remove oxygen.
   C. inflate the tire with air.
   D. inflate the tire once is all that is needed.

_____ 5. Jack needs to perform tire rotation on a car that is an all-wheel drive with directional, differently sized tires. Which of these methods should he follow?
   A. Forward-cross pattern
   B. X pattern
   C. Front-to-rear pattern
   D. Dismount and remount on the wheels from the other side

_____ 6. Which among the following tire and wheel balancing methods gives the best ride quality?
   A. Road force balancing
   B. Dynamic balancing
   C. Static balancing
   D. Bubble balancing

_____ 7. Which of the following valve cores are recommended for use in TPMS sensors?
   A. Unplated brass caps
   B. Brass valve cores
   C. Nickel-plated valve cores
   D. Aluminum valve cores

_____ 8. Which of the following tools can act as a safety measure in the event of a tire explosion during inflation?
   A. Tire inflation cage
   B. TPMS torque wrench
   C. Air tire buffer
   D. Tire dunk tank

_____ 9. All of the following statements are true *except*:
   A. excessive loaded radial runout on the tire can be corrected by replacing the tire.
   B. the only method for fixing excessive lateral runout on the tire is to replace the tire.
   C. a wheel balancer is used to identify and correct wheel imbalances.
   D. the most common issue with tires is a broken belt.

_____ 10. Heavy pulling of a vehicle to either the left or the right could be due to any of the following *except*:
   A. mismatched tire sizes or pressures.
   B. out-of-alignment wheels.
   C. nitrogen filled tires.
   D. a dragging front brake assembly.

ASE Technician A/Technician B Style Questions

_____ 1. Tech A says that when checking tire pressure, the tires should be "cold." Tech B says that the tires should be driven more than 3 miles before checking tire pressure. Who is correct?
   A. Tech A
   B. Tech B
   C. Both Tech A and B
   D. Neither Tech A nor B

_____ 2. Tech A says that tires should be rotated every 20,000 miles. Tech B says that when performing a tire rotation, each tire should be moved to the next clockwise position on the vehicle. Who is correct?
   A. Tech A
   B. Tech B
   C. Both Tech A and B
   D. Neither Tech A nor B

_____ 3. Tech A says that a static imbalance condition is centered within the width of the tire. Tech B says that a dynamic imbalance condition can be anywhere within the width of the tire. Who is correct?
   A. Tech A
   B. Tech B
   C. Both Tech A and B
   D. Neither Tech A nor B

_____ 4. Tech A says that a tire with more wear on the center of the tread is caused by under-inflation of the tire. Tech B says that feathering of the tire tread is most commonly a result of excessive toe-in or toe-out. Who is correct?
   A. Tech A
   B. Tech B
   C. Both Tech A and B
   D. Neither Tech A nor B

_____ 5. Tech A says that you should apply tire lubricant to the bead of the tire when removing the tire from the rim. Tech B says that the turntable jaws on many tire changers can hold the rim by grasping it from the outside or the inside. Who is correct?
   A. Tech A
   B. Tech B
   C. Both Tech A and B
   D. Neither Tech A nor B

_____ 6. Tech A says that lead wheel weights have been outlawed in some States. Tech B says that when balancing a tire, it is good practice to reuse the wheel weights to cut down on waste. Who is correct?
   A. Tech A
   B. Tech B
   C. Both Tech A and B
   D. Neither Tech A nor B

_____ 7. Tech A says that some TPMS sensors are part of the tire's valve stem. Tech B says that some TPMS sensors are held on by a large band that fits around the center of the rim. Who is correct?
   A. Tech A
   B. Tech B
   C. Both Tech A and B
   D. Neither Tech A nor B

_____ 8. Tech A says that when repairing a leaky tire with a plug patch, the patch goes on the outside of the tire. Tech B says that the plug patch must be applied while the glue is still wet. Who is correct?
   A. Tech A
   B. Tech B
   C. Both Tech A and B
   D. Neither Tech A nor B

_____ **9.** Tech A says that it is a good practice to cover the buffed area and newly applied plug patch with a rubber patch sealant. Tech B says that it is good practice to use the mechanical buffer tool to smooth the plug patch after it has been applied. Who is correct?
   A. Tech A
   B. Tech B
   C. Both Tech A and B
   D. Neither Tech A nor B

_____ **10.** Tech A says that an outside micrometer is used to measure axle flange runout. Tech B says that lateral runout of the tire, wheel, or axle flange causes the wheels to jiggle side to side. Who is correct?
   A. Tech A
   B. Tech B
   C. Both Tech A and B
   D. Neither Tech A nor B

Steering System Theory

At the start of each chapter you'll find the NATEF Tasks, Knowledge Objectives, and Skills Objectives from the textbook. These are your objectives as you make your way through the exercises in this workbook and the chapter in your textbook. The following activities have been designed to help you refresh your knowledge of the material in this chapter.

NATEF Tasks

- N38001 Describe the function of suspension and steering control systems and components (i.e., active suspension and stability control). (MLR/AST/MAST)
- N38002 Identify hybrid vehicle power steering system electrical circuits and safety precautions. (MLR/AST/MAST)

Knowledge Objectives

After reading this chapter, you will be able to:

- K38001 Describe the purpose, function, and main types of steering systems.
- K38002 Describe the purpose of steering geometry and explain how the Ackermann principle applies.
- K38003 Describe the purpose and function of rack-and-pinion steering components.
- K38004 Describe the purpose and function of parallelogram steering components.
- K38005 Describe the purpose and function of steering columns.
- K38006 Describe the purpose, function, and variety of four-wheel steering systems.
- K38007 Describe the purpose, function, and variations of steering boxes.
- K38008 Describe the purpose, function, and components of the rack-and-pinion gearbox.
- K38009 Describe the purpose, function, and variety of worm gearboxes.
- K38010 Describe the purpose and function of a worm-and-sector gearbox.
- K38011 Describe the purpose and function of the worm-and-roller gearbox.
- K38012 Describe the purpose and function of a recirculating ball gearbox.
- K38013 Describe the purpose, function, and variety of power steering systems.
- K38014 Describe the purpose and function of the hydraulically assisted power steering system.
- K38015 Describe the purpose and function of power steering fluid and hoses.
- K38016 Describe the hydraulically controlled steering process.
- K38017 Describe the purpose and function of the flow control valve.
- K38018 Describe the purpose, function, and variety of electric power steering systems.
- K38019 Describe the basic operation of basic electric power steering operation.

Skills Objectives

There are no Skills Objectives in this chapter.

Matching

Match the following terms with the correct description or example.

A. Active control
B. Beam axle
C. Adjustable bushing
D. Adjustment sleeve
E. Ball-return guide

F. Bump steer
G. Clock spring
H. Constant mesh
I. Chassis
J. Drag link

_____ **1.** A component that connects the tie rods together and to the center link on some applications and provides the adjustment point for toe-in or toe-out.

_____ **2.** A brace or nylon part that pushes against the rack to adjust the mesh of the rack teeth to the pinion teeth.

_____ **3.** A system of providing constant feedback from sensors in the vehicle to the control unit.

_____ **4.** A special passage or metal tube through which the balls move in recirculating ball steering boxes.

_____ **5.** The undesired condition produced when hitting a bump.

_____ **6.** A suspension system in which one set of wheels is connected laterally by a single beam or shaft.

_____ **7.** The frame of a vehicle, to which the suspension pieces attach.

_____ **8.** A steel or iron rod that transfers movement of the pitman arm to a relay lever.

_____ **9.** A term used to describe two or more parts, such as gears, that are in constant contact with each other.

_____ **10.** A special rotary electrical connector located between the steering wheel and the steering column

Multiple Choice

Read each item carefully, and then select the best response.

_____ **1.** A _____ transmits the driver's steering effort from the steering wheel down to the steering box.
  A. steering column
  B. steering arm
  C. pitman arm
  D. tie-rod assembly

_____ **2.** In a _____ steering system, the center link and axle, if equipped, along with the pitman arm and idler arm always move parallel to each other.
  A. rack-and-pinion
  B. electric power
  C. electrically powered hydraulic
  D. parallelogram

_____ **3.** Identify the component of a rack-and-pinion steering system that has an inline ball-and-socket joint on one end of a shaft and is threaded on the other end of the shaft.
  A. Rack
  B. Pinion
  C. Inner tie rod
  D. Rubber bellows

_____ **4.** In a rack-and-pinion steering system, a(n) _____ protects the inner joints from dirt and contaminants.
  A. outer tie-rod
  B. rubber bellow
  C. socket
  D. meshed pinion

_____ **5.** A _____ keeps the steering wheel of a vehicle from shaking when the driver hits a pothole or other road irregularity.
  A. relay level
  B. rubber below
  C. worm shaft
  D. steering damper

_____ **6.** In a rack-and-pinion gearbox, a(n) _____ holds the rack against the pinion gear.
  A. clock spring
  B. spring-loaded rack guide yoke
  C. idler arm
  D. nylon brush

_____ **7.** A _____ has worm gear inside a block with a threaded hole in it and gear teeth cut into its outside that engage the sector shaft to move the pitman arm.
  A. worm-and-roller gearbox
  B. worm-and-sector gearbox
  C. cam and lever steering box
  D. recirculating ball steering box

_____ **8.** A(n) _____ sensor is a device used to measure the load on the steering wheel.
   A. wheel speed
   B. MAF
   C. torque
   D. camshaft position

_____ **9.** The flow-control valve of a power steering pump regulates pressures to as high as _____ pounds per square inch (psi).
   A. 800 to 1000
   B. 500 to 700
   C. 1200 to 1500
   D. 2000 to 2500

_____ **10.** Identify the type of electric power assist steering systems in which the power assist unit is attached to the steering gear pinion shaft.
   A. Pinion-assist type
   B. Column-assist type
   C. Rack-assist type
   D. Direct-drive type

True/False

If you believe the statement to be more true than false, write the letter "T" in the space provided. If you believe the statement to be more false than true, write the letter "F."

_____ **1.** A steering box also uses principles of gear reduction to give the driver mechanical advantage over the wheels.

_____ **2.** Steering geometry and suspension geometry must be within the manufacturer's specifications for a vehicle to operate correctly.

_____ **3.** The steering response of a rack-and-pinion steering system is very dull.

_____ **4.** In a rack-and-pinion steering system, the pinion is in constant mesh with the rack.

_____ **5.** The parallelogram steering linkage is less complicated than the rack-and-pinion linkage.

_____ **6.** The center link of a parallelogram steering system may also be called a track rod or drag link.

_____ **7.** A four-wheel steering system improves high-speed handling and increases maneuverability.

_____ **8.** The value of reduction ratio is not affected by the size of the pinion of a rack-and-pinion gearbox.

_____ **9.** In a rack-and-pinion steering, the rack is connected to the tie-rod assembly through an idler gear.

_____ **10.** Power steering hoses are usually made of flexible, high-pressure hose material.

Fill in the Blank

Read each item carefully, and then complete the statement by filling in the missing word(s).

1. _____ _____ _____ system uses an electric motor and sensors
to provide feedback to the vehicle's computer systems to decrease steering effort.

2. _____ _____ _____ system is a power-assist system that uses an electric motor to replace the hydraulic pump to decrease steering effort.

3. A(n) _____ - _____ _____ _____ is a power steering pump driven by a belt or gear off the crankshaft.

4. A(n) _____ - _____ valve is used in power steering pumps to control the amount of flow out of the power steering pump.

5. A(n) _____ _____ converts the rotary motion of the steering wheel to the linear motion needed to pivot the wheels.

6. In a parallelogram steering system, the _____ _____ connects the pitman arm to the idler arm.

7. A(n) _____ / _____ mechanism allows drivers to control the steering wheel position to best suit their preferences.

8. _____ _____ is the ratio between the turns of the steering wheel and the angle turn of the wheel.

9. The _____ _____ mode of an electric power steering system adjusts the amount of assist according to the vehicle speed to improve road feel and dampen kickback.

10. A(n) _____ _____ is a spring-loaded piece of steel connected to the pinion gear at its bottom end and the input shaft at its top.

Labeling

Label the following diagrams with the correct terms.

1. Components of a rack-and-pinion steering system:

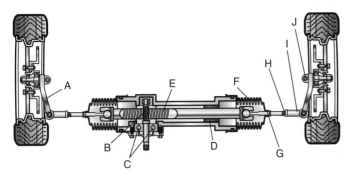

A. _____

B. _____

C. _____

D. _____

E. _____

F. _____

G. _____

H. _____

I. _____

J. _____

2. Components of a typical tilt steering wheel mechanism:

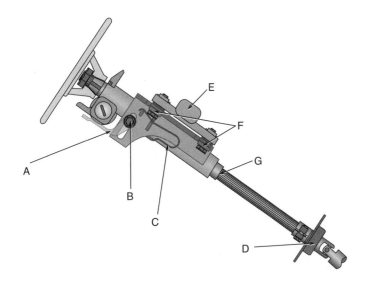

A. _____

B. _____

C. _____

D. _____

E. _____

F. _____

G. _____

3. Components of a worm-and-sector type of worm gear steering box:

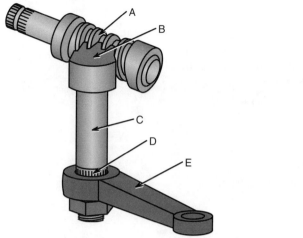

A. _____

B. _____

C. _____

D. _____

E. _____

4. Components of a power-assisted recirculating ball gearbox:

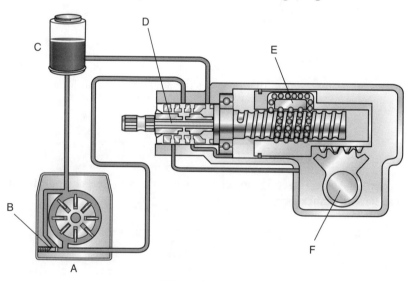

A. _____

B. _____

C. _____

D. _____

E. _____

F. _____

Review Questions

_____ 1. All of the following statements are true *except*:
   A. the steering box converts the rotary motion of the steering wheel to angular motion.
   B. steering linkage connects the steering box to the steering arm.
   C. the steering system provides control over the vehicle's direction of travel.
   D. the steering knuckle pivots on bushings.

_____ 2. In an electronic power steering system, PCM stands for:
   A. powertrain control module.
   B. portable control mechanism.
   C. power cutting mechanism.
   D. power control module.

_____ 3. The Ackermann principle is applied in steering geometry to:
   A. reduce vibration of the vehicle.
   B. reduce wobbling of the vehicle.
   C. navigate a corner without scrubbing.
   D. make steering response sharper.

_____ 4. Which of the following components is the inner tie rod socket connected to in a rack-and-pinion steering system?
   A. Rack
   B. Pinion
   C. Nylon brushes
   D. Intermediate shaft

_____ 5. The part of the parallelogram steering mechanism that provides the adjustment point for adjusting the toe setting is the:
   A. pitman arm.
   B. tie rod.
   C. idler arm.
   D. adjustment sleeve.

_____ 6. In modern computer-controlled four-wheel steering, an actuator similar to a front rack-and-pinion assembly attaches to the rear steering knuckles with:
   A. center arm ends.
   B. tie-rod ends.
   C. bushes.
   D. clock spring.

_____ 7. The steering box converts the rotary motion of the steering wheel into:
   A. reciprocating motion.
   B. angular motion.
   C. up and down motion.
   D. tangential motion.

_____ 8. Choose the correct statement.
   A. Turning the steering wheel rotates the pinion and moves the rack up and down.
   B. The teeth on both the pinion and the rack are helical gears.
   C. A large pinion means the number of turns of the steering wheel is increased.
   D. The steering ratio is the same on all vehicles.

_____ 9. Which type of gear box uses a recirculating ball steering box in it?
   A. Worm-and-sector
   B. Worm-and-roller
   C. Worm-and-nut
   D. Worm-and-steering

_____ 10. Which of the following electric power assist steering systems has the power assist unit, controller, and torque sensor connected to the steering column?
   A. Pinion-assist type
   B. Rack-assist type
   C. Column-assist type
   D. Direct drive type

ASE Technician A/Technician B Style Questions

_____ **1.** Tech A says that the steering column uses one or more flexible joints to connect to the steering gearbox. Tech B says that the pitman arm is bolted to the frame and relays the steering linkage movement to the opposite wheel from the steering gearbox. Who is correct?
   A. Tech A
   B. Tech B
   C. Both A and B
   D. Neither A nor B

_____ **2.** Tech A says that the clock spring (spiral cable) assists the turning of the steering wheel on vehicles with EPS. Tech B says that the clock spring is used to transmit an electrical signal to the driver's side airbag. Who is correct?
   A. Tech A
   B. Tech B
   C. Both A and B
   D. Neither A nor B

_____ **3.** Tech A says that some manufacturers specify automatic transmission fluid in their power steering system. Tech B says that the parts of higher voltage electrically assisted power steering systems are similar to an electrically assisted power steering system. Who is correct?
   A. Tech A
   B. Tech B
   C. Both A and B
   D. Neither A nor B

_____ **4.** Tech A says that rack-and-pinion steering systems generally do not use power steering due to their lighter duty construction. Tech B says that rack and-pinion steering systems use a worm gear arrangement to move the rack. Who is correct?
   A. Tech A
   B. Tech B
   C. Both A and B
   D. Neither A nor B

_____ **5.** Tech A says that when the flow-control valve of a hydraulically assisted power steering is forced open at a steering stop, usually an audible whine is heard due to its high operating pressure Tech B says that in the neutral position, the pressure in the power steering system is very high. Who is correct?
   A. Tech A
   B. Tech B
   C. Both A and B
   D. Neither A nor B

_____ **6.** Tech A says that most high-pressure power steering hoses use an O-ring to seal the end of each hose to the pump and steering gear. Tech B says that the return hose goes from the steering gear to the power steering pump reservoir. Who is correct?
   A. Tech A
   B. Tech B
   C. Both A and B
   D. Neither A nor B

_____ **7.** Tech A says that when the vehicle is being driven straight ahead, a belt-driven power steering pump will pump fluid continuously, placing a minimal load on the engine. Tech B says that a belt-driven power steering pump is activated by an electromagnetic clutch, so it only pumps fluid when the wheels are being steered. Who is correct?
   A. Tech A
   B. Tech B
   C. Both A and B
   D. Neither A nor B

_____ **8.** Tech A says that the pressure relief valve maintains a preset minimum pressure in the system. Tech B says that the pressure relief valve prevents excessive pressure. Who is correct?
   A. Tech A
   B. Tech B

    C. Both A and B

    D. Neither A nor B

_____ **9.** Tech A says that on a hydraulic power steering system the power steering switch turns off the power steering pump if the pressure gets too high. Tech B says that on the same system, the power steering switch is used to turn on the pump if the pressure gets too low. Who is correct?

    A. Tech A

    B. Tech B

    C. Both A and B

    D. Neither A nor B

_____ **10** Tech A says that no matter which way the vehicle turns, the inside wheel must always turn less sharply than the outside wheel. Tech B says that the Ackermann principle angles the steering arms toward the center of the rear axle. Who is correct?

    A. Tech A

    B. Tech B

    C. Both A and B

    D. Neither A nor B

Servicing Steering Systems

At the start of each chapter you'll find the NATEF Tasks, Knowledge Objectives, and Skills Objectives from the textbook. These are your objectives as you make your way through the exercises in this workbook and the chapter in your textbook. The following activities have been designed to help you refresh your knowledge of the material in this chapter.

NATEF Tasks

- N39001 Inspect for power steering fluid leakage; determine needed action. (MLR/AST/MAST)
- N39002 Diagnose power steering gear (non–rack-and-pinion) binding, uneven turning effort, looseness, hard steering, and noise concerns; determine needed action. (AST/MAST)
- N39003 Diagnose power steering gear (rack-and-pinion) binding, uneven turning effort, looseness, hard steering, and noise concerns; determine needed action. (AST/MAST)
- N39004 Diagnose steering column noises, looseness, and binding concerns (including tilt/telescoping mechanisms); determine needed action. (AST/MAST)
- N39005 Flush, fill, and bleed power steering system; use proper fluid type per manufacturer specification. (MLR/AST/MAST)
- N39006 Remove and reinstall power steering pump. (AST/MAST)
- N39007 Remove and reinstall press-fit power steering pump pulley; check pulley and belt alignment. (AST/MAST)
- N39008 Inspect, remove, and/or replace power steering hoses and fittings. (MLR/AST/MAST)
- N39009 Remove and replace rack-and-pinion steering gear; inspect mounting bushings and brackets. (AST/MAST)
- N39010 Inspect rack-and-pinion steering gear inner tie-rod ends (sockets) and bellows boots; replace as needed. (MLR/AST/MAST)
- N39011 Inspect, remove, and/or replace pitman arm, relay (center link/intermediate) rod, idler arm, mountings, and steering linkage damper. (MLR/AST/MAST)
- N39012 Inspect, replace, and/or adjust tie-rod ends (sockets), tie-rod sleeves, and clamps. (MLR/AST/MAST)
- N39013 Inspect electric power steering assist system. (MLR/AST)
- N39014 Inspect, test, and diagnose electrically assisted power steering systems (including using a scan tool); determine needed action. (MAST)
- N39015 Identify hybrid vehicle power steering system electrical circuits and service and safety precautions. (MLR/AST/MAST)
- N39016 Disable and enable supplemental restraint system (SRS); verify indicator lamp operation. (MLR/AST/MAST)
- N39017 Remove and replace steering wheel; center/time supplemental restraint system SRS coil (clock spring). (AST/MAST)
- N39018 Inspect steering shaft universal joint(s), flexible coupling(s), collapsible column, lock cylinder mechanism, and steering wheel; determine needed action. (AST/MAST)

Knowledge Objectives

After reading this chapter, you will be able to:

- K39001 Describe the purpose and function of tools used in steering system service.

Skills Objectives

After reading this chapter, you will be able to:

- S39001 Perform basic steering system diagnosis.
- S39002 Perform maintenance and repair tasks on the power steering system.
- S39003 Pressure test a power steering system.
- S39004 Perform maintenance and repair on rack-and-pinion steering systems.

- S39005 Perform maintenance and repair on parallelogram steering systems.
- S39006 Inspect and service electric power steering.
- S39007 Perform maintenance and repair on steering columns equipped with SRS.

Matching

Match the following terms with the correct description or example.

A. Dial indicator

B. Tools for mechanical diagnosis

C. Pitman arm puller

D. Safety stand

E. Tools for electrical diagnosis

F. Pry bar

_____ **1.** Tools include the factory scanner and the digital multimeter (DMM).

_____ **2.** A tool that provides stability while working on a raised vehicle.

_____ **3.** A tool made especially for removing the pressed-on pitman arm from the sector shaft.

_____ **4.** Tools include a power steering system pressure tester and various measuring devices, such as dial indicators and belt tension gauges.

_____ **5.** A lever used to apply pressure for testing purposes or to move various components.

_____ **6.** A tool used to measure the runout or movement on different parts of the steering system.

Multiple Choice

Read each item carefully, and then select the best response.

_____ **1.** Identify the tool that has a tab designed to grab the slot in the sleeve and is used to turn the sleeve when adjusting the toe setting.
A. Pitman arm puller
B. Inner tie-rod end tool
C. Tie-rod sleeve adjusting tool
D. Pickle fork

_____ **2.** A _____ is used to check volume of fluid flow, maximum pressure, and leaks internal to the steering gear.
A. scan tool
B. DMM
C. belt tension gauge
D. power steering system analyzer

_____ **3.** A _____ is used to read codes and data from the vehicle's powertrain control module.
A. scan tool
B. DMM
C. belt tension gauge
D. power steering system analyzer

_____ **4.** Identify the tool that is used to measure voltage and ohms in a vehicle's electrical systems.
A. Circuit tester
B. Power steering system analyzer
C. Scan tool
D. DMM

_____ **5.** When checking for binding issues, it may be necessary to _____ to verify where the binding is located.
A. check the universal joint
B. test the steering gearbox
C. separate the steering linkage
D. wind the clock spring

_____ **6.** A _____ carries all the electrical signals that flow to the components on the steering wheel and allows the steering wheel to rotate.
A. clock spring
B. steering knuckle
C. tie-rod end
D. sprag clutch

_____ **7.** Winding a clock spring in the opposite direction will _____.
  A. center the clock spring
  B. greatly shorten its life
  C. increase the winding speed without breaking the wires
  D. require steering angle sensor recalibration

_____ **8.** Power steering pump pulleys are typically held in place by a _____.
  A. bushing
  B. press fit
  C. threaded fastener
  D. sleeve bearing

_____ **9.** _____ make the final connection between the steering linkage and the steering arms.
  A. Ball joints
  B. Zerk fittings
  C. Clock springs
  D. Tie rods

_____ **10.** Looseness in tie-rod ends may be felt as loose steering and is frequently mistaken as a _____.
  A. steering knuckle wear
  B. flexible coupler play
  C. steering gearbox problem
  D. steering fluid leak

True/False

If you believe the statement to be more true than false, write the letter "T" in the space provided. If you believe the statement to be more false than true, write the letter "F."

_____ **1.** In a steering system, play generally results from worn ball sockets and bushings.

_____ **2.** Power steering fluid leaks are not a fire hazard.

_____ **3.** Diagnosing steering gear issues in a rack-and-pinion system is similar to a non–rack-and-pinion system.

_____ **4.** When servicing the steering column of a vehicle, a steering angle sensor calibration is typically not required.

_____ **5.** Rack-and-pinion steering gear removal is fairly simple as all vehicle types use the same procedure for removal and replacement.

_____ **6.** A pickle fork can be used to remove a tie rod from an aluminum steering knuckle.

_____ **7.** Electrically assisted steering systems have very little allowance for adjustment or repair in the face of problems.

_____ **8.** A uniform color designation is used for high-voltage wires in hybrid vehicles across all manufacturers.

_____ **9.** A memory minder can be used on a vehicle when disabling an airbag to retain DTCs.

_____ **10.** Teardown of the steering column or replacement may be necessary to correct play in the steering column assembly.

Fill in the Blank

Read each item carefully, and then complete the statement by filling in the missing word(s).

1. A(n) _____ - _____ _____ _____ is used to pull the tapered shaft on a tie-rod end from its mating steering component.

2. A(n) _____ _____ is a test light used to diagnose electrical problems.

3. A(n) _____ _____ _____ is designed to measure the amount of flex in a drive belt and used by some manufacturers to adjust proper belt tension.

4. _____ _____ of the power steering system checks the operation of the power steering pump, pressure relief valve, control valve, power piston, and hoses when the driver complains of hard or inconsistent steering.

5. Whenever a power steering pump is removed or replaced, typically the _____ must also be removed from the old pump and installed on the new pump.

6. Looseness in the _____ _____ may cause excessive toe change on rough road surfaces and lead to a wandering condition.

7. The two basic types of tie-rod ends are _____ _____ and _____.

8. The flexible coupler or steering shaft universal joint should always have _____ play.

9. _____ _____ are small wires with clips on the ends that are used to diagnose electrical problems.

10. A(n) _____ _____ and _____ _____ uses ultraviolet light and dye to pinpoint steering fluid leaks.

Labeling

Label the following diagrams with the correct terms.

1. Steering system specialty tools:

A.

A. _____

B.

B. _____

C.

C. _____

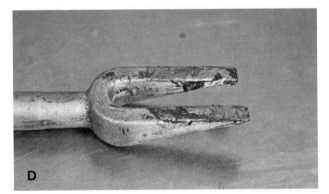

D.

D. _____

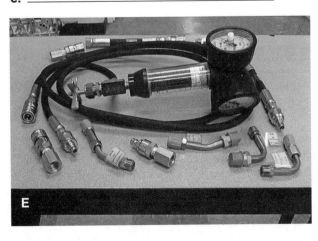

E.

E. _____

F.

F. _____

2. Types of tie-rod end:

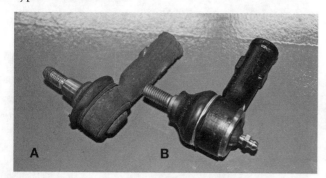

A. _____

B. _____

3. Types of power steering pump filter:

A. _____

B. _____

Skill Drills

Place the skill drill steps in the correct order.

1. Removing and Reinstalling a Power Steering Pump:

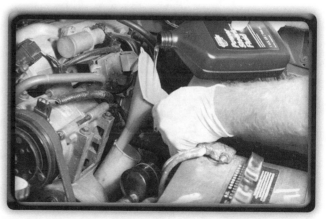

_____ **A.** Disconnect the drive belt(s) and inspect for cracking or groove depth with a belt groove depth gauge. Replace any belt that is cracked or worn beyond specifications.

_____ **B.** To reinstall the new or overhauled power steering pump, reinstall in the reverse order. Fill and bleed the system with the specified power steering fluid.

_____ **C.** Disconnect the power steering hoses from the pump, and check for damage or leaks. Replace hoses if needed. New O-rings should be used on hose ends on reassembly, if the vehicle is so equipped.

_____ **D.** After researching the specified procedure for removing the power steering pump, raise the vehicle on a lift or support it on safety stands. Drain the power steering system's fluid by disconnecting the power steering return line, and dispose of the fluid in accordance with environmental legislation.

_____ **E.** Remove the pump retaining bolts, and remove the power steering pump.

2. Removing and Reinstalling a Press-Fit Power Steering Pump Pulley:

_____ **A.** Tighten the center bolt (while holding the outer nut) to press off the old drive pulley. If replacing the pump, remove the old one and install the new one.

_____ **B.** Reinstall the drive belt, or replace it with a new one if needed. Refill and bleed the power steering system with the specified fluid.

_____ **C.** Place the pulley onto the power steering pump shaft, with the removal flange facing forward. Using the install portion of the pulley puller tool kit, thread the bolt portion of the tool all the way into the shaft of the new power steering pump.

_____ **D.** Tighten the outer nut (while holding the center bolt) until the pulley bottoms on the shaft. Remove the puller.

_____ **E.** Assuming the pump is removed from the vehicle, install the correct power steering pulley puller on the pulley, making sure the puller is installed in the correct direction.

_____ **F.** Thread the outer nut down so that the bearing or washer is against the pulley.

3. Inspecting and Replacing the Center Link:

_____ **A.** Install the new center link in reverse order of removal.

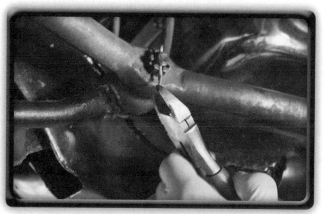

_____ **B.** Push and pull the tire/wheel assembly from side to side, checking each of the center link joints for excess movement. If the movement is out of specifications, the joint(s) will have to be replaced. Remove the cotter pin and nuts from the taper studs of the pitman arm, idler arm, and inner tie-rod ends.

_____ **C.** Separate the taper studs, using the double-hammer method, a pickle fork, or the approved puller. Remove the center link.

Review Questions

_____ **1.** When confronted with a steering system problem, all of the following should be taken into consideration *except*:
   A. mechanical components.
   B. the suspension system.
   C. electrical components.
   D. the cooling system.

_____ **2.** Choose the correct statement.
   A. Steering systems are mostly automatic.
   B. Sensors do not cause steering faults.
   C. As more electronic power steering systems are produced, electrical faults are becoming more common.
   D. The suspension system does not interfere with the steering system.

_____ **3.** Which tool is particularly useful in performing a continuity test on any opens or shorts in an EPS system and help determine where the problem is located?
   A. TPMS tool
   B. Factory scanner
   C. DMM
   D. Digital SPM tool

_____ **4.** The pickle fork tool can be used for:
   A. removing rod ends.
   B. checking the continuity of the electronic circuit.
   C. removing pitman arms.
   D. centering the clock spring.

_____ **5.** Which of the following devices is used to measure the runout or movement on different parts of the steering system, such as play in tie-rod ends?
   A. Dial indicator
   B. Pickle fork
   C. Pitman arm puller
   D. Tie-rod sleeve adjusting tool

_____ **6.** All of the following statements with respect to power steering fluid are true *except*:
   A. It transmits pressure throughout a vehicle's power steering system.
   B. It provides lubrication to the moving parts.
   C. It does not get contaminated so only its level needs checking.
   D. It must be able to perform in any weather conditions.

_____ **7.** Pressure testing a power steering system checks all of the following *except*:
   A. operating pressure.
   B. maximum pressure.

C. fluid flow.
D. steering linkage faults.

_____ **8.** All of the following can create play in the steering wheel *except*:
A. worn steering gears.
B. worn tie-rod ends.
C. bent steering arm.
D. looseness in the idler arm.

_____ **9.** If the EPS lamp indicates a fault:
A. check the electrical components of the system.
B. dismantle the steering system to check for issues.
C. hook up a scan tool to the vehicle's data link connector.
D. check the mechanical components of the system.

_____ **10.** Which of the following systems should be disabled while working on or around the steering column, any of the airbags, or other pyrotechnic devices?
A. EPS
B. ABS
C. SRS
D. TRW

ASE Technician A/Technician B Style Questions

_____ **1.** Tech A says that power steering fluid leaks can cause a vehicle to catch fire. Tech B says that fluorescent
dye can be added to power steering fluid to locate the source of a leak. Who is correct?
A. Tech A
B. Tech B
C. Both A and B
D. Neither A nor B

_____ **2.** Tech A says that in the steering system, play generally results from worn ball sockets and bushings. Tech B says that hard steering is typically caused by tire pressure that is too high. Who is correct?
A. Tech A
B. Tech B
C. Both A and B
D. Neither A nor B

_____ **3.** Tech A says that when flushing power steering fluid, you should run the engine for a few minutes after all of the old fluid has drained out of the system. Tech B says that power steering fluid should be flushed if a major part of the hydraulic steering system is being replaced. Who is correct?
A. Tech A
B. Tech B
C. Both A and B
D. Neither A nor B

_____ **4.** Tech A says that many power steering pump pulleys are typically held in place by a press fit. Tech B says that some power steering pump pulleys are made out of plastic. Who is correct?
A. Tech A
B. Tech B
C. Both A and B
D. Neither A nor B

_____ **5.** Tech A says that to properly check a tie-rod end, the technician should twist the tie-rod end, and any rotational movement means the joint is bad. Tech B says that when checking a tie rod, any side-to-side movement in the joint means the tie rod is bad. Who is correct?
A. Tech A
B. Tech B
C. Both A and B
D. Neither A nor B

_____ **6.** Tech A says that worn rack-and-pinion mount bushings can cause excessive play in the steering system. Tech B says that a worn idler arm can cause excessive play in the steering system. Who is correct?
- **A.** Tech A
- **B.** Tech B
- **C.** Both A and B
- **D.** Neither A nor B

_____ **7.** Tech A says that a pickle fork is used to hold a tie rod while it is being tightened. Tech B says that an outer tie-rod end should have a noticeable side-to-side play if it is okay. Who is correct?
- **A.** Tech A
- **B.** Tech B
- **C.** Both A and B
- **D.** Neither A nor B

_____ **8.** Tech A says that worn tie-rod ends can cause a steering wandering complaint. Tech B says that a hard steering complaint could be caused by a worn power steering pump. Who is correct?
- **A.** Tech A
- **B.** Tech B
- **C.** Both A and B
- **D.** Neither A nor B

_____ **9.** Tech A says that when disabling the SRS system, verify that the correct fuse was removed by turning the key on and observing that the SRS light remains lit for at least 30 seconds and does not go out. Tech B says that after enabling the SRS system, you should test the system by turning the key to the run position while sitting in the driver's seat. Who is correct?
- **A.** Tech A
- **B.** Tech B
- **C.** Both A and B
- **D.** Neither A nor B

_____ **10.** Tech A says that when replacing the clock spring, you should turn it all the way to either end and then install it in the steering column. Tech B says that clock springs are used to return the steering wheel to its centered position. Who is correct?
- **A.** Tech A
- **B.** Tech B
- **C.** Both A and B
- **D.** Neither A nor B

Suspension System Theory

At the start of each chapter you'll find the NATEF Tasks, Knowledge Objectives, and Skills Objectives from the textbook. These are your objectives as you make your way through the exercises in this workbook and the chapter in your textbook. The following activities have been designed to help you refresh your knowledge of the material in this chapter.

NATEF Tasks

There are no NATEF tasks in this chapter.

Knowledge Objectives

After reading this chapter, you will be able to:

- K40001 Describe the purpose, function, and forces acting on suspension systems.
- K40002 Explain the principles of sprung and unsprung weight and how dampening is affected by them.
- K40003 Describe the function of the suspension system.
- K40004 Describe the forces in suspension systems and how they are controlled.
- K40005 Describe yaw, pitch, and roll as they relate to the vehicle.
- K40006 Describe the purpose and function of suspension system components.
- K40007 Describe the purpose, types, and function of springs.
- K40008 Describe the purpose and function of shock absorbers and struts.
- K40009 Describe the purpose and function of control arms and rods.
- K40010 Describe the purpose and function of the steering knuckle.
- K40011 Describe the purpose and function of ball joints.
- K40012 Describe the purpose and function of bushings.
- K40013 Describe the various types of suspension systems.
- K40014 Describe the purpose and function of dead and live axles.
- K40015 Describe the purpose and function of a solid axle.
- K40016 Describe the purpose and types of an independent suspension system.
- K40017 Describe the main types of front suspension systems.
- K40018 Describe the components and layout of a strut suspension.
- K40019 Describe the components and layout of a modified strut suspension.
- K40020 Describe the components and layout of the SLA suspension.
- K40021 Describe the components and layout of a twin I-beam suspension.
- K40022 Describe the main types of rear suspension systems.
- K40023 Describe the components and layout of rigid-axle leaf-spring suspensions.
- K40024 Describe the components and layout of rigid-axle coil-spring suspensions.
- K40025 Describe the components and layout of rigid-axle suspensions.
- K40026 Describe the components and layout of rear independent suspension (dead axle) suspensions.
- K40027 Describe the components and layout of rear-wheel drive independent suspensions.
- K40028 Describe the purpose and function of active and adaptive suspension systems.
- K40029 Describe the operation of the adaptive air suspension system.

Skills Objectives

There are no Skills Objectives in this chapter.

Matching

Match the following terms with the correct description or example.

A. Adaptive air suspension   **F.** Independent suspension
B. Control arm   **G.** Leaf spring
C. Coil spring   **H.** MacPherson strut
D. Axle   **I.** Magneto-rheological fluid
E. Ball joint   **J.** Overshoot

_____ **1.** A swivel connection mounted in the outer end of the front control arm.

_____ **2.** A spring steel wire, heated and wound into a coil, which is used to support the weight of a vehicle.

_____ **3.** A system that uses rubber bags or bladders filled with air to support the weight of the vehicle.

_____ **4.** The primary load-bearing element of a vehicle's suspension system, commonly referred to as wishbone.

_____ **5.** A system that allows the up-and-down movement of one tire without affecting the other tire on the axle.

_____ **6.** The shaft of the suspension system to which the tires and wheels are attached.

_____ **7.** A component made of one or more flat, tempered steel springs that are bracketed together.

_____ **8.** The amount a spring extends past its original length following compression.

_____ **9.** A fluid that has the unique characteristic of changing viscosity when exposed to a magnetic field.

_____ **10.** A component that is used on an independent suspension where the spring and shock are joined together.

Multiple Choice

Read each item carefully, and then select the best response.

_____ **1.** Identify the type of rubber bushing that has a voided section molded in it that allows component movement under torque application.
     A. Rubber-bonded bushing
     B. Resin bushing
     C. Compliance bushing
     D. Spring shackle bushing

_____ **2.** A _____ is used to hold the dead axle and keep it from moving from side to side through corners.
     A. panhard rod
     B. single-point control arm
     C. rubber seal
     D. compliance bushing

_____ **3.** Pitch is the movement of a vehicle around its _____.
     A. centerline
     B. z-axis
     C. x-axis
     D. y-axis

_____ **4.** In a _____, the coil spring is mounted between the axle housing and the vehicle body.
     A. rigid dead axle suspension
     B. rigid-axle coil-spring suspension
     C. rear independent suspension
     D. rear-wheel drive independent suspension

_____ **5.** A _____ bushing has a steel outer housing and inner sleeve with rubber inside.
     A. compliance
     B. resin
     C. rubber-bonded
     D. brass

_____ **6.** Identify a true statement with respect to an independent suspension system.
     A. In an independent suspension, unsprung mass can be kept low.
     B. In an independent suspension, a center axle housing can be used efficiently.

    C. An independent suspension forms a dependent suspension.
    D. An independent suspension does not handle as well as a solid axle.

_____ **7.** In a strut suspension, the shock absorber is contained inside the _____.
    A. control arm
    B. strut
    C. steering knuckle
    D. extension housing

_____ **8.** A _____ is connected to the rear of the multi-leaf spring and allows the leaf spring to move downward when a load is placed on the rear of the vehicle.
    A. rebound clip
    B. rigid spring hanger
    C. spring eye
    D. swinging shackle

_____ **9.** In a leaf spring, the longest leaf, called the main leaf, is rolled at both ends to form _____.
    A. spring hangers
    B. spring eyes
    C. swinging shackles
    D. spring arms

_____ **10.** A spring that has evenly space coils is said to have a(n) _____.
    A. variable pitch
    B. uniform pitch
    C. barrel pitch
    D. progressive rate of deflection

True/False

If you believe the statement to be more true than false, write the letter "T" in the space provided. If you believe the statement to be more false than true, write the letter "F."

_____ **1.** A dead axle does not drive a vehicle.
_____ **2.** In light vehicle applications, air is used primarily for ride height control.
_____ **3.** Oscillation is the fluctuation of an object between two states.
_____ **4.** An overshoot is the amount a spring compresses under a load.
_____ **5.** A spring with a progressive rate of deflection will deflect easily under heavy loads.
_____ **6.** A reaction force acts in the same direction as the applied force.
_____ **7.** A rubber-bonded bushing also known as a metalastic bushing.
_____ **8.** Sintering is the process of using pressure and heat to bond metal particles.
_____ **9.** A solid axle forms a dependent suspension.
_____ **10.** The ball joint on a MacPherson strut is a loaded joint.

Fill in the Blank

Read each item carefully, and then complete the statement by filling in the missing word(s).

1. A(n) _____ _____ - _____ shock absorber is used in an automatic load-sensing system that adjusts ride height automatically.
2. A _____ acts as a pivot point and cushion at suspension fulcrum points and allows for movement while maintaining alignment.
3. A(n) _____ force moves an object in a different direction or into a different shape.
4. _____ is the vehicular movement along its x-axis.
5. A(n) _____ _____ - _____ shock absorber allows manual adjustment of the dampening rate.
6. With regard to suspension springs, _____ refers to the uncontrolled compression and decompression of the spring following overshoot.

7. A panhard rod is mounted on the body or frame of the vehicle and the _____ is also referred to as a _____ _____.

8. _____ causes a vehicle to lower or rise on the front end during quick braking or acceleration.

9. A(n) _____ _____ is a metal strap that is warped around the leaf spring to prevent excessive flexing of the main leaf during rebound.

10. The amount of ground clearance a vehicle has, measured from a point on the body or frame is called _____ _____.

Labeling

Label the following diagrams with the correct terms.

1. Components of a suspension system:

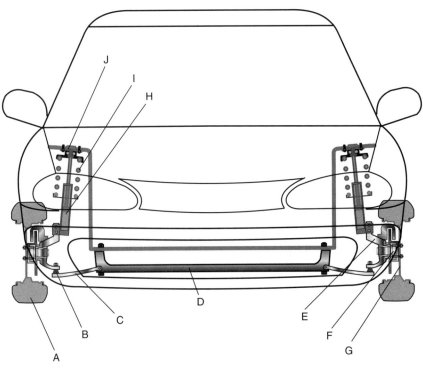

A. _____

B. _____

C. _____

D. _____

E. _____

F. _____

G. _____

H. _____

I. _____

J. _____

2. Types of springs:

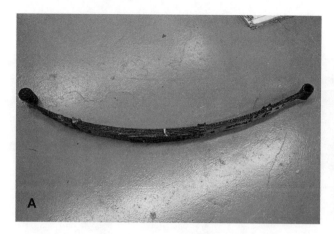

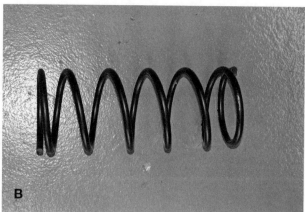

A. _____

B. _____

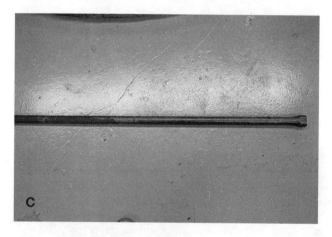

C. _____

3. Forces acting on a vehicle:

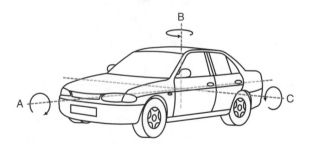

A. _____

B. _____

C. _____

4. Components of a direct-acting telescopic type shock absorber:

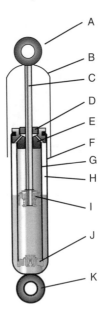

A. _____

B. _____

C. _____

D. _____

E. _____

F. _____

G. _____

H. _____

I. _____

J. _____

K. _____

5. Types of ball joint:

A. _____

B. _____

Review Questions

_____ 1. All of these act as common indicators for the problems in the suspension system *except*:
   A. a bouncy ride.
   B. a reduction in steering control.
   C. noises when going over a bump.
   D. improper transmission shifting.

_____ 2. For the vehicle to operate properly and safely, suspension and steering components should be aligned with each other and also with the:
   A. engine centerline.
   B. wheels' centerline.
   C. vehicle centerline.
   D. axle centerline.

_____ 3. The components that are part of the sprung weight of a vehicle are:
   A. axles.
   B. brakes.
   C. steering parts not supported by springs.
   D. suspension parts supported by springs.

_____ 4. The suspension system performs all of the following functions *except*:
   A. absorbing the large road forces generated while driving on non-perfect roads.
   B. holding the wheels and tires in the proper orientation.
   C. monitoring the tread wear of each tire.
   D. supporting the weight of the chassis, drivetrain, passenger compartment, occupants, and any additional load.

_____ 5. Which of the following places a twisting pressure on the suspension members that push the vehicle along the road?
   A. Driving thrust
   B. Breaking torque
   C. Cornering force
   D. Centrifugal force

_____ 6. The movement around an imaginary line drawn down the center of the vehicle from front to back is called:
   A. yaw.
   B. roll.
   C. pitch.
   D. rock.

_____ 7. Which of the following dampen spring oscillations by forcing oil through small holes in a piston?
   A. Springs
   B. Shock absorbers
   C. Control arms
   D. Axles

_____ 8. When the pitch is varied, the deflection rate varies in the spring. Then, the spring is said to have a:
   A. uniform pitch.
   B. cylindrical pitch.
   C. barrel pitch.
   D. progressive rate of deflection.

_____ 9. Which of the following shock absorbers is also called self-leveling?
   A. Automatic load-adjustable shock absorbers
   B. Electronic adjustable-rate shock absorbers
   C. Manual adjustable-rate shock absorbers
   D. Gas-pressurized shock absorbers

_____ 10. All of the following statements are true *except*:
   A. the solid axle provides a simple means of mounting the hub and wheel units.
   B. SLA uses upper and lower control arms to control the movement of the knuckle.
   C. in strut suspension, the shock absorber is contained outside the strut.
   D. solid axle systems are inexpensive and good for hauling heavy loads.

ASE Technician A/Technician B Style Questions

_____ 1. Tech A says that the wheel and tire are examples of unsprung weight. Tech B says that the exhaust system is an example of sprung weight. Who is correct?
   A. Tech A
   B. Tech B
   C. Both A and B
   D. Neither A nor B

_____ 2. Tech A says that one purpose of the suspension system is to keep the tires in contact with the road. Tech B says that the heavier the weight of the unsprung components, the smaller the reaction force they will generate. Who is correct?
   A. Tech A
   B. Tech B
   C. Both A and B
   D. Neither A nor B

_____ 3. Tech A says that yaw is when a vehicle deviates from its straight path. Tech B says that roll is when the front of the vehicle noses down or rises up. Who is correct?
   A. Tech A
   B. Tech B
   C. Both A and B
   D. Neither A nor B

_____ 4. Tech A says that leaf springs are made from a single length of special wire, which is heated and wound on a former in the shape of a coil. Tech B says that a progressive-rate spring offers a soft ride but can also carry a heavier load. Who is correct?
   A. Tech A
   B. Tech B
   C. Both A and B
   D. Neither A nor B

_____ 5. Tech A says that shock absorbers dampen in the downward direction. Tech B says that shock absorbers dampen in the upward direction. Who is correct?
   A. Tech A
   B. Tech B
   C. Both A and B
   D. Neither A nor B

_____ 6. Tech A says that in a MacPherson strut suspension, the hydraulic strut supports the top of the steering knuckle, so it must be much stronger than an ordinary shock absorber. Tech B says that gas-pressurized shock absorbers don't use hydraulic fluid; they use pressurized nitrogen gas only. Who is correct?
   A. Tech A
   B. Tech B
   C. Both A and B
   D. Neither A nor B

_____ 7. Tech A says that a loaded ball joint supports the weight of the vehicle. Tech B says that a ball joint in a MacPherson strut suspension is a follower joint (not loaded). Who is correct?
   A. Tech A
   B. Tech B
   C. Both A and B
   D. Neither A nor B

_____ 8. Tech A says that a dead axle is designed to carry the weight of the vehicle, with no drive capability. Tech B says that live axles transmit power to the wheels. Who is correct?
   A. Tech A
   B. Tech B
   C. Both A and B
   D. Neither A nor B

_____ **9.** Tech A says that control arms serve as primary load-bearing elements of a vehicle's suspension system. Tech B says that an A-arm is a relatively flat triangular part that mounts to the frame or subframe at each leg of the A. Who is correct?

    A. Tech A

    B. Tech B

    C. Both A and B

    D. Neither A nor B

_____ **10.** Tech A says that on short-/long-arm (SLA) suspension systems, the upper control arm is the long one. Tech B says that on SLA suspension systems, the control arms are connected to the frame by ball joints. Who is correct?

    A. Tech A

    B. Tech B

    C. Both A and B

    D. Neither A nor B

Servicing Suspension Systems

At the start of each chapter you'll find the NATEF Tasks, Knowledge Objectives, and Skills Objectives from the textbook. These are your objectives as you make your way through the exercises in this workbook and the chapter in your textbook. The following activities have been designed to help you refresh your knowledge of the material in this chapter.

NATEF Tasks

- N41001 Diagnose vehicle wander, drift, pull, hard steering, bump steer, memory steer, torque steer, and steering return concerns; determine needed action. (AST/MAST)
- N41002 Diagnose short- and long-arm suspension system noises, body sway, and uneven ride height concerns; determine needed action. (AST/MAST)
- N41003 Diagnose strut suspension system noises, body sway, and uneven ride height concerns; determine needed action. (AST/MAST)
- N41004 Inspect, remove, and/or replace front/rear stabilizer bar (sway bar) bushings, brackets, and links. (MLR/AST/MAST)
- N41005 Inspect, remove, and/or replace shock absorbers; inspect mounts and bushings. (MLR/AST/MAST)
- N41006 Inspect, remove, and/or replace short- and long-arm suspension system coil springs and spring insulators. (AST/MAST)
- N41007 Inspect, remove, and/or replace steering knuckle assemblies. (AST/MAST)
- N41008 Inspect, remove, and/or replace upper and lower control arms, bushings, shafts, and rebound bumpers. (MLR/AST/MAST)
- N41009 Inspect, remove, and/or replace upper and/or lower ball joints (with or without wear indicators). (MLR/AST/MAST)
- N41010 Inspect, remove, and/or replace strut cartridge or assembly, strut coil spring, insulators (silencers), and upper strut bearing mount. (MLR/AST/MAST)
- N41011 Inspect rear suspension system leaf spring(s), spring insulators (silencers), shackles, brackets, bushings, center pins/bolts, and mounts. (MLR/AST/MAST)
- N41012 Inspect, remove, and/or replace strut rods and bushings. (AST/MAST)
- N41013 Inspect, remove, and/or replace track bar, strut rods/radius arms, and related mounts and bushings. (MLR/AST/MAST)
- N41014 Inspect, remove, and/or replace torsion bars and mounts. (MLR/AST/MAST)

Knowledge Objectives

After reading this chapter, you will be able to:

- K41001 Describe an overview of servicing suspension systems.
- K41002 Describe the purpose of tools used to service suspension systems.
- K41003 Describe the diagnostic process for suspension systems.
- K41004 Describe common issues with suspension systems.

Skills Objectives

After reading this chapter, you will be able to:

- S41001 Perform maintenance and repair on suspension systems.
- S41002 Lubricate steering and suspension systems.

Matching

Match the following terms with the correct description or example.

A. Dial indicator

B. Excessive play

C. Vehicle wander

D. Chassis ear

E. Drift

_____ **1.** The vehicle is not driving in exactly the direction the driver is steering it.

_____ **2.** A tool used to measure play in ball joints.

_____ **3.** Occurs when the driver is holding the steering wheel steady and straight, but the vehicle slowly begins to move either to the right or left.

_____ **4.** A tool that involves microphones that can be placed at various locations on the vehicle and a set of earphones worn by the technician.

_____ **5.** Magnifies the feel of road imperfections and makes the steering less responsive to steering wheel input.

Multiple Choice

Read each item carefully, and then select the best response.

_____ **1.** Identify the first step of the strategy-based diagnostic process of suspension system problems.
  A. Verifying the repair
  B. Focused testing
  C. Verifying the customer's concern
  D. Researching possible faults and gathering information

_____ **2.** Identify the third step of the strategy-based diagnostic process of suspension system problems.
  A. Verifying the repair
  B. Focused testing
  C. Verifying the customer's concern
  D. Performing the repair

_____ **3.** Identify the condition that requires correction from the driver to keep the vehicle straight.
  A. Vehicle wander
  B. Torque steer
  C. Hard steering
  D. Drift

_____ **4.** _____ is a pull that occurs during heavy acceleration.
  A. Torque steer
  B. Hard steering
  C. Drift
  D. Bump steer

_____ **5.** The ride height of a vehicle can only be measured if _____.
  A. the vehicle is equipped with an electronically controlled suspension
  B. the vehicle has matching tires that are properly inflated
  C. additional weight is placed in the vehicle
  D. the vehicle is cold

_____ **6.** Most ride height specifications require the measurement to be within _____ side to side.
  A. two inches
  B. three inches
  C. half an inch
  D. five inches

_____ **7.** Testing a strut-type suspension or conventional shock absorber involves performing a _____.
  A. bounce test
  B. noise test
  C. scan tool test
  D. DMM test

_____ **8.** To measure ball joint play of a suspension, the joint must be _____.
  A. cold
  B. hot

     C. loaded

     D. unloaded

_____ **9.** Identify a true statement with respect to removing and replacing shock absorbers.

     A. When replacing shock absorbers, the old rubber bushings can be reused.

     B. Even a slight oil film on the shock absorber is an indication of fluid leak.

     C. If a shock absorber must be replaced, it is industry practice to replace them as pairs.

     D. Loose or damaged shock absorbers need to be visually inspected and cannot be distinguished by noises.

_____ **10.** In a torsion bar, a large bolt in the torque arm helps change the amount of pressure it places on the _____ to raise or lower the suspension.

     A. control arm

     B. sprag clutch

     C. extension housing

     D. anchor bolt protrusion

True/False

If you believe the statement to be more true than false, write the letter "T" in the space provided. If you believe the statement to be more false than true, write the letter "F."

_____ **1.** After any suspension system components are replaced, the vehicle will most likely need a wheel alignment.

_____ **2.** A tie-rod end puller should always be used on aluminum steering arms.

_____ **3.** Operation of chassis ear during a road test should be performed by the driver to accurately diagnose the source of noise.

_____ **4.** During a bounce test, slight dampness on the shock and fluid drips on the shock are normal.

_____ **5.** The method of unloading the suspension ball joints depends on the layout of the suspension.

_____ **6.** Overfilling a lubricated joint with grease can rupture the seal or rubber boot or bellows.

_____ **7.** A torsion bar will have the same spring force even if twisted in the opposite direction.

_____ **8.** If a torsion bar is not marked, then a mark must be scribed on the torsion bar and corresponding arm to identify left and right.

_____ **9.** A faulty shock absorber cannot dampen the spring oscillations to promote a smoother ride.

_____ **10.** In a vehicle with adjustable shock absorbers, the shock absorber adjustments should be the same for the left- and right-hand sides.

Fill in the Blank

Read each item carefully, and then complete the statement by filling in the missing word(s).

1. An electronic stethoscope is sometimes called a(n) _____ _____.

2. When diagnosing suspension system problems, you may need to perform a road test to _____ the customer concern.

3. A(n) _____ is felt when the driver feels the steering wheel wanting to go to one side due to a bad tire.

4. _____ _____ can result from binding conditions in any pivot points in the steering or suspension system and can also result from unbalanced power steering assist.

5. The ride height of a vehicle can be measured with the help of a(n) _____ _____.

6. When removing leaf springs, the axle must be supported with the help of a(n) _____ _____.

7. In case of chopped tire wear or if the driver complains of ride comfort problems, the parts of the _____ _____ should be checked.

8. The ball joint of a suspension connects the upper and lower control arms to the _____ _____.

9. If the top of a shock absorber is held in by a stud and nut, a(n) _____ should be used to hold the top of the stud while unthreading the nut.

10. A(n) _____ _____ _____ is the only way to see inside an electronically controlled suspension system and to determine the problems.

Skill Drills

Place the skill drill steps in the correct order.

   1. Performing Ride Height Diagnosis:

_____ **A.** Check for properly sized, matching, and inflated tires. Correct any issues found.

_____ **B.** Inspect for bent components or a weak or broken spring if any measurements are not correct. If working with a torsion bar suspension, you may have to adjust ride height to correct the condition.

_____ **C.** Refer to the manufacturer's service information for correct measurement points and specifications.

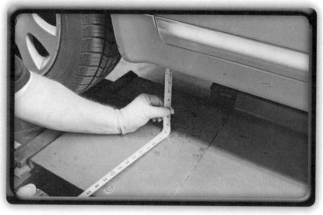

_____ **D.** Measure from points specified, such as from frame to ground on all four corners of the vehicle, and compare measurements to specifications.

_____ **E.** Check the vehicle for any nonstandard loads in the trunk or luggage area. Remove them temporarily while measuring ride height.

2. Measuring Play in the Suspension System: Loaded Lower Ball Joint:

_____ **A.** Rock the tire in and out at the top, watching for any play in the upper ball joint, and compare to specifications.

_____ **B.** Place a dial indicator on the lower control arm and vertically against the steering knuckle.

_____ **C.** Place a pry bar under the tire and pry it upward, watching the dial indicator reading as you pry and release. Record the total amount of movement in the joint and compare to the manufacturer's specifications.

3. Replacing a Shock Absorber:

_____ **A.** Pull the shock out by hand. Replace with new shock. Repeat on the other side.

_____ **B.** Raise the vehicle on a lift, and support the axle/control arm with a jack stand. With a socket and box-end wrench, remove the upper bolts holding the shocks in place.

_____ **C.** Remove the lower bolts holding the shock in place.

Review Questions

_____ **1.** Which of these tools is appropriate for changing coil springs on struts?
  A. Strut compressor
  B. Pitman arm puller
  C. Air chisel
  D. Ball joint socket

_____ **2.** Incorrect angles in the steering linkage due to a component being bent can result in:
  A. noise.
  B. bump steer.
  C. pull.
  D. hard steering.

_____ **3.** When the driver feels the steering wheel pulling to one side, which of the following should be checked first?
  A. Looseness in the suspension system
  B. Problems in the braking system
  C. Tire pressure
  D. Four-wheel alignment

_____ **4.** Which of the following can be used to diagnose the source of noise?
  A. Strut servicing kit
  B. Air chisel
  C. Chassis ear
  D. Scan tool

_____ **5.** All of the following statements with respect to suspension systems are true *except*:
  A. an electronic stethoscope is the best tool for diagnosing caster angle problems.
  B. if one of the front tires is low, it may cause the vehicle to pull to one side.
  C. a four-wheel alignment is needed to verify the alignment angles.
  D. torque steer is a pull that occurs during heavy acceleration.

_____ **6.** Which of the following statements is *correct*?
  A. Worn shock absorbers will not cause any problems on good roads.
  B. Shock absorbers use plastic bushings to isolate them from the vehicle body.
  C. If there is a slight oil film on the shock absorber, corrective action should be taken.
  D. The stabilizer components help prevent body roll when cornering.

_____ **7.** When testing a shock absorber, and releasing at the bottom of the stroke, what is the maximum times the vehicle should rebound?
  A. Zero
  B. Once
  C. Twice
  D. Three times

_____ **8.** The best method for testing the lower ball joint on a MacPherson strut suspension is to:
  A. raise the vehicle by the frame and allow the suspension to hang free.
  B. test it at the floor level.
  C. place a floor jack under the lower control arm and raise the wheel off the ground.
  D. fit a wooden block between the arm and the frame.

_____ **9.** In the suspension and steering systems of most modern vehicles:
  A. the joints need to be lubricated every month.
  B. there may be no grease fittings present.
  C. lubricated joints should be overfilled with grease.
  D. the joints need to be lubricated every fuel stop.

_____ **10.** Which of the following should be inspected when the ride height does not match the manufacturer's specifications?
  A. Shock absorbers
  B. Suspension springs
  C. Upper ball joints
  D. Lower ball joints

ASE Technician A/Technician B Style Questions

_____ **1.** Tech A says that suspension faults involving wear can often times be located during a visual inspection and confirmed as faulty with a measuring tool if necessary. Tech B says that damaged components may require an alignment machine to identify damaged parts. Who is correct?
  A. Tech A
  B. Tech B
  C. Both A and B
  D. Neither A nor B

_____ **2.** Tech A says that a road test is always part of focused testing. Tech B says that a road test is part of verifying the repair. Who is correct?
  A. Tech A
  B. Tech B
  C. Both A and B
  D. Neither A nor B

_____ **3.** Tech A says that worn sway bar bushings, brackets, and link bushings can cause excessive body sway. Tech B says that unmatched tires can cause ride height to be out of specs. Who is correct?
  A. Tech A
  B. Tech B
  C. Both A and B
  D. Neither A nor B

_____ **4.** Tech A says that when unloading a suspension where the coil spring or torsion bar is pushing against the lower control arm, a wood block must be placed between the upper control arm and the frame. Tech B says when unloading a MacPherson strut suspension with only a lower control arm, raise the vehicle by the frame, and allow the suspension to hang free. Who is correct?
  A. Tech A
  B. Tech B
  C. Both A and B
  D. Neither A nor B

_____ **5.** Tech A says that shock absorbers can be tested with a "bounce test." Tech B says that it is industry standard to replace an individual faulty shock absorber. Who is correct?
  A. Tech A
  B. Tech B
  C. Both A and B
  D. Neither A nor B

___ **6.** Tech A says that cotter pins should never be installed in ball joints. Tech B says that ball joints are typically welded into the control arm. Who is correct?

   A. Tech A

   B. Tech B

   C. Both A and B

   D. Neither A nor B

___ **7.** Tech A says that on most modern vehicles, the joints are sealed and lubricated for life, so there may be no grease fittings present. Tech B says that you should add grease to the ball joint until all the old grease is pushed out past the rubber boot on the joint. Who is correct?

   A. Tech A

   B. Tech B

   C. Both A and B

   D. Neither A nor B

___ **8.** Tech A says that both halves of the strut rod bushings go on the back side of the frame. Tech B says that on some vehicles the strut rod is the adjustment point for caster. Who is correct?

   A. Tech A

   B. Tech B

   C. Both A and B

   D. Neither A nor B

___ **9.** Tech A says that loose ball joints can cause the vehicle to wander. Tech B says that loose control arm bushings can cause a vehicle to wander. Who is correct?

   A. Tech A

   B. Tech B

   C. Both A and B

   D. Neither A nor B

___ **10.** Tech A says that when removing a MacPherson strut assembly from a vehicle, you must use a strut compressor to keep the spring compressed. Tech B says that a strut compressor is used only after the strut assembly has been removed from the vehicle. Who is correct?

   A. Tech A

   B. Tech B

   C. Both A and B

   D. Neither A nor B

Wheel Alignment

At the start of each chapter you'll find the NATEF Tasks, Knowledge Objectives, and Skills Objectives from the textbook. These are your objectives as you make your way through the exercises in this workbook and the chapter in your textbook. The following activities have been designed to help you refresh your knowledge of the material in this chapter.

NATEF Tasks

- N42001 Perform pre-alignment inspection; measure vehicle ride height; determine needed action. (MLR/AST/MAST)
- N42002 Prepare vehicle for wheel alignment on alignment machine; perform four-wheel alignment by checking and adjusting front- and rear-wheel caster, camber, and toe as required; center steering wheel. (AST/MAST)
- N42003 Reset steering angle sensor. (AST/MAST)
- N42004 Check toe-out on turns (turning radius); determine needed action. (AST/MAST)
- N42005 Check steering axis inclination (SAI) and included angle; determine needed action. (AST/MAST)
- N42006 Check rear wheel thrust angle; determine needed action. (AST/MAST)
- N42007 Check front and/or rear cradle (subframe) alignment; determine needed action. (AST/MAST)

Knowledge Objectives

After reading this chapter, you will be able to:

- K42001 Explain the purpose and function of wheel alignment and the alignment angles.
- K42002 Explain camber, its purpose, and effects.
- K42003 Explain caster, its purpose, and effects.
- K42004 Explain toe, its purpose, and effects.
- K42005 Explain toe-out on turns, its purpose, and effects.
- K42006 Explain steering axis inclination, its purpose, and effects.
- K42007 Explain included angle and its purpose.
- K42008 Explain scrub radius, its purpose, and effects.
- K42009 Explain turning radius, its purpose, and effects.
- K42010 Explain thrust angle, centerlines, and setbacks, their purpose, and effects.
- K42011 Explain ride height, its purpose, and effects.
- K42012 Identify tools used in wheel alignment and their function.

Skills Objectives

After reading this chapter, you will be able to:

- S42001 Perform a wheel alignment.

Matching

Match the following terms with the correct description or example.

- **A.** Ackermann angle
- **B.** Camber
- **C.** Ackermann principle
- **D.** Included angle
- **E.** Caster
- **F.** Centerline
- **G.** Positive caster
- **H.** Scrub radius
- **I.** Negative caster
- **J.** Zero scrub radius

_____ 1. The geometric alignment of linkages in a vehicle's steering such that the wheels on the inside of a turn are able to move in a smaller circle radius than the wheels on the outside.

_____ 2. The angle formed through the wheel pivot points when viewed from the side in comparison to a vertical line through the wheel.

_____ 3. The angle the steering arms make with the steering axis, projected toward the center of the rear axle.

_____ 4. The side-to-side vertical tilt of the wheel.

_____ 5. The angle formed between the SAI and the camber line.

_____ 6. Forward tilt of the steering knuckle pivot points from the vertical line.

_____ 7. A condition in which the camber line intersects the SAI line at the road surface.

_____ 8. The imaginary line drawn down the exact center of the vehicle from front to back.

_____ 9. The distance between two imaginary lines—the camber line and the SAI line.

_____ 10. Backward tilt of the steering knuckle pivot points from the vertical line.

Multiple Choice

Read each item carefully, and then select the best response.

_____ 1. _____ is viewed from the front of the vehicle and measured in degrees.
   A. Camber
   B. Caster
   C. Toe-in
   D. Toe-out

_____ 2. A wheel that leans away from the center of the vehicle at the top is said to have _____.
   A. positive caster
   B. negative camber
   C. negative caster
   D. positive camber

_____ 3. Identify the condition in which the camber line is inside the SAI line.
   A. Positive scrub radius
   B. Negative scrub radius
   C. Positive included angle
   D. Negative included angle

_____ 4. A tire with no tilt to provide maximum tire patch contact with the road is said to have _____.
   A. positive caster
   B. zero camber
   C. positive toe-in
   D. zero included angle

_____ 5. During braking, _____ causes the vehicle to veer toward the side with the greater braking effort.
   A. included angle
   B. toe-in
   C. positive scrub radius
   D. diagnostic angle

_____ 6. _____ refers to the relationship between the centerline of the vehicle and the angle of the rear tires.
   A. Diagnostic angle
   B. Included angle axis
   C. Steering axis
   D. Thrust angle

_____ 7. In a vehicle, setback should be no more than _____ from side to side.
   A. quarter of an inch
   B. half an inch
   C. inch
   D. 2 inches

_____ **8.** Identify a true statement with respect to ground clearance.
  A. Ground clearance is the amount of distance between the ground and a specified part of the vehicle such as the fender well.
  B. Increasing ground clearance has no effect on scrub radius.
  C. Increasing ground clearance increases the risk of an accident in several ways.
  D. Changing ground clearance has very little effect on the vehicle's center of gravity

_____ **9.** The condition in which the fronts of the wheels are closer together than the rears of the wheels, when viewed from above is called _____.
  A. caster
  B. toe-in
  C. camber
  D. toe-out

_____ **10.** The condition in which the fronts of the wheels are farther apart than the rears of the wheels, when viewed from above is called _____.
  A. caster
  B. toe-in
  C. camber
  D. toe-out

True/False

If you believe the statement to be more true than false, write the letter "T" in the space provided. If you believe the statement to be more false than true, write the letter "F."

_____ **1.** Camber tends to pull in the direction of the most positive camber.

_____ **2.** When calculating the included angle, if the camber angle is specified as negative, then it is added to the SAI angle.

_____ **3.** Less effort is needed to turn the steering wheel of a vehicle as the positive caster increases.

_____ **4.** Scrub radius can be changed accidentally in a number of ways.

_____ **5.** If a rear-wheel drive vehicle has negative scrub radius, the vehicle's forward motion and the friction between the tire and the road cause a force that tends to move the front wheels backward.

_____ **6.** The term thrust line refers to the direction in which the rear wheels are pointing.

_____ **7.** Thrust angle cannot be adjusted on vehicles with adjustable rear suspensions.

_____ **8.** Setback is a diagnostic measurement because it is generally not adjustable.

_____ **9.** Steering axis inclination (SAI) angle can be adjusted.

_____ **10.** Generally, SAI and included angles should not vary more than half a degree from side-to-side, plus or minus.

Fill in the Blank

Read each item carefully, and then complete the statement by filling in the missing word(s).

  1. A wheel that leans toward the center of the vehicle is said to have _____ _____.

  2. _____ _____ is calculated by the addition of SAI angle and the camber angle.

  3. When an angle is referred to as a(n) _____ _____, it means the angle cannot be changed, but is measured to determine if any parts are bent, such as a spindle, control arm, or steering arm.

  4. _____ _____ causes the tires of a vehicle to travel in a straight line with minimal driver input.

  5. In a vehicle, differences in caster cause a pull to the side with the most _____ caster.

  6. _____ _____ is also known as steering offset and scrub geometry.

  7. On front-wheel drive vehicles, positive scrub radius causes _____ - _____.

  8. The distance one wheel is set back from the wheel on the opposite side of the axle is called _____.

  9. On rear-wheel drive vehicles, positive scrub radius causes _____ - _____.

  10. _____ _____ is a measure of how small a circle the vehicle can turn in when the steering wheel is turned to the limit.

Labeling

Label the following diagrams with the correct terms.

1. Types of camber:

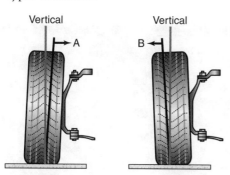

A. _____

B. _____

2. Types of caster:

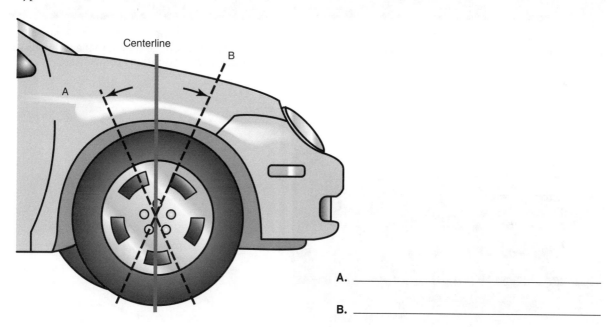

A. _____

B. _____

3. Types of toe:

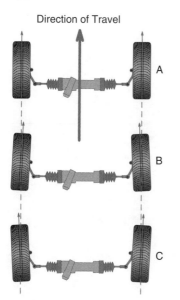

A. _____

B. _____

C. _____

Skill Drills

Place the skill drill steps in the correct order.

1. Checking SAI and Included Angle:

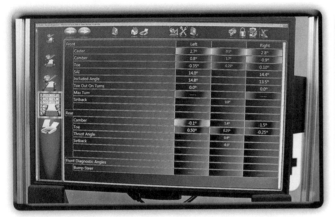

_____ **A.** Calculate the included angle, if the alignment machine doesn't, by adding the camber reading of each wheel to the SAI of each wheel, and compare to specifications. Remember that if camber is a negative number, you need to subtract the camber from the SAI to get the included angle.

_____ **B.** Position the vehicle on the alignment rack. Attach the wheel sensors on the vehicle to the locations specified by the sensor manufacturer, and compensate.

_____ **C.** Follow the alignment machine instructions for taking the SAI measurements, and compare them to the vehicle manufacturer's specifications. Typically, the SAI reading will require a caster sweep to be performed. SAI is a nonadjustable angle. No changes can be made; the angle helps the technician to verify that suspension components are bent.

2. Checking Front and/or Rear Cradle Alignment:

_____ **A.** If the parts are not bent, check the positioning of the cradle. Loosen cradle bolts and shift in the necessary direction to correct alignment angles.

_____ **B.** If adjustment is still not possible, check for a bent cradle or cradle mounting points by measuring from fixed points on one side compared to the same points on the other side. If they are different, the cradle needs adjusting.

_____ **C.** Position the vehicle on the alignment rack. Attach the wheel sensors on the vehicle, and compensate. Take the alignment readings and compare to the specifications. If camber and caster are incorrect and not adjustable, check for bent parts.

3. Preparing a Vehicle for a Wheel Alignment:

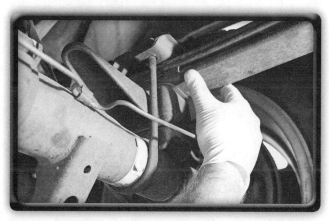

_____ **A.** With the vehicle raised, inspect all suspension and steering components, including the wheel bearings. Repair or replace all damaged or worn suspension components.

_____ **B.** Position the rear wheels on the slip plates or rear turntables.

_____ **C.** Check the play of the steering wheel. Correct any excess play before undertaking the wheel alignment.

_____ **D.** Position the vehicle on the wheel alignment ramp making sure the front tires are positioned correctly on the turntables.

_____ **E.** Check the size and condition of all four tires. Adjust the air pressure to specifications.

_____ **F.** Attach the wheel units of the wheel alignment machine.

_____ **G.** Remove any heavy items from the trunk and passenger compartments.

_____ **H.** Measure the vehicle's ride height.

_____ **I.** Bounce each corner of the vehicle to check the correct functioning of the shock absorbers.

Review Questions

_____ **1.** Wheel alignments should be performed for all of the following reasons *except*:
   A. when the vehicle has covered a long distance with low tire pressure.
   B. when tire wear shows any tire wearing angle issue.
   C. when components are replaced that could affect the alignment.
   D. whenever new tires are being installed.

_____ **2.** All of the following statements with respect to camber are true *except*:
   A. it is the side-to-side vertical tilt of the wheel.
   B. it tends to pull in the opposite direction of the most positive camber.
   C. it is affected by ride height.
   D. in modern vehicles, large positive number angles would cause the tire to ride on the outer edges of the tires.

_____ **3.** When a vehicle has negative caster:
   A. the center of the tire contact point is in front of the steering axis centerline.
   B. it causes the tires to travel in a straight line with minimal driver input.
   C. it causes the spindle to tilt as the wheel is steered.
   D. it can become unstable as speed increases.

_____ **4.** All of the following statements are true *except*:
   A. the condition in which the front of the wheels are closer together than the rear of the wheels is called toe-in.
   B. the condition in which the front of the wheels are farther apart than the rear is called toe-out.
   C. toe-out on turns is the relative toe setting of the rear wheels as the vehicle turns.
   D. improper toe settings cause much faster tire wear than camber or caster.

_____ **5.** The axis around which the wheel assembly swivels as it turns to the right or left is called the:
   A. steering axis.
   B. included angle axis.
   C. diagnostic angle.
   D. inclination angle.

_____ **6.** On front-wheel drive vehicles, negative scrub radius will cause:
   A. toe-in.
   B. greater torque steer.
   C. toe-out.
   D. the front wheels to move backward.

_____ **7.** If the camber line is outside of the SAI line (or they intersect below the road surface), then it has:
   A. positive offset.
   B. zero scrub radius.
   C. negative offset.
   D. zero offset.

_____ **8.** Which of the following statements is correct?
   A. Most front-wheel drive vehicles use a positive scrub radius.
   B. Scrub radius is a measure of how small a circle the vehicle can turn in when the steering wheel is turned to the limit.
   C. Ideally, the thrust line and the vehicle's geometric centerline should line up closely.
   D. A setback issue in the rear will pull toward the side with the maximum setback.

_____ **9.** A tool that is used to hold alignment targets to the wheels is a:
   A. wheel alignment machine.
   B. turntable.
   C. steering wheel holder.
   D. wheel clamp and extension.

_____ **10.** Which of the following tools is used to keep the steering wheel from turning when centering the steering wheel during an alignment?
   A. Brake pedal depressor tool
   B. Wheel alignment machine
   C. Steering wheel holder
   D. Scan tool

ASE Technician A/Technician B Style Questions

_____ **1.** Tech A says that thrust angle refers to the direction the front wheels are pointing. Tech B says that scrub radius refers to the intersection of the tire's camber line in relation to an imaginary line through the steering knuckle pivots. Who is correct?
   A. Tech A
   B. Tech B
   C. Both A and B
   D. Neither A nor B

_____ **2.** Tech A says that a vehicle will tend to pull toward the side with the most positive camber. Tech B says that camber is the forward and backward tilt of the steering axis from vertical when viewed from the side. Who is correct?
   A. Tech A
   B. Tech B
   C. Both A and B
   D. Neither A nor B

_____ **3.** Tech A says that caster is when the distance between the fronts of the tires are closer together than the rears of the tires. Tech B says that a vehicle will pull toward the side with the most positive caster. Who is correct?
   A. Tech A
   B. Tech B
   C. Both A and B
   D. Neither A nor B

_____ **4.** Tech A says that toe-in is when the front of the tires are farther apart than the rear of the tires. Tech B says that excessive toe causes faster tire wear than camber or caster. Who is correct?
   A. Tech A
   B. Tech B
   C. Both A and B
   D. Neither A nor B

_____ **5.** Tech A says that worn ball joints can affect alignment angles. Tech B says that worn control arm bushings can affect alignment angles. Who is correct?
   A. Tech A
   B. Tech B
   C. Both A and B
   D. Neither A nor B

_____ **6.** Tech A says that the front wheels should be aligned before the rear wheels. Tech B says that front wheel toe should be adjusted after front wheel caster and camber. Who is correct?
  A. Tech A
  B. Tech B
  C. Both A and B
  D. Neither A nor B

_____ **7.** Tech A says that when the front wheels are being steered around a corner, the fronts of the tires are further apart than the rears. Tech B says that steering axis inclination is formed by drawing a line through the center of the upper and lower pivot points of the suspension assembly. Who is correct?
  A. Tech A
  B. Tech B
  C. Both A and B
  D. Neither A nor B

_____ **8.** Tech A says that changing the diameter of the wheels and tires can affect scrub radius. Tech B says that the vehicle's thrust angle is the same as the rear wheels' camber angle. Who is correct?
  A. Tech A
  B. Tech B
  C. Both A and B
  D. Neither A nor B

_____ **9.** Tech A says that checking tire size and pressure is a part of the pre-alignment inspection. Tech B says that the alignment machine requires a compensation process for the wheel adapters. Who is correct?
  A. Tech A
  B. Tech B
  C. Both A and B
  D. Neither A nor B

_____ **10.** Tech A says that most all vehicles have adjustable caster and camber. Tech B says that when performing a four-wheel alignment, the rear wheels are adjusted first so they conform to the vehicle's centerline. Who is correct?
  A. Tech A
  B. Tech B
  C. Both A and B
  D. Neither A nor B

Principles of Braking

At the start of each chapter you'll find the NATEF tasks, Knowledge Objectives, and Skills Objectives from the textbook. These are your objectives as you make your way through the exercises in this workbook and the chapter in your textbook. The following activities have been designed to help you refresh your knowledge of the material in this chapter.

NATEF Tasks

- N3001 Describe the operation of a regenerative braking system. (MLR/AST/MAST)

Knowledge Objectives

After reading this chapter, you will be able to:

- K43001 Describe the evolution of braking systems over time.
- K43002 Explain braking system fundamentals.
- K43003 Describe the factors that affect braking.
- K43004 Describe kinetic energy.
- K43005 Describe acceleration and deceleration.
- K43006 Describe energy transformation.
- K43007 Describe the purpose and function of friction and friction brakes.
- K43008 Describe the process of heat transfer.
- K43009 Explain the types of brake fade.
- K43010 Describe rotational force and its effect.
- K43011 Describe levers and mechanical advantage, and provide examples.
- K43012 Describe the purpose and operation of the various types of brake systems.
- K43013 Describe the operation of hydraulic brakes.
- K43014 Describe the operation of air brakes.
- K43015 Describe the operation of exhaust brakes.
- K43016 Describe the operation of compression brakes.
- K43017 Describe the operation of electric brakes.
- K43018 Describe the operation and components of parking brakes.
- K43019 Describe the operation of brake-by-wire brake systems.

Skills Objectives

There are no Skills Objectives for this chapter.

Matching

Match the following terms with the correct description or example.

A. Exhaust brake
B. Band brake
C. Brake assist
D. Brake fade
E. Brakes
F. Conservation of energy
G. Disc brakes
H. Drum brakes
I. Friction
J. Fulcrum

K. Jake brake
L. Kinetic energy
M. Master cylinder
N. Mechanical advantage
O. Mechanical disadvantage
P. Parking brake
Q. Regenerative braking
R. Scrub brakes
S. Top hat parking brake
T. Weight transfer

_____ **1.** A type of brake system that forces stationary brake pads against the outside of a rotating brake rotor.

_____ **2.** A brake system that uses leverage to force a friction block against one or more wheels.

_____ **3.** When the load distance on a lever is greater than the effort distance, which means the effort required to move the load is greater than the load itself.

_____ **4.** A physical law that states that energy cannot be created or destroyed.

_____ **5.** A drum brake that is located inside a disc brake rotor in order to act as a parking brake.

_____ **6.** A type of brake system that forces brake shoes against the inside of a brake drum.

_____ **7.** An enhanced safety system built in to some ABS systems that anticipates a panic stop and applies maximum braking force to slow the vehicle as quickly as possible.

_____ **8.** Technology that allows a vehicle to recapture and store part of the kinetic energy in a reusable form when braking.

_____ **9.** The reduction in stopping power caused by a change in the brake system such as overheating, water, or overheated brake fluid.

_____ **10.** The ratio of load and effort for any simple machine such as a lever.

_____ **11.** A braking system that uses a metal band lined with friction material to clamp around the outside of a wheel or drum.

_____ **12.** The point around which a lever rotates and that supports the lever and the load.

_____ **13.** A brake that works by restricting the flow of exhaust gases through the engine by closing a butterfly valve located in the exhaust manifold.

_____ **14.** Weight moving from one set of wheels to the other set of wheels during braking, acceleration, or cornering.

_____ **15.** A brake system that consists of an extra exhaust valve on a diesel engine, which releases compressed gases from the combustion chamber at the top of the compression stroke; also called a compression brake.

_____ **16.** The resistance created by surfaces in contact.

_____ **17.** Converts the brake pedal force into hydraulic pressure, which is then transmitted via brake lines and hoses to one or more pistons at each wheel brake unit.

_____ **18.** A brake system used for holding the vehicle when it is stationary.

_____ **19.** A system made up of hydraulic and mechanical components designed to slow or stop a vehicle.

_____ **20.** The energy of an object in motion; it increases by the square of the speed.

Multiple Choice

Read each item carefully, and then select the best response.

_____ **1.** Which type of brake is commonly used to activate drum-type friction brakes on the trailer?
   A. Air brake
   B. Exhaust brake
   C. Compression brake
   D. Electric brake

_____ **2.** What type of system uses a computer to monitor the speed of each wheel and control the hydraulic pressure to each wheel to prevent wheel lockup?
   A. Brake assist
   B. Antilock brake system
   C. Brake-by-wire
   D. Brake pedal emulator

_____ **3.** In a brake-by-wire system a _____ tells the computer how firmly the driver intends to brake which then sends control signals to the appropriate brake actuators.
   A. brake pedal emulator
   B. service brake
   C. hydraulic actuator
   D. kinetic sensor

_____ **4.** Which of the following factors influence a vehicle's ability to brake effectively?
   A. Weight of the vehicle
   B. Height of the vehicle

         C. Tire composition

         D. All of the above

_____ **5.** What law states that an object will stay at rest or at uniform speed unless it is acted on by an outside force?

         A. Euler's first law of motion

         B. The law of conservation of energy

         C. Newton's first law of motion

         D. Kirchhoff's law

_____ **6.** The amount of friction between two moving surfaces in contact with each other is expressed as a ratio and is called the _____.

         A. law of conservation of energy

         B. coefficient of friction

         C. rate of heat transfer

         D. second law of motion

_____ **7.** When brakes are operated on a moving vehicle, a _____ force is generated.

         A. cornering

         B. directional

         C. deflecting

         D. rotational

_____ **8.** Brake pedals are usually a _____. They pivot at the top end (fulcrum). The foot pressure (effort) is applied to the bottom end. And the master cylinder (load) is applied between the two.

         A. lever of the first order

         B. lever of the second order

         C. lever of the third order

         D. lever of the fourth order

_____ **9.** What type of braking system is used on trailers towed by light vehicles if their gross weight exceeds a certain value?

         A. Jake brake

         B. Exhaust braking system

         C. Electric braking system

         D. Air-operated braking system

_____ **10.** What type of parking brake uses a small drum brake to prevent the driveshaft from turning?

         A. Drum-style parking brake

         B. Transmission-mounted parking brake

         C. Top hat parking brake

         D. Electric parking brake

True/False

If you believe the statement to be more true than false, write the letter "T" in the space provided. If you believe the statement to be more false than true, write the letter "F."

_____ **1.** The band braking system was used for more than 2,000 years with virtually no change.

_____ **2.** Giving greater control of the braking system to the computer increases driving safety.

_____ **3.** Aggressive driving causes tires to become hot and possibly overheated, thus reducing the tire's ability to obtain maximum traction.

_____ **4.** The service brake is usually operated by hand, but some vehicles use a foot-activated pedal.

_____ **5.** Faster-moving objects have more kinetic energy than slower-moving objects of the same weight.

_____ **6.** An outside force needs to act upon a vehicle to cause it to decelerate, that force comes from the mass of the Earth.

_____ **7.** Static friction is resistance between moving surfaces and is present in standard brakes.

_____ **8.** Most of the heat generated by the braking process radiates into the atmosphere.

_____ **9.** Water fade is caused by water-soaked brake linings acting like a lubricant and lowering the coefficient of friction between the braking surfaces.

_____ **10.** Modern drum and disc brake systems are regularly fitted with an ABS that monitors the speed of each wheel and prevents wheel lock-up or skidding, no matter how hard brakes are applied or how slippery the road surface.

_____ **11.** Air-operated braking systems use an extra lobe on the camshaft to control an auxiliary exhaust valve at the top of each cylinder.

_____ **12.** When engaged, the jake brake releases the compression stroke pressure before it can be transmitted back to the power stroke of the piston.

_____ **13.** Parking brake systems incorporate an automatic method of adjustment.

_____ **14.** Regenerative braking is accomplished by causing the hybrid vehicle's electric motor to act as a battery.

_____ **15.** Some current hybrid vehicles use brake-by-wire technology during regeneration but with a hydraulic backup brake system.

Fill in the Blank

Read each item carefully, and then complete the statement by filling in the missing word(s).

1. A(n) _____-_____-_____ system does away with the hydraulic portion of the brake system and replaces it with sensors, wires, an electronic control unit, and electrically actuated motors to apply individual brake units at each wheel.

2. In a(n) _____ braking system the amount of stopping power is controlled by how much electricity is being generated.

3. There are two brake systems on all vehicles—a _____ brake and a _____ brake.

4. By using _____ of different sizes, hydraulic forces can be increased or reduced, allowing designers to obtain the desired braking force for each wheel.

5. Heavier objects have more _____ energy than lighter objects moving at the same speed.

6. In an automobile, _____, or an increase in kinetic energy, is caused by the power from the engine.

7. The energy used to cause a vehicle to accelerate and decelerate must be _____ from one form of energy to another.

8. _____ _____ is caused by the buildup of heat in the braking surfaces, which get so hot they cannot create any additional heat, leading to a loss of friction.

9. _____ fade is caused by the brake fluid becoming so hot that it boils.

10. Brake systems use _____ and mechanical advantage to apply service and parking brakes.

11. An _____ _____ may be used in addition to friction brakes in medium and heavy vehicles, which creates engine braking by restricting the exhaust flow.

12. On articulated vehicles, such as tractor/trailers, any delays in applying the trailer brakes are minimized by using a relay valve and a separate _____ _____ on the trailer.

13. A(n) _____ brake works by restricting the flow of exhaust gases through the engine by closing a butterfly valve located in the exhaust manifold.

14. On drum brakes, a drum-style parking brake _____ applies the brake shoes against the drum.

15. Part of the _____ _____ cable is inside a wound steel housing, which allows it to be somewhat flexible, yet noncompressible to guide the cable and hold everything in place.

Labeling

Label the following diagrams with the correct terms.

1. Weight transfer during braking:

A. _____

B. _____

C. _____

D. _____

2. Basic types of levers:

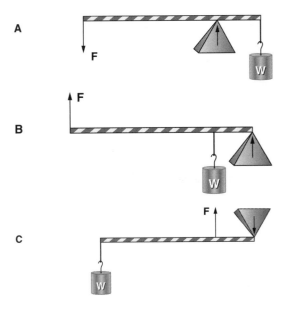

A. _____

B. _____

C. _____

3. The hydraulic brake system:

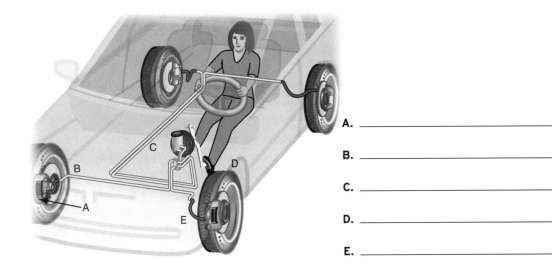

A. _____

B. _____

C. _____

D. _____

E. _____

4. Power brake booster:

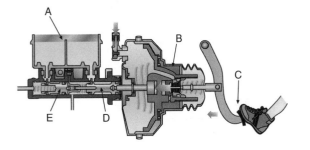

A. _____

B. _____

C. _____

D. _____

E. _____

5. The air brake system:

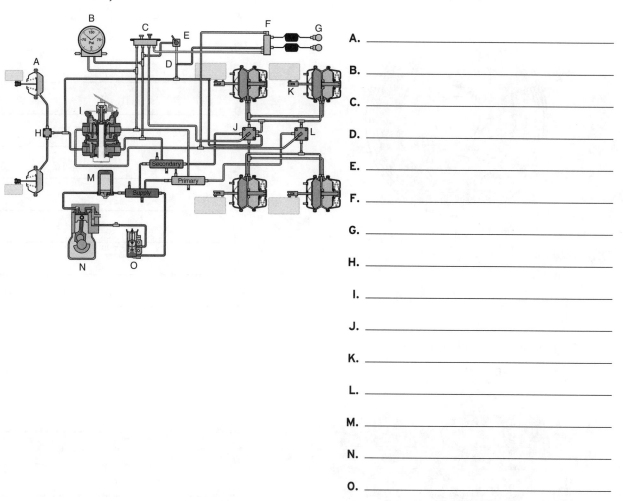

A. _____

B. _____

C. _____

D. _____

E. _____

F. _____

G. _____

H. _____

I. _____

J. _____

K. _____

L. _____

M. _____

N. _____

O. _____

6. Air brake canister:

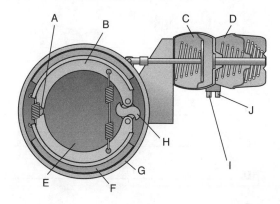

A. _____

B. _____

C. _____

D. _____

E. _____

F. _____

G. _____

H. _____

I. _____

J. _____

7. Electric braking system:

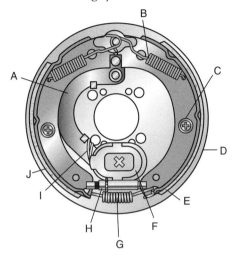

A. _____

B. _____

C. _____

D. _____

E. _____

F. _____

G. _____

H. _____

I. _____

J. _____

8. Top hat design parking brake:

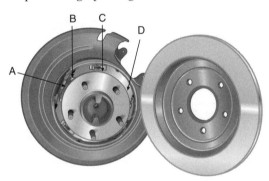

A. _____

B. _____

C. _____

D. _____

9. Drum-style parking brake:

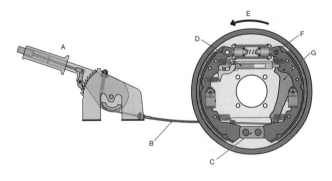

A. _____

B. _____

C. _____

D. _____

E. _____

F. _____

G. _____

10. Electrohydraulic brake-by-wire system:

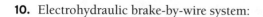

A. _____

B. _____

C. _____

D. _____

E. _____

F. _____

G. _____

H. _____

I. _____

J. _____

K. _____

L. _____

M. _____

N. _____

O. _____

Review Questions

_____ **1.** Which of these is a simple mechanical system that uses leverage to force a friction block against one or more wheels?
   A. Drum brake
   B. Band brake
   C. Scrub brake
   D. Disc brake

_____ **2.** All of the below statements are true *except*:
   A. Service brakes consist of drum and/or disc brakes and are operated by hand.
   B. The parking brake is used for holding the vehicle in place when it is stationary.
   C. In disc brakes, pads are forced against the outside of a brake disc.
   D. Modern braking systems are hydraulically operated.

_____ **3.** If we triple the speed of an object, the kinetic energy will:
   A. increase by three times.
   B. increase by nine times.
   C. decrease by three times.
   D. increase by six times.

_____ **4.** The cycle of energy transformation in a typical vehicle is:
   A. Chemical energy→Heat energy→Mechanical energy→Kinetic energy
   B. Kinetic energy→Heat energy→Mechanical energy→Chemical energy

    C. Chemical energy→Mechanical energy→Heat energy→Kinetic energy

    D. Mechanical energy→Heat energy→Chemical energy→Kinetic energy

_____ **5.** All of the following statements are true *except*:

    A. Heat transfers from a hot area to a cool area.

    B. Friction is the resistance created by surfaces in contact.

    C. Kinetic friction is resistance between non-moving surfaces.

    D. In drum brakes, the heat is created outside of the drum and transferred to the inner surface.

_____ **6.** The kind of brake fade caused by the brake fluid becoming so hot that it boils is:

    A. heat fade.

    B. water fade.

    C. hydraulic fade.

    D. hard fade.

_____ **7.** The brake pedal uses leverage:

    A. for weight transfer.

    B. to multiply the force applied to the master cylinder.

    C. to increase traction.

    D. to decrease heat generation.

_____ **8.** Which of the following is used on heavy vehicles and is commonly called air brake?

    A. Hydraulic control unit

    B. Hydraulic brake

    C. Air operated braking system

    D. Electric brake

_____ **9.** Medium and heavy duty vehicles often require increased braking in situations where friction brakes overheat and fail. This can be addressed by using a(n):

    A. parking brake.

    B. air brake.

    C. electric brake.

    D. exhaust brake.

_____ **10.** Vehicles equipped with disc brakes incorporate a mechanically operated drum-style parking brake in the center of the rear disc brake rotors, commonly called a:

    A. drum-style parking brake.

    B. top hat parking brake.

    C. electric braking system.

    D. transmission mounted parking brake.

ASE Technician A/Technician B Style Questions

_____ **1.** Tech A says that regenerative braking converts brake heat from friction into electricity. Tech B says that regenerative braking converts electrical energy from the battery into braking energy. Who is correct?

    A. Tech A

    B. Tech B

    C. Both A and B

    D. Neither A nor B

_____ **2.** Tech A says that antilock brake systems (ABS) were the first versions of EBC systems. Tech B says that ABS sensors apply or release hydraulic pressure to the wheel brake units during ABS brake events. Who is correct?

    A. Tech A

    B. Tech B

    C. Both A and B

    D. Neither A nor B

_____ **3.** Tech A says that water soaked brake shoes can be a cause of brake fade. Tech B says that disc brakes dissipate heat faster than drum brakes. Who is correct?

    A. Tech A

    B. Tech B

    C. Both A and B
    D. Neither A nor B

_____ **4.** Tech A says that a disc brake operates by clamping friction materials to the outside of a disc. Tech B says that a drum brake operates by clamping friction materials to the outside of a drum. Who is correct?
    A. Tech A
    B. Tech B
    C. Both A and B
    D. Neither A nor B

_____ **5.** Tech A says that tire pressure does not affect braking. Tech B says that heavy vehicle loads increase stopping distance. Who is correct?
    A. Tech A
    B. Tech B
    C. Both A and B
    D. Neither A nor B

_____ **6.** Tech A says that light-duty service brakes are typically applied hydraulically. Tech B says that light-duty parking brakes are typically applied hydraulically. Who is correct?
    A. Tech A
    B. Tech B
    C. Both A and B
    D. Neither A nor B

_____ **7.** Tech A says that the heavier the vehicle, the more stopping power is needed. Tech B says that the faster a vehicle is moving, the more braking power is needed. Who is correct?
    A. Tech A
    B. Tech B
    C. Both A and B
    D. Neither A nor B

_____ **8.** Tech A says that kinetic energy is created during braking to stop the vehicle. Tech B says that kinetic energy is converted to heat energy during braking. Who is correct?
    A. Tech A
    B. Tech B
    C. Both A and B
    D. Neither A nor B

_____ **9.** Tech A says that the brake pedal uses leverage to multiply foot pressure. Tech B says that when braking hard while moving forward, the vehicle's weight transfers to the rear wheels, increasing their traction. Who is correct?
    A. Tech A
    B. Tech B
    C. Both A and B
    D. Neither A nor B

_____ **10.** Tech A says that friction brakes can fade due to overheating of the brake lining. Tech B says that friction brakes can fade due to overheating of the brake fluid. Who is correct?
    A. Tech A
    B. Tech B
    C. Both A and B
    D. Neither A nor B

Hydraulic and Power Brakes Theory

At the start of each chapter you'll find the NATEF tasks, Knowledge Objectives, and Skills Objectives from the textbook. These are your objectives as you make your way through the exercises in this workbook and the chapter in your textbook. The following activities have been designed to help you refresh your knowledge of the material in this chapter.

NATEF Tasks

There are no NATEF tasks in this chapter.

Knowledge Objectives

After reading this chapter, you will be able to:

- K44001 Describe the principles behind the hydraulic braking system.
- K44002 Describe the principles of hydraulic pressure and force.
- K44003 Describe the principles of input force, working pressures, and output force.
- K44004 Describe the purpose and function of brake system hydraulic components.
- K44005 Describe the purpose and characteristics of brake fluid.
- K44006 Describe the types, purpose, and operation of master cylinders.
- K44007 Describe the operation of single-piston master cylinders.
- K44008 Describe the operation of tandem master cylinders.
- K44009 Describe the operation of quick take-up master cylinders.
- K44010 Describe the operation of ABS master cylinders.
- K44011 Describe the purpose and operation of master cylinder reservoirs and float switches.
- K44012 Describe the purpose and function of brake pedals.
- K44013 Describe the types of divided hydraulic systems and their function.
- K44014 Describe the purpose, construction, and function of brake lines and hoses.
- K44015 Describe the purpose and function of sealing washers and fittings.
- K44016 Describe the purpose and function of hydraulic braking system control components.
- K44017 Describe the purpose and function of proportioning valves.
- K44018 Describe the purpose and function of metering valves.
- K44019 Describe the purpose and function of pressure differential valves.
- K44020 Describe the purpose and function of combination valves.
- K44021 Describe the purpose and operation of brake warning lights and stop lights.
- K44022 Describe the types, purpose, and operation of power brake systems.
- K44023 Describe the components and operation of vacuum brake boosters.
- K44024 Describe the components and operation of hydraulic brake boosters.
- K44025 Describe the components and operation of electrohydraulic brake boosters.

Skills Objectives

There are no Skills Objectives in this chapter.

Matching

Match the following terms with the correct description or example.

- **A.** Bleeding
- **B.** Brake fluid
- **C.** Brake hose
- **D.** Brake lines
- **E.** Compensating port
- **F.** Aerate

G. Inlet port
H. Input force
I. Load transfer
J. Metering valve
K. Output force
L. Outlet port
M. Poppet valve

N. Primary cup
O. Primary piston
P. Quick take-up valve
Q. Residual pressure valve
R. Secondary cup
S. Secondary piston
T. Working pressure

_____ **1.** A brake piston in the master cylinder moved directly by the pushrod or the power booster; it generates hydraulic pressure to move the secondary piston.

_____ **2.** The tendency of silicone-based fluid to create air bubbles when forced at high pressure through small passages.

_____ **3.** Force that equals the working pressure multiplied by the surface area of the output piston, expressed as pounds, newtons, or kilograms.

_____ **4.** In drum brake systems, a valve that maintains pressure in the wheel cylinders slightly above atmospheric pressure so air does not enter the system through the seals in the wheel cylinders.

_____ **5.** The process of removing air from a hydraulic braking system.

_____ **6.** The force applied to the input piston, measured in either pounds or kilograms.

_____ **7.** A valve used on vehicles equipped with older rear drum/front disc brakes to delay application of the front disc brakes until the rear drum brakes are applied. Located in line with the front disc brakes.

_____ **8.** Hydraulic fluid that transfers forces under pressure through the hydraulic lines to the wheel braking units.

_____ **9.** Links the cylinder to the brake lines.

_____ **10.** Made of seamless, double-walled steel, and able to transmit over 1,000 psi (6895 kPa) of hydraulic pressure through the hydraulic brake system.

_____ **11.** A piston that is moved by hydraulic pressure generated by the primary piston in the master cylinder.

_____ **12.** Connects the reservoir with the space around the piston and between the piston cups in a brake master cylinder.

_____ **13.** The pressure within a hydraulic system while the system is being operated.

_____ **14.** A valve used to release excess pressure from the larger piston in a quick take-up master cylinder once the brake pads have contacted the brake rotors.

_____ **15.** A valve that controls the flow of brake fluid at usually preset pressures.

_____ **16.** Connects the brake fluid reservoir to the master cylinder bore when the piston is fully retracted, allowing for expansion and contraction of the brake fluid.

_____ **17.** A seal that prevents loss of fluid from the rear of each piston in the master cylinder.

_____ **18.** A seal that holds pressure in the master cylinder when force is applied to the piston.

_____ **19.** A flexible section of the brake lines between the body and suspension to allow for steering and suspension movement.

_____ **20.** Weight transfer from one set of wheels to the other set of wheels during braking, acceleration, or cornering.

Multiple Choice

Read each item carefully, and then select the best response.

_____ **1.** What law states that pressure applied to a fluid in one part of a closed system will be transmitted without loss to all other areas of the system?
A. Newton's law
B. Pascal's law
C. Kirchhoff's law
D. Ohm's law

_____ **2.** All of the following are variables to consider when talking about pressure and force in hydraulic systems, *except*:
A. input force
B. fluid type

    C. output force

    D. working pressure

_____ **3.** Standard brake fluid is _____, which means it absorbs water.

    A. hydrotropic

    B. aerated

    C. hygroscopic

    D. hydraulic

_____ **4.** Brake fluids are tested to ensure they meet the standards of quality for _____.

    A. stability

    B. resistance to oxidation

    C. boiling point

    D. all of the above

_____ **5.** What type of brake fluid is silicone-based?

    A. DOT 2

    B. DOT 3

    C. DOT 4

    D. DOT 5

_____ **6.** When the brake pedal is released quickly, the use of small holes drilled in the piston so that brake fluid from the reservoir can pass through the inlet port and past the edge of the primary cup, thus preventing a vacuum from being created is called _____.

    A. recuperation

    B. compensating

    C. aeration

    D. residual pressure release

_____ **7.** The _____ master cylinder is a tandem master cylinder used in divided systems.

    A. single-piston

    B. dual-piston

    C. ABS

    D. quick take-up

_____ **8.** What type of flare is sometimes called a bubble flare?

    A. Inverted double flare

    B. International Standards Organization flare

    C. Mushroom flare

    D. DIN flare

_____ **9.** Which of the following components is used to modify pressures within the hydraulic braking system?

    A. Proportioning valves

    B. Pressure differential valves

    C. Antilock hydraulic control units

    D. All of the above

_____ **10.** All of the following conditions will cause the brake warning light to illuminate, *except*:

    A. Parking brake is engaged

    B. Brake fluid is low

    C. Brake pedal is pressed

    D. Prove out circuit

True/False

If you believe the statement to be more true than false, write the letter "T" in the space provided. If you believe the statement to be more false than true, write the letter "F".

_____ **1.** In a closed system, hydraulic pressure is transmitted equally in all directions throughout the system.

_____ **2.** Because silicone-based fluid tends to aerate when forced at high pressure through small passages, it is not to be used in any vehicle equipped with antilock brakes.

_____ **3.** The outlet port adjusts for changes in the volume of the brake fluid ahead of the piston.

_____ **4.** Quick take-up master cylinders are used on disc brake systems that are equipped with low-drag brake calipers.

_____ **5.** Master cylinder reservoirs can be built into the master cylinder housing or can be a separate unit.

_____ **6.** The master cylinder converts the brake pedal force into hydraulic pressure that is transferred to the wheel brake units.

_____ **7.** A front-engine rear-wheel drive car has around 40% of its load on its rear wheels and 60% on its front wheels.

_____ **8.** While brake hoses are designed to be flexible, they should never be pinched, kinked, or bent tighter than a specified radius.

_____ **9.** During heavy braking, master cylinder pressure can reach the poppet valve's crack point.

_____ **10.** Adjustable proportioning valves are not recommended for most applications due to the amount of trial and error necessary to set them properly.

_____ **11.** The combination valve can combine the pressure differential valve, metering valve, and proportioning valve(s) in one unit.

_____ **12.** The brake warning light is activated by a normally closed switch located on the brake pedal assembly.

_____ **13.** The vacuum-assisted power booster uses the difference between engine vacuum and atmospheric pressure to increase the force that acts on the master cylinder pistons.

_____ **14.** Dual-diaphragm power boosters work on the same principle of operation as the single-diaphragm power booster but are much larger in diameter.

_____ **15.** While hydraulic brake boosters use power steering fluid to operate the booster, the master cylinder portion of the system still uses brake fluid.

Fill in the Blank

Read each item carefully, and then complete the statement by filling in the missing word(s).

1. The same _____ applied over different-sized surface areas will produce different levels of force.

2. If brake fluid boils, it turns from a liquid to a _____, which is compressible.

3. Brake fluids are graded against compliance standards set by the United States _____ _____ _____.

4. _____-_____ master cylinders have one piston with two cups: a primary cup and a secondary cup.

5. _____ master cylinders combine two master cylinders within a common housing that share a common cylinder bore.

6. The _____ piston of a tandem master cylinder is in the rear of the cylinder.

7. _____ _____-_____ master cylinders are used on disc brake systems that are equipped with low-drag brake calipers.

8. The _____ _____ uses leverage to multiply the effort from the driver's foot to the master cylinder.

9. The _____ _____ must be able to transmit considerable hydraulic pressure, 1500 psi (10,342 kPa) or more, during panic stops.

10. The _____ _____ flare is created by first flaring the end of the tube outward in a Y shape. Then about half of the flared end is folded inside of itself, leaving a double-thick section of brake line on the flared portion of the Y.

11. Many brake hoses use _____ fittings to connect the hose to the wheel unit.

12. _____ valves reduce brake pressure to the rear wheels when their load is reduced during moderate to severe braking.

13. A _____ _____ valve monitors any pressure difference between the two separate hydraulic brake circuits.

14. During hydraulic braking system bleeding, the pressure differential valve may need to be _____.

15. The less common _____ braking system gets rid of the vacuum booster and replaces it with an electrically driven hydraulic pump.

Labeling

Label the following diagrams with the correct terms.

1. Single piston master cylinder with primary and secondary cups:

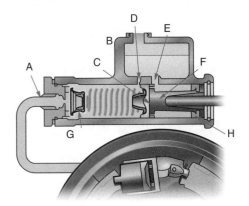

A. _____

B. _____

C. _____

D. _____

E. _____

F. _____

G. _____

H. _____

2. Single piston master cylinder with small holes in the piston to allow for recuperation:

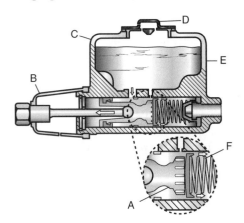

A. _____

B. _____

C. _____

D. _____

E. _____

F. _____

3. Divided hydraulic systems:

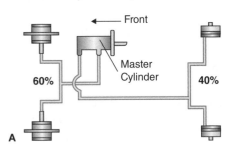

A. _____

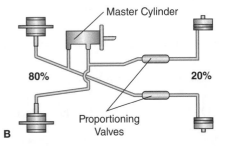

B. _____

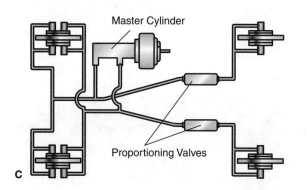

C. _____

4. Flexible brake hose construction:

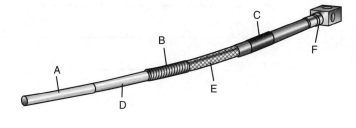

A. _____

B. _____

C. _____

D. _____

E. _____

F. _____

5. Pressure differential valve with a leak in the hydraulic braking system:

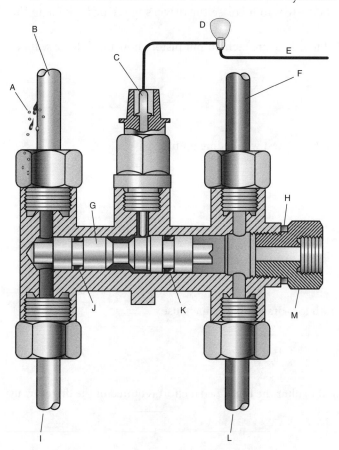

A. _____

B. _____

C. _____

D. _____

E. _____

F. _____

G. _____

H. _____

I. _____

J. _____

K. _____

L. _____

M. _____

6. Combination valve:

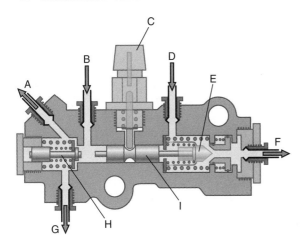

A. _____

B. _____

C. _____

D. _____

E. _____

F. _____

G. _____

H. _____

I. _____

Review Questions

_____ **1.** All of the statements are true *except*:
   A. Pascal's law is the principle behind hydraulic brakes.
   B. varying amounts of mechanical force can be extracted from a single amount of hydraulic pressure.
   C. the smaller brake caliper pistons on the front wheels give greater mechanical force and braking power to the front wheels.
   D. a power booster is fitted to the brake system to increase the driver's brake pedal force to the master cylinder.

_____ **2.** If 100 psi of working pressure is applied to a 2 square inch output piston, how much force will be created?
   A. 50 lb
   B. 100 lb
   C. 200 lb
   D. 400 lb

_____ **3.** Which of the following brake fluids has the highest wet boiling point?
   A. DOT 2
   B. DOT 4
   C. DOT 3
   D. DOT 5

_____ **4.** The port that connects the reservoir to the cylinder, just barely ahead of the primary cup is the:
   A. compensating port.
   B. inlet port.
   C. outlet port.
   D. primary port.

_____ **5.** Disc brake systems that are equipped with low-drag brake calipers use:
   A. tandem master cylinders.
   B. quick take-up master cylinders.
   C. single-piston master cylinders.
   D. modern master cylinders.

_____ **6.** Different lever designs can be engineered to alter the brake pedal effort required of the driver by using different levels of:
   A. input force.
   B. output force.
   C. working pressure.
   D. mechanical advantage.

_____ **7.** A wheel's braking ability depends most on:
  A. engine speed.
  B. the type of brake fluid used.
  C. the load it is carrying.
  D. the type of transmission used.

_____ **8.** Which of the following flares is created by first flaring the end of the tube outward in a Y shape?
  A. Straight flare
  B. Bubble flare
  C. Inverted double flare
  D. ISO flare

_____ **9.** Which of the following is used to hold off the application of the front brakes on vehicles with disc brakes on the front wheels and drum brakes on the rear wheels?
  A. Load-sensitive proportioning valve
  B. Metering valve
  C. Pressure differential valve
  D. Combination valve

_____ **10.** The valve that reduces rear brake pressure when the vehicle is lightly loaded and allows higher pressure when it is heavily loaded is:
  A. load-sensitive proportioning valve.
  B. metering valve.
  C. pressure differential valve.
  D. combination valve.

ASE Technician A/Technician B Style Questions

_____ **1.** Tech A says that hydraulic pressure is applied equally in all directions throughout a closed system. Tech B says that air in the hydraulic system will cause the brake pedal to be spongy. Who is correct?
  A. Tech A
  B. Tech B
  C. Both A and B
  D. Neither A nor B

_____ **2.** Tech A says that a brake pedal that does not return all the way causes the brake warning light on the instrument panel to stay on. Tech B says that a brake pedal that does not return causes the brake lights to stay on. Who is correct?
  A. Tech A
  B. Tech B
  C. Both A and B
  D. Neither A nor B

_____ **3.** Tech A says that brake fluid should have a low freezing point. Tech B says that brake fluid should be replaced every 12,000 miles. Who is correct?
  A. Tech A
  B. Tech B
  C. Both A and B
  D. Neither A nor B

_____ **4.** Tech A says that DOT 5 brake fluid should be used in all vehicles today because it is silicone based and will not absorb water. Tech B says that DOT 4 and DOT 3 are not recommended for use in ABS systems. Who is correct?
  A. Tech A
  B. Tech B
  C. Both A and B
  D. Neither A nor B

_____ **5.** Tech A says that the secondary piston in a master cylinder is operated by hydraulic pressure. Tech B says that the brake pedal return spring returns the master cylinder pistons to their original position. Who is correct?
  A. Tech A
  B. Tech B

      C. Both A and B

      D. Neither A nor B

_____ 6. Tech A says that the low level brake fluid switch on a master cylinder turns on the brake warning light when the system is low on fluid. Tech B says that the low level switch also monitors the condition of the fluid and activates the warning light when the brake fluid needs to be replaced. Who is correct?

      A. Tech A

      B. Tech B

      C. Both A and B

      D. Neither A nor B

_____ 7. Tech A says that the metering valve controls pressure to the rear brakes. Tech B says that the proportioning valve controls pressure to the front brakes. Who is correct?

      A. Tech A

      B. Tech B

      C. Both A and B

      D. Neither A nor B

_____ 8. Tech A says that the vacuum booster increases the vacuum in the brake system. Tech B says that the vacuum booster uses vacuum and atmospheric pressure to multiply the driver's foot pressure applied to the master cylinder push rod. Who is correct?

      A. Tech A

      B. Tech B

      C. Both A and B

      D. Neither A nor B

_____ 9. Tech A says that input force divided by the area of the input gives working pressure. Tech B says that working pressure multiplied by the surface area of the output piston gives output force. Who is correct?

      A. Tech A

      B. Tech B

      C. Both A and B

      D. Neither A nor B

_____ 10. Tech A says that quick take-up master cylinders use two additional pistons to move brake fluid faster. Tech B says that banjo fittings are commonly used to connect brake hoses to wheel brake units. Who is correct?

      A. Tech A

      B. Tech B

      C. Both A and B

      D. Neither A nor B

Servicing Hydraulic Systems and Power Brakes

At the start of each chapter you'll find the NATEF Tasks, Knowledge Objectives, and Skills Objectives from the textbook. These are your objectives as you make your way through the exercises in this workbook and the chapter in your textbook. The following activities have been designed to help you refresh your knowledge of the material in this chapter.

NATEF Tasks

- N45001 Select, handle, store, and fill brake fluids to proper level; use proper fluid type per manufacturer specification. (MLR/AST/MAST)
- N45002 Test brake fluid for contamination. (MLR/AST/MAST)
- N45003 Bleed and/or flush brake system. (MLR/AST/MAST)
- N45004 Measure brake pedal height, travel, and free play (as applicable); determine needed action. (AST/MAST)
- N45005 Check brake pedal travel with and without engine running to verify proper power booster operation. (MLR/AST/MAST)
- N45006 Diagnose pressure concerns in the brake system using hydraulic principles (Pascal's law). (AST/MAST)
- N45007 Check master cylinder for internal/external leaks and proper operation; determine needed action. (MLR/AST/MAST)
- N45008 Remove, bench bleed, and reinstall master cylinder. (AST/MAST)
- N45009 Measure and adjust master cylinder pushrod length. (AST/MAST)
- N45010 Inspect vacuum type power booster unit for leaks; inspect the check valve for proper operation; determine needed action. (AST/MAST)
- N45011 Inspect and test hydraulically assisted power brake system for leaks and proper operation; determine needed action. (AST/MAST)
- N45012 Inspect brake lines, flexible hoses, and fittings for leaks, dents, kinks, rust, cracks, bulging, wear; and loose fittings/supports; determine needed action. (MLR/AST/MAST)
- N45013 Replace brake lines, hoses, fittings, and supports. (AST/MAST)
- N45014 Fabricate brake lines using proper material and flaring procedures (double-flare and ISO types). (AST/MAST)
- N45015 Inspect, test, and/or replace components of brake warning light system. (AST/MAST)
- N45016 Check parking brake operation and parking brake indicator light system operation; determine needed action. (MLR/AST/MAST)
- N45017 Check parking brake system and components for wear, binding, and corrosion; clean, lubricate, adjust, and/or replace as needed. (MLR/AST/MAST)
- N45018 Check operation of brake stop light system. (MLR/AST/MAST)

Knowledge Objectives

After reading this chapter, you will be able to:

- K45001 Describe hydraulic system service and liability concerns.

Skills Objectives

After reading this chapter, you will be able to:

- S45001 Perform hydraulic system maintenance.
- S45002 Perform hydraulic system component diagnosis and repair.

Matching

Match the following terms with the correct description or example.

A. Bleeding

B. Free play

C. ISO flare method

D. CANbus circuit

E. Brake bleeder wrench

F. Flare nut wrench

_____ **1.** A two-wire communication network that transmits status and command signals between control modules in a vehicle.

_____ **2.** A method for joining brake lines.

_____ **3.** The amount of clearance between the brake pedal linkage and the master cylinder piston.

_____ **4.** The process of removing air from a hydraulic braking system.

_____ **5.** A tool used to loosen and tighten fittings on brake lines.

_____ **6.** A tool used to open and close bleeder screws.

Multiple Choice

Read each item carefully, and then select the best response.

_____ **1.** _____ brake bleeders provide a reservoir of brake fluid under pressure.

A. Vacuum

B. Hydraulic

C. Pressure

D. Mechanical

_____ **2.** In humid or wet climates, the brake fluid may need to be flushed every _____.

A. five years

B. five months

C. two months

D. two years

_____ **3.** A(n) _____ measures specific chemicals/metals in a brake fluid and can indicate whether there is a chemical breakdown of the brake fluid.

A. aerosol flushing kit

B. test strip

C. gas analyzer

D. hydrometer

_____ **4.** Identify the bleeding method in which one person operates the brake pedal while the other person opens and closes the bleeder screws on the wheel brake units to allow the air and old brake fluid to be pushed out.

A. Manual bleeding

B. Vacuum bleeding

C. Pressure bleeding

D. Bench bleeding

_____ **5.** _____ uses clean brake fluid under pressure from an auxiliary tool or piece of equipment, to force the air and old brake fluid from a hydraulic braking system.

A. Bench bleeding

B. Manual bleeding

C. Vacuum bleeding

D. Pressure bleeding

_____ **6.** Identify a true statement with respect to manual bleeding.

A. It requires very less time to bleed the brake fluid.

B. It is less effective at removing trapped air in systems that have high spots in the brake lines.

C. It is best only when a large amount of brake fluid has to be bled.

D. It is less efficient in vehicles that have a small vertical drop between the master cylinder and the wheel brake units.

_____ **7.** If the brake pedal height of a vehicle is 10" and the travel takes it down to 4", then the brake pedal travel is _____.
   A. 14"
   B. 40"
   C. 6"
   D. 2.5"

_____ **8.** Identify the test in a vacuum booster diagnosis that tests for leaks between the booster chambers.
   A. Brake pedal free travel test
   B. External leak test
   C. Performance test
   D. Internal leak test

_____ **9.** A(n) _____ test checks the brake pedal linkage clearance.
   A. external leak
   B. brake pedal free travel
   C. vacuum brake bleeder
   D. operation

_____ **10.** Generally, manufacturers specify a minimum of _____ of mercury of intake manifold vacuum.
   A. 16"
   B. 24"
   C. 10"
   D. 32"

True/False

If you believe the statement to be more true than false, write the letter "T" in the space provided. If you believe the statement to be more false than true, write the letter "F."

_____ **1.** ISO flare method is also called a bubble flare.

_____ **2.** Brake failure that leads to an accident due to improperly tightening brake components can lead to criminal liability.

_____ **3.** The best way to clean brake fluid that may have been spilled is to rub the brake fluid with cloth.

_____ **4.** As the moisture content in a brake fluid increases, the chances of galvanic reaction reduces.

_____ **5.** High levels of moisture content in a brake fluid reduce the boiling point of the brake fluid.

_____ **6.** The manual bleeding method requires the most amount of equipment and tools as compared to other brake bleeding methods.

_____ **7.** When performing a vacuum bleed, the master cylinder should not be allowed to run dry.

_____ **8.** Removing and bench bleeding the master cylinder are usually only performed when the master cylinder is being replaced.

_____ **9.** Replacing the master cylinder normally requires pushrod length adjustment.

_____ **10.** Single-diaphragm and dual-diaphragm vacuum brake boosters have completely different diagnostic procedures.

Fill in the Blank

Read each item carefully, and then complete the statement by filling in the missing word(s).

1. _____ _____/_____ _____ _____ _____ are used to test the operation of the proportioning valve and metering valve.

2. In very dry climates, the brake fluid may need to be flushed every _____ _____.

3. A(n) _____-_____ _____ _____ uses a DMM to measure the voltage created by the galvanic reaction due to the level of moisture in the brake fluid.

4. Brake fluid _____ _____ contain special color-changing pads that react in the presence of moisture or specific chemicals that have built up in the fluid.

5. The bleeding process that uses a vacuum bleeder to pull the air and old brake fluid from the system is called _____ _____.

6. Brake pedal travel is sometimes called _____ _____.

7. Brake pedal travel is measured by reading brake pedal height and _____ the height from the floor.

8. _____ _____ represents how much reserve is left for the brake pedal to travel if needed.

9. In a vacuum booster diagnosis, a(n) _____ _____ _____ tests for leaks to the atmosphere.

10. Power booster testing starts with a brake pedal free travel test and then follows up with a(n) _____ _____.

Labeling

Label the following diagrams with the correct terms.

1. Common tools used to repair brakes:

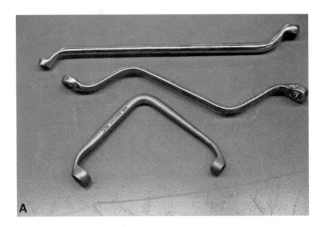

A. _____

B. _____

C. _____

D. _____

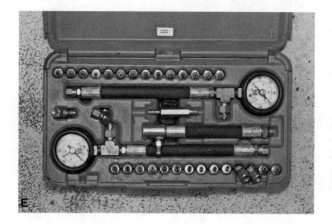

E.

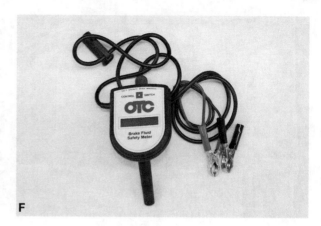

E. _____

F. _____

2. Components of a typical non-CANbus stop light circuit:

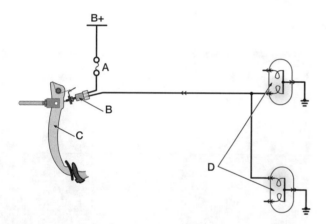

A. _____

B. _____

C. _____

D. _____

Skill Drills

Place the skill drill steps in the correct order.

1. Selecting, Handling, Storing, and Filling Brake Fluid:

_____ A. Only add the manufacturer's recommended brake fluid to bring the level to the full mark once all brake faults have been resolved. Replace the cover, and check that it is properly seated. Check for any leaks around the master cylinder. Dilute with fresh clean water any brake fluid that may have been spilled.

_____ B. Research the specified type of brake fluid in the appropriate service information. Wipe around the master cylinder reservoir cover to prevent any dirt from entering the system. Remove the reservoir cover.

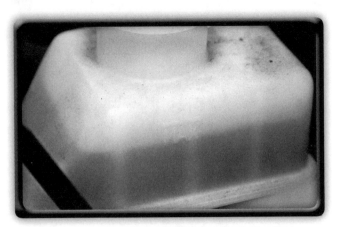

_____ **C.** Check the fluid level in the reservoir. The fluid should be near the full mark on the side of the cylinder or within half an inch of the top of each chamber if there are no marks.

2. Performing Master Cylinder Service and Bench Bleeding:

_____ **A.** Place the master cylinder on the power booster, and install the nuts just far enough to hold it from falling off.

_____ **B.** Install the bleeder lines into the master cylinder outlet ports with the ends of the lines deep within the master cylinder reservoir. Fill the reservoir about half full with clean brake fluid. With an appropriate tool, slowly push the master cylinder piston into the bore. Allow the piston to return to its rest position. Repeat until all air bubbles have been removed from the master cylinder.

_____ **C.** Tighten the bolts connecting the master cylinder to the power booster to their proper torque. Tighten the brake line fittings using a flare nut or line wrench. Use the double wrench method if the master cylinder is fitted with an adapter. Top off the master cylinder, and bleed all wheel brake units to remove any remaining air. Start the engine, and check brake pedal feel to verify proper height and firmness. Visually inspect all fittings and bleeder screws for leaks.

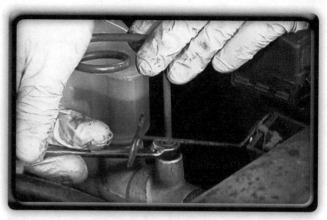

_____ **D.** Compare the new unit to the old one to verify that it is the correct replacement. Remove all of the old brake fluid from the master cylinder reservoir. Remove the master cylinder brake lines, using a flare wrench and, if necessary, the double wrench method.

_____ **E.** Carefully line up the brake lines, and start them by using your fingers to thread them into the master cylinder outlet ports at least four or five threads from when they first catch. Do not use a wrench to start the threads.

_____ **F.** Remove the nuts holding the master cylinder to the power brake booster. Remove the master cylinder. Mount the master cylinder in a vise with the reservoir facing up. Now is a good time to perform the next task: measure and adjust pushrod length.

3. Fabricating Brake Lines, Using the Inverted Double Flare Method:

_____ **A.** Remove the flaring tool, and inspect the flare to see if it has been formed correctly. Remove the flared line from the clamp, and inspect it.

_____ **B.** Tighten down the flaring tool until the adapter touches the clamp. This forms a widening and narrowing of the tube.

_____ **C.** Remove the adapter, and reinstall the flaring tool. Tighten down the flaring tool to fold the narrowed portion back into the widened portion of the flare. Stop when the tool starts to get hard to tighten.

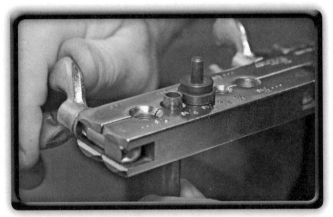

_____ **D.** Install the proper fitting onto the brake line. Use a bench vise to hold the brake line clamping tool. Select the proper adapter to match the tubing size. Use it to set the height of the tube in the clamp. Tighten down the clamp securely.

_____ **E.** Insert the adapter into the tubing, and install the flaring tool onto the clamp and over the adapter.

Review Questions

_____ **1.** Brake fluid testers are used to test the:
   A. level of the brake fluid.
   B. type of the brake fluid.
   C. current temperature of the brake fluid.
   D. moisture content of the brake fluid.

_____ **2.** All of the following statements are true with respect to brake fluid handling _except_:
   A. Brake fluid is considered to be a top-off fluid.
   B. Brake fluid levels should be inspected during every oil change.
   C. The fluid should be near the full mark on the side of the cylinder or within half of an inch of the top of each chamber if there are no marks.
   D. The cause of the low brake fluid level needs to be identified and corrected before topping off.

_____ **3.** All of the following can be used to determine if the brake fluid should be flushed _except_:
   A. manufacturer's time/mileage specification.
   B. boiling point test.
   C. metering valve gauge.
   D. using the test strip.

_____ **4.** When performing a DMM-galvanic reaction test, the fluid should be flushed if it is:
   A. not equal to 0 V.
   B. below 0.3 V.
   C. above 0.3 V.
   D. above 3 V.

_____ **5.** What happens when bleeding is not done?
   A. The brakes will feel spongy and will not be fully functional.
   B. The brake fluid gets contaminated.
   C. The brake pedal is harder to push than normal.
   D. The brakes will drag.

_____ **6.** In the case of possible petroleum contamination, which of the following can be used to flush brake fluid?
   A. Compressed air
   B. Alcohol
   C. Gasoline
   D. Mineral-based products

_____ **7.** The master cylinder should be inspected for internal and external leaks in all of the following scenarios _except_:
   A. the brake fluid is low in the reservoir.
   B. the brake warning light is on.
   C. the brake pedal reserve height is too low.
   D. the brake pedal is harder to push than normal.

_____ **8.** When a vacuum-type power booster is used, the driver will be required to increase foot pressure to activate the brakes if there is:
   A. insufficient vacuum.
   B. excess air.
   C. excess vacuum.
   D. excess brake fluid.

_____ **9.** Which of the following tests is used to verify brake booster operation and involves starting the engine while measuring pedal height?
   A. Brake pedal free travel test
   B. Performance test
   C. External leak test
   D. Internal leak test

_____ **10.** All of the following statements with respect to replacing brake lines, brake hoses, fittings, and supports are true *except*:

   A. depress the brake pedal with a brake pedal depressor to prevent brake fluid from draining out of the vehicle.

   B. using flare nut wrenches and the double wrench method, carefully remove any brake lines, hoses, fittings, and supports that are to be replaced.

   C. reassemble the removed components using tools only.

   D. bleed any trapped air from the system.

ASE Technician A/Technician B Style Questions

_____ **1.** Tech A says that technicians have been successfully sued for improper brake repairs, resulting in large cash settlements. Tech B says that to reduce liability, good technicians create processes to help ensure steps of the job are not forgotten. Who is correct?

   A. Tech A

   B. Tech B

   C. Both A and B

   D. Neither A nor B

_____ **2.** Tech A says that a service brake pedal that does not return all the way causes the brake warning light on the instrument panel to stay on. Tech B says that a service brake pedal that does not return causes the brake lights to stay on. Who is correct?

   A. Tech A

   B. Tech B

   C. Both A and B

   D. Neither A nor B

_____ **3.** Tech A says that brake fluid should periodically be checked for excessive moisture content. Tech B says that brake fluid should be replaced every year. Who is correct?

   A. Tech A

   B. Tech B

   C. Both A and B

   D. Neither A nor B

_____ **4.** Tech A says that brake pedal free play is the amount of clearance between the brake pedal linkage and the master cylinder piston. Tech B says that brake pedal travel is sometimes called reserve pedal. Who is correct?

   A. Tech A

   B. Tech B

   C. Both A and B

   D. Neither A nor B

_____ **5.** Tech A says that a sinking brake pedal is an indication of a faulty vacuum booster. Tech B says that the master cylinder can only have external leaks, not internal leaks. Who is correct?

   A. Tech A

   B. Tech B

   C. Both A and B

   D. Neither A nor B

_____ **6.** Tech A says that part of the hydraulic system diagnostic process could require disassembly and visual inspection or measurements of the suspected component or system. Tech B says that may involve performing tests in the shop with a scan tool, pressure gauges, or a DMM. Who is correct?

   A. Tech A

   B. Tech B

   C. Both A and B

   D. Neither A nor B

_____ **7.** Tech A says that to performance test a vacuum booster; start with the engine off, apply the brakes several times, hold the pedal down, start the engine, and observe the brake pedal action. Tech B says that to check a vacuum booster for internal leaks, you should pressurize the booster with compressed air and listen for leaks. Who is correct?

　A. Tech A

　B. Tech B

　C. Both A and B

　D. Neither A nor B

_____ **8.** Tech A says that when flaring a brake line, you should install the fitting onto the line after the line has been flared. Tech B says that when fabricating a double flare, the adapter widens and narrows the line, and then the flaring tool folds the narrowed portion back into the widened portion of the flare. Who is correct?

　A. Tech A

　B. Tech B

　C. Both A and B

　D. Neither A nor B

_____ **9.** Tech A says that bench bleeding a master cylinder prevents having to bleed air from the brake lines during replacement. Tech B says that bench bleeding the master cylinder makes bleeding the brakes on the vehicle easier. Who is correct?

　A. Tech A

　B. Tech B

　C. Both A and B

　D. Neither A nor B

_____ **10.** Tech A says that a faulty vacuum booster can affect engine operation. Tech B says that steel brake line can be replaced with a copper line, as it is easier to bend into shape. Who is correct?

　A. Tech A

　B. Tech B

　C. Both A and B

　D. Neither A nor B

Disc Brake Systems

At the start of each chapter you'll find the NATEF tasks, Knowledge Objectives, and Skills Objectives from the textbook. These are your objectives as you make your way through the exercises in this workbook and the chapter in your textbook. The following activities have been designed to help you refresh your knowledge of the material in this chapter.

NATEF Tasks

- N46001 Identify and interpret brake system concerns; determine needed action. (AST/MAST)
- N46002 Describe procedure for performing a road test to check brake system operation including an antilock brake system (ABS). (MLR/AST/MAST)
- N46003 Diagnose poor stopping, noise, vibration, pulling, grabbing, dragging or pedal pulsation concerns; determine needed action. (AST/MAST)
- N46004 Remove and clean caliper assembly; inspect for leaks, damage, and wear; determine needed action. (MLR/AST/MAST)
- N46005 Inspect caliper mounting and slides/pins for proper operation, wear, and damage; determine needed action. (MLR/AST/MAST)
- N46006 Check brake pad wear indicator; determine needed action. (MLR/AST/MAST)
- N46007 Remove, inspect, and/or replace brake pads and retaining hardware; determine needed action. (MLR/AST/MAST)
- N46008 Lubricate and reinstall caliper, brake pads, and related hardware; seat brake pads; inspect for leaks. (MLR/AST/MAST)
- N46009 Retract and readjust caliper piston on an integrated parking brake system. (MLR/AST/MAST)
- N46010 Clean and inspect rotor and mounting surface; measure rotor thickness, thickness variation, and lateral runout; determine needed action. (MLR/AST/MAST)
- N46011 Remove and reinstall/replace rotor. (MLR/AST/MAST)
- N46012 Refinish rotor on vehicle; measure final rotor thickness and compare with specification. (MLR/AST/MAST)
- N46013 Refinish rotor off vehicle; measure final rotor thickness and compare with specification. (MLR/AST/MAST)
- N46014 Inspect and replace drive axle wheel studs. (MLR/AST/MAST)
- N46015 Install wheel and torque lug nuts. (MLR/AST/MAST)
- N46016 Describe importance of operating vehicle to burnish/break-in replacement brake pads according to manufacturer's recommendations. (MLR/AST/MAST)

Knowledge Objectives

After reading this chapter, you will be able to:

- K46001 Describe the theory of operation of disc brakes.
- K46002 Describe the components of the disc brake system.
- K46003 Describe how the components of the disc brake system work together during braking operations.
- K46004 Describe the advantages and disadvantages of the disc brake system.
- K46005 Describe the types, purpose, and function of disc brake calipers.
- K46006 Describe the purpose, type, and function of disc brake pads.
- K46007 Describe the principle of the coefficient of friction and how it affects brake lining materials.
- K46008 Describe the methods used to reduce noise in disc brakes.
- K46009 Describe the types of wear indicators for disc brakes.
- K46010 Describe types of disc brake rotors and their function.
- K46011 Describe the types, purpose, and operation of parking brakes in a disc brake system.

Skills Objectives

After reading this chapter, you will be able to:

- S46001 Perform disc brake diagnosis, service, and repair.
- S46002 Perform caliper and pad service.
- S46003 Perform rotor service.

Matching

Match the following terms with the correct description or example.

A. Backing plate
B. Bearing races
C. Bonded linings
D. Brake booster
E. Brake wash station
F. Caliper
G. Dial indicator
H. Drawing-in method
I. Electronic control module
J. Independent rear suspension

K. Lateral runout
L. Low-drag caliper
M. Off-car brake lathe
N. Fixed caliper
O. Pushrod
P. Riveted linings
Q. Rotor
R. Sliding or floating caliper
S. Edge code
T. Ventilated rotor

_____ 1. A method for replacing wheel studs that uses the lug nut to draw the wheel stud into the hub or flange.

_____ 2. Also called warpage, the side-to-side movement of the rotor surfaces as the rotor turns.

_____ 3. A piece of equipment designed to safely clean brake dust from drum and disc brake components.

_____ 4. A type of brake caliper that only has piston(s) on the inboard side of the rotor. The caliper is free to slide or float, thus pulling the outboard brake pad into the rotor when braking force is applied.

_____ 5. A caliper designed to maintain a larger brake pad-to-rotor clearance by retracting the pistons farther than normal.

_____ 6. Brake linings riveted to the brake pad backing plate with metal rivets and used on heavier-duty or high-performance vehicles.

_____ 7. Brake linings that are essentially glued to the brake pad backing plate; more common on light-duty vehicles.

_____ 8. A type of brake rotor with passages between the rotor surfaces that are used to improve heat transfer to the atmosphere.

_____ 9. A hydraulic device that uses pressure from the master cylinder to apply the brake pads against the rotor.

_____ 10. A vacuum or hydraulically operated device that increases the driver's braking effort.

_____ 11. A type of suspension system where each rear wheel is capable of moving independently of the other.

_____ 12. A metal plate to which the brake lining is fixed.

_____ 13. A two-digit code printed on the edge of a friction lining that describes its coefficient of friction.

_____ 14. A tool used to machine (refinish) drums and rotors after they have been removed from the vehicle.

_____ 15. Tool used to measure the lateral runout of the rotor.

_____ 16. A mechanism used to transmit force from the brake pedal to the master cylinder.

_____ 17. Hardened metal surfaces that roller or ball bearings fit into when a bearing is properly assembled.

_____ 18. The main rotating part of a disc brake system.

_____ 19. A type of brake caliper bolted firmly to the steering knuckle or axle housing and having at least one piston on each side of the rotor.

_____ 20. A computer that receives signals from input sensors, compares that information with preloaded software, and sends an appropriate command signal to output devices; used to manage the antilock brake system.

Multiple Choice

Read each item carefully, and then select the best response.

_____ 1. In high-performance vehicles, the _____ are made from composite materials, ceramics, or carbon fiber; otherwise, they are usually made of cast iron.
   A. brake pads
   B. calipers
   C. rotors
   D. all of the above

_____ 2. Disc brake caliper assemblies are bolted to the _____.
   A. axle housing
   B. wheel hub
   C. steering knuckle
   D. either A or C

_____ 3. Disc brake caliper pistons are sealed by a stationary square section sealing ring, also called a _____.
   A. square cut O-ring
   B. caliper gasket
   C. square-to-round gasket
   D. square oil seal

_____ 4. Manufacturers have dealt with the corrosion issue by making caliper pistons out of _____, which does not corrode or rust.
   A. aluminum
   B. carbon fiber
   C. phenolic resin
   D. rubber

_____ 5. The backing plate has _____ that correctly positions the pad in the caliper assembly and helps the backing plate maintain the proper position to the rotor.
   A. rivets
   B. tabs
   C. bolts
   D. lugs

_____ 6. The amount of friction between two surfaces is expressed as a ratio and is called the _____.
   A. sliding resistance
   B. coefficient of friction
   C. friction ratio
   D. drag factor

_____ 7. Today, brakes are manufactured from a variety of different materials including all of the following, _except_:
   A. Kevlar
   B. semimetallic materials
   C. asbestos
   D. ceramic materials

_____ 8. A spring steel _____ mounted to the brake pad may be used to notify the driver that the brake pads are worn to their minimum limit.
   A. rivet
   B. scratcher
   C. needle
   D. squealer

_____ 9. Which type of rotors are less expensive and usually found on smaller vehicles?
   A. Solid
   B. Ventilated
   C. Stainless steel
   D. Phenolic resin

_____ 10. Which type of parking brake is engaged by pushing a button on the dash?
   A. Top hat
   B. Integrated mechanical
   C. Electric
   D. Automatic

True/False

If you believe the statement to be more true than false, write the letter "T" in the space provided. If you believe the statement to be more false than true, write the letter "F."

_____ **1.** The hub can be part of the brake rotor or a separate assembly that the rotor slips over and is bolted to by the lug nuts.

_____ **2.** Disc brake pads require much lower application pressures to operate than drum brake shoes because they are self-energizing.

_____ **3.** The sliding or floating caliper has brake pads located on each side of the rotor, but all of the pistons are only on one side, usually the inside of the rotor.

_____ **4.** Bonded linings are less susceptible to failure under high temperatures.

_____ **5.** The lower the edge code letter, the less friction the material has, and the harder the brake pedal must be applied to achieve a given amount of stopping power.

_____ **6.** Society of Automotive Engineers standards assure that an EE-rated lining from one manufacturer will have the same braking characteristics as an EE-rated lining from another manufacturer.

_____ **7.** Technicians can apply a high-temperature liquid rubber compound to the back of the brake pad that stays flexible, absorbs brake pad vibrations, and helps reduce brake noise.

_____ **8.** Lateral runout tends to move the caliper pistons in the same direction as each other, so brake fluid is not pushed back to the master cylinder.

_____ **9.** Solid rotors are used to improve heat transfer to the atmosphere.

_____ **10.** Most disc brake rotors are stamped with the manufacturer's minimum thickness specification.

Fill in the Blank

Read each item carefully, and then complete the statement by filling in the missing word(s).

1. The purpose of the _____ _____ system is to provide an effective means to slow the vehicle under a variety of conditions in an acceptable distance and manner.

2. Calipers use hydraulic pressure from the _____ _____ to apply the brake pads.

3. Disc brake pads consist of friction material bonded or riveted onto a steel _____ _____.

4. A(n) _____ _____ on the top of the piston bore allows for the removal of air within the disc brake system as well as helping with performing routine brake fluid changes.

5. _____-_____ calipers are designed to maintain a larger brake pad-to-rotor clearance by retracting the pistons a little bit farther.

6. Floating calipers are mounted in place by _____ _____ and _____.

7. The Society of Automotive Engineers (SAE) has adopted letter codes to rate the coefficient of friction of brake lining materials. The rating is written on the edge of the friction linings and is called the _____ _____.

8. Adding brake pad _____ and _____ to the brake pads help cushion the brake pad and absorb some of the vibration.

9. Incorporating _____ tangs on the brake pad backing plate allow technicians to crimp the tangs so they are more firmly mounted in the caliper.

10. Most _____ _____ are mechanically applied by use of a cable and ratcheting lever assembly.

Labeling

Label the following diagrams with the correct terms.

1. Disc versus drum brakes:

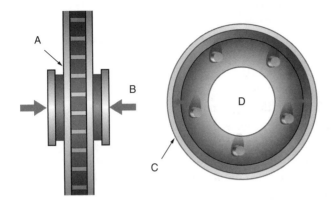

A. _____

B. _____

C. _____

D. _____

2. The master cylinder converts the pedal force into hydraulic pressure:

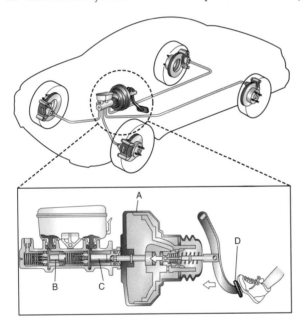

A. _____

B. _____

C. _____

D. _____

3. Identify the disc brake tools:

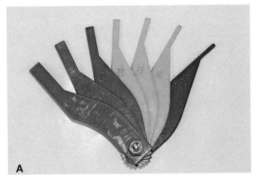

A. _____   B. _____

C. _____

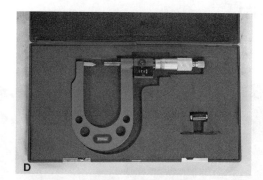

D. _____

E. _____

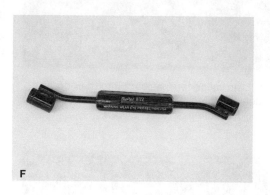

F. _____

G. _____

H. _____

I. _____

J. _____

Skill Drills

Place the skill drill steps in the correct order.

1. Removing and Inspecting Calipers:

_____ **A.** Push the caliper pistons back into their bores slightly. Although many technicians use a screwdriver, as shown, a pry bar or C-clamp is a safer choice.

_____ **B.** Inspect the caliper, including the piston dust boot for leaks or damage. Determine any necessary actions.

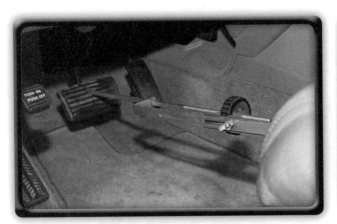

_____ **C.** Use a brake pedal holding tool to slightly apply the brakes and block off the compensating ports in the master cylinder to avoid excess fluid leakage.

_____ **D.** Research the procedure for removing the caliper in the appropriate service information. Loosen the bleeder screws slightly, and then retighten them.

_____ **E.** Remove the brake line or hose from the caliper. Be careful not to lose any sealing rings.

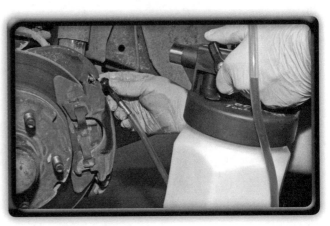

_____ **F.** If the caliper is being rebuilt or a new caliper will be installed, it is good practice to flush the old brake fluid from the system at this time.

_____ **G.** Remove the caliper assembly from its mountings.

2. Disassembling Calipers:

_____ **A.** Clean all of the caliper parts, including the seal grooves, following the service manual procedure.

_____ **B.** Measure the caliper bore-to-piston clearance with a feeler gauge, and compare to specifications. Determine any necessary actions.

_____ **C.** Inspect each of the parts for damage, rust, and wear. Also check the caliper pin bores or bushings for wear or damage. Replace if they cannot be cleaned up.

_____ **D.** Disassemble the caliper, following the service manual procedure.

3. Inspecting and Measuring Disc Brake Rotors:

_____ **A.** Measure the thickness of the rotor in five to eight places around the face of the rotor. Calculate the maximum thickness variation, and compare to specifications.

_____ **B.** Slowly rotate the rotor to find the highest spot on the rotor. Read the dial indicator showing maximum runout.

_____ **C.** Inspect the rotor for hard spots or hot spots, scoring, cracks, and damage.

_____ **D.** Keep turning the rotor to make sure the dial indicator does not read below zero. If it does, rezero the dial caliper on the lowest spot. Keep turning the rotor to find the highest spot and reread the dial indicator. Compare all of your readings to the specifications and determine if the rotor is fit for service, is machinable, or needs to be replaced.

_____ **E.** Research the procedure and specifications for inspecting the rotor. If you have not already done so, remove the caliper assembly, brake pads, and any hardware. Clean the rotor with approved asbestos removal equipment.

_____ **F.** Set up a dial indicator to measure lateral runout. Rotate the rotor and find the lowest spot on the rotor, then zero the dial indicator.

_____ **G.** Measure the rotor thickness at the deepest groove or thinnest part of the rotor and compare to specifications.

4. Refinishing Hubless Rotors on Vehicle:

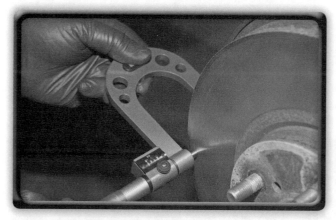

_____ **A.** Remeasure the rotor thickness to determine if the rotor is above minimum thickness specifications. Readjust the wheel bearings if necessary.

_____ **B.** Engage the automatic feed, and watch for proper machining action. If necessary, repeat this step until all damaged surface areas have been removed on both sides of the rotor.

_____ **C.** Install the antichatter device, if specified.

_____ **D.** Adjust the cutting bits, and cut off any lip at the edge of the rotor.

_____ **E.** Research the brake lathe manufacturer's procedure for properly refinishing the rotor. Mount the on-car brake lathe to the rotor after cleaning the rust and dirt from between the rotor and hub or adjusting the wheel bearing so there is no end play.

_____ **F.** Make sure the cutting bits will not contact the rotor face, and move the cutting head toward the inner diameter of the rotor face. Set the cutting bits to the proper cutting depth for machining.

_____ **G.** If necessary, perform a finish cut on the rotor.

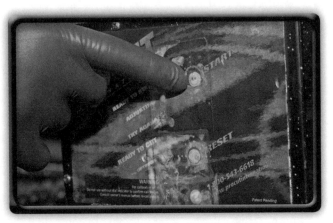

_____ **H.** Perform the runout calibration on the brake lathe. Some brake lathes require manual compensation, whereas other machines can perform this automatically.

5. Installing Wheels, Torquing Lug Nuts, and Making Final Checks:

_____ **A.** Carefully run all of the lug nuts down so they are seated in the wheel.

_____ **B.** Once all of the lug nuts have been torqued, go around them again, this time in a circular pattern to ensure that you did not miss any in the previous pattern.

_____ **C.** Check the brake fluid level in the master cylinder reservoir. Start the vehicle, and check the brake pedal for proper feel and height. Check the parking brake for proper operation. Also inspect the system for any brake fluid leaks and loose or missing fasteners.

_____ **D.** Use a torque wrench to tighten each lug nut to the proper torque in the proper sequence.

_____ **E.** If the vehicle was equipped with hubcaps and valve stem caps, reinstall them.

_____ **F.** Lower the vehicle so the tires are partially on the ground to keep them from turning while tightening the lug nuts.

_____ **G.** Start the lug nuts on the wheel studs, being careful to match up the surfaces.

Review Questions

_____ **1.** All of the following statements with respect to the disc brake system are true *except*:
   A. the disc brake rotor is bolted to the wheel hub flange.
   B. the hydraulic pressure from the master cylinder causes the caliper to create a mechanical clamping action.
   C. drum brakes require higher applied forces than disc brakes.
   D. the heat generated on the outside surfaces of the rotor is transferred to the atmosphere.

_____ **2.** Which of the following primary components of the disc brake system uses hydraulic pressure from the master cylinder to apply the brake pads?
   A. Rotor
   B. Caliper
   C. Proportioning valve
   D. Brake pads

_____ **3.** When the brake pedal is depressed, a pushrod transfers the force to a hydraulic master cylinder through the:
   A. brake booster.
   B. brake liner.
   C. hoses.
   D. pistons.

_____ **4.** Which of these is an advantage of the disc brake system over drum brakes?
   A. Disc brakes transfer less heat to the atmosphere.
   B. Disc brakes reduce the likelihood of brake fade.
   C. Disc brakes do not need maintenance.
   D. Disc brakes do not create annoying squeals and squeaks.

_____ **5.** All of the following statements referring to disc brake calipers are true *except*:
   A. disc brake caliper assembly clamps the brake pads onto the rotors to slow the vehicle.
   B. calipers are fitted with a bleeder screw on the top of the piston bore.
   C. the O-ring is compressed between the piston and caliper housing, creating a positive seal to keep the high-pressure brake fluid from leaking out.
   D. fixed calipers are the most common type used in passenger vehicles.

_____ **6.** Which of the following materials have the highest coefficient of friction?
   A. Leather and oak
   B. Brass and cast iron
   C. Rubber and concrete
   D. Copper and cast iron

_____ **7.** The following edge code letters correspond to four different brake friction materials. Which of these has the lowest coefficient of friction?
   A. EE
   B. FF
   C. GG
   D. HH

_____ **8.** All of the following statements with respect to wear indicators are true *except*:
   A. a spring steel scratcher is a mechanically operated wear indicator.
   B. when the scratcher makes a squealing noise, it means the brakes must be serviced.
   C. on a sensor type system, contact with the rotor will light a warning light or warning message.
   D. electrical contacts cannot be manufactured into the pad, so they have to be clipped to the pad.

_____ **9.** Which of the following statements is true with respect to parallelism?
   A. It causes the steering wheel to shimmy.
   B. It results when the rotor's thickness varies by as little as 0.0003".
   C. It causes the brake pedal to pulsate.
   D. It should be inspected using a brake micrometer.

_____ **10.** In which type of parking brake does the rotor have a deeper offset than normal?
   A. Foot-operated parking brake
   B. Integrated parking brake

C. Top hat design parking brake
D. Electric parking brake

ASE Technician A/Technician B Style Questions

_____ 1. Tech A says that disc brakes operate on the principle of friction. Tech B says that disc brakes operate on the principle of regeneration. Who is correct?
   A. Tech A
   B. Tech B
   C. Both A and B
   D. Neither A nor B

_____ 2. Tech A says that some vehicles use fixed calipers. Tech B says that some vehicles use sliding/floating calipers. Who is correct?
   A. Tech A
   B. Tech B
   C. Both A and B
   D. Neither A nor B

_____ 3. Tech A says that disc brake pads require higher application force than drum brake shoes. Tech B says that disc brakes are self-energizing. Who is correct?
   A. Tech A
   B. Tech B
   C. Both A and B
   D. Neither A nor B

_____ 4. Tech A says that fixed calipers use one or more pistons only on one side of the rotor. Tech B says that sliding/fixed calipers use one or more pistons on both sides of the rotor. Who is correct?
   A. Tech A
   B. Tech B
   C. Both A and B
   D. Neither A nor B

_____ 5. Tech A says that calipers use steel piston rings to seal each piston. Tech B says that calipers use a square section O-ring to seal each piston. Who is correct?
   A. Tech A
   B. Tech B
   C. Both A and B
   D. Neither A nor B

_____ 6. Tech A says that chrome plated pistons resist rust. Tech B says that pistons made of phenolic resin do not corrode and transmit less heat. Who is correct?
   A. Tech A
   B. Tech B
   C. Both A and B
   D. Neither A nor B

_____ 7. Tech A says that some vehicles are equipped with a spring steel brake pad wear indicator that drags on the rotor when the lining thickness is low. Tech B says that some vehicles are equipped with an electric brake pad wear sensor that activates a warning on the dash. Who is correct?
   A. Tech A
   B. Tech B
   C. Both A and B
   D. Neither A nor B

_____ 8. Tech A says that rotors should be measured for thickness variation (parallelism). Tech B says that rotors should be measured for lateral runout. Who is correct?
   A. Tech A
   B. Tech B
   C. Both A and B
   D. Neither A nor B

_____ **9.** Tech A says that rotors that are too thin cannot handle as much heat and will experience brake fade sooner. Tech B says that brake pedal pulsation is the result of air in the hydraulic system. Who is correct?
  A. Tech A
  B. Tech B
  C. Both A and B
  D. Neither A nor B

_____ **10.** Tech A says that a micrometer is used to measure rotor thickness variation. Tech B says that a micrometer is used to measure rotor lateral runout. Who is correct?
  A. Tech A
  B. Tech B
  C. Both A and B
  D. Neither A nor B

Drum Brake Systems

At the start of each chapter you'll find the NATEF tasks, Knowledge Objectives, and Skills Objectives from the textbook. These are your objectives as you make your way through the exercises in this workbook and the chapter in your textbook. The following activities have been designed to help you refresh your knowledge of the material in this chapter.

NATEF Tasks

- N47001 Diagnose poor stopping, noise, vibration, pulling, grabbing, dragging, or pedal pulsation concerns; determine needed action. (AST/MAST)
- N47002 Remove, clean, and inspect brake drum; measure brake drum diameter; determine serviceability. (MLR/AST/MAST)
- N47003 Refinish brake drum and measure final drum diameter; compare with specification. (MLR/AST/MAST)
- N47004 Remove, clean, inspect, and/or replace brake shoes, springs, pins, clips, levers, adjusters/self-adjusters, other related brake hardware, and backing support plates; lubricate and reassemble. (MLR/AST/MAST)
- N47005 Inspect wheel cylinders for leaks and proper operation; remove and replace as needed. (MLR/AST/MAST)
- N47006 Pre-adjust brake shoes and parking brake; install brake drums or drum/hub assemblies and wheel bearings; perform final checks and adjustments. (MLR/AST/MAST)
- N47007 Install wheel and torque lug nuts. (MLR/AST/MAST)

Knowledge Objectives

After reading this chapter, you will be able to:

- K47001 Explain the purpose, operation, and components of the drum brake system.
- K47002 Describe the operation of drum brakes.
- K47003 Describe the process of self-energization and servo action.
- K47004 Describe the operation of the different types of drum brakes.
- K47005 Describe the purpose and function of drum brake components.
- K47006 Describe the purpose, types, and function of brake drums.
- K47007 Describe the purpose and function of the backing plate.
- K47008 Describe the purpose, types, and function of wheel cylinders.
- K47009 Describe the purpose, types, and function of brake shoes and linings.
- K47010 Describe the purpose and function of drum brake springs and hardware.
- K47011 Describe the operation of the drum parking brake system.
- K47012 Describe the types and purpose of brake tools.

Skills Objectives

After reading this chapter, you will be able to:

- S47001 Perform maintenance and repair on drum brake systems.

Matching

Match the following terms with the correct description or example.

A. Anchor pin
B. Automatic brake self-adjuster
C. Backing plate
D. Brake drum
E. Duo-servo drum brake system

F. Hold-down springs
G. Hold-down spring tool
H. Leading/trailing shoe drum brake system
I. Parking brake mechanism
J. Self-energizing

K. Servo action

L. Specialty springs

M. Springs and clips

N. Twin leading shoe drum brake system

O. Wheel cylinder

_____ **1.** Type of brake shoe arrangement where one shoe is positioned in a leading manner and the other shoe in a trailing manner.

_____ **2.** A drum brake design where one brake shoe, when activated, applies an increased activating force to the other brake shoe, in proportion to the initial activating force; further enhances the self-energizing feature of some drum brakes.

_____ **3.** Springs that hold the brake shoes against the backing plate.

_____ **4.** A mechanism that operates the brake shoes or pads to hold the vehicle stationary when the parking brake is applied.

_____ **5.** Brake shoe arrangement in which both brake shoes are self-energizing in the forward direction.

_____ **6.** A short, wide, hollow cylinder that is capped on one end and bolted to a vehicle's wheel; it has an inner friction surface that the brake shoe is forced against.

_____ **7.** A hydraulic cylinder with one or two pistons, seals, dust boots, and a bleeder screw that pushes the brake shoes into contact with the brake drum to slow or stop the vehicle.

_____ **8.** Springs used to return links and levers on the parking brake system or the self-adjuster mechanism.

_____ **9.** A system on drum brakes that automatically adjusts the brakes to maintain a specified amount of running clearance between the shoes and drum.

_____ **10.** A system that uses servo action in both the forward and reverse direction.

_____ **11.** Various devices that hold the brake shoes in place or return them to their proper place.

_____ **12.** A tool used for removing and installing hold-down springs.

_____ **13.** A component of the backing plate that takes all of the braking force from the brake shoes.

_____ **14.** A stamped steel plate, bolted to the steering or suspension, which supports the wheel cylinder, brake shoes, and other hardware.

_____ **15.** The property of drum brakes that assists the driver in applying the brakes; when brake shoes come into contact with the moving drum, the friction tends to wedge the shoes against the drum, thus increasing the braking force.

Multiple Choice

Read each item carefully, and then select the best response.

_____ **1.** All of the following are main components of the drum brake system, _except_:

    A. wheel cylinder

    B. brake shoes

    C. rotor

    D. parking brake mechanism

_____ **2.** In drum brake systems, when the brake pedal is depressed, a _____ transfers the force to a hydraulic master cylinder.

    A. linkage

    B. pushrod

    C. cable

    D. brake line

_____ **3.** All of the following are types of drum brake systems, _except_:

    A. twin leading shoe

    B. leading/trailing shoe

    C. twin trailing shoe

    D. duo-servo

_____ **4.** Brake drums are usually made out of _____ due to its ability to withstand high temperatures, absorb a lot of heat, and maintain its shape.

    A. cast iron

    B. stainless steel

    C. chrome

    D. phenolic resin

_____ **5.** The _____ must be able to take all of the braking force when the brakes are applied, so it must be strong and firmly attached to the backing plate.

    A. wheel cylinder

    B. anchor pin

    C. brake drum

    D. primary shoe

_____ **6.** A reduction in the coefficient of friction capability as the heat in brake pads and linings builds up is called _____.

    A. bonding fail

    B. slippage

    C. brake fade

    D. wear

_____ **7.** Which of the following can cause drum brakes to make a groaning noise?

    A. Excessive brake dust

    B. Overheating

    C. Fluid leak

    D. Worn brake pads

_____ **8.** What type of brake springs are generally quite stiff, making them a challenge to install?

    A. Specialty springs

    B. Hold-down springs

    C. Torsion springs

    D. Return springs

_____ **9.** What type of brake springs can be of all different shapes and sizes and can be used to push or pull components into their proper position?

    A. Torsion springs

    B. Return springs

    C. Specialty springs

    D. Hold-down springs

_____ **10.** What type of self-adjuster uses two toothed pieces held in contact with each other by spring pressure that can slide over each other in one direction, but hold in the other direction?

    A. Star wheel type

    B. Ratcheting-style

    C. Servo-style

    D. Cable-style

True/False

If you believe the statement to be more true than false, write the letter "T" in the space provided. If you believe the statement to be more false than true, write the letter "F."

_____ **1.** The master cylinder converts brake pedal force into hydraulic pressure.

_____ **2.** Trailing shoes are self-energizing.

_____ **3.** Brake drums provide the rotating friction surface that the brake lining contacts.

_____ **4.** Hubless-style drums have a one-piece integrated hub/drum assembly.

_____ **5.** Cylinder bores on aluminum wheel cylinders are usually honed to help them resist corrosion.

_____ **6.** Drum brakes are usually designed so that the condition of the lining can only be checked once the drum has been removed.

_____ **7.** In a duo-servo brake installation the matching shoes belong on the same side of the vehicle.

_____ **8.** The lining on brake shoes is much thinner than on disc brake pads.

_____ **9.** If you switch a self-adjuster from one side of the vehicle to the other it will retract the adjustment, causing the brake shoe clearance to increase as the brakes adjust.

_____ **10.** Drum parking brake systems mechanically apply the regular service brake shoes.

Fill in the Blank

Read each item carefully, and then complete the statement by filling in the missing word(s).

1. The drum is bolted to the vehicle's axle _____ by the lug nuts.
2. Each drum brake has two brake shoes with a friction material called a(n) _____ attached.
3. Manufacturers might use linings with different _____ _____ _____ for each of the shoes to get the desired braking load between the two shoes.
4. Brake drums are machined to a specific diameter from the manufacturer, which is called its _____ diameter.
5. All of the brake unit components, except the _____ _____, are mounted on a backing plate bolted to the vehicle axle housing or suspension.
6. The cylinder bore, or inside diameter of the cylinder, is created by drawing a properly sized _____ _____ through the bore.
7. The _____ _____ is a hollow screw with a taper on the end that mates with a matching tapered seat in the wheel cylinder.
8. Most modern vehicles use _____-_____ wheel cylinders because they are simpler to design, install, and bleed.
9. The terms primary and secondary refer to the _____ _____ in a duo-servo brake system.
10. Since 1968 manufacturers have incorporated a _____-_____ mechanism into their drum brake systems that is capable of maintaining proper shoe-to-drum clearance.

Labeling

Label the following diagrams with the correct terms.

1. The main components of a drum brake system:

A. _____
B. _____
C. _____
D. _____
E. _____
F. _____
G. _____
H. _____
I. _____
J. _____
K. _____
L. _____

2. A twin leading shoe drum brake:

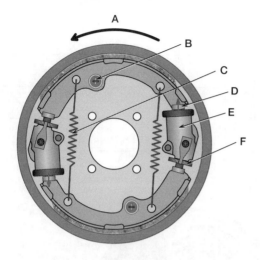

A. _____

B. _____

C. _____

D. _____

E. _____

F. _____

3. The duo-servo drum brake system:

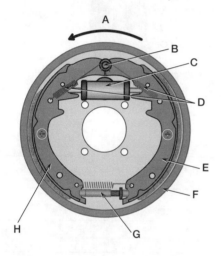

A. _____

B. _____

C. _____

D. _____

E. _____

F. _____

G. _____

H. _____

4. Double-acting wheel cylinder (cross section):

Double Acting (Cross section)

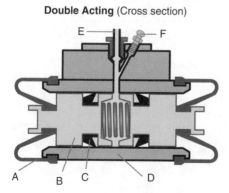

A. _____

B. _____

C. _____

D. _____

E. _____

F. _____

5. Star wheel assembly:

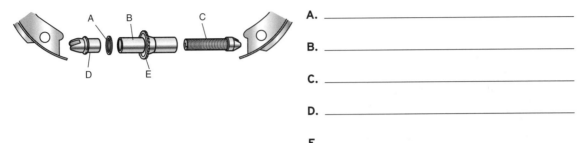

A. _____

B. _____

C. _____

D. _____

E. _____

6. Parking brake assembly for a drum brake:

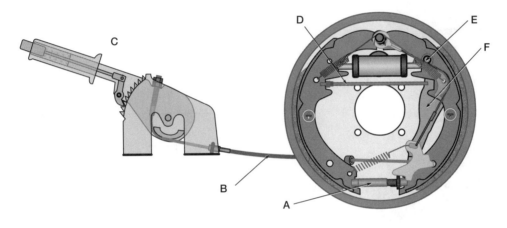

A. _____

B. _____

C. _____

D. _____

E. _____

F. _____

7. Drum brake tools:

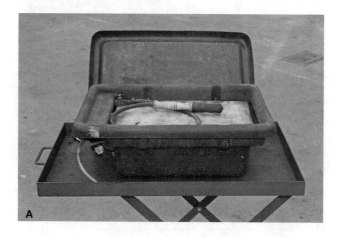

A. _____

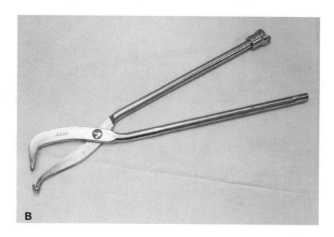

B. _____

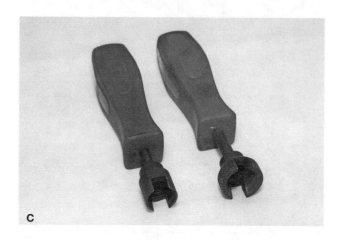

C. _____

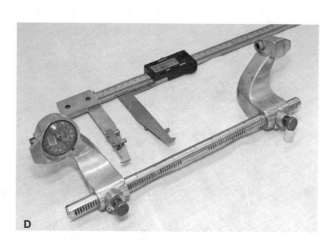

D. _____

E. _____

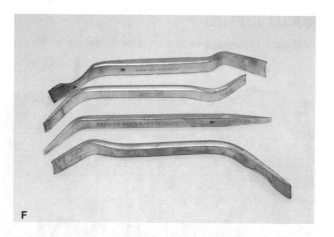

F. _____

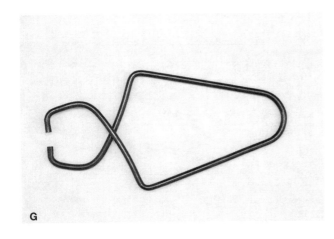

G.

H.

I.

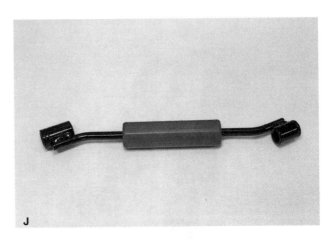

J.

Skill Drills

Test your knowledge of skill drills by filling in the correct words in the photo captions.

1. Removing, Inspecting, and Installing Wheel Cylinders:

Step 1: Peel back the _____ _____, and check for brake fluid behind them. Determine any necessary actions.

Step 2: Use a _____ nut or line wrench to unscrew the brake line from the wheel cylinder.

Step 3: Remove wheel cylinder mounting _____ and wheel cylinder from the _____ _____.

Step 4: _____ the wheel cylinder, and _____ each part. Determine any necessary actions.

Step 5: If the cylinder can be reused, _____ it, preferably with new _____ and dust boots. If not, replace it with a new wheel cylinder. Reinstall the _____ _____ by hand.

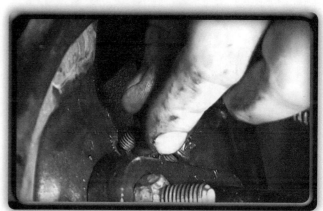

Step 6: Install and tighten any mounting screws. After that, tighten the brake line with a flare nut or _____ _____.

2. Pre-Adjusting Brakes and Installing Drums and Wheel Bearings:

Step 1: Make sure the brake shoes are fully up against their stops and _____ on the backing plate.

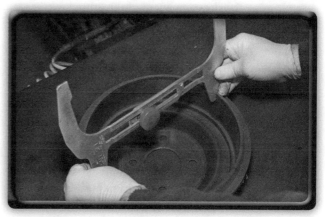

Step 2: Set the _____ _____ gauge to the drum _____, and lock it in place.

Step 3: Place the pre-adjustment gauge over the _____ of the _____ _____.

Step 4: Adjust the _____ _____ until the centers of the brake shoes just _____ the pre-adjustment gauge.

Step 5: Test install the _____ _____ to verify the drum fits. Adjust the _____ as necessary.

Step 6: Adjust the _____ _____ according to the manufacturer's procedure. If the drum has serviceable wheel _____, repack, install, adjust, and secure them.

Review Questions

_____ 1. The component of the drum brake system attached to the backing plate is the:
   A. automatic self-adjuster.
   B. brake shoes.
   C. wheel cylinder.
   D. parking brake lever.

_____ 2. All of the following statements with respect to brake systems are true *except*:
   A. drum brakes are self-energizing.
   B. trailing shoes are self-energizing.
   C. leading shoes are self-energizing.
   D. wedging effect assists the driver in applying the brakes.

_____ 3. Which of these drum brake systems uses servo action in both directions?
   A. Leading shoe drum brake system
   B. Trailing shoe drum brake system
   C. Twin leading shoe drum brake system
   D. Duo-servo drum brake systems

_____ 4. Choose the correct statement.
   A. Brake drums are usually made from fiber.
   B. Hubless drums are more expensive than hub-style drums.
   C. Brake drums can be refinished on the vehicle.
   D. The backing plate has holes stamped in it.

_____ **5.** The component that prevents a direct path for water spray and dirt to enter the brake drum is the:
  A. labyrinth seal.
  B. wheel bearing.
  C. axle seal.
  D. wheel cylinder dust boot.

_____ **6.** All of the following statements with respect to a wheel cylinder and piston are true *except*:
  A. It is standard practice to hone out deep pits in the wheel cylinder bore.
  B. The piston is usually made of anodized aluminum.
  C. The wheel cylinder uses a seal to seal the wheel cylinder.
  D. The wheel cylinder is fitted with a bleeder screw to allow bleeding of air.

_____ **7.** Choose the correct statement.
  A. The composition of the lining material does not affect brake operation.
  B. The primary shoe is responsible for doing most of the braking work.
  C. Riveted linings are used on heavier duty or high-performance vehicles.
  D. Drum brakes create more noise than disc brakes.

_____ **8.** When the driver releases the brake pedal, the brake shoes are withdrawn by the:
  A. hold-down spring.
  B. return spring.
  C. specialty spring.
  D. coil spring.

_____ **9.** Among the tools used to diagnose and repair drum brake systems, the wheel cylinder piston clamp is used to:
  A. install parking brake cables on the parking brake lever.
  B. hold the pistons in the wheel cylinder while the brake shoes are removed.
  C. pre-adjust brake shoes before installing the drum.
  D. remove and install hold-down springs.

_____ **10.** Which of the following brake tools is used to adjust brake shoes when the drum is installed?
  A. Flare nut wrench
  B. Brake spring pliers
  C. Brake spoon
  D. Wheel cylinder piston clamp

ASE Technician A/Technician B Style Questions

_____ **1.** Tech A says that parking brakes on drum brake vehicles use separate brake shoes for backup in an emergency. Tech B says that parking brakes on drum brake vehicles mechanically operate the standard drum brake shoes. Who is correct?
  A. Tech A
  B. Tech B
  C. Both A and B
  D. Neither A nor B

_____ **2.** Tech A says that most brake drums are designed to be machined if minor surface issues are present. Tech B says that brake drums can be reused if they are machined larger than specifications, as long as the surface is smooth. Who is correct?
  A. Tech A
  B. Tech B
  C. Both A and B
  D. Neither A nor B

_____ **3.** Tech A says that duo-servo brake shoes are only anchored on the top. Tech B says that duo-servo brakes typically use single-piston wheel cylinders. Who is correct?
  A. Tech A
  B. Tech B
  C. Both A and B
  D. Neither A nor B

_____ **4.** Tech A says that both secondary shoes should be installed on the passenger side of the vehicle. Tech B says that the lining on the primary shoe is typically shorter in length than the lining on the secondary shoe. Who is correct?
  A. Tech A
  B. Tech B
  C. Both A and B
  D. Neither A nor B

_____ **5.** Tech A says that a cleaned-up self-adjuster can be installed on either side of the vehicle. Tech B says that grease seals are meant to be reusable. Who is correct?
  A. Tech A
  B. Tech B
  C. Both A and B
  D. Neither A nor B

_____ **6.** Tech A says to use an air hose to clean the backing plate of dust and contamination. Tech B says to use a water-based cleaning solution to clean the backing plate of dust and contamination. Who is correct?
  A. Tech A
  B. Tech B
  C. Both A and B
  D. Neither A nor B

_____ **7.** Tech A says that riveted lining is usually for heavy-duty or high-performance vehicles. Tech B says that bonded lining is glued to the metal brake shoe. Who is correct?
  A. Tech A
  B. Tech B
  C. Both A and B
  D. Neither A nor B

_____ **8.** Tech A says that a metal-on-metal grinding noise in drum brakes generally requires replacing the brake shoes and resurfacing or replacing the drums. Tech B says that one way to help identify whether a problem is coming from the front or rear brakes is to test-drive the vehicle in a safe place at a relatively low speed and lightly apply the parking brake. Who is correct?
  A. Tech A
  B. Tech B
  C. Both A and B
  D. Neither A nor B

_____ **9.** Tech A says that brake shoe linings saturated with brake fluid from a leaky wheel cylinder can be cleaned with brake cleaner and reused as long as they aren't worn out. Tech B says that brake shoes should be replaced in axle sets. Who is correct?
  A. Tech A
  B. Tech B
  C. Both A and B
  D. Neither A nor B

_____ **10.** Tech A says that when performing a brake job on the rear axle of an older vehicle, inspection finds brake fluid under the dust boot; the wheel cylinder should be replaced. Tech B says that when a drum brake return spring has failed, springs on both rear wheels need to be replaced. Who is correct?
  A. Tech A
  B. Tech B
  C. Both A and B
  D. Neither A nor B

Wheel Bearings

At the start of each chapter you'll find the NATEF tasks, Knowledge Objectives, and Skills Objectives from the textbook. These are your objectives as you make your way through the exercises in this workbook and the chapter in your textbook. The following activities have been designed to help you refresh your knowledge of the material in this chapter.

NATEF Tasks

- N48001 Diagnose wheel bearing noises, wheel shimmy, and vibration concerns; determine needed action. (AST/MAST)
- N48002 Remove, clean, inspect, repack, and install wheel bearings; replace seals; install hub and adjust bearings. (MLR/AST/MAST)
- N48003 Remove, inspect, service and/or replace front and rear wheel bearings. (AST/MAST)
- N48004 Replace wheel bearing and race. (MLR/AST/MAST)
- N48005 Remove, reinstall, and/or replace sealed wheel bearing assembly. (AST/MAST)

Knowledge Objectives

After reading this chapter, you will be able to:

- K48001 Explain basic wheel bearing theory.
- K48002 Describe the components of wheel bearings.
- K48003 Describe the types of wheel bearings.
- K48004 Describe cylindrical roller bearings.
- K48005 Describe tapered roller bearings.
- K48006 Describe ball bearings.
- K48007 Explain how sealed bearings are different from serviceable bearings.
- K48008 Explain the purpose and function of grease and axle seals.
- K48009 Describe the differences between rear drive axle wheel bearing arrangements.
- K48010 Describe bearing lubricants and their application.
- K48011 Explain the process of adjusting wheel bearings.

Skills Objectives

After reading this chapter, you will be able to:

- S48001 Perform wheel bearing maintenance and repair.

Matching

Match the following terms with the correct description or example.

A. Antifriction bearing

B. Ball bearings

C. Bearing packer

D. Castellated nut

E. Cylindrical roller bearing assembly

F. End play

G. Grease seal

H. Interference fit

I. Lithium soap

J. Outer race

K. Preload

L. Running clearance

M. Tapered roller bearing assembly

N. Unitized wheel bearing hub

O. Wheel bearing

_____ **1.** A component that is designed to keep grease from leaking out and contaminants from leaking in.

_____ **2.** A condition where the wheel bearing components are forced together under pressure and therefore have no end play.

_____ **3.** An adjusting nut with slots cut into the top such that it resembles a castle; used with a cotter pin to prevent the nut from turning.

_____ **4.** An assembly consisting of the hub, wheel bearing(s), and possibly the wheel flange, which is preassembled and ready to be installed on a vehicle.

_____ **5.** The outside component of a wheel bearing that has a smooth, hardened surface for rollers or balls to ride on.

_____ **6.** A component that allows the wheels to rotate freely while supporting the weight of the vehicle, made up of an inner race, outer race, rollers or balls, and a cage.

_____ **7.** Wheel bearing assemblies that use surfaces that are in rolling contact with each other to greatly reduce friction compared to surfaces in sliding contact.

_____ **8.** A condition when two parts are held together by friction because the outside diameter of the inner component is slightly larger than the inside diameter of the outer component.

_____ **9.** A tool that forces grease into the spaces between the bearing rollers.

_____ **10.** A type of wheel bearing with races and rollers that are tapered in such a manner that all of the tapered angles meet at a common point, which allows them to roll freely and yet control thrust.

_____ **11.** A thickening agent for grease to give it the proper consistency.

_____ **12.** The in-and-out movement of the hub caused by clearance within the wheel bearing assembly.

_____ **13.** The amount of space between wheel bearing components while in operation.

_____ **14.** The rolling components of a wheel bearing consisting of hardened balls that roll in matching grooves in the inner and outer races.

_____ **15.** A type of wheel bearing with races and rollers that are cylindrical in shape and roll between inner and outer races, which are parallel to each other.

Multiple Choice

Read each item carefully, and then select the best response.

_____ **1.** What type of bearings must be serviced periodically by disassembling, cleaning, inspecting, and repacking them with the specified lubricant?
  A. Sealed bearings
  B. Serviceable bearings
  C. Ball bearings
  D. Unitized bearings

_____ **2.** What type of wheel bearing assembly is used where heavier loads need to be supported and the wheel bearings are put under a side load condition?
  A. Tapered roller bearing assemblies
  B. Unitized bearings
  C. Cylindrical roller bearing assemblies
  D. Either A or C

_____ **3.** Lubrication of serviceable tapered wheel bearing assemblies is usually accomplished by using _____.
  A. wheel bearing grease
  B. lithium soap
  C. gear lube
  D. either A or C

_____ **4.** Many seals use a(n) _____ to help hold the lips of the seal in contact with the shaft it is sealing.
  A. O-ring
  B. garter spring
  C. rubber gasket
  D. sealing bushing

_____ **5.** In a _____ the weight of the vehicle is fully carried by a pair of tapered roller bearing assemblies, which ride between the hub and axle tube.
   A. semifloating axle
   B. ¾ floating axle
   C. full-floating axle
   D. ½ floating axle

_____ **6.** In a(n) _____, the wheel flange is part of the axle, which is supported by a single bearing assembly near the flange end of the axle.
   A. ¾ floating axle
   B. semifloating axle
   C. full-floating axle
   D. solid axle

_____ **7.** In a _____ design, there is a single bearing assembly between the outside of the axle tube and the hub.
   A. ¾ floating axle
   B. full floating axle
   C. semifloating axle
   D. splined axle

_____ **8.** The level of gear lube should normally be within _____ of the bottom of the fill plug hole.
   A. 0.25"
   B. 0.50"
   C. 0.75"
   D. none of the above

_____ **9.** Grease is made out of a base oil, plus a thickening agent such as _____.
   A. lithium soap
   B. polysaccharides
   C. molybdenum thickening agents
   D. either A or C

_____ **10.** On adjustable wheel bearings, the proper clearance must be set using the _____.
   A. keyed washer
   B. adjusting nut
   C. lock cage
   D. lock nut

True/False

If you believe the statement to be more true than false, write the letter "T" in the space provided. If you believe the statement to be more false than true, write the letter "F."

_____ **1.** Sealed bearings are designed so they cannot be disassembled or adjusted.

_____ **2.** The outer bearing assembly is typically larger than the inner bearing assembly.

_____ **3.** Packing is best performed with a bearing packing tool, but it can be successfully performed by hand.

_____ **4.** Roller bearings roll easier than ball bearings since they have a smaller contact area; thus, they provide a small increase in vehicle efficiency.

_____ **5.** Sealed wheel bearings need to be adjusted for proper running clearance after installation.

_____ **6.** On some vehicles equipped with ABS brakes, the ABS sensor is integrated into the unitized wheel bearing assembly.

_____ **7.** Gear lube is somewhat thicker than bearing grease.

_____ **8.** Automotive wheel bearing grease is a thickened lubricant, designated as a plastic solid.

_____ **9.** Sealed bearings and double-row bearing assemblies come from the manufacturer with the proper clearance machined into them.

_____ **10.** On four-wheel drive vehicles, the adjustable wheel bearing locking mechanism commonly includes a keyed washer, adjusting nut, keyed lock washer, and lock nut.

Fill in the Blank

Read each item carefully, and then complete the statement by filling in the missing word(s).

1. In many instances, _____ roller bearing assemblies use the surface of the axle as the inner bearing race.

2. _____ a bearing means that the spaces between the rollers and races are completely filled with grease.

3. Virtually all wheel bearings using a ball bearing assembly are of the _____-_____ ball bearing variety, and they are commonly used in automotive light vehicle applications.

4. In some applications, the _____ _____ is press-fit into the axle housing, which is stationary, and seals against the axle shaft, which is rotating.

5. A(n) _____ _____ is a soft metal pin that can be bent into shape and is used to retain the bearing adjusting nut.

6. In many rear-wheel drive vehicles, the wheel bearing assemblies are open to the axle housing, which is partially filled with _____ _____ that also lubricates the differential assembly.

7. A(n) _____ _____ is usually threaded and can be removed to allow the level of a fluid to be checked and filled.

8. _____ refers to the thickness of the gear lube; the higher the number, the thicker the gear lube.

9. The thickness of grease is graded by the _____ _____ _____ _____.

10. _____ refers to the absence of clearance in the bearing and the specified amount of pressure forcing the bearing components together.

Labeling

Label the following diagrams with the correct terms.

1. Components of a wheel bearing:

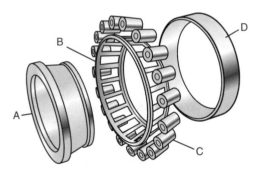

A. _____

B. _____

C. _____

D. _____

2. Identify the following components:

A. _____

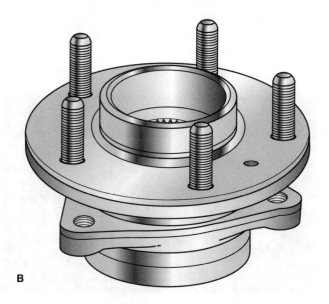

B

B. _____

C

C. _____

3. Lock nut-style wheel bearing locking mechanism:

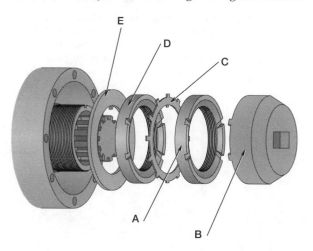

A. _____

B. _____

C. _____

D. _____

E. _____

Skill Drills

Place the skill drill steps in the correct order.

1. Removing, Cleaning, and Inspecting Wheel Bearings:

_____ **A.** Wipe any old grease off of the wheel bearings, races, and spindle with a rag, and give them a quick visual inspection. Consult the bearing diagnosis chart to identify any faults.

_____ **B.** Remove the locking mechanism. Remove the adjusting nut, keyed washer, and outer bearing. Reinstall the adjusting nut approximately five turns back onto the spindle.

_____ **C.** Remove the wheel bearing dust cap with dust cap pliers or a narrow cold chisel and hammer.

_____ **D.** Give the parts a final inspection, and consult the bearing diagnosis chart if there are any signs of damage. Using the specified grease, pack both wheel bearings, being careful to keep dirt and debris out of the grease.

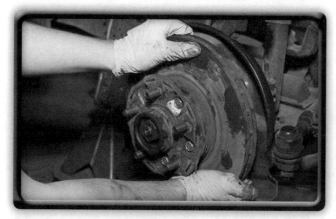

_____ **E.** Grasp the drum/rotor at the 1 o'clock and 7 o'clock positions or 11 o'clock and 5 o'clock positions. While holding downward pressure, quickly pull the drum/rotor toward you. The adjusting nut should catch the inner bearing race and pop the grease seal and bearing out of the hub, leaving them sitting on the spindle.

_____ **F.** If the wheel bearings are in serviceable condition, completely clean the wheel bearings, races, and hub. If using solvent to clean any of the components, make sure there is no solvent-contaminated grease left on the parts.

2. Packing Grease by Hand:

_____ **A.** Smear some grease around the outside of the bearing. Repeat this process on the other bearing.

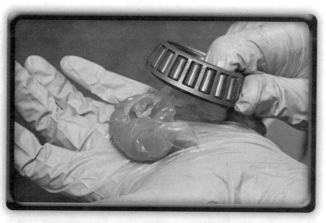

_____ **B.** Using a pair of latex or nitrile (nitro) gloves, place a small glob of grease in the palm of your nondominant hand. Place the index finger of your other hand through the bearing center hole with the larger diameter facing down.

_____ **C.** Carefully turn the bearing as a unit to a new space, and keep forcing grease between the bearings. Do this until all of the spaces are full.

_____ **D.** Push the large diameter of the bearing down the edge of the grease into your palm. This should force grease into the space between the bearings and races. Continue this process until grease comes out of the top of the bearing.

3. Installing the Locking Mechanism:

_____ **A.** If it is a locking nut style, then tighten the lock nut to the specified torque. This is usually a substantial torque of 50 ft-lb (67.79 N·m) or more.

_____ **B.** If it is a pin and hole style, or a bendable tang locking style, then place the washer against the adjusting nut (with the pin lined up, if that style) and thread the locking nut up against it. Torque the locking nut to the specified torque, and if a bendable tang style, bend the appropriate tang out toward you against the flat side of the locking nut with a small pry bar to lock the adjustment in place.

_____ **C.** Install the dust cap, being sure it is fully seated in the hub. Make sure the drum/rotor turns freely without binding or making any unusual noises.

_____ **D.** If the locking mechanism is a cotter pin, insert the new cotter pin through the castellated nut or locking cage, and the spindle. The short leg of the cotter pin should be against the castellated nut, and the long leg should be toward you. With the cotter pin fully engaged in the notch, bend the outer leg toward you and up over the end of the spindle. Cut it off just beyond the spindle. Also cut the short leg off at the nut or cage. Make sure the cotter pin will not hit the inside of the dust cap.

4. Replacing Wheel Bearings and Races:

_____ **A.** Using a hydraulic press or a hammer and bearing race installer, carefully drive the race until it is fully seated in the hub. When using a hammer and punch, a distinct sharp metallic sound should be produced when it seats. Inspect the race to verify that it is fully seated. Also check for any damage caused by installation. If everything is good, pack the new bearing and install it.

_____ **B.** With the wheel bearings removed from the wheel hub, clean and inspect the bearing and race for damage. Determine which bearing and race need to be replaced. Using a hydraulic press or a hammer and punch from the opposite side of the hub, carefully force the race from the hub. Keep it as straight as possible while removing it.

_____ **C.** Remove any burrs with a fine file or Dremel™, and remove any debris from the seat. Lightly lubricate the outside surface of the new race, and set it thick side down in the hub.

5. Removing and Reinstalling Sealed Wheel Bearings Using the Unitized Wheel Bearing Hub Style:

_____ **A.** If the wheel you are working on is a drive wheel, remove the axle hub nut and tap the drive axle loose with a dead blow hammer.

_____ **B.** Carefully compare the new hub to the old one, then fit the new hub assembly (over the axle shaft, if equipped) to the knuckle, making sure it is fully seated in place, and torque the mounting bolts to the specified torque.

_____ **C.** Loosen the axle hub nut, if equipped, while the tire is still on the ground. Remove the wheel and brake assembly following the specified procedure. Also disconnect the ABS connector and/or sensor if mounted to the hub.

_____ **D.** Unbolt and remove the hub assembly from the steering knuckle. Clean the knuckle assembly, and check the hub seat for nicks, burrs, or other damage.

_____ **E.** Reassemble the brake assembly and ABS sensor, if removed, following the specified procedure; install the wheel, and torque the lug nuts. Be sure the correct ends of the lug nuts are facing the wheel.

_____ **F.** Install the drive axle nut, if equipped. Use a new hub nut if called for by the manufacturer, and torque to specifications.

Review Questions

_____ **1.** Which component of wheel bearings holds the rollers or balls in place?
   A. An outer race
   B. An inner race
   C. A bearing cage
   D. Interference fit

_____ **2.** In most situations, serviceable wheel bearing races are held in place by:
   A. bolts
   B. an interference fit
   C. snap rings
   D. set screws

_____ **3.** Which type of bearing has an inner race called cone and an outer race called cup?
   A. Cylindrical roller bearings
   B. Double-row ball bearings
   C. Ball bearing
   D. Tapered roller bearing

_____ **4.** When packing a serviceable wheel bearing:
   A. make sure to fill all of the space in the hub with grease.
   B. make sure to fill the bearing grease cap full of grease.
   C. make sure to fill the spaces between the rollers with grease.
   D. only smear grease on the outside surfaces of the bearings.

_____ **5.** When installing a cotter pin in a wheel bearing locknut:
   A. adjust the wheel bearing and then install the cotter pin.
   B. install the cotter pin and then adjust the wheel bearing.
   C. install the dust cap and then install the cotter pin.
   D. install the cotter pin and then install the wheel bearing.

_____ **6.** All of the following statements regarding sealed and serviceable bearings are true _except_:
   A. Sealed bearing assemblies are prefilled with lubricant and have integrated grease seals, unlike serviceable bearings.
   B. In serviceable bearings, proper running clearance must be adjusted, whereas sealed bearings are manufactured with the proper clearance.
   C. Sealed bearing assemblies do not need periodic maintenance, unlike serviceable bearings.
   D. Sealed bearing assemblies never fail whereas serviceable bearings can fail.

_____ **7.** Choose the correct statement.
   A. All wheel bearings have the seal built right into the bearing assembly.
   B. A garter spring helps maintain an adequate seal if the parts are slightly out of alignment.
   C. Grease seals are designed so they can be reused.
   D. When installing a seal, the sealing lip need not be pre-lubed as it comes with a small amount of oil or grease.

_____ **8.** In which of the following rear drive axle designations is a pair of tapered roller bearing assemblies used on each side?
   A. Full floating axle
   B. Semi-floating axle
   C. ¾-floating axle
   D. ½-floating axle

_____ **9.** All of the following statements with respect to lubricants and their application are true _except_:
   A. Gear lube is somewhat thicker than engine oil.
   B. The level of gear lube should normally be within 0.25" (6.35 mm) of the bottom of the fill plug hole.
   C. The higher the viscosity number, the thinner the gear lube.
   D. A bearing packer is a tool that forces grease into the spaces between the bearing rollers.

_____ **10.** When adjusting serviceable wheel bearings, the final adjustment (2nd adjustment) should be approximately:
   A. 20 ft-lb (27.1 N.m)
   B. 15–25 in-lb (1.69–2.82 N.m)

C. 0.020" (0.508 mm)

D. 0.050" (1.27 mm)

ASE Technician A/Technician B Style Questions

_____ **1.** Tech A says that cylindrical roller bearings can carry more weight than similarly sized ball bearings. Tech B says that tapered roller bearings used in opposing pairs control side thrust in both directions. Who is correct?

A. Tech A

B. Tech B

C. Both A and B

D. Neither A nor B

_____ **2.** Tech A says that a tapered roller bearing assembly has less rolling resistance than a similarly sized ball bearing assembly. Tech B says that the bearing assembly in a unitized wheel bearing assembly can normally be disassembled, cleaned, and repacked. Who is correct?

A. Tech A

B. Tech B

C. Both A and B

D. Neither A nor B

_____ **3.** Tech A says that over time a grease seal can wear a groove in the sealing surface of the axle or shaft that may require replacement of the axle or shaft. Tech B says that grease seals need to be replaced every time the bearing is removed. Who is correct?

A. Tech A

B. Tech B

C. Both A and B

D. Neither A nor B

_____ **4.** Tech A says that in a full floating axle, the axle does not support the weight of the vehicle. Tech B says that when adjusting tapered wheel bearings, the final torque should be about 20 ft-lb. Who is correct?

A. Tech A

B. Tech B

C. Both A and B

D. Neither A nor B

_____ **5.** Tech A says that serviceable wheel bearings can be repacked by removing the dust cap, filling it with grease, and reinstalling it. Tech B says that the cotter pin must be replaced with a new one every time it is removed. Who is correct?

A. Tech A

B. Tech B

C. Both A and B

D. Neither A nor B

_____ **6.** Tech A says that the gear lube level in the final drive is okay as long as you can touch the level with your finger. Tech B says that the gear lube level should normally be no more than ¼" below the bottom threads on the fill plug hole. Who is correct?

A. Tech A

B. Tech B

C. Both A and B

D. Neither A nor B

_____ **7.** Tech A says that wheel bearings must be replaced as a set, bearing, and race. Tech B says that the wheel bearings and races on both sides of the vehicle must be replaced if one side fails. Who is correct?

A. Tech A

B. Tech B

C. Both A and B

D. Neither A nor B

_____ **8.** Tech A says that unitized wheel bearing hubs are virtually zero maintenance systems until they wear out. Tech B says that unitized wheel bearing hubs are usually replaced as a unit. Who is correct?
   A. Tech A
   B. Tech B
   C. Both A and B
   D. Neither A nor B

_____ **9.** Tech A says that when installing a bearing race, it should only take finger pressure to install it. Tech B says that on a tapered roller bearing, the race is also called the cup. Who is correct?
   A. Tech A
   B. Tech B
   C. Both A and B
   D. Neither A nor B

_____ **10.** Tech A says that when a race is fully seated, a sharp metallic sound is produced when installation is complete. Tech B says that to be sure a race is fully seated, the wheel bearing adjusting nut should be tightened to at least 100 ft-lb of torque, which will finish seating it. Who is correct?
   A. Tech A
   B. Tech B
   C. Both A and B
   D. Neither A nor B

Electronic Brake Control Systems

At the start of each chapter you'll find the NATEF tasks, Knowledge Objectives, and Skills Objectives from the textbook. These are your objectives as you make your way through the exercises in this workbook and the chapter in your textbook. The following activities have been designed to help you refresh your knowledge of the material in this chapter.

NATEF Tasks

- N49001 Bleed the electronic brake control system hydraulic circuits. (MAST)
- N49002 Depressurize high-pressure components of an electronic brake control system. (MAST)
- N49003 Diagnose poor stopping, wheel lockup, abnormal pedal feel, unwanted application, and noise concerns associated with the electronic brake control system; determine needed action. (MAST)
- N49004 Diagnose electronic brake control system electronic control(s) and components by retrieving diagnostic trouble codes, and/or using recommended test equipment; determine needed action. (MAST)
- N49005 Identify and inspect electronic brake control system components (ABS, TCS, ESC); determine needed action. (AST/MAST)
- N49006 Test, diagnose, and service electronic brake control system speed sensors (digital and analog), toothed ring (tone wheel), and circuits using a graphing multimeter (GMM)/digital storage oscilloscope (DSO) (includes output signal, resistance, shorts to voltage/ground, and frequency data). (MAST)
- N49007 Diagnose electronic brake control system braking concerns caused by vehicle modifications (tire size, curb height, final drive ratio, etc.). (MAST)

Knowledge Objectives

After reading this chapter, you will be able to:

- K49001 Explain the progression and operating principles of electronic brake control systems.
- K49002 Describe the three most common EBC systems.
- K49003 Explain the principles of operation of antilock brake systems.
- K49004 Explain the principles of operation of traction control.
- K49005 Describe the basic principles of operation of electronic stability control.

Skills Objectives

After reading this chapter, you will be able to:

- S49001 Perform maintenance and repair tasks on EBC systems.
- S49002 Remove and install electric and hydraulic EBC components.
- S49003 Perform diagnostic tasks on electronic brake controlled systems.

Matching

Match the following terms with the correct description or example.

A. ABS proportioning valve depressor
B. Accumulator
C. Body control module (BCM)
D. Channel
E. Common bore
F. Fault codes
G. High-pressure accumulator

H. Integral ABS system
I. Isolation valve
J. Magneto-resistive sensor
K. Nonintegral ABS systems
L. Oversteer
M. Roll-rate sensor
N. Steering angle sensor

O. Steering wheel position sensor
P. Tone wheel
Q. Understeer

R. Variable reluctance sensor
S. Vehicle speed sensor
T. Wheel speed sensor

_____ **1.** A type of wheel speed sensor that uses the principle of magnetic induction to create its signal.

_____ **2.** A brake system in which the master cylinder, power booster, and HCU are all combined in a common unit.

_____ **3.** A sensor that measures the amount of turning a driver desires. This information is used by the ESC system to know the driver's directional intent.

_____ **4.** An alphanumeric code system used to identify potential problems in a vehicle system.

_____ **5.** A storage container that holds pressurized brake fluid.

_____ **6.** The valve in the HCU that either allows or blocks brake fluid that comes from the master cylinder from entering the HCU hydraulic circuit.

_____ **7.** A brake system in which the master cylinder, power booster, and HCU are all separate units.

_____ **8.** The computer that controls the electrical system in the body of a vehicle, including power windows, door locks, heating and A/C systems, and in some cases the EBC system.

_____ **9.** The component that creates an electrical signal based on the speed of the vehicle, which is sent to the EBCM.

_____ **10.** A sensor that measures the amount of roll around the vehicle's horizontal axis that a vehicle is experiencing.

_____ **11.** A device that creates an analog or digital signal according to the speed of the wheel.

_____ **12.** A storage container designed to contain high-pressure liquids such as brake fluid.

_____ **13.** A sensor that signals to the EBCM both the position and speed of the steering wheel.

_____ **14.** A tool used to hold the proportioning valve open on some ABS HCUs.

_____ **15.** The number of wheel speed sensor circuits and hydraulic circuits the EBCM monitors and controls.

_____ **16.** A condition in which the front wheels are turned further than the direction the vehicle is moving and the front tires are slipping sideways toward the outside of the turn.

_____ **17.** A condition in which the rear wheels are slipping sideways toward the outside of the turn.

_____ **18.** The part of the wheel speed sensor that has ribs and valleys used to create an electrical signal inside of the pick-up assembly.

_____ **19.** When a single cylinder is used for two pistons. A tandem master cylinder would be an example of two pistons in one bore.

_____ **20.** A type of wheel speed sensor that uses an effect similar to a Hall effect sensor to create its signal.

Multiple Choice

Read each item carefully, and then select the best response.

_____ **1.** ABS systems use a computer that sends electrical signals to the _____ that momentarily hold or release hydraulic pressure to that wheel until it speeds up and starts rolling again.
   A. wheel speed sensors
   B. master cylinder
   C. solenoid valves
   D. spool valves

_____ **2.** Which component of the ABS system contains electric solenoid valves controlled by the EBCM to modify hydraulic pressure in each hydraulic circuit?
   A. Master cylinder
   B. Hydraulic control unit
   C. Power booster
   D. Accumulator

_____ **3.** Which of these is used to control the flow of brake fluid in the hydraulic system?
   A. Electric solenoid
   B. Spool valve
   C. Check valve
   D. Brake pedal sensor

_____ **4.** A _____ system uses separate speed sensors and hydraulic control circuits for each of the four wheels.
  A. single-channel
  B. two-channel
  C. three-channel
  D. four-channel

_____ **5.** If the high-pressure pump fails for any reason, the _____ holds enough brake fluid at high pressure to apply the brakes 10 to 20 times before the boost is used up.
  A. hydraulic control unit
  B. accumulator
  C. master cylinder
  D. reservoir

_____ **6.** A wheel sensor assembly consists of a toothed tone wheel (or tone ring) that rotates with the wheels and a stationary _____ attached to the hub or axle housing.
  A. pick-up assembly
  B. resistor
  C. tooth
  D. relay

_____ **7.** The height of the sine wave is called its _____.
  A. peak
  B. amplitude
  C. phase
  D. duration

_____ **8.** What style of speed sensor is sometimes called a passive system since it is self-contained and needs no outside power to function?
  A. Variable reluctance
  B. Magneto-resistive
  C. Hall effect
  D. Either A or C

_____ **9.** Some ABS systems provide _____ through the ABS warning lamp when a specific terminal is grounded or two specific terminals are shorted together.
  A. blink codes
  B. Morse codes
  C. flash codes
  D. either A or C

_____ **10.** An electronic stability control system may integrate a(n) _____ into the basic ABS and TCS systems.
  A. yaw sensor
  B. steering angle sensor
  C. roll-rate sensor
  D. all of the above

True/False

If you believe the statement to be more true than false, write the letter "T" in the space provided. If you believe the statement to be more false than true, write the letter "F."

_____ **1.** Electronic stability control systems take the ABS and TCS systems to the next level by adding sensor information regarding the driver's directional intent.

_____ **2.** Understeer occurs when the vehicle is turning more sharply than the front wheels are being steered.

_____ **3.** Applying the brakes too hard or on a slippery surface can cause the wheels to lock.

_____ **4.** Maximum braking traction occurs when the wheels are rotating 20–25% slower than the vehicle speed.

_____ **5.** Nonintegral ABS systems use a fairly standard tandem master cylinder and a typical vacuum or hydraulic power booster.

_____ **6.** Some hydraulic control units use a single, three-position solenoid valve per circuit, while others use dual, two-position valves per hydraulic circuit.

_____ **7.** The pick-up assembly and tone wheel do not touch each other; a small gap, called an air gap, must be maintained at the specified clearance.

_____ **8.** The magneto-resistive sensor does not function effectively below vehicle speeds of around 5 mph.

_____ **9.** The brake switch is a normally open switch, meaning that if the switch is not affected by any outside force, electrical current will flow through it.

_____ **10.** Many electronic stability control system-equipped vehicles also monitor signals from the throttle position sensor, vehicle speed sensor, and brake pedal position sensor to help prevent a loss of control of the vehicle.

Fill in the Blank

Read each item carefully, and then complete the statement by filling in the missing word(s).

1. In the quest for increased safety, manufacturers developed a series of electronic _____ _____ systems; the first-generation was the antilock brake system.

2. The _____ _____ system applies brake pressure to the slipping tire, which causes more of the engine's torque to be transmitted to the wheel or wheels with the most traction.

3. The _____-_____ _____ system is designed to prevent wheels locking or skidding, no matter how hard the brakes are applied or how slippery the road surface, and to maintain steering control of the vehicle.

4. When the ignition switch is turned on, the ABS controller illuminates the yellow ABS warning lamp and performs an automatic _____-_____ of the system.

5. Drivers need to be taught to expect ABS brake pedal _____ when in a panic stop.

6. The ABS control module (or EBCM) sends commands in the form of _____ _____ to the hydraulic control unit.

7. A(n) _____-_____ system uses one sensor circuit with the speed sensor typically located in the differential and one hydraulic control circuit to control both rear wheels.

8. _____-_____ accumulators hold brake fluid in a spring-loaded chamber when it is released by the dump valves during an EBC event.

9. The electronic brake control module supplies the magneto-resistive or Hall effect sensor systems with a _____ _____ of between 5 and 12 volts, depending on the manufacturer.

10. On a traction control system _____ _____ direct hydraulic pressure from the accumulator to the ABS solenoid valves so individual wheel brake units can be applied independently.

Labeling

Label the following diagrams with the correct terms.

1. HCU solenoid valve arrangement:

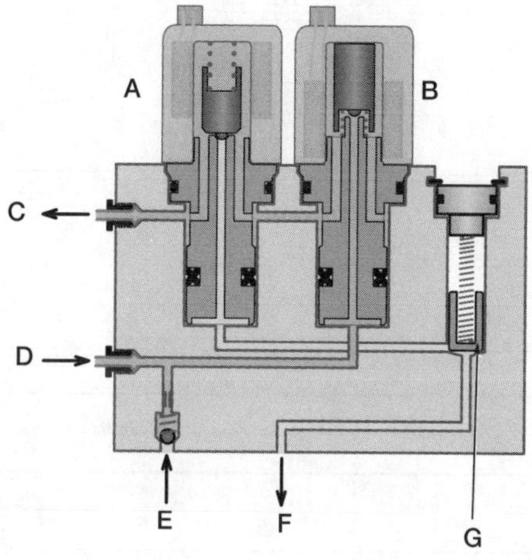

A. _____

B. _____

C. _____

D. _____

E. _____

F. _____

G. _____

2. Portless ABS master cylinder:

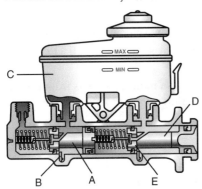

A. _____

B. _____

C. _____

D. _____

E. _____

3. The four types of ABS channels:

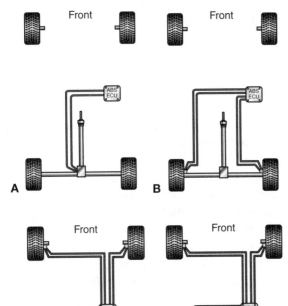

A. _____

B. _____

C. _____

D. _____

4. Wheel speed sensor sine wave:

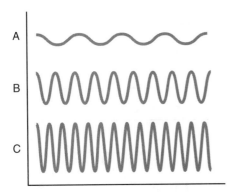

A. _____

B. _____

C. _____

5. Tools used to diagnose electronic brake systems:

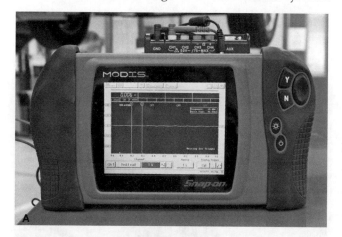

A. _____

B. _____

C. _____

Skill Drills

Test your knowledge of skill drills by filling in the correct words in the photo captions.

   1. Testing Variable Reluctance Sensors:

Step 1: Disconnect the suspect sensor, measure its _____, and _____ the reading to the specifications. If the resistance does not meet the manufacturer's specifications, _____ the sensor.

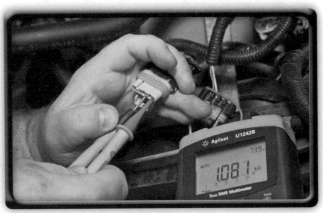

Step 2: If it is within specifications, test the two-wire circuit back to the EBCM for _____, _____, _____ _____, and _____. Repair as necessary.

Step 3: If the circuit is good, reconnect the _____ _____ connector and attach a GMM or DSO to one of the sensor _____.

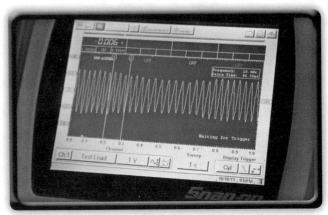

Step 4: Spin the _____ _____, and observe the pattern. It should be a clean _____ analog pattern of sufficient _____ (voltage).

Step 5: If the _____ is not correct, _____ the tone wheel for _____, and replace as necessary.

Step 6: If the tone wheel is good, replace the _____ _____ _____. If the pattern looks OK, you may have to compare it to the other wheel speed sensor _____ while _____ the vehicle. After repair, clear the _____ _____, if directed by the service information.

Review Questions

_____ 1. Magnetic induction type wheel speed sensors create which type of signal?
   A. 12 volt DC voltage
   B. Analog AC voltage
   C. Digital DC voltage
   D. 12 volt AC voltage

_____ 2. Which EBC system uses sensor information regarding the vehicle's actual direction?
   A. ABS system
   B. TCS system
   C. ESC system
   D. Base brake system

_____ 3. Choose the correct statement regarding ABS solenoids.
   A. During "hold," the brake pressure is prevented from returning to the master cylinder.
   B. During "release," the brake pressure is directed to the wheel brake unit.
   C. During "hold," the brake pressure is being increased to the wheel brake unit.
   D. During "release," the brake pressure is held steady.

_____ 4. Which primary component in an ABS system sends output control signals to electronic solenoid valves?
   A. Brake pedal switch
   B. Hydraulic control unit
   C. Wheel speed sensor
   D. Electronic control unit

_____ 5. All of the following statements referring to the principles of ABS braking are true _except_:
   A. During normal braking, the EBCM does not energize the solenoid valves in the hydraulic unit.
   B. If the wheel speed sensors indicate that the wheel is still decelerating too rapidly after the pressure has been held, the EBCM commands the appropriate solenoid valve to release braking pressure.
   C. If the wheels are not skidding, the EBCM does not monitor the speed of each wheel.
   D. Changes in HCU valve position normally cause rapid hydraulic pulsations.

_____ 6. Choose the correct statement with respect to the principles of operation of traction control.
   A. The TCS system was developed to prevent the drive wheels from slipping while the vehicle is being accelerated.
   B. Traction control is active at all speeds.
   C. When the TCS is active, the EBCM monitors only the speed of the drive wheels.
   D. If the driver deactivates the TCS, the ABS system will also be deactivated.

_____ 7. Which sensor in the ESC system tells the EBCM the rate at which the vehicle is actually turning?
   A. Steering angle sensor
   B. Roll-rate sensor
   C. Yaw sensor
   D. Wheel speed sensor

_____ 8. All of the following statements with respect to the operation of the ESC system are true _except_:
   A. The ECBM monitors the yaw sensor signal, the steering angle sensor signal, and the roll-rate sensor signal as well as the wheel speed sensor signals.
   B. The EBCM detects understeer, oversteer, or roll in the signal values and then applies up to three wheel brake units to help bring the vehicle back within proper stability parameters.
   C. The EBCM requests a reduction in engine power through the powertrain control module (PCM) to help slow the vehicle further.
   D. No matter the driving conditions or driver actions, ESC will prevent a loss of control of the vehicle.

_____ 9. Which of the following features designed into ESC systems holds the brake pressure until the throttle is depressed and the vehicle starts to move forward?
   A. Hill assist
   B. Hill descent control
   C. Engine braking control
   D. Panic stop assist

_____ **10.** All of the following are likely to turn the ABS light on except:

    A. replacing a faulty wheel speed sensor

    B. mismatched tires

    C. low tire pressure on one or more tires

    D. installing a different ration final drive

ASE Technician A/Technician B Style Questions

_____ **1.** Tech A says that an antilock brake system (ABS) helps shorten the stopping distance during a panic stop. Tech B says that antilock brake systems work by increasing the hydraulic pressure in the brake system so the brakes can be applied harder. Who is correct?

    A. Tech A

    B. Tech B

    C. Both A and B

    D. Neither A nor B

_____ **2.** Tech A says that traction control can reduce the power output of the engine to increase traction. Tech B says that electronic stability control increases the risk of rollover. Who is correct?

    A. Tech A

    B. Tech B

    C. Both A and B

    D. Neither A nor B

_____ **3.** Tech A says that an electronic braking system has sensors that monitor wheel speed. Tech B says that understeer is generally easier to recover from than oversteer. Who is correct?

    A. Tech A

    B. Tech B

    C. Both A and B

    D. Neither A nor B

_____ **4.** Tech A says that ABS controls braking every time the brakes are applied. Tech B says that during an ABS event, it is normal for the brake pedal to pulsate. Who is correct?

    A. Tech A

    B. Tech B

    C. Both A and B

    D. Neither A nor B

_____ **5.** Tech A says that during antilock braking, brake fluid may be returned to the master cylinder. Tech B says that solenoid valves in the hydraulic control unit will isolate the master cylinder from the brake circuit when it is in the Hold mode. Who is correct?

    A. Tech A

    B. Tech B

    C. Both A and B

    D. Neither A nor B

_____ **6.** Tech A says that mismatched tires may cause the ABS system to register a fault code. Tech B says that a traction control system may automatically apply brake pressure to a wheel brake unit even if the vehicle is not being braked. Who is correct?

    A. Tech A

    B. Tech B

    C. Both A and B

    D. Neither A nor B

_____ **7.** Tech A says that an ABS key-on system test checks for faults in the vehicle's base brake system. Tech B says that on most vehicles ABS DTCs are stored in memory for later retrieval. Who is correct?

    A. Tech A

    B. Tech B

    C. Both A and B

    D. Neither A nor B

_____ **8.** Tech A says that a yaw sensor tells the computer the vehicle's actual direction. Tech B says that raising a vehicle's curb height has no effect on the electronic stability control system. Who is correct?
   A. Tech A
   B. Tech B
   C. Both A and B
   D. Neither A nor B

_____ **9.** Tech A says that a scan tool may be required to bleed air from the ABS brake system. Tech B says that some vehicles have a high-pressure accumulator that may need to have the pressure bled off before hydraulic brake repairs are made. Who is correct?
   A. Tech A
   B. Tech B
   C. Both A and B
   D. Neither A nor B

_____ **10.** Tech A says that some ABS wheel speed sensors create a square wave digital pattern. Tech B says that some wheel speed sensors create an AC sine wave pattern. Who is correct?
   A. Tech A
   B. Tech B
   C. Both A and B
   D. Neither A nor B

Principles of Electrical Systems

At the start of each chapter you'll find the NATEF tasks, Knowledge Objectives, and Skills Objectives from the textbook. These are your objectives as you make your way through the exercises in this workbook and the chapter in your textbook. The following activities have been designed to help you refresh your knowledge of the material in this chapter.

NATEF Tasks

- N50001 Demonstrate knowledge of the causes and effects from shorts, grounds, opens, and resistance problems in electrical/electronic circuits. (MLR/AST/MAST)
- N50002 Demonstrate knowledge of electrical/electronic series, parallel, and series-parallel circuits using principles of electricity (Ohm's law). (MLR/AST/MAST)

Knowledge Objectives

After reading this chapter, you will be able to:

- K50001 Explain the basic fundamentals of electricity.
- K50002 Define units of electrical measurement.
- K50003 Define electrical circuit terminology.
- K50004 Explain the sources and effects of electricity.
- K50005 Explain the application of basic electrical laws.

Skills Objectives

There are no Skills Objectives for this chapter.

Matching

Match the following terms with the correct description or example.

A. Alternating current (AC)	**K.** Ohm
B. Amp	**L.** Hole theory
C. Relay	**M.** Polarity
D. Current flow	**N.** Semiconductor
E. Ammeter	**O.** Short
F. Electromagnet	**P.** Silicon
G. Energy	**Q.** Electron theory
H. Ground	**R.** Voltage drop
I. Insulator	**S.** Hot junction
J. Sine wave	**T.** Volt

_____ **1.** The theory that as electrons flow from negative to positive, holes flow from positive to negative.

_____ **2.** A material that has properties that prevent the easy flow of electricity. These materials are made up of atoms with five to eight electrons in the valance ring.

_____ **3.** The theory that electrons, being negatively charged, repel other electrons and are attracted to positively charged objects; thus electrons flow from negative to positive.

_____ **4.** A conductor wound in a coil that produces a magnetic field when current flows through it.

_____ **5.** The state of charge, positive or negative.

_____ **6.** A device used to measure current flow.

_____ **7.** A material commonly used to make semiconductors.

_____ **8.** A type of current flow that flows back and forth.

_____ **9.** The heating point of a thermocouple.

_____ **10.** The ability to do work.

_____ **11.** Also called a short circuit, the flow of current along an unintended route.

_____ **12.** An electromechanical switching device whereby the magnetism from a coil winding acts on a lever that switches a set of contacts.

_____ **13.** The amount of potential difference between two points in a circuit.

_____ **14.** A mathematical function that describes a repetitive waveform such as an alternating current signal.

_____ **15.** An abbreviation for amperes, the unit for current measurement.

_____ **16.** The unit for measuring electrical resistance.

_____ **17.** The unit used to measure potential difference or electrical pressure.

_____ **18.** A material used to make microchips, transistors, and diodes.

_____ **19.** The flow of electrons, typically within a circuit or component.

_____ **20.** The return path for electrical current in a vehicle chassis, other metal of the vehicle, or dedicated wire.

Multiple Choice

Read each item carefully, and then select the best response.

_____ **1.** Electromotive force is also referred to as _____.
   A. voltage
   B. resistance
   C. amperage
   D. electrons

_____ **2.** The electrical resistance of a circuit is measured in _____.
   A. A
   B. Ω
   C. V
   D. W

_____ **3.** What materials make a good insulator?
   A. Copper and aluminum
   B. Ceramic and plastic
   C. Copper and silicon
   D. Argon and silicon

_____ **4.** If a 15-volt circuit with a single light has a current flow of 2 amps, then what is the power in watts in the circuit?
   A. 17
   B. 30
   C. 7.5
   D. 13

_____ **5.** Which type of current flow is produced by a battery?
   A. Alternating current
   B. Three phase
   C. Direct current
   D. Sine wave

_____ **6.** What is meant by the term "continuity"?
   A. A low-voltage circuit that does not have a complete circuit and therefore cannot conduct current
   B. A circuit fault in which current takes a shorter path, in terms of resistance, through an accidental or unintended route
   C. An electrical circuit that has a continuous and uninterrupted connection
   D. An electric circuit that has a break, and current cannot flow past the break

_____ **7.** The term _____ describes a low-voltage circuit that does not have a complete circuit and therefore cannot conduct current.
   A. closed
   B. open
   C. short
   D. grounded

_____ **8.** When two dissimilar metals are immersed in an electrolyte, the breakdown of chemicals into charged particles that results in a flow of electricity is called _____.
   A. photovoltaic effect
   B. induction
   C. electrolysis
   D. electrostatic energy

_____ **9.** All of the following are effects of the flow of electricity, except:
   A. Chemical reactions
   B. Mechanical action
   C. Heat
   D. Magnetism

_____ **10.** Which of the following Ohm's law formulas is correct?
   A. A = V/R
   B. V = A × R
   C. R = V ÷ A
   D. All of the above

_____ **11.** The rate of transforming energy is also known as _____.
   A. power
   B. voltage
   C. work
   D. magnetism

_____ **12.** In a(n) _____ circuit, all components are connected directly to the voltage supply.
   A. series
   B. parallel
   C. series/ parallel
   D. all of the above

_____ **13.** Which law states that current entering any junction is equal to the sum of the current flowing out of the junction?
   A. Ohm's law
   B. Kirchhoff's current law
   C. The law of conservation of energy
   D. Newton's first law of energy

_____ **14.** A _____ is an electromechanical switching device whereby the magnetism from a coil winding acts on a lever that switches a set of contacts.
   A. thermocouple
   B. solenoid
   C. diode
   D. relay

_____ **15.** Electrochemical energy is produced when _____.
   A. sunlight falls on photocells
   B. steam builds up
   C. when two dissimilar metals are heated
   D. two dissimilar metals are immersed in an acidic liquid

_____ **16.** What of these is a by-product of the flow of electricity?
   A. Heat
   B. Water
   C. Oil
   D. Steam

_____ **17.** If a person has a 4 ohm resistor and the battery is charged to 12 volts, how many amps will flow in the circuit?
  A. 1 amp
  B. 2 amps
  C. 3 amps
  D. 4 amps

_____ **18.** How many paths are there in a series circuit?
  A. One
  B. Two
  C. Three
  D. Four

_____ **19.** Which of these cannot conduct electrons easily?
  A. Conductors
  B. Superconductors
  C. Insulators
  D. Semi-conductors

_____ **20.** What can be the number of valence ring electrons of conductors?
  A. Two
  B. Four
  C. Six
  D. Eight

True/False

If you believe the statement to be more true than false, write the letter "T" in the space provided. If you believe the statement to be more false than true, write the letter "F."

_____ **1.** A deficiency of electrons gives an atom an overall positive charge.

_____ **2.** Most wiring diagrams are written from the conventional theory perspective, while electronic circuits are typically designed and operate on the electron theory perspective.

_____ **3.** Volts, amps, and ohms are three basic units of electrical measurement.

_____ **4.** Hertz is the measurement of frequency and indicates the number of cycles per second.

_____ **5.** If voltage stays the same and resistance doubles, half as much amperage can be pushed through the resistance.

_____ **6.** A potential electrical difference across a crystal that will physically distort the crystal is called electromagnetic induction.

_____ **7.** When negative ions in a solution are attracted to the negative plate and positive ions to the positive plate, a chemical reaction can occur.

_____ **8.** Ohm's law is a relationship between volts, amps, and ohms, and because they must always balance out, if we know any two of the values, then we can calculate the third.

_____ **9.** A light bulb uses a certain amount of electrical power, but the power used is not an indication of brightness.

_____ **10.** A typical incandescent light bulb creates light, but only about 10% of the electricity is converted to light; about 90% is wasted as heat.

Fill in the Blank

Read each item carefully, and then complete the statement by filling in the missing word(s).

1. _____ _____ are only loosely held by the nucleus and are free to move from one atom to another when an electrical potential (pressure) is applied.

2. Electrical _____, measured in ohms, affects the current flow in a circuit.

3. _____ _____ tells us that if we increase current flow through a resistance, the voltage used by that resistance will increase.

4. The PN junction of a semiconductor is located in the _____ layer.

5. The unit of _____ _____ is the watt.

6. A(n) _____ is constructed by winding a conductor wire, many hundreds or thousands of times, around a soft iron or metal core and passing a current through the coil.

7. The transfer of electrical energy from one coil to another through induction in a transformer is known as _____ _____.

8. _____ is achieved when an electrical circuit has a continuous and uninterrupted electrical connection and is thereby capable of conducting current and working as designed.

9. In its purest definition, the term _____ describes a circuit fault in which current takes a shorter path, resistance-wise, through an accidental or unintended route.

10. One _____ is produced when 1 volt causes 1 amp of current to flow.

Labeling

Label the following diagrams with the correct terms.

1. Parts of an atom (including charge):

A. _____   Charge _____

B. _____   Charge _____

C. _____   Charge _____

2. Ions:

A

B

A. _____

B. _____

3. Insulators:

A   B   C

A. _____

B. _____

C. _____

4. Short circuit:

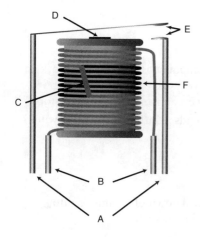

A. _____

B. _____

C. _____

D. _____

E. _____

F. _____

Review Questions

_____ **1.** All of the following statements describing the basic principles of electricity are true *except*:
  A. An atom with less/deficiency of electrons than protons has an overall positive charge and is called a positive ion.
  B. An atom with more electrons than protons has an overall negative charge and is called a negative ion.
  C. A positive ion exerts a repelling force on the extra electron.
  D. The flow of electrons from atom to atom is called current flow.

_____ **2.** Which of the following materials is typically used in the construction of semiconductors?
  A. Silicon
  B. Copper
  C. Plastic
  D. Ceramic

_____ **3.** Electromotive force can be best described as the:
  A. force of electrons repelling each other.
  B. repelling force of the negative terminal.
  C. attracting force of the positive terminal.
  D. force of attraction/repelling which drives the electrons to move along.

_____ **4.** The degree to which a material opposes the passage of electrical current through it is called:
  A. voltage.
  B. resistance.
  C. discharge.
  D. insulation.

_____ **5.** Which of the following is a measure of the number of electrons flowing past a given point in 1 second?
  A. Volt
  B. Watt
  C. Ohm
  D. Amp

_____ **6.** The device which is used to measure the amount of resistance in a component or a circuit is a(n):
  A. ohmmeter.
  B. ammeter.
  C. voltmeter.
  D. multimeter.

_____ **7.** The force with which the positive terminal pulls the free electrons toward it in a circuit is measured in:
  A. volts.
  B. amperage.

    C. current.
    D. ohms.

_____ **8.** All of the following statements describing an electrical circuit are true *except*:
    A. An open circuit does not have continuity.
    B. Current flows through the fuse into the circuit wires.
    C. Electrical circuits consist of a power source, a fuse, a switch, a component that performs work, and wires connecting them all together.
    D. When the switch is moved to closed position, the current path is broken and current flow stops.

_____ **9.** Which side of a circuit starts at the negative post of the battery and ends at either a load or a switch?
    A. Positive side
    B. Ground side
    C. Supply side
    D. Power side

_____ **10.** When two dissimilar metals are immersed in an acidic liquid, the breakdown of chemicals into charged particles results in a flow of electricity. This principle is used in a(n):
    A. HVAC system.
    B. battery.
    C. sensor.
    D. LED.

ASE Technician A/Technician B Style Questions

_____ **1.** Tech A says that a pure short circuit is the only type of short circuit. Tech B says that a short causes abnormally high current flow in the circuit and may cause the circuit protection devices to open the circuit. Who is correct?
    A. Tech A
    B. Tech B
    C. Both A and B
    D. Neither A nor B

_____ **2.** Tech A says that the movement of electrons in a circuit is called current flow. Tech B says that the movement of electrons in a circuit is measured in amps. Who is correct?
    A. Tech A
    B. Tech B
    C. Both A and B
    D. Neither A nor B

_____ **3.** Tech A says that electromotive force is also known as voltage. Tech B says that when electrons flow in one direction only, this is DC. Who is correct?
    A. Tech A
    B. Tech B
    C. Both A and B
    D. Neither A nor B

_____ **4.** Tech A says that an unintended resistance results in a voltage drop. Tech B says that one of the factors that determines the level of electrical resistance is the weight of the conductor. Who is correct?
    A. Tech A
    B. Tech B
    C. Both A and B
    D. Neither A nor B

_____ **5.** Tech A says that if resistance stays the same and voltage goes up, then amperage goes down. Tech B says that if voltage stays the same and resistance goes down, then amperage goes down. Who is correct?
    A. Tech A
    B. Tech B
    C. Both A and B
    D. Neither A nor B

_____ **6.** Tech A says that a series circuit has only one path for current to flow. Tech B says that a parallel circuit current flows through one resistor before getting to the next resistor. Who is correct?
   A. Tech A
   B. Tech B
   C. Both A and B
   D. Neither A nor B

_____ **7.** Two technicians are discussing a series circuit with four resistors of various resistances. Tech A says that current flow is different in each resistor. Tech B says that current flow is the same in each resistor. Who is correct?
   A. Tech A
   B. Tech B
   C. Both A and B
   D. Neither A nor B

_____ **8.** Tech A says that an ohm is a unit of measurement of resistance. Tech B says that high resistance creates heat at the point of resistance in the circuit. Who is correct?
   A. Tech A
   B. Tech B
   C. Both A and B
   D. Neither A nor B

_____ **9.** Tech A says that in a series circuit with two resistors of 120 ohms each, the total circuit resistance is 240 ohms. Tech B says that in a parallel circuit with two resistors of 120 ohms each, the total circuit resistance is 240 ohms. Who is correct?
   A. Tech A
   B. Tech B
   C. Both A and B
   D. Neither A nor B

_____ **10.** Tech A says that if a 12-volt light has 10 amps flowing through it, it is using 22 watts of electricity. Tech B says that watts are units of electrical power. Who is correct?
   A. Tech A
   B. Tech B
   C. Both A and B
   D. Neither A nor B

Electrical Components and Wiring

At the start of each chapter you'll find the NATEF tasks, Knowledge Objectives, and Skills Objectives from the textbook. These are your objectives as you make your way through the exercises in this workbook and the chapter in your text-book. The following activities have been designed to help you refresh your knowledge of the material in this chapter.

NATEF Tasks

- N51001 Use wiring diagrams during the diagnosis (troubleshooting) of electrical/electronic circuit problems. (AST/MAST)
- N51002 Use wiring diagrams to trace electrical/electronic circuits. (MLR)
- N51003 Inspect, test, repair, and/or replace components, connectors, terminals, harnesses, and wiring in electrical/ electronic systems (including solder repairs); determine needed action. (MLR/AST/MAST)
- N51004 Repair data bus wiring harness. (MAST)

Knowledge Objectives

After reading this chapter, you will be able to:

- K51001 Describe the function and purpose of electronic components.
- K51002 Describe wires and wire harnesses.
- K51003 Repair wiring harness.

Skills Objectives

There are no Skills Objectives for this chapter.

Matching

Match the following terms with the correct description or example.

A. American wire gauge (AWG)
B. Breakdown
C. Armature
D. Butt connector
E. P-N junction
F. P-NP transistor
G. Commutator
H. Mylar tape
I. Normally open (NO)
J. Circuit breaker

K. Controlled area network bus (CANbus)
L. Potentiometer
M. Primary winding
N. Printed circuit
O. Normally closed (NC)
P. Negative temperature coefficient (NTC)
Q. Bus
R. Doping
S. Drain line
T. Diode

_____ 1. A wire included in a harness, with one end grounded to reduce interference or noise being induced into the harness.

_____ 2. A device that trips and opens a circuit, preventing excessive current flow in a circuit. It can be reset to allow for reuse.

_____ 3. A two-lead electronic component that allows current flow in one direction only.

_____ 4. An electrical contact that is open in the at-rest position.

_____ **5.** A device made on armatures of electric generators and motors to control the direction of current flow in the armature windings.

_____ **6.** Polyester film that may be metalized and incorporated into a wiring harness to provide electrical shielding.

_____ **7.** A wire data network found in vehicles to connect control modules so they can communicate quickly and easily.

_____ **8.** A standard used to identify different wire sizes.

_____ **9.** The rotating wire coils in motors and generators. It is also the moving part of a solenoid or relay, and the pole piece in a permanent magnet generator.

_____ **10.** A three-terminal resistive device with one terminal connected to the input of the resistor, one terminal connected to the output of the resistor, and the third terminal connected to a movable wiper arm that moves up and down the resistor.

_____ **11.** A crimp or solder joint that creates a permanent connection.

_____ **12.** The junction between N- and P-type semiconductor materials.

_____ **13.** The loss of electrical insulation properties.

_____ **14.** A transistor in which N-type material is sandwiched between two layers of P-type material. This type of semiconductor material has holes, meaning it is missing electrons.

_____ **15.** The coil of wire in the low voltage circuit that creates the magnetic field in a step-up transformer

_____ **16.** An electrical circuit for distributing electrical signals bi-directionally.

_____ **17.** An electrical contact that is closed in the at-rest position.

_____ **18.** The fine copper strip or track attached to an insulated board for mounting and connecting electronic components

_____ **19.** The introduction of impurities to pure semiconductor materials to provide N- and P-type semiconductors.

_____ **20.** A characteristic of materials whereby resistance decreases as temperature increases.

Multiple Choice

Read each item carefully, and then select the best response.

_____ **1.** The point where P-type and N-type semiconductors join is called the _____.
   A. depletion area
   B. hole
   C. pn junction
   D. carrier

_____ **2.** All of the following are materials used to make semiconductors, *except*:
   A. germanium
   B. mica
   C. silicon
   D. gallium-arsenide

_____ **3.** A _____ is made up of an electromagnet, a set of switch contacts, terminals, and the case.
   A. thermocouple
   B. solenoid
   C. diode
   D. relay

_____ **4.** An ignition coil can be described as a _____.
   A. solenoid
   B. relay
   C. step-up transformer
   D. step-down transformer

_____ **5.** Mechanical variable resistors with three connections, two fixed and one moveable, are called _____.
   A. thermistors
   B. rheostats

_____ **C.** potentiometers

           D. transistor

_____ **6.** A _____ can be thought of as the electronic version of a one-way check valve.

           A. transistor

           B. diode

           C. resistor

           D. capacitor

_____ **7.** A _____ is a semiconductor device used as a switch and to amplify currents.

           A. diode

           B. capacitor

           C. resistor

           D. transistor

_____ **8.** All of the following are examples of the type of shielding used in shielded wiring harnesses, *except*:

           A. Twisted pair

           B. Drain lines

           C. Seamless plastic

           D. Mylar tape

_____ **9.** Which of the following terminals accommodate screws?

           A. Push-on spade terminals

           B. Butt connectors

           C. Male and female terminals

           D. Eye ring terminals

_____ **10.** Coloring the wires on the wiring diagram does all of the following, *except*:

           A. forces you to determine what each wire in the diagram does.

           B. helps to organize your thoughts so that you can understand how electricity flows through the circuit.

           C. helps to keep you from forgetting what a particular wire does.

           D. makes the circuit diagram appear to be more clear.

True/False

If you believe the statement to be more true than false, write the letter "T" in the space provided. If you believe the statement to be more false than true, write the letter "F."

_____ **1.** Gallium-arsenide has been used to create blue light-emitting diodes, and it can withstand high operating temperatures.

_____ **2.** Some capacitors, and most semiconductor components, are polarity sensitive.

_____ **3.** Flasher cans are electronic devices, while flasher controls are mechanical devices.

_____ **4.** A solenoid is an electromechanical device that converts electrical energy into mechanical linear movement.

_____ **5.** In a motor, the armature and brushes act as switches to control the current flow through the windings of the commutator.

_____ **6.** A thermistor is a mechanical variable resistor with two connections.

_____ **7.** When a capacitor is charged, one surface is positively charged and the other is negatively charged.

_____ **8.** A PNP transistor has an N-type semiconductor between two P-types.

_____ **9.** A control module or unit is a generic term that identifies an electronic unit that controls one or more electrical systems in the vehicle.

_____ **10.** Most speed control systems use pulse-width modulation to control motor speed.

_____ **11.** Printed circuits are essentially a map of all of the electrical components and their connections.

_____ **12.** A controlled area network bus uses two thin wires to connect, or multiplex, many of the control units and their sensors to each other.

Fill in the Blank

Read each item carefully, and then complete the statement by filling in the missing word(s).

1. A doped semiconductor always has an excess of one type of charge carrier; electrons in excess make it an _____-_____ semiconductor, and holes in excess make it a _____-_____ semiconductor.

2. Within the PN junction some electrons and holes cancel each other out and few charge carriers are present; this very thin _____ _____ acts like an insulator.

3. A(n) _____-_____ relay acts like a mechanical relay but does not have any moving parts.

4. The metal core of a solenoid, used by the electromagnet to strengthen the magnetic field, is referred to as a(n) _____.

5. As _____ voltage is reached, the Zener diode's resistance suddenly collapses.

6. _____ _____ are added to vehicles to build in specific time delays in turning on or off electrical devices.

7. There are many different types of sensors installed in the modern vehicle; they are used to provide information to the _____ on the vehicle.

8. There are two scales used to measure the sizes of wires: the metric wire gauge and the _____ _____ _____.

9. Wiring _____, also known as wiring looms or cable harnesses, are used throughout the vehicle to group two or more wires together within a sheath of either insulating tape or tubing.

10. A _____ _____ is used throughout the vehicle to group two or more wires together within a sheath of either insulating tape or tubing.

Labeling

Label the following diagrams with the correct terms.

1. Diode symbols:

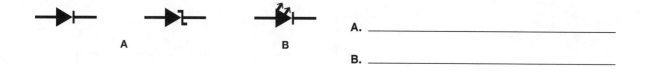

A
B

A. _____

B. _____

2. Wiring diagram symbols:

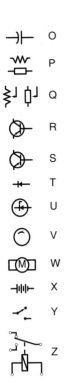

A. _____

B. _____

C. _____

D. _____

E. _____

F. _____

G. _____

H. _____

I. _____

J. _____

K. _____

L. _____

M. _____

N. _____

O. _____

P. _____

Q. _____

R. _____

S. _____

T. _____

U. _____

V. _____

W. _____

X. _____

Y. _____

Z. _____

3. Transistors:

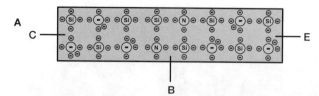

A. _____

B. _____

Skill Drills

Test your knowledge of skill drills by filling in the correct words in the photo captions.

    1. Stripping Wire Insulation:

Step 1: Choose the correct _____ _____.

Step 2: Select the hole that matches the _____ of the wire to be stripped. Place the wire in the hole, and close the _____ firmly around it to cut the _____.

Step 3: Remove the insulation. To keep the _____ together, give them a light _____.

2. Installing a Solderless Terminal:

Step 1: Make sure you have the correct size of _____ for the wire to be terminated and the terminal has the correct volt/amp _____. Remove an appropriate amount of the protective _____ from the wire.

Step 2: Lightly _____ the wire _____ and place the terminal onto the _____.

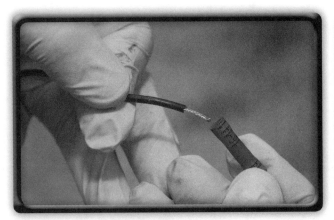

Step 3: Use a proper _____ _____ for the terminal you are crimping. Do not use _____, as they have a tendency to cut through the connection. Select the proper _____.

Step 4: Crimp the _____ section first. Use firm _____ so a good electrical contact will be made, but not _____ force, as this can _____ the pin or terminal.

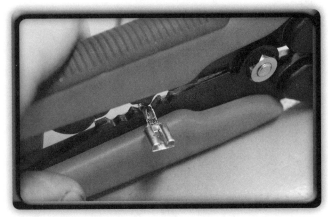

Step 5: If crimping an _____ terminal, lightly crimp the insulation _____ so they hold the _____ firmly.

Step 6: If crimping a _____ terminal, use the proper tool and follow the instructions.

3. Soldering Wires and Connectors:

Step 1: Safely position the soldering iron while it is _____. While the soldering iron is heating, use wire strippers to _____ an appropriate amount of the _____ insulation from the wires.

Step 2: _____ the wires together to make a good _____ _____ between them.

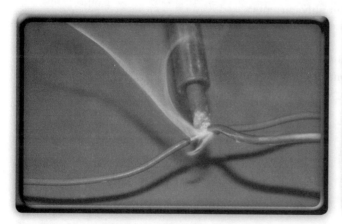

Step 3: _____ the soldering iron tip, and gently heat up the _____ while placing the _____ opposite of the soldering iron. Allow the solder to be _____ into the joint.

Step 4: Pictured is a good _____ _____ where the solder has been _____ in.

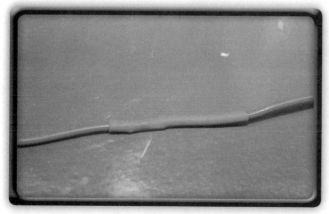

Step 5: Once the electrical connection has been made and it has _____ enough for you to handle it, slide the insulator _____ cover over the joint and use a _____ _____ to shrink the tubing around the _____.

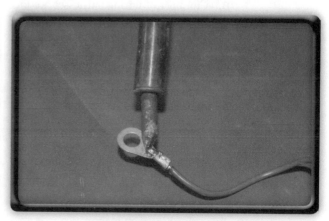

Step 6: To solder a wire to a terminal _____, it is best to _____ it in place as before and use the solder to "glue" the joint together. Place the heated iron onto the _____ to get it hot enough to _____ the solder applied to the end of the crimped wire tabs. Some solder will be _____ between the terminal and the wire. Cover the terminal with _____ _____ tubing.

Review Questions

_____ **1.** Which of the following components can be programmed and are an integral part of other electrical components?
  A. Sensors
  B. Zener diodes
  C. Microprocessors
  D. Actuators

_____ **2.** Choose the correct statement.
  A. Semiconductor devices use high operating voltages.
  B. Semiconductor devices are sensitive to heat and voltage spikes.
  C. Semiconductor devices are not reliable.
  D. Semiconductor devices need regular maintenance.

_____ **3.** Which of the following materials is widely used to build high-speed semiconductors?
  A. Silicon
  B. Germanium
  C. Gallium-arsenide
  D. Silicon carbide

_____ **4.** All of the following statements about transistors are correct _except_:
  A. Transistors are used as a switch and to amplify currents.
  B. They are made up of two sections of different polarity.
  C. Transistors have two PN junctions.
  D. Transistor symbols always have an emitter, base, and a collector.

_____ **5.** What is the most common use of speed control units in vehicles?
  A. To control the fan speed in the HVAC system and the radiator
  B. To control the speed of the windshield
  C. To control the speed of the car
  D. To control the speed of the engine

_____ **6.** Which of the following types of shielding is used in wiring to prevent electromagnetic interference (EMI)?
  A. Special plastic coated wires
  B. Silicon tape
  C. Nylon tape
  D. Mylar tape

_____ **7.** All of the following statements are true _except_:
  A. Wires are the dominant signal carriers in a vehicle.
  B. A number of wiring harnesses are located throughout the vehicle.
  C. As technology has developed, usage of wires and cables has reduced.
  D. Wires and wiring harnesses are the arteries of the vehicle's electrical system.

_____ **8.** Fiber optic cable has all of the following advantages over a conventional copper cable _except_:
  A. It can carry much more data than copper wires.
  B. It is less affected by interference.
  C. Light in one fiber does not interfere with light in another fiber.
  D. It is more expensive when compared to conventional cables.

_____ **9.** If both wires in the twisted pair CANbus need to be repaired, it is best to:
  A. replace both wires.
  B. replace one of the wires.
  C. stagger the joints.
  D. repair without removing the insulation.

_____ **10.** Excessive bare wire may:
  A. expose the wire to a potential short circuit.
  B. reduce the current-carrying capacity of the wire.
  C. not achieve a good connection.
  D. result in a poor wire-to-terminal connection.

ASE Technician A/Technician B Style Questions

_____ **1.** Tech A says that if the specified fuse keeps blowing, it is generally okay to replace it with a larger fuse. Tech B says that a fusible link is one type of circuit protection device. Who is correct?
  A. Tech A
  B. Tech B
  C. Both A and B
  D. Neither A nor B

_____ **2.** Tech A says that 18 AWG wire is larger than 12 AWG wire. Tech B says that the larger the diameter of the conductor, the more electrical resistance it has. Who is correct?
  A. Tech A
  B. Tech B
  C. Both A and B
  D. Neither A nor B

_____ **3.** Tech A says that some relays are equipped with a suppression diode in parallel with the winding. Tech B says that some relays are equipped with a resistor in parallel with the winding. Who is correct?
  A. Tech A
  B. Tech B
  C. Both A and B
  D. Neither A nor B

_____ **4.** Tech A says that NTC thermistors alter their resistance value inversely to temperature (as the temperature increases, resistance value decreases). Tech B says that PTC thermistors are used as throttle position sensors. Who is correct?
  A. Tech A
  B. Tech B
  C. Both A and B
  D. Neither A nor B

_____ **5.** Tech A says that a transistor has a single P–N junction. Tech B says that a transistor is a semiconductor device used as a switch and to amplify currents. Who is correct?
  A. Tech A
  B. Tech B
  C. Both A and B
  D. Neither A nor B

_____ **6.** Tech A says that wiring diagrams are essentially a map of all of the electrical components and their connections. Tech B says that in many cases, each wire in wire harnesses use two colors; the first one is the solid color, and the second one is the stripe. Who is correct?
  A. Tech A
  B. Tech B
  C. Both A and B
  D. Neither A nor B

_____ **7.** Tech A says that a twisted pair is two wires, twisted together, that deliver signals between common components. Tech B says that in many cases, wiring diagrams are set up with power on the top of the diagram and ground on the bottom. Who is correct?
  A. Tech A
  B. Tech B
  C. Both A and B
  D. Neither A nor B

_____ **8.** Tech A says that it is best to use a knife or other type of sharp tool to cut away the insulation when stripping a wire. Tech B says that any issues with wiring are more likely to be with the terminals than with the wires themselves. Who is correct?
  A. Tech A
  B. Tech B
  C. Both A and B
  D. Neither A nor B

_____ **9.** Tech A says that while soldering wires, apply the solder to the wire opposite the soldering iron. Tech B says that you should heat the wire up until the plastic insulation melts. Who is correct?

    A. Tech A

    B. Tech B

    C. Both A and B

    D. Neither A nor B

_____ **10.** Tech A says that a relay is a one-way electrical check valve used in alternators to change AC into DC. Tech B says that a relay uses electromagnetism to open or close a switch. Who is correct?

    A. Tech A

    B. Tech B

    C. Both A and B

    D. Neither A nor B

Meter Usage and Circuit Diagnosis

At the start of each chapter you'll find the NATEF tasks, Knowledge Objectives, and Skills Objectives from the textbook. These are your objectives as you make your way through the exercises in this workbook and the chapter in your textbook. The following activities have been designed to help you refresh your knowledge of the material in this chapter.

NATEF Tasks

- N52001 Demonstrate the proper use of a digital multimeter (DMM) when measuring source voltage, voltage drop (including grounds), current flow, and resistance. (MLR/AST/MAST)
- N52002 Demonstrate knowledge of electrical/electronic series, parallel, and series-parallel circuits using principles of electricity (Ohm's law). (MLR/AST/MAST)
- N52003 Demonstrate proper use of a test light on an electrical circuit. (MLR/AST/MAST)
- N52004 Use fused jumper wires to check operation of electrical circuits. (MLR/AST/MAST)
- N52005 Inspect and test fusible links, circuit breakers, and fuses; determine needed action. (MLR/AST/MAST)
- N52006 Inspect and test switches, connectors, and wires of starter control circuits; determine needed action. (AST/MAST)
- N52007 Check electrical/electronic circuit waveforms; interpret readings and determine needed action. (MAST)

Knowledge Objectives

After reading this chapter, you will be able to:

- K52001 Explain the purpose, function, and layout of a DMM.
- K52002 Describe the ranges, settings, and setup of a DMM.
- K52003 Explain the process of measuring volts, ohms, and amps.

Skills Objectives

After reading this chapter, you will be able to:

- S52001 Perform series circuit measurements.
- S52002 Perform parallel circuit measurements.
- S52003 Perform series-parallel circuit measurements.
- S52004 Perform basic electrical circuit testing and diagnosis.
- S52005 Locate opens, shorts, grounds, and high resistance.
- S52006 Inspect a circuit with jumper leads and/or a test light.
- S52007 Inspect circuit protection and control devices.

Matching

Match the following terms with the correct description or example.

A. Attenuator

B. High resistance

C. Min/max setting

D. Oscilloscope

E. Probing technique

F. Short to power

_____ **1.** A setting on a DMM to display the maximum and minimum readings.

_____ **2.** A term that describes a circuit or components with unintended resistance, which causes the circuit not to perform properly.

_____ **3.** A condition in which current flows from one circuit into another.

_____ **4.** An electrical measuring tool used to diagnose and repair electrical faults.

_____ **5.** The way in which test probes are connected to a circuit.

_____ **6.** A device that reduces the power of a signal without distorting its waveform.

Multiple Choice

Read each item carefully, and then select the best response.

_____ **1.** A digital multimeter is used to measure _____.
   A. voltage
   B. amperage
   C. resistance
   D. all of the above

_____ **2.** A digital multimeter for three-phase fixed equipment and single-phase commercial lighting would have a _____ rating.
   A. CAT I
   B. CAT II
   C. CAT III
   D. CAT IV

_____ **3.** The _____ setting is often used to measure vehicle battery voltage while the engine is cranking or the battery is charging.
   A. hold
   B. sample
   C. min/max
   D. save

_____ **4.** The red lead for the DMM is labeled with the _____ symbol.
   A. +
   B. V/Ω
   C. –
   D. ±

_____ **5.** All of the following are examples of common types of DMM probes, _except_:
   A. ground probes
   B. alligator clips
   C. fine-pin probes
   D. insulation piercing probes

_____ **6.** The sum of all the _____ in a series circuit equals the supply voltage.
   A. resistors
   B. batteries
   C. voltage drops
   D. loads

_____ **7.** The _____ is the same in all parts of a properly working series circuit.
   A. voltage
   B. current
   C. resistance
   D. all of the above

_____ **8.** A break in the electrical circuit where either the power supply or ground circuit has been interrupted is known as:
   A. capacitance.
   B. voltage drop.
   C. short circuit.
   D. open circuit.

_____ **9.** As the position of the wiper of a potentiometer is changed, so is the _____ to a load connected to the potentiometer.
   A. voltage
   B. ground
   C. current flow
   D. both A and C

_____ **10.** _____ can be fitted to the probe leads to reduce the maximum voltage to safe levels for the oscilloscope to measure.
   A. Attenuators
   B. Cuffs
   C. Alligator clips
   D. Current clamps

True/False

If you believe the statement to be more true than false, write the letter "T" in the space provided. If you believe the statement to be more false than true, write the letter "F."

_____ **1.** Hybrid vehicles typically require meters and test leads rated as CAT III or CAT IV.

_____ **2.** 5208 mV is the same as 5208 millivolts. It could also be called 52.08 volts.

_____ **3.** The red lead is the positive lead, and the black lead is the negative lead.

_____ **4.** After back-probing always reinsulate the hole that the probe makes with room temperature vulcanizing silicone to prevent any corrosion.

_____ **5.** To accurately measure the resistance of a component, you should remove or isolate the component from the circuit.

_____ **6.** A voltage drop occurs when current flows through a resistance.

_____ **7.** Voltage drop can be measured across components, connectors, or cables, but current has to be flowing to get an accurate measurement.

_____ **8.** Parallel circuits are commonly used in the vehicle's electrical system, especially for lights.

_____ **9.** Oscilloscopes display time on the vertical axis, and voltage is displayed on the horizontal axis, or from left to right across the screen.

_____ **10.** If the resistance and voltage of a circuit are known, then the theoretical current can be calculated using Ohm's law.

Fill in the Blank

Read each item carefully, and then complete the statement by filling in the missing word(s).

1. A basic _____ can measure alternating current (AC) and direct current (DC) voltage, AC and DC amperage, and resistance.

2. _____ _____ are used to connect the DMM to the circuit being tested and come in pairs: one red, the other black.

3. When the _____ function is activated, the display will hold the value on the display until the function or DMM is turned off.

4. _____-_____ occurs when the probe is pushed in from the back of a connector to make a connection.

5. The _____ _____ fastens around the conductor and measures the strength of the magnetic field produced from current flowing through the conductor.

6. _____ _____ is a setting on a DMM to store the present reading.

7. Current flow is _____ proportional to resistance.

8. The sum of the current flow in each branch is equal to the total _____ circuit current flow.

9. As a _____ charges, the voltage drop across it increases and the current flow decreases.

10. _____ _____ can occur anywhere in the circuit and can be difficult to locate, especially if it is intermittent.

Labeling

Label the following diagrams with the correct terms.

1. Electrical behavior in a series circuit:

Simple Series Circuit

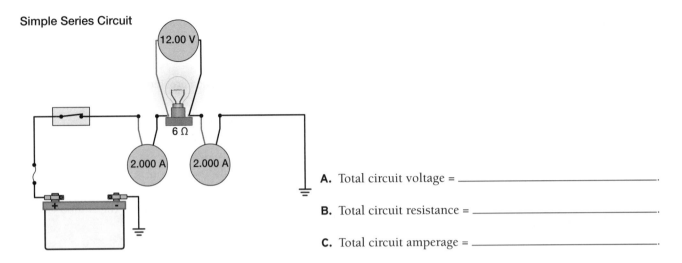

A. Total circuit voltage = _____.

B. Total circuit resistance = _____.

C. Total circuit amperage = _____.

2. Electrical values in a parallel circuit with equal-resistance bulbs:

Simple Parallel Circuit

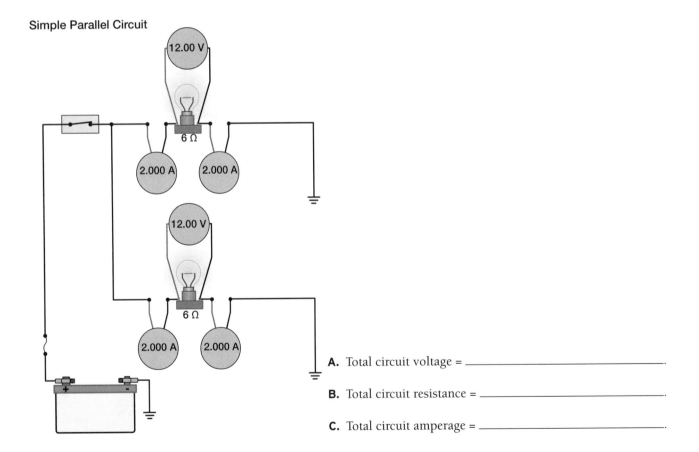

A. Total circuit voltage = _____.

B. Total circuit resistance = _____.

C. Total circuit amperage = _____.

3. Measuring amperage in a circuit with a relay controlled by a switch and a single lightbulb with a 12-volt DC supply:

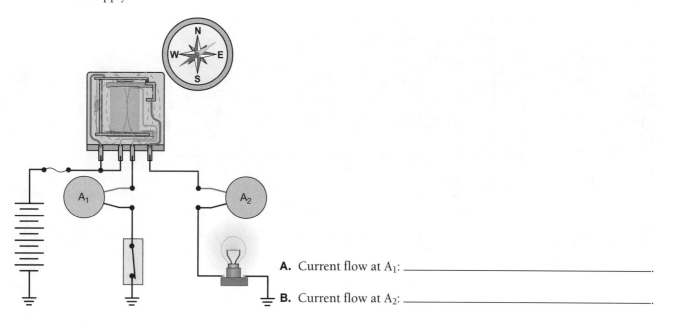

A. Current flow at A_1: _____.

B. Current flow at A_2: _____.

4. Components of a DMM:

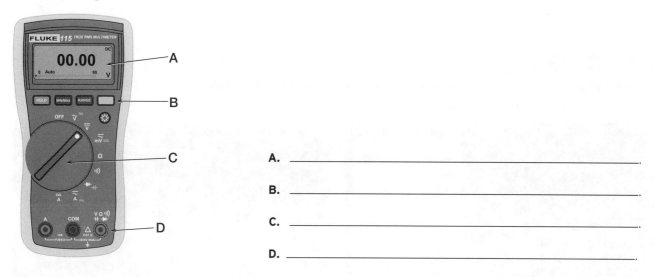

A. _____.

B. _____.

C. _____.

D. _____.

5. DMM values:

Factor	Prefix	Symbol
1,000,000	Mega	A. _____
1000	Kilo	B. _____
1	No prefix	
0.001	milli	C. _____
0.000001	Micro	D. _____

A. _____ .

B. _____ .

C. _____ .

D. _____ .

Skill Drills

Test your knowledge of skill drills by filling in the correct words in the photo captions.

   1. Checking Circuit Waveforms:

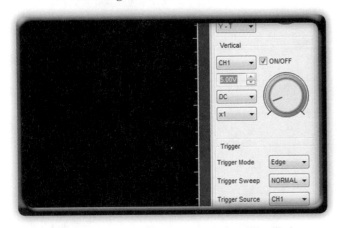 

Step 1: Determine the circuit to be tested and the likely _____ and frequency of the _____ to be measured. Set the voltage level per division and _____ _____.

Step 2: Connect the _____ to the _____ in the circuit to be measured.

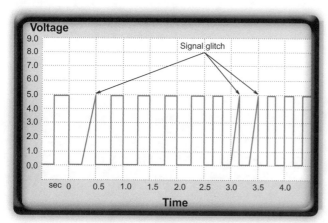

Step 3: _____ waveforms from the circuit being tested. _____ the waveform, comparing it to the manufacturer's specifications or _____ good waveforms.

2. Checking Circuits with Fused Jumper Leads:

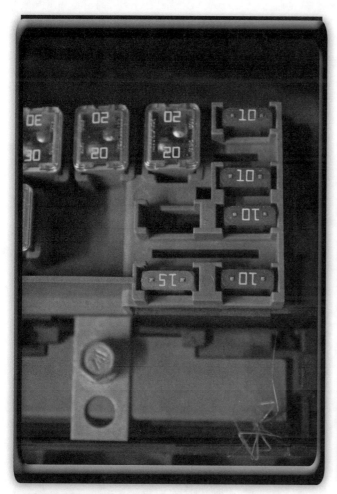

Step 1: Identify the _____ to be checked, and determine the fuse rating for the circuit.

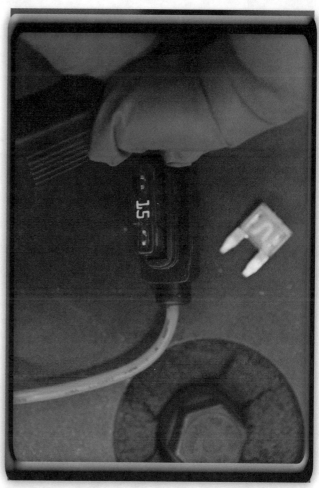

Step 2: Select the appropriate _____ lead, install the correct _____ in it, and connect one end to the battery _____ terminal.

Step 3: Touch the jumper lead quickly to the _____ _____ terminal. Never jump across a load; doing so bypasses circuit resistance, causing excessive _____ in the circuit and damaging it.

3. Checking a Circuit with a Test Light:

Step 1: Connect the end of the light with the _____ on it to the negative battery _____. Touch the _____ end of the test light to the positive battery terminal. The _____ should come on.

Step 2: Connect the clip to a known good _____. A typical known good ground is any unpainted _____ surface on the vehicle that is directly _____ to the battery ground return system.

Step 3: Place the _____ on the terminal to be _____. If _____ is present, the light will come on.

Review Questions

_____ **1.** DMM is used to measure all of the following in a circuit *except*:
  A. voltage.
  B. resistance.
  C. current.
  D. specific gravity.

_____ **2.** All of the following statements are true *except*:
  A. Measuring source voltage is accomplished with both meter leads on the positive terminal of the battery.
  B. The DMM on the volt setting is measuring the difference in voltage between the positive test lead and the ground.
  C. Measuring available voltage and voltage drop in the circuit are performed as part of the diagnostic process.
  D. Most modern DMMs can display minimum and maximum readings.

_____ **3.** Which of the following is the recommended range to be set on a DMM to get the most accurate reading?
  A. Highest range possible for the value being measured
  B. Lowest range possible for the value being measured
  C. Always the highest range on the DMM
  D. Always the lowest range on the DMM

_____ **4.** Which category of DMM is the minimum required when working on hybrid vehicles?
  A. CAT I
  B. CAT II
  C. CAT III
  D. CAT IV

_____ **5.** Choose the correct statement.
  A. The COM slot is always used for the black lead.
  B. The meter screen will always read what the COM lead is touching.
  C. The standard probe leads that are supplied with a DMM are both black.
  D. To take voltage measurements, the probing lead (red) is connected to the "A" slot.

_____ **6.** Which of the following is used to designate a reading of 400 megavolts?
  A. 400 mv
  B. 400 MV
  C. 400 kV
  D. 400 µV

_____ **7.** Which of the following precautions should be taken while measuring the resistance in a series circuit using a DMM?
  A. The switch should be on.
  B. The components should be disconnected from the circuit.
  C. Class "0" gloves shouldn't be worn.
  D. Start by using the lowest meter range.

_____ **8.** Conducting a voltage drop test on the power and ground circuits is best for locating:
  A. high resistance faults.
  B. capacitance faults.
  C. short circuit.
  D. parasitic draw.

_____ **9.** What is the total resistance for two 2-ohm resistors connected in parallel?
  A. 1 ohm
  B. 2 ohms
  C. 3 ohms
  D. 4 ohms

_____ **10.** Which of the following can be fitted to probe leads to reduce the maximum voltage to safe levels for an oscilloscope to measure?
  A. TPS
  B. Attenuator
  C. Capacitor
  D. Resistor

ASE Technician A/Technician B Style Questions

_____ **1.** Tech A says that total resistance goes up as more parallel paths are added. Tech B says that total amperage goes up as more parallel paths are added. Who is correct?
  A. Tech A
  B. Tech B
  C. Both A and B
  D. Neither A nor B

_____ **2.** Tech A says that when reading DC voltage on a meter, a "+" before the number means that there is a higher voltage at the red lead than the black lead. Tech B says that a "–" before the number means that there is a lower voltage at the red lead than the black lead. Who is correct?
  A. Tech A
  B. Tech B
  C. Both A and B
  D. Neither A nor B

_____ **3.** Tech A says that to read amperage, the meter must be hooked up in series in a circuit. Tech B says that to read amperage at a load, you should place one lead of the ammeter on the input side of the load and the other lead on the output. Who is correct?
  A. Tech A
  B. Tech B
  C. Both A and B
  D. Neither A nor B

_____ **4.** Tech A says that when measuring available voltage, the common (black) lead should be on a good ground. Tech B says that a resistance reading on a lightbulb requires the DMM to be hooked to each side of the bulb and the switch turned on. Who is correct?
  A. Tech A
  B. Tech B
  C. Both A and B
  D. Neither A nor B

_____ **5.** Tech A says that when checking a voltage drop across an open switch, a measurement of 12 volts is normal. Tech B says that when checking voltage drop across an open switch, a measurement of 12 volts means there are 12 volts on each side of the switch. Who is correct?
  A. Tech A
  B. Tech B
  C. Both A and B
  D. Neither A nor B

_____ **6.** A customer complains of a weak horn. Tech A says that the horn is faulty and should be replaced. Tech B says that performing a voltage drop test on the horn circuit is a valid test in this situation. Who is correct?
A. Tech A
B. Tech B
C. Both A and B
D. Neither A nor B

_____ **7.** Tech A says that when resistance increases, current flow decreases. Tech B says that when voltage decreases, current increases. Who is correct?
A. Tech A
B. Tech B
C. Both A and B
D. Neither A nor B

_____ **8.** Tech A says that an open circuit typically causes higher current flow, which will blow the fuse. Tech B says that a short to ground can typically be found by checking voltage at different points in the circuit. Who is correct?
A. Tech A
B. Tech B
C. Both A and B
D. Neither A nor B

_____ **9.** Tech A says that when a fuse has blown, it just has to be replaced, because it performed its job. Tech B says that when a fuse has blown, the circuit has to be diagnosed because the fuse was probably not the problem. Who is correct?
A. Tech A
B. Tech B
C. Both A and B
D. Neither A nor B

_____ **10.** Two technicians are discussing scope testing. Tech A says that the vertical axis of the screen shows voltage. Tech B says that the horizontal axis shows time. Who is correct?
A. Tech A
B. Tech B
C. Both A and B
D. Neither A nor B

Battery Systems

At the start of each chapter you'll find the NATEF tasks, Knowledge Objectives, and Skills Objectives from the textbook. These are your objectives as you make your way through the exercises in this workbook and the chapter in your textbook. The following activities have been designed to help you refresh your knowledge of the material in this chapter.

NATEF Tasks

- N53001 Inspect and clean battery; fill battery cells; check battery cables, connectors, clamps, and hold-downs. (MLR/AST/MAST)
- N53002 Perform slow/fast battery charge according to manufacturer's recommendations. (MLR/AST/MAST)
- N53003 Jump-start vehicle using jumper cables and a booster battery or an auxiliary power supply. (MLR/AST/MAST)
- N53004 Perform battery state-of-charge test; determine needed action. (MLR/AST/MAST)
- N53005 Confirm proper battery capacity for vehicle application; perform battery capacity and load test; determine needed action. (MLR/AST/MAST)
- N53006 Identify electrical/ electronic modules, security systems, radios, and other accessories that require reinitialization or code entry after reconnecting vehicle battery. (MLR/AST/MAST)
- N53007 Maintain or restore electronic memory functions. (MLR/AST/MAST)
- N53008 Diagnose the cause(s) of excessive key-off battery drain (parasitic draw); determine needed action. (AST/MAST)

Knowledge Objectives

After reading this chapter, you will be able to:

- K53001 Describe battery types and construction.
- K53002 Explain battery sizing, configurations, and ratings.
- K53003 Describe lead/acid batteries' charging and discharging process.

Skills Objectives

After reading this chapter, you will be able to:

- S53001 Perform battery-related service.
- S53002 Perform battery tests while maintaining memory.

Matching

Match the following terms with the correct description or example.

A. Absorbed glass mat
B. Battery terminal configuration
C. Cold cranking amps (CCA)
D. Electrical capacity

E. Cranking amps (CA)
F. Gassing
G. Keep alive memory (KAM)
H. Parasitic draw

_____ 1. The escape of gas from the battery.
_____ 2. A standard for rating the ability of a vehicle battery to supply high current under cold operating conditions.
_____ 3. The placement of positive and negative battery terminals.
_____ 4. A certain minimum amount of parasitic current draw that is used by the vehicle's circuits to maintain memory functions and monitor systems.
_____ 5. The ability of a circuit or component to carry electrical loads.

_____ **6.** Unwanted drain on the vehicle battery when the vehicle is off.

_____ **7.** A type of lead-acid battery.

_____ **8.** A standard similar to CCA but that measures the battery's function at a higher temperature—32°F (0°C).

Multiple Choice

Read each item carefully, and then select the best response.

_____ **1.** A standard 12-volt car battery consists of _____ cells connected in series.
- **A.** one
- **B.** two
- **C.** six
- **D.** twelve

_____ **2.** All of the following are methods used to rate automotive battery capacity, *except*:
- **A.** cold cranking amps
- **B.** voltage output
- **C.** cranking amps
- **D.** reserve capacity

_____ **3.** A(n) _____ battery typically has no removable cell covers, so you cannot adjust or test the fluid levels inside.
- **A.** deep cycle
- **B.** lead-acid
- **C.** low-maintenance
- **D.** reserve capacity

_____ **4.** Which of the following is a type of rechargeable cell battery?
- **A.** Lead-acid
- **B.** Nickel-cadmium
- **C.** Lithium ion
- **D.** All of the above

_____ **5.** All of the following are advantages of lithium-ion batteries, *except*:
- **A.** high energy density
- **B.** shelf life
- **C.** low internal resistance
- **D.** low self-discharge

_____ **6.** Which tool is commonly used to measure parasitic draw from the battery?
- **A.** Low-amp current clamp
- **B.** Scan tool
- **C.** Ammeter
- **D.** Either A or C

_____ **7.** Performing a battery state-of-charge test with a(n) _____ will give a good indication of whether the battery needs to be charged or not.
- **A.** refractometer
- **B.** hydrometer
- **C.** DMM
- **D.** any of the above

_____ **8.** The higher the _____, the higher the percentage of acid in the electrolyte, which corresponds to a high battery state of charge.
- **A.** specific gravity
- **B.** water level
- **C.** temperature
- **D.** amperage

_____ **9.** Batteries were first developed in the early _____.
- **A.** 1700s
- **B.** 1800s
- **C.** 1900s
- **D.** 2000s

_____ **10.** The traditional automobile battery type is the _____ _____ battery.
- **A.** lead-acid
- **B.** lithium-ion
- **C.** zinc-bromine
- **D.** nickel-cadmium

True/False

If you believe the statement to be more true than false, write the letter "T" in the space provided. If you believe the statement to be more false than true, write the letter "F."

_____ **1.** Batteries store electricity in chemical form.

_____ **2.** Electrolyte is made up of sulfuric acid and water.

_____ **3.** Sizing has to do with the electrical specifications of the battery, while ratings have to do with the battery's physical attributes.

_____ **4.** Reserve capacity is the time in minutes that a new fully charged battery at 80°F (27°C) will supply a constant load of 25 amps without its voltage dropping below 10.5 volts for a 12-volt battery.

_____ **5.** The typical cell voltage of a lithium-ion battery is 1.2 volts.

_____ **6.** Installing a battery into a vehicle backward can instantly destroy on-board electronics.

_____ **7.** Placing a load on the charged battery by turning on an accessory such as the headlights helps absorb any sudden rise in voltage that may occur as the load on the alternator is suddenly decreased.

_____ **8.** Many municipalities require battery recycling and levy a "core charge" on every new automotive battery sold.

_____ **9.** State-of-charge testing tells us how much capacity the battery has left.

_____ **10.** In some cases, it may be possible to use a 9-volt memory minder or memory saver to maintain the vehicle's memory while the vehicle battery is disconnected.

Fill in the Blank

Read each item carefully, and then complete the statement by filling in the missing word(s).

1. Each cell of a fully charged "12-volt" battery has a nominal _____ volts, for a total of _____ volts.

2. The more plate _____ _____ there is, the higher the electrical capacity of the battery.

3. Because the electrolyte in _____ _____ _____ batteries is a gel, which does not spill, this type of battery is especially handy for rough handling or tipping.

4. The charging process increases the amount of _____ in the electrolyte, making the electrolyte stronger.

5. The _____ the battery temperature, the higher the rate of charging.

6. Lithium-ion batteries may suffer from _____ _____ and cell rupture if overheated or overcharged.

7. Battery cables and terminals are designed to carry _____ _____ currents that are required during cranking of the automotive engine.

8. Battery terminals are usually _____ or _____ onto the battery cables to ensure strong, low-resistance connections.

9. Always remove the _____ or ground terminal first when disconnecting battery cables.

10. Some manufacturers say that their batteries should not be load tested, and instead should be _____ tested.

Labeling

Label the following diagrams with the correct terms.

1. Components of a simple battery:

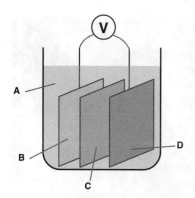

A. _____

B. _____

C. _____

D. _____

2. Typical plate arrangement in a wet cell battery:

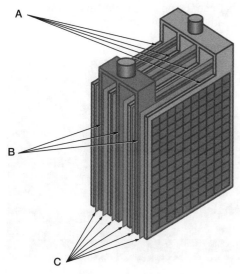

A. _____

B. _____

C. _____

Skill Drills

Place the skill drill steps in the correct order.

    1. Inspecting, Cleaning, Filling, and Replacing the Battery and Cables:

_____ **A.** Carefully clean the battery case and the battery tray.

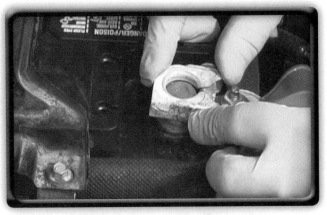

_____ **B.** Reconnect the positive battery terminal and tighten it in place. Once the positive terminal is finished, reconnect the negative terminal and tighten it.

_____ **C.** Measure the voltage on the top of the battery with a DMM. Place the black lead on the negative post, and move the red lead across the top of the battery until you find the highest reading.

_____ **D.** Coat the terminal connections with anticorrosive paste or spray to keep oxygen from the terminal connections. Test that you have a good electrical connection by starting the vehicle.

_____ **E.** Keeping it upright, remove the battery from its tray and place it on a clean work surface. Inspect the battery for damage.

_____ **F.** Reinstall the cleaned and serviced battery. Replace the hold-downs, and make sure the battery is securely held in position. If installing a new battery, ensure that it meets the original manufacturer's specifications.

_____ **G.** Remove the battery hold-downs or other hardware securing the battery.

_____ **H.** Clean the battery posts with a battery terminal tool. Clean the cable terminals with the same battery terminal tool. Examine the battery cables for fraying or corrosion.

_____ **I.** Remove the cable clamp from the negative terminal first. Then remove the positive terminal. Bend the cables back out of the way so that they cannot fall back and touch the battery terminals accidentally.

2. Jump-Starting a Vehicle:

_____ **A.** Connect the other end of this lead to the positive terminal of the charged battery or the remote terminal.

_____ **B.** Position the charged battery close enough to the discharged battery that it is within comfortable range of your jumper cables. If the charged battery is in another vehicle, make sure the two vehicles are not touching.

_____ **C.** Connect the other end of the negative lead to a good ground on the engine block of the vehicle with the discharged battery, and as far away as possible from the battery.

_____ **D.** Connect the red jumper lead to the positive terminal of the discharged battery in the vehicle you are trying to start.

_____ **E.** Connect the black jumper lead to the negative terminal of the charged battery or the battery remote terminal.

_____ **F.** Do not connect the lead to the negative terminal of the discharged battery itself; doing so may cause a dangerous spark. Also, do not connect the negative lead to the body or chassis as the ground wire from the body back to the negative battery terminal is usually too small to carry current needed for jump starting the vehicle.

_____ **G.** Disconnect the leads in the reverse order of connecting them.

_____ **H.** Try to start the vehicle with the discharged battery. If the booster battery does not have enough charge or the jumper cables are too small in diameter to do this, start the engine in the booster vehicle, and allow it to partially charge the discharged battery for several minutes. Turn on the headlights on the booster vehicle to reduce the possibility of a voltage spike damaging electronic equipment, and try starting the first vehicle again.

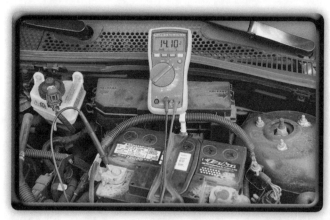

_____ **I.** If the charging system is working correctly and the battery is in good condition, the battery will be recharged while the engine is running, although it could end up over-heating and damaging the alternator.

3. Charging a Battery:

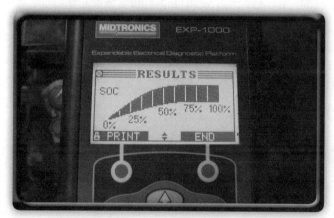

_____ **A.** Once the battery is charged, turn the charger off. Remove the surface charge by turning on the headlights for three to five minutes. Using a conductance tester, load tester, DMM, refractometer, or hydrometer, test the battery's state of charge and capacity.

_____ **B.** Calculate the ideal and maximum charge rates. Plug in the charger, and turn it to the appropriate charge rate. Monitor the battery voltage while charging.

_____ **C.** Ensure that the battery has not been frozen. Install a memory saver into the DLC, and disconnect the negative terminal. Verify that the charger is unplugged and off. Connect the red lead to the positive terminal and the black lead to the negative terminal.

4. Load Testing a Battery:

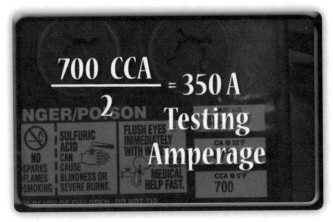

_____ **A.** Verify that the temperature of the battery is within the testing parameters. Use an infrared temperature gun to determine the temperature by measuring the temperature of the side of the battery. If you are using an automatic load tester, enter the battery's CCA and select "Test" or "Start." If you are using a manual load tester, calculate the test load, which is usually half of the CCA.

_____ **B.** Maintain this load for 15 seconds while watching the voltmeter. Read the voltmeter, and immediately turn the control knob off. At room temperature, the voltage should be 9.6 volts or higher at the end of the 15-second draw. If the battery is colder than room temperature, look up the compensated minimum voltage. Determine any necessary action.

_____ **C.** With the tester controls off and the load control turned to the Off position, connect the tester leads to the battery. Place the inductive amps clamp around either the black or the red tester cables in the correct orientation.

5. Maintaining or Restoring Electronic Memory Functions:

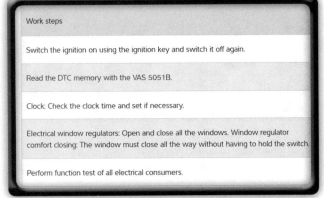

_____ **A.** Identify the correct procedure and any needed tools, and verify that initialization codes are available.

_____ **B.** Identify which modules, if any, require reinitialization or code entry when the battery is disconnected.

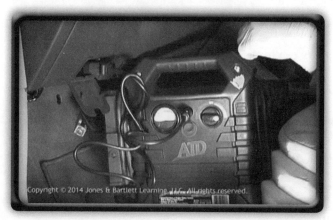

_____ **C.** If maintaining memory function, install a memory minder prior to the vehicle battery being disconnected. If reinitializing the electronic systems, use the correct codes to reinitialize the modules if required.

Review Questions

_____ **1.** Which of the following does a battery convert into electrical energy?
- **A.** Heat energy
- **B.** Mechanical energy
- **C.** Chemical energy
- **D.** Light energy

_____ **2.** The type of battery that is most common in automobiles is a:
- **A.** lithium-ion battery.
- **B.** lead-acid battery.
- **C.** nickel-cadmium battery.
- **D.** zinc-bromine battery.

_____ **3.** All of the following statements are true *except*:
- **A.** A battery consists of two similar metals.
- **B.** An automotive battery can supply very high discharge currents while maintaining a high voltage.
- **C.** The fundamental components and operation of the battery remain the same irrespective of the size and usage.
- **D.** Batteries store electricity in chemical form.

_____ **4.** Which of the following batteries are most suited for off-road and all-terrain vehicles?
- **A.** Low-maintenance batteries
- **B.** Lead-acid batteries
- **C.** Lithium-ion batteries
- **D.** Absorbed glass mat batteries

_____ **5.** Automotive battery capacity is rated based on all of the following *except*:
- **A.** cold cranking amps (CCA).
- **B.** cranking amps (CA).
- **C.** reserve capacity.
- **D.** terminal style.

_____ **6.** The lead plates of the lead-acid batteries are immersed in:
- **A.** diluted sulfuric acid solution.
- **B.** distilled water.
- **C.** mineral water.
- **D.** brine solution.

_____ **7.** All of the following are factors in shortening battery life *except*:
- **A.** having deep discharge cycles.
- **B.** excessive vibration.

    C. a moderate external temperature.

    D. developing corrosion.

_____ **8.** Status-of-the charge of a no-maintenance battery can be determined using a(n):

    A. single cell hydrometer float.

    B. TPS.

    C. oscilloscope.

    D. hygrometer.

_____ **9.** Which of the following is the best and safest method to clean the battery when there is a voltage of more than 0.2 volts on top of the battery?

    A. Clean it in a solvent tank.

    B. Clean it in a hot-water cleaning machine.

    C. Clean it with a steam cleaner.

    D. Clean with baking soda and water mixture

_____ **10.** Which the following tests is performed to determine the capacity and life left in the battery?

    A. Leak test

    B. Hydrometer test

    C. Conductance test

    D. Vacuum test

ASE Technician A/Technician B Style Questions

_____ **1.** Tech A says that a battery stores electrical energy in chemical form. Tech B says that a battery provides the initial electrical power for the engine starting system. Who is correct?

    A. Tech A

    B. Tech B

    C. Both A and B

    D. Neither A nor B

_____ **2.** Tech A says that a 12-volt battery has six cells. Tech B says that the more plates a cell in a battery has, the more voltage it creates. Who is correct?

    A. Tech A

    B. Tech B

    C. Both A and B

    D. Neither A nor B

_____ **3.** Tech A says that a parasitic draw is measured in volts. Tech B says that pulling fuses one at a time can help locate a parasitic draw. Who is correct?

    A. Tech A

    B. Tech B

    C. Both A and B

    D. Neither A nor B

_____ **4.** Tech A says that when disconnecting the battery, the negative terminal should be disconnected first. Tech B says that baking soda and water will remove lead oxide from battery terminals. Who is correct?

    A. Tech A

    B. Tech B

    C. Both A and B

    D. Neither A nor B

_____ **5.** Tech A says that checking the specific gravity will indicate the battery's cold cranking amps. Tech B says that a battery load test should be performed when the battery is heavily discharged. Who is correct?

    A. Tech A

    B. Tech B

    C. Both A and B

    D. Neither A nor B

_____ **6.** Tech A says that lead oxide acts as an insulator on the battery posts and has to be scraped away. Tech B says that current can leak across the dirt on the surface of the battery. Who is correct?

    A. Tech A

    B. Tech B

    C. Both A and B

    D. Neither A nor B

_____ **7.** Tech A says that batteries should be charged as fast as possible. Tech B says that the ideal charging rate is the CCA divided by 70. Who is correct?

    A. Tech A

    B. Tech B

    C. Both A and B

    D. Neither A nor B

_____ **8.** Tech A says that the surface of the battery can be cleaned with baking soda and water. Tech B says that the electrolyte level should be below the top surface of the plates. Who is correct?

    A. Tech A

    B. Tech B

    C. Both A and B

    D. Neither A nor B

_____ **9.** Tech A says that the specific gravity of the electrolyte can be checked with a hydrometer. Tech B says that the specific gravity of the electrolyte can be checked with a refractometer. Who is correct?

    A. Tech A

    B. Tech B

    C. Both A and B

    D. Neither A nor B

_____ **10.** Tech A says that all vehicles have a specified CCA rating for the battery. Tech B says that reserve capacity indicates how many times the engine can be started by the battery. Who is correct?

    A. Tech A

    B. Tech B

    C. Both A and B

    D. Neither A nor B

Starting and Charging Systems

At the start of each chapter you'll find the NATEF tasks, Knowledge Objectives, and Skills Objectives from the textbook. These are your objectives as you make your way through the exercises in this workbook and the chapter in your textbook. The following activities have been designed to help you refresh your knowledge of the material in this chapter.

NATEF Tasks

- N54001 Demonstrate knowledge of an automatic idle-stop/start-stop system. (MLR/AST/MAST)
- N54002 Perform starter current draw tests; determine needed action. (MLR/AST/MAST)
- N54003 Perform starter circuit voltage drop tests; determine needed action. (MLR/AST/MAST)
- N54004 Inspect and test switches, connectors, and wires of starter control circuits; determine needed action. (MLR/AST/MAST)
- N54005 Inspect and test starter relays and solenoids; determine needed action. (MLR/AST/MAST)
- N54006 Differentiate between electrical and engine mechanical problems that cause a slow-crank or a no-crank condition. (AST/MAST)
- N 54007 Remove and install starter in a vehicle. (MLR/AST/MAST)
- N54008 Perform charging system output test; determine needed action. (MLR/AST/MAST)
- N54009 Perform charging circuit voltage drop tests; determine needed action. (MLR/AST/MAST)
- N54010 Diagnose (troubleshoot) charging system for causes of undercharge, no-charge, or overcharge conditions. (AST/MAST)
- N54011 Remove, inspect, and/or replace generator (alternator). (MLR/AST/MAST)

Knowledge Objectives

After reading this chapter, you will be able to:

- K54001 Describe the purpose, operation, and types of starter systems.
- K54002 Explain the function of starter motor components.
- K54003 Explain the operation of the starter solenoid and control circuit.
- K54004 Describe the purpose and function of the charging system.
- K54005 Explain the purpose and function of alternator components.
- K54006 Explain rectification and the operation of the rectifier.
- K54007 Explain the process of controlling charging system output.

Skills Objectives

After reading this chapter, you will be able to:

- S54001 Perform starting system inspections.
- S54002 Perform charging system inspections.

Matching

Match the following terms with the correct description or example.

A. Rectification

B. Counter-electromotive force (CEMF)

C. Alternator

D. Hold-in winding

E. Starter drive

F. Pull-in winding

_____ **1.** A low-current winding found in starter solenoids that holds the plunger in the activated position.

_____ **2.** A process of converting AC into DC required by the battery and nearly all of the automobile systems.

_____ **3.** A device that transmits the rotational drive from the starter armature to the engine via the ring gear that is mounted on the engine flywheel, flexplate, or torque converter.

_____ **4.** Voltage created in the field windings as the motor rotates, which opposes battery voltage and limits motor speed.

_____ **5.** A high-current winding found in starter solenoids that pulls the solenoid plunger into the activated position.

_____ **6.** A device that supplies the electrical energy required for modern vehicles whenever the engine is operating.

Multiple Choice

Read each item carefully, and then select the best response.

_____ **1.** The starter motor is mounted on the transmission or cylinder block in a position to engage a _____ around the outside edge of the engine flywheel, flex plate, or torque converter.
  A. magnet
  B. commutator
  C. ring gear
  D. sleeve

_____ **2.** In the direct-drive system, the starter drive is mounted directly on one end of the _____.
  A. flywheel
  B. armature shaft
  C. transmission
  D. reduction gear

_____ **3.** The commutator end frame carries copper-impregnated carbon _____, which conduct current through the armature when it is being rotated in operation.
  A. spur gears
  B. brushes
  C. coils
  D. strips

_____ **4.** A(n) _____ consists of two semicircular segments that are connected to the two ends of the loop and are insulated from each other.
  A. helix
  B. armature
  C. commutator
  D. electromagnet

_____ **5.** The _____ is typically a cylindrical device mounted on the starter motor that switches the high current flow required by the starter motor on and off and engages the starter drive with the ring gear.
  A. solenoid
  B. armature
  C. commutator
  D. pinion

_____ **6.** For many years, manufacturers have placed switches in _____ with the starter solenoid windings, which prevents the starter from being activated.
  A. parallel
  B. series
  C. series/parallel
  D. either A or C

_____ **7.** The _____ prevents the starter motor from being driven by the engine once the engine starts, which would spin the armature faster than it could handle.
  A. flywheel
  B. starter control circuit
  C. pole shoe
  D. overrunning clutch

_____ **8.** The _____ converts mechanical energy into electrical energy by electromagnetic induction.
   A. DC generator
   B. inverter
   C. alternator
   D. rectifier

_____ **9.** The voltage potential induced by an AC generator is called _____.
   A. electromotive force
   B. electromagnetic induction
   C. counter-electromotive force
   D. either A or B

_____ **10.** To change AC to DC, automotive alternators use a rectifier assembly consisting of _____ in a specific configuration.
   A. transistors
   B. diodes
   C. resistors
   D. semiconductors

_____ **11.** In the _____ method of connection, one end of each phase winding is taken to a central point where the ends are connected together.
   A. wye
   B. delta
   C. triangle
   D. square

_____ **12.** The _____ is an electromagnet that rotates freely in the alternator and is supported on each end by ball bearings.
   A. stator
   B. slip ring
   C. voltage regulator
   D. rotor

True/False

If you believe the statement to be more true than false, write the letter "T" in the space provided. If you believe the statement to be more false than true, write the letter "F."

_____ **1.** All vehicles equipped with an automatic transmission use a neutral safety switch or a similar device.

_____ **2.** The starter motor converts mechanical energy to electrical energy for the purpose of cranking the engine over.

_____ **3.** A conductor loop that can freely rotate within the magnetic field is the most efficient motor design.

_____ **4.** The hold-in winding draws a higher current and creates a stronger magnetic field than the pull-in winding.

_____ **5.** Some Ford vehicles use a separate starter relay in the engine compartment, instead of a solenoid, to control the high current for the starter motor.

_____ **6.** Some immobilizer systems now use keyless starting. The vehicle has a start button on the dash and does not require the key to be inserted into an ignition switch.

_____ **7.** A diode bridge gets its name from two diodes in series bridged with a wire.

_____ **8.** In the wye method, the windings are connected in the shape of a triangle.

_____ **9.** Alternator decoupling pulleys are prone to wear just like the tensioner and belt, so they need to be inspected and replaced when faulty.

_____ **10.** The alternator's cooling fan is mounted on the rotor shaft and may be an integral part of the drive pulley or part of the rotor.

Fill in the Blank

Read each item carefully, and then complete the statement by filling in the missing word(s).

1. The _____ system provides a method of rotating the vehicle's internal combustion engine to begin the combustion cycle.

2. _____ _____ starters use an extra gear between the armature and the starter drive mechanism.

3. The _____ _____ _____ activates the solenoid winding to draw the plunger forward.

4. A(n) _____ _____ system is a computer-managed security system that disables the vehicle starter and engine systems by using an electronic system to uniquely identify each vehicle key by a security code system.

5. Most hybrid vehicles use a _____-_____ electric motor for engine start-up, auxiliary power, and regenerative braking functions.

6. A _____-_____ AC generator has only one stationary coil, which creates a single sine wave.

7. The _____ _____ monitors battery voltage and adjusts the current flow through the rotor appropriately.

8. Many alternators are designed with A-type circuits and a(n) _____ _____ on the regulator that provides a method of full-fielding the charging system with the engine running.

9. The _____ consists of a cylindrical, laminated iron core, which carries the three (or four) phase windings in slots on the inside.

10. The diodes for rectification are mounted on _____ _____ to assist in dissipating the heat generated in the diodes.

Labeling

Label the following diagrams with the correct terms.

1. A typical starter motor, solenoid, and starter drive:

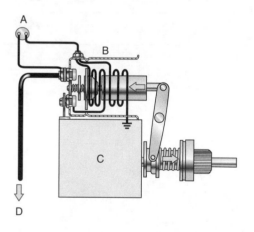

A. _____

B. _____

C. _____

D. _____

2. Series-wound starter:

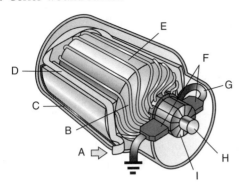

A. _____

B. _____

C. _____

D. _____

E. _____

F. _____

G. _____

H. _____

I. _____

3. Simple single-loop motor and electromagnetic fields—with commutator and brushes:

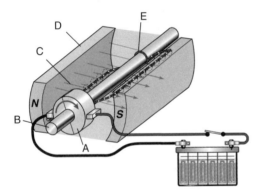

A. _____

B. _____

C. _____

D. _____

E. _____

4. Ford moveable pole shoe starter:

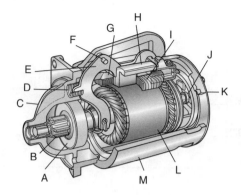

A. _____

B. _____

C. _____

D. _____

E. _____

F. _____

G. _____

H. _____

I. _____

J. _____

K. _____

L. _____

M. _____

5. Basic starter control circuit:

Automatic Transmission

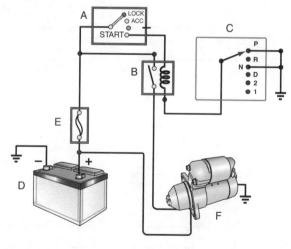

A. _____

B. _____

C. _____

D. _____

E. _____

F. _____

Manual Transmission

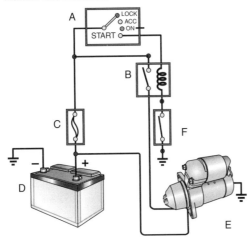

A. _____

B. _____

C. _____

D. _____

E. _____

F. _____

6. Starter drive one-way clutch:

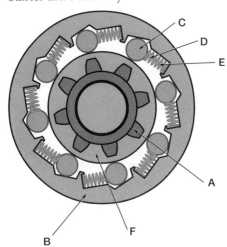

A. _____

B. _____

C. _____

D. _____

E. _____

F. _____

7. The alternator:

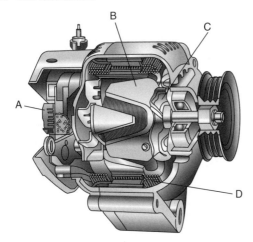

A. _____

B. _____

C. _____

D. _____

Skill Drills

Place the skill drill steps in the correct order.

1. Testing the Starter Draw:

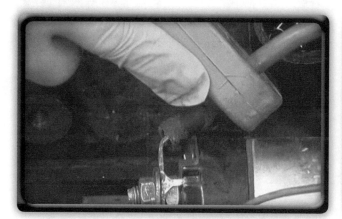

_____ **A.** Connect the amps clamp around either the positive or the negative battery lead in the correct orientation. Make sure all of the appropriate wires are inside the clamp and the clamp is completely closed.

_____ **B.** Disable the engine from starting by one of the following methods:
- Clear flood mode: This mode is programmed by manufacturers on many electronic fuel injection vehicles. It can be activated by holding the throttle down to the floor before turning the key. If the engine starts, lift your foot off the throttle and try another method.
- Pull the fuel pump relay and run the engine until it dies.
- Disconnect the fuel injectors or ignition coils.
- Disconnect the spark plug wires.

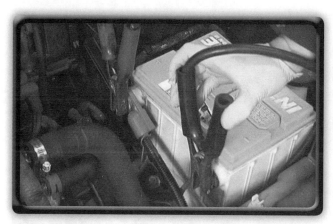

_____ **C.** Research the specifications for the starter draw test. Prepare the starter tester by setting it up to measure starter current. Connect the red lead to the positive terminal of the battery and the black lead to the negative terminal of the battery.

_____ **D.** With the engine disabled, crank the engine and read the amps and volts as soon as the amps stabilize. Compare the readings to specifications and determine any necessary actions.

2. Testing Starter Circuit Voltage Drop:

_____ **A.** Set the DMM to volts. Connect the black lead to the positive battery post and the red lead to the input of the starter (not the input of the solenoid unless that is the only accessible terminal).

_____ **B.** Connect the black lead to the negative battery post and the red lead to the starter housing. Crank the engine and read the voltage drop. If the voltage drop is more than 0.5 volts on either side of the circuit, use the voltmeter and wiring diagram to isolate the voltage drop. Determine any necessary actions.

_____ **C.** Crank the engine and read the maximum voltage drop for the positive side of the circuit.

3. Inspecting and Testing Relays and Solenoids:

_____ **A.** If the solenoid does *not* click with the key in the crank position, remove the electrical connection for the control circuit at the solenoid.

_____ **B.** Measure the voltage across the contacts with the relay *not* activated. This should read near battery voltage if both sides of the switched circuit are OK. If not, perform voltage drop tests on each side of the switch circuit. Activate the relay while measuring the voltage drop across the contacts. If it is more than 0.5 volts, the relay will need to be replaced.

_____ **C.** Use a relay adapter to mount the relay on top of the relay socket so you can check the control circuit wiring and perform voltage drop tests on the contacts. Activate the relay while measuring the voltage across the relay winding. If it is near battery voltage, the control circuit wiring is okay.

_____ **D.** Use a jumper wire to apply battery voltage to the control circuit terminal on the solenoid and see if the solenoid clicks. Determine any necessary actions.

_____ **E.** To test a relay, measure the resistance of the relay winding and compare to specifications. If out of specifications, replace the relay.

_____ **F.** To test a starter solenoid, measure the voltage drop across the solenoid contact terminals with the key in the crank position. If more than 0.5 volts, replace the solenoid or starter assembly.

4. Removing and Installing a Starter:

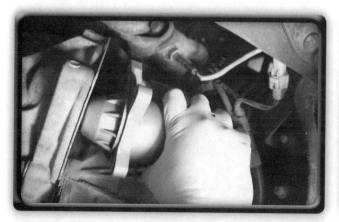

_____ **A.** Remove the starter motor, being careful to catch any shims that might be between the starter and the block. Reinstall the starter motor by reversing these steps, and verify its proper operation.

_____ **B.** Disconnect the negative terminal of the battery after determining whether a memory minder is required.

_____ **C.** Loosen the starter motor mounting bolts, and remove them while holding the starter so it does not fall.

_____ **D.** Remove any engine covers or components required to gain access to the starter. Remove starter motor electrical connections, noting how the wires were routed. In some vehicles, the wires cannot be accessed until the starter is removed.

5. Replacing an Alternator:

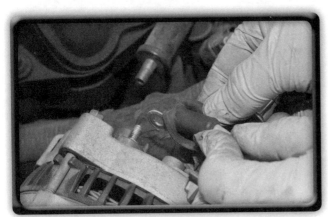

_____ **A.** Locate the electrical connections at the rear of the alternator, and note their positions. Loosen any securing fasteners or covers, and remove terminals one at a time.

_____ **B.** Turn the ignition to the on position, and make sure the charge light on the instrument panel illuminates. Start the engine to see if the charge light goes off. Measure the regulated voltage and maximum alternator amperage output. Remove the fender covers, and return any tools used to their correct place.

_____ **C.** Reinstall the electrical wires to their correct terminals, referring to the manufacturer's information. Check the security of any fastening devices.

_____ **D.** Reattach to the negative post of the battery. Make sure the fastener is tight, and replace any battery terminal covers.

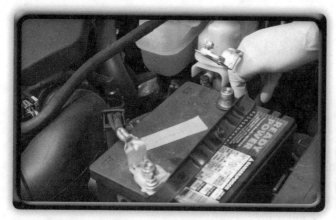

_____ **E.** Install fender covers. Verify any memory issues, and remove the negative terminal of the battery.

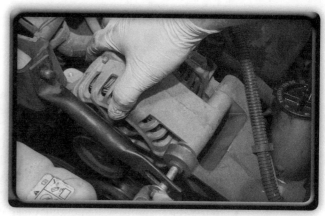

_____ **F.** Reinstall the alternator. Situate the alternator in the mounting bracket(s) and, while still supporting the alternator, loosely start the securing fasteners that hold the alternator to its mounting bracket(s).

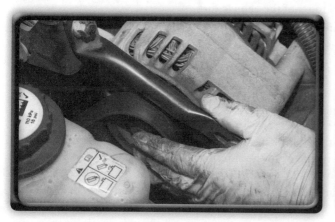

_____ **G.** Install the drive belt over the alternator drive pulley, and, using the correct tools, adjust the belt to the correct tension.

_____ **H.** Loosen the drive belt, and remove it from the alternator pulley. Check the condition of the belt to see if it is still serviceable.

_____ **I.** Loosen the securing fasteners that hold the alternator to its mounting bracket(s), making sure the alternator is supported. Remove the alternator.

Review Questions

_____ 1. What is the main purpose of the starter system in a vehicle?
   A. To provide a method of rotating the vehicle's internal combustion engine to begin the combustion cycle
   B. To start the vehicle's charging system.
   C. To start all the other systems of the vehicle
   D. To start the conversion of chemical energy into electrical energy

_____ 2. A starter draw test measures:
   A. the amount of voltage dropped across the solenoid contacts.
   B. the amount of current a starter draws during cranking.
   C. the amount of current draw in the starter control circuit.
   D. the amount of time it takes for the starter to crank the engine over.

_____ 3. To test the charging system output do all of the following EXCEPT:
   A. Connect a charging system tester to the battery, and the amps clamp around the alternator output wire.
   B. Raise the engine RPM to approximately 1.500 RPM.
   C. manually or automatically load down the battery just enough to obtain the maximum amperage output without pulling battery voltage below 12.0 volts.
   D. disconnect the negative battery terminal to see if the vehicle dies.

_____ 4. Which component slows down the armature when the starter motor is disengaged?
   A. Shift fork
   B. Copper-impregnated carbon brushes
   C. Tensioned spiral springs
   D. Brake washer

_____ 5. What is the purpose of the diodes in an alternator rectifier?
   A. to control the voltage output of the alternator.
   B. to control the amount of current going through the rotor winding.
   C. to transfer the current from the voltage regulator to the slip rings on the rotor.
   D. to transform the alternating current into direct current.

_____ 6. What is the main purpose of the fork in starter motor engagement?
   A. It activates a starter-mounted solenoid.
   B. It transmits drive in one direction only and freewheels in the opposite direction.
   C. It helps more current to flow in the circuit.
   D. It engages the starter drive.

_____ 7. All of the following statements with respect to the operational function of a starter solenoid are true _except_:
   A. It switches the high current flow required by the starter motor on and off.
   B. It engages the starter drive with the ring gear.
   C. It is typically a cylindrical device mounted on the starter motor.
   D. It conducts electricity from the starter motor to the control circuit.

_____ 8. All of the following statements with respect to the operation of a starter solenoid are true _except_:
   A. A pull-in winding draws a higher current and creates a stronger magnetic field than the other winding—the hold-in winding.
   B. The output of the pull-in winding is connected to the main starter terminal.
   C. The movement of the solenoid windings engages the drive pinion with the flywheel ring gear.
   D. The output of the hold-in winding is connected to ground on the starter casing.

_____ 9. Alternators have all of the following characteristics _except_:
   A. greater wattage output at lower rpm.
   B. lower maximum RPM.
   C. smaller physical size and weight for a given output.
   D. greater reliability and longer service life.

_____ 10. Which component in the alternator controls the strength of the magnetic field of the rotating magnet?
   A. Voltage regulator
   B. Diode assembly
   C. Rectifier assembly
   D. A cooling fan

ASE Technician A/Technician B Style Questions

_____ **1.** Tech A says that some starters use gear reduction to improve efficiency. Tech B says that a starter converts electrical energy to mechanical energy. Who is correct?
  A. Tech A
  B. Tech B
  C. Both A and B
  D. Neither A nor B

_____ **2.** Tech A says that the pull-in winding is short-circuited when the solenoid is fully engaged. Tech B says that the starter drive has a built-in one-way clutch. Who is correct?
  A. Tech A
  B. Tech B
  C. Both A and B
  D. Neither A nor B

_____ **3.** Tech A says that a voltage drop of 0.8 volt on the starter ground circuit is within specifications. Tech B says that high starter draw current could be caused by a spun main bearing in the engine. Who is correct?
  A. Tech A
  B. Tech B
  C. Both A and B
  D. Neither A nor B

_____ **4.** Tech A says that when testing a relay winding with an ohmmeter, it should show the winding is open. Tech B says that the solenoid closes a set of heavy contacts that send current flow to the starter motor. Who is correct?
  A. Tech A
  B. Tech B
  C. Both A and B
  D. Neither A nor B

_____ **5.** Tech A says that most hybrid vehicles use the high-voltage electric motor to start the engine. Tech B says that most hybrid engines need to crank over more slowly than regular engines. Who is correct?
  A. Tech A
  B. Tech B
  C. Both A and B
  D. Neither A nor B

_____ **6.** Tech A says that some alternator pulleys are designed to freewheel in one direction. Tech B says that the alternator output terminal is connected to one of the slip rings on the rotor. Who is correct?
  A. Tech A
  B. Tech B
  C. Both A and B
  D. Neither A nor B

_____ **7.** Tech A says that the stator rotates inside a magnetic field. Tech B says that the rotor is bolted between the two end housings. Who is correct?
  A. Tech A
  B. Tech B
  C. Both A and B
  D. Neither A nor B

_____ **8.** Tech A says that the voltage regulator controls the strength of the rotor's magnetic field. Tech B says that the voltage regulator is installed between the output terminal of the alternator and the positive terminal of the battery. Who is correct?
  A. Tech A
  B. Tech B
  C. Both A and B
  D. Neither A nor B

_____ **9.** Tech A says that overcharging can lead to short life of bulbs and other electrical devices. Tech B says that the charging system regulated voltage is checked with maximum load on the battery. Who is correct?

   A. Tech A

   B. Tech B

   C. Both A and B

   D. Neither A nor B

_____ **10.** Tech A says that the rectifier assembly controls the output of the alternator. Tech B says that the alternator output circuit voltage drop must be checked with the charging system under a heavy load. Who is correct?

   A. Tech A

   B. Tech B

   C. Both A and B

   D. Neither A nor B

CHAPTER

Lighting Systems

55

At the start of each chapter you'll find the NATEF tasks, Knowledge Objectives, and Skills Objectives from the textbook. These are your objectives as you make your way through the exercises in this workbook and the chapter in your textbook. The following activities have been designed to help you refresh your knowledge of the material in this chapter.

NATEF Tasks

- N55001 Identify system voltage and safety precautions associated with high-intensity discharge headlights. (MLR/AST/MAST)
- N55002 Aim headlights. (MLR/AST/MAST)
- N55003 Diagnose (troubleshoot) the causes of incorrect operation of warning devices and other driver information systems; determine needed action. (AST/MAST)

Knowledge Objectives

After reading this chapter, you will be able to:

- K55001 Describe the function of the lighting systems and types of lightbulbs.
- K55002 Explain the purpose of each of the convenience and safety light systems.
- K55003 Explain the purpose of each of the driver's intention indicator light systems.
- K55004 Explain the function of common headlight systems.
- K55005 Describe electronically controlled lighting systems.

Skills Objectives

After reading this chapter, you will be able to:

- S55001 Perform lighting system inspection, testing, and service.
- S55002 Measure headlight intensity.
- S55003 Diagnose failures in driver information display systems.

Matching

Match the following terms with the correct description or example.

A. Ballast
B. High-intensity discharge (HID)
C. Incandescent lamp

D. Light-emitting diode (LED)
E. Vacuum tube fluorescent (VTF)

_____ **1.** A type of lighting that produces light with an electric arc rather than a glowing filament.

_____ **2.** A type of lighting used for instrumentation displays on vehicle instrument panel clusters. This type of lighting emits a very bright light with high contrast and can shine in various colors. Also called vacuum fluorescent display (VFD).

_____ **3.** A device that increases lighting voltage substantially and controls the current to the bulb.

_____ **4.** A type of lighting used in various automotive applications, such as warning indicators and alphanumeric displays.

_____ **5.** The traditional bulb that uses a heated filament to produce light.

Multiple Choice

Read each item carefully, and then select the best response.

_____ 1. Incandescent bulbs are inefficient, converting only about _____ of the electricity to visible light.
   A. 10%
   B. 15%
   C. 25%
   D. 30%

_____ 2. What kind of incandescent lamps are filled with bromine or iodine gas?
   A. Incandescent
   B. Vacuum tube fluorescent
   C. Halogen
   D. High-intensity discharge

_____ 3. LEDs are often required to give off a specified amount of light; to achieve this they are usually connected in groups called _____.
   A. clusters
   B. series strings
   C. parallel sets
   D. packs

_____ 4. Which type of bulb works well as a combination taillight and brake light because it has one filament that emits a small amount of light, and a second filament that emits more light?
   A. LED cluster
   B. Festoon-style bulb
   C. Tandem bulb
   D. Dual-filament bulb

_____ 5. Which type of lamp base gets its name from the two retaining pins on the side of the base?
   A. Bayonet-style
   B. Festoon-style
   C. Wedge-style
   D. Pin-type

_____ 6. Which type of lights usually light up as part of a self-test when the ignition initially comes on to show they are in working order?
   A. Marker lights
   B. Warning lamps
   C. Tail lights
   D. Courtesy lights

_____ 7. For safety reasons, _____ continue to operate when the light switch is moved to the headlight position.
   A. park lights
   B. signal lamps
   C. taillights
   D. both A and C

_____ 8. Many vehicles by law now have a higher additional third brake light mounted on top of the trunk lid or on the rear window called a _____ light.
   A. pedestal light
   B. courtesy light
   C. center high mount stop light
   D. festoon light

_____ 9. White lights mounted at the rear of a vehicle that provides the driver with vision behind the vehicle at night are called _____.
   A. back-up lights
   B. tail lights
   C. reverse lights,
   D. either A or C

_____ **10.** Which type of lights simultaneously cause a pulsing in all exterior indicator lights and both indicator lights on the instrument panel?
   A. Hazard warning lights
   B. Turn signal lights
   C. Backup lights
   D. Driving lights

_____ **11.** Existing lights that turn on when the vehicle is running and turn off when the engine stops in order to improve the vehicle's visibility to other drivers in all weather conditions are called _____.
   A. hazard warning lights
   B. dual-filament lights
   C. courtesy lights
   D. daytime running lights

_____ **12.** A(n) _____ headlight has a highly polished aluminized glass reflector that is fused to the optically designed lens.
   A. dual-filament
   B. semi-sealed beam
   C. sealed-beam
   D. HID

_____ **13.** Which type of headlight produces light with an electric arc rather than a glowing filament?
   A. LED
   B. HID
   C. Sealed-beam
   D. Halogen

_____ **14.** Which type of lights are used with other vehicle lighting in poor weather such as thick fog, driving rain, or blowing snow?
   A. Driving lights
   B. Cornering lights
   C. Fog lights
   D. Smart lights

_____ **15.** In comprehensive adaptive lighting systems, otherwise known as smart lighting, all lighting system decisions are determined by the _____.
   A. Driver
   B. CAN-bus
   C. Power control module
   D. Body control module

True/False

If you believe the statement to be more true than false, write the letter "T" in the space provided. If you believe the statement to be more false than true, write the letter "F."

_____ **1.** Wattage is found by multiplying the voltage used by the lamp by the current flowing through it.

_____ **2.** High-intensity halogen lamp light comes from metallic salts that are vaporized within an arc chamber.

_____ **3.** Some countries mandate that HID headlamps may only be installed on vehicles with lens-cleaning systems and automatic self-leveling systems.

_____ **4.** Wattage is an indication of light output.

_____ **5.** Dome lights use festoon-style lights, which have a base on each end of a cylindrical light bulb.

_____ **6.** Government regulations control the height of taillights and their brightness.

_____ **7.** Taillights are the only white lights on the rear of the vehicle.

_____ **8.** Imported vehicles tend to have separate amber-colored turn signal lamps on both the front and the rear of the vehicle.

_____ **9.** The beam selector switch is a double-pole, single-throw switch, meaning it has two movable poles but makes contact in one position.

_____ **10.** Some vehicles use LED lights as headlights.

_____ **11.** Passive night vision systems use a heat-sensing camera to pick up thermal radiation emitted by objects.

_____ **12.** Cornering lights are white lights usually installed into the bumper or fender and are designed to provide side lighting when the vehicle is turning corners.

_____ **13.** Automatic headlight-leveling systems ensure the headlights are always correctly aligned, regardless of the load the vehicle is carrying.

_____ **14.** To reduce the amount of wiring required, a system is used that integrates sensors into a common wiring harness, called a BCM.

_____ **15.** Not all wiring diagrams use the same symbols or the same numbering system.

Fill in the Blank

Read each item carefully, and then complete the statement by filling in the missing word(s).

1. Modern vehicles use many different kinds and sizes of _____, also known in some places as light bulbs or light globes.

2. One of the advantages of a(n) _____ is that it turns on instantly.

3. In a bulb marked 12V/21W, the _____ will consume 21 watts of power when 12 volts is applied across it.

4. Many newer bulbs use a _____ base either made from the glass bulb itself or with a built-in plastic base.

5. _____ lights are usually controlled by the vehicle body computer with inputs from the ignition and door switches either in the handle, latch, or door pillar.

6. _____ lights are used to mark the sides of some vehicles and are often located down the sides of the vehicle or trailer.

7. Today's computer-controlled brake lights are activated by the _____ _____ _____ when the computer senses an input from the brake pedal switch.

8. The cancelling mechanism of the _____ _____ lights operates to return the switch to its central or "off" position after a turn has been completed and the steering wheel is returned to the straight-ahead position.

9. Some domestic vehicles use the rear brake lamps as turn signals by flashing the _____ _____ on one side to indicate the turn.

10. Most vehicle _____ require two beams to provide for a high beam and low beam operation.

11. A(n) _____-_____ headlight system produces a high-intensity forward beam and uses a lens system to project the light forward, rather than the traditional reflector system.

12. Active _____ _____ systems use an infrared light generator that projects infrared light in front of and to the side of the roadway ahead.

13. _____ _____ are installed on the front of the vehicle and provide higher intensity illumination over longer distances than standard headlight systems.

14. _____ headlights have the ability to adjust the length of the headlight beam based on the distance of oncoming traffic.

15. Manufacturers design the circuits to operate in specific ways and then create schematics or _____ _____, which are a diagrammatic layout of the entire circuit.

Labeling

Label the following diagrams with the correct terms.

1. Typical CANbus diagram:

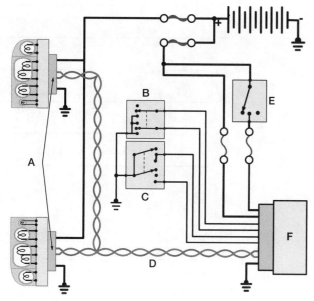

A. _____

B. _____

C. _____

D. _____

E. _____

F. _____

2. Automatic headlight system:

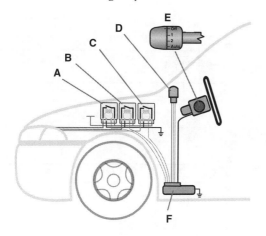

A. _____

B. _____

C. _____

D. _____

E. _____

F. _____

3. Battery and fuse symbols:

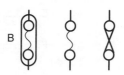

A. _____

B. _____

C. _____

D. _____

4. Ground and connector symbols:

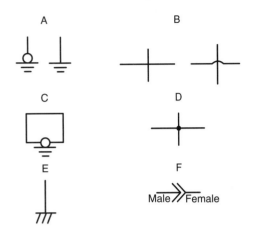

A. _____

B. _____

C. _____

D. _____

E. _____

F. _____

5. Switch symbols:

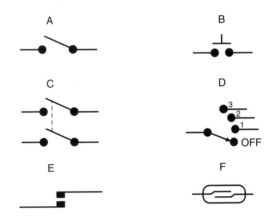

A. _____

B. _____

C. _____

D. _____

E. _____

F. _____

6. Resistors, coils, and relay symbols:

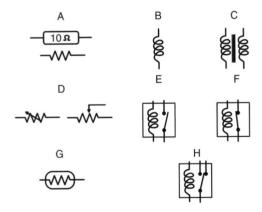

A. _____

B. _____

C. _____

D. _____

E. _____

F. _____

G. _____

H. _____

7. Semiconductor symbols:

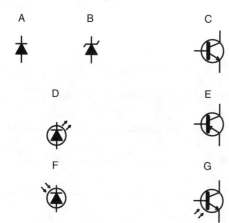

A. _____

B. _____

C. _____

D. _____

E. _____

F. _____

G. _____

8. Capacitor and device symbols:

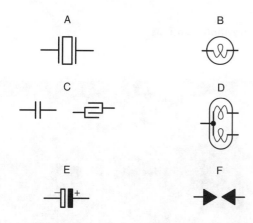

A. _____

B. _____

C. _____

D. _____

E. _____

F. _____

9. Motors, generators, and solenoid symbols:

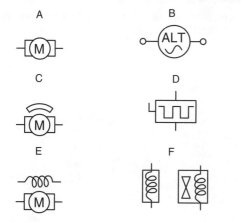

A. _____

B. _____

C. _____

D. _____

E. _____

F. _____

10. Gauges and warning device symbols:

A

V

B

♪

C

A

D

E

F

A. _____

B. _____

C. _____

D. _____

E. _____

F. _____

Skill Drills

Test your knowledge of skill drills by filling in the correct words in the photo captions.

1. Checking and Changing an Exterior Light Bulb:

Step 1: Remove the _____ to expose the bulb. If the bulb is _____ mounted, gently grip the bulb and push it inward. Turn the bulb slightly _____, and remove it from the bulb holder. Some bulbs pull straight out.

Step 2: Inspect the bulb holder to make sure there is no _____. If there is, clean it with a bulb socket _____ _____ or _____ _____.

Step 3: Insert the new bulb into the bulb holder, _____ it fully, turn it slightly _____, and release it. Test it by _____ it on and off. Then replace the cover, and _____ it again.

2. Checking and Changing a Headlight Bulb:

Step 1: Switch the headlights on at _____ beam, then to _____ beam. Check that the _____ - _____ indicator is operating. If one of the lights does not operate or is dim, that headlight will have to be diagnosed and potentially replaced.

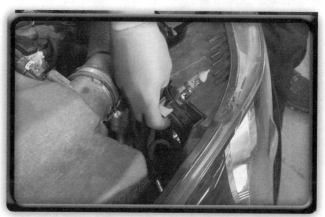

Step 2: Test the vehicle headlights. Obtain the replacement _____ for the vehicle. Unplug the _____ _____ at the _____ of the lamp unit.

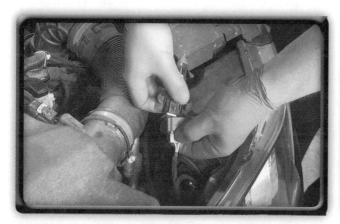

Step 3: _____ the old bulb, and _____ it with the new one. Handle the new bulb only by its _____ or, if supplied, by the _____ cover.

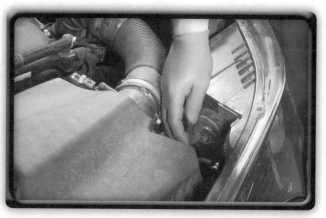

Step 4: Replace the unit and the _____ _____ or bulb assembly, and then plug in the _____. Switch on the lights again to _____ that they are both operating correctly.

3. Aiming Headlights:

Step 1: Make sure the tires are _____ properly, the _____ point straight ahead, and there is no extra _____ in the vehicle. Position the vehicle correctly in relation to the headlamp _____ unit following the equipment manufacturer's instructions. Calibrate the aligner for any _____ _____ and for the vehicle being tested.

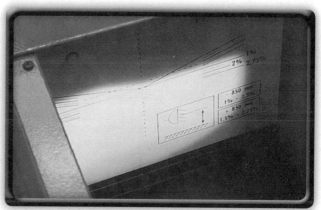

Step 2: On the types of _____ that require the headlights to be on during alignment, turn the headlights on to a _____ _____ setting. The _____ of the illuminating beams should be in the _____ _____ quadrants of the chart or wall markings or as specified by the manufacturer.

Step 3: The high beam should be _____, falling on the _____ of the horizontal and vertical marks or as specified by the manufacturer. If necessary, turn the _____ _____ on the headlight so the lights _____ to the correct places or _____ on the levels are centered, depending on the type of aligner equipment you are using.

Review Questions

_____ **1.** Which of the following alert(s) the other drivers of a change in direction?
  A. Red or amber turn signals
  B. Beam selector
  C. Brake lights
  D. Emergency flasher light

_____ **2.** Which lightbulbs are very efficient and sensitive, and can be damaged even by finger oil residue?
  A. Incandescent lamps
  B. Halogen lamps
  C. Xenon lamps
  D. VTF lamps

_____ **3.** Which of the following lamps produce more lumens with a bluish tinge for the given wattage when compared with all other lamps?
  A. Incandescent lamps
  B. Halogen lamps
  C. High intensity discharge lamps
  D. VTF lamps

_____ **4.** Which lights are wired in parallel with the taillights and operate whenever the taillights are switched on?
  A. Headlights
  B. Turn signal lights
  C. Backup lights
  D. License plate lights

_____ **5.** All of the following statements referring to driving lights are true *except*:
  A. Driving lights typically use quartz halogen bulbs in the 55- to 120-watt range.
  B. The quality of reflector is extremely important in driving lights to get the optimum performance.
  C. Driving lights are wired so that they operate only when the high beam is operating.
  D. Driving lights turn off when the headlights are switched from low to high beam.

_____ **6.** Which of the following statements describes the purpose of backup lights?
  A. It indicates to other drivers that the vehicle is stopping.
  B. It provides the driver with vision behind the vehicle.
  C. It alerts other drivers that the vehicle is about to turn.
  D. It provides vision to other drivers who are approaching.

7. Choose the correct statement with respect to turn signal lights.
- **A.** They serve a decorative purpose.
- **B.** They warn the other drivers that the vehicle is about to stop.
- **C.** They warn the drivers in front to slow down.
- **D.** They warn other road users of the driver's intended change of direction.

8. Which of the following lights use flashing control and also warn other road users if the vehicle is parked in a dangerous position on the side of the road?
- **A.** High intensity flashing beam lights
- **B.** Turn signal lights
- **C.** Hazard warning lights
- **D.** Parking lights

9. All of the following statements with respect to the function of headlights are true *except*:
- **A.** They illuminate the road ahead.
- **B.** They help drivers at the time of reduced visibility.
- **C.** They provide two beams, high and low, to serve different purposes.
- **D.** They are connected in series with each other.

10. All of the following statements with respect to electronically controlled lighting systems are true *except*:
- **A.** The bus combines all the individual systems wherever possible into a multiplexed serial communications network.
- **B.** The common wiring harness increases the weight of the electronic system used.
- **C.** Troubleshooting a networked system requires more training and more tools than a simple digital multimeter.
- **D.** An advantage of such a system is less wire and fewer connections.

ASE Technician A/Technician B Style Questions

1. Tech A says that a voltage drop on the ground side of a bulb won't affect its brightness because the electricity has already been used up. Tech B says that measuring voltage drop is a good way to determine if there is unwanted resistance in a circuit. Who is correct?
- **A.** Tech A
- **B.** Tech B
- **C.** Both A and B
- **D.** Neither A nor B

2. Tech A says that incandescent bulbs resist vibration well. Tech B says that HID headlamps require up to approximately 25,000 volts to start. Who is correct?
- **A.** Tech A
- **B.** Tech B
- **C.** Both A and B
- **D.** Neither A nor B

3. Tech A says that some automotive lightbulbs have more than one filament inside. Tech B says that before aligning headlights, make sure the tires are inflated properly. Who is correct?
- **A.** Tech A
- **B.** Tech B
- **C.** Both A and B
- **D.** Neither A nor B

4. Tech A says that LED brake lights illuminate faster than incandescent bulbs. Tech B says that LED brake lights have more visibility and last longer. Who is correct?
- **A.** Tech A
- **B.** Tech B
- **C.** Both A and B
- **D.** Neither A nor B

5. Tech A says that if the brake light switch is open, neither brake light will illuminate. Tech B says that the backup lights operate when taillights operate. Who is correct?
- **A.** Tech A
- **B.** Tech B

C. Both A and B

D. Neither A nor B

_____ 6. Tech A says that some brake lights get power from the brake switch through the turn signal switch. Tech B says many turn signals use amber lights. Who is correct?

A. Tech A

B. Tech B

C. Both A and B

D. Neither A nor B

_____ 7. Tech A says that some vehicles automatically "dim" the headlights when light is detected from oncoming vehicles. Tech B says that the CHMSL is illuminated when the taillights are activated. Who is correct?

A. Tech A

B. Tech B

C. Both A and B

D. Neither A nor B

_____ 8. Tech A says that some turn signals are flashed by a flasher can. Tech B says that some turn signals are flashed by the BCM. Who is correct?

A. Tech A

B. Tech B

C. Both A and B

D. Neither A nor B

_____ 9. Tech A says that a light intensity meter is used to measure the brightness of headlights. Tech B says that some headlights can automatically adjust side to side when the vehicle is cornering. Who is correct?

A. Tech A

B. Tech B

C. Both A and B

D. Neither A nor B

_____ 10. Tech A says that if the oil pressure warning light is on, the first thing you should do is replace the oil pressure sending unit. Tech B says that if a bulb is dim, you should perform a voltage drop test on the power and ground side of the bulb. Who is correct?

A. Tech A

B. Tech B

C. Both A and B

D. Neither A nor B

Network Communications and Body Accessories

At the start of each chapter you'll find the NATEF tasks, Knowledge Objectives, and Skills Objectives from the textbook. These are your objectives as you make your way through the exercises in this workbook and the chapter in your textbook. The following activities have been designed to help you refresh your knowledge of the material in this chapter.

NATEF Tasks

- N56001 Diagnose body electronic systems circuits using a scan tool; check for module communication errors (data communication bus systems); determine needed action. (AST/MAST)
- N56002 Describe the process for software transfer, software updates, or reprogramming of electronic modules. (AST/MAST)
- N56003 Diagnose operation of comfort and convenience accessories and related circuits (such as: power window, power seats, pedal height, power locks, truck locks, remote start, moon roof, sun roof, sun shade, remote keyless entry, voice activation, steering wheel controls, back-up camera, park assist, cruise control, and auto dimming headlamps); determine needed repairs. (AST/MAST)
- N56004 Diagnose operation of safety systems and related circuits (such as: horn, airbags, seat belt pretensioners, occupancy classification, wipers, washers, speed control/collision avoidance, heads-up display, park assist, and back-up camera); determine needed repairs. (AST/MAST)
- N56005 Diagnose operation of security/anti-theft systems and related circuits (such as: theft deterrent, door locks, remote keyless entry, remote start, and starter/fuel disable); determine needed repairs. (AST/MAST)
- N56006 Remove and reinstall door panel. (MLR)

Knowledge Objectives

After reading this chapter, you will be able to:

- K56001 Explain the purpose, function, and types of vehicle networks.
- K56002 Explain the layout and operation of a LIN-bus network.
- K56003 Explain the layout and operation of a CANbus network.
- K56004 Explain the purpose and types of DC accessory motors.

Skills Objectives

After reading this chapter, you will be able to:

- S56001 Diagnose CANbus network faults.
- S56002 Diagnose a DC accessory motor fault.
- S56003 Diagnose horn systems failure.
- S56004 Diagnose faults in the power door lock systems.
- S56005 Diagnose faults in the wiper/washer systems.
- S56006 Diagnose faults in heated accessory circuits.

Matching

Match the following terms with the correct description or example.

- **A.** Blower motor
- **B.** Body control module (BCM)
- **C.** Brushless DC motor
- **D.** Data link connector (DLC)
- **E.** Passive keyless entry (PKE)
- **F.** Permanent magnet electric motor
- **G.** Remote keyless entry (RKE)
- **H.** Stepper motor

_____ **1.** A type of brushless motor with a key difference: It is designed to rotate in fixed steps through a set number of degrees.

_____ **2.** An active system that senses the proximity of a fob and locks or unlocks the vehicle.

_____ **3.** The port to which a scan tool can be connected.

_____ **4.** An electric motor that does not have any brushes and is sometimes called an "electronically commutated motor." In this type of motor, an electronic control module replaces the brushes and commutator.

_____ **5.** A system that remotely unlocks and locks the vehicle without the use of a traditional key.

_____ **6.** An electronic control module for body electrical systems.

_____ **7.** An electric motor, usually the permanent magnet type that moves air over the air-conditioning evaporator and heater core.

_____ **8.** An electric motor in which the magnetic field in the casing is produced by permanent magnets, while the armature has an electromagnetic field generated by passing electrical current through loops or windings, thereby producing the motor action.

Multiple Choice

Read each item carefully, and then select the best response.

_____ **1.** Which of the following is a high-speed network used for critical data such as supplemental restraint systems, antilock brake systems, and engine controls?
  A. CANbus A
  B. CANbus B
  C. CANbus C
  D. CANbus D

_____ **2.** A group of eight bits of binary data is called a _____.
  A. microbyte
  B. byte
  C. kilobyte
  D. megabyte

_____ **3.** Which of the following is a standard CANbus network configuration?
  A. Bus parallel
  B. Star parallel
  C. Looped series
  D. All of the above

_____ **4.** What type of motor can be used to rotate a short distance and then stop or go in the reverse direction for a set number of degrees by controlling each coil individually through the microcontroller?
  A. Brush-type motor
  B. Potentiometer
  C. Stepper motors
  D. Induction motor

_____ **5.** The horn switch on vehicles with a driver's side airbag is usually mounted in the steering wheel and requires a _____ to maintain an electrical connection to the circuit as the steering wheel rotates.
  A. clock spring
  B. slot switch
  C. slip ring and brush assembly
  D. transmitter

_____ **6.** What type of keyless entry system uses a fob transmitter but does not require any action by the user?
  A. Remote keyless entry
  B. Passive keyless entry
  C. Magnetic proximity entry
  D. Either A or C

_____ **7.** What controls the intermittent operation of a windshield wiper timer circuit?
  A. Discrete electronic timer
  B. Time-delay cube relay

C. Vehicle body computer
D. Either A or C

_____ **8.** Most power mirrors use _____ for control of up-and-down and in-and-out movements.
   A. sensors
   B. electric motors
   C. hydraulic systems
   D. mechanical systems

True/False

If you believe the statement to be more true than false, write the letter "T" in the space provided. If you believe the statement to be more false than true, write the letter "F."

_____ **1.** CANbus-compliant diagnostic systems have been required on all vehicles sold in the United States since 2008.

_____ **2.** Some networks transmit and receive signals over a single wire, but most have dual wires and are commonly called "CANbus high (H)" and "CANbus low (L)," with the same message sent on both lines.

_____ **3.** Using the scan tool may require the vehicle's ignition system to be on for an extended period of time. Use a standard battery charger to support the battery when the engine is not running.

_____ **4.** Two magnetic fields are required for motor action, one in the casing and the other in the rotating armature.

_____ **5.** Blower motor speed can be controlled by using a number of resistors connected in series and a switch to select between combinations of resistors or a more complex electronic speed control module.

_____ **6.** More sophisticated electric seat systems are controlled by an electronic control unit and can "remember" seat and mirror positions for each driver.

_____ **7.** The clock spring is a device within the steering wheel with a flexible ribbon cable that can rotate endlessly in a single direction.

_____ **8.** Keyless entry systems and the engine immobilizer or security systems are two parts of the same system.

Fill in the Blank

Read each item carefully, and then complete the statement by filling in the missing word(s).

1. In electrical and electronic systems, a _____ is a means of connecting many electrical or electronic components for either data or power sharing.

2. Regardless of how the network is physically connected, the CANbus-H and CANbus-L systems will have terminating resistors connected to the data lines to form a(n) _____ through the resistors.

3. Diagnosing and repairing vehicles may require software transfers, software updates, or _____ reprogramming of the vehicle's electronic modules with the manufacturer's latest update.

4. _____ _____ in modern vehicles are usually switched by relays, which are controlled by an electronic control unit based on information from the coolant temperature sensor.

5. The electric motors used for power mirrors and widows are _____ so they can provide the movements in either direction.

6. Electric pedal height adjustment is achieved by using a reversible motor driven adjustment _____ that moves the pedals in toward the firewall or out toward the driver.

7. The driver's side door is usually a _____ door lock, which means that when it is locked or unlocked with the key (or the remote fob) the other locks follow suit.

8. The CANbus system uses digital data, called binary data, which have only two states: _____ or _____.

Labeling

Label the following diagrams with the correct terms.

1. CANbus configurations:

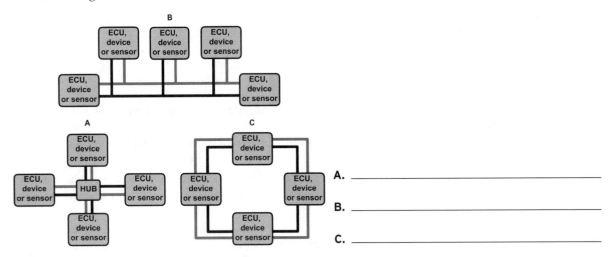

A. _____

B. _____

C. _____

2. Brush-type motor:

Series Wound DC Motor

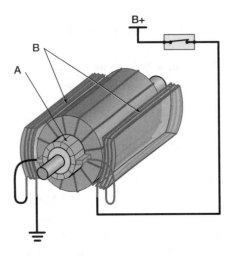

A. _____

B. _____

3. Stepper motor:

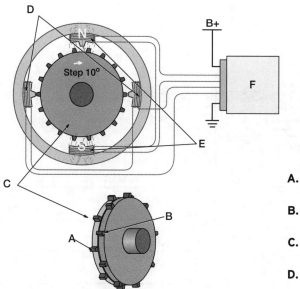

When a pair of coils are energized, the magnetic field both attracts and repels the north and south poles of the rotor causing it to rotate by a set amount.

A. _____

B. _____

C. _____

D. _____

E. _____

F. _____

4. A typical MOST network:

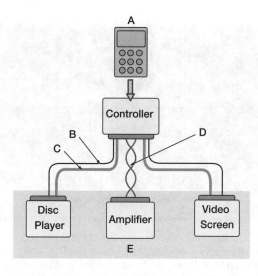

A. _____

B. _____

C. _____

D. _____

E. _____

5. A typical brushless electric motor:

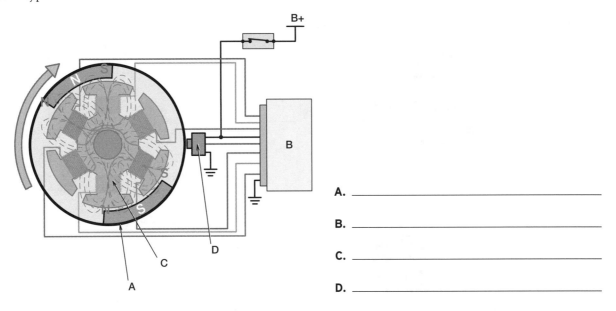

A. _____

B. _____

C. _____

D. _____

Skill Drills

Place the skill drill steps in the correct order.

1. Checking for Module Communication Errors Using a Scan Tool:

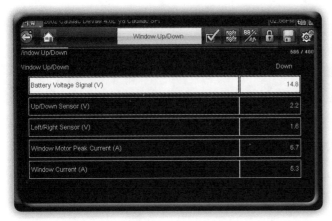

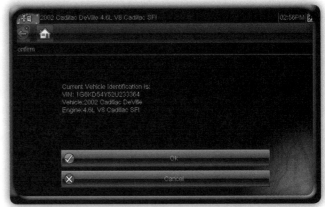

_____ **A.** Command the module to take the appropriate action, and observe the response. If you do not receive the proper response, refer to the service information for the diagnostic procedure.

_____ **B.** After researching the correct procedure in the manufacturer's information, locate the DLC and connect the scan tool. Power on the scan tool, and turn the ignition on. Establish scan tool communications with the vehicle.

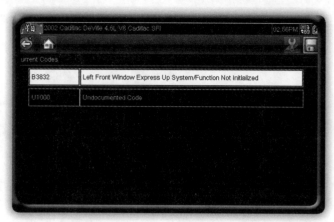

_____ **C.** Check fault codes using the scan tool, and follow the diagnostic procedure in the service information. Check to see if any modules are inactive, or not listed as active, that should be.

2. Performing Software Transfers, Software Updates, or Flash Reprogramming on Modules:

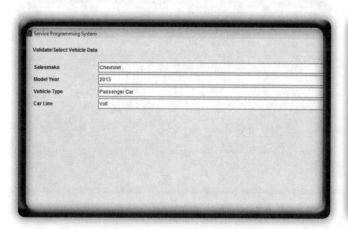

_____ **A.** Establish flash program tool communication with the vehicle.

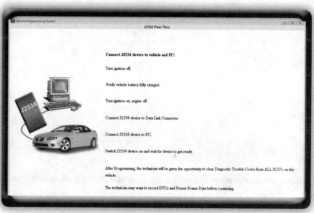

_____ **B.** Locate the DLC. Connect and power on the flash program tool. Turn the ignition on.

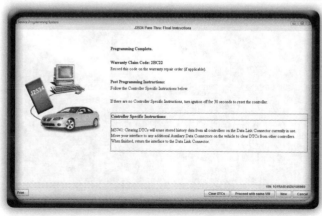

_____ **C.** Disconnect the flash programmer, and check the vehicle's functionality.

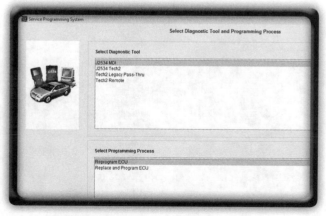

_____ **D.** Obtain the latest vehicle software program updates from the manufacturer, and load the updates into the flash programmer. Connect a battery support unit to the vehicle.

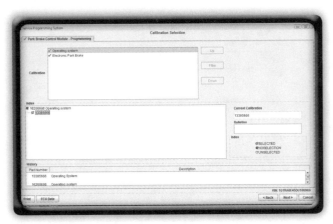

_____ **E.** Identify the vehicle modules to be updated, and use the flash program tool to perform software transfers, software updates, or flash reprogramming.

3. Testing the Horn System:

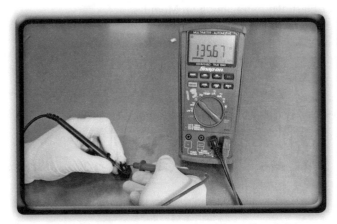

_____ **A.** If the switch leg is good, measure the resistance between terminals 85 and 86 on the horn relay itself. The resistance should be between about 40 and 100 ohms. If not, replace the relay.

_____ **B.** If the horn now honks, check that either terminal 85 (1) or 86 (2) has battery voltage. If 85 has battery voltage then 86 is controlled by the horn switch, or vice-versa.

_____ **C.** Confirm that the horn does not operate. Research circuit operation and circuit diagrams for the horn from the service information. Check for power and ground at horn when the horn switch is operated. If power and ground are present, the horn is faulty and needs to be replaced.

_____ **D.** If battery voltage is present, jump terminal 30 (or 3) to terminal 87 (or 5). The horn should honk. If it does not, check for an open wire between terminal 87 and the horn with a DMM.

_____ **E.** If there is no power to the horn, remove the relay and check for battery voltage at terminal 30 (or 3). If battery voltage is not present, check the horn fuse and the rest of the feed circuit.

_____ **F.** If the resistance is good, either measure the voltage drop across the switch contacts of the relay (30 and 87) or substitute a known good relay.

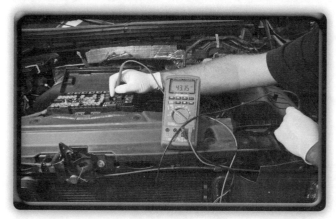

_____ **G.** Connect a DMM between the switch leg terminal and ground. Operate the horn switch; resistance should decrease to less than an ohm. If it does not, search out the high resistance or open circuit back to the horn switch. Suspect either the clock spring or the horn switch itself.

4. Removing the Door Panel:

_____ **A.** Peel back the inner liner from the frame, preserving it for reuse.

_____ **B.** Research removal and reinstallation of the door panel from the manufacturer's service information. Remove fixtures such as the arm rest.

_____ **C.** Remove the cables, and carefully pry the panel from the frame.

_____ **D.** Reinstall the door panel using the reverse procedure while ensuring all electrical connections are reinstalled.

_____ **E.** Remove the switch panel.

5. Testing the Washer System:

_____ **A.** If an electrical fault is indicated by lack of a washer motor sound, check for battery voltage and ground at the pump, when it is activated.

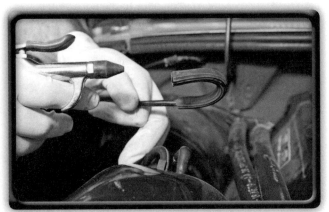

_____ **B.** If the pump spins when activated but does not pump washer fluid, check the hoses and nozzles for obstructions. Blow out with compressed air if necessary.

_____ **C.** Check for the correct solution level in tanks, and listen for washer pump operation.

_____ **D.** If the power and ground circuits are good, measure the resistance of the pump motor and compare to specifications.

_____ **E.** If the power or ground circuit is faulty, perform voltage drop tests on the faulty side, until the fault is located.

Review Questions

_____ **1.** What is the function of a multiplexed system in a vehicle?
  A. It transmits information across one or two wires.
  B. It interprets information.
  C. It sends the information only to the module that needs it.
  D. It processes the information travelling through it.

_____ **2.** Choose the correct statement.
  A. Many vehicles use only one type of networking system.
  B. Usually more than one type of networking system is incorporated in vehicles.
  C. The faster the network, the less expensive it is.
  D. Different networks do not share information between them.

_____ **3.** The communication network system most likely used to transmit high-speed audio and video is:
  A. CAN network.
  B. LIN network.
  C. MOST network.
  D. CAN FD network.

_____ **4.** All of the following statements with respect to MOST networks are true *except*:
  A. They can be plug and play devices that can be added even after servicing.
  B. They can use electrical conductors for sending data signals.
  C. They can use plastic optic fiber for sending data signals.
  D. The highest transfer rate in this network is 25 kbps.

_____ **5.** The horn switch is typically connected:
    A. the ground side of the relay winding.
    B. the power side of the relay winding.
    C. the power side of the horn.
    D. the ground side of the horn.

_____ **6.** One of the best things you can do when checking for module communication on a network is to:
    A. trace out the circuit starting at the battery.
    B. connect a scan tool to the network DLC and check to see if there are any modules that are missing or not communicating.
    C. measure the voltage on CAN-H.
    D. measure the voltage on CAN-L

_____ **7.** When updating the software in the vehicle's PCM:
    A. the vehicle should be running at full operating temperature.
    B. a battery support unit needs to be connected to ensure that the vehicle's battery does not discharge.
    C. the PCM should be disconnected from the vehilce.
    D. the vehicle's negative battery terminal must be disconnected.

_____ **8.** The communication line system used for high-speed controller area network bus (CANbus) systems is:
    A. two-wire.
    B. twisted-pair two-wire.
    C. two-wire shielded.
    D. single-wire.

_____ **9.** The network system that is ideal for the entertainment systems on a vehicle is the:
    A. CAN.
    B. LIN.
    C. MOST.
    D. Ethernet.

_____ **10.** Which of these motors is used to open and close the throttle plate one step at a time, as directed by the powertrain control module (PCM)?
    A. Brushless motor
    B. Permanent magnet motor
    C. Stepper motor
    D. Blower motor

ASE Technician A/Technician B Style Questions

_____ **1.** Tech A says that CANbus A is a low-speed data network. Tech B says that CANbus C is a high-speed network. Who is correct?
    A. Tech A
    B. Tech B
    C. Both A and B
    D. Neither A nor B

_____ **2.** Tech A says that CANbus systems typically use two 120-ohm terminating resistors with a total circuit resistance of 60 ohms. Tech B says that CANbus systems use two 120-ohm terminating resistors with a total circuit resistance of 240 ohms. Who is correct?
    A. Tech A
    B. Tech B
    C. Both A and B
    D. Neither A nor B

_____ **3.** Tech A says that a twisted pair of wires in a wire loom makes it easier to route wires to their destination. Tech B says that the twisted pair of wires transmit differential signals of opposite polarity on the two lines. Who is correct?
    A. Tech A
    B. Tech B
    C. Both A and B
    D. Neither A nor B

_____ **4.** Tech A says that flashing an electronic control module with updated software can solve customer concerns. Tech B says that when flashing an electronic control unit or module, make sure no power loss or disconnect occurs, as the electronic control unit or module may be damaged. Who is correct?
  A. Tech A
  B. Tech B
  C. Both A and B
  D. Neither A nor B

_____ **5.** Tech A says that stepper motors are used as blower motors to achieve various speeds controlled by the driver. Tech B says that stepper motors are used where precise movement must occur, such as in electronic throttle controls. Who is correct?
  A. Tech A
  B. Tech B
  C. Both A and B
  D. Neither A nor B

_____ **6.** Tech A says that resistors are used to control the speed of the blower motor on some vehicles. Tech B says that high speed is obtained when current flows through all of the resistors, to the motor. Who is correct?
  A. Tech A
  B. Tech B
  C. Both A and B
  D. Neither A nor B

_____ **7.** Tech A says that the clock spring is a device used in the steering wheel to transmit signals across the rotating electrical connection. Tech B says that the clock spring must be centered during installation, as it only allows turning both ways a certain number of rotations. Who is correct?
  A. Tech A
  B. Tech B
  C. Both A and B
  D. Neither A nor B

_____ **8.** Tech A says that the horn typically gets its power directly from the horn switch. Tech B says that the horn switch activates a relay. Who is correct?
  A. Tech A
  B. Tech B
  C. Both A and B
  D. Neither A nor B

_____ **9.** Tech A says that if the washer pump operates, but no washer fluid sprays out the nozzles, the windshield wiper motor is faulty. Tech B says that many wiper motors use a low speed brush and a high-speed brush to control wiper speed. Who is correct?
  A. Tech A
  B. Tech B
  C. Both A and B
  D. Neither A nor B

_____ **10.** Tech A says that a heated window grid can be tested for breaks with a voltmeter or test light. Tech B says that heated seats have special tubes in which heated coolant is circulated to heat them up, just like the vehicle's regular heater. Who is correct?
  A. Tech A
  B. Tech B
  C. Both A and B
  D. Neither A nor B

57 Safety, Entertainment, and Antitheft Systems

At the start of each chapter you'll find the NATEF tasks, Knowledge Objectives, and Skills Objectives from the textbook. These are your objectives as you make your way through the exercises in this workbook and the chapter in your textbook. The following activities have been designed to help you refresh your knowledge of the material in this chapter.

NATEF Tasks

- N57001 Diagnose operation of comfort and convenience accessories and related circuits (such as: power window, power seats, pedal height, power locks, truck locks, remote start, moon roof, sun roof, sun shade, remote keyless entry, voice activation, steering wheel controls, back-up camera, park assist, cruise control, and auto dimming headlamps); determine needed repairs. (AST/MAST)
- N57002 Diagnose operation of safety systems and related circuits (such as: horn, airbags, seat belt pretensioners, occupancy classification, wipers, washers, speed control/collision avoidance, heads-up display, park assist, and back-up camera); determine needed repairs. (AST/MAST)
- N57003 Diagnose operation of entertainment and related circuits (such as: radio, DVD, remote CD changer, navigation, amplifiers, speakers, antennas, and voice-activated accessories); determine needed repairs. (AST/MAST)
- N57004 Diagnose operation of security/anti-theft systems and related circuits (such as: theft deterrent, door locks, remote keyless entry, remote start, and starter/fuel disable); determine needed repairs. (AST/MAST)

Knowledge Objectives

After reading this chapter, you will be able to:

- K57001 Describe the purpose, function, and types of cruise control systems.
- K57002 Describe the purpose and function of various collision avoidance systems.
- K57003 Explain the purpose, function, and operation of supplemental restraint systems and components.
- K57004 Describe the types of components and the features that make up the entertainment system.
- K57005 Describe the process of diagnosing the entertainment system.
- K57006 Describe the purpose and function of mobile Global Positioning Systems.
- K57007 Describe the types and function of vehicle antitheft systems.

Skills Objectives

There are no Skills Objectives for this chapter.

Matching

Match the following terms with the correct description or example.

A. System components
B. Driver control components of cruise control
C. Supplemental restraint system
D. Night vision system
E. Drive-by-wire

_____ 1. Components such as On/Off switch, dash indicator lamp, and control switches.
_____ 2. A system that uses a DC stepper motor directly connected to the throttle shaft.
_____ 3. Components such as electronic control module, speed sensor, clutch switch or transmission range sensor.
_____ 4. A system that includes passenger safety devices such as airbags and seat belt pretensioners.
_____ 5. A system that uses special infrared or low-light cameras mounted on the front of the vehicle.

Multiple Choice

Read each item carefully, and then select the best response.

_____ 1. Identify the cruise control actuator that uses a reversible motor and a reduction gear to pull a cable, which moves the throttle plate.
   A. Hydraulic actuator
   B. Electric actuator
   C. Vacuum actuator
   D. Electronic actuator

_____ 2. _____ control systems have no physical connection between the accelerator pedal and the throttle.
   A. Vacuum actuator
   B. Pneumatic actuator
   C. Electronic throttle
   D. Hydraulic actuator

_____ 3. In an adaptive cruise control, _____ sensors are used to determine the vehicle direction.
   A. steering angle
   B. vehicle speed
   C. throttle position
   D. torque

_____ 4. Identify the collision avoidance system that uses radar, laser, or cameras to monitor the space beside the vehicle.
   A. Active headlight system
   B. Lane departure warning system
   C. Night vision system
   D. Side collision avoidance system

_____ 5. _____ systems monitor the lines on the road and warn the driver of imminent departure.
   A. Active headlight
   B. Side collision avoidance
   C. Night vision
   D. Lane departure warning

_____ 6. Identify the gas that is used to rapidly inflate an airbag when a vehicle experiences severe collision.
   A. Helium
   B. Nitrogen
   C. Oxygen
   D. Carbon dioxide

_____ 7. Typically, air bag inflation under a collision takes no longer than _____ second.
   A. 0.70
   B. 0.50
   C. 0.03
   D. 0.09

_____ 8. A(n) _____ pretensioner relies on an explosive charge to tighten the seat belt in a severe frontal accident.
   A. ballistic
   B. electric
   C. mechanical
   D. hydraulic

_____ 9. Identify the type of seat belt pretensioner that is reusable and can be activated repeatedly.
   A. Ballistic pretensioner
   B. Electric pretensioner
   C. Mechanical pretensioner
   D. Hydraulic pretensioner

_____ 10. _____ pretensioner systems rely on inertia to move a sensing mass.
   A. Ballistic
   B. Electric
   C. Pneumatic
   D. Mechanical

True/False

If you believe the statement to be more true than false, write the letter "T" in the space provided. If you believe the statement to be more false than true, write the letter "F."

_____ 1. Cruise control does not have any minimum speed that must be met before it can be set.

_____ 2. A vehicle equipped with electronic throttle control requires an additional throttle actuator.

_____ 3. Some driver fatigue monitoring systems tug on the seat belt to alert the driver.

_____ 4. A secondary safety system has to be activated to work and is only necessary in severe accidents.

_____ 5. An airbag is designed to act as a strong counterforce against the inertia of the occupants.

_____ 6. Airbags are designed to replace seat belts.

_____ 7. Mechanically deployed airbags do not have any electrical circuitry.

_____ 8. If any of the SRS-related devices are deployed, most manufacturers require all of the deployed devices, the crash sensors, and the control module to be replaced.

_____ 9. Most vehicle tracking systems can work very accurately without satellite communication.

_____ 10. When keyless entry is used, personalization of systems is possible.

Fill in the Blank

Read each item carefully, and then complete the statement by filling in the missing word(s).

1. _____ _____ allows the driver to set a cruise speed for the vehicle, which it then memorizes and maintains without throttle input from the driver.

2. Cruise control is deactivated when the driver touches the _____ _____ in an automatic transmission vehicle.

3. A(n) _____ - _____ cruise control uses vacuum to operate a vacuum servo, which is connected to the throttle linkage by a cable.

4. In a(n) _____ _____ _____ the driver does not have to constantly adjust the cruise control in heavier traffic conditions.

5. _____ _____ systems identify pedestrians and animals that pose a hazard to a vehicle when driving.

6. _____ safety systems are ready to operate in any accident and include bumper bars, body panels, seat belts, crumple zones, and collapsible steering columns.

7. A(n) _____ assembly consists of a nylon bag, squib, igniter, gas generator, and airbag triggering mechanism.

8. Airbags in systems with _____ _____ _____ are capable of varying the deployment force of the airbag as needed.

9. A(n) _____ _____ _____ is used to determine the exact location of a vehicle on the Earth's surface.

10. _____ is the method of locating an object using mathematics based on forming a triangle with two known points.

Labeling

Label the following diagrams with the correct terms.

1. Components of a vacuum operated cruise control actuator:

Vacuum Actuator

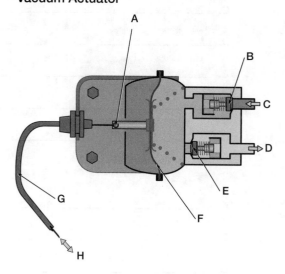

A. _____

B. _____

C. _____

D. _____

E. _____

F. _____

G. _____

H. _____

2. Typical SRS injury reduction devices:

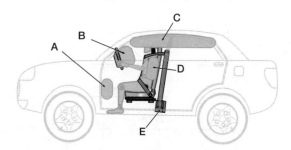

A. _____

B. _____

C. _____

D. _____

E. _____

3. Parts of an airbag assembly:

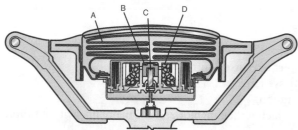

A. _____

B. _____

C. _____

D. _____

4. Components of a smart airbag system:

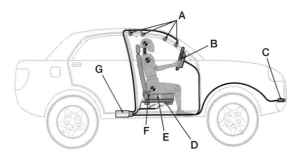

A. _____

B. _____

C. _____

D. _____

E. _____

F. _____

G. _____

5. Dual-stage airbag (60% deployment):

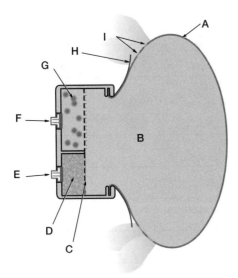

A. _____

B. _____

C. _____

D. _____

E. _____

F. _____

G. _____

H. _____

I. _____

Review Questions

_____ **1.** Choose the correct statement with respect to cruise control.
   A. It is not an integral part of the safety system.
   B. It controls the vehicle's steering operation.
   C. It sets a cruise speed for the vehicle, which it then memorizes and maintains without throttle input from the driver.
   D. Once the speed of the vehicle is set, it cannot be changed manually.

_____ **2.** All of the following are types of cruise control acutators *except*:
   A. hydraulic actuator
   B. electric actuator
   C. electronic throttle actuator
   D. vacuum actuator

_____ **3.** All of the following actions will be performed by a vehicle pre-crash system *except*:
   A. pretensioning the seat belts.
   B. prepositioning the seats.
   C. warning audio for the incoming vehicle.
   D. rolling up the windows and sunroof.

_____ **4.** Which of the following is the purpose of active headlight systems in a vehicle?
- **A.** They warn the driver of imminent departure.
- **B.** They illuminate the road around the corner.
- **C.** They monitor vehicles and objects behind the vehicle.
- **D.** They enhance the image of the road and project it on the windshield.

_____ **5.** Which of the following components are a part of secondary (active) safety systems designed to protect occupants?
- **A.** Seat belt pretensioners
- **B.** Body panels
- **C.** Crumple zones
- **D.** Collapsible steering columns

_____ **6.** Choose the correct statement with respect to the deployment of air bags in the vehicle.
- **A.** All airbags are triggered electrically.
- **B.** A steel ball releases a firing pin into the squib in the case of an electrically deployed airbag.
- **C.** The air bags are filled with air.
- **D.** the airbag deploys due to simultaneous actions occurring within the squib, the igniter, and the gas generator.

_____ **7.** Each of the following are categories of theft-deterrent systems *except*:
- **A.** Component identification
- **B.** Vehicle locking
- **C.** Seat belt pretensioners.
- **D.** Engine and transmission immobilization

_____ **8.** The radio reception issue is to be checked by verifying all of the following *except* by:
- **A.** selecting a station that you know comes in well in your location.
- **B.** checking for good power and ground connections.
- **C.** detecting any unwanted ripple or noise in the power circuit.
- **D.** checking Internet connectivity of the vehicle.

_____ **9.** The GPS unit establishes its own location:
- **A.** by transmitting signals to satellites.
- **B.** by the time it takes for signals to arrive from satellites.
- **C.** by contacting the nearest radio tower.
- **D.** with the help of the CPU.

_____ **10.** Dead locking adds a further level of security by:
- **A.** requiring manual locking in addition to automatic locking.
- **B.** locking each door with a different code.
- **C.** activating small electric motors in each door lock mechanism, mechanically locking them.
- **D.** requiring a password be entered before the doors unlock.

ASE Technician A/Technician B Style Questions

_____ **1.** Tech A says that the cruise control disengages when the driver steps on the brake pedal. Tech B says that adaptive cruise control uses radar or laser systems to sense the distance and speed of the vehicle in front. Who is correct?
- **A.** Tech A
- **B.** Tech B
- **C.** Both A and B
- **D.** Neither A nor B

_____ **2.** Tech A says that some night vision systems display an enhanced image of the road, in front of the vehicle, on the windshield. Tech B says that pre-crash systems are designed to make it faster for a person to exit a vehicle after a crash. Who is correct?
- **A.** Tech A
- **B.** Tech B
- **C.** Both A and B
- **D.** Neither A nor B

_____ **3.** Tech A says that SRS air bags stay inflated until rescue people arrive on the scene. Tech B says that in severe collisions, wearing seat belts is not important if the vehicle is equipped with SRS airbags. Who is correct?
  A. Tech A
  B. Tech B
  C. Both A and B
  D. Neither A nor B

_____ **4.** Tech A says that in a collision, SRS air bags are quickly inflated by an electric air compressor. Tech B says that SRS air bags can be repacked and reused after a collision. Who is correct?
  A. Tech A
  B. Tech B
  C. Both A and B
  D. Neither A nor B

_____ **5.** Tech A says that some entertainment systems have speed-dependent volume, which changes the volume of the radio based on vehicle speed. Tech B says that some warning messages can be broadcast over the audio system. Who is correct?
  A. Tech A
  B. Tech B
  C. Both A and B
  D. Neither A nor B

_____ **6.** Tech A says that microdots are used as a theft deterrent in some vehicles. Tech B says that microdot is the name given to a single datum transmitted over a vehicle network. Who is correct?
  A. Tech A
  B. Tech B
  C. Both A and B
  D. Neither A nor B

_____ **7.** Tech A says that immobilization occurs when the theft-deterrent system prevents the vehicle's engine from starting or the transmission from operating without the properly authorized key. Tech B says that on some vehicles, when the driver leaves the vehicle and the key is beyond a certain range, the theft-deterrent module automatically locks the vehicle. Who is correct?
  A. Tech A
  B. Tech B
  C. Both A and B
  D. Neither A nor B

_____ **8.** Tech A says that most SRS systems use a safing sensor to reduce the possibility of accidental deployment of the airbags. Tech B says that airbags are designed to act like a nice, soft pillow in an accident. Who is correct?
  A. Tech A
  B. Tech B
  C. Both A and B
  D. Neither A nor B

_____ **9.** Tech A says that If any of the SRS-related devices are deployed for any reason, most manufacturers require all of the deployed devices, the crash sensors, and the control module to be replaced. Tech B says that there are relatively large holes in the rear of an airbag that allow it to quickly deflate after deployment. Who is correct?
  A. Tech A
  B. Tech B
  C. Both A and B
  D. Neither A nor B

_____ **10.** Tech A says that in some vehicles, airbag deployment can be based on the speed of the impact and the weight of the seat occupant. Tech B says that the SRS seat belt pretensioners tighten the seat belt when you connect the seat belt. Who is correct?
  A. Tech A
  B. Tech B
  C. Both A and B
  D. Neither A nor B

Principles of Heating and Air-Conditioning Systems

At the start of each chapter you'll find the NATEF tasks, Knowledge Objectives, and Skills Objectives from the textbook. These are your objectives as you make your way through the exercises in this workbook and the chapter in your textbook. The following activities have been designed to help you refresh your knowledge of the material in this chapter.

NATEF Tasks

There are no NATEF Tasks for this chapter.

Knowledge Objectives

After reading this chapter, you will be able to:

- K58001 Describe the history and regulations of automotive HVAC systems.
- K58002 Explain the basic principles of HVAC systems.
- K58003 Explain the purpose and function of AC components and controls.
- K58004 Explain the purpose, function, and types of HVAC restrictions.
- K58005 Explain the purpose, function, and types of switches and control circuits.
- K58006 Explain the purpose and function of hoses, pipes, lines, and O-rings.
- K58007 Explain the purpose and function of driers.
- K58008 Explain the purpose, function, and types of HVAC compressors and clutches.
- K58009 Explain the purpose function and types of HVAC heat exchangers (condenser and evaporator).
- K58010 Explain the purpose, function, and types of refrigerants and refrigerant oils.
- K58011 Explain the operation of each type of AC system.
- K58012 Explain the operation of the fixed orifice tube system.
- K58013 Explain the operation of the thermal expansion valve system.
- K58014 Explain the purpose and function of heating system.
- K58015 Describe the purpose and function of the heating and ventilation system components.

Skills Objectives

There are no Skills Objectives in this chapter.

Matching

Match the following terms with the correct description or example.

A. Externally equalized valve
B. Axial piston compressor
C. Barrier-type hose
D. Chlorofluorocarbon (CFC)
E. Closed-loop system
F. Condensation
G. Convection
H. Double crimping
I. Electric servo
J. Evaporator

K. Filter media
L. Fixed-orifice tube system
M. Heat transfer
N. High-pressure switch
O. Parallel flow condenser
P. Refrigerant
Q. Restriction
R. Swash plate
S. Tubes
T. Vaporization

_____ **1.** The name given to a chemical compound designed to meet the needs of the refrigeration system.

_____ **2.** The process of transferring heat by the circulatory movement that occurs in a gas or fluid as areas of differing temperatures exchange places due to variations in density and the action of gravity.

_____ **3.** A system with a fixed-orifice tube that uses an accumulator between the evaporator and the compressor.

_____ **4.** An air-conditioning door actuator controlled by electricity.

_____ **5.** Metal pipes running side to side or up and down that the coolant or refrigerant travels through.

_____ **6.** A totally self-contained system with no materials entering or exiting.

_____ **7.** A condenser with multiple parallel tubes flowing from one side tank to the other.

_____ **8.** The changing of a gas into a liquid through cooling.

_____ **9.** The changing of a liquid to a gas through boiling.

_____ **10.** Overcrimping or recrimping a fitting to keep it from leaking. It normally results in a bigger leak and is not recommended.

_____ **11.** Another name for an axial plate.

_____ **12.** A design of compressor that uses an angled plate (swash plate) to create the piston movement.

_____ **13.** A screen designed to keep debris from the TXV that is normally located in the receiver dryer.

_____ **14.** The flow of heat from a hotter part to a cooler part; it can occur in solids, liquids, or gases.

_____ **15.** A manufactured compound designed to be used as a refrigerant. It is now illegal due to the high chlorine content.

_____ **16.** A style of TXV where the external valve uses the sensing bulb on the outlet side to overcome spring pressure to open the valve.

_____ **17.** The air-conditioning component normally located in the passenger compartment designed to allow low-pressure refrigerant liquid to change states to a gas.

_____ **18.** A blockage that partially stops or slows the flow of a material such as refrigerant.

_____ **19.** A switch designed to open at a predetermined high pressure to protect the compressor; it is normally located on the high-side line near the compressor.

_____ **20.** A rubber hose made with a nylon bladder inside to contain substances with small molecular structures, such as R-134a.

Multiple Choice

Read each item carefully, and then select the best response.

_____ **1.** The federal law that regulates air emissions from stationary and mobile sources and contains all of the motor vehicle air-conditioning requirements and laws is called the _____.
   A. National Air Quality Standards Act
   B. Clean Air Act
   C. Air Conditioning Act
   D. Environmental Protection Act

_____ **2.** The amount of water vapor in the air expressed as a percentage is called _____.
   A. saturation level
   B. condensation point
   C. relative humidity
   D. evaporation point

_____ **3.** The process of transferring heat through matter by the movement of heat energy through solids from one particle to another is called _____.
   A. convection
   B. conduction
   C. radiation
   D. evaporation

_____ **4.** Heat energy is measured in _____.
   A. degrees Fahrenheit
   B. degrees Celsius
   C. British thermal units
   D. relative humidity

_____ 5. The heat required to change the water at its maximum temperature from a liquid to a gas is called _____.
   A. latent heat of evaporation
   B. latent heat of condensation
   C. latent heat of freezing
   D. latent heat of vaporization

_____ 6. The _____ changes a low-pressure refrigerant gas to a high-pressure gas and provides the needed refrigerant movement in the system.
   A. condenser
   B. compressor
   C. evaporator
   D. restrictor

_____ 7. Hot high-pressure gas enters the _____ from the compressor; the gas flows through a series of coils, ambient air removes the heat from the hot high-pressure gas, which begins to change into a liquid.
   A. condenser
   B. evaporator
   C. restriction
   D. orifice tube

_____ 8. Dichlorodifluoromethane, commonly known as _____, is a member of the CFC family of gases and was the first common refrigerant to be used in an automotive air conditioner.
   A. R-10
   B. R-12
   C. R-124b
   D. R-134a

_____ 9. All of the following are common oils used in refrigeration systems, _except_:
   A. POE oil
   B. mineral oil
   C. PAG oil
   D. copaiba oil

_____ 10. The _____ compressor works in much the same way as the axial piston compressor except that it has only a single row of pistons instead of two opposing rows of pistons.
   A. rotary vane
   B. scroll-type
   C. swash plate
   D. wobble plate

_____ 11. The air-conditioning system may use a _____ to dampen pulsations and noise from the compressor.
   A. muffler
   B. restrictor
   C. noise damper
   D. serpentine condenser

_____ 12. A _____ has a sensing device on the outlet side of the evaporator that senses changes in temperature and a valve that can vary the amount of opening to allow more or less gaseous refrigerant through.
   A. Bernoulli valve
   B. thermal expansion valve
   C. fixed-orifice tube
   D. velocity restrictor

_____ 13. According to the automotive industry numbering system a ½" air-conditioning hose would be referred to as a(n) _____ hose.
   A. #4
   B. #6
   C. #8
   D. #10

_____ 14. Nitrile butadiene rubber and hydrogenated nitrile butadiene rubber have both been used to make _____ for air-conditioning systems.
   A. gaskets
   B. barrier hose cores

    C. O-rings
    D. all of the above

_____ **15.** Fixed-orifice tube systems use a(n) _____ to ensure that a pure gas is delivered to the compressor.
    A. receiver filter drier
    B. accumulator
    C. Schrader valve
    D. Bernoulli filter

_____ **16.** The _____ is designed to ensure that the temperature of the refrigerant leaving the evaporator is between 5°F and 20°F higher than the boiling point of the refrigerant at the current operating pressure.
    A. superheat spring
    B. accumulator
    C. desiccant
    D. Schrader valve

_____ **17.** The thermal expansion valve uses an _____ to open and close the port.
    A. internally equalized valve
    B. externally equalized valve
    C. H block valve
    D. any of the above

_____ **18.** The _____ is located inside the cabin in the plastic box with the air-conditioning evaporator.
    A. defroster
    B. heater core
    C. condenser
    D. accumulator

_____ **19.** Air doors are controlled by _____.
    A. cables
    B. vacuum servos
    C. electric servos
    D. any of the above

_____ **20.** A common type of blower motor control is a(n) _____ that uses resistors in series to regulate the speed of the fan.
    A. resistor pack
    B. potentiometer
    C. resistor block
    D. either A or C

True/False

If you believe the statement to be more true than false, write the letter "T" in the space provided. If you believe the statement to be more false than true, write the letter "F."

_____ **1.** Automotive air-conditioning service and repair technicians need to have a special license.

_____ **2.** When pressure is lowered on a gas, its temperature rises; when pressure is raised, its temperature drops.

_____ **3.** The amount of heat given up by steam to turn back into a liquid is 970 Btu and is called latent heat of condensation.

_____ **4.** With the use of refrigerants, maintaining vaporization and condensing points at normal ambient temperatures is simply done by raising or reducing the pressure of the refrigerant.

_____ **5.** PAG oil mixed with mineral oil creates a hazardous gas that can corrode the air-conditioning system.

_____ **6.** When the volume above a compressor piston reduces, the refrigerant is forced out of the cylinder through the suction reed valves.

_____ **7.** Sanden scroll-type compressors are used as air-conditioning compressors as well as transmission oil pumps and power steering pumps.

_____ **8.** The clutch electrical winding typically has a resistance value of 3–5 ohms on a 12-volt DC air-conditioning compressor.

_____ **9.** The condenser fan is designed to pull or push air from in front of the vehicle through the condenser to remove heat and reduce the pressure on the high side.

_____ 10. Some vehicles, such as conversion vans, minivans, and SUVs, use a dual evaporator system composed of two different units to cool the vehicle.

_____ 11. The site glass is a glass portal used only with R-134a refrigerant that allows you to look into the air-conditioning system and see the liquid refrigerant flow.

_____ 12. A fixed-orifice tube with a diameter of 0.057" (1.4 mm) would be blue in color.

_____ 13. Desiccant is a chemical compound that can absorb moisture and help keep the air-conditioning system dry.

_____ 14. The receiver filter drier is located between the condenser outlet and the TXV inlet.

_____ 15. The heater core is a small radiator consisting of tubes, fins, and tanks.

Fill in the Blank

Read each item carefully, and then complete the statement by filling in the missing word(s).

1. Automotive air conditioning is federally regulated by the _____ _____ _____.

2. Heat always transfers from _____ objects to _____ objects.

3. The transfer of heat through the emission of energy in the form of invisible waves is called _____.

4. One pound of water at _____ _____ and at a temperature of 32°F (0°C) would require 1 Btu of energy added to increase the temperature 1 degree Fahrenheit.

5. At 32°F, the latent heat of _____ begins.

6. If the velocity of a liquid rises, the pressure of the liquid must drop according to the _____ principle.

7. Tetrafluoroethane, commonly known as _____, was the replacement for R-12 refrigerant.

8. When the piston is drawn away from the compressor head, the pumping chamber volume increases and the _____ _____ _____ allows low-pressure refrigerant to enter the pumping chamber.

9. The air-conditioning _____ _____ is an electromagnetic device that uses a metal plate with no friction material and spring steel to engage and disengage the compressor to the drive pulley.

10. The condenser is normally positioned in front of the radiator where it is exposed to maximum _____ _____ when the vehicle is in motion.

11. A(n) _____ condenser is constructed from a single tube that snakes back and forth across the condenser.

12. The job of the _____ is to take a low-pressure liquid and transform it to a low-pressure gas.

13. Barrier-type hose is constructed with a nylon inner core to prevent moisture _____ and permeation of refrigerant from the air-conditioning system.

14. _____ _____ are placed on both the low and the high side of an air-conditioning system to allow an entry point for checking pressures.

15. If the air-conditioning system loses all refrigerant, the _____ _____ cycling switch will turn off the compressor clutch and possibly save the compressor from failure due to no refrigerant and oil.

16. The _____ _____ valve is located at the entry to the evaporator and provides a throttling or restricting function to control the quantity of refrigerant entering the evaporator.

17. The _____ _____ switch is a normally closed, temperature-controlled switch that controls the compressor clutch.

18. Attached to the spinning shaft of the blower motor is a plastic cage with fins to pull or push air called a(n) _____ _____.

19. Some blower motor systems use _____ _____ _____ to control fan speed, this is done by controlling "on" time compared to "off" time on the ground side of the circuit.

20. Some manufacturers use an activated charcoal cabin _____ _____, which helps trap odors and airborne pollutants such as carbon monoxide and oxides of nitrogen.

Labeling

Label the following diagrams with the correct terms.

1. Components of an air-conditioning unit:

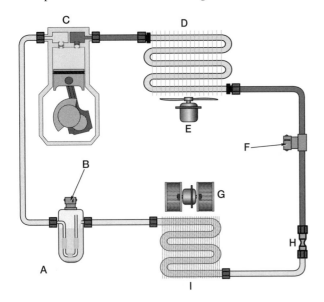

A. _____

B. _____

C. _____

D. _____

E. _____

F. _____

G. _____

H. _____

I. _____

2. Axial piston compressor:

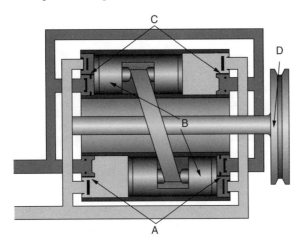

A. _____

B. _____

C. _____

D. _____

3. Rotary vane compressor:

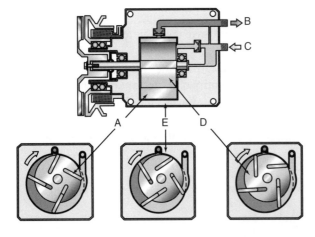

A. _____

B. _____

C. _____

D. _____

E. _____

4. Sanden scroll-type air-conditioning compressor and clutch:

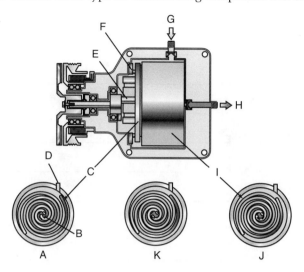

A. _____

B. _____

C. _____

D. _____

E. _____

F. _____

G. _____

H. _____

I. _____

J. _____

K. _____

5. Pressure drop and speed increase through a restriction:

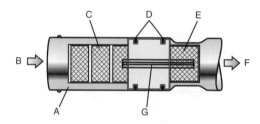

A. _____

B. _____

C. _____

D. _____

E. _____

F. _____

G. _____

6. Accumulator:

A. _____

B. _____

C. _____

D. _____

E. _____

F. _____

G. _____

H. _____

I. _____

J. _____

7. Thermal expansion valve:

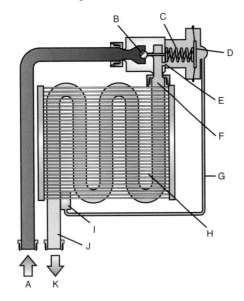

A. _____

B. _____

C. _____

D. _____

E. _____

F. _____

G. _____

H. _____

I. _____

J. _____

K. _____

8. TXV block:

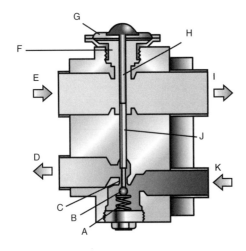

A. _____

B. _____

C. _____

D. _____

E. _____

F. _____

G. _____

H. _____

I. _____

J. _____

K. _____

9. Receiver filter drier:

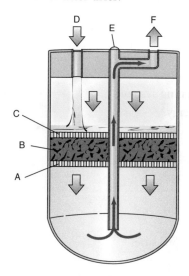

A. _____

B. _____

C. _____

D. _____

E. _____

F. _____

10. Heater controls:

Heater control valve:

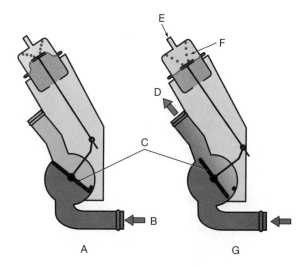

A. _____

B. _____

C. _____

D. _____

E. _____

F. _____

G. _____

Blend door in the "Mixing" position:

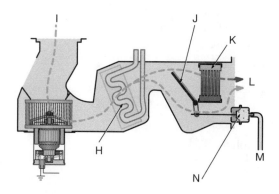

H. _____

I. _____

J. _____

K. _____

L. _____

M. _____

N. _____

Review Questions

_____ 1. Automotive air-conditioning service and repair technicians need to have which special license?
  A. Hazardous materials license
  B. Master Technician license
  C. 609 license
  D. No license is required to work on automotive air-conditioning systems.

_____ 2. How does air-conditioning absorb a large amount of heat energy?
  A. By evaporating a liquid
  B. By freezing a liquid
  C. By cooling a liquid
  D. By cooling a gas

_____ 3. All of the following are properties of a refrigerant _except_:
  A. It has a super low boiling point.
  B. It changes its state without breaking down.
  C. It vaporizes and condenses at the correct temperature and pressure.
  D. Its pressure remains unchanged during the cooling cycle.

_____ 4. Which of the following components provides the needed refrigerant movement in the system?
  A. Compressor
  B. Condenser
  C. Restriction
  D. Evaporator

_____ 5. Which of the following components in the AC transforms low-pressure fluid to low-pressure gas?
  A. Compressor
  B. Condenser
  C. Restriction
  D. Evaporator

_____ 6. The fixed orifice tube is used for:
  A. sensing changes in temperature.
  B. blocking the flow of liquid refrigerant through the system.
  C. adjusting heat in the cabin.
  D. allowing only a specific amount of liquid refrigerant through at a time.

_____ 7. Choose the correct statement with respect to pressure switches.
  A. They are used to display the pressure drop and rise in the system.
  B. They are in parallel connection with the AC compressor.
  C. They send inputs to the control module to vary the compressor speed.
  D. They are used to engage and disengage the compressor clutch.

_____ 8. All of the following statements with respect to hoses, pipes, and tubes are true _except_:
  A. Heater hose can substitute for air-conditioning hose if needed.
  B. Pipes are used particularly where no give or movement is necessary.
  C. Hoses are slid into the pipes and a crimp is used to fasten them.
  D. All air-conditioning hoses must be a barrier-type hose.

_____ 9. Choose the correct statement with respect to driers.
  A. Driers are circulated in the system.
  B. They absorb any moisture in the system.
  C. They are left open to absorb the moisture.
  D. They are placed in the restriction.

_____ 10. What type of compressor uses two interwoven scrolls?
  A. Variable displacement compressor
  B. Sanden scroll-type compressor
  C. Rotary vane compressor
  D. Sanden wobble plate compressor

ASE Technician A/Technician B Style Questions

_____ **1.** Tech A says that one advantage of an air conditioner is that the system removes water from the air. Tech B says that an AC compressor clutch is activated by a magnetic field. Who is correct?
   A. Tech A
   B. Tech B
   C. Both A and B
   D. Neither A nor B

_____ **2.** Tech A says that automotive air-conditioning is regulated by the EPA. Tech B says that EPA tests air-conditioning systems every five years. Who is correct?
   A. Tech A
   B. Tech B
   C. Both A and B
   D. Neither A nor B

_____ **3.** Tech A says that an accumulator creates the pressure needed for the air-conditioning system to operate.
Tech B says that the high side refers to refrigerant entering the compressor. Who is correct?
   A. Tech A
   B. Tech B
   C. Both A and B
   D. Neither A nor B

_____ **4.** Tech A says that heat is removed from the passenger compartment by the heater core. Tech B says that heat in the cab is absorbed by the refrigerant and is transferred to the outside air at the condenser. Who is correct?
   A. Tech A
   B. Tech B
   C. Both A and B
   D. Neither A nor B

_____ **5.** Tech A says that conduction is when heat transfers through solids. Tech B says that radiation is when heat travels through space. Who is correct?
   A. Tech A
   B. Tech B
   C. Both A and B
   D. Neither A nor B

_____ **6.** Tech A says that the air-conditioning compressor creates high-pressure liquid. Tech B says that the restriction creates a physical change in refrigerant from a liquid to a gas. Who is correct?
   A. Tech A
   B. Tech B
   C. Both A and B
   D. Neither A nor B

_____ **7.** Tech A says that when an air-conditioning system freezes up, the refrigerant freezes and stops the cooling process. Tech B says that when an air-conditioning system freezes up, the evaporator coils are covered with frozen water molecules that stop airflow across the coils, thus preventing cooling. Who is correct?
   A. Tech A
   B. Tech B
   C. Both A and B
   D. Neither A nor B

_____ **8.** Tech A says that the evaporator is on the high side of the system. Tech B says that the condenser transfers heat to the atmosphere. Who is correct?
   A. Tech A
   B. Tech B
   C. Both A and B
   D. Neither A nor B

_____ **9.** Tech A says that R-134a replaced R-12 as an approved refrigerant. Tech B says that HFO-1234yf refrigerant is flammable. Who is correct?

A. Tech A

B. Tech B

C. Both A and B

D. Neither A nor B

_____ **10.** Tech A says that the engine thermostat controls the flow of coolant through the heater system. Tech B says that the heater core can have engine coolant or refrigerant flowing through it, depending on whether heat or cool is commanded. Who is correct?

A. Tech A

B. Tech B

C. Both A and B

D. Neither A nor B

Heating and Air-Conditioning Systems and Service

At the start of each chapter you'll find the NATEF tasks, Knowledge Objectives, and Skills Objectives from the textbook. These are your objectives as you make your way through the exercises in this workbook and the chapter in your textbook. The following activities have been designed to help you refresh your knowledge of the material in this chapter.

NATEF Tasks

- N59001 Identify and interpret heating and air conditioning problems; determine needed action. (AST/MAST)
- N59002 Performance test A/C system; identify problems. (AST/MAST)
- N59003 Identify abnormal operating noises in the A/C system; determine needed action. (AST/MAST)
- N59004 Inspect A/C condenser for airflow restrictions; perform necessary action. (MLR/AST/MAST)
- N59005 Inspect evaporator housing water drain; perform needed action. (AST/MAST)
- N59006 Identify the source of HVAC system odors. (MLR/AST/MAST)
- N59007 Diagnose A/C system conditions that cause the protection devices (pressure, thermal, and/or control module) to interrupt system operation; determine needed action. (MAST)
- N59008 Leak test A/C system; determine needed action. (AST/MAST)
- N59009 Identify refrigerant type; select and connect proper gauge set/test equipment; record temperature and pressure readings. (AST/MAST)
- N59010 Identify A/C system refrigerant; test for sealants; recover, evacuate, and charge A/C system; add refrigerant oil as required.
- N59011 Recycle, label, and store refrigerant. (AST/MAST)
- N59012 Inspect, remove, and/or replace A/C compressor drive belts, pulleys, tensioners, and visually inspect A/C components for signs of leaks; determine needed action. (MLR/AST/MAST)
- N59013 Remove, inspect, reinstall and/or replace A/C compressor and mountings; determine recommended oil type and quantity. (AST/MAST)
- N59014 Determine need for an additional A/C system filter; perform needed action. (AST/MAST)
- N59015 Remove and inspect A/C system mufflers, hoses, lines, fittings, O-rings, seals, and service valves; perform needed action. (AST/MAST)
- N59016 Remove, inspect, reinstall, and/or replace condenser; determine required oil type and quantity. (MAST)
- N59017 Remove, inspect, and replace receiver/drier or accumulator/drier; determine recommended oil type and quantity. (AST/MAST)
- N59018 Remove, inspect, and install expansion valve or orifice (expansion) tube. (AST/MAST)
- N59019 Determine procedure to remove and reinstall evaporator; determine required oil type and quantity. (AST/MAST)
- N59020 Inspect condition of refrigerant oil removed from A/C system; determine needed action. (AST/MAST)
- N59021 Determine recommended oil and oil capacity for system application. (AST/MAST)
- N59022 Perform correct use and maintenance of refrigerant handling equipment according to equipment manufacturer's standards. (AST/MAST)

Knowledge Objectives

After reading this chapter, you will be able to:

- K59001 Describe the process of servicing the air-conditioning system.
- K59002 Describe AC system refrigerant capacity and how to identify overcharge and undercharge conditions.
- K59003 Identify common AC services and tools.

Skills Objectives

After reading this chapter, you will be able to:

- S59001 Perform A/C system component inspections.
- S59002 Inspect and Handle system refrigerant.
- S59003 Repair compressor failure.
- S59004 Repair heat exchanger, expansion device, or refrigerant line failure.
- S59005 Evaluate condition of refrigerant system oil.

Matching

Match the following terms with the correct description or example.

A. Accumulator
B. Air-conditioning compressor clutch
C. Air-conditioning machine
D. Anemometer
E. Charge
F. Heated diode
G. Microleak detector
H. Micron gauge
I. Muffler
J. Oiler

K. Overcharging
L. Performance testing
M. Pressure transients
N. Reclaim/recycle machine
O. Reclaiming
P. Refrigerant identifiers
Q. Sniffer
R. State of charge
S. Ultrasonic
T. Vacuum pump

_____ 1. A device to quiet the pipes of the air-conditioning system with baffles placed inside to deaden the sound of refrigerant moving.

_____ 2. Minor fluctuations on the gauges that may indicate a problem.

_____ 3. The process of recreating a driving situation to check air-conditioning performance and vent temperature.

_____ 4. A pump used to evacuate the air-conditioning system and put it into a deep vacuum or low pressure to remove moisture.

_____ 5. A solution used to detect refrigeration leaks.

_____ 6. An electronic device used to determine the source of leaks.

_____ 7. A method of leak detection that uses a sensitive microphone to hear small refrigerant leaks by amplifying the hissing noise.

_____ 8. A machine designed to recover, recycle, evacuate, leak test, and recharge (R/R/R) the air-conditioning system.

_____ 9. Overfilling of the air-conditioning system; may result in poor cooling or mechanical failure of the system.

_____ 10. A device placed between the evaporator and the compressor to collect liquid refrigerant and prevent it from entering the compressor.

_____ 11. A device designed to measure vacuum very precisely.

_____ 12. The process of removing refrigerant from the air-conditioning system by using an air-conditioning machine; also called recovering.

_____ 13. A device that measures airflow in feet per minute (fpm).

_____ 14. Devices used to check for impurities in the air-conditioning system.

_____ 15. The amount of refrigerant present in the system or the process of installing refrigerant in the system.

_____ 16. An engagement device connected to the compressor crankshaft to engage the crankshaft with a belt-driven pulley.

_____ 17. The amount of refrigerant in a system compared to how much should be in it.

_____ 18. An air-conditioning machine designed to remove and recycle refrigerant for reuse.

_____ 19. A sniffer that uses electricity to determine if there is a refrigerant leak.

_____ 20. A device used to add oil to the air-conditioning system.

Multiple Choice

Read each item carefully, and then select the best response.

_____ 1. The only way to determine the type of refrigerant in a system is with the aid of a(n) _____.
   A. refrigerant identifier
   B. performance test
   C. pressure gauge set
   D. anemometer

_____ 2. The _____ test is used to check refrigerant for acidic contaminants and water intrusion.
   A. purity
   B. acid
   C. refrigerant identification
   D. contaminant

_____ 3. When testing the air-conditioning system, an engine's revolutions per minute should be at _____, which is the ideal and average rpm for the majority of air-conditioning systems on vehicles.
   A. 600
   B. 1200
   C. 1800
   D. 2400

_____ 4. Generally, if a(n) _____ is triggered, the cause is overcurrent, meaning the current flow has become elevated.
   A. circuit breaker
   B. thermal unit
   C. fuse
   D. any of the above

_____ 5. A(n) _____ comes in both mechanical and digital styles and has a low-side and a high-side gauge connected to a common manifold that can be used for manual servicing of the air-conditioning system.
   A. air-conditioning machine
   B. reclaim/recycle machine
   C. sealant detector
   D. pressure gauge set

_____ 6. A(n) _____ is used to determine what the high- and low-side pressures should be at a given outside temperature and humidity in a properly functioning system.
   A. vacuum pump
   B. anemometer
   C. PT chart
   D. relative humidity chart

_____ 7. What type of gauge is designed to read negative pressure?
   A. Pressure gauge
   B. Vacuum gauge
   C. Oil-filled gauge
   D. Transient gauge

_____ 8. Supersensitive microphones that can pick up the hiss of a leak that is too small to be heard by human ears are called _____ sniffers.
   A. corona-suppression
   B. heated diode
   C. ultrasonic
   D. supersonic

_____ 9. What type of sniffer is considered the best for working with R-134a refrigerant?
   A. Heated diode
   B. Ultrasonic
   C. Corona-suppression
   D. Ultraviolet

_____ **10.** While performing a dye test to find a leak, ultraviolet light will cause the refrigerant dye to glow with a(n) _____ color.
   A. orange
   B. blue
   C. green
   D. either A or C

_____ **11.** What type of testing works great for testing discharged systems or for prechecking for a leak after repairs have been made and before recharging the system?
   A. Ultraviolet
   B. Nitrogen
   C. Ultrasonic
   D. Heated diode

_____ **12.** The reclaiming or recovering process uses a(n) _____ to remove refrigerant from the system.
   A. vacuum pump
   B. air-conditioning machine
   C. oiler
   D. drier

_____ **13.** While thoroughly flushing a system usually removes all debris and contaminants, installing a(n) _____ provides an extra level of protection for the compressor and expansion valve or orifice tube.
   A. desiccant bag
   B. drier
   C. additional filter
   D. Schrader valve

_____ **14.** The _____ needs to be removed and inspected whenever there are leaks or the desiccant is failing to dry the refrigerant.
   A. receiver/drier
   B. condenser
   C. accumulator
   D. either A or C

_____ **15.** With a micron gauge, the pressure is measured in microns, or _____ of 1 millimeter.
   A. one-tenth
   B. one-hundredth
   C. one-thousandth
   D. one-hundred thousandth

True/False

If you believe the statement to be more true than false, write the letter "T" in the space provided. If you believe the statement to be more false than true, write the letter "F."

_____ **1.** The proper charge for the air conditioner can be found under the hood on the air-conditioning identification sticker.

_____ **2.** Overcharging the air-conditioning system will affect the orifice tube and TXV systems in the same manner.

_____ **3.** An undercharged air-conditioning system will cause an unusual smell throughout the cabin when running the air conditioner.

_____ **4.** A high-pressure switch may have a cutoff pressure of 400 psi; at that pressure the switch opens because the pressure is high enough to cause the hoses and lines to rupture.

_____ **5.** Allowing sealant to be drawn into a refrigerant identifier or air-conditioning machine can ruin them.

_____ **6.** Oil-filled pressure gauges do not allow the needle to move fast enough for you to see pressure transients.

_____ **7.** The air-conditioning technician should perform maintenance and repair of the air-conditioning machine after every use.

_____ **8.** An air-conditioning machine allows you to remove and store the old refrigerant by refilling the same tank that the new refrigerant came in.

_____ **9.** The air-conditioning system should be flushed if the compressor comes apart or if the desiccant bag breaks open.

_____ **10.** Any time lines are loosened, the O-rings in the fittings must be replaced or there is potential for leaks.

_____ **11.** Typically, the TXV is mounted on the front of the evaporator.

_____ **12.** The refrigerant R-12 used a mineral oil, while the refrigerant R-134a uses a polyalkylene glycol (PAG) oil.

_____ **13.** Charging an air-conditioning system is performed after the air-conditioning system has been evacuated and before any oil is replaced.

_____ **14.** Changing the vacuum pump oil regularly will extend the life of the pump and make it reach maximum vacuum quicker.

_____ **15.** Leaks from the heater core can result in coolant misting out of the vents or coolant dripping onto the passenger-side carpet, or both.

Fill in the Blank

Read each item carefully, and then complete the statement by filling in the missing word(s).

1. Carrying out a (n) _____ _____ of the HVAC system is the way we verify the customer concern.

2. The _____ _____ _____ is best tested by removing all of the refrigerant from the air-conditioning system and comparing that amount to the manufacturer's specifications.

3. If the _____ _____ becomes clogged with leaves or debris over time, the water will not be able to drain, it will stagnate and begin growing bacteria, creating an unpleasant odor.

4. When charging an air-conditioning system on the high side only, if the low side gauge does not reach zero before _____ _____, the TXV or orifice tube is bad.

5. An aftermarket _____ _____ has the fittings and oil to change an R-12 unit over to an R-134a unit.

6. With a(n) _____-_____ sniffer, refrigerant gas is used as an insulator to slow current between electrodes.

7. To inspect the air gap of the compressor clutch use feeler gauges to measure the air gap between the _____ _____ and the clutch drive plate with the clutch disengaged.

8. Often, the entire dash assembly must be removed before the air-conditioning _____ box can be accessed.

9. After all repairs are made, the air-conditioning system needs to be _____ to remove all of the moisture from the air introduced into the lines from opening up the air-conditioning system.

10. The oiler uses _____ _____ to push oil into the air-conditioning system.

Labeling

Label the following diagrams with the correct terms.

Identify the following tools used in the service of heating and air-conditioning systems:

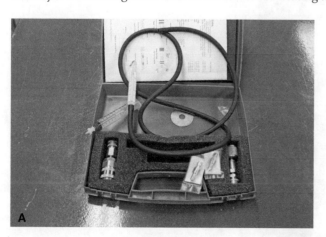

A.

A. _____

B. _____

C. _____

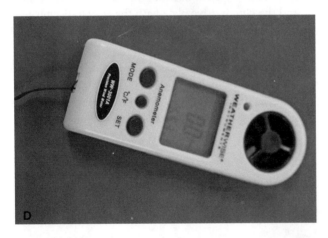

D. _____

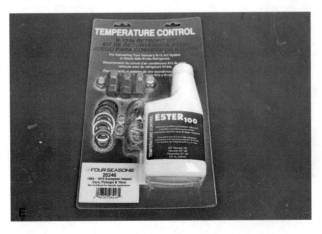

E. _____

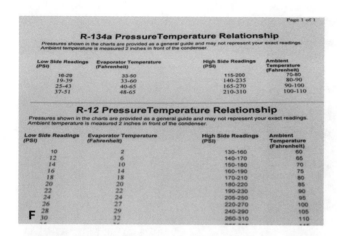

F. _____

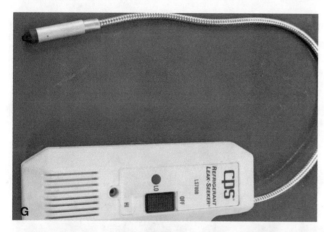

G. _____

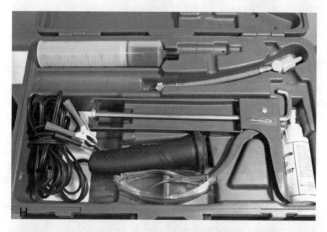

H. _____

I. _____

J.

J. _____

Skill Drills

Place the skill drill steps in the correct order.

1. Identifying the Refrigerant Type:

_____ **A.** After selecting the pressure gauge set, make sure the service valves on the gauges are in the off or shut position.

_____ **B.** Measure the ambient temperature (6" to 8" [15 to 20 cm] in front of the condenser) and the pressure on the pressure gauge set. Compare the pressure to the PT chart for that type of refrigerant.

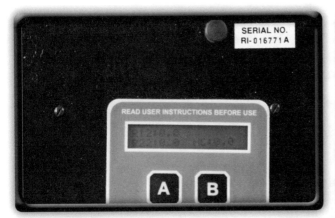

_____ **C.** Turn off the valve, and disconnect the refrigerant identifier. If the refrigerant does not match the under-the-hood sticker, reclaim the contaminated refrigerant into a contaminated tank and label the refrigerant for disposal. If the refrigerant is 100% pure and matches the under-the-hood sticker, continue to the next step.

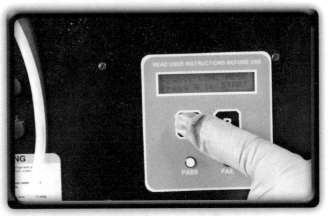

_____ **D.** Use a sealant identifier to check whether there is any sealant in the system. If there is, notify your supervisor. Turn on the refrigerant identifier, and allow the machine to warm up.

_____ **E.** Connect the service chuck of the pressure gauge to the air-conditioning system. Open the valves, watch the high- and low-pressure gauges, and record the pressure. If the high- and low side gauges are the same pressure and you could not check for noncondensable gasses, use the PT chart to determine that as follows.

_____ **F.** Connect the refrigerant identifier to the low side of the air-conditioning system, and open the service valve. Follow the prompts on the refrigerant identifier, and record the refrigerant type and amount of air, if any.

2. Removing, Inspecting, and Reinstalling the Compressor:

_____ **A.** Unplug the compressor clutch.

_____ **B.** Plug in the compressor clutch, and install the drive belt. Proceed to the evacuation procedure.

_____ **C.** Check the resistance of the clutch coil, and check the pulley bearing. Check the terminals for corrosion. Check the tag on the new compressor to see if it came with oil installed. If not, install the specified amount of new oil.

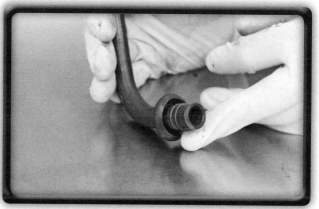

_____ **D.** Install the air-conditioning lines with new sealing rings.

_____ **E.** Remove the hoses from the air-conditioning system. Cap the lines.

_____ **F.** Install the new compressor; tighten the mounting hardware to specifications.

_____ **G.** Reclaim the refrigerant, making note of the amount removed. Compare this amount to the factory specifications. Remove the belt using a serpentine belt tool or the proper wrench. Remove tension from the tensioner, and slide the belt off, noting routing for reinstallation.

_____ **H.** Remove the mounting bolts following the manufacturer's specifications. Pour oil from the compressor into a graduated cylinder, and check the oil for acid using acid test strips.

3. Removing, Inspecting, and Reinstalling the Condenser:

_____ **A.** Remove the inlet and outlet lines on the condenser.

_____ **B.** Install the inlet and outlet lines. Replace all of the components in reverse order from removal. Evacuate the air-conditioning system if all other air-conditioning repairs are complete.

_____ **C.** Install the new condenser. Fasten the condenser with the mounting hardware.

_____ **D.** After reclaiming the air-conditioning system, remove all necessary components to access the condenser. Refer to the manufacturer's specific procedures on component removal.

_____ **E.** Install new O-rings on the air-conditioning lines.

_____ **F.** Remove the hold-down bolts for the condenser.

4. Removing, Inspecting, and Installing a TXV:

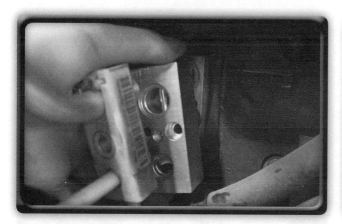

_____ **A.** Install the new expansion valve and torque the bolts to specification.

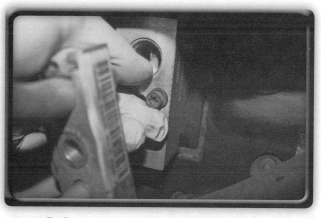

_____ **B.** Remove the bolts holding the expansion valve to the evaporator inlet.

_____ **C.** Install a new mounting stud. Reinstall the lines to the expansion valve, and tighten retaining nut. Evacuate the system if all other repairs were made.

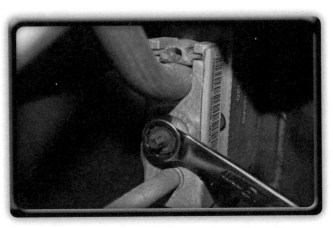

_____ **D.** After reclaiming the air-conditioning system, use a wrench to loosen the bolt holding the liquid and suction line block to the expansion valve.

_____ **E.** Install new gaskets or O-rings onto the new expansion valve and the suction and liquid lines.

_____ **F.** Remove the center stud going through the expansion valve. Gently remove the lines from the expansion valve.

5. Removing, Inspecting, and Installing an Orifice Tube:

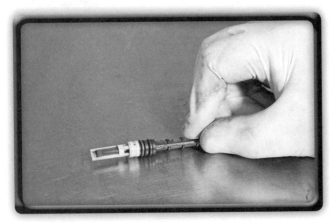

_____ **A.** Select the new orifice tube, making sure to replace with the properly colored tube. Lubricate the orifice tube O-rings, and install the new one with the direction arrow pointing in the direction of refrigerant flow.

_____ **B.** Locate the orifice tube, and determine whether it is serviceable. After locating the serviceable orifice tube, remove the line where the orifice tube is housed.

_____ **C.** Lubricate and install new O-rings on the line, and reinstall the line. Proceed to the evacuation if all other repairs were made.

_____ **D.** Using small needle-nose pliers or the orifice tube removal tool, pull out the old orifice tube from the housing. Note the color of the old orifice tube.

Review Questions

_____ **1.** All of the following statements are true with respect to performance testing the air-conditioning system *except*:
   A. The heater fan needs to be on the lowest speed.
   B. The heater control knob should be on the coldest setting.
   C. The airflow should be set to the dash vents.
   D. An external fan should be used to supply air to the condenser to simulate driving conditions.

_____ **2.** Which is the most common source of abnormal noises in an air conditioner?
   A. Evaporator
   B. Condenser
   C. Compressor
   D. Expansion valve

_____ **3.** Which of the following types of testing requires an empty air-conditioning system?
   A. Corona suppression
   B. Heated diode testing
   C. Dye testing
   D. Nitrogen testing

_____ **4.** Choose the correct statement.
   A. Experts recommend the usage of a sealant to fix a leak.
   B. A refrigerant identifier is used to determine the type of refrigerant.
   C. A contaminated refrigerant can be recycled using a reclaiming machine and reused.
   D. The reclaimed refrigerant can be stored in the virgin disposable tank that the new refrigerant came in.

_____ **5.** All of the following can cause the compressor clutch to not engage *except*:
   A. The clutch coil receives full power and ground.
   B. Resistance of clutch coil is more than specifications.
   C. The gap between the clutch assembly and air-conditioning pulley is too large.
   D. A voltage drop is present in the electrical circuit that energizes the clutch coil.

_____ **6.** Which of the following refrigerants uses mineral oil?
   A. R-410a
   B. R-134a
   C. R-12
   D. HFO-1234yf

_____ **7.** When charging an air-conditioning system, if the pressure reaches a positive pressure number too rapidly, what does it indicate?
   A. The reed valves in the compressor are likely bad.
   B. The TXV or orifice tube is restricted.
   C. The refrigerant is contaminated.
   D. The desiccant bag is broken.

_____ **8.** When removing the heater core, how should the heater hoses be removed?
  A. By using a wrench
  B. By slitting the hoses lengthwise
  C. By heating to loosen them
  D. By twisting the heater hoses

_____ **9.** In a typical orifice tube system, which of the following indicates an undercharge of refrigerant?
  A. Both the low and the high side gauges are running higher than normal.
  B. The air-conditioning compressor clutch runs for a long time before it shuts off.
  C. The air in the ducts feels cold.
  D. The air-conditioning clutch has a rapid cycle time.

_____ **10.** If the pressure gauges read low pressure on the high side, high pressure on the low side, or about equal pressures, what might it indicate?
  A. The system may be low on refrigerant.
  B. The compressor is not working fully.
  C. There is a blockage in the low side of the system that is not allowing refrigerant to pass.
  D. There is a blockage on the high side or an airflow restriction across the condenser.

ASE Technician A/Technician B Style Questions

_____ **1.** Tech A states that the wider the gap on an air-conditioning clutch, the greater the ohm reading when checking the windings. Tech B states that the air-conditioning clutch is electromagnetically operated. Who is correct?
  A. Tech A
  B. Tech B
  C. Both A and B
  D. Neither A nor B

_____ **2.** Tech A states that an air-conditioning performance test usually requires that an auxiliary condenser fan be used during the test. Tech B states that a performance test will show if the air-conditioning system is contaminated with sealer. Who is correct?
  A. Tech A
  B. Tech B
  C. Both A and B
  D. Neither A nor B

_____ **3.** Tech A states that refrigerant in a vehicle should be identified before recovering the refrigerant. Tech B states that refrigerant doesn't need to be identified if you are only topping up a system with refrigerant. Who is correct?
  A. Tech A
  B. Tech B
  C. Both A and B
  D. Neither A nor B

_____ **4.** Tech A states that when evacuating an air-conditioning system, the vacuum should be maintained for approximately 10–15 minutes (but as long as 30 minutes) after the system reaches the boiling point pressure of water. Tech B states that one main purpose of evacuating an air-conditioning system is to remove any moisture from the system. Who is correct?
  A. Tech A
  B. Tech B
  C. Both A and B
  D. Neither A nor B

_____ **5.** Tech A states that the system should be flushed if the compressor came apart. Tech B states that the system should be flushed if the oil is contaminated. Who is correct?
  A. Tech A
  B. Tech B
  C. Both A and B
  D. Neither A nor B

_____ **6.** Tech A states that when using pressurized nitrogen to locate a leak, an electronic sniffer should be used. Tech B states that electronic sniffers are used when the system has at least a minimal refrigerant charge. Who is correct?
   A. Tech A
   B. Tech B
   C. Both A and B
   D. Neither A nor B

_____ **7.** Tech A states that microns are a much more accurate unit of measuring vacuum than inches of mercury (Hg). Tech B states that microns are a much more accurate measure of time than seconds. Who is correct?
   A. Tech A
   B. Tech B
   C. Both A and B
   D. Neither A nor B

_____ **8.** Tech A states that to determine how much refrigerant is needed in a system, you must refer to identifying labels on the vehicle or the service information. Tech B states that to determine the amount of refrigerant needed, you just charge the system until the pressures look correct. Who is correct?
   A. Tech A
   B. Tech B
   C. Both A and B
   D. Neither A nor B

_____ **9.** Tech A states that when removing any component of an air-conditioning system, the oil should be drained from it and measured so that the same amount of new oil can be reinstalled. Tech B states that oil should only be in the compressor, and if any oil is found in any other components, it means that the receiver drier is faulty. Who is correct?
   A. Tech A
   B. Tech B
   C. Both A and B
   D. Neither A nor B

_____ **10.** Tech A states that if moisture enters the air-conditioning system, acid will be created. Tech B states that evacuating an air-conditioning system will boil moisture, which will be removed from the system as a gas. Who is correct?
   A. Tech A
   B. Tech B
   C. Both A and B
   D. Neither A nor B

Electronic Climate Control

At the start of each chapter you'll find the NATEF tasks, Knowledge Objectives, and Skills Objectives from the textbook. These are your objectives as you make your way through the exercises in this workbook and the chapter in your textbook. The following activities have been designed to help you refresh your knowledge of the material in this chapter.

NATEF Tasks

- N60001 Identify hybrid vehicle A/C system electrical circuits and service/safety precautions. (MLR/AST/MAST)
- N60002 Check operation of automatic or semiautomatic heating, ventilation, and air-conditioning (HVAC) control systems; determine needed action. (AST/MAST)
- N60003 Using a scan tool, observe and record related heating, ventilation, and air-conditioning (HVAC) data and trouble codes. (AST/MAST)
- N60004 Inspect and test HVAC system control panel assembly; determine needed action. (AST/MAST)
- N60005 Inspect and test HVAC system control cables, motors, and linkages; perform needed action. (AST/MAST)
- N60006 Diagnose temperature control problems in the HVAC system; determine needed action. (MAST)
- N60007 Inspect HVAC system ducts, doors, hoses, cabin filters, and outlets; perform needed action. (MLR/AST/MAST)
- N60008 Inspect and test HVAC system blower motors, resistors, switches, relays, wiring, and protection devices; determine needed action. (AST/MAST)
- N60009 Diagnose A/C compressor clutch control systems; determine needed action. (AST/MAST)
- N60010 Diagnose malfunctions in the vacuum, mechanical, and electrical components and controls of the heating, ventilation, and A/C HVAC system; determine needed action. (AST/MAST)

Knowledge Objectives

After reading this chapter, you will be able to:

- K60001 Describe the purpose and operation of climate control sensors.
- K60002 Describe the purpose and operation of HVAC control panels.
- K60003 Describe the operation of climate control system devices.
- K60004 Describe the unique components of hybrid vehicle HVAC systems.
- K60005 Describe the testing and diagnosis process on HVAC systems.

Skills Objectives

After reading this chapter, you will be able to:

- S60001 Diagnose failures in the HVAC system controls.
- S60002 Diagnose HVAC system control devices and actuators.

Matching

Match the following terms with the correct description or example.

- **A.** Actuator
- **B.** Air-conditioning compressor clutch
- **C.** Air-conditioning pressure sensor
- **D.** Ambient air temperature sensor
- **E.** Aspirator
- **F.** Cabin air temperature sensor
- **G.** Dual-drive air-conditioning compressor

- **H.** Electric servo motor
- **I.** Engine coolant temperature sensor
- **J.** Evaporator temperature sensor
- **K.** Feedback signal
- **L.** Heater control cables
- **M.** Limit switches
- **N.** Manual climate control system

O. Negative temperature coefficient (NTC) thermistor
P. Photodiode
Q. Printed circuitry

R. Semiautomatic climate control system
S. Sun load (solar) sensor
T. Vacuum servo

_____ **1.** Circuitry that holds resistors, capacitors, transistors, and integrated circuits that are soldered into place to create the control module or computer.

_____ **2.** A voltage signal sent back to an electronic control unit and enables the control module to interpret temperature or other information from its sensors.

_____ **3.** A thermistor that measures air temperature inside the vehicle.

_____ **4.** A climate control system fully controlled by the operator.

_____ **5.** A photodiode that varies voltage based on light. It is used to determine the radiant heat coming from the sun into the passenger cabin and gives an input signal of sunlight load to the ECU.

_____ **6.** A thermistor that is used to measure the air temperature outside the vehicle.

_____ **7.** A vacuum-controlled device that uses vacuum on a diaphragm to pull a link or lever that is connected to the air box door.

_____ **8.** An air compressor drive used on some hybrid vehicles. The compressor can be driven by the accessory belt or by an electric motor.

_____ **9.** Switches that turn off power flow to an electric motor when a particular limit is reached.

_____ **10.** A tube that is used to direct airflow across the cabin air temperature sensor.

_____ **11.** A thermistor that measures the temperature of the engine coolant.

_____ **12.** A sensor that gives an input signal of refrigerant pressure in the air-conditioning system to the ECU.

_____ **13.** A system that provides automatic function of the heater or cooling only, leaving fan speed and mode selection to the operator.

_____ **14.** A device that moves the air doors of the air box. It is controlled by input from the climate control panel.

_____ **15.** Also referred to as an electric actuator, a motor that provides movement to operate the air doors in an air box to control air temperature and air movement.

_____ **16.** Cables that control the air doors in an air box as part of the air distribution system.

_____ **17.** The mechanical coupler that is electromagnetically engaged and provides a way of uncoupling the compressor from the accessory drive belt.

_____ **18.** A thermistor that reads the temperature of the evaporator, used to ensure that the evaporator does not freeze.

_____ **19.** An electronic component that creates a varying voltage or current output based on the amount of light striking it.

_____ **20.** A thermistor that gains resistance as temperature goes down and loses resistance as temperature goes up.

Multiple Choice

Read each item carefully, and then select the best response.

_____ **1.** The climate control system of an automobile manages all of the following subsystems, _except_:
A. heating
B. refrigeration
C. ventilation
D. air conditioning

_____ **2.** The electronic control unit compares the _____ from the temperature sensors with values stored in its memory, programmed in when the module is installed into the vehicle.
A. signal voltage values
B. feedback signals
C. reference voltages
D. pulse-width

_____ **3.** The ECU can control a blower motor's speed by sending a(n) _____ signal that works by repeatedly turning on and off the current flow to the component.
A. analog
B. high frequency

     C. pulse-width–modulated

     D. low frequency

_____ **4.** Which sensor is usually located in front of the air-conditioning condenser where the forward motion of the vehicle and the action of the condenser fans force air over the sensor?

     A. Ambient air temperature sensor

     B. Engine coolant temperature sensor

     C. Air-conditioning pressure sensor

     D. Cabin air temperature sensor

_____ **5.** The _____ sensor is a photodiode.

     A. evaporator

     B. sun load

     C. engine coolant

     D. cabin air

_____ **6.** Either the low-pressure sensor or the high-pressure sensor can send a(n) _____ signal to the ECU based on the pressure in the system.

     A. pulse-width–modulated

     B. resistance

     C. analog

     D. variable voltage

_____ **7.** The _____ sensor is located in the airstream where the air leaves the evaporator and signals to the ECU the temperature of the air.

     A. ambient air temperature

     B. evaporator temperature

     C. air-conditioning pressure

     D. cabin air temperature sensor

_____ **8.** The operator can tell the ECU where to deliver air and at what temperature, using switches that produce a(n) _____ signal.

     A. on/off–type

     B. pulse-width–modulated

     C. variable voltage

     D. resistance

_____ **9.** The _____ temperature control panel is designed to allow the driver and passenger to control the temperature delivered to their side of the vehicle.

     A. manual

     B. semiautomatic

     C. fully automatic

     D. dual-zone

_____ **10.** The vacuum _____ is installed on the vacuum system to ensure vacuum is present for the control panel to use even when the engine is at wide open throttle.

     A. switch

     B. canister

     C. servo

     D. relay

_____ **11.** In a manual air conditioner, the fan control switch connects _____ with the blower motor to control its speed.

     A. resistors in series

     B. resistors in parallel

     C. resistors in series and parallel

     D. none of the above

_____ **12.** The _____ is a plastic housing that holds other components of the climate control system, such as the heater core and the evaporator.

     A. blend box

     B. plenum

     C. air box

     D. air duct

_____ **13.** The _____ is a sealed container with a spring and diaphragm inside.
    A. vacuum servo
    B. electric actuator
    C. solenoid actuator
    D. recirculation door

_____ **14.** Some electric servo motors use a _____ to signal to the ECU the position of the blend door and, if it is moving, the direction in which it is traveling.
    A. thermistor
    B. variable voltage resistor
    C. potentiometer
    D. limit switch

_____ **15.** Most hybrids now use a _____ motor, which directly drives the compressor.
    A. single-phase
    B. high-voltage electric
    C. low-voltage
    D. servo

True/False

If you believe the statement to be more true than false, write the letter "T" in the space provided. If you believe the statement to be more false than true, write the letter "F."

_____ **1.** The manual climate control system gives the operator full control of the climate control system and does not use a computer or electronic control unit.

_____ **2.** The resistance value of a positive temperature coefficient thermistor goes down as it is heated.

_____ **3.** Negative temperature coefficient thermistors are usually used in automotive applications.

_____ **4.** The actuator is a tube that directs airflow to the in-vehicle temperature sensor.

_____ **5.** Typically, air-conditioning systems will use two pressure sensors to monitor refrigerant pressure.

_____ **6.** Transducers are electronic devices that convert one form of energy to another.

_____ **7.** All of the buttons used with the manual control panel are present on the automatic panel as well.

_____ **8.** Most manual air-conditioning systems use four resistors to give three operator-selectable speeds of the blower motor.

_____ **9.** The mode door directs air through or around the heater core to deliver hot or cold air into the passenger cabin, and the blend door changes the location of air delivery to floor, defrost, or vent.

_____ **10.** Geared motor actuators are used in HVAC systems, while solenoid actuators are used in systems such as door locks and fuel door latches.

Fill in the Blank

Read each item carefully, and then complete the statement by filling in the missing word(s).

1. The _____ _____ _____ controls the speed of the blower motor automatically depending on the difference between the interior cabin temperature and the operator-selected temperature.

2. The _____ loaded into the electronic control unit contains all the data to make the system operate properly.

3. The electronic control unit receives signals in the form of _____ from each of the sensors.

4. A typical resistor pack blower motor has only _____ speeds.

5. The _____ _____ is a safety device built into the compressor by manufacturers to ensure pressures cannot get too high in the system and rupture a line.

6. A _____ _____ _____ has a rotary or linear switch for fan speed, modes, and temperature.

7. Relay windings are normally equipped with a mechanism to reduce _____ _____, which are induced in the windings when the relay is deactivated.

8. The _____ _____ is an electric motor that is attached to a circular fan sometimes referred to by technicians as a squirrel cage fan.

9. The higher the resistance connected in line with the blower motor, the _____ the blower motor will operate.

10. The _____ _____ directs air through or around the heater core to deliver hot or cold air into the passenger cabin.

11. The _____ door is designed to work with the maximum air-conditioning button or switch and will shut airflow off from outside the vehicle and instead recirculate air from inside the passenger compartment back through the evaporator.

12. Older electric actuators may incorporate _____ _____ to stop current to the electric actuator when the maximum travel of the door has been reached.

13. Most hybrids now use a high-voltage electric motor, which directly drives the _____.

14. Some hybrids use _____-_____ air-conditioning compressors that can be belt driven by the ICE or by a high-voltage motor.

15. The compressor in the hybrid air-conditioning system may be driven by the internal combustion engine through a standard belt and _____ clutch arrangement, just like a standard air-conditioning compressor clutch arrangement.

Labeling

Label the following diagrams with the correct terms.

1. Blend door:

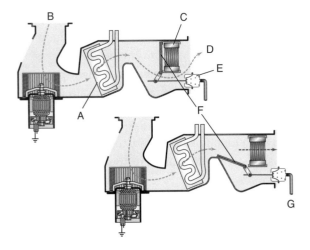

A. _____

B. _____

C. _____

D. _____

E. _____

F. _____

G. _____

2. Recirculation door:

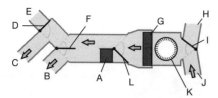

A. _____

B. _____

C. _____

D. _____

E. _____

F. _____

G. _____

H. _____

I. _____

J. _____

K. _____

L. _____

3. Vacuum solenoid:

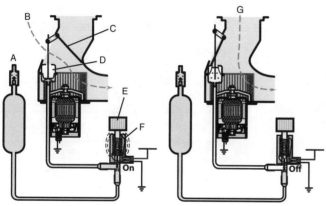

A. _____

A. _____

B. _____

C. _____

D. _____

E. _____

F. _____

4. Electrically driven air-conditioning compressor:

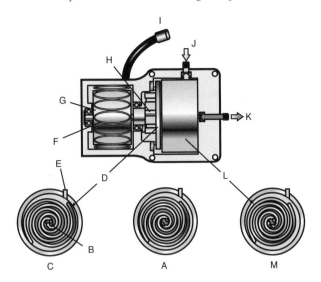

A. _____

B. _____

C. _____

D. _____

E. _____

F. _____

G. _____

H. _____

I. _____

J. _____

K. _____

L. _____

M. _____

5. Dual-drive air-conditioning compressor:

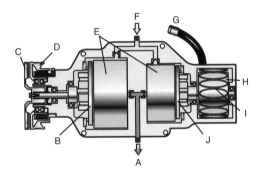

A. _____

B. _____

C. _____

D. _____

E. _____

F. _____

G. _____

H. _____

I. _____

J. _____

Skill Drills

Test your knowledge of skill drills by filling in the correct words in the photo captions.

1. Inspecting and Testing the Electric Cooling Fan:

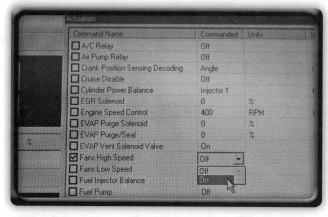

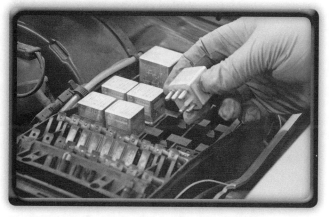

Step 1: If the cooling fan does not come on when the system is turned on, install the _____ _____, and find the _____ controls for the cooling fan; then turn the cooling fan on.

Step 2: If the cooling fan still does not run, find the coolant _____ relay, _____ the relay, and find terminals _____ and _____.

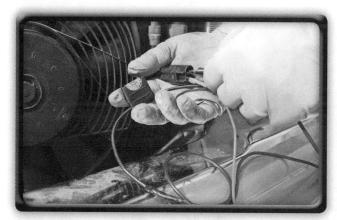

Step 3: Install the _____ _____ wire to the connections to provide power to the cooling fan. CAUTION: Make sure you _____ the _____ _____ (30 and 87) and not the control circuit. Jumping the _____ _____ can burn up the ECU, even with fused jumper wires!

Step 4: Inspect the cooling fan for operation. If the fan is still not operating, _____-_____ the connector at the cooling fan with the jumper wire _____ _____ from the previous step. Connect the _____ leads to both back-probed wires (power and ground); the meter should read _____ voltage.

Step 5: If battery voltage is present, _____ the faulty _____ _____. If battery voltage is not present, use the _____ to locate the _____ or high _____ in the circuit.

2. Inspecting and Testing a Blower Motor:

Step 1: Turn on the blower motor, and check whether the motor is _____ on each _____. Research the _____ _____ for the condition found.

Step 2: Use a _____ to test for _____ and _____ by back-probing the wires at the _____ of the blower motor. Turn the _____ switch to Run and the _____ switch to the speed that does not operate, and _____ the meter. If the meter reads more than about _____ _____, the fan should be operating. If it isn't, the blower motor needs to be _____.

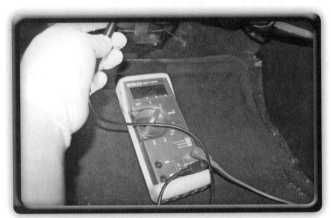

Step 3: If the reading is less than 3 volts, then perform a _____ _____ test on the power and ground sides of the _____. If the voltage drop is excessive, use a wiring _____ and voltmeter to track down the high _____ or opening in the circuit, and _____ as necessary.

Step 4: If the control circuit tests _____, but the fan is making unusual _____ or is not operating correctly, remove the blower motor by _____ the electrical connector and removing any _____, nuts, or _____ retaining the blower motor to the _____ _____.

Step 5: Inspect the fan _____ and fins for _____ objects or _____.

Step 6: If the fan is in good operating condition, measure the _____ _____ with the blower motor _____ from the vehicle, either (1) with a low-amp _____ (inductive clamp) around the _____ to or from the motor, or (2) with an _____ set to 20 amps and wired in _____ with the motor. Run the motor while _____ the amperage. If necessary, _____ the blower motor and retest.

3. Testing Air-Conditioning Compressor Clutch Control Systems:

Step 1: _____ the testing procedure and specifications in the appropriate service information. Unplug the compressor _____ electrical two-wire _____ located at the front of the air-conditioning _____. Check the _____ of the clutch windings. If the resistance does not match the manufacturer's specifications, replace the _____ _____.

Step 2: Check supply _____ and ground to the compressor clutch _____. Place the _____ lead on the _____ side of the clutch connector, and place the _____ lead on the _____ side of the clutch connector. Ensure that the air-conditioning _____ is turned on. Your meter should display near battery _____.

Step 3: Perform a _____ _____ test of power and ground. Connect the red lead of your voltmeter to the positive terminal of the _____ _____ _____. Connect the black lead to _____ positive. Ensure the air-conditioning clutch is turned on with the _____ panel. Look for a _____ or loss of voltage on the _____ wire of no more than 0.4 volts. If more than 0.4 volts is found, the power wire has _____ resistance in it. Repeat the step for the _____ side by connecting the _____ lead to the negative terminal and the _____ lead to the battery _____.

4. Inspecting and Testing the HVAC Control Panel Assembly:

Step 1: After researching the operation and _____ procedure for the control panel _____, start by _____ all of the heater and air-conditioning _____. Note any _____. Remove clips and bolts holding _____ _____ under the _____.

Step 2: Move the _____ control switch from maximum to _____.

Step 3: Observe the blend door _____ for movement. If no movement is detected, test the _____ system according to service information. If movement is present, _____ the actuator by undoing the _____ securing it to the air box.

Step 4: Move the _____ door by hand, and check whether it is _____ at the _____ or is _____. If the blend door is broken, the entire _____ _____ must be removed. Refer to service information for removal and repair.

Step 5: Move each _____, and watch the appropriate _____ for proper _____.

5. Diagnosing Temperature Control Problems in the HVAC System:

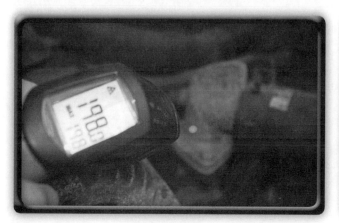 

Step 1: Research the operation and diagnostic procedure for the control panel assembly, and _____ the customer _____. Check for full operating temperature of the _____ by pointing an infrared _____ at the thermostat housing. If the temperature is not hot enough, the _____ is likely in need of replacement.

Step 2: Test for _____ with the _____ tool. If a code is set, follow the _____ chart for the code pulled. If no code is set, follow the _____-_____ troubleshooting chart.

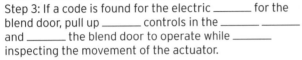

Step 3: If a code is found for the electric _____ for the blend door, pull up _____ controls in the _____ _____ and _____ the blend door to operate while _____ inspecting the movement of the actuator.

Step 4: If _____ is found at the actuator, inspect for a _____ or binding door by turning the _____ by hand. If no movement is found at the actuator, perform the test for _____ (power and ground) at the actuator while _____ it.

Step 5: If no power and ground are found, _____-_____ the wires for the actuator at the connector of the _____ voltage (power and ground) while commanding the _____. If no power and ground are coming from the ECU, the ECU will have to be _____.

Review Questions

_____ **1.** The ECU sends output commands to which type of component to control fan speed, heater core coolant flow, air-conditioning clutch activation, and so on?
- **A.** Transistor
- **B.** Actuator
- **C.** Integrated circuit
- **D.** Capacitor

_____ **2.** Which of these systems is able to control the air doors and fan speed to match the climate inside the vehicle to the settings selected?
- **A.** Manual
- **B.** Semiautomatic
- **C.** Automatic
- **D.** Remote

_____ **3.** Which of the following sensors signals to the ECU the temperature of the coolant which flows through the heater core?
- **A.** Ambient air temperature sensor
- **B.** Cabin air temperature sensor

C. Engine coolant temperature sensor
D. Sun load, or solar, sensor

_____ **4.** The ECU receives instructions regarding the desired cabin temperature from the:
A. relative humidity sensor.
B. evaporator temperature sensor.
C. air-conditioning pressure sensor.
D. HVAC control panel.

_____ **5.** Which of the following control a relatively large current flow in one part of a circuit by a much smaller current flow?
A. Relays
B. Blower motor speed controls
C. Air boxes
D. Limit switches

_____ **6.** Which of these is a function of the blower motor?
A. Controlling electric components such as the air-conditioning compressor clutch and condenser fan
B. Providing the desired amount of airflow in the cabin
C. Controlling temperature and position of the airflow from the air distribution system
D. Movement of air box doors

_____ **7.** Which of these is the most common issue a technician might encounter with the automatic HVAC system?
A. Failure of electric actuators
B. Vacuum leaks
C. Sensor failure
D. Jammed fans

_____ **8.** Negative temperature coefficient (NTC) thermistors:
A. increase resistance as they warm up.
B. are a form of transistor.
C. decrease resistance as they warm up.
D. are a form of diode.

_____ **9.** When there is a difference in the speed of the vent airflow with the system in recirculation mode compared to fresh air mode, may indicate:
A. restricted cabin air filter.
B. failure of the blower motor.
C. a jammed fan.
D. a bad clutch coil.

_____ **10.** What should be one of the first steps when diagnosing automatic or semiautomatic HVAC systems?
A. Researching the system's operation in the service information
B. Recovering and recharging the refrigerant in the system.
C. Changing the settings to manual mode
D. Checking by replacing with another ECU system

ASE Technician A/Technician B Style Questions

_____ **1.** Tech A says that a temperature blend air door controls how much air bypasses the heater core. Tech B says that the recirculation blend air door controls fresh air. Who is correct?
A. Tech A
B. Tech B
C. Both A and B
D. Neither A nor B

_____ **2.** Tech A says that in a temperature blend air system, the air conditioner runs continuously. Tech B says that in a temperature blend air system, a blend door moves to direct all of the airflow either across the heater core for maximum heat or around the heater core for cold. Who is correct?
A. Tech A
B. Tech B
C. Both A and B
D. Neither A nor B

_____ 3. Tech A says that air flow in the vents is controlled by adding or removing a second or third motor to increase or decrease air flow. Tech B says that blower motor speed is controlled by controlling voltage and current to make the blower motor run faster or slower. Who is correct?
   A. Tech A
   B. Tech B
   C. Both A and B
   D. Neither A nor B

_____ 4. Tech A says that the fresh air setting pulls air from the cabin. Tech B says that when the outside temperature is very hot, the recirculate setting will cool the cabin further. Who is correct?
   A. Tech A
   B. Tech B
   C. Both A and B
   D. Neither A nor B

_____ 5. Tech A says that when an air door operated by an electric actuator doesn't move, replace the actuator. Tech B says that when a door operated by a vacuum actuator doesn't move, always verify the door moves freely, and there are no vacuum leaks. Who is correct?
   A. Tech A
   B. Tech B
   C. Both A and B
   D. Neither A nor B

_____ 6. Tech A says that some electric actuators are positioned by an HVAC ECU which checks the air flow with sensors. Tech B says that some electric actuators are positioned by an HVAC ECU and some actuators have a potentiometer to tell the HVAC ECU the position of the door. Who is correct?
   A. Tech A
   B. Tech B
   C. Both A and B
   D. Neither A nor B

_____ 7. Tech A says some newer vehicles use pulse width modulation (duty cycle) to control blower motor speeds, which leads to smooth changes in speeds. Tech B says that the evaporator temperature sensor is used to measure the temperature in the passenger compartment. Who is correct?
   A. Tech A
   B. Tech B
   C. Both A and B
   D. Neither A nor B

_____ 8. Tech A says that most hybrids now use a high-voltage electric motor that directly drives the A/C compressor. Tech B says that some hybrids use dual-drive air-conditioning compressors. Who is correct?
   A. Tech A
   B. Tech B
   C. Both A and B
   D. Neither A nor B

_____ 9. Tech A says that if the air gap between the compressor clutch and the pulley is too large, the clutch may not engage. Tech B says that if system voltage is too low, the compressor clutch will not engage. Who is correct?
   A. Tech A
   B. Tech B
   C. Both A and B
   D. Neither A nor B

_____ 10. Tech A says that in HVAC systems that do not use computer controls, it is important to check the engine computer for issues relating to how the vehicle runs that could affect HVAC performance. Tech B says that codes should only be consulted if you get stuck during diagnosis. Who is correct?
   A. Tech A
   B. Tech B
   C. Both A and B
   D. Neither A nor B

Ignition Systems

At the start of each chapter you'll find the NATEF tasks, Knowledge Objectives, and Skills Objectives from the textbook. These are your objectives as you make your way through the exercises in this workbook and the chapter in your textbook. The following activities have been designed to help you refresh your knowledge of the material in this chapter.

NATEF Tasks

- N61001 Access and use service information to perform step-by-step (troubleshooting) diagnosis. (AST/MAST)
- N61002 Remove and replace spark plugs; inspect secondary ignition components for wear and damage. (AST/MAST)
- N61003 Diagnose (troubleshoot) ignition system related problems such as no-starting, hard starting, engine misfire, poor drivability, spark knock, power loss, poor mileage, and emissions concerns; determine needed action. (AST/MAST)
- N61004 Inspect and test crankshaft and camshaft position sensor(s); determine needed action. (AST/MAST)
- N61005 Inspect, test, and/or replace ignition control module and powertrain/engine control module; reprogram/ initialize as needed. (AST/MAST)

Knowledge Objectives

After reading this chapter, you will be able to:

- K61001 Explain the basic principles of a modern ignition system.
- K61002 Explain the need to vary ignition timing during engine operation.
- K61003 Describe the purpose and functions of the components in an ignition system.
- K61004 Describe the breaker points ignition system.
- K61005 Describe the electronic ignition system.
- K61006 Describe the distributorless ignition system.

Skills Objectives

After reading this chapter, you will be able to:

- S61001 Perform ignition system maintenance.
- S61002 Inspect and test ignition system components.
- S61003 Inspect and test primary and secondary circuits.
- S61004 Inspect and test ignition coils.
- S61005 Inspect and test ignition pickup assemblies.
- S61006 Inspect and test spark plug wires.
- S61007 Inspect distributor caps and rotors.

Matching

Match the following terms with the correct description or example.

- **A.** Ballast resistor
- **B.** Breaker plate
- **C.** Center electrode
- **D.** Cranking
- **E.** Direct ignition system
- **F.** Dwell angle
- **G.** Electronic ignition system
- **H.** Firing line
- **I.** Heat range
- **J.** Ignition coil
- **K.** Ignition switch
- **L.** Inductive current
- **M.** Oscilloscope
- **N.** Primary circuit

O. Rotor
P. Secondary winding
Q. Spark plug

R. Spark timing
S. Throttle body
T. Waste cylinder

_____ **1.** The low-voltage circuit that turns the coil on and off.

_____ **2.** The cylinder in a waste spark ignition system that receives a spark near the top of its exhaust stroke.

_____ **3.** A high-voltage rotating switch that transfers voltage from the distributor cap's center terminal to the outer terminals.

_____ **4.** The point at which a spark occurs at the spark plug relative to the position of the piston.

_____ **5.** A device used to amplify an input voltage into the much higher voltage needed to jump the electrodes of a spark plug.

_____ **6.** A tool that shows graphically what is happening to voltage over a period of time; it is used to diagnose electrical faults.

_____ **7.** The housing on an intake manifold that is used to control the amount of filtered air that enters the cylinders.

_____ **8.** The rating of a spark plug's operating temperature.

_____ **9.** Used to limit the amount of current flowing in the ignition primary circuit.

_____ **10.** An ignition system that uses a nonmechanical method of triggering the ignition coil's primary circuit.

_____ **11.** The high-voltage copper wiring found in an ignition coil.

_____ **12.** The movable plate the breaker points are mounted on that pivots as the vacuum advance pulls on it.

_____ **13.** May refer to a waste spark ignition or a coil-on-plug ignition system, in which the coils are directly attached to the spark plugs.

_____ **14.** The current that has been created across a conductor by moving it through a magnetic field.

_____ **15.** The electrode located in the center of a spark plug. It is the hottest part of the spark plug.

_____ **16.** The amount of time that the primary circuit is energized, measured in degrees of distributor rotation.

_____ **17.** Rotating the engine by turning the ignition key to the start position.

_____ **18.** A switch operated by a key or start/stop button and used to turn on or off a vehicle's electrical and ignition system.

_____ **19.** The tall lines on a parade pattern that indicate the voltage required to initially jump the spark plug gap.

_____ **20.** A device that provides a gap for the high-voltage spark to occur in each cylinder.

Multiple Choice

Read each item carefully, and then select the best response.

_____ **1.** For an engine to run smoothly and efficiently, the high-voltage spark must cross the spark plug electrode as the piston approaches top dead center of the _____.
A. intake stroke
B. compression stroke
C. power stroke
D. exhaust stroke

_____ **2.** What type of ignition system eliminates the distributor by using dedicated ignition coils—one coil for each pair of cylinders?
A. Contact breaker point ignition system
B. Electronic ignition system
C. Waste spark ignition system
D. Direct ignition system

_____ **3.** The _____ replaced the contact breaker points with an electronic switching device but still used a distributor to dispense the spark to the various cylinders.
A. electronic ignition system—distributor type
B. waste spark ignition system
C. direct ignition system
D. coil-on-plug ignition system

_____ **4.** The ignition system uses a(n) _____ to convert relatively low-voltage and high-current flow into very high-voltage and very low-current flow.
   A. spark plug
   B. ignition module
   C. induction coil
   D. reluctor

_____ **5.** Faraday's law states that relative movement between a conductor and a magnetic field allows _____ ways by which voltage can be induced in a conductor.
   A. three
   B. four
   C. five
   D. six

_____ **6.** The correct spark timing varies according to _____.
   A. transmission gear selected
   B. detected knock
   C. engine temperature
   D. all of the above

_____ **7.** The powertrain control module may also be called a(n) _____.
   A. engine control module
   B. body control module
   C. electronic control unit
   D. either A or C

_____ **8.** When the ignition switch is turned to the _____ position, most warning lamps on the instrument panel should illuminate.
   A. accessory
   B. on/run
   C. start/crank
   D. lock and off

_____ **9.** When battery voltage pushes current through the _____ of an ignition coil, a magnetic field is created.
   A. primary winding
   B. secondary winding
   C. iron core
   D. high-tension terminal

_____ **10.** Spark plugs are identified by _____.
   A. thread size or diameter
   B. reach or length of the thread
   C. heat range or operating temperature
   D. all of the above

_____ **11.** Contact breaker points are opened by _____ on the distributor shaft, and closed by a spring.
   A. rubbing blocks
   B. sensors
   C. cam lobes
   D. gears

_____ **12.** The _____ is made up of two plates constructed from narrow strips of aluminum foil that are insulated from each other by a special waxed paper, called a dielectric.
   A. rotor
   B. condenser
   C. contact breaker
   D. ballast resistor

_____ **13.** It is the main function of the _____ to distribute the spark to the spark plugs in the correct sequence and at the correct time in the engine cycle.
   A. condenser
   B. ballast resistor
   C. distributor
   D. high-tension terminal

_____ **14.** The vacuum advance mechanism is designed to operate on _____ vacuum.
   A. ported
   B. manifold
   C. venturi
   D. any of the above

_____ **15.** In Hall-effect systems, a _____ can be located inside the distributor to signal an ignition module to turn the primary circuit on and off.
   A. Hall-effect switch
   B. throttle position sensor
   C. mass airflow sensor
   D. manifold absolute pressure sensor

_____ **16.** Ignition coils employed with electronic systems are referred to as _____ because their primary winding resistance and number of turns are low.
   A. low-inductance coils
   B. high-inductance coils
   C. dual-inductance coils
   D. stators

_____ **17.** The _____ is shaped like a very shallow cup with slits, or windows, cut into it at evenly spaced intervals and made of a ferrous metal.
   A. optical-type sensor
   B. interrupter ring
   C. reluctor
   D. stator

_____ **18.** What type of sensor, located inside the distributor, can be used to sense the position of the crankshaft and send an appropriate voltage signal to the ignition module or PCM?
   A. Hall-effect
   B. Induction-type
   C. Optical-type
   D. Variable-resistance

_____ **19.** A distributorless ignition system uses a _____ to calculate engine speed and determine engine position.
   A. crankshaft position sensor
   B. cam lobe
   C. camshaft position sensor
   D. both A and C

_____ **20.** A _____ on an oscilloscope or lab scope shows all the cylinders firing in sequence.
   A. parade pattern
   B. firing line
   C. raster
   D. spark line

True/False

If you believe the statement to be more true than false, write the letter "T" in the space provided. If you believe the statement to be more false than true, write the letter "F."

_____ **1.** The ignition coil's function is to amplify the battery's low voltage and high current into very high voltage and low current.

_____ **2.** The low-voltage side of the induction coil is called the secondary circuit, and the high-voltage side is called the primary circuit.

_____ **3.** Available voltage is the maximum amount of voltage available to try to push current to jump the spark plug gap if the gap were infinite.

_____ **4.** In early vehicles that used a distributor, base spark timing was set at idle speeds by positioning the distributor body in relation to its rotating cam.

_____ **5.** Ignition coils are basically step-up transformers.

_____ **6.** The secondary ignition coil winding has 15,000 to 30,000 turns of very thin insulated aluminum wire wound around its core.

_____ **7.** High-tension leads conduct the high-output voltage generated in the secondary ignition circuit between the high-tension terminal(s) of the ignition coil, the distributor cap, and the spark plugs.

_____ **8.** The same spark plug can sometimes be used in different engines with different gap settings.

_____ **9.** The condenser absorbs the surge of inductive current that occurs when the contact breaker points begin to separate.

_____ **10.** The most common automotive use for a ballast resistor is to reduce the voltage and current to the ignition coil by being inserted in series in the primary circuit between the ignition switch and the positive terminal of the ignition coil.

_____ **11.** The distributor cap covers the end of the distributor to protect the components and provides a connection point between the rotor and the spark plug leads.

_____ **12.** The centrifugal advance mechanism controls ignition advance in relation to engine load.

_____ **13.** In electronic ignition systems, the contact breaker points are eliminated and the primary circuit is switched or triggered electronically with a power transistor located in the ignition module.

_____ **14.** The stator has one tooth for each cylinder; as it spins the teeth interact with the reluctor to trigger the ignition module.

_____ **15.** The dwell control section of the ignition module determines when the primary circuit will be switched on and for how long current will flow in the primary winding.

_____ **16.** The switching transistor acts as a relay; when activated, it allows current to flow through the ignition coil primary winding and through the collector/emitter to ground.

_____ **17.** In direct ignition systems, there is one ignition coil for each pair of companion cylinders.

_____ **18.** In a waste spark system the cylinder on the compression stroke is said to be the event cylinder and the cylinder on the exhaust stroke is the waste cylinder.

_____ **19.** The spark timing on a distributorless ignition system is controlled by the powertrain control module.

_____ **20.** Raster allows a technician to compare each spark line to each other, which tells how much voltage it takes to keep the spark burning and for how long.

Fill in the Blank

Read each item carefully, and then complete the statement by filling in the missing word(s).

1. The purpose of the ignition system is to create the _____-_____ _____ and deliver it at the right time to each cylinder.

2. The original ignition system was called the _____ _____ _____ ignition system, a mechanical system with a switch that was opened and closed as the engine was running.

3. The amount of voltage required to initially get current to jump the spark plug gap is called _____ voltage.

4. Spark timing is almost always indexed to the _____-_____ cylinder.

5. The _____ _____ plate, also called a breaker plate, is a moveable metal plate located in the distributor, beneath the distributor cap on which the contact breaker points are mounted.

6. The _____ supplies the electrical energy to the ignition circuit during start-up.

7. A(n) _____ _____ disables the ignition, fuel, and starter systems unless a transponder device with the correct code is within close range of a receiver in the vehicle.

8. _____-_____ _____ connect the secondary ignition components together, such as the coil to the distributor cap and the distributor cap to the spark plugs.

9. If the insulation around the cable is insufficient and the leads are not spaced far enough apart and run parallel to each other, then a(n) _____ _____ can be generated in the other wires.

10. Spark plug _____ is the distance from the seat of the spark plug to the end of the spark plug threads.

11. The setting of the contact breaker gap influences the _____ _____.

12. The _____ advance mechanism controls ignition timing in relation to engine speed.

13. Ignition _____ are used in virtually every type of ignition system except the contact breaker point system.

14. _____-_____ systems are electronic systems that use a magnetic pulse generator, also called a variable reluctor sensor, to generate an AC signal.

15. A(n) _____ winding is an extended length of wire wrapped into a circle.

16. The pickup coil winding is connected to the ignition module and forms part of a(n) _____ _____ _____ _____ _____.

17. In a distributor, the Hall-effect generator and its _____ _____ are located on one leg of a U-shaped assembly mounted on the distributor base plate.

18. In _____ ignition systems, the distributor is eliminated and replaced by multiple ignition coils.

19. A(n) _____ or lab scope can be used to observe the electrical patterns created by the triggering devices and ignition coil.

20. Many oscilloscopes have the ability to stack each spark plug's ignition pattern vertically, which is called _____.

Labeling

Label the following diagrams with the correct terms.

1. Contact breaker point ignition system:

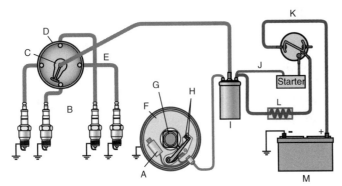

A. _____

B. _____

C. _____

D. _____

E. _____

F. _____

G. _____

H. _____

I. _____

J. _____

K. _____

L. _____

M. _____

2. Electronic ignition system—distributor type:

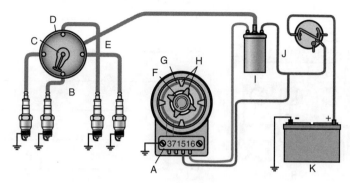

A. _____

B. _____

C. _____

D. _____

E. _____

F. _____

G. _____

H. _____

I. _____

J. _____

K. _____

3. Waste spark ignition system:

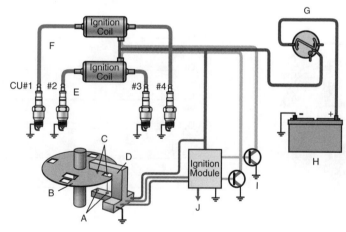

A. _____

B. _____

C. _____

D. _____

E. _____

F. _____

G. _____

H. _____

I. _____

J. _____

4. Coil-on-plug ignition system:

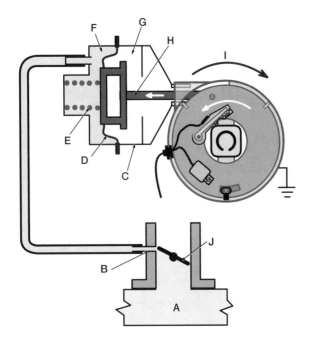

A. _____

B. _____

C. _____

D. _____

E. _____

F. _____

G. _____

H. _____

I. _____

J. _____

5. Vacuum advance mechanism:

A. _____

B. _____

C. _____

D. _____

E. _____

F. _____

G. _____

H. _____

I. _____

J. _____

6. Ignition coil:

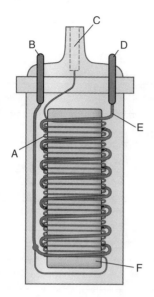

A. _____

B. _____

C. _____

D. _____

E. _____

F. _____

7. Parts of a high-tension lead:

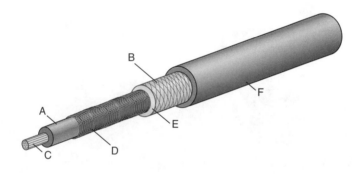

A. _____

B. _____

C. _____

D. _____

E. _____

F. _____

8. Spark plug:

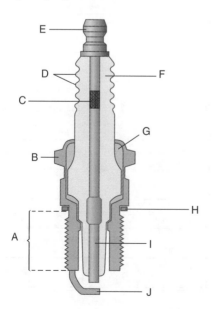

A. _____

B. _____

C. _____

D. _____

E. _____

F. _____

G. _____

H. _____

I. _____

J. _____

9. Contact breaker point operation:

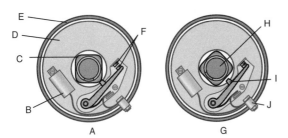

A. _____

B. _____

C. _____

D. _____

E. _____

F. _____

G. _____

H. _____

I. _____

J. _____

10. Distributor:

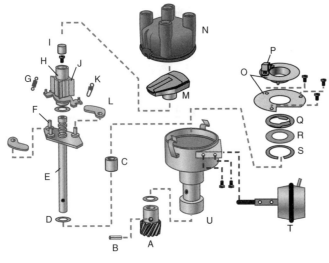

A. _____

B. _____

C. _____

D. _____

E. _____

F. _____

G. _____

H. _____

I. _____

J. _____

K. _____

L. _____

M. _____

N. _____

O. _____

P. _____

Q. _____

R. _____

S. _____

T. _____

U. _____

11. Vacuum sources:

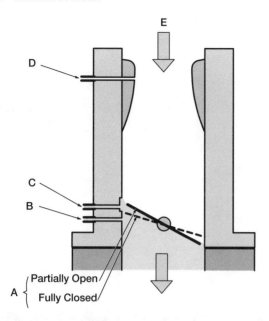

A. _____

B. _____

C. _____

D. _____

E. _____

Skill Drills

Test your knowledge of skill drills by filling in the correct words in the photo captions.

1. Performing a Spark Test:

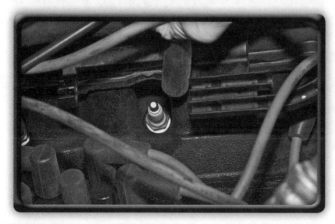

Step 1: Remove the high-tension _____ or _____ from the end of the _____ _____.

Step 2: Connect a _____ _____ to the _____ of the coil or high-tension lead, and attach the _____ to a good _____.

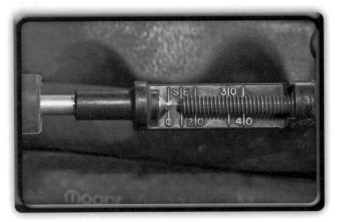

Step 3: Crank the engine, and watch for a _____ _____ the tester _____. If there is no spark present, continue on to the next skill drill.

2. Testing the Ignition Coil:

Step 1: Visually inspect the ignition coil(s) and wires. All the coil _____ should be clean, secure, and free of _____.

Step 2: To test the _____ of the primary windings, place the _____ leads on each of the two primary winding _____. If the reading is not within specifications, the coil is _____ and must be _____.

Step 3: To test the _____ windings, place one ohmmeter _____ on the secondary _____ terminal and the other to the _____ _____ terminal, or the coil secondary _____, if equipped. If the reading is not within specifications, the _____ is faulty and must be replaced.

3. Testing a Spark Plug Wire:

Step 1: Disconnect the spark plug _____ at both ends by grasping the _____ on the ends and _____ while pulling the wire off. _____ each wire for _____, brittleness, or _____ spots.

Step 2: Place one lead of the _____ on each _____ of the spark plug wire. _____ the wire while _____ the ohmmeter.

Step 3: Replace the _____ _____ _____, start the engine, and lightly _____ water on the spark plug wires or run a grounded _____ _____ along each wire. If the readings are not within specifications or if the wires _____, replace the spark plug wires, making sure to _____ them in their factory positions to prevent damage.

4. Testing the Crankshaft and Camshaft Position Sensors:

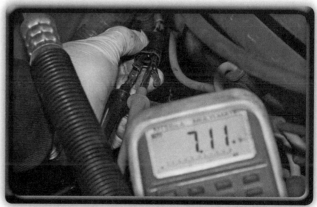

Step 1: Remove the connector from the _____ by removing any _____ _____ that may be present, and _____ the connector off.

Step 2: If it is an _____-_____ sensor, use an ohmmeter to read the _____, and compare the readings to the _____. Replace the sensor if its resistance is too _____ or too low, indicating that it is _____.

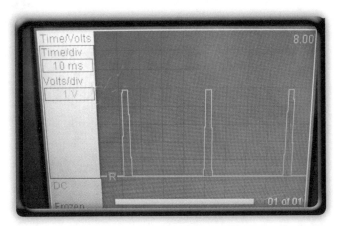

Step 3: If the sensor is a _____-_____ or _____ sensor, or the previous reading is normal, use a _____ _____ to observe the sensor signal and compare to a known good _____. If faulty, replace the sensor.

5. Testing an Ignition Module:

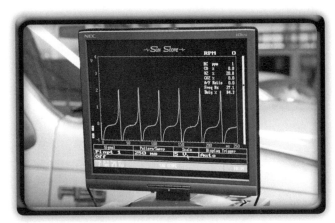

Step 1: Test all the _____ wires leading to the _____ module for proper _____ and _____ signals.

Step 2: Check for proper _____ signals from the ignition module with the _____ set to _____ and while _____. If the specified _____ are present but the ignition module will not produce the proper output _____, the ignition module should be replaced.

Step 3: Check the _____ _____ between the ignition module and the engine _____ with a DMM. If the voltage drop is more than 0.1 volt, check for _____ or rust between the ignition module and the _____ _____. Clean and _____ the ignition module.

Review Questions

_____ 1. All of the following components are common to all ignition systems *except*:
   A. spark plugs.
   B. the ignition coil.
   C. a device for triggering the ignition coil.
   D. a distributor.

_____ 2. Which of the following does the ignition system use to convert relatively low-voltage and high-current flow into very high-voltage and very low-current flow?
   A. Induction coil
   B. Ignition switch
   C. Ignition module
   D. Spark plugs

_____ 3. Which of these usually increases primarily because of the growing gap of the spark plug as it wears over time?
   A. Required voltage
   B. Available voltage
   C. Reserve voltage
   D. Primary voltage

_____ 4. In electronically triggered ignition systems, the spark timing is engineered into the design of the engine and is not adjustable. Which component measures engine speed?
   A. Throttle position sensor
   B. Manifold absolute pressure sensor
   C. Crankshaft position sensor
   D. Mass airflow sensor

_____ 5. Which of the following ignition switch positions unlocks the steering column but does not enable any electrical systems or disable the engine immobilizer or theft-deterrent system?
   A. Lock
   B. Off
   C. Accessory
   D. On

_____ 6. Which of the following systems has the fewest parts, which reduces failures and maintenance the most?
   A. Waste spark ignition system
   B. Coil-on-plug ignition system
   C. Contact breaker point ignition system
   D. Distributor-type electronic ignition system

_____ 7. Which of the following equipment is used to test for voltage drops and high resistance within the primary circuit?
   A. Spark testers
   B. LED test light
   C. Digital multimeter
   D. Standard test light

_____ 8. On distributor type vehicles, when testing the secondary side of the circuit, the oscilloscope can display several scope patterns. A high firing line on just one cylinder may indicate:
   A. low resistance.
   B. a short in the circuit.
   C. an open spark plug wire.
   D. low compression.

_____ 9. If there is a slight drag between the gapping tool gauge and the spark plug electrodes as the gauge is installed and removed, it means:
   A. the gap of the spark plug is correct.
   B. the gap of the spark plug is too high.
   C. the gap of the spark plug is too low.
   D. the spark plug was not pre-gapped.

_____ **10.** If the coil primary circuit has continuity, the reading should be 12 volts or more when:
- **A.** the ignition switch is on, and the red lead of the multimeter is connected to the secondary output terminal of the coil and the black lead to engine ground.
- **B.** the ignition switch is off, and the red lead of the multimeter is connected to the positive terminal of the coil and the black lead to engine ground.
- **C.** the ignition switch is in the run position, and the red lead or test light is connected to the negative side of the coil and the black lead to a good ground.
- **D.** the ignition switch is off, and the red lead or test light is connected to the negative side of the coil and the black lead to a good ground.

ASE Technician A/Technician B Style Questions

_____ **1.** Tech A says that contact breaker points are a mechanical switch that opens and closes once for every ignition spark that is created. Tech B says that contact breaker points send high voltage directly from the points to the spark plugs. Who is correct?
- **A.** Tech A
- **B.** Tech B
- **C.** Both A and B
- **D.** Neither A nor B

_____ **2.** Tech A says that as engines gain miles, the spark plug gap increases, which raises the ignition system's available voltage. Tech B says that misfire occurs when required voltage is higher than available voltage. Who is correct?
- **A.** Tech A
- **B.** Tech B
- **C.** Both A and B
- **D.** Neither A nor B

_____ **3.** Tech A says that as engine RPM increases, spark timing generally increases. Tech B says that as engine load increases, spark timing generally decreases. Who is correct?
- **A.** Tech A
- **B.** Tech B
- **C.** Both A and B
- **D.** Neither A nor B

_____ **4.** Tech A says that a Hall-effect switch uses light to turn a circuit on and off. Tech B says that waste spark systems don't need distributors. Who is correct?
- **A.** Tech A
- **B.** Tech B
- **C.** Both A and B
- **D.** Neither A nor B

_____ **5.** Tech A says that coil-on-plug ignition systems use one coil to fire two cylinders. Tech B says that you should twist spark plug boots before removing them. Who is correct?
- **A.** Tech A
- **B.** Tech B
- **C.** Both A and B
- **D.** Neither A nor B

_____ **6.** Tech A says that the ignition system will maintain spark at the spark plug for approximately 23 degrees of crankshaft rotation. Tech B says that the duration of spark in the spark plug only lasts 2 to 3 degrees of crankshaft rotation. Who is correct?
- **A.** Tech A
- **B.** Tech B
- **C.** Both A and B
- **D.** Neither A nor B

_____ **7.** Tech A says that the positive side of the coil primary circuit is typically switched by the ignition module. Tech B says that on two-wire COP coils, the coil is switched by an external ignition module or the PCM. Who is correct?
   A. Tech A
   B. Tech B
   C. Both A and B
   D. Neither A nor B

_____ **8.** Tech A says that one advantage of distributorless ignition systems is no moving parts to maintain. Tech B says that the resistance of the coil primary winding can best be tested with a voltmeter. Who is correct?
   A. Tech A
   B. Tech B
   C. Both A and B
   D. Neither A nor B

_____ **9.** Tech A says that an inductive pickup coil can be tested for shorts and grounds with an ohmmeter. Tech B says that an inductive pickup coil pattern can be tested with a lab scope. Who is correct?
   A. Tech A
   B. Tech B
   C. Both A and B
   D. Neither A nor B

_____ **10.** Tech A says that on a secondary ignition pattern, the firing line shows how much voltage it takes to jump the spark plug gap. Tech B says that the spark line on a secondary pattern tells the length of the spark plug reach. Who is correct?
   A. Tech A
   B. Tech B
   C. Both A and B
   D. Neither A nor B

Gasoline Fuel Systems

At the start of each chapter you'll find the NATEF tasks, Knowledge Objectives, and Skills Objectives from the textbook. These are your objectives as you make your way through the exercises in this workbook and the chapter in your textbook. The following activities have been designed to help you refresh your knowledge of the material in this chapter.

NATEF Tasks

- N62001 Replace fuel filter(s) where applicable. (MLR/AST/MAST)
- N62002 Inspect and test fuel pump(s) and pump control system for pressure, regulation, and volume; determine needed action. (AST/MAST)
- N62003 Check fuel for contaminants; determine needed action. (AST/MAST)
- N62004 Inspect, test, and/or replace fuel injectors. (AST/MAST)

Knowledge Objectives

After reading this chapter, you will be able to:

- K62001 Explain the principles related to gasoline fuel systems.
- K62002 Explain the purpose and function of the fuel supply system components.
- K62003 Explain the principles EFI fuel systems.
- K62004 Explain the types and operation of carbureted fuel systems.

Skills Objectives

After reading this chapter, you will be able to:

- S62001 Perform maintenance and preliminary testing of fuel systems.

Matching

Match the following terms with the correct description or example.

A. Accelerator pump	**K.** Idle
B. Accelerator pump circuit	**L.** Injector
C. Air supply system	**M.** Knocking
D. Choke	**N.** Misfire
E. Dieseling	**O.** Pressure
F. Element	**P.** Octane rating
G. Float chamber	**Q.** Relay
H. Fuel rail	**R.** Throttle
I. Fuel metering system	**S.** Vacuum
J. Fuel system	**T.** Vapor lock

_____ **1.** A condition in which the engine continues to run after the ignition key is turned off. Also referred to as run-on.

_____ **2.** A standard measure of the performance of a motor or aviation fuel.

_____ **3.** The speed at which an engine runs without any throttle applied.

_____ **4.** Equipment in a motor vehicle that delivers the proper amount of fuel to each cylinder.

_____ **5.** A device used to produce acceleration by controlling the air/fuel mixture.

_____ **6.** A situation in which vapor forms in the fuel line, and the bubbles of vapor block the flow of fuel and stop the engine.

_____ **7.** The carburetor circuit involved with heavy acceleration, directly connected to the accelerator pump.

_____ **8.** The force per unit area applied to the surface of an object.

_____ **9.** Tubing that connects several injectors to the main fuel.

_____ **10.** A magnetically operated switch used to make or break current flow in a circuit.

_____ **11.** A small pump usually located inside the carburetor that sprays an extra amount of fuel into the carburetor air horn during acceleration.

_____ **12.** Equipment in a motor vehicle that delivers fuel to the engine.

_____ **13.** The replaceable portion of a filter, such as an air filter or oil filter.

_____ **14.** A pressure in an enclosed area that is lower than atmospheric pressure.

_____ **15.** A device that provides a rich air/fuel mixture until the engine warms up by restricting the flow of air at the entrance to the carburetor, before the venturi.

_____ **16.** A noise heard when the air/fuel mixture spontaneously ignites before the spark plug is fired at the optimum ignition moment.

_____ **17.** Equipment in a motor vehicle that delivers air to the engine.

_____ **18.** Failure of one or more cylinders to fire or complete combustion.

_____ **19.** A chamber that holds a quantity of fuel at atmospheric pressure ready for use.

_____ **20.** A valve that is controlled by a solenoid or spring pressure to inject fuel into the engine.

Multiple Choice

Read each item carefully, and then select the best response.

_____ **1.** _____ occurs before normal combustion, when something in the combustion chamber heats up enough to ignite the mixture before the spark plug fires.
   A. Vapor lock
   B. Dieseling
   C. Choking
   D. Pre-ignition

_____ **2.** A violent collision of flame fronts in the cylinder, caused by uncontrolled combustion is called _____.
   A. dieseling
   B. detonation
   C. misfire
   D. throttling

_____ **3.** The stoichiometric air/fuel ratio is represented by the Greek letter _____.
   A. alpha
   B. delta
   C. omega
   D. lambda

_____ **4.** The optimum ratio of air to fuel for combustion is known as _____.
   A. injection ratio
   B. computer-controlled ratio
   C. stoichiometric ratio
   D. pressure/vacuum ratio

_____ **5.** Atmospheric pressure at sea level is calculated as _____.
   A. 14.7 psi
   B. 1 lambda
   C. 101 kilopascals
   D. either A or C

_____ **6.** In a carburetor power circuit the size of the main _____ is selected to provide the best mixture for economy under cruising conditions.
   A. venturi
   B. metering jet

          C. barrel

          D. float bowl

_____ **7.** The _____ should operate as briefly as possible; overuse produces rich mixtures that cause exhaust pollution and increases fuel consumption.

          A. choke

          B. accelerator pump

          C. metering jet

          D. fuel pump

_____ **8.** Extra carburetor _____ (as many as four) improve performance, particularly at high speeds, by letting more air and fuel enter the cylinders.

          A. injectors

          B. metering jets

          C. float bowls

          D. barrels

_____ **9.** Vapor from the fuel tank is vented through a _____ where fuel vapors are stored until they are burned in the engine.

          A. drier

          B. charcoal canister

          C. desiccant

          D. filter sock

_____ **10.** The _____ is a variable resistor that is attached to a float mechanism in the fuel tank.

          A. sending unit

          B. fuel pump relay

          C. pressure regulator

          D. accelerometer

_____ **11.** A _____ is incorporated into the end of the fuel pickup tube and is the first line of defense against fuel contamination.

          A. fuel filter

          B. fuel rail

          C. filter sock

          D. fuel separator

_____ **12.** The _____ system uses one or two fuel injectors located centrally on the intake manifold, right above the throttle plates.

          A. throttle body injection

          B. fuel rail injection

          C. diesel fuel direct injection

          D. gasoline direct injection

_____ **13.** The _____ system uses a fuel injector for each cylinder located in the intake manifold near each intake valve that sprays fuel toward the valve.

          A. single-point injection

          B. multipoint fuel injection

          C. gasoline direct injection

          D. throttle body injection

_____ **14.** The exhaust gas oxygen sensor is also called the _____ sensor.

          A. optical

          B. ultrasonic

          C. pressure

          D. lambda

_____ **15.** Many engine management systems use a _____ to detect detonation.

          A. potentiometer

          B. thermistor

          C. position sensor

          D. knock sensor

True/False

If you believe the statement to be more true than false, write the letter "T" in the space provided. If you believe the statement to be more false than true, write the letter "F."

_____ 1. The more effectively liquid gasoline is changed into vapor, the more efficiently it burns in the engine.

_____ 2. There are two different methods used to measure the octane rating of a fuel—the Research Octane Number and the Motor Octane Number.

_____ 3. A lean air/fuel mixture has less air in proportion to the amount of fuel.

_____ 4. Dieseling may cause an engine to run backward for a brief time when it comes to a stop.

_____ 5. A vacuum gauge can be calibrated in inches of mercury in a scale reading from 0" to 30", or if using millimeters of mercury, the scale reads from 0 to 760 mm.

_____ 6. The off idle circuit enables the engine to keep running when there is not enough air speed through the venturi to create a vacuum.

_____ 7. The fuel pump on a carbureted system can be either electric or mechanical.

_____ 8. Modern vehicles are required by the Environmental Protection Agency to have a vented gas cap.

_____ 9. The fuel filter typically consists of a pleated paper filter housed in a sealed container, and its primary function is to prevent contaminants from reaching the injectors.

_____ 10. Some vehicles use a pressure regulator on the fuel rail, some are in the fuel tank, and others control fuel pressure by controlling the speed of the fuel pump.

_____ 11. Gasoline direct injection engines can run fuel mixtures as lean as 65 to 1, much leaner than the stoichiometric ratio.

_____ 12. Sequential injection means that the injectors operate twice per cycle, once each crankshaft revolution, each time delivering half the fuel for the cycle.

_____ 13. A homogeneous mixture results in good power and a very clean burn.

_____ 14. Gasoline is mainly a mixture of paraffins, naphthenes, aromatics, and olefins, together with some other organic compounds and contaminants such as sulfur.

_____ 15. Higher compression engines are more susceptible to engine knock.

_____ 16. An air-fuel mixture that is too lean can make an engine run smooth.

Fill in the Blank

Read each item carefully, and then complete the statement by filling in the missing word(s).

1. The _____ _____ system draws in gasoline from the gas tank (fuel cell) and delivers it under pressure to a fuel metering device.

2. The less easily the fuel ignites, the higher the _____ _____.

3. The term _____ _____ describes the chemically correct air/fuel ratio necessary to achieve complete combustion of the fuel and air.

4. Fuel-injected vehicles do not experience _____ unless there is a leaking injector when the ignition is turned off.

5. When an extra squirt of fuel is needed for a burst of speed, the _____ _____ circuit comes into play.

6. A(n) _____-_____ carburetor normally uses an electronically controlled solenoid valve called a mixture control solenoid to respond to the PCM commands.

7. The fuel _____ _____ can incorporate the use of a blowback ball valve to prevent fuel from leaking from the vehicle during fill-ups and to deter gas theft.

8. The primary job of the _____ _____ is to send constant electrical signals to the gas gauge located in the driver information center or to the BCM, which then controls the gas gauge.

9. A(n) _____ _____ is a special manifold designed to provide a reservoir of pressurized fuel for the fuel injectors.

10. The modern _____ _____ is simply a spring-loaded, electric-solenoid spray nozzle.

11. There are two types of _____ fuel injection systems. One uses a pressure regulator in the fuel tank, and the other controls the speed of the fuel pump to modify pressure.

12. _____-_____ are also commonly used to seal the injector to the fuel rail.

13. The powertrain control module monitors the air/fuel ratio by using a(n) _____ sensor.

14. _____ _____ _____ is also known as single-point injection or central-point injection.

15. The _____/_____ test measures the fuel pressure being delivered to the fuel rail along with the volume of the fuel pump.

Labeling

Label the following diagrams with the correct terms.

1. Fractional distillation tower:

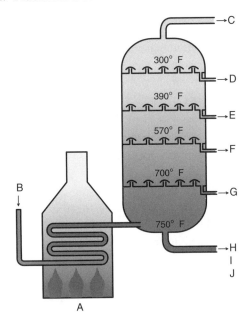

A. _____

B. _____

C. _____

D. _____

E. _____

F. _____

G. _____

H. _____

I. _____

J. _____

2. Types of carburetors:

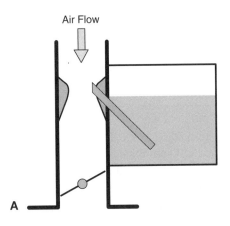

A. _____

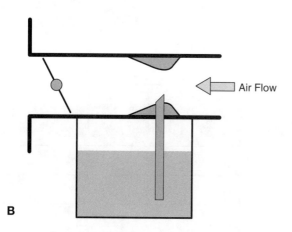

B   Air Flow

B. _____

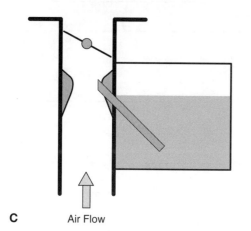

C   Air Flow

C. _____

3. Float bowl, float, and needle and seat:

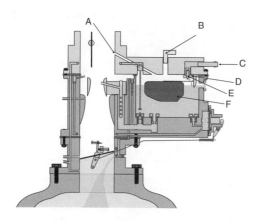

A. _____

B. _____

C. _____

D. _____

E. _____

F. _____

4. Main metering jet and discharge nozzle:

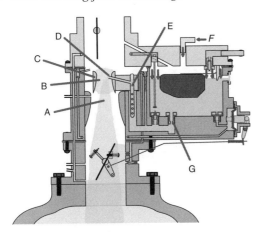

A. _____

B. _____

C. _____

D. _____

E. _____

F. _____

G. _____

5. The choke:

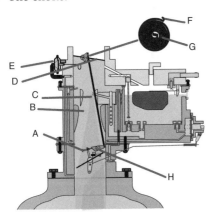

A. _____

B. _____

C. _____

D. _____

E. _____

F. _____

G. _____

H. _____

6. Mechanical fuel pump:

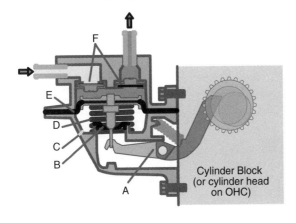

A. _____

B. _____

C. _____

D. _____

E. _____

F. _____

7. Diaphragm-type electric fuel pump:

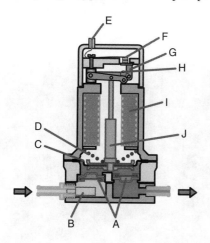

A. _____

B. _____

C. _____

D. _____

E. _____

F. _____

G. _____

H. _____

I. _____

J. _____

8. Fuel tank:

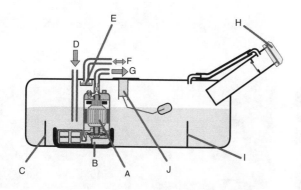

A. _____

B. _____

C. _____

D. _____

E. _____

F. _____

G. _____

H. _____

I. _____

J. _____

Skill Drills

Place the skill drill steps in the correct order.

1. Replacing a Fuel Filter:

_____ **A.** Reinstall the filter, with the flow indicator arrow pointing toward the engine, and fully engage the lines, making sure they are secure.

_____ **B.** For a quick disconnect filter: Using the correct tool, release the quick disconnect connectors from the outlet end of the filter, catching any leaking fuel in a fuel-proof container.

_____ **C.** Turn the key to the on position for 5 seconds, but do not start the engine, and then turn it back to off. Repeat the process two more times, checking the filter connections for leaks. If no leaks are found, start the vehicle, letting it run for 2 to 3 minutes before shutting it off. Recheck the filter connections for leaks.

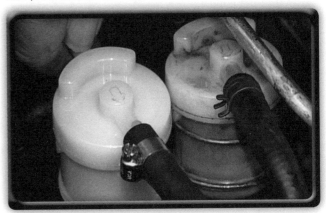

_____ **D.** Reinstall the filter, making sure you have the filter facing in the right direction, with the flow indicator arrow pointing toward the engine. Tighten the fittings on both ends using the double wrench method.

_____ **E.** Obtain the correct replacement filter and components. Loosen the bracket holding the filter in place, if equipped. Follow the steps below according to the type of filter you are replacing.

_____ **F.** Some low pressure types use clamps to seal the connections.

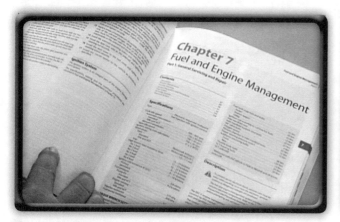

_____ **G.** Refer to the service information to identify the location and type of fuel filter and the correct procedure for removing and replacing it. If the engine is equipped with an electric fuel pump, release the pressure according to the service information.

_____ **H.** Wipe any residual fuel off with a clean shop rag, and write the date and mileage on the filter. Remember to replace the fuel pump fuse, if removed.

_____ **I.** For a flared fitting type of filter: A number of connection types are used on filters. On flared fitting types, disconnect the fuel line on the engine side of the filter, using the double wrench method. If necessary, drain any excess fuel into a fuel-proof container.

_____ **J.** Release the quick disconnect connectors from the inlet end of the filter, and remove the filter from the lines.

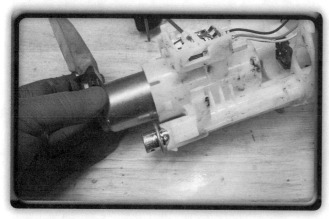

_____ **K.** Carefully remove the in-tank fuel filter from the pump assembly, and replace it with a new one, if it is a replaceable type.

_____ **L.** On vehicles with the filter in the tank, remove the fuel pump assembly.

2. Inspecting and Testing Fuel Pumps:

_____ **A.** Start the engine, measure the pressure, and compare to specifications. With the engine running and the end of the fuel line from the fuel pressure gauge in a 1-quart plastic bottle, open the valve on the gauge and stop the fuel flow after 15 seconds.

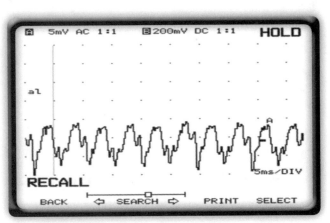

_____ **B.** Start the engine, look at the lab scope pattern, and compare the pattern to the service information.

_____ **C.** Turn the key to the run position and measure the pressure. If none, test the fuel pump's electrical circuit.

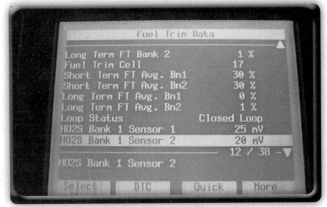

_____ **D.** After repair, reconnect the scan tool and test drive the vehicle to verify the repair by monitoring the oxygen sensors and fuel trim.

_____ **E.** If the pressure test or volume test was less than specified, you can use a lab scope and low-amps clamp to graph the current flow going to the fuel pump. Remove the fuel pump fuse, and connect a jumper lead between the terminals in the fuse box. Place the amps clamp around the jumper lead.

_____ **F.** After researching the procedure for testing the fuel pump in the service information, install a fuel pump gauge on the fuel rail test port.

_____ **G.** Measure the amount of fuel delivered in that time, and compare to specifications.

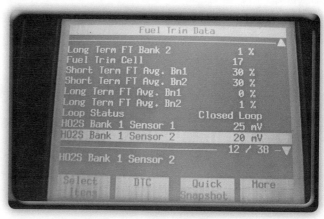

_____ **H.** Connect a scan tool to the DLC and record rpm, VSS, front oxygen sensors, both fuel trims, and fuel pressure, if equipped, under heavy load and at higher rpm. After returning to the shop, look at your recording; if you see a low fuel pressure or a lean oxygen signal with a large increase in fuel trim, the vehicle has a fuel delivery problem.

3. Checking Fuel for Contaminants and Quality:

_____ **A.** Allow the mixture to settle. Observe the level of the water in the bottom of the test tube. Anything higher than the initial 10 mL is the amount of alcohol in the fuel. List your observations and determine any necessary actions.

_____ **B.** Add 90 mL of gasoline, bringing the total volume to 100 mL.

_____ **C.** Carefully pour off the fuel in the test tube back into the fuel container. Make sure no water leaves the test tube. Properly dispose of the remaining water–fuel mixture.

_____ **D.** Pour 10 mL of water into the 100 mL graduated test tube.

_____ **E.** Cap the test tube tightly. Slowly agitate the fuel-water mixture for 30 seconds. If there is any alcohol in the fuel, this motion will allow the water to be absorbed by the alcohol.

_____ **F.** Collect a quantity of fuel from the vehicle's fuel rail in a clear plastic fuel container. Let it settle and check for contaminants, cloudiness, or improper odor.

4. Inspecting and Testing Fuel Injectors:

_____ **A.** Activate the injector pulsing tool for the appropriate amount of time. Watch the pressure gauge, and record the pressure after the injector has been pulsed.

_____ **B.** Pressurize the fuel rail by turning on the ignition switch for a few seconds. Then turn the ignition switch off. Record the fuel pressure.

_____ **C.** Repeat this test on each fuel injector, pressurizing the fuel rail each time before activating the injector pulsing tool. Record the pressure readings before and after each test. Compare all readings to specifications and to each other. Determine any necessary actions.

_____ **D.** Install the fuel pressure gauge on the fuel rail. Connect the injector pulsing tool to one fuel injector, according to the tool maker's instructions, and set it for the appropriate number and time of pulses.

_____ **E.** Measure the resistance of the suspect fuel injector, and compare to specifications. If the resistance is not in specifications, replace the injector.

Review Questions

_____ **1.** All of the following statements with respect to the fuel system are true *except*:
   A. It provides the ideal air-fuel mixture for the operating conditions of the engine.
   B. Fuel has to be vaporized, turning from a liquid to a gas.
   C. The larger the liquid droplets, the faster they can be vaporized.
   D. It takes time and temperature for fuel to vaporize fully.

_____ **2.** Which of these air-fuel mixtures gives good fuel economy and low exhaust emissions suitable for cruising conditions?
   A. A slightly lean mixture
   B. A rich mixture
   C. A slightly rich mixture
   D. An extremely rich mixture

_____ **3.** Which of the following temporarily stores fuel vapors until they can be burned in the engine?
   A. Fuel tank
   B. Fuel pump
   C. Fuel rail
   D. Evaporative emission control system (EVAP)

_____ **4.** Which of these fuel injection systems operates with fuel injectors located only in the intake manifold near each intake valve and sprays fuel toward the valve?
   A. Central-point injection
   B. Throttle body injection
   C. Multipoint fuel injection
   D. Gasoline direct injection

_____ **5.** Choose the correct statement with respect to the stoichiometric mode of operation.
   A. It is designed to be used during light throttle, cruise conditions.
   B. It is designed for moderate engine load conditions when a bit more power is needed than for light cruising.
   C. It is designed for heavy engine load conditions when full power is needed.
   D. It is designed to quickly heat the catalytic converter.

_____ **6.** In GDI engines, which of the following is the least risky way to remove the carbon on intake valves and runners, especially if the buildup is very heavy?
   A. Removing the cylinder head, disassembling it, and cleaning it
   B. Removing the intake manifold and using a crushed walnut shell blaster to blast away the carbon
   C. Removing the intake manifold and using a chemical cleaner to soften and dissolve the carbon so it can be removed
   D. Induction cleaning

_____ 7. Which tool is used when measuring fuel pump volume?
   A. Digital multimeter
   B. Fuel pressure gauge
   C. Lab scope
   D. Pulse tester

_____ 8. All of the following are valid ways to relieve the static pressure in the fuel system before removing the fuel lines *except*:
   A. removing the fuel pump relay or the fuel pump fuse and running the engine until it dies.
   B. connecting a fuel pump pressure gauge (that has a bleed valve) to the fuel rail test point, and releasing the excess pressure from the system into a gas can.
   C. on GDI equipped engines, using a scan tool to release the fuel pressure.
   D. using fuel filter lines.

_____ 9. The alcohol content that can be tolerated by flex vehicle and non-flex vehicles, respectively, without causing any drivability issues are in the range of:
   A. 25%; 45%.
   B. 85%; 10%.
   C. 35%; 95%.
   D. 50%; 50%.

_____ 10. An injector pressure drop test to see if the injector is restricted with deposits can be done using a(n):
   A. oscilloscope.
   B. pulse tool.
   C. digital multimeter.
   D. fuel line release tool.

ASE Technician A/Technician B Style Questions

_____ 1. Tech A says that most electric fuel pumps are now mounted inside of the fuel tank. Tech B says that fuel flows through the center of the electric pump and is used to cool the pump. Who is correct?
   A. Tech A
   B. Tech B
   C. Both A and B
   D. Neither A nor B

_____ 2. Tech A says that the stoichiometric ratio is 14.7 gallons of air to 1 gallon of fuel. Tech B says it is 14.7 parts air to 1 part fuel by mass. Who is correct?
   A. Tech A
   B. Tech B
   C. Both A and B
   D. Neither A nor B

_____ 3. Tech A says that some fuel pressure regulators are connected to the throttle plate. Tech B says that too much alcohol in gasoline can cause the engine to run improperly. Who is correct?
   A. Tech A
   B. Tech B
   C. Both A and B
   D. Neither A nor B

_____ 4. Tech A says that high octane fuel is harder to ignite than lower octane. Tech B says that using high octane fuel in an engine designed for lower octane will produce better fuel economy and power. Who is correct?
   A. Tech A
   B. Tech B
   C. Both A and B
   D. Neither A nor B

_____ **5.** Tech A says that dieseling in a car today indicates a possible leaking injector. Tech B says that fuel filters with flared fittings need to be loosened and tightened with the double wrench method. Who is correct?
   A. Tech A
   B. Tech B
   C. Both A and B
   D. Neither A nor B

_____ **6.** Tech A says that a lambda greater than 1 means the engine is running rich. Tech B says that the amount of oxygen in the exhaust indicates how rich or lean the mixture is. Who is correct?
   A. Tech A
   B. Tech B
   C. Both A and B
   D. Neither A nor B

_____ **7.** Tech A says that gauge pressure indicates pressure above atmospheric pressure. Tech B says that atmospheric pressure increases as elevation increases. Who is correct?
   A. Tech A
   B. Tech B
   C. Both A and B
   D. Neither A nor B

_____ **8.** Tech A says that fuel pressure is regulated by a fuel pressure regulator on some vehicles. Tech B says that fuel pressure is regulated by controlling the speed of the fuel pump on some vehicles. Who is correct?
   A. Tech A
   B. Tech B
   C. Both A and B
   D. Neither A nor B

_____ **9.** Tech A says that measuring the alcohol content in gasoline involves using water. Tech B says that as long as the fuel pressure is correct, you don't have to worry about fuel pump volume. Who is correct?
   A. Tech A
   B. Tech B
   C. Both A and B
   D. Neither A nor B

_____ **10.** Tech A says that fuel injectors can be checked for the specified amount of resistance. Tech B says that an injector pressure drop test can determine if an injector is restricted with deposits. Who is correct?
   A. Tech A
   B. Tech B
   C. Both A and B
   D. Neither A nor B

Engine Management System

At the start of each chapter you'll find the NATEF tasks, Knowledge Objectives, and Skills Objectives from the textbook. These are your objectives as you make your way through the exercises in this workbook and the chapter in your textbook. The following activities have been designed to help you refresh your knowledge of the material in this chapter.

NATEF Tasks

There are no NATEF tasks in this chapter.

Knowledge Objectives

After reading this chapter, you will be able to:

- K63001 Explain the purpose and function of engine management sensors.
- K63002 Explain the purpose and operation of potentiometer-based sensors.
- K63003 Explain the purpose and operation of thermistor-based sensors.
- K63004 Explain the purpose and function of inductive and Hall-effect sensors.
- K63005 Explain the purpose and operation of oxygen sensors.
- K63006 Explain the purpose and operation of air measurement sensors.
- K63007 Explain the purpose and operation of pressure sensors.
- K63008 Explain the purpose and operation of switches as sensors.
- K63009 Explain the purpose and function of the PCM.
- K63010 Explain the purpose and function of the controlled devices.
- K63011 Explain the purpose, function, and application of relays as controlled devices.
- K63012 Explain the purpose, function, and application of solenoids as controlled devices.
- K63013 Explain the purpose, function, and application of control modules as controlled devices.
- K63014 Explain the purpose, function, and application of electric motors as controlled devices.
- K63015 Explain the engine management system control strategies.
- K63016 Describe the operation of speed density and mass airflow systems.
- K63017 Explain feedback and looping.
- K63018 Explain short- and long-term fuel trim.
- K63019 Explain fuel shutoff mode and clear flood mode.

Skills Objectives

There are no Skills Objectives in this chapter.

Matching

Match the following terms with the correct description or example.

A. Adaptive learning
B. EGR valve
C. Frequency
D. Camshaft position sensor
E. Electronically controlled throttle

_____ 1. A detection device that signals to the PCM the rotational position of the camshaft.

_____ 2. A system that uses a pedal position sensor to calculate the driver's desired throttle position and sends commands to the PCM.

_____ 3. Monitoring sensor data over time also allows the base fuel settings to be updated in the PCM memory as components age.

_____ **4.** The rate of change in direction, oscillation, or cycles in a given time.

_____ **5.** A device that allows a controlled amount of exhaust gas into the intake manifold during a certain period of engine operation.

Multiple Choice

Read each item carefully, and then select the best response.

_____ **1.** A _____ is a variable resistor that can be used to adjust voltage in a circuit.
   A. relay
   B. potentiometer
   C. rheostat
   D. reed switch

_____ **2.** To test a throttle position sensor, the voltage on the signal return wire is measured with the vehicle in _____ mode.
   A. key on, engine off
   B. clear flood
   C. key on, engine on
   D. fuel shutoff

_____ **3.** In an engine, a(n) _____ sensor measures the temperature of the incoming air through the air filtration system.
   A. manifold absolute pressure
   B. oxygen
   C. mass airflow
   D. intake air temperature

_____ **4.** A(n) _____ is mounted on the crankcase housing and is used to sense the movement of the ring gear teeth on the flywheel.
   A. reed switch
   B. potentiometer
   C. inductive-type sensor
   D. thermistor

_____ **5.** A(n) _____ can be used to send constant data to the computer to determine when the number-one piston of an engine is on the compression stroke.
   A. camshaft position sensor
   B. fuel pressure sensors
   C. engine coolant temperature sensor
   D. accelerator pedal position sensor

_____ **6.** Identify the sensor that is positioned in the exhaust pipe and is used to measure the amount of oxygen in the exhaust gases produced by the engine to determine fuel mixture and spark timing.
   A. Intake air temperature sensor
   B. Mass airflow sensor
   C. Oxygen sensor
   D. Manifold absolute pressure sensor

_____ **7.** What is the switching point of most oxygen sensors that is used to indicate whether the air-fuel ratio is rich or lean?
   A. 0.45 volts
   B. 0.60 volts
   C. 0.20 volts
   D. 0.85 volts

_____ **8.** What is the required operating temperature of a Nernst cell?
   A. 200°F
   B. 300°F
   C. 400°F
   D. 600°F

_____ **9.** A mass airflow sensor is typically installed in the _____.
- **A.** firewall or along the fender in the engine bay
- **B.** fuel rail
- **C.** air intake hose leading to the throttle body assembly
- **D.** exhaust pipe near the catalytic converter

_____ **10.** Identify the type of Karman vortex airflow sensor in which the air vortices cause a mirror to oscillate and interrupt an infrared signal.
- **A.** Ultrasonic type
- **B.** Optical type
- **C.** Pressure type
- **D.** Temperature type

True/False

If you believe the statement to be more true than false, write the letter "T" in the space provided. If you believe the statement to be more false than true, write the letter "F."

_____ **1.** An electronically controlled throttle system is also called drive-by-wire.

_____ **2.** A digital signal is a direct on/off with no in-between transition.

_____ **3.** The resistance of a positive temperature coefficient thermistor is inversely proportional to temperature.

_____ **4.** To maintain the air-fuel ratio within an optimum range extra fuel is needed when the engine is cold.

_____ **5.** The ignition pickup-style position sensor is primarily a Ford design.

_____ **6.** Stoichiometric sensors indicate the exact value of the air-fuel ratio of an engine.

_____ **7.** The temperature of the air entering the engine has no effect on the density of the air-fuel mixture.

_____ **8.** A solenoid is an electromechanical device similar to a relay and moves a valve or linkage.

_____ **9.** An active feedback loop is called an open loop.

_____ **10.** Clear flood mode is activated when the throttle position sensor indicates a wide-open throttle when the ignition is cranked.

Fill in the Blank

Read each item carefully, and then complete the statement by filling in the missing word(s).

1. A(n) _____ _____ sensor measures atmospheric pressure.

2. A(n) _____ _____ sensor is used to monitor crankshaft position and speed.

3. An exhaust gas recirculation valve is used to lower _____ _____ exhaust emissions.

4. _____ signals are continuously variable, typically changing in strength and time.

5. A resistor that changes its resistance with the changes in temperature is called a(n) _____.

6. In negative temperature coefficient thermistors, the _____ goes down as the temperature goes up.

7. A(n) _____ _____ is a type of speed sensor that uses a magnetic field to open and close a movable set of contacts.

8. A mass airflow (MAF) sensor directly measures the mass of filtered air entering the engine in _____ per second.

9. The PCM can adjust the ignition timing of an engine to help reduce the knocking with the input from a(n) _____ sensor.

10. _____ _____ _____ is a safety precaution in which fuel is shut off when certain conditions are met during a vehicle crash.

Labeling

Label the following diagrams with the correct terms.

1. Types of signal:

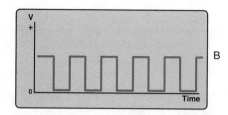

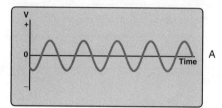

A. _____

B. _____

2. Components of a reed switch:

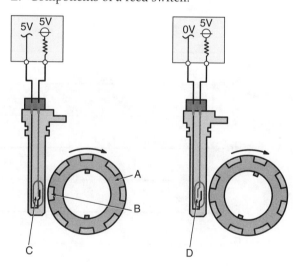

A. _____

B. _____

C. _____

D. _____

3. Components of a typical vane-type airflow meter:

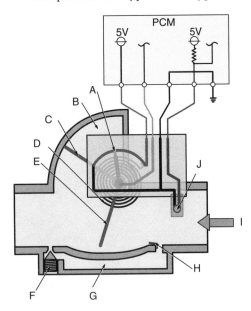

A. _____

B. _____

C. _____

D. _____

E. _____

F. _____

G. _____

H. _____

I. _____

J. _____

4. Components of a solenoid-type air control valve:

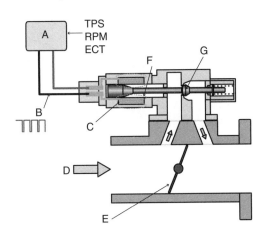

A. _____

B. _____

C. _____

D. _____

E. _____

F. _____

G. _____

5. Components of a coil-on-plug ignition module built into the coil:

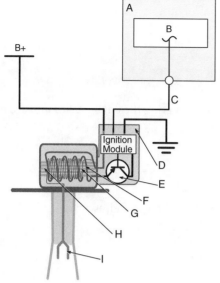

A. _____

B. _____

C. _____

D. _____

E. _____

F. _____

G. _____

H. _____

I. _____

Review Questions

_____ **1.** In the engine management system, which of the following create input signals to the PCM?
   A. Sensors
   B. Relays
   C. Control modules
   D. Solenoids

_____ **2.** Which of the following is the best tool to measure the voltage output from a throttle position sensor?
   A. Scan tool
   B. DVOM
   C. DMM
   D. Digital storage oscilloscope (DSO)

_____ **3.** In a vehicle, thermistors are used in various sensors related to:
   A. pressure.
   B. temperature.
   C. voltage.
   D. speed.

_____ **4.** Which of the following sensors are most involved in the control of ignition timing and injection sequencing?
   A. Fuel temperature sensor
   B. Accelerator pedal position sensor
   C. Crankshaft position sensor
   D. Oxygen sensor

_____ **5.** Which of the following sensors provides information that is the most critical for proper air-fuel mixture, as well as ignition timing?
   A. Manifold absolute pressure (MAP) sensor
   B. Barometric pressure (BARO) sensor
   C. Fuel pressure sensor
   D. Knock sensor

_____ **6.** Which part of a powertrain control module retains diagnostic trouble codes (DTCs), freeze-frame data, and learned data?
   A. Memory and storage section
   B. Sensor input/output signal processing section

    C. Data processing section
    D. Output drivers section

_____ **7.** Which of the following is often used as an actuator to control other actuators when the computer needs to control a high-current load?
    A. Solenoids
    B. Thermistors
    C. Motors
    D. Relays

_____ **8.** The speed-density method of determining the amount of air entering the engine takes into account all of the following *except*:
    A. engine rpm.
    B. manifold absolute pressure.
    C. air temperature.
    D. spark knock.

_____ **9.** The feedback looping system in a three-way catalytic converter serves to adjust:
    A. the air-fuel ratio.
    B. engine speed.
    C. the temperature in the passenger cabin.
    D. fuel consumption.

_____ **10.** Which of the following modes is used by technicians to fool the engine into cranking without starting during a cranking sound diagnosis test?
    A. Fuel shutoff mode
    B. Clear flood mode
    C. Key on, engine off mode
    D. Stoichiometric mode

ASE Technician A/Technician B Style Questions

_____ **1.** Tech A says that analog signals are continuously variable signals. Tech B says that digital signals are direct on/off signals with no in-between transition. Who is correct?
    A. Tech A
    B. Tech B
    C. Both A and B
    D. Neither A nor B

_____ **2.** Tech A says that potentiometer type sensors use a variable resistance to create a variable voltage signal that corresponds to a specific condition. Tech B says that oxygen sensors are the potentiometer type. Who is correct?
    A. Tech A
    B. Tech B
    C. Both A and B
    D. Neither A nor B

_____ **3.** Tech A says that the oxygen sensor measures the amount of oxygen entering the intake manifold. Tech B says that many oxygen sensors have a built-in heater to warm them up more quickly. Who is correct?
    A. Tech A
    B. Tech B
    C. Both A and B
    D. Neither A nor B

_____ **4.** Tech A says that mass airflow sensors determine mass airflow based on engine speed and manifold pressure. Tech B says that some airflow sensors use a hot wire to determine mass airflow. Who is correct?
    A. Tech A
    B. Tech B
    C. Both A and B
    D. Neither A nor B

_____ **5.** Tech A says that the output drivers in the PCM typically send either simple on/off signals, or pulse-width-modulated signals to the actuators, depending on the actuator being controlled. Tech B says that in many cases, the software in the PCM's memory can be updated by uploading software updates, called a reflash process. Who is correct?
   A. Tech A
   B. Tech B
   C. Both A and B
   D. Neither A nor B

_____ **6.** Tech A says that speed density systems use vehicle speed and fuel density to determine injector pulse width. Tech B says that mass airflow systems use a sensor to measure the mass of the air entering the engine. Who is correct?
   A. Tech A
   B. Tech B
   C. Both A and B
   D. Neither A nor B

_____ **7.** Tech A says that open loop is when the PCM pretty much ignores the oxygen sensor signals. Tech B says that closed loop is when the PCM shuts off the fuel injectors during a collision. Who is correct?
   A. Tech A
   B. Tech B
   C. Both A and B
   D. Neither A nor B

_____ **8.** Tech A says that the difference between the stored pulse width and the actual pulse width required to keep the mixture at the correct ratio is called fuel trim. Tech B says that long-term fuel trim values can be positive or negative. Who is correct?
   A. Tech A
   B. Tech B
   C. Both A and B
   D. Neither A nor B

_____ **9.** Tech A says that fuel shutoff mode is when the PCM shuts off the fuel pump when the fuel tank is overfull. Tech B says that clear flood mode is activated by holding the throttle to the floor with the key off and then cranking the engine. Who is correct?
   A. Tech A
   B. Tech B
   C. Both A and B
   D. Neither A nor B

_____ **10.** Tech A says that the oxygen sensor is part of the feedback system for the engine management system. Tech B says that long-term fuel trims that are positive means that the PCM is leaning out the fuel mixture from the base pulse-width setting. Who is correct?
   A. Tech A
   B. Tech B
   C. Both A and B
   D. Neither A nor B

Onboard Diagnostics

At the start of each chapter you'll find the NATEF tasks, Knowledge Objectives, and Skills Objectives from the textbook. These are your objectives as you make your way through the exercises in this workbook and the chapter in your textbook. The following activities have been designed to help you refresh your knowledge of the material in this chapter.

NATEF Tasks

- N64001 Describe the use of OBD monitors for repair verification. (MLR/AST/MAST)
- N64002 Retrieve and record diagnostic trouble codes (DTC), OBD monitor status, and freeze-frame data; clear codes when applicable. (MLR/AST/MAST)
- N64003 Inspect and test computerized engine control system sensors, powertrain/engine control module (PCM/ECM), actuators, and circuits using a graphing multimeter (GMM)/digital storage oscilloscope (DSO); perform needed action. (MAST)
- N64004 Perform active tests of actuators using a scan tool; determine needed action. (AST/MAST)
- N64005 Interpret diagnostic trouble codes (DTCs) and scan tool data related to the emissions control systems; determine needed action. (AST/MAST)
- N64006 Diagnose the causes of emissions or driveability concerns with stored or active diagnostic trouble codes (DTC); obtain, graph, and interpret scan tool data. (MAST)
- N64007 Diagnose emissions or drivability concerns without stored or active diagnostic trouble codes; determine needed action. (MAST)
- N64008 Diagnose drive ability and emissions problems resulting from malfunctions of interrelated systems (cruise control, security alarms, suspension controls, traction controls, HVAC, automatic transmissions, non-OEM-installed accessories, or similar systems); determine needed action. (MAST)

Knowledge Objectives

After reading this chapter, you will be able to:

- K64001 Describe the reasons for onboard diagnostic systems.
- K64002 Explain the two main generations of onboard diagnostic systems.
- K64003 Decode and explain diagnostic trouble codes and freeze-frame data.
- K64004 Explain the purpose and function of the system readiness monitors.
- K64005 Describe the purpose and function of scan tools.
- K64006 Explain the role of the scan tool in the diagnostic process.

Skills Objectives

After reading this chapter, you will be able to:

- S64001 Diagnose emissions or drivability concerns.

Matching

Match the following terms with the correct description or example.

A. Aftermarket
B. Bidirectional scanners
C. Exhaust gas recirculation (EGR)
D. Clean Air Act
E. Continuous monitoring

F. Controller area network (CAN)
G. Data link connector (DLC)
H. Diagnostic trouble code (DTC)
I. Drive cycle
J. Electronic brake control module (EBCM)

K. Emissions

L. Emission analyzer

M. Freeze-frame

N. Pending code

O. Malfunction indicator lamp (MIL)

P. Module

Q. Monitor

R. Powertrain control module (PCM)

S. Scan tool

T. Volatile organic compound

_____ **1.** Tailpipe and volatile organic compound pollutants emitted by the automobile.

_____ **2.** An OBD II test run to ensure that a specific component or system is working properly.

_____ **3.** A series of prescribed automobile operating conditions during which emissions testing is performed.

_____ **4.** A device able to electronically communicate with and extract data from the vehicle's one or more onboard computers.

_____ **5.** A localized (on-board) vehicle network that enables computers and components to send and receive signals across a shielded twisted pair of wires.

_____ **6.** The hydrocarbons in petroleum products that contribute to combustion.

_____ **7.** Code that indicates the component or circuit in which a fault has been detected.

_____ **8.** An electronic computer or circuit board that controls specific functions.

_____ **9.** The module that controls and monitors the anti-lock braking system.

_____ **10.** Federal legislation enacted in the United States to help curb emissions from automobiles.

_____ **11.** A feature of OBD II that records sensor data when a fault occurs.

_____ **12.** Scanners used to cause various components and systems to operate for test purposes.

_____ **13.** The module that runs the engine management systems through self-tests at engine start-up and continues to monitor the systems once underway.

_____ **14.** A term that describes OBD II monitors that run continuously throughout the drive cycle.

_____ **15.** That segment of the trade that supplies parts, services, and repair for vehicles outside of the original equipment manufacturer (OEM) or the dealer network.

_____ **16.** A fault code that has not been validated by failing a second consecutive test.

_____ **17.** A device that enables a scan tool to access data stored in the vehicle's various computers.

_____ **18.** A service bay or lab device used for detecting/measuring vehicle emissions.

_____ **19.** A system that reduces NOx emissions by introducing burned exhaust gases back into the intake manifold to dilute the air-fuel mixture.

_____ **20.** An indicator located in the instrument cluster that illuminates when the powertrain control module (PCM) detects a fault in one of the vehicle systems.

Multiple Choice

Read each item carefully, and then select the best response.

_____ **1.** When a vehicle's _____ is illuminated it means the vehicle is not complying with clean air regulations.

    A. malfunction indicator lamp

    B. VOC indicator light

    C. check engine light

    D. emission indicator lamp

_____ **2.** Which of the following pollutants are monitored and controlled by on-board systems using state-of-the-art electronics?

    A. Hydrocarbons

    B. Carbon dioxide

    C. Oxides of nitrogen

    D. All of the above

_____ **3.** Oxidizing catalytic converters were introduced in _____.

    A. 1968

    B. 1971

    C. 1975

    D. 1981

_____ **4.** The second generation of on-board diagnostic (OBD II) systems operates under standards set by _____.
  A. Association des Constructeurs Européens d'Automobiles
  B. Society of Automotive Engineers
  C. Japanese Automotive Standards Organization
  D. all of the above

_____ **5.** The complete listing of OBD I and OBD II standardized nomenclature for parts and systems used by engineers and technicians is known as _____.
  A. SAE J2012
  B. SAE J1930
  C. SAE J1962
  D. SAE J1968

_____ **6.** To simplify wiring, _____ have become common place in today's vehicles.
  A. controller area networks
  B. data link connectors
  C. OBD I systems
  D. closed-loop systems

_____ **7.** All diagnostic trouble codes have been standardized by the Society of Automotive Engineers and are listed in _____.
  A. SAE J1972
  B. SAE J1930
  C. SAE J2012
  D. SAE J1962

_____ **8.** If the first character of an OBD II diagnostic code is the letter *U*, then the fault is located in the _____.
  A. body
  B. communication system
  C. chassis controller
  D. emission system

_____ **9.** Snapshots that are automatically recorded in the vehicle's powertrain control module when a vehicle fault occurs are referred to as _____ data.
  A. freeze-frame
  B. continuously monitored
  C. keep alive
  D. OBD I

_____ **10.** A _____ includes the following events: A vehicle starts, warms up, is accelerated, cruises, slows down, accelerates once more, decelerates, stops, and cools down.
  A. warm-up cycle
  B. scan cycle
  C. drive cycle
  D. fault cycle

True/False

If you believe the statement to be more true than false, write the letter "T" in the space provided. If you believe the statement to be more false than true, write the letter "F."

_____ **1.** Carbon monoxide and sulfur dioxide react together to create ground-level ozone.

_____ **2.** Evaporative emission control systems were first introduced in 1971.

_____ **3.** OBD I monitored mainly hard electrical circuit malfunctions, whereas OBD II is an enhanced diagnostic system that identifies faults in anything that may affect the vehicle's emission system.

_____ **4.** Emission-related diagnostic trouble codes are the same across all OBD II equipped vehicle makes and models, as are the SAE-recommended names used to describe components and systems.

_____ **5.** If the catalytic converter is at risk, such as from overfueling or a continuous misfire, the malfunction indicator lamp will flash.

_____ **6.** For newer vehicles, diagnostic trouble codes are saved even if the vehicle's battery is disconnected.

_____ **7.** OBD I systems monitor all emission-related components and circuits for opens, shorts, and abnormal operation.

_____ **8.** There are hundreds of possible diagnostic trouble codes, and the list grows constantly as on-board systems become more sophisticated and unique.

_____ **9.** An evaporative emission monitor will not run if the fuel tank is nearly full or nearly empty.

_____ **10.** The bidirectional scan tool is like a "magic bullet." The fault code points directly to the problem.

Fill in the Blank

Read each item carefully, and then complete the statement by filling in the missing word(s).

1. _____ _____ compounds may be fuel or oil vapors emitted from the fuel tank, fuel lines, engine crankcase, or elsewhere.

2. OBD II faults and background data can be accessed and read by original equipment manufacturer (OEM) test equipment or by _____ test equipment made by other companies.

3. The first generation of _____ diagnostic systems operated under manufacturer standards, starting with California vehicles and becoming nationwide in 1981.

4. The _____ _____ _____ is a 16-pin connector with a common (SAE J1962) size and shape.

5. Diagnostic trouble _____ are "set" in one or more of the vehicle's powertrain control modules (PCMs) once a fault is detected.

6. A _____ _____ is designed to operate the vehicle in such a manner as to meet the enabling criteria to cause the PCM to perform the readiness monitor tests.

7. Lower-priority faults are monitored with _____ monitors, meaning they are checked only once during each engine warm-up cycle, or even less often, depending on certain circumstances such as ambient temperatures or fuel level.

8. A _____-_____ cycle is when the engine is started and run until the engine operating temperature reaches 160°F (71.1°C) and has increased in temperature at least 40°F (22°C), and the engine is turned off again.

9. A(n) _____ _____ is a device able to electronically communicate with and extract data from the vehicle's one or more onboard computers.

10. A(n) _____ _____ _____ monitors how long it takes for an oxygen sensor to start operating reliably from cold start-up.

Skill Drills

Test your knowledge of skill drills by filling in the correct words in the photo captions.

1. Retrieving and Recording DTCs, OBD Monitor Status, and Freeze-Frame Data:

Step 1: Select the _____ _____ to provide the best coverage for the _____ and _____ of vehicle. Locate the _____, and connect the scan tool.

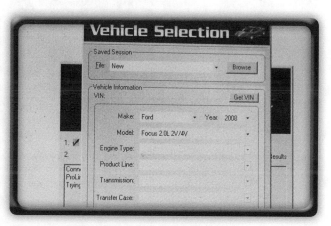

Step 2: Power on the scan tool, and turn the _____ on. Establish scan tool _____ with the _____.

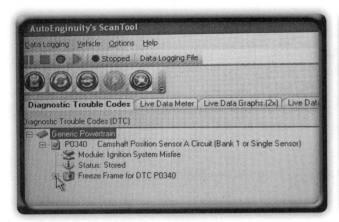

Step 3: _____ and _____ the DTCs.

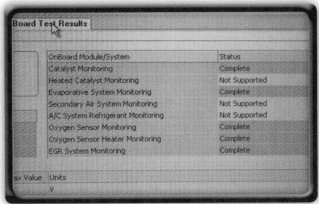

Step 4: Retrieve and record _____ _____ status.

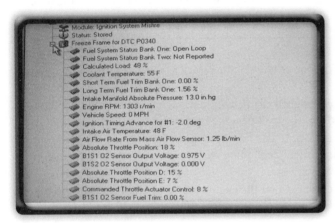

Step 5: Retrieve and record _____-_____ data applicable to DTCs and _____.

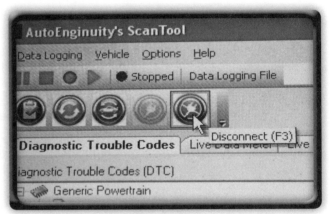

Step 6: Power _____ the scan tool, turn the _____ off, and _____ the scan tool.

2. Testing Engine Control System Sensors, the PCM, Actuators, and Circuits:

Step 1: Determine the _____ to be tested and the likely _____ and frequency of the _____ to be measured. Set up the _____ multimeter or _____, setting the voltage level and time base to commence measurements.

Step 2: Connect the _____ to the _____ to be measured.

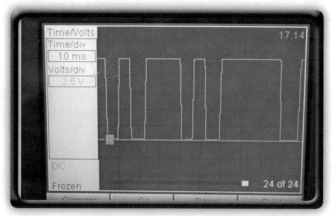

Step 3: _____ the waveforms from the circuit under test. _____ the waveform, _____ it to the manufacturer's specifications or _____ _____ waveforms. Determine the necessary actions.

Review Questions

_____ **1.** Why is it important to run the monitors after repair?
  A. To ensure that the fault doesn't immediately reoccur.
  B. So that the vehicle will operate in closed loop.
  C. So that the vehicle will operate in open loop.
  D. To ensure that the PCM is updated to the latest software.

_____ **2.** All of the following statements regarding DLC are true *except*:
  A. Scan tools serve to access OBD information via the DLC.
  B. Its location is also now fairly standardized as being within 2' of the engine.
  C. The DLC enables the scanner to access data stored in the vehicle's various computers.
  D. It is a 16-pin connector with a common (SAE J1962) size, shape, and pin layout.

_____ **3.** If the MIL flashes, it indicates that the:
  A. engine needs to be serviced within the next 100 miles.
  B. driver should stop the vehicle as soon as safely possible.
  C. vehicle needs refueling.
  D. PCM is malfunctioning.

_____ **4.** Pending or current codes that have happened in the past but haven't been cleared manually with a scan tool, or automatically after approximately 40 warm-up cycles without the code reoccurring, are known as:
  A. current DTCs.
  B. pending codes.
  C. history codes.
  D. generic codes.

_____ **5.** If the first character of the DTC is U, it indicates that the fault is located within the:
  A. powertrain.
  B. body.
  C. chassis controller.
  D. network communication system.

_____ **6.** All of the following statements with respect to freeze-frame data are true *except*:
  A. Freeze-frame data are automatically recorded in the vehicle's PCM when a vehicle DTC is stored.
  B. Freeze-frame data are a list of sensor data that are associated with the specific DTC.
  C. Freeze-frame data is saved for all DTCs stored in memory.
  D. Difficult-to-find intermittent faults can be diagnosed by carefully reviewing the freeze-frame data for clues to the location of the fault.

_____ **7.** Which of the following is a continuous monitor?
  A. Fuel system monitor
  B. Catalytic converter monitor
  C. Evaporative system monitor
  D. EGR system monitor

_____ **8.** Bidirectional scanners:
  A. can be used to cause various components to operate on many vehicles.
  B. can only extract data from the vehicle's one or more on-board computers.
  C. are used to place a fault in a computer system.
  D. can only be used to detect engine faults.

_____ **9.** How can you make sure that the system isn't about to turn on the MIL due to pending codes?
  A. Checking the results of the monitors on Mode 6 and Mode 7
  B. Reassembling the engine
  C. Erasing the codes
  D. Checking freeze-frame data

_____ **10.** Which of the following are used to make precise electrical measurements over time and display the results on a graph as a waveform?
  A. Digital storage oscilloscopes
  B. Scan tools
  C. Continuous monitors
  D. DMM

ASE Technician A/Technician B Style Questions

_____ **1.** Tech A says that on OBD II vehicles, it is a good idea to clear the codes before diagnosis and see if they reset. Tech B says that the DTC indicates which part needs to be changed. Who is correct?
  A. Tech A
  B. Tech B
  C. Both A and B
  D. Neither A nor B

_____ **2.** Tech A says that OBD I and OBD II DLC connectors are different from each other. Tech B says that OBD II standardizes the designations for diagnostic trouble codes (DTCs). Who is correct?
  A. Tech A
  B. Tech B
  C. Both A and B
  D. Neither A nor B

_____ **3.** Tech A says that monitors are designed to test whether emission systems are working properly. Tech B says that monitors are designed to store sensor data about a fault if a DTC is set. Who is correct?
  A. Tech A
  B. Tech B
  C. Both A and B
  D. Neither A nor B

_____ **4.** Tech A says that a CANbus network communicates over a bundle of many individual wires, specially designed for fast communication speed. Tech B says that OBD II mandates that a DTC must be set if the emissions are more than 1.5 times the EPA FTP. Who is correct?
  A. Tech A
  B. Tech B
  C. Both A and B
  D. Neither A nor B

_____ **5.** Tech A says that OBD II allows a technician to hook up a generic scan tool to read DTCs and clear DTCs. Tech B says that when the MIL is on, the vehicle should not be driven. Who is correct?
  A. Tech A
  B. Tech B
  C. Both A and B
  D. Neither A nor B

_____ **6.** Tech A says that something as simple as a loose gas tank fill cap will turn on the MIL. Tech B says that some DTCs require two trips to set a "current" code. Who is correct?
   A. Tech A
   B. Tech B
   C. Both A and B
   D. Neither A nor B

_____ **7.** Tech A says that a "P" in the DTC stands for a powertrain code. Tech B says a "U" stands for an undetermined code. Who is correct?
   A. Tech A
   B. Tech B
   C. Both A and B
   D. Neither A nor B

_____ **8.** Tech A says that if the MIL is blinking, it indicates a catalyst-damaging fault. Tech B says that the EGR readiness monitor can use the MAP sensor to verify the EGR gases are flowing. Who is correct?
   A. Tech A
   B. Tech B
   C. Both A and B
   D. Neither A nor B

_____ **9.** Tech A says that the MIL can turn off if the fault doesn't reappear in three consecutive trips when the monitor is run. Tech B says that when an MIL is activated, the PCM stores the DTC until a predetermined number of drive cycles automatically erase the DTC or if cleared manually by a scan tool. Who is correct?
   A. Tech A
   B. Tech B
   C. Both A and B
   D. Neither A nor B

_____ **10.** Tech A says OBD I mainly monitored hard electrical circuit malfunctions. Tech B says that OBD II codes only monitor non-powertrain components. Who is correct?
   A. Tech A
   B. Tech B
   C. Both A and B
   D. Neither A nor B

Intake and Exhaust Systems

At the start of each chapter you'll find the NATEF tasks, Knowledge Objectives, and Skills Objectives from the textbook. These are your objectives as you make your way through the exercises in this workbook and the chapter in your textbook. The following activities have been designed to help you refresh your knowledge of the material in this chapter.

NATEF Tasks

- N65001 Inspect throttle body, air induction system, intake manifold, and gaskets for vacuum leaks and/or unmetered air. (AST/MAST)
- N65002 Verify idle control operation. (AST/MAST)
- N65003 Inspect integrity of the exhaust manifold, exhaust pipes, muffler(s), catalytic converter(s), resonator(s), tailpipe(s), and heat shield(s); perform needed action. (MLR/AST/MAST)
- N65004 Inspect condition of exhaust system hangers, brackets, clamps, and heat shields; determine needed action (MLR/AST/MAST).
- N65005 Perform exhaust system back-pressure test; determine needed action. (AST/MAST)
- N65006 Test the operation of turbocharger/supercharger systems; determine needed action. (MAST)

Knowledge Objectives

After reading this chapter, you will be able to:

- K65001 Explain the purpose and function of the intake system and components.
- K65002 Explain the components and function of intake manifolds.
- K65003 Explain forced induction.
- K65004 Explain the purpose and function of the exhaust system and components.
- K65005 Explain the purpose and function of the muffler system.

Skills Objectives

After reading this chapter, you will be able to:

- S65001 Perform intake and exhaust inspection and testing.

Matching

Match the following terms with the correct description or example.

- **A.** Blow-off valve
- **B.** Compressor surge
- **C.** Forced induction
- **D.** Helmholtz resonator
- **E.** Mandrel forming
- **F.** Mass airflow (MAF) sensor
- **G.** Plenum chamber

_____ **1.** The pressurization of airflow going into the cylinder through the use of a turbocharger or supercharger.

_____ **2.** The special bending of pipe to ensure the pipe does not collapse. The use of this pipe bender allows for very tight bends without creating kinks or reducing the size of the pipe.

_____ **3.** The PCM input sensor that can measure air entering the engine down to tenths of a gram per second.

_____ **4.** The backup of air against the throttle plate as it is closed. The turbocharger is still spinning, pressurizing air, when the throttle plate is closed. Air will stack up, creating a rapid slowing of the turbocharger compressor wheel. This can damage the compressor wheel.

_____ **5.** A valve that allows the release of excessive boost pressure from the turbocharger when the throttle plate is quickly closed.

_____ **6.** A device that uses the principle of noise cancellation through the collision of sound waves. When necessary, it is used in addition to the muffler to cancel additional sounds. This device may also be used on the induction system to muffle noise of airflow through the induction system.

_____ **7.** A large portion of the intake manifold after the throttle plate and before the intake runner tubes. The manifold provides a reservoir of air and helps prevent interference with the flow of air between individual branches.

Multiple Choice

Read each item carefully, and then select the best response.

_____ **1.** The air cleaner element or filter is manufactured using _____.
   A. pleated paper
   B. oil-impregnated cloth or felt
   C. an oil bath configuration
   D. any of the above

_____ **2.** A(n) _____ is a container that is sealed and specially shaped to cancel noise created by pressure waves.
   A. air cleaner
   B. baffle
   C. Helmholtz resonator
   D. intake manifold

_____ **3.** Cylinder heads that have intake and exhaust manifolds on opposite sides of the engine are known as _____ heads.
   A. parallel
   B. cross-flow
   C. in-line
   D. variable-intake

_____ **4.** Manifolds that respond to changes in engine load and speed by changing their effective length in two or three stages are called _____ systems.
   A. variable inertia
   B. cross-flow
   C. variable intake
   D. either A or C

_____ **5.** The method of warming the incoming air by passing it through a shroud around the exhaust manifold is called a(n) _____ system.
   A. early fuel evaporation
   B. manifold preheating
   C. mass airflow heating
   D. heated induction

_____ **6.** The volume of air entering a cylinder during intake in relation to the internal volume of the cylinder when the piston is at bottom dead center is called _____ and is usually expressed as a percentage.
   A. cylinder volume
   B. induction volume
   C. volumetric efficiency
   D. compression efficiency

_____ **7.** _____ increases air pressure in the intake manifold above atmospheric pressure.
   A. Back-pressure
   B. Forced induction
   C. Intake air heating
   D. Both A and C

_____ **8.** In a turbocharged engine when air pressure in the intake manifold reaches a preset level, the _____ automatically directs the exhaust gases so they bypass the turbine.
   A. wastegate
   B. bypass valve

    C. blow-by valve

    D. aspirator

_____ **9.** When manifold pressure rises above normal and works against the spinning exhaust turbine wheel, slowing it considerably, it is called _____.

    A. back-pressure

    B. blow-back

    C. forced induction

    D. compressor surge

_____ **10.** When the outgoing pulse from one cylinder is timed to arrive at the header junction at exactly the right time to help draw out the pulse from another cylinder, it is known as a _____ exhaust.

    A. balanced

    B. cross-flow

    C. tuned

    D. mandrel-formed

_____ **11.** The _____ is attached to the exhaust manifold and connects to the catalytic converter.

    A. engine pipe

    B. flexible connector

    C. down pipe

    D. either A or C

_____ **12.** The _____ allows movement between the engine and the rest of the exhaust system, and keeps the pipes aligned under a load.

    A. engine pipe

    B. flexible connector

    C. exhaust manifold

    D. intermediate pipe

_____ **13.** A _____ catalytic converter converts oxides of nitrogen back into nitrogen and oxygen, and the hydrocarbons and carbon monoxide to water and carbon dioxide.

    A. two-way

    B. three-way

    C. four-way

    D. all of the above

_____ **14.** The _____ connects the catalytic converter to the muffler.

    A. flexible connector

    B. exhaust bracket

    C. intermediate pipe

    D. engine pipe

_____ **15.** A(n) _____ is sometimes used between the muffler and the exhaust outlet to reduce any resonance levels that the muffler could not adequately suppress.

    A. baffle chamber

    B. intermediate pipe

    C. resonator

    D. secondary muffler

True/False

If you believe the statement to be more true than false, write the letter "T" in the space provided. If you believe the statement to be more false than true, write the letter "F."

_____ **1.** Vaporization starts when the fuel system atomizes the fuel by breaking it up into very small particles by using high pressure to spray it into the charge of air.

_____ **2.** The throttle body controls airflow with a butterfly valve or valves, also called throttle valves.

_____ **3.** On most heavy-duty diesel engines and a few gasoline engines, the air cleaner assembly uses an air filter indicator to tell the operator whether the filter needs to be cleaned or replaced.

_____ **4.** The two main components of the four-stroke intake system are the air cleaner and the throttle body.

_____ **5.** Diesel engines may have more than one air cleaner.

_____ **6.** The air intake manifold for an electronic fuel injection multipoint engine normally has short branches of variable length.

_____ **7.** Port fuel-injected or gasoline direct-injected intake manifolds do not normally need to be heated, since the manifold does not carry fuel.

_____ **8.** Electric heaters can be placed between the intake manifold and the throttle body and used to preheat the air.

_____ **9.** In a stock naturally aspirated engine, one without forced induction, volumetric efficiency can almost never be 100%.

_____ **10.** In a turbocharged engine a bypass valve may be installed so if the wastegate should fail, it can prevent an abnormal rise in manifold pressure.

_____ **11.** On many current vehicles, the exhaust manifold is often replaced with a header.

_____ **12.** Leaded fuel must not be used in an engine with a catalytic converter, because lead will coat the catalyst and prevent it from doing its job.

_____ **13.** Noise cancellation refers to putting a sound material around a perforated pipe that the exhaust gases flow through.

_____ **14.** Adding a variable-flow exhaust to the baffle or chamber system reduces emission noise.

_____ **15.** Exhaust gaskets can be found between the engine cylinder head and the exhaust manifold, the engine pipe and the catalytic converter, and possibly the catalytic converter and the muffler.

Fill in the Blank

Read each item carefully, and then complete the statement by filling in the missing word(s).

1. The _____ system ensures that clean, dry air is supplied to the engine.

2. The _____ system provides a path for the burned exhaust gases to safely exit the engine and travel out the rear of the vehicle.

3. The _____ _____ filters the incoming air.

4. An efficient cyclone precleaner can remove up to _____% of particles before they reach the main filter element, greatly extending its life.

5. The _____ precleaner system uses angled vanes that give the incoming air a swirling motion.

6. The _____ _____ has several tubular branches and carries air and/or air/fuel mixture from the air cleaner to the cylinder head.

7. On vehicles with emission controls, air cleaners use a(n) _____ valve to control how much hot air enters the air cleaner.

8. A buildup of pressure in the system that interferes with the outward flow of exhaust gases is known as _____-_____.

9. A(n) _____ compresses the air in the intake system to above atmospheric pressure, which increases the density of the air entering the engine.

10. A(n) _____ is a forced induction system that uses wasted kinetic energy from the exhaust gases to increase the intake pressure.

11. The purpose of a(n) _____ is to reduce the intake air temperature up to a few hundred degrees Fahrenheit before it enters the intake manifold.

12. Headers provide a(n) _____ effect to help remove exhaust gases from the cylinders.

13. The engine pipe is usually made of a _____ _____ material.

14. The exhaust components are supported by _____-mounted exhaust brackets that help isolate the vibrations of the exhaust from the main body of the vehicle.

15. The function of a vehicle's _____ is to manage the sound coming from the exhaust system.

16. Noise _____ is a system that prevents the sound waves from leaving the exhaust system by canceling them out inside the muffler.

17. The _____-type muffler uses a perforated tube or baffle that is wrapped in fiberglass material, and this will absorb the noise of combustion as gases flow past.

18. A(n) _____ muffler is designed to produce anti-noise without restricting exhaust flow.

19. The _____ takes the exhaust gases away from the vehicle and must not allow any of the exhaust gases to enter the vehicle.

20. Applying a(n) _____ _____ to the cylinder head's combustion chamber and exhaust ports has the effect of creating a thermal barrier from the hot gases to the cylinder head itself.

Labeling

Label the following diagrams with the correct terms.

1. Air induction system:

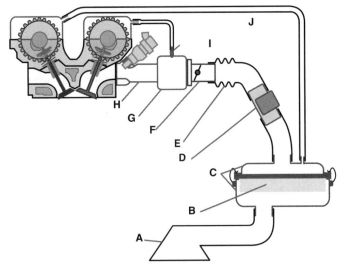

A. _____

B. _____

C. _____

D. _____

E. _____

F. _____

G. _____

H. _____

I. _____

J. _____

2. Using hot engine coolant to heat the manifold:

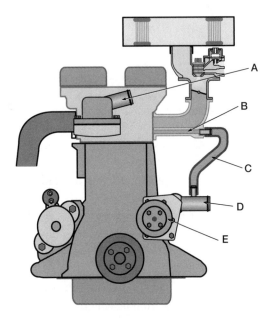

A. _____

B. _____

C. _____

D. _____

E. _____

3. Volumetric efficiency of a normally aspirated engine:

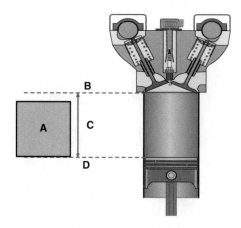

A. _____

B. _____

C. _____

D. _____

4. Volumetric efficiency of a forced-induction engine:

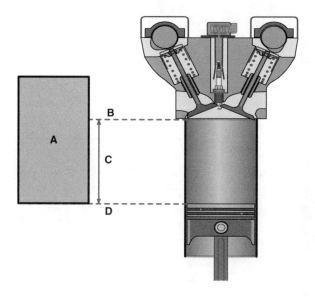

A. _____

B. _____

C. _____

D. _____

5. Identify the following intake and exhaust system components:

A. _____

B. _____

C. _____

D. _____

E. _____

F. _____

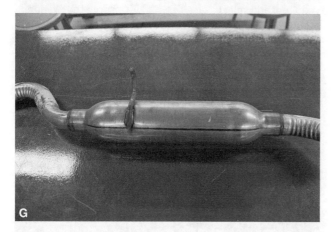

G. _____

Skill Drills

Test your knowledge of skill drills by filling in the correct words in the photo captions.

1. Inspecting the Throttle Body, Air Induction System, and Intake Manifold:

Step 1: Start the _____, and let the _____ stabilize. Using an _____ or _____ testing tool, place the hose near the suspected _____ area.

Step 2: Open the _____ _____ to slowly _____ the acetylene or propane.

Step 3: On vehicles _____ an idle control system, observe the rpm and smoothness of the engine. If the engine speed _____ or smooths out, then a _____ leak is present. Determine any necessary repairs.

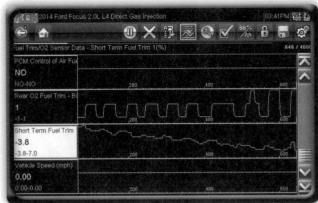

Step 4: On vehicles with an _____ _____ system, connect a scan tool and select _____ _____. Observe the oxygen, short-term fuel trims, and _____ _____ width as you are _____ the acetylene or propane around.

Step 5: Shut off the _____, and connect a _____ _____ to the _____ manifold. Start the smoke machine, and _____ smoke into the intake manifold.

Step 6: Using a bright _____, look around the engine compartment for _____ of _____. Any smoke coming from the _____ _____ inlet is normal. Determine any necessary action(s).

2. Inspecting the Exhaust System for Leaks:

Step 1: Safely lift and secure the vehicle on a _____. Inspect for _____ or _____ _____ in the exhaust system, including the exhaust _____. Inspect brackets, hangers, and clamps.

Step 2: Have a helper hold a _____ against the exhaust pipe(s) while the engine is _____ to increase the _____ in the system. _____ and _____ for any leaks.

Step 3: Use large adjustable _____ to test the _____ of the pipes by moderately _____ the pipes. Determine necessary repairs.

3. Testing the Exhaust System for Back-Pressure:

Step 1: Remove the _____ _____. Install an _____ to the oxygen sensor _____, and connect a _____-_____ gauge.

Step 2: Start the engine, and _____ any exhaust _____-_____, which should be no more than 1.5 psi (10.3 kPa) at _____ and no more than 3 psi (20.7 kPa) at 2000 rpm. Increase the engine _____ to 2000 rpm, and observe the _____. Determine any necessary actions.

Step 3: Inspect the oxygen sensor _____, put _____-_____ on the sensor _____, and _____ to the proper specifications.

Review Questions

_____ 1. The intake system does all of the following *except*:
- **A.** prevent carbon dioxide from entering the engine.
- **B.** ensure that clean, dry air is supplied to the engine.
- **C.** provide a sealed passageway to the combustion chambers.
- **D.** control the amount of air entering the engine.

_____ 2. Choose the correct statement with respect to the exhaust system.
- **A.** It stores the exhaust gases until the catalytic converter heats up.
- **B.** It blocks the air rushing into the engine.
- **C.** It helps reduce the harmful emissions.
- **D.** It is used to warm up the fuel tank.

_____ 3. Which of the following is one of the functions of an air cleaner?
- **A.** Preventing harmful gases from entering the passenger compartment
- **B.** Muffling the noise of the intake pulses
- **C.** Restricting the airflow to the engine at higher speeds
- **D.** Reducing the noise of combustion

_____ 4. In cross-flow heads:
- **A.** the design produces lesser power.
- **B.** the intake and exhaust manifolds are on the opposite sides of the engine.
- **C.** air and fuel are carried on the same branch.
- **D.** the intake and exhaust manifolds are beside each other.

_____ 5. Which of the following components in the exhaust system helps in the reduction of exhaust emissions?
- **A.** Manifold
- **B.** Catalytic converter
- **C.** Muffler
- **D.** Resonator

_____ 6. Which of these is attached to the exhaust manifold and connects to the catalytic converter?
- **A.** Resonator
- **B.** Heat shield
- **C.** Muffler
- **D.** Flex pipe

_____ 7. A catalytic converter converts all of the following gases into less harmful gases *except*:
- **A.** carbon monoxide.
- **B.** hydrocarbons.
- **C.** oxides of nitrogen.
- **D.** sulfur oxides.

_____ 8. To inspect an exhaust system, technicians do all of the following except:
- **A.** block off the exhaust pipe with the engine running and look for leaks.
- **B.** use large adjustable pliers to test the integrity of the pipes by moderately squeezing the pipes.
- **C.** spray the exhaust system with dye check and use a florescent light to locate leaks.
- **D.** inspect for leaks or rust holes in the exhaust system.

_____ 9. An exhaust system back-pressure test is used to:
- **A.** determine whether there is a restriction that will create low power.
- **B.** test the boost pressures that the system can produce.
- **C.** test the integrity of the exhaust pipes.
- **D.** test for exhaust leaks.

_____ 10. Air leaks in the induction system can be tested by all of the following methods *except*:
- **A.** using a substitute fuel to artificially enrich the mixture at the point of the leak.
- **B.** using a smoke machine to fill the intake system and show any external leaks.
- **C.** using an electronic stethoscope to listen for and pinpoint the source of the leak.
- **D.** submerging the system in water and looking for air bubbles.

ASE Technician A/Technician B Style Questions

_____ **1.** Tech A says that coolant circulates through some intake manifolds to help warm them up. Tech B says that some intake manifolds use an electric heater grid to warm up the intake air. Who is correct?
   A. Tech A
   B. Tech B
   C. Both A and B
   D. Neither A nor B

_____ **2.** Tech A says that in some gas engines, the intake manifold runner length can be varied. Tech B says that some intake systems use resonators to quiet intake noise. Who is correct?
   A. Tech A
   B. Tech B
   C. Both A and B
   D. Neither A nor B

_____ **3.** Tech A says that the fuel injectors are mounted in the throttle body on gas direct injection engines. Tech B says that air and fuel are mixed in the intake manifold on gas direct engines. Who is correct?
   A. Tech A
   B. Tech B
   C. Both A and B
   D. Neither A nor B

_____ **4.** Tech A says that scavenging creates a low pressure in the cylinder by means of the exhaust gases flowing through the exhaust pipe. Tech B says that increased back pressure in the exhaust system increases the scavenging effect. Who is correct?
   A. Tech A
   B. Tech B
   C. Both A and B
   D. Neither A nor B

_____ **5.** Tech A says that shorter intake manifolds produce higher torque at lower rpm. Tech B says that longer intake manifolds produce higher torque at high engine speeds. Who is correct?
   A. Tech A
   B. Tech B
   C. Both A and B
   D. Neither A nor B

_____ **6.** Tech A says that air becomes heated as a supercharger compresses it. Tech B says that a turbocharger is designed to pull the exhaust gases out of the engine more effectively. Who is correct?
   A. Tech A
   B. Tech B
   C. Both A and B
   D. Neither A nor B

_____ **7.** Tech A says that a wastegate is designed to direct waste gases to the intake manifold. Tech B says that a blow-off valve allows excess boost pressure to "blow off" into the atmosphere. Who is correct?
   A. Tech A
   B. Tech B
   C. Both A and B
   D. Neither A nor B

_____ **8.** Tech A says that most engines with a turbocharger have turbo lag. Tech B says that a variable-geometry turbocharger will overcome most turbo lag. Who is correct?
   A. Tech A
   B. Tech B
   C. Both A and B
   D. Neither A nor B

_____ **9.** Tech A says that a catalytic converter operates best at cold temperatures. Tech B says that the catalytic converter is typically located before the muffler. Who is correct?
   A. Tech A
   B. Tech B
   C. Both A and B
   D. Neither A nor B

_____ **10.** Tech A says that small vacuum leaks can be found with a smoke machine. Tech B says that stepper motors are used to control idle speed in some vehicles. Who is correct?
   A. Tech A
   B. Tech B
   C. Both A and B
   D. Neither A nor B

Emission Control Systems

At the start of each chapter you'll find the NATEF tasks, Knowledge Objectives, and Skills Objectives from the textbook. These are your objectives as you make your way through the exercises in this workbook and the chapter in your textbook. The following activities have been designed to help you refresh your knowledge of the material in this chapter.

NATEF Tasks

- N66001 Diagnose emission and driveability concerns caused by catalytic converter system; determine needed action. (AST/MAST)
- N66002 Diagnose emissions and driveability concerns caused by the evaporative emissions control (EVAP) system; determine needed action. (MAST)
- N66003 Diagnose oil leaks, emissions, and driveability concerns caused by the positive crankcase ventilation (PCV) system; determine needed action. (AST/MAST)
- N66004 Inspect, test, service, and/or replace positive crankcase ventilation (PCV) filter/breather, valve, tubes, orifices, and hoses; perform needed action. (MLR/AST/MAST)
- N66005 Diagnose the cause of excessive oil consumption, coolant consumption, unusual exhaust color, odor, and sound; determine needed action. (AST/MAST)
- N66006 Diagnose emissions and driveability concerns caused by the exhaust gas recirculation (EGR) system; inspect, test, service, and/or replace electrical/electronic sensors, controls, wiring, tubing, exhaust passages, vacuum/pressure controls, filters, and hoses of exhaust gas recirculation (EGR) systems; determine needed action. (AST/MAST)
- N66007 Diagnose emissions and driveability concerns caused by the secondary air injection system; inspect, test, repair, and/or replace electrical/electronically operated components and circuits of secondary air injection systems; determine needed action. (MAST)

Knowledge Objectives

After reading this chapter, you will be able to:

- K66001 Explain the composition of air, regulated emissions, and their sources.
- K66002 Explain each type of vehicle emissions.
- K66003 Explain the various ways that emissions are controlled in an engine.
- K66004 Explain the purpose and function of each emission control system.
- K66005 Diagnose faults related to PCV system or fluid consumption.

Skills Objectives

There are no Skills Objectives in this chapter.

Matching

Match the following terms with the correct description or example.

A.	Activated charcoal	**H.**	Hydrocarbon
B.	Blow-by pressure	**I.**	Lambda
C.	Carbon monoxide	**J.**	Particulate matter
D.	Compression-ignition engine	**K.**	PCV valve
E.	Emission	**L.**	Pintle
F.	Exhaust gas recirculation (EGR) system	**M.**	Pressure relief valve
G.	Flame front	**N.**	Pulse air system

O. Purging
P. Reed valve
Q. Quenched

R. Two-way catalytic converter
S. Vaporization
T. Vent solenoid

_____ **1.** A flexible valve made from spring steel that flexes to open or close, usually due to pressure changes.

_____ **2.** A valve that controls the amount of crankcase ventilation flow that is allowed and varies with changes in manifold pressure.

_____ **3.** The rapid burning of the air/fuel mixture that moves outward from the spark plug across the cylinder.

_____ **4.** Pressure that leaks past the compression rings during compression and combustion.

_____ **5.** The process of pulling stored fuel vapors from the charcoal canister and moving them into the engine to be burned.

_____ **6.** A valve that is designed to release pressure if it gets above a calibrated level; used in a gas cap as a safety device.

_____ **7.** A converter that changes only hydrocarbons and carbon monoxide into harmless elements.

_____ **8.** A system that recirculates a portion of burned gases back into the combustion chamber to displace air and fuel and cool combustion temperatures.

_____ **9.** A solenoid that allows fresh air to enter the evaporative system during a purge event. Also used for an evaporative system monitoring test.

_____ **10.** An emission created when raw fuel evaporates into the atmosphere or when it does not burn at all in the combustion chamber and is exhausted out the tailpipe.

_____ **11.** An engine that uses the heat of compression to ignite the air/fuel mixture; also known as a diesel engine.

_____ **12.** Tiny particles of solid or liquid suspended in the air and graded in a size range from 10 nanometers to 100 micrometers in diameter.

_____ **13.** A substance that will absorb large amounts of vapor, used in charcoal canisters to store and release fuel vapors.

_____ **14.** A tapered valve that sits in a tapered seat to seal a passageway for air or fuel.

_____ **15.** The changing of a liquid to a gas through boiling.

_____ **16.** A colorless, odorless, tasteless, flammable, and highly toxic gas that is heavier than air and is a product of the incomplete combustion of carbon and oxygen.

_____ **17.** The use of normal exhaust engine pulses to draw air into the exhaust stream.

_____ **18.** The release of substances into the atmosphere that can occur naturally and can also be human-made.

_____ **19.** The state in a combustion chamber in which the flame cannot burn due to cold surfaces or poor distribution of the fuel mixture.

_____ **20.** The ratio of air to fuel at which all of the oxygen in the air and all of the fuel are completely burned.

Multiple Choice

Read each item carefully, and then select the best response.

_____ **1.** The _____ standard is an automotive self-diagnostic system mandated by the EPA that requires a warning light to alert the driver of an emission system fault.
A. clean air
B. emission control
C. OBD I
D. OBD II

_____ **2.** Oxides of _____ are major contributors to photochemical smog, along with hydrocarbons and sunlight.
A. helium
B. nitrogen
C. carbon
D. hydrogen

_____ **3.** _____ is a natural by-product of complete combustion.
   A. Water
   B. Carbon monoxide
   C. Carbon dioxide
   D. Both A and C

_____ **4.** Since carbon monoxide is absorbed so easily by red blood cells, the _____ has set a permissible exposure limit in the workplace of 35 ppm for an 8-hour shift with a ceiling of 200 ppm for any length of time.
   A. Occupational Safety and Health Administration
   B. National Institute for Occupational Safety and Health
   C. American Conference of Governmental Industrial Hygienists
   D. Society of Automotive Engineers

_____ **5.** Which corrosive compound, emitted into the atmosphere through exhaust, is a major environmental pollutant, coming back to earth in contaminated rainwater, called acid rain?
   A. Oxides of nitrogen
   B. Carbon monoxide
   C. Sulfur dioxide
   D. Hydrocarbons

_____ **6.** What is produced in the atmosphere when unburned hydrocarbons and oxides of nitrogen react chemically with sunlight?
   A. Smog
   B. Acid rain
   C. Sulfur dioxide
   D. Carbon monoxide

_____ **7.** The stoichiometric ratio for compressed natural gas is _____.
   A. 14.7:1
   B. 17.2:1
   C. 6.45:1
   D. 34.3:1

_____ **8.** Readings of _____ of carbon dioxide in the exhaust indicate proper combustion efficiency.
   A. 6% to 8%
   B. 12% to 15%
   C. 2% to 5%
   D. 8% to 9%

_____ **9.** The _____ is an example of a precombustion emission control system.
   A. exhaust gas recirculation system
   B. secondary air injection system
   C. heated air intake system
   D. both A and C

_____ **10.** _____ catalytic converters contain both a reduction catalyst and an oxidizing catalyst.
   A. Two-way
   B. Three-way
   C. Four-way
   D. All of the above

_____ **11.** The _____ is a type of positive crankcase ventilation system.
   A. fixed orifice
   B. variable orifice
   C. separator
   D. all of the above

_____ **12.** The _____ is an example of an electrically operated exhaust gas recirculation valve.
   A. negative back pressure EGR valve
   B. positive back pressure EGR valve
   C. stepper motor EGR valve
   D. single-diaphragm EGR valve

_____ **13.** The _____ system is designed to ensure hydrocarbons are not released into the atmosphere when fuel in the fuel tank begins to vaporize and build pressure.
   A. evaporative emission
   B. positive crankcase ventilation
   C. exhaust gas recirculation
   D. secondary air injection

_____ **14.** The fuel cap may incorporate a(n) _____ to release a small amount of pressure to prevent the fuel tank from rupturing.
   A. expansion valve
   B. vacuum relief valve
   C. pressure relief valve
   D. positive back-pressure valve

_____ **15.** Secondary air injection systems use a(n) _____ to control airflow in the system.
   A. air-switching valve
   B. air diverter valve
   C. check valve
   D. all of the above

True/False

If you believe the statement to be more true than false, write the letter "T" in the space provided. If you believe the statement to be more false than true, write the letter "F."

_____ **1.** Humans breathe in oxygen and exhale carbon dioxide; trees and plants take in carbon dioxide and give back oxygen.

_____ **2.** The EPA requires that when a vehicle's emissions deviate from the federal test procedure limit by 3.5 times, the malfunction indicator lamp must turn on and one or more specific diagnostic trouble codes be set in memory.

_____ **3.** Particulate matter is graded in a size range from 10 nanometers to 100 micrometers in diameter; particulates of less than 10 micrometers are dangerous to humans.

_____ **4.** Gasoline, diesel, LPG, and natural gas are all hydrocarbon compounds.

_____ **5.** Exposure to carbon monoxide levels of 400 ppm may be fatal in as little as 30 minutes.

_____ **6.** Sulfur reduces catalyst efficiency in modern vehicles, and vehicles operating with higher sulfur gasoline have higher emissions than vehicles operating on lower sulfur gasoline.

_____ **7.** Keeping the air/fuel ratio close to the stoichiometric point produces minimal hydrocarbon and carbon monoxide emissions.

_____ **8.** The exhaust gas recirculation system is a postcombustion emission control system.

_____ **9.** Any vehicle produced after 1996 monitors catalyst efficiency by using two oxygen sensors, one in front of the catalytic converter and one after the catalytic converter.

_____ **10.** The positive crankcase ventilation system regulates the flow of blow-by gases between the crankcase and the intake manifold.

_____ **11.** A PCV valve connects the exhaust port, or manifold, and the intake manifold.

_____ **12.** The negative back-pressure exhaust gas recirculation valve has a single, spring-loaded diaphragm that seals off the vacuum chamber.

_____ **13.** Older vehicles used vacuum controls solely to operate the exhaust gas recirculation system.

_____ **14.** Before 1971, vehicles vented the fuel tank through the filler cap into the atmosphere.

_____ **15.** A vented filler cap allows air to enter the fuel tank to relieve the low pressure as the fuel is drawn out of the tank or when the fuel contracts as the temperature drops.

_____ **16.** In some earlier carbureted engine designs, the charcoal canister had a vapor line connected to the carburetor float bowl to absorb any fuel vapors from it.

_____ **17.** Some manufacturers use dedicated sensors such as a purge switch, which is located in the purge line and senses the flow of gases or the pressure drop caused by the flow of gases that are being purged.

_____ **18.** Aspirated air injection systems use an air pump to help facilitate the moving of air in the system.

_____ **19.** Pinging can be referred to as the sound of marbles being shaken in a glass jar and is damaging to the engine if it is allowed to continue.

_____ **20.** A five-gas analyzer is a diagnostic tool that uses sensors to measure the level of gases in the exhaust stream.

Fill in the Blank

Read each item carefully, and then complete the statement by filling in the missing word(s).

1. _____ _____ systems are designed to limit the pollution caused by the storing and burning of various fuels.

2. The _____ _____ is the maximum amount of emissions that a vehicle is permitted to emit.

3. The _____ _____ completes the combustion process by adding another oxygen molecule to the carbon monoxide to convert it to carbon dioxide.

4. Victims of _____ _____ poisoning can sometimes look healthy and pink-cheeked because concentrations of carbon monoxide in the bloodstream give the blood a brighter red color than normal.

5. _____ _____ _____ irritate the eyes, nose, and throat.

6. In spark-ignition engines, _____ are caused by incomplete combustion of rich air/fuel mixtures.

7. In a combustion chamber where surface temperatures are low, the combustion flame can go out or be _____.

8. Reducing the valve overlap reduces the _____ _____, which is when the exhaust gases moving out of the combustion chamber create a low-pressure area in the exhaust manifold, helping to pull air and fuel into the cylinder.

9. The _____ _____, also referred to as lambda, is the ratio of air to fuel at which all of the oxygen in the air and all of the fuel are completely burned.

10. An exhaust gas oxygen (EGO) sensor is also known as a _____ sensor.

11. _____ _____ is a brown haze that hangs in the sky, typically seen over large cities and is caused by oxides of nitrogen.

12. In older vehicles, crankcase vapors were vented directly to the atmosphere through a(n) _____ _____ or road-draft tube.

13. The _____ _____ _____ system was designed by automotive engineers in the 1970s to control the emission of oxides of nitrogen.

14. If the EVAP system of a vehicle passes the purge flow test, the PCM performs a _____ test.

15. Modern fuel tanks contain a(n) _____ _____, which is an air chamber that allows for the expansion of liquid fuel on hot days.

16. A(n) _____ _____ is connected to the vapor space in the fuel tank or the liquid vapor separator and carries fuel vapors from the fuel tank to a storage container called a charcoal canister.

17. Older vehicles use vacuum to control the opening and closing of the canister _____ _____, which is spring-loaded in the closed position.

18. Newer EVAP systems monitor purge operation by reading a _____ _____ pressure sensor while pulling a vacuum on the system.

19. The pulse air system uses the pulsations of the exhaust gas to open and close a(n) _____ _____, which is a flat metal valve that flexes when pressure is applied against it.

20. The _____ _____ intake system collects hot air from around the exhaust manifold and mixes it with outside air entering the air cleaner assembly.

Labeling

Label the following diagrams with the correct terms.

   1. PCV system:

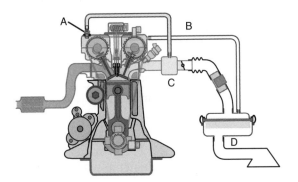

A. _____

B. _____

C. _____

D. _____

   2. Computer-controlled EGR system:

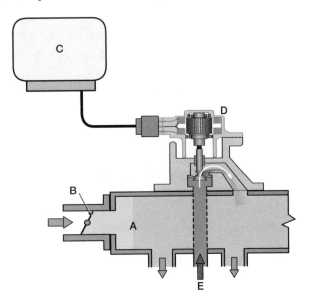

A. _____

B. _____

C. _____

D. _____

E. _____

3. Negative back-pressure EGR valve:

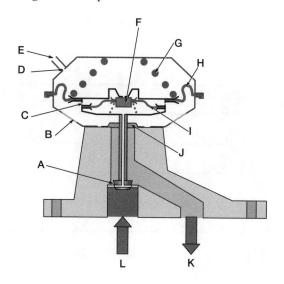

A. _____

B. _____

C. _____

D. _____

E. _____

F. _____

G. _____

H. _____

I. _____

J. _____

K. _____

L. _____

4. Pulse-width-modulated EGR valve and stepper motor EGR valve:

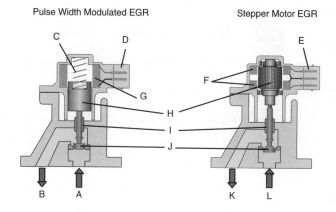

A. _____

B. _____

C. _____

D. _____

E. _____

F. _____

G. _____

H. _____

I. _____

J. _____

K. _____

L. _____

5. EGR vacuum control system:

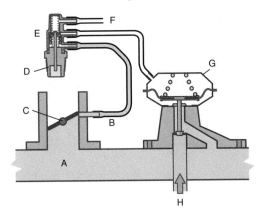

A. _____

B. _____

C. _____

D. _____

E. _____

F. _____

G. _____

H. _____

6. EVAP system:

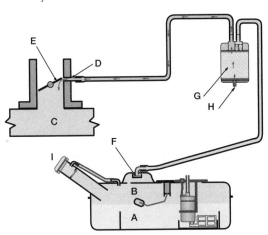

A. _____

B. _____

C. _____

D. _____

E. _____

F. _____

G. _____

H. _____

I. _____

7. Charcoal canister:

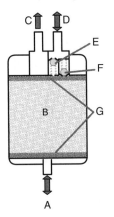

A. _____

B. _____

C. _____

D. _____

E. _____

F. _____

G. _____

8. Electrically operated vacuum purge system:

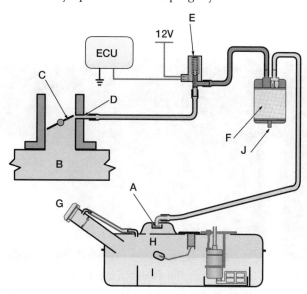

A. _____

B. _____

C. _____

D. _____

E. _____

F. _____

G. _____

H. _____

I. _____

J. _____

9. Secondary air injection system:

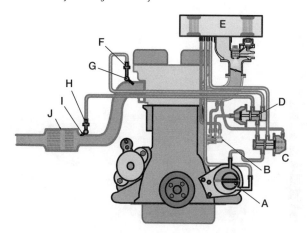

A. _____

B. _____

C. _____

D. _____

E. _____

F. _____

G. _____

H. _____

I. _____

J. _____

10. Heated air intake system:

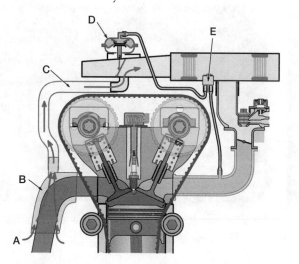

A. _____

B. _____

C. _____

D. _____

E. _____

Skill Drills

Test your knowledge of skill drills by filling in the correct words in the photo captions.

1. Using a Five-Gas Analyzer:

Step 1: Research the local _____ _____ for this vehicle in the applicable _____ or online sources. Warm up both the _____ and the exhaust gas _____. Leak test the analyzer _____ and _____.

Step 2: _____ the analyzer, if applicable. _____ the exhaust analyzer _____ in the vehicle's _____ _____ at least 18" (46 cm).

Step 3: Allow the vehicle to _____ and record the _____ readings. Compare your readings to the _____ and determine any necessary action(s).

2. Inspecting and Servicing the PCV System:

Step 1: Locate the _____ _____. With the engine idling, _____ the PCV _____ and check for the presence of a strong _____.

Step 2: Remove the _____ and check that it is still pliable and not _____ with _____ deposits.

Step 3: Remove the PCV valve and _____ it for _____ If there are any issues, _____ it with a new one of the same type. If fixed orifice style, make sure the _____ is clean.

Step 4: Reinstall the PCV valve into the _____ _____.

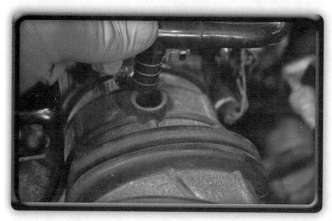

Step 5: Remove the _____ hose from the _____ _____ assembly.

Step 6: With the engine _____, block off the breather hose and _____ for vacuum _____ up in the breather hose and _____, indicating that the PCV system can handle the amount of _____-_____ gases. There should also be a slight amount of measurable vacuum in the crankcase at _____, typically measurable at the dipstick tube as _____ "-2" H_2O. This would indicate that the PCV system is operating and adequate for the blowby produced by the engine.

3. Inspecting and Servicing the EVAP System:

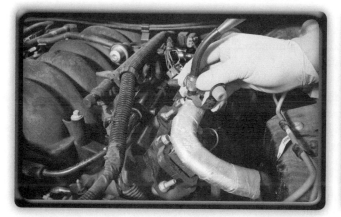

Step 1: Use a _____ _____ and check for _____ related to the EVAP system. If a code is found, follow the _____ procedures for that code. If the diagnostic code indicates a _____, connect an _____ tester to the EVAP test port.

Step 2: Use the EVAP system _____ _____ to determine if the _____ is in fact_____ and, if so, the _____ of the leak.

Step 3: Use a _____ _____ to help locate the leak. If smoke is detected, look in the area of the smoke to _____ the cause of the _____. If no smoke is detected, the system could be leaking _____ through a stuck-open _____ _____ or a _____ vent valve. Repair according to the manufacturer's procedure.

Review Questions

_____ **1.** All of the following are sources of emissions from current gasoline-fuelled motor vehicles *except*:
  A. the fuel system.
  B. the crankcase.
  C. the HVAC system.
  D. the tailpipe.

_____ **2.** The EPA requires that the malfunction indicator lamp (MIL) turn on and one or more specific diagnostic trouble codes (DTCs) be set in memory:
  A. whenever emissions are released.
  B. when emissions cross the FTP limit.
  C. when emissions are twice the FTP limit.
  D. when emissions are 1.5 times the FTP limit.

_____ **3.** Which of the following is a nonharmful emission?
  A. Nitrogen
  B. Carbon monoxide (CO)
  C. Oxides of nitrogen (NOx)
  D. Sulfur dioxide (SO_2)

_____ **4.** The reduction catalyst in a catalytic converter helps to:
  A. reduce the oxides of nitrogen molecules into their base compounds.
  B. oxidize any unburned hydrocarbons and carbon monoxide.
  C. convert exhaust water to oxygen and hydrogen.
  D. oxidize nitrogen before releasing it into the atmosphere.

_____ **5.** Which of the following is a function of the positive crankcase ventilation (PCV) system?
  A. It burns fuel vapors from the charcoal canister.
  B. It directs blowby gases and vapors back into the intake manifold.
  C. It prevents exhaust gases from entering into the engine.
  D. It ensures that the ventilation capacity is less than the amount of blowby.

_____ **6.** Choose the correct statement with respect to the exhaust gas recirculation system.
  A. It recirculates gases from the crankcase to the exhaust system.
  B. The EGR valve opens only during full throttle.
  C. The EGR valve is open during idle.
  D. Most PCM-controlled EGR systems incorporate a feedback loop, called a monitor, to ensure that the valve is working properly and EGR gases are flowing in the system.

_____ 7. Which of the following ensures that hydrocarbons are not released into the atmosphere when fuel in the fuel tank begins to vaporize and build pressure?
A. Catalytic converter
B. EVAP system
C. EGR system
D. PCV system

_____ 8. Which of the following uses oxygen sensors to measure the level of gases in the exhaust stream?
A. Idling five-gas test
B. Catalytic converter testing
C. Intrusive test
D. Purge flow test

_____ 9. In which of these cases is the catalytic converter most likely to be saved?
A. When the catalyst is severely overheated
B. When contaminated by lead and silicone
C. When contaminated by carbon
D. When the converter is physically damaged

_____ 10. Black exhaust represents:
A. a blown head gasket.
B. oil that is being burned in the combustion chamber.
C. an overly rich air-fuel mixture.
D. a leaky intake manifold gasket.

ASE Technician A/Technician B Style Questions

_____ 1. Tech A says that the purge valve is part of the evaporative emission system. Tech B says that OBD II systems must illuminate the MIL when the emissions exceed 1.5 times the FTP. Who is correct?
A. Tech A
B. Tech B
C. Both A and B
D. Neither A nor B

_____ 2. Tech A says that carbon monoxide is partially burned fuel. Tech B says that oxides of nitrogen are unburned fuel. Who is correct?
A. Tech A
B. Tech B
C. Both A and B
D. Neither A nor B

_____ 3. Tech A says that hydrocarbons are a result of complete combustion. Tech B says that a catalytic converter creates a chemical reaction, changing carbon monoxide and hydrocarbons to water and carbon dioxide. Who is correct?
A. Tech A
B. Tech B
C. Both A and B
D. Neither A nor B

_____ 4. Tech A says that allowing hot exhaust gases into the engine through the EGR valve helps to warm up the engine during warm-up. Tech B says that rich fuel mixtures create low amounts of carbon monoxide. Who is correct?
A. Tech A
B. Tech B
C. Both A and B
D. Neither A nor B

_____ 5. Tech A says that burning gasoline in an engine creates water as a by-product of combustion. Tech B says that variable valve timing can be used to reduce oxides of nitrogen, eliminating the need for an EGR valve on some engines. Who is correct?
A. Tech A
B. Tech B

      C. Both A and B

      D. Neither A nor B

_____ **6.** Tech A says that the PCV system recirculates exhaust gases into the intake manifold. Tech B says that the PCV system recirculates blowby gases into the intake manifold. Who is correct?

      A. Tech A

      B. Tech B

      C. Both A and B

      D. Neither A nor B

_____ **7.** Tech A says that the PCM monitors the pre-cat and post-cat oxygen sensors to determine catalytic converter efficiency. Tech B says that a catalytic converter can be tested by graphing the oxygen sensor readings on a scan tool or lab scope and comparing them. Who is correct?

      A. Tech A

      B. Tech B

      C. Both A and B

      D. Neither A nor B

_____ **8.** Tech A says that the EVAP system stores escaping hydrocarbons until the engine can burn them. Tech B says that catalytic converters were designed for regular leaded gas. Who is correct?

      A. Tech A

      B. Tech B

      C. Both A and B

      D. Neither A nor B

_____ **9.** Tech A says that the EGR valve is open fully at idle so that the engine will not die. Tech B says that oxides of nitrogen are created in large amounts when the combustion temperature is above 2500°F (1400°C). Who is correct?

      A. Tech A

      B. Tech B

      C. Both A and B

      D. Neither A nor B

_____ **10.** Tech A says that black exhaust indicates a very rich-running engine. Tech B says that white exhaust can indicate coolant in the exhaust. Who is correct?

      A. Tech A

      B. Tech B

      C. Both A and B

      D. Neither A nor B

Alternative Fuel Systems

At the start of each chapter you'll find the NATEF tasks, Knowledge Objectives, and Skills Objectives from the textbook. These are your objectives as you make your way through the exercises in this workbook and the chapter in your textbook. The following activities have been designed to help you refresh your knowledge of the material in this chapter.

NATEF Tasks

- N67001 Identify safety precautions for high-voltage systems on electric, hybrid, hybrid electric, and diesel vehicles. (MLR/AST/MAST)
- N67002 Identify service precautions related to service of the internal combustion engine of a hybrid vehicle. (MLR/AST/MAST)
- N67003 Identify hybrid vehicle A/C system electrical circuits and service/safety precautions. (MLR/AST/MAST)
- N67004 Identify hybrid vehicle auxiliary (12 V) battery service, repair, and test procedures. (MLR/AST/MAST)

Knowledge Objectives

After reading this chapter, you will be able to:

- K67001 Describe alternative fuel and the conditions favorable for its use.
- K67002 Describe common alternative fuels.
- K67003 Explain the purpose and function of the various types of gaseous fuel storage system.
- K67004 Explain the applications of biofuels.
- K67005 Explain fuel cell operation.
- K67006 Explain battery electric vehicles and their components.
- K67007 Describe hybrid electric vehicles.
- K67008 Explain hybrid drive configurations and operation.
- K67009 Describe the safety and service precautions for servicing hybrid and electric vehicles.

Skills Objectives

There are no Skills Objectives in this chapter.

Matching

Match the following terms with the correct description or example.

A. Alternative fuel

B. Biodiesel

C. Burn rate

D. Catalyst

E. Electronically continuously variable transmission

F. Emission standards

G. Anode

H. Hydrocarbon (HC)

I. Hygroscopic

J. Inverter

K. Mercaptan

L. Multiphase

M. Nitrogen oxides

N. Particulate matter (PM)

O. Pour point

P. Town gas

Q. M85 vehicle

R. Slow-fill

S. Ethanol

T. Wood gas

_____ **1.** Volatile organic compounds (VOCs) of unburned fuel that contribute to photochemical smog.

_____ **2.** The various compounds of nitrogen that contribute to the creation of smog in the presence of sunlight.

_____ **3.** Locally available gas used to power early internal combustion engines that is mostly methane.

_____ **4.** A transmission without individual gears or gear ratios.

_____ **5.** A hydrogen and methane gas created by a process of thermal gasification of wood or some other biomass.

_____ **6.** The temperature at which diesel fuel is not gelled.

_____ **7.** Alcohol-based motor fuel made from starches and sugars.

_____ **8.** The rate of flame spread for liquid or gaseous fuel.

_____ **9.** A device that converts direct current to alternating current.

_____ **10.** The method of filling a compressed natural gas vehicle (such as overnight) so the cylinders are completely filled.

_____ **11.** An electric motor that operates through more than one phase.

_____ **12.** Renewable fuel made from organic feedstocks.

_____ **13.** Mainly produced by diesel engines, becomes trapped in the lungs and causes health issues.

_____ **14.** A nonpetroleum-based motor fuel.

_____ **15.** A positively charged electrode or plate.

_____ **16.** A flexible-fuel vehicle, meaning any mixture of methanol and gasoline/petrol in the fuel tank can be used by the engine.

_____ **17.** A device that changes chemical composition without self-destruction.

_____ **18.** Cutoff points set by governmental agencies to limit tailpipe emissions.

_____ **19.** An agent that smells like sulfur that is added to liquefied petroleum or natural gas to aid in detecting leaks.

_____ **20.** The ability of a substance to attract and hold water molecules.

Multiple Choice

Read each item carefully, and then select the best response.

_____ **1.** In 1992, Congress passed the _____, the intent of which was to advance, through mandates, the use of vehicles capable of using alternatives to gasoline and diesel.
   A. Clean Air Act
   B. Energy Policy Act
   C. Environmental Protection Act
   D. Alternative Fuel Act

_____ **2.** What product of partially burned fuel displaces oxygen in the bloodstream and causes asphyxiation?
   A. Carbon dioxide
   B. Nitrogen oxides
   C. Hydrocarbons
   D. Carbon monoxide

_____ **3.** In the United States, the _____ controls federally mandated emission standards.
   A. Emission Standards Agency
   B. Environmental Protection Agency
   C. Clean Air Agency
   D. Clean Energy Agency

_____ **4.** Vehicles that are designed to operate on two different fuels blended together in various mixture amounts by percentage are called _____.
   A. LPG vehicles
   B. biodiesel vehicles
   C. flexible-fuel vehicles
   D. CNG vehicles

_____ **5.** Which fossil fuel is primarily methane, but may also include ethane, propane, butane, and other gases such as carbon dioxide, nitrogen, and helium?
   A. Liquefied petroleum gas
   B. Natural gas

    C. Syngas
    D. Biodiesel

_____ **6.** What type of fuel was used for lighting and internal combustion engine vehicles during the very early days before petroleum became the fuel of choice?
    A. Wood gas
    B. Natural gas
    C. Diesel
    D. Town gas

_____ **7.** What type of gas consists mainly of varying combinations of hydrogen and carbon monoxide, and it can be produced in a number of different ways, including the Fischer-Tropsch method for the gasification of coal?
    A. Town gas
    B. Wood gas
    C. Compressed natural gas
    D. Syngas

_____ **8.** What type of vehicle runs on two different fuels that are injected directly into the combustion chamber, almost at the same time?
    A. Dual-fuel
    B. Bi-fuel
    C. Hybrid
    D. Fuel cell

_____ **9.** What kind of renewable fuel is made by chemically combining natural oils from soybeans, cottonseeds, canola, animal fats, algae, jatropha seeds, or even recycled cooking oil with an alcohol such as methanol or ethanol, and a catalyst like lye?
    A. Producer gas
    B. Biodiesel
    C. Syngas
    D. Bi-fuel

_____ **10.** Some diesel engines can run on _____, but only if it has been properly treated to remove the glycerin, which could otherwise gunk up injectors and engine parts like piston rings.
    A. straight vegetable oil
    B. wood fuel
    C. waste vegetable oil
    D. either A or C

_____ **11.** The _____ is the temperature below which diesel fuel will not flow at all.
    A. cloud point
    B. pour point
    C. boiling point
    D. viscosity threshold

_____ **12.** Second-generation _____ is derived from a variety of cellulose-based plants such as switchgrass.
    A. biodiesel
    B. bio-ethanol
    C. methanol
    D. biomass

_____ **13.** All of the following are basic elements of a fuel cell, *except*:
    A. anode.
    B. cathode.
    C. electrode.
    D. catalyst.

_____ **14.** A device called a(n) _____ is used to separate hydrogen from other fuels, such as gasoline.
    A. splitter
    B. inverter
    C. rectifier
    D. reformer

_____ **15.** The "exhaust" produced by a fuel cell vehicle is _____.

    A. methane

    B. water

    C. carbon monoxide

    D. nitrogen

_____ **16.** What type of electric motor does not use brushes or commutators?

    A. Permanent magnet

    B. Multiphase

    C. Brushless

    D. Synchronous

_____ **17.** What type of vehicle uses a combination of electric power and an internal combustion engine?

    A. Fuel cell vehicle

    B. Hybrid electric vehicle

    C. Battery electric vehicle

    D. Flexible-fuel vehicle

_____ **18.** In what type of hybrid drive configuration is the gasoline engine used only to drive a generator and charge a battery, which produces power to drive an electric motor?

    A. Series hybrid

    B. Parallel hybrid

    C. Series-parallel hybrid

    D. All of the above

_____ **19.** In a hybrid vehicle the _____ feature temporarily shuts off the internal combustion engine when it is not needed, such as when idling or coasting.

    A. regenerative braking

    B. displacement-on-demand

    C. idle stop

    D. power-on-demand

_____ **20.** What type of vehicle uses only one power source, the battery, to propel the vehicle for a certain distance before the batteries need charging and the internal combustion engine is needed?

    A. Plug-in hybrid electric vehicle

    B. Fuel cell vehicle

    C. Series-parallel hybrid vehicle

    D. Flexible-fuel vehicle

True/False

If you believe the statement to be more true than false, write the letter "T" in the space provided. If you believe the statement to be more false than true, write the letter "F."

_____ **1.** Transitioning to cleaner alternative energy and fuel choices can help reduce the effects of pollution.

_____ **2.** Although harmless in small amounts, too much carbon monoxide is a serious atmospheric concern. It is considered a greenhouse gas.

_____ **3.** Emission standards set cutoff points for the amount of pollutants that vehicles may release into the environment.

_____ **4.** Since methane has no odor, an odorant called mercaptan is added so humans may detect leaks.

_____ **5.** Compressed natural gas vehicles make use of light weight cylinders that offer long range.

_____ **6.** Producer gas is a generic term that refers to a number of manufactured gases such as wood gas, town gas, and syngas.

_____ **7.** Dual-fuel engines and vehicles are capable of running on either gasoline or natural gas, though some engine modifications are required for them to run efficiently.

_____ **8.** In a dedicated natural gas conversion, the diesel injectors are replaced with spark plugs and the natural gas fuel is premixed with air before intake occurs.

_____ **9.** There are two types of LPG storage container: portable universal cylinders and permanently mounted tanks.

_____ **10.** Compressed natural gas valve installation and inspection specifications are contained in the National Fire Protection Association (NFPA) standards and published in their NFPA-52 document.

_____ **11.** B100 fuel, the blend most commonly available, contains 10% biodiesel and 90% petrodiesel.

_____ **12.** Methanol is highly poisonous and dangerous to the environment.

_____ **13.** M85 vehicles are flex-fuel vehicles that can run on any mixture of methanol and gasoline/petrol, though the limit of methanol in the mixture is 85% in the United States.

_____ **14.** Hydrogen is the lightest element, yet it has the highest energy content per unit weight/mass of all energy-based fuels—three times the energy of gasoline/petrol.

_____ **15.** Each fuel cell consists of a membrane electrode assembly sandwiched between plates.

_____ **16.** A parallel hybrid allows both the engine and the electric motor to drive the vehicle together, or either one by itself.

_____ **17.** Displacement-on-demand deactivates cylinders when operating under cruise or coasting conditions to save fuel.

_____ **18.** Idle stop turns off the internal combustion engine when the vehicle is at a standstill.

_____ **19.** The retarding effect (vehicle slowing) caused by regenerative braking provides the same deceleration as normal engine braking would.

_____ **20.** Fuel cell vehicles are considered hybrid vehicles because they have two power sources.

Fill in the Blank

Read each item carefully, and then complete the statement by filling in the missing word(s).

1. The co-products of _____ production, such as dried distiller grains, are sold as feed for livestock.

2. _____ _____ is literally fine soot that measured in microns, or millionths of an inch.

3. California's _____-_____ _____ standard includes six major emission categories, each with several targets depending on vehicle weight and cargo capacity.

4. _____ _____ _____ is heavier than air and is the least carbon-emitting hydrocarbon fuel available.

5. _____ _____ _____ vehicles use methane compressed for storage and use in light-duty passenger vehicles, delivery trucks, and buses.

6. A(n) _____-_____ fuel gauge is placed in the tank and raises or lowers in a tube for fuel level calculation.

7. _____ is the solution in a battery, such as sulfuric acid and water used in a lead-acid battery.

8. _____ gas is mostly hydrogen and carbon monoxide, and it is created by passing steam over red-hot coke.

9. A(n) _____ _____ _____ ensures that an LPG fuel storage tank cannot be filled past the safe fill limit of 80%.

10. The volume of space required for _____ _____ _____ storage tanks is almost twice that required for LNG tanks for delivering the equivalent mileage range.

11. Biodiesel burns with less particulate and with no _____ or _____, thus producing less harmful and irritating emissions.

12. Biodiesel, depending on the feedstock and process used, is a light yellow to dark gold liquid, with a(n) _____ very similar to petrodiesel fuel.

13. The cloud point is the temperature at which diesel fuel starts to appear cloudy, indicating that _____ crystals have begun to form.

14. _____ is a renewable energy source, plant, or animal material used as a source of fuel.

15. A fuel _____ sensor tells the engine computer what percentage of methanol is in the fuel, and it adjusts the injection quantity ignition timing accordingly.

16. A fuel cell is a(n) _____-_____ device that combines hydrogen and oxygen to produce water and in the process it produces electricity and heat.

17. When coupled with sustainable or renewable energy sources, the _____ _____ vehicle can truly serve as an emissions-free vehicle.

18. _____ braking occurs when the drive motor(s) act as generators to recharge the traction batteries during deceleration or when braking.

19. The internal combustion engine in a hybrid vehicle is designed to operate only within its most efficient operating range, typically somewhere between 2000 and 4500 rpm, where engine peak _____ efficiency and peak torque are developed.

20. The Chevy Volt is known as an _____-_____ electric vehicle.

Labeling

Label the following diagrams with the correct terms.

   1. Liquefied natural gas fuel tank:

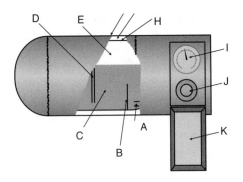

A. _____

B. _____

C. _____

D. _____

E. _____

F. _____

G. _____

H. _____

I. _____

J. _____

K. _____

   2. Fuel cell creating electricity:

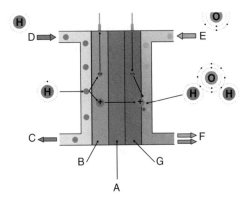

A. _____

B. _____

C. _____

D. _____

E. _____

F. _____

G. _____

3. Fuel cells in a stack:

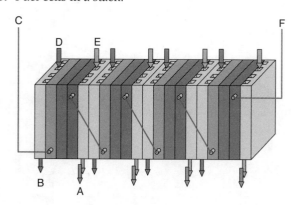

A. _____

B. _____

C. _____

D. _____

E. _____

F. _____

4. Power splitting transmission:

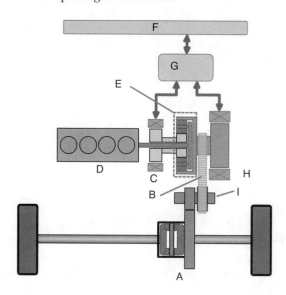

A. _____

B. _____

C. _____

D. _____

E. _____

F. _____

G. _____

H. _____

I. _____

Review Questions

_____ 1. Alternative fuels advance all of the following *except*:
- **A.** energy security.
- **B.** environmental concerns.
- **C.** economy.
- **D.** elegance.

_____ 2. Which of the following is derived from other forms of fuel such as wood or coal?
- **A.** Manufactured gas
- **B.** Liquefied natural gas
- **C.** Compressed natural gas
- **D.** Liquefied petroleum gas

_____ 3. Choose the correct statement.
- **A.** CNG is compressed and stored at low pressures.
- **B.** The volume of space required for LNG storage tanks is almost twice that required for CNG tanks for delivering the equivalent mileage range.
- **C.** Because CNG is a gas, not a liquid, it does not matter whether the container is standing up or lying down.
- **D.** CNG cylinders come in two types (heavy and light).

_____ 4. Bio-alcohol is used primarily:
- **A.** as a blend with traditional petrodiesel.
- **B.** by itself.
- **C.** as a blend with liquefied natural gas.
- **D.** as a blend with gasoline.

_____ 5. When compared to petrodiesel, biodiesel:
- **A.** has a lower cetane rating.
- **B.** has a lower cloud point and pour point.
- **C.** produces significantly fewer emissions.
- **D.** produces more harmful emissions.

_____ 6. Choose the correct statement with respect to a fuel cell.
- **A.** It produces higher emissions than biodiesel-powered vehicles.
- **B.** It combines hydrogen and oxygen to produce water and in the process it produces electricity and heat.
- **C.** A fuel cell produces a voltage of about 1000 volts.
- **D.** Fuel cells are heavy and increase vehicle load.

_____ 7. Which of the following is a rechargeable battery with the highest energy density currently in use?
- **A.** Lead-acid
- **B.** Nickel-cadmium
- **C.** Nickel-metal hydride
- **D.** Lithium-ion

_____ 8. Which of the following hybrid drive configurations is where the ICE only drives a generator to charge the batteries, which then power the electric motor to drive the wheels?
- **A.** Series hybrid
- **B.** Parallel hybrid
- **C.** Series-parallel hybrid
- **D.** Battery-electric hybrid

_____ 9. Hybrid vehicles that can be driven short distances and at low speeds using only the (high-voltage) batteries are classified as:
- **A.** full hybrids.
- **B.** partial hybrids.
- **C.** micro hybrids.
- **D.** macro hybrids.

_____ 10. All of the following statements are true with respect to servicing hybrid and electric vehicles *except*:
- **A.** Pierce a high-voltage wire when testing for voltage.
- **B.** Avoid working on the high-voltage areas of a hybrid vehicle without first having the proper training.

C. Disconnect the main high-voltage battery pack before service is performed on or around the high-voltage components.

D. Never assume that the vehicle is turned off because it is silent or still.

ASE Technician A/Technician B Style Questions

_____ 1. Tech A says that fuel cells only emit CO_2 to the atmosphere. Tech B says that fuel cells run on water. Who is correct?
   A. Tech A
   B. Tech B
   C. Both A and B
   D. Neither A nor B

_____ 2. Tech A says that ethanol-blended gas at 10% is a nationwide standard. Tech B says that 15% ethanol-blended gas has been approved for 2001 vehicles and newer. Who is correct?
   A. Tech A
   B. Tech B
   C. Both A and B
   D. Neither A nor B

_____ 3. Tech A says that high-voltage wires in hybrid and electric vehicles are usually a special color. Tech B says that special high-voltage gloves should be worn when working on high-voltage vehicles. Who is correct?
   A. Tech A
   B. Tech B
   C. Both A and B
   D. Neither A nor B

_____ 4. Tech A says that E85 vehicles are designed to use 85% ethanol efficiently. Tech B says that hydrogen cars are not zero-emission vehicles. Who is correct?
   A. Tech A
   B. Tech B
   C. Both A and B
   D. Neither A nor B

_____ 5. Tech A says that lithium-ion batteries currently have the highest energy density of batteries used in HEVs. Tech B says that nickel–metal hydride batteries are less expensive than lithium-ion batteries. Who is correct?
   A. Tech A
   B. Tech B
   C. Both A and B
   D. Neither A nor B

_____ 6. Tech A says that CNG fuel tanks hold 3600 psi (24,800 kPa). Tech B says that CNG engines tend to emit white smoke, which is water vapor. Who is correct?
   A. Tech A
   B. Tech B
   C. Both A and B
   D. Neither A nor B

_____ 7. Tech A says that some hybrid battery packs are cooled by a cooling system. Tech B says that regenerative braking in a hybrid vehicle uses electricity from the high-voltage battery to slow the vehicle. Who is correct?
   A. Tech A
   B. Tech B
   C. Both A and B
   D. Neither A nor B

_____ **8.** Tech A says that prior to working on a hybrid vehicle, make sure the "Ready" indicator is on. Tech B says that once the service plug is removed, you can immediately start working on the high-voltage system. Who is correct?
- **A.** Tech A
- **B.** Tech B
- **C.** Both A and B
- **D.** Neither A nor B

_____ **9.** Tech A says that a CAT III meter is required when working on the EV or HEV high-voltage system. Tech B says that a HEV can start the ICE on its own if the "Ready" indicator is on. Who is correct?
- **A.** Tech A
- **B.** Tech B
- **C.** Both A and B
- **D.** Neither A nor B

_____ **10.** Tech A says that biodiesel mixed with diesel fuel does not reduce emissions. Tech B says that a 1% or more blend of biodiesel extends the life of injectors. Who is correct?
- **A.** Tech A
- **B.** Tech B
- **C.** Both A and B
- **D.** Neither A nor B

Credits